ROUTLEDGE LIBRARY EDITIONS:
DEMOGRAPHY

Volume 3

MICRO-APPROACHES TO DEMOGRAPHIC RESEARCH

MICRO-APPROACHES TO DEMOGRAPHIC RESEARCH

Edited by
JOHN C. CALDWELL,
ALLAN G. HILL
AND
VALERIE J. HULL

Routledge
Taylor & Francis Group
LONDON AND NEW YORK

First published in 1988 by Kegan Paul International

This edition first published in 2024
by Routledge
4 Park Square, Milton Park, Abingdon, Oxon OX14 4RN

and by Routledge
605 Third Avenue, New York, NY 10158

Routledge is an imprint of the Taylor & Francis Group, an informa business

British Library Cataloguing in Publication Data
A catalogue record for this book is available from the British Library

ISBN: 978-1-032-53819-8 (Set)
ISBN: 978-1-032-54902-6 (Volume 3) (hbk)
ISBN: 978-1-032-54911-8 (Volume 3) (pbk)
ISBN: 978-1-003-42803-9 (Volume 3) (ebk)

DOI: 10.4324/9781003428039

Micro-Approaches to Demographic Research

John C. Caldwell, Allan G. Hill
& Valerie J. Hull

KEGAN PAUL INTERNATIONAL
LONDON AND NEW YORK
in association with
Australian International Development Assistance Bureau
Seminars for Development Program
International Union for the Scientific Study of the Population

First published in 1988 by Kegan Paul International Limited
11 New Fetter Lane, London EC4P 4EE

Distributed by
Associated Book Publishers (UK) Ltd
11 New Fetter Lane, London EC4P 4EE

Routledge, Chapman & Hall Inc.
29 West 35th Street
New York, NY 10001, USA

J.M. Dent Pty Ltd
112 Lewis Road
Knoxfield 3180
Victoria, Australia

Printed in Great Britain by
Whitstable Litho Printers Ltd.

ISBN 0-7103-0297-5

Contents

Tables

Figures

List of papers presented at the Canberra Seminar but not included in this book

HILL, A.	'The Aim of the IUSSP Working Group on the Micro-Approach to Demographic Research'
CAMERON, J.	'Contrasts and Contradictions in Fertility Behaviour: A Consequence of Method'
GARENNE, M.	'The Use of a Computerized Questionnaire for Improving the Recording of Early Deaths in Rural Senegal'
GURUSWAMY, M.	'Nature of Activity in a Village Setting: Methods of Data Collection'
HETLER, C.	'Female-Headed Households in Indonesia'
LARSON, A.	'Life Course Transitions of Girls in Late Nineteenth Century Melbourne: An Outline of a Micro-Approach to Historical Demography'
O'NEILL, B.	'Nuptiality and Illegitimacy in Twentieth Century Portugal: An Anthropological Case Study'
PREMI, M.	'A Case for Micro-Level Studies on Internal Migration in India'
SUHARSO, LAM & PADMANABHA	'Comments from Policy Makers'

Preface

In recent years an increasing number of demographers have become concerned as to the adequacy of the methods of data collection employed by population researchers. Questions have been raised about the possibility of supplementing traditional census and survey techniques with more intensive field studies drawing upon both anthropological and small scale survey methodologies. The IUSSP moved toward meeting this new demand by establishing in 1982 a Working Group on Micro-Approaches to Demographic Research, chaired by Allan Hill.

The first major activity of this working group was the organization of a conference on the subject held at the Australian National University, Canberra, in September 1984 with John Caldwell as local organizer. The conference aimed both at presenting and examining the new field methodologies and at learning the results obtained from the use of these methodologies in the field. This book presents selected papers from that conference both for their own value but also as an encouragement and guide for others who attempt to discover not only the parameters of demographic behaviour but why such behaviour occurs and how and why it is changing.

The conference was made possible by generous grants from AIDAB, the Australian International Development Assistance Bureau, which nominated the meeting for support as a contribution to its Research for Development Seminar program, and from the Population Council, under its International Research Awards Program on the Determinants of Fertility in Developing Countries (funded by the United States Agency for International Development under subordinate Agreement No.CP84.08A). In addition a wide range of support services and meeting accommodation was provided by the Australian National University, and, especially, by the Department of Demography and its parent body, the Research School of Social Sciences. In London, Allan Hill's activities were made possible by the Centre for Population Studies, London School of Hygiene and Tropical Medicine, University of London.

We should also note that, fired by the feeling of doing something new and different, the members of the IUSSP Working Group, throughout four years, and the conferees in Canberra in September 1984 all developed a strong group spirit which augurs well for the future of micro-approach research in the population field. Unfortunately, due to publisher's constrictions, nine of the original papers presented at the conference are not included in this book. However, a list of the titles omitted, together with their authors, appears on page xiv.

Since the meeting, Valerie Hull, a participant in the conference, has joined the organizers in editing this book. In addition, much of the work in getting an acceptable manuscript to the publishers has been undertaken by Daphne Broers-Freeman, with the assistance of Elizabeth Baker, both of the A.N.U. Department of Demography, and the word processing was carried out by Jean Davitt.

We hope that this book will encourage more experimental work and believe that it fills the need for a textbook as to what might be done and how the researcher can begin in a very new sub-field.

September 1987

John Caldwell
Allan Hill
Valerie Hull

Introduction

Recent Developments Using Micro-Approaches to Demographic Research

John C. Caldwell and Allan G. Hill

Social science research on demographic issues is surprisingly deficient in theory for two main reasons: one is the overweening but understandable concern with measurement of the principal demographic parameters. The other is the reluctance of demographers to engage in research whose methods are unconventional and whose output cannot be measured in numerical terms. The reasons for this demise of demographic research on the 'remote' determinants of fertility, mortality and migration are manifold but one component is the success and dominance of a single methodology (the sample survey) and its accompanying panoply of semi-standardized analysis techniques (e.g. 'direct' and 'indirect' methods for calculating the basic demographic parameters; regression analysis of varying levels of sophistication). The survey is good at describing patterns and for the analysis of simple associations, but it has to be selective with reference to the respondents contacted and the topics to be explored. The sampling design itself often means that individuals are not seen in the setting of families, nor households in the context of their neighbours. Techniques such as mapping or re-survey of the same population can produce a provocative description of a single phenomenon but such descriptive work based on survey material is unlikely to generate an original body of theory.

Theoretical Issues

Demographic research shares with social science generally several major unsolved theoretical problems. One difficulty which dogs all social scientists is the problem of linking observations obtained from different levels, a variant of the long-standing dispute between those who believe in 'social facts' and the individualists. A central problem in micro-level research is how 'social facts' or at least community and possibly national level forces can be observed at the local level. An empirical problem linked to this difficulty is the choice of appropriate measurement units. Whilst the problem of misleading statistical associations deriving from choice of inappropriate measurement units has been known for some time, (e.g. Blalock and Blalock, 1968), very few have tried to demonstrate statistically how the influence of factors at one level can be detected at other levels in the system. Some progress on this front in a largely non-statistical format is demonstrated in papers by Arthur and McNicoll (1978); Cain (1978); and Das Gupta (ch.6). Rarely do we see true community level attributes used in the analysis of relationships at other levels although there are some exceptions to this generalization (e.g. Lesthaeghe *et al.*, 1983). The micro-level approach may offer a partial solution to this problem in that thorough immersion in the society studied, coupled with a central interest in all phases of the work from design to final analysis, does encourage a more holistic view.

A second theoretical problem which appears amenable to treatment by micro-approaches is the search for alternatives to the single variable model. Whilst first Davis and Blake (1956), then Bongaarts and Potter (1983) and Mosely (1980) advanced our knowledge of a small set of factors affecting fertility and to a lesser extent mortality, their 'proximate determinants' framework has had a stultifying effect on the search for the 'remote determinants' first because the models deal separately with the effects of single 'determinants' (e.g. marriage; contraception; abortion) which are clearly interdependent; and second because the model itself is deterministic and uni-directional, thus discouraging researchers from consideration of complicated effects involving feedback. The researcher working with a micro-approach is more likely to find, for example, the family a more natural unit of observation and analysis for fertility studies than an individual woman, and qualitative changes are more likely to be noticed when quasi-anthropological methods, including collection of biographies, are employed.

Apart from caution, what can 'pocket' research contribute to theoretical developments in demography? The pressure to produce conceptual schemes or typologies containing 'lawlike propositions that interrelate the concepts or variables two or more at a time' (Blalock, 1969, p.2) means that the researcher must translate his ideas into theoretical models consisting of networks of refutable hypotheses. We must temporarily suspend discussion of the theory-dependence of all observations (Papineau, 1978, p.29ff). These models are often difficult to evaluate against field observations but micro-simulation is at least one option, particularly if the models used are stochastic (producing variances rather than simply means).

A further theoretical area where micro-level research might be expected to advance our understanding of social systems is related to the more general need for more experimentation in the social sciences. Whether we are using an algorithm based on verification (Ayer, 1946) or on falsifiability (Popper, 1959), there is a crying need for some acid tests of demographic theory. It is unthinkable that any very radical experiments will be conducted by governments with the necessary scientific controls at a national scale. Most of us are not certain enough of our theory to allow this. But all around the world, some small and other large attempts at social engineering are underway in the guise of development projects. Frequently, only a few variables are being manipulated in each case, since our capacity to engender radical change is limited even with the full coercive power of the modern state. Where such interventions are in hand would seem ideal testing grounds for bodies of theory, ensuring that experiments in one context are replicable elsewhere, and for development of thinking about 'facts' and the nature of evidence generally.

Methodology

Clearly, no single methodology will suffice in view of the diverse aims of demographic research, including work that adopts the micro-approach because of the generally accepted view that observations and therefore the systems needed to make them are theory-dependent. Several empirical results have emerged, however, from the micro-level work completed in demography so far.

First, accepting that single factor, single level models of any significant demographic process will be inadequate, some sort of more complex observational system will be necessary. Supplementing the probably indispensable household survey will be other more time consuming studies collecting marriage histories, work histories, indeed whole biographies. Data on economic transactions including labour use are also likely to be added but again only for small populations because of practical considerations. Still lacking is a clear idea of how societal factors can be observed at the local level although McNicoll (ch.1) has indicated how tracing the local effects of centrally decided administrative reforms may be a productive line of enquiry in this context.

Following on from this is the implication that more thought is needed in connection with the choice of units for survey and analysis. In North America and Northwest Europe, the choice of the co-residential family as an almost independent economic unit or 'firm' may be justified for certain restricted forms of demographic analysis but elsewhere the network of kinship and economic ties stretches far beyond the household. Much of micro-economic theory concerning fertility and broader generalizations such as the intergenerational wealth flows concept (Caldwell, 1983b) are both examples of theories whose verification or falsification first demands a resolution of the problem of choosing the appropriate accounting units. Which group of people stands to gain as a result of, for example, a reduction of fertility by young couples? Again, there is no perfect theoretical answer to this question of the choice of the appropriate units but the best informed empirical response is sure to stem from a close personal knowledge of the society under study.

A more mundane methodological bonus accruing from research using a micro-approach concerns the ability to separate rules from practice in a much clearer way. Several studies have demonstrated how questions both on intentions 'Do you want another child?' and on behaviour e.g. contraceptive effectiveness varying with intention (Bumpass and Westoff, 1970, ch.5) evoke varying responses during interview depending on the respondents' circumstances at the time of interview. Survey responses give a misleading average picture of attitudes and behaviour in the society.

In surveys, particularly large surveys, the tendency is to obtain normative responses or reflections of the rules, particularly on sensitive topics (e.g. post-natal taboos on intercourse). More intensive studies commonly reveal contradictory findings at the individual level although a surprising consistency often emerges when the data are aggregated.

Finally, we should mention the importance of continuous or at least extended observation as a method of collecting information during crises or periods of stress. When under strain, social and political systems at all levels are at their most revealing. For operational reasons, most large surveys and censuses are deliberately postponed during such difficult periods so there is a systematic bias against survey work conducted then. But the resident observer, or even the researcher with data for a preceding period and the capacity to make further observations later, may gain considerable insights during a period of stress. Relative losses of body weight during a famine tabulated by age and sex may reveal more about intergenerational wealth or income flows than several years observation during better times. Clearly, the case here is for research designs which explicitly consider change and its assessment at the outset rather than assuming a steady state at least in the period immediately preceding the survey.

Applications

The most fruitful way to demonstrate some of the output from the rich diversity of current research is to present a summary of recent findings, most of which were presented at the first meeting of the IUSSP Micro-Approaches Working Group in Canberra during September 1984 and are included in this book.

One group of micro-approach users has worked much as do anthropologists, concentrating on a single community and emphasizing the need for understanding the society as a whole. They differ from pure anthropologists in that the focus of the former is primarily demographic in contrast to say, kinship or inheritance systems examined for their own sake. At present, the body of demographic theory pertaining to the micro-scale is very limited but some substantial results are emerging from major projects such as the one on the value of children (Fawcett, 1983), leading on to some more focused research on particular hypotheses. Nonetheless, demographers, even those working at the micro-scale, still prefer to work with quantifiable information including that obtained from written records and archives.

Examples of this kind of approach are provided by the work undertaken by the Vlassoffs in Maharashtra, India in 1975-6 (Vlassoff, ch.5), by that of Mougne in Ban Pong, Northern Thailand in 1972-4 and again later (Mougne, ch.7), and by the Jefferys in Uttar Pradesh, India in 1982-3 (Jeffery, Jeffery and Lyon, ch.18). The Jefferys interestingly state that they wished to study people as such as a reaction not against the disintegrating effect of surveys but against the pre-occupation of anthropologists with 'kinship algebra and discussion of abstract structures'. This integrative kind of approach was the one adopted from the outset by the Caldwells and Reddy in Karnataka, India from 1979 (Caldwell, Reddy and Caldwell, ch.2) and by others connected to the Population Centre, Bangalore and the Department of Demography, Australian National University, Canberra.

A closely related group are those who use similar methods but with a narrower focus. Some of the best examples of this genre are the work on labour use by Peet in Nepal and White in Java in 1972-3 in a joint project with Nag (Nag, Peet and White, 1977); by Khuda on Bangladesh (Khuda, 1979); and by Guruswamy in Tamil Nadu, India (Guruswamy, 1984). Cain spans both groups in that his 1976-8 program in Char Gopalpur, Bangladesh, examined labour inputs within the larger framework of the household life cycle, economic mobility and security (Cain, 1977; 1978). Myntti concentrated largely on women's health although her detailed knowledge of rural North Yemen allowed her to relate this to reproduction (Myntti, ch.24). Hetler deliberately focused on female-headed households in Indonesia but found that this later led her to a detailed study of migration and its local effects (Hetler, 1984). Cameron, while attempting to show that New Zealand society was different from the impression given by a large scale survey, found herself concentrating on what she regarded as the common-sense biological interpretations offered by the population which differed markedly from those of the survey researchers (Cameron, 1984).

One variant of the micro-method is offered, as Chen (ch.15) has pointed out, by the laboratory situation of the few large surveillance systems in existence such as that of the International Diaorrhoeal Research Centre at Matlab in Bangladesh where the collection of data on a quarter of a million people has inevitably resulted in a micro-macro mix in which some studies have been largely quantitative and others, such as that by Lindenbaum (1983) almost entirely anthropological although focused on the relationship between maternal education and child mortality. Garenne has shown how findings from micro-work can improve the quality of questionnaire-based surveys through the development of forms tailor-made for each respondent (Garenne, 1984).

A further group employs a combination of methods, sometimes built around a single-round survey or a longitudinal study in a single community. Examples are the work of Hull, Hull and Singarimbun between 1969 and 1980 in Sriharjo and Maguwoharjo, Java concentrating largely on fertility (Hull, Hull and Singarimbun, ch.4); as reported by Orubuloye and Caldwell (1975) for two villages in Nigeria in 1973-4 with a focus on health; and by Caldwell and Caldwell in Nigeria in 1974 with a very specific focus on post-partum sexual abstinence (Caldwell and Caldwell, 1977; 1981). Other work of this type is carried out by Oppong and Abu (ch.9) on family size in Tamale, Ghana; by Nag and Kak (ch.14) in the Punjab; and by Pison (ch.17) in Eastern Senegal. The Nag and Kak chapter is unique in demographic studies but not in anthropology in that it is a re-study of an area examined by another researcher with similar interests looking in turn at a third person's results. Das Gupta too was also able to look again at a village near Delhi examined by Oscar Lewis some 20 years earlier to ascertain the nature of change in the intervening period (Das Gupta, ch.6).

A slightly different tradition has been described for a program in Mali by a varied group of investigators which remains closer to demographic data and population measures but uses supplementary data and approaches to interpret these results, taking a small sample of the population for study through flexible, non-questionnaire based investigation (Hill, Randall and van den Eerenbeemt, 1983; Hill and Randall, 1984; Hilderbrand *et al.*, 1984; Randall, 1984; Fulton and Randall, ch.12). This type of approach has been adopted as part of a further project on marriage and household formation amongst Fulani in central Mali (Hill and Thiam, ch.19). The use of a survey approach as the major instrument, with personal involvement, participant observation and interviews in depth as an illuminating supplementary strategy has also characterized the work of some migration researchers in the Pacific: Chapman in the Solomons in the early 1960s (Chapman, ch.20); Hugo in West Java a decade later (Hugo, ch.21); and Haberkorn (ch.22) in Vanuatu recently. One of their reasons was the difficulty experienced in bringing out the complexity of migration movements from the survey alone. Premi (1984) has outlined a great number of questions raised by macro-approach studies in India and, he maintains, unanswerable except by micro-approach research. Essentially the same approach was adopted by MacCormack when studying women's knowledge of reproductive biology in Jamaica (MacCormack, ch.25). Van de Walle worked in conjunction with a multi-round demographic survey in Burkina-Faso (formerly Upper Volta) but concentrated her own work on long interviews elucidating attitudes towards reproduction and family size (van de Walle, ch.10). The other extreme of this approach is represented by the work of Pison who utilized a participant approach to improve demographic data collection in eastern Senegal (Pison, ch.17). Freedman experimented in Taiwan with a small team of anthropologists who sought to explore a range of questions which had been raised by a long program of demographic research based largely on surveys (Freedman and Hermalin, 1975; Freedman, Fan, Wei and Weinberger, 1977).

Another approach in an area where there had been a considerable history of demographic survey work was that adopted by Knodel and Pramualratana (ch.3) in Thailand. Their focus group research was carried out by arranging group discussions in a series of locations where a moderator led the discussions on topics which were pre-designed but in such a way that leads could be followed up in an open-ended fashion. Interestingly, this approach in Thailand and that of the Caldwells and Reddy in South India drew some quite similar conclusions on the nature of demographic change of a type not readily investigated by the survey approach.

In terms of its intensity and personal involvement, a related type of research is that which carries out a number of small scale surveys or collects demographic data by other methods in a single culture area and where the principal investigators participate to a major extent in all the work. Such research usually has a sharp focus. Examples are the examination of the timing of additional children amongst the Yoruba of Nigeria by Adeokun (ch.8); the work of Carael on breastfeeding in three localities in Zaire (Carael, ch.11); and that by Aaby on the incidence, transmission and impact of measles in six localities of Guinea Bissau (Aaby, ch.16).

A micro-approach has been attempted by historians working in the localities in which past events originally took place. They employ recorded information about individuals which they can relate to other persons, to the institutions then in existence, to the geographical context and even to continuing cultural traditions. An example of this is the work of Smith who has drawn on the records of English manorial courts during the thirteenth, fourteenth and fifteenth centuries which he is now using for comparison with the institutional determinants of fertility in South Asia by Cain (Smith, ch.13). Other historical work is that of Larson on the life course transition of girls and young women in nineteenth century Melbourne, Australia (Larson, 1984), and O'Neill who has related historical material to present-day behaviour in the study of nuptiality and illegitimacy in northeast Portugal (O'Neill, 1984).

Finally, there are those who have employed personal experience together with a wide range of material drawn from others to produce a synthesis. Kreager (1982) has done this with anthropological studies of the Sudan and of the Mayans of Central America (Kreager, ch.23). Employing different materials but adopting a similar approach, Arthur and McNicoll (1978) and McNicoll (ch.1) looked at the institutional determinants of fertility. Within this emerging tradition, it is probably worthwhile to describe in a little detail the sequence of activities followed by the Caldwells and Reddy in South India which because of their wide compass have served as a template for others. In India, the research began with an initial census of the study population which serves as the baseline data for all future work. Many of the original results are mapped. Vital events are recorded. As new information becomes available, smaller surveys are conducted to examine particular sets of relationships. Yet the core of the work is essentially anthropological, involving participant observation and a great deal of familiarization with the community, its families and its individuals. The principal investigators carry out long, probing interviews with individuals and groups exploring aspects of demographic behaviour and broader aspects of social life. Unlike many anthropologists they work with a small team of assistants in order to build up files of information and observations about each household and the whole community. They and their assistants hold regular discussions comparing ideas and building hypotheses. These hypotheses are not hidden from the community but, whenever possible, respondents are invited to participate in the testing of these hypotheses and in the suggestion of alternative theories. There is an emphasis on change, its nature and causes. Special attention is given to the elderly and to comparing responses between generations. Village histories are constructed and published and archival material especially from the last two centuries is assembled. The particular focus of the work has varied from year to year: fertility change (Caldwell, Reddy and Caldwell, 1982b) and family planning (Caldwell *et al.*, ch.2); marriage (Caldwell *et al.*, 1983b) and family structure (Caldwell *et al.*, 1984a); sickness and death (Caldwell *et al.*, 1983a); risk insurance (Caldwell *et al.*, 1986) and education (Caldwell *et al.*, 1985).

Conclusions

One of the questions to ask at the end of this brief review of an active and developing field of research is whether we have yet progressed beyond the common-sense position that there is a need for a mix of both macro- and micro-approaches in demographic research. The Canberra meeting provided a resounding 'yes' to this for a number of reasons. First, several researchers showed that micro-approach work produced findings which conflicted with conventional wisdom derived from surveys and aggregate analysis; Aaby's paper on measles is a perfect illustration of this point. Secondly, the meeting showed that we were not simply discussing the relative merits of quantitative versus qualitative research methods; instead, the issue was the collection of evidence, its nature and its confrontation with theory. This point is still under active discussion since it is possible to build convincing cases for the operation of certain social systems without the formality of sets of testable hypotheses. Much of the work by Jack Goody on production and reproduction, for example, is based on normative statements but there is a cohesiveness to his explanations which is itself convincing (Goody and Tambiah, 1973; Goody, 1958). Neither Goody nor the practitioners of the micro-approach in demography can cease the search for exceptions which prove the rule and this is in a sense the principal check on the rightness of explanations at this level. Possibly a harder task faces users of the micro-approach in demography than those from other disciplines since demography is amongst the most numerical of the social sciences. The demographic audience remains largely sceptical of wordy explanations since their standards of proof and evidence are conditioned by an awesome respect for the often quite erroneous 'meter reading' (Bronowski, 1951) characteristic of the physical sciences.

This review has indicated that the empirical side of the field is active and capable of original thought, but the yawning gap is still the lack of a body of theory which will help with the difficult problems of contrasting levels of operation of the causal variables, the isolation of independent variables, the nature of evidence, and the task of constructing general theory from particular cases. The positive side is that some new techniques are emerging for dealing with measurements made on small numbers of people and for capturing change in the short term (e.g. Brass and Macrae, 1984). An active frontier of research is sure to be micro-simulation of more than just simple economic processes which will give us some feel for the range of possible alternatives as well as a form of sensitivity analysis of small communities to change in some key variables.

1

On the Local Context of Demographic Change*

Geoffrey McNicoll

For a number of years, many would agree, survey research on demographic behaviour has been experiencing diminishing returns. We learn the same kinds of things about more and more societies, while important and interesting questions on the theoretical frontier remain out of reach - lying, so to speak, below the focal length of this instrument. Theory-building proceeds through increasingly sophisticated causal modelling tested not against social reality in the rough, but against that recorded, imputed, cleaned and recorded version of reality that is the 'data set' of modern demography. The micro-approaches to demographic research that are the subject of this volume promise ways out of the impasse. The survey-generated demographic accounting system is retained, but the crude correlates of demographic change can now be refined to reveal the inner logic of survey-based relationships; the ambivalences suppressed in multiple-choice responses can be explored. A new, deeper empirical understanding of population change is attained.

That, at any rate, is what may be imagined. Performance, however, tends to fall short. What will it take to make the micro-studies enterprise genuinely productive for the field? Two things, in my view. First, a much less casual tie between data gathering and theory development than has existed for the most part thus far - present seminar participants, I hasten to add, surely excepted. And second, research that is informed by immediate and pressing concerns of public policy - that shows some exasperation with a time scale of expected outcomes measured in decades or in whole careers. All the future remains to make sense of the past, but efforts to initiate, speed up, and ease the pain of demographic transition in the present allow no such leisureliness. In this essay I have tried to set out some empirical research directions for the case of fertility that satisfy these criteria.

Conditions For Fertility Decline: Locus of Debate

The twin prongs of the antinatalist strategy adopted by most governments concerned with high fertility and endorsed in most

---

* An earlier version of this chapter, cast in terms of comments on the UN World Population Plan of Action, was presented at the UN Expert Group Meeting on Fertility and Family, New Delhi, January 1983.

writing on population policy are first, actions that directly or indirectly raise the new costs of children to parents, and second, measures that reduce the monetary and psychic costs to individuals, of fertility regulation. Families under this strategy, however, exist in a curiously empty world - autonomous entities exercising their rights to reproduce under the influence of disembodied forces of economy and culture. Largely ignored is another group of factors that also impinge on fertility and where government interventions, for better or worse, have profound effects on demographic outcomes: the local economic, social and administrative arrangements of the society above the level of the family. Conceptually, of course, the fertility effects of these arrangements can ultimately be assessed in terms of the economics (if broadly enough construed) of marriage, of children, and of fertility regulation; but both in interpreting country experience and in discussing policy issues a separate treatment of them is valuable.

Until the 1970s there would probably have been a fairly wide consensus as to the social and economic conditions that support a low-fertility regime. Success in economic development could be tied more directly to demographic change: fertility decline was promoted by, for example, increased private costs of children - especially in terms of education; higher rates of female participation in the formal labour force - both before marriage and after childbearing; and the emergence of institutional alternatives to family support networks in smoothing life-cycle fluctuations of income and coping with risk. The identification of such constituent factors provided detailed guidance for policy; in the rhetoric of the 1974 Bucharest conference, it was not development itself that was the best contraceptive but the diminished economic value of children, more female employment, or state provision of social security. Yet something was lost in this move from the general to the specific. The separate conditions supposedly conducive to low fertility were of course not individually sufficient; but nor were they assuredly individually necessary. Striking exceptions came too readily to mind.

There had always been cases - historically, France was the classic one - where low fertility had been attained seemingly against many social and economic odds (sometimes in the face of vigorous government efforts to oppose it). Usually, explanations could be framed in terms of economic exigencies, especially as a consequence of gradually raised and then dashed aspirations. And France, everyone could agree, was *sui generis*. Other apparent anomalies - a number of Caribbean countries with fairly low fertility as early as the 1950s, for example - largely escaped notice. But China, showing large fertility declines since the late 1960s, was a startling new fact - and with 30 per cent of the Third World's population, could not be classified as an exception. Nor could other low-fertility regions: Kerala and Tamil Nadu in India, East Java in Indonesia, virtually all of Thailand, or Sri Lanka, to mention only some of the more striking instances. Fertility decline in such regions among poor, predominantly rural populations, suggested that straightforward linking of demographic and economic change left out important parts of the truth.

Candidates for such omissions were many. Three of the most popular, each with strong support on other grounds, were expansion of formal education, reduction of inequality in income distribution, and enhancement of the economic position of women. In each of these cases, however, and in others too where congenial statistical associations could be found with fertility (although in the case of income distribution even the statistical conclusion was controversial), the likelihood is that the specific characteristic, in addition to whatever direct influence it has on fertility, is also a reflection of some of the same conditions that have made for lowered fertility. For education, the sources of demand for schooling are a large part of what calls for investigation if we are to understand the fertility connection; for income distribution, the same is true for the underlying features of economy and polity that generate observed distributions; for women's status, our attention should focus on the supports for an existing pattern of power relationships within the family and for a gender-segmented labour market outside it. Moving the debate to these grounds makes the analytical task at once both more coherent and less accessible to familiar quantitative methodologies. The territory thus defined - mapped only sketchily in the discussion that follows under headings of locality, administration and mentalités - is the proper domain of micro-studies of fertility change.

Locality: Economic and Social Configurations

Shifts in territorial social organization, in the ways and degrees to which individuals are linked to local community and to other kinds of social grouping with a territorial basis, are among the most familiar institutional changes that accompany development and demographic transition. The stereotypical picture is of a cohesive, all-embracing village community gradually losing its members through urban migration and losing authority over those who remain. In essentials, this picture survives the fairly drastic revisions that have punctured whatever Elysian qualities observers once attached to the intitial state: the village as a hotbed of class struggle, factional strife and interpersonal feuds lends itself less readily to casual personification than did the idyllic village republic, but may still have been no less a source of rigorous social control over most members' individual behaviour.

The reasons for the weakening of village authority structures are well known. They include the geographical widening of labour markets allowed by improvements in transport, making extensive rural-based commuting a common-place; the growth of rural non-agricultural occupations, that leaves full-time farmers and farm workers a diminishing minority of the labour force even in what are still thought of as agrarian economies; pervasive monetization of exchange relations, that coverts localized patron-client ties into more anonymous contractual arrangements; the penetration of urban consumer values and consumption patterns into rural hinterlands; and so on. Countless village studies around the world document such trends and changes.

The demographic implications of these past and prospective changes are complex and variegated. Unlike the historical situation in Europe or Japan, in most of the contemporary Third World community influence over demographic behaviour has not been directed toward control over marriage or establishment of a household. Indeed in many societies the emphasis is quite the opposite - social pressures have compelled very early female marriage and early start of childbearing. The community control, such as it was, applied rather to birth intervals, with breastfeeding or postpartum taboos on sexual intercourse as the instrument, and net reproduction rather than fertility as the perhaps unrecognized goal.

Such an arrangement may have been needed in coping with very high mortality, but it meshes also with the requirements of sustaining patriarchal social systems, with lineage dominating conjugal ties. (See the illuminating analyses of West African examples in Lesthaeghe, 1980 and Caldwell, 1982 ch.3). It was however by no means limited to those societies. In much of East and Southeast Asia and South India, for example, families have for long been essentially nuclear in form, with women not typically subjugated to the husband's family or tightly constrained in occupational choice. Yet there too the fine-tuned control of local demography through marriage in the European/Japanese pattern did not emerge.

As social control at the community level recedes, families and their individual members gain greater autonomy while losing whatever informal insurance function (minimal though it may have been) the former regime supported. For fertility, decisions may well have to be made on a more narrowly economic basis than before. The timing of this process has varied widely by region, located generations ago in some and only begun in the last two decades in others. There are similarly wide differences in the nature of the rural economy into which families are cast - in terms of its technological level and the alternative kinds of institutional arrangements it offers, and hence in terms of the economic incentives influencing fertility that it contains.

The variety of situations here has been the fly in the ointment of classical demographic theory. Fertility decline is by no means a necessary consequence of attenuated patronage and community roles; continued high fertility reflecting an income-diversification strategy by families is one plausible outcome, for example. An economy's employment structure (in particular, the opportunities it offers for female and for child employment), the returns it confers on education, and the degree of employment security it affords are important factors in characterizing fertility incentives. Any comprehensive analysis of the determinants of rural fertility trends must take these factors into account. Development policies that try to impose new organizational forms on rural labour have potentially significant fertility implications.

Communities may of course lose any significant control over the economic life of their members while retaining it in certain other domains - such as in defining appropriate marriage ages or asserting standards of morality. This situation arises especially when work is largely located outside the community's boundaries - as, for example, in the case of fringe settlements providing daily workers to urban labour markets. Economic interest here would likely militate against population control even if it were a feasible social policy. Rural villages or urban settlements in effect might individually benefit by exploiting the rest of the economy through migrant labour (commuting, short-term migration, or even long-term migration provided remittances continue), in a classic 'prisoner's dilemma' situation analogous to that usually defined at the individual or family level, with no expected gain from fertility limitation.

Administration: Non-programmatic Government

The main institutions that have picked up functions that once were the province of the local community are of course those of government, national and local. In any country, there is an in-built tension and potential for conflict between vertically-structured, sectorally-defined government activities, extending down to individual families or citizens, and horizontally-organized units of local government. In developing countries, the former tend to get more publicity (and control contacts with international agencies) while the latter turn out to be more crucial in determining results. As development proceeds, at least in the contemporary world, modern information and control technology enables national governments to bypass this local involvement when they wish, and the role of local government tends to become increasingly trivial.

The withering of local government over the course of development should have important benefits for the economy. It removes a potentially damaging impediment to innovation and easy factor mobility at a time when those characteristics are increasingly needed for vigorous economic growth. Conversely, where political choice dictates a continued strong role for local administration, there is likely to be considerable economic cost in foregone growth. The recent administrative history of China provides an interesting case in point. One main thrust of the Dengist reforms has been to pull back local administration from the commune to the county level. The communes were initially superimposed on market areas (usually with headquarters in market towns); at the short-lived peak of Maoist radicalism in 1958 there were fruitless efforts to make these gangling units into cohesive, solidary groups; since that time the commune has gradually yielded authority and the latest changes have virtually left it a market town again. The retreat all along was for hard-nosed economic reasons.

But how does demographic change fit into this picture? The suggested incompatibility between the style of local administration that is most conducive to economic growth and the style that in effect has evolved for political control has important implications for population growth and population policy. To the extent fertility is a part of parental economic strategy, local government sets the ground-rules within which planning has to be undertaken and defines the contingencies that need to be allowed for. Where the system limits upward economic mobility, the second-best strategies that families resort to may well involve different (presumably higher) fertility outcomes - a trade-off recognized in classical demographic theorizing.

Population policy as a national programmatic activity also typically seeks to work through local administration in some measures. Its achievements thus can be constrained by the nature and scope of that system. In particular, as discussed below, some of the most effective antinatalist policies have been those that allied themselves closely with local government and succeeded in mobilizing its energies to their program goals. Here proposals for administrative reform can pose a conflict between economic and demographic ends in an acute form.

Mentalités: Traditions Great and Small

It would simplify matters greatly to believe (as many social scientists do believe) that cultural influences on behaviour are merely a kind of aura surrounding material realities, creating a slight interference for hard-headed analysis - adding to the error term of one's regressions - but basically a peripheral concern. The history of research on peasant economy lends some support to this view: there, efforts to portray peasant farmers as operating outside a straightforward economic calculus, seeking a 'limited good', clinging to tradition-bound behaviour, and so on, have been largely discredited. In some ways the model of the peasant as a fine-tuned profit-maximizer is not more firmly ensconced in the economic literature than the analogous assumption applied to the modern corporation - trends in the theory of the firm are decidedly in the opposite direction. But it does not follow, even if the 'rational peasant' turned out to be more rational than the rest of us in economic dealings, that demographic behaviour too is thereby taken care of. Becker's dictum that 'all human behaviour can be viewed as involving participants who maximize their utility from a stable set of preferences and accumulate an optimal amount of information and other inputs in a variety of markets' (Becker, 1976) becomes progressively less helpful as the subject moves further away from getting and spending. Fertility is quite far removed.

This said, one can go a long way in explaining demographic change without having to draw on the cloudy techniques of cultural analysis. That does not mean that the cultural content here is slight, but rather that cultural change can lead to concomitant changes in social organization that have a convenient tangibility when it comes to analysis (the direction of causality can also of course be the opposite). Thus, the important cultural change associated with the 'opening' of village communities - the gradual loss of the localized 'little tradition' and its replacement by a more uniform set of values of an urban-based popular culture - can be treated as if it were a by-product of the organizational change.

More problematic is the case of cultural change that does not seem to have a social structural counterpart. It can sometimes be argued that this is a lag phenomenon: fertility, for example, remains at a previous high level for some time after socioeconomic conditions shift toward favouring lower fertility, but the reaction time, perhaps because of the internal coherence and thus stability of the values involved, is long. Conceding such a cultural system, however, even if loosely articulated and not free of inconsistencies, identifies a potentially important subject for study. The widespread casual use of the term 'diffusion' in fertility analysis as if it were explanatory rather than simply descriptive, underlines the need for pursuing that research direction. The reasons that some ideas 'diffuse' and not others must be sought in specific local cultural and social structural environments.

Posing still more difficulty is the case where fertility change seems to occur simultaneously over widely different economies and societies. Bourgeois-Pichat (1981) has pointed to this happening in Europe in the reversals of fertility trends occurring around 1942, 1965 and possibly 1980, and argues that it presents a phenomenon calling for a wholly new (and as yet undeveloped) approach to understanding demographic change. Even here, however, the starting point is held to be a thorough knowledge of local situations.

Premises About the Determinants of Fertility

The preceding demarcation of content does little to set operational guidelines for micro-level research on fertility change. For that purpose I return to the desiderata proposed earlier of research closely informed by theory and policy. What is our theory? Unfortunately there is no well-agreed answer: vigorous arguments persist over the nature of fertility determination. Many disputes over strategies to regulate fertility originate in such differences of view. The problem is not, of course, the immediate biological and behavioural factors accounting for variations among fertility rates - the so-called proximate determinants: those are comparatively well understood, and the unresolved issues are mostly technical. The source of disagreement concerns rather the nature of the influence of socioeconomic and cultural factors on fertility and the nature of fertility decision making. It would be a diversion from the purpose of this chapter to discuss the intricacies that surround the subject of fertility determinants (they form the content, for example, of the massive study recently conducted by the U.S. National Academy of Sciences - (see Bulatao *et al*., 1983), but a very brief statement of the theoretical position taken here is a necessary basis for the later comments on research directions (see McNicoll, 1980a for a fuller account).

Four propositions describe the broad framework:

1. The factors that are consciously taken into account and thus implicitly traded off against each other in making fertility decisions define a person's domain of adaptive behaviour for fertility. Within such a domain the economist's consumer-choice model or its psychological equivalent is appropriate for analyzing fertility outcomes (aside from the element of chance that is always present). Such a domain may be so narrow as to leave little scope for deliberate choice (as in a situation of so-called 'natural' fertility), or be so large that the boundaries are irrevelant.

2. The boundaries of such a domain are governed by the particular institutional and cultural setting experienced by the individual, which brings certain factors into apposition with fertility and not others. Changes in this setting may indirectly elicit changes in individual behaviour, but not through a simple one-to-one mapping. Exploration of the dynamics of changes in this setting is likely to play a major part in the explanation of fertility change.

3. Fertility decline may entail a radical widening of domain boundaries (as in the natural fertility to fully controlled fertility model), a shift in boundaries (possibly a narrowing), or a change in the economics of fertility within a constant domain.

4. Different groups in a population (particularly groups defined by cultural or economic setting, but possibly also men and women) may experience different routes of fertility transition. (Changes in the relative sizes of such groups are obviously one source of overall fertility change.)

The major task of analysis of fertility change in the terms of this framework is to explore the shifting pattern of constraints on adaptive behaviour in fertility over time, and in particular over the course of economic development, relating this pattern to economic, institutional and cultural change in the society. Accommodated within this framework are various familiar models of fertility change, here greatly simplified:

The 'Coale Transition'

Fertility decline in this model is seen as a shift from a 'natural fertility' regime to a regime of deliberate individual birth control by parents, induced by unspecified cultural or institutional changes in the society - in effect, expanding the domain of adaptive behaviour (or moving away from a boundary solution). See Coale (1973).

The 'Chicago Transition'

This is a cutback in the demand for children resulting from a straightforward rise in their relative cost, typically associated with an increasing value of time. No domain shifts are posited. See Nerlove (1974).

The 'Caldwell Transition'

In this model a decisive change in the constraints on adaptive behaviour is proposed. Children, from being associated with parental - and especially patriarchal - consumption, come to be linked instead to patterns of sentiment within the nuclear family group. See Caldwell (1982, chs.4,5).

The framework evidently allows for other kinds of fertility transition as well. Not all feasible or even historically-observed transitions are of equal policy interest, and hence warrant the same effort at comprehension. Considerations of practicability and of welfare costs, not to mention ethical scruples, presumably should influence research emphases.

Scope For Population Policy

A government's role in development is not necessarily ineffectual when it entails promoting grass-roots change, but rather success or failure in that endeavour hinges largely on the way in which the effort makes use of, rather than conflicts with the realities of local social organization. Notwithstanding this fact, the temptation to evade the complexities of the local setting in designing policy is obviously great, and in the case of fertility is rarely resisted. Two courses of action, covering the majority of antinatalist policies in the Third World today (and, for that matter, the pronatalist policies in the First and, more particularly, Second Worlds), illustrate this evasion.

The first course has been to limit programmatic action to management of an efficient distribution system for modern contraceptive supplies and services, together with attendant publicity. Local-level social organization is recognized only by offering a mixture of methods. The empirical justification for this policy course is found in responses to survey questions asking reproductive-age women about their desired completed family size, questions which routinely reveal a substantial gap between stated fertility desires and likely fertility outcomes - an 'unmet need' that a family planning program endeavours to fill. As market research, the surveys yielding these findings are singularly unenlightening (it is hard to imagine a corporate client being satisfied with such a basis for investment in a distribution network). Yet for them to go further - in exploring the depth of demand, its price elasticity, and the countervailing constraints that might deflect individual behaviour from declared desires or intentions - would take them deep into the dimensions of local society discussed earlier.

The second broad course of action in population policy that has equally sought to skirt these intricacies has been derived from the aggregate statistical associations of education, child mortality, women's status, and so on, with low fertility. Reading causality into these relationships yields policy recommendations that call for wholly unexceptionable measures well within the mainstream development program of any even moderately progressive government. What is not usually part of the policy content is specification of the local-level detail of the program intervention. Yet in virtually each case (mortality reduction is probably the sole exception) the fertility impact depends in large measure precisely on that detail. Here is the likely source of the considerable statistical 'noise' in the aggregate relationship. The broad similarities of program action in the particular policy area among countries account for the relationship being detected through that noise, but the policy instrument thus derived is extremely blunt. To hone it calls for grubbing about in the 'unexplained' variance.

A curious feature of these two dominant policy courses should be noted. Both are largely free of political costs. Family planning programs obviously absorb resources that have an opportunity cost, but their share of the budget tends to be trivial; moral objections, with fairly few exceptions, have proven evanescent and readily catered to by adjustments of method mix. Development programs that have a hoped-for fertility payoff are generally seen as goods in themselves, and political battles over them, if needed at all, are fought well away from demographic territory. This situation should probably arouse suspicion: can a social change as profound as, say a halving of average family size be attained through policy measures that exact no appreciable costs? A free lunch of this sort is on the face of it implausible. Perhaps the policy bite here is less than meets the eye.

Both these policy directions have claimed substantial successes, and in combination are taken by many observers to account for most of the current fertility declines in the Third World. Yet a case can be made that such 'success' has been in fair degree accidental - an outcome of changes in society and economy that owe little to awakened government concerns with rapid population growth. Even where government action has been influential, an element of fortuitousness probably remains: the reasons may have as much to do with the happenstance of local conditions that are conducive to fertility decline as to the intervention itself.

The argument, in other words, comes down to this: a lack of close attention to the local-level content of policy action, and to how that content meshes with existing features of local policy and culture, leads to an erratic record of accomplishment. Even when positive results can be convincingly claimed, very likely they have far from fully exploited the existing potentialities for change, or have been attained at higher social cost than was necessary. A corollary is that an analytical focus on local setting rather than on vertically-defined program activity (whether in family planning or development) will better illuminate the range of options for population policy and may well point to directions not yet explored.

Some examples will help to give substance to this argument.

Increasing the Salience of the Economic Calculus of Fertility

There is evidence in many Third World settings that children confer net economic benefits on their parents or on others (such as husband's lineage) in a position to influence fertility patterns. Even if children imposed a net burden, moreover, they may still be economically valued in the absence of any more secure means of storing value for the parents' old age or of hedging against misfortune. In these settings any increase in the salience of fertility decisions as an aspect of family economic strategy would merely reinforce high fertility levels.

Yet in other situations this may well not be the case. The conventional 'family planner's view' of fertility transition is of natural fertility slowly supplanted by individual awareness of the manifold benefits (among them, economic benefits) of smaller families, converting a latent unmet need for contraception into effective demand - a Coale transition. Making demand effective, in this congenial world, simply calls for publicity campaigns promoting family planning methods. Such an expectation has been scornfully dismissed both by those who put store in the economic logic of individual fertility strategies and by those who analogously point to fertility as being determined within a more or less coherent and resilient cultural system. Recent highly-intriguing evidence from a major series of family planning experiments in Bangladesh, however, argues for careful consideration of that dismissal (see below).

Other initial states in which economic decision making is impeded by countervailing cultural or institutional circumstances may equally be cases where the issue is the salience of the fertility calculus rather than the net balance of incentives. An illustration of such a situation would be Indonesia in the 1960s: there it can be argued that a combination of the extreme politicization of day-to-day life, where every local dispute or policy debate was cast in terms of increasingly violent party politics, and the uncertainties of an economy sliding into hyper-inflation precluded the necessary degree of stability of setting that is plausibly required for long-range family economic planning to make sense. Stability was attained following a resolution of the political impasse, creating a setting in which the economics of fertility could come to the forefront as a matter for individual decision making. (See McNicoll and Singarimbun, 1983). Analogous if less striking cases than this particular one are probably common.

Linking Fertility Policy to Local Administration

Earlier in this chapter I distinguished between administration systems that while functioning to maintain political stability incidentally quenched economic innovation, and those that were intentionally minimalist as a means of promoting growth and technological advance. Where the pace of economic growth is rapid, the chances are, on the one hand, that fertility (if not population growth) is moving sharply downward anyway under the socioeconomic changes taking place and, on the other hand, that the relative burden of population growth is not unduly heavy - absorbing, say, two percentage points out of a GNP growth rate of 6 - 8 per cent or more, as in South Korea or Malaysia. In extreme cases of government population concern (Singapore is the main example) explicit efforts to administer economic disincentives nevertheless mounted, but more commonly policy action is a good deal less strenuous.

Where, in contrast, economic growth is comparatively slow and population expansion takes a large proportion of it, one evident option for an antinatalist policy is to ally itself to local government in an effort to use administrative pressures to achieve results. China in the 1970s would be a case in point. The potential problem is that the administrative apparatus thus enlisted in the antinatalist effort may be part of the reason for slow economic growth in the first place. Administrative reforms that are designed to release economic energies may at the same time relax pressures on fertility.

There are, of course, solutions to such difficulties, each with its own social costs. A fine-grained assessment of how local administration in fact operates, with a sensitivity to demographic as well as economic incentive structures, is the basic requirement for identifying low-cost routes.

Ad hoc, Specialized Institutional Design

In its modern guise local government is a specialized institution. Its concerns may range across provision of primary and secondary education, water supply, enforcement of building codes, and police and fire protection, but in total the content is quite narrow. Large areas of activity, especially in the economy, lie outside its scope. In earlier stages of development, less is excluded from its concerns - often at some cost (as argued above) to economic performance.

In devising institutional arrangements conducive to a moderating of population growth, there are simple alternatives to all-embracing local authority that nevertheless avoid what are sometimes seen as symmetrically distasteful *laissez faire* approaches. These entail the design of specialized institutions (governmental or not) to counter the pronatalist incentives faced by particular groups in the population - groups in the main not defined in terms of residence so that the institution is less at risk of merging with the pre-existing government structure. In rural development, for example, the economic security problems of marginal landholders and landless agricultural workers are properly seen as calling for this kind of attention. Co-operative organization of various kinds is the mainline approach here. The 1976 Asian Agricultural Survey, for example, called for formation of 'semi-spontaneous, small, primary organizations operating on the basis of direct participation and serving well defined common interests... [and able to] generate measurable private gains for their participants' (Asian Development Bank, 1978, pp.228-9). A different option, lacking the potential solidarity element but still with important impact on individual and family economic security, is the guaranteed employment scheme - the best known example of which is that of Maharashtra state in India. Enhanced economic security has a plausible downward influence on fertility in many settings (for a strong argument on these lines in the case of employment guarantee schemes, see Cain and Lieberman, 1982).

Community-Level Demographic Control

Although community influence on family and individual behaviour is progressively weakened and narrowed over the course of economic development, a residual role for it in the demographic sphere may still be feasible. The possibility mentioned earlier of a community's economic interests being served by a 'remittance' strategy, or, if permanent outmigration is significant, the possible need for high fertility in order to maintain population size, provide reasons why fertility control may not be socially favoured at this level. Policy options that seek to internalize part of the social costs of high fertility within small communities as a means of stimulating antinatalist social pressures nevertheless may warrant consideration in some settings. (For a discussion of such policies see McNicoll, 1975).

One objection to this policy direction is that it seems to assume a commonality of interest that simply does not exist in many communities. There may however still be prospects for generating common interests that in some domains (women's status might be an example) could override existing division. Interestingly, although community level policies appear to be most relevant for rural areas, where territorial boundaries have evident meaning, the 'common interest' problem is in some ways more easily addressed in urban settings where communities are generally more homogeneous by social class.

Micro-Approaches to Fertility Research

What then is the research agenda implied by the above discussion of fertility theory and policy? What should we most be trying to find out, and how?

Much work I believe remains to be done in what can be termed comparative institutional analysis of the local context of fertility behaviour. A persuasive institutional explanation for an observed pattern of fertility change is hard to improve upon. I have argued elsewhere (McNicoll, 1980a) that it is a good way short of conclusive, but it nevertheless takes us far. Yet efforts to construct such explanations frequently come up against sheer ignorance of institutional forms and dynamics - even, sometimes, the lack of fairly elementary mapping of social organization. Filling in such gaps is a form of micro-level research that may well be comparatively undemanding.

A view of society that emphasizes institutional arrangements does have a certain crudity. To its disparagers, it presents a picture of 'well-trained sheep-dogs picking their way through institutional mazes' (Cicourel, 1973). Yet as the focus of attention narrows down to individuals, attempting to comprehend the actor's behaviour in terms of his thinking and perception, it is all too easy to lose sight of the institutional setting that to a possibly large extent constrains that behaviour. Getting into people's heads is fine if one can get out again. Of course the subjectivity of an observer is never total: the categories brought to bear, in the field setting or in later interpretive analysis, inevitably entail pre-suppositions, some no doubt unrecognized.

Achieving a balance between institutional and cognitive depictions of fertility change would clearly be highly desirable. On a non-operational level, both of these enter the framework of fertility transition I described earlier. A potentially promising route to give substance to this framework is Cicourel's (1974, p.204) suggested strategy of 'controlled indefinite triangulation' - an iterative procedure whereby respondents are given an opportunity to react to their own previous accounts, the accounts of others, and the interpretations of the researcher. Independently, Leibenstein has suggested a somewhat similar research plan.

Much more could of course be accomplished, and much more rapidly, were there situations where proper experimental procedures could be applied. The singular importance of the work of the International Centre for Diarrhoeal Disease Research, Bangladesh in family planning research is that it comprises carefully controlled experiments on a scale sufficient to detect induced demographic responses. Some of the findings are close to being startling, suggesting as they do that fairly slight differences in health and family planning delivery patterns can have substantially different effects on fertility (see Phillips *et al.*, 1982). The possibility that a cognitive shift in the fertility decision-making domain could occur, so to speak, almost casually is discomfiting to a broad range of social scientists.

Any discussion of micro-approaches to demographic research involving field practitioners of various sorts is likely to generate vigorous debates on the relative merits of quasi-anthropological studies, focus groups, in-depth surveys, and no doubt a number of other data-gathering procedures. Not being a party to such debates, I would conclude this chapter by expressing the hope that equal attention will be given to epistemological aspects of these approaches. 'The real micro-level,' Garfinkel (1981, p.73) writes, 'consists of a set of individuals together with a non-trivial sociology.' Research that can perceive and retain that non-triviality is the real micro-level approach.

2

Investigating the Nature of Population Change in South India: Experimenting with a Micro-Approach

John C. Caldwell, P.H. Reddy, and Pat Caldwell

This chapter will neither focus on the problems encountered when attempting to examine the context of population change by employing large scale surveys nor report on the findings of the 1979-83 project on the Origins of Population Change in South India. The former has been treated in two papers (Caldwell, Reddy and Caldwell, 1982a; Caldwell, 1985) and the latter in a series of reports.[1] The aim here will be to reflect in retrospect on what we tried to do and why we chose that course, and then to consider the degree of success attained.

In 1979 we knew that there was something worth investigating in South India. The National Sample Survey claimed that rural fertility in Karnataka was low, with a crude birth rate less than thirty per thousand, more than one-sixth below that estimated for rural India as a whole, and probably over one-quarter lower than what it had been 20 years earlier (Registrar General of India, 1983; Department of Family Welfare, 1982a). We wished to ascertain whether this was true even in areas not affected by the Green Revolution, and we also wished to explore suggestions that there were socioeconomic and religious differentials in the acceptance of family planning. Accordingly, census and other records were employed to identify dry-farming areas over 100 kilometres from either Bangalore or Mysore, with a population containing a substantial number of both the poorer Harijan (formerly, the 'untouchables') group and Muslims. It seemed preferable that our main centre should contain a primary health unit. It had to be in one of the large areas covered by the Indian Population Project (a program of the World Bank, Government of India and State Government of Karnataka which had established the Population Centre in Bangalore) but we believed it should not have been subject to an intensive campaign by that project. We randomly chose one centre which fulfilled these criteria.

A research site, when only one is chosen, can hardly be said to be typical except in terms of the criteria employed. This is a continuing problem of anthropology and can be justified both on the grounds that it is better to know one place well than all places superficially and also that many interrelations found in one centre probably hold more generally even in contrasting areas. Ultimately, associated work was carried out in six very different localities and we increasingly had the opportunity to discern what was a purely local phenomenon and what was much more general.[2]

The choice of locality had both its strengths and its weaknesses. The local birth rate had come down to about 32 per thousand, a decline of around 13 points over 20 years. There was something to explain. The different situations of the Muslims and the Harijans were important and we were able to investigate these smaller communities to a satisfactory extent only because they were sufficiently strongly represented in the area. On the other hand, this decision meant that we were restricted to a multi-caste village with a population of around 2,500. We soon found that the surrounding smaller hamlets were very different in their social, economic and occupational structures. In these hamlets fewer than 10 per cent of adult males work outside agriculture (compared with 50 per cent in the larger village), education is more recent and at lower levels, and most of the population is usually of a single caste. Almost half the population of India live in small hamlets of this kind. We soon added eight of them to our study, totalling another 2,500 persons. This raises an important question of interpretation with regard to anthropological studies in India, and perhaps elsewhere. Most of the anthropological research seems to have been done in larger villages where there is a greater diversity to study and where it is often easier to find somewhere to stay. Nevertheless, clearly much is lost by ignoring the smaller, simpler centres.

Our first focus was on changing fertility, although we later found that this cannot be fully understood without a substantial knowledge of changes in family structure, marriage, morbidity and mortality. The single-theme survey or investigation has very serious limitations.

The Method of Investigation

There were important decisions about how to start such an investigation, who would do it, and how to do it.

We retained much of the demographer's armoury. We carried out initial mapping for census and sampling purposes. The maps became more important than we had anticipated because we subsequently employed them to show distributions of characteristics and behavioural phenomena that tended to generate hypotheses for testing. We carried out a full initial census which identified all the population and permitted the employment of retrospective data to determine demographic trends. Because subequent household research vastly increased our knowledge, the initial census data were to be considerably modified. This was a salutary lesson in terms of reliance on one-time census or survey findings. One of the greatest problems is securing adherence to definitions of who actually constitutes a household and normally resides in it; even some of the most sophisticated households, who seemed to have fully understood our definitions, were later found to have erred, generally by including members who usually live elsewhere. A few deliberately misreport because of apprehension about land reform and other fears.

We also made records of vital events and annual censuses, but probably did not devote as great a proportion of our resources to this effort as would have been the case if our major focus had been there rather than on the social and economic context of demographic behaviour. Nevertheless, the continual checking and updating of household schedules on every visit made it difficult for vital events to pass unrecorded even if they had been missed by the vital registration surveys.

Our demographic background also played a part in the decisions taken about investigators. The three principal investigators could have carried out a typical anthropological investigation, but we decided that we wished to increase the scale of the work and usually collaborated with about eight to ten assistants. The original assistants came from a variety of backgrounds but were selected because of rural origins and training, usually a graduate degree, in the social sciences. Most of the training for the research project was essentially apprenticeship on the job.

The central aspect of such research is that the research assistants should not become either survey interviewers or independent investigators. The responsibility for formulating new hypotheses, or at least for identifying those that should be explored further, and for exactly specifying them, must remain with the principal investigators. This is achieved partly by placing substantial emphasis on the importance of ideas and hypotheses and encouraging assistants to report all their ideas and hunches. This can be institutionalized in the form of nightly sessions where the whole team discusses the experiences of the day and the new ideas which have surfaced. To some extent, it also happens when the principal investigators de-brief assistants after household visits. Nevertheless, the chief instrument for developing new hypotheses is long investigatory interviews by the principal investigators themselves. It is during these interviews that new leads are identified and followed, even those relating to themes which had not previously been strictly specified as part of the investigation. Thus, the body of hypotheses expands continually, with a mounting feeling of excitement in the survey team, and each day is clearly a new one and more advanced than those that preceded it. Obviously the original body of hypotheses owes much to reading, and field demographers miss a great deal, and undertake much unnecessary work, if they start their research without being saturated with the anthropological, historical, economic and agricultural literature on the region.

Even at best, a team of assistants cannot fully communicate all their thoughts to each other, and even a team of eight or twelve cannot cope with getting to know well more than a fraction of 800 families. We have constantly wondered how the single anthropologist can do much more than scratch the surface. Does a man, for instance, largely get to know those adult males who often appear in public places? Does he get to know well a small selection of families who are atypical in that they are easily accessible? We were determined that this would not happen and accordingly used a sampling approach to determine which households we would investigate. Thus, at the outset our enquiry into fertility control adopted a deterministic approach, namely the investigation of all households characterized by having at least one woman 30-39 years of age, currently married and living with her husband, and with at least three living children. This was fairly satisfactory until we wished to extend the enquiry to cover other aspects of demographic behaviour; it became clear that we had devoted a great deal of effort to familiarizing ourselves with an atypical cross-section as far as these additional studies were concerned. Even when we studied fertility control and decision-making, restricting selection of families had the drawback that we could not get to know the small but important group who begin to think of fertility control or practise it at lower parities. However, there were always other families outside our sample whom we came to know well from everyday contact. They were often above average in education, loquacity or self-analysis and necessarily contributed to our hypotheses if not to our detailed study files.

With our expanding range of hypotheses and matters to investigate, we interviewed households repeatedly, often for hours at a time. At first we intended to talk to each individual separately, but such interviews formed only a small proportion of the total. More often we spoke to a group whose number and composition changed over time according to work needs. Our suspicion of group interviewing lessened as it became obvious that the interaction of a number of people led far more often to the memory of newer or more exact information than it did to the suppression of lesser personalities by more forceful ones. Where necessary we followed into the fields individuals who appeared to have something more to disclose or we made a later separate appointment. Often the group sent for someone who had specialized knowledge.

At first we tended to maintain the distinction between interviewer and interviewee and not to disclose our full hand with regard to the research. As we became more experienced, and on subsequent interviews, we tended more and more to take them into our confidence. We revealed our working hypotheses and our lines of thought and they either provided additional information or produced evidence to show why these ideas were untenable. Often they worried about interpretation, consulted other people, and came back with new ideas.

Interviewers kept notes, to be later written into household files which were periodically synthesized and summarized. The principal investigators also kept anthropologists' notebooks which proved to be indispensible not only for recording important points but more significantly for providing the material from which many hypotheses were later developed. The original census in the larger village was not extensive because we wished to obtain as much material as possible from the in-depth interviews and because we did not wish to force people to adopt fixed responses before the more flexible discussions. Both these concepts proved to be wrong. Unless one employs a fixed schedule in the anthropological interviews then the simpler and more quantifiable data are not always collected completely or in a uniform way. There was also little evidence that previous responses were either remembered or consciously adopted. Consequently, we expanded the baseline census-survey for the smaller villages and supplemented that of the large village. This proved to be invaluable for obtaining an ecological perspective of the whole area, for obtaining a pattern of systematic responses, and for testing such responses against the evidence obtained from the alternative approach.

As we began to examine new selected topics, we increasingly undertook small highly-focused surveys on such matters as the arrangement of marriage, the partitioning of households, and the enrolment in and withdrawal of children from school. In all cases, such focused surveys were preceded by anthropological approaches and were followed up by more work of this type.

The heart of much of the work was the participant observation enshrined in anthropological methodology. We found that only some aspects of matters which interested us occurred sufficiently frequently or sufficiently publicly for the method to work without a good deal of contrivance, especially in the form of the directing of conversations. The team lived in a range of households and this provided different participatory experiences. We decided against the employment of paid informants, but their role was replaced by various constant companions who took an increasing interest in finding out exactly what had happened in their community and how change had taken place.

On occasion, we took the opportunity of some unusual event to redirect research in the hope of understanding that event and drawing some more general truths from the experience. Perhaps the best example of this was the redeployment of research resources during 1983 as the drought in the southern Deccan worsened, in order to understand the nature of risk and the implications of risk aversion in more normal times.

Our central concern was with change, both demographic and related socioeconomic change. We necessarily had an historical perspective. Increasingly, we found it of value to discuss all our topics with the more elderly people and the very old became constant contacts. In this type of investigation, supported as they were by much about the past that had already been learnt, they became articulate and often provided better descriptions of the situation decades ago than of the present.

In all our questions, there was a continuing emphasis on change, on the sequence of events, and on the reasons that things altered. There is very little distinction between good social science and social history.

The Nature of Evidence and Proof

The more detailed fieldwork of this type that one does, the more everything begins to fit into place. The proof of this lies in the fact that the investigator can eventually provide reasonably accurate answers when new questions are posited about the society without having to rush off to find respondents. This knowledge of the society comes from a preceding density of questions that no survey can possibly approach. It also arises from the flexibility of the interviewing method whereby new leads can at once be followed. One increasingly wonders whether the relationships shown by the statistical associations between variables in a large scale survey are much more than abstractions associating pairs of reflections or proxies with each other.

Two other problems associated with the survey approach become ever more apparent. The first is the inevitable tendency to identify the respondent as the chief actor in the events. Usually, the respondent has been forced to supply evidence and views about matters which are regarded by the patriarch or his wife as none of the respondent's business and as outside the area where she could make decisions and act. Increasingly, one wonders how the survey can understand anything without a family, neighbourhood and community context. The second is that the necessary rapid interviewing and the search for a limited number of answers, usually in some priority order, mean that respondents give a completely artificial impression of conflicting with each other in their testimonies. It is the mechanism of the survey itself which produces the wide distribution of evidence. Thus, in the work on the 1983 drought, we found a surprising consensus, but no large scale survey would have achieved this.

The most important issue is whether we just receive and record a body of impressions or whether we can establish some findings with a high degree of probability. Our census-surveys or subsequent surveys of much larger populations can produce some satisfactory significant statistical associations, although even in this case it is the micro-approach work which will provide the best evidence on the direction of causation.

However, the justification for much of the effort expended on micro-approach investigations must be of a different type, that which justifies anthropological research. This method of proof is a form of the scientific method. It rests upon the formulation of hypotheses and the subsequent attempt to disprove them by accumulating evidence. It rests also upon prediction based on the reasonably secure informational base already established and the investigation to ascertain whether the predictions hold good.

One problem is the type of evidence adduced for proof or disproof. Much, although not all of it, is necessarily subjective and judgemental. Nevertheless, its total mass can be very convincing. Nor does one fall into the survey trap of basing proof only on the most quantifiable evidence when such data are often of only secondary relevance.

Perhaps a more serious problem is the generation of hypotheses. One solution adopted by anthropology has been to focus on a limited number of questions and to build up a major body of knowledge. This may one day be possible also in the area of the cause of demographic change but as yet there is nothing comparable with the body of research findings and resultant theory which has been amassed, for instance, on kinship. One solution is to mine the literature available on demographic change in the writings on the region (or further afield) by anthropologists and others. Nor should one underestimate historical or religious writings. In South India there is a body of social analysis which extends back for 200 years, much of it connected with the need of the East India Company to understand the society. Much can also be gleaned from religious writings, which, in India, stretch back for 4 millennia.

Nevertheless, we found that the major source for our hypotheses had to be our own research. Some were generated from conversation and chance discoveries during a single interview. However, the most important source was the files which were accumulating on each family. Originally, we had regarded these files much as demographers are prone to do, and had thought of coding their contents. Fortunately, we realized that their information was too important for this. We repeatedly browsed through them, recalling as frequently as not the discussions which had given rise to them, and jotted down rudimentary hypotheses. We sharpened these in group discussions and in our next interviews until we had a formulation which could be fitted into our checklists for use in household discussions. These checklists were never employed as a list of questions but sooner or later we got around to all of them in probing discussions.

Some hypotheses were discarded as they proved to be incorrect or insufficiently general. Most were made more specific. Some were used as the basis for questions in small focused interviews. Ultimately, the intellectual responsibility for deciding upon the extent to which hypotheses have been disproved or still largely stand must be borne by the principal investigators and reported by them.

It is also possible to test the reconstruction of the past and of change which has occurred with historical and archival material. In India these sources are massive and are under-used by social scientists.

When we began the work, we did it with a strong conviction that one of our major purposes and justifications was to build a better questionnaire for large scale sample surveys. We still think that all such surveys should be preceded by and accompanied with micro-approach work. Nevertheless, we have increasingly come to agree with the anthropologists that the findings of the micro-approach work are an end in themselves. The minute examination and the interrelations shown build up a body of knowledge that is valid in itself and probably can be predicted to be largely true for other areas with changes arising from local circumstance. Other local work at a later date may confirm this but it is not the resonsibility of the initial investigators to have to organize this work. Similarly, the investigators can search survey and other official data for patterns which could be predicted or explained by their findings, taking equally careful note where they seem to be negated. The primary subsequent task of the investigators is to contribute to the building of theoretical frameworks which can be employed by themselves or by others for designing further research and tests or for constructing more general theory.

This is not to say that such investigators may not also have an interest in designing micro-macro-mix research where both components can throw light on each other and contribute to the other's research design in the one program. Such work can help elucidate the extent to which the small area studies can be generalized. If an archival component is also built in, it can help to assess the retrospective data derived from both the micro- and macro-approaches. Often it can provide guidance for the interpretation of those retrospective data; it cannot replace them because many of the concerns of those interested in demographic change are about matters which are almost entirely omitted from the written historical record.

Some Findings, with Attention to the Extent to which a Micro-Approach was Necessary

The most important finding of the micro work was the extent to which many types of change are interrelated. Social, political, economic and educational forces exist in the one context and affect each other and eventually produce demographic change. There was a not unconnected parallel between mortality and fertility decline, and significant statistical associations could be shown, but the connections were common relationships to factors like increased schooling, related to the Independence Movement's determination to put all children into school, and to the greater development of an exchange economy at the expense of the subsistence economy with its fatal dependence on the cycle of plenty and deprivation. We built up a significant picture of changing relations between the generations, especially the erosion of patriarchal authority, as education, transport, the growth of non-agricultural employment and the coming of the mass cinema changed expectations and opportunities. We followed among a still religious people a transformation of religious interpretation as a broadening spectrum of behaviour was felt to be significant only in the secular sphere. These are matters which may later be probed by the survey but which necessarily must have their forms delineated previously by more intimate work.

Among the older respondents we were able to view an earlier society where sexual relations were postponed after marriage among Hindus so that no birth could take place during the first year and where sex was infrequent or non-existent between spouses long before the wife reached menopause. It was a society where weaning decisions were usually dictated by the next pregnancy and where that pregnancy was postponed not only by lactational amenorrhoea but also by post-partum sexual abstinence. This was a society where the state had few views on any of these matters, but where religion, especially in its most local manifestation, certainly did, and where relatives, particularly of the older generation, were the instruments for policing that morality. That policing weakened, first in the area of the control of coitus. It was changes of this kind that made it easier for the older generation among Hindus to withdraw to an agnostic position once the state intervened with a new morality with regard to fertility control. Among the Muslims, who held that they had a revealed and written morality that impinged on these specific questions, the old did not abdicate so readily and Muslim fertility remained well above that of Hindus. Their resistance to what they regarded as the blind Hindu acceptance of a state-led socio-theological morality explained the religous fertility differential which we found in the area and which we believed threw light on such differentials reported across India.

It was first through our work on marriage and the desired arrangements that we learnt just how deep was the fear of periodic adversity and the desire to link some of the family fortunes to non-agricultural sources of income. Given this new lead, we were able to relate declining farm size, arising in general from population growth and in specific cases from land reform, to the increased desire and opportunity for some family members to work outside agriculture; we could then trace the links to rising levels of education and a stronger demand for fertility control. We understood the local people's fear of life-cycle bottlenecks threatening their plans to educate children and to secure the desired jobs or marriages for them. It was only the 1983 drought which starkly threw into unusually high relief the operating of all these processes. The micro-approach allowed us to distinguish between the ideal and the actual in the performance of the family planning program. It revealed the role played by the program in intervening in family decision-making and in making concrete vague feelings of economic apprehension. It made more concrete our own feelings about the role in fertility decline played by the program when we found how few local people doubted the primacy of their intervention as a causal mechanism. We understood too the resistance to the program when we found that not only ordinary people but also the elites, and even those in the program when not acting in their official capacity, believed that it was only too probable that sterilization would maim a woman for life and could easily kill a man.

We had come to the investigation with apparent strong evidence that fertility had declined steeply in the second half of the 1970s in South India even though the Emergency had not impinged strongly in the area. We found that there had been sufficient additional pressure to explain the steepened fertility decline and we found also why the public picture of events in the region during those times was different.

Perhaps the most revealing fertility discoveries were in the area of family planning decision-making. It became possible to document the first suggestions of sterilization, and of the hints, nagging and pressures. It was clear just how pressures could build up on the daughter-in-law, how she might fear her husband's vigour, health and employment being endangered by vasectomy, how his death would profoundly alter her position, and how a sacrificial role, well in keeping with social and religious tradition, might appeal to some. Yet, in most families the ultimate decision was hers, as was so often and so relentlessly stressed, and a situation as simple as this was all that was likely to be reported to a survey interviewer enquiring about who made the decision. The survey analyst would then report an autonomy of females of the younger generation greatly at odds with the actual situation.

Only participation in the community could reveal just how strong the pressure of the 'establishment' was in ensuring that only the family planning message was heard in public, whether at a school meeting or that of the *panchayat* (village council). Even complaints about family planning are quickly stifled by the bureaucrats, the educated and the rich, who frequently publicly advocate the use of the program. They partly regard themselves as the representatives of the government or of the national interest and they partly have been convinced by the population debate of the truth of earlier lurking fears, namely that they have much to lose from the unbridled reproduction of the already numerous poor. During the Emergency the landlords of the larger village agreed not to employ agricultural labourers who had been targeted by the family planning program for having three or more living children but still resisted sterilization. It is this same group, close to those who control the health unit, who are likely to experiment with the IUD while agreeing that there is little point in the program advocating any method other than sterilization to the feckless poor.

It was soon clear that any study of either fertility change or the decision-making structure of families had to take into account the persistent rise in average female age at marriage, now nearing 19 years. Only detailed enquiry about successive marriages within families revealed the persistent evolution from a nominal bride-price to a kind of open market dowry system within each caste. This had first appeared among Brahmin families, then among peasant castes, and was now invading the backward castes, though not as yet the Harijans. The reports of the late eighteenth and early nineteenth centuries revealed a time when bride-price had been sufficiently high to deter many marriages. The elites, well aware of the opposition of government and of the nationalist movement to dowry, told us that they paid none, and certainly would have reported this way in a survey. Only when we questioned them about their obvious financial worries over a forthcoming marriage or the lavishness of the marriage when it occurred, did they explain that they gave presents rather than dowry. They were proud of the expenditure in comparison to that which their peers made, but most regretted that the situation had come about and few offered any argument along the lines of *Sanskritization* that it improved the religious or social standing of their caste. They explained the rise of dowry in terms of a marriage squeeze rendering bridegrooms more scarce (a demographically plausible argument) and the greater market value of the educated young men now becoming available in larger numbers. It was the endless discussions on this latter point that proved to us just how valuable was a relative with a secure income from outside agriculture and how apprehensive were families of facing periods of crisis with only agricultural incomes.

If it had not been our experience over the years that only one non-arranged marriage had taken place, an occurrence which gave rise to profound problems not yet solved, we might have looked at the data for evidence to support a tendency to regard arranged marriage as an institution likely to collapse.

Marriage was seen in a new light when its need was expressed most commonly in discussions of the household labour force and of why it was the departure of a daughter-in-law or the sickness of her mother-in-law that meant a new marriage must be arranged. Meeting the dowry for such a marriage was an argument understood by all as to why the partition of the larger family should be postponed longer so as to retain a single economic unit with maximum efficiency for saving.

It was conversations with teachers, lamenting the withdrawal of their best girl students just before the important senior school leaving certificate examination, which brought home to us the strength of the fear still felt over freedom for a girl who has reached menarche and is not yet married. One family consulted a member of the team, as an outsider, about whether, in such circumstances, menarche could or should be hidden for a short time by postponing the related ceremonies.

Observation and conversation with regard to specific marriages revealed financial aspects which should be quantifiable but where full disclosure might be impossible to obtain. Clearly one should attempt to distinguish between wedding costs and those constituting the dowry, and also between dowry costs before or at the time of the wedding and other subsequent payment of gifts. It is also clear that much of the payment finds its way to those who provide services or goods for the wedding and increasingly to the younger generation who are marrying, so marriage payments are not merely a rotating fund that subsequently allows another marriage as is largely the case, for instance, among many pastoral people of the African Savannah.

The research where the micro-approach had the clearest margin over the survey, and where we concluded that most surveys must yield close to meaningless data, was in the area of morbidity and mortality, especially the former. So many sick people believed themselves to be experiencing either hot-cold imbalance from incautious eating or other behaviour, or thought that they were suffering from divine punishments or other inflictions of extra-human origin, that even the most careful cross-questioning failed to secure a statement of much of the illness. People who were clearly very sick reported that they were not ill, and babies died even though they were said to be in good health. Indeed, the term for describing a complex of infantile disorders, including diarrhoea and infantile cirrhosis of the liver, was *balagraha* (divine visition upon children). Not only were the causes of much sickness deeply embedded in religion, but, as a consequence, so was the treatment. It was a long time - far longer than most surveys are in a specific area - before we convinced most people that we were also interested in afflictions that were not the kind appropriate for treatment in the health centre and that we were interested in alternative treatments. They believed their reaction to be just common sense and politeness, for researchers from the modern segment of society are likely to be concerned only with the institutions deriving from that segment. Indeed, one reason why those institutions are used is that those who have gone to school believe that they have entered a world of such institutions. Some refusal arises from a fear of modern medicine and a belief that the interviewers would order such treatment. Sometimes it is the investigators who are wrong. Survey workers in India often assume that the alternatives to modern medicine are the practices associated with the Hindu or Muslim religions, *Ayurvedic* or *Unani* medicine. In our district the input from practitioners of these therapies was trivial compared with temple rites, charms, herbalism, and a wide range of magical practices and services offered by a new type of 'quack'.

These are not the only difficulties in explaining the under-utilization of modern health services. There are costs in terms of payments and presents which are not officially supposed to be made, of income foregone not only by the sufferer but also by those who accompany him or her, as well as transport and food costs. It is difficult to obtain adequate quantification even by methods much more tedious than those employed by surveys because of a reluctance to count a present given reciprocally in return for assistance as tradition dictates, let alone to estimate for the sick how much income they really did forego.

There are matters of fundamental importance when assessing morbidity and mortality which can only be examined by a participatory approach but which are exceedingly difficult even by these means. Feeding occurs in successive order by time so that the men who eat first do not know either what is left for the women or whether they ate anything during food preparation. Children may be given the same amount at first but little girls are restrained from demanding more to a greater extent than little boys as part of their training for femininity rather than as a conscious effort to achieve feeding differentials. Mothers traditionally did not draw attention to their sick children or demand treatment until their mothers-in-law or husbands took notice and action. In terms of mothers-in-law this makes some sense as they care for young children when the mothers are in the field. The more education the daughters-in-law have the more the balance of decision-making changes but this is regarded as so inevitable and obvious that it is very rarely reported to investigators.

Attitudes towards health and treatment change with secularization as some spheres of action are removed from the religious domain. This may well happen as a person becomes apparently more religious in a movement toward greater devotion to a major Hindu god at the expense of adherence to the village goddess. Most survey measures of religiosity would fail to record this as a secular shift. With the secular shift, there may be no intensification of pollution avoidance but that avoidance will be more closely related to bacterial rather than spiritual pollution. Whether this shows up in a survey as greater cleanliness depends very much on the number and type of questions asked.

The work on family structure brought out clearly the life cycle movements from more complex to nuclear families and the persistence of one stem household in each larger family to provide for the older parents. It showed how the proportion of nuclear families gives little indication of the family situation when most conceptions and the first movements toward fertility control take place. Much of this work can be done by well constructed surveys provided that they find ways of accurately measuring family and residence by more than crude cooking-pot measures.

Concluding Note

Much of what is in surveys is not wholly wrong. Nevertheless, the picture is usually so marred by important omissions that it gives a completely wrong impression. What the survey does contain is a kind of lowest common denominator measuring those phenomena which occur everywhere. What it leaves out is the cultural and social diversity which really explains why fertility or mortality levels persist in one place rather than another. What they lack is not only a sense of place but also a sense of time which is disastrous because adequate explanations of social change are essentially historical ones.

It is impossible to undertake any intensive micro-approach work without increasingly wondering what a large scale survey moving quickly through the area would pick up. Yet even the micro-approach researcher is tempted by a curiosity about larger patterns and numbers (convincing by their very size) to employ the small scale findings for designing better sets of questions for the surveys. However, this is done in the knowledge that much of the interpretation will depend on an understanding from alternative sources of just how the family and community operate so as to produce this result.

However, the prime object of micro-approach research, beyond reporting immediate findings, should be the building of a better body of theory, which has a value both in its own right and as a stepping stone to more generalized theory or other micro research or more satisfactory macro research.

Notes

1. General findings have been reported in Caldwell, Reddy and Caldwell, 1982b. Results dealing with fertility and family planning are found in Caldwell, 1983a; Caldwell and Caldwell, 1985; Caldwell, Reddy and Caldwell, 1984b; those on family structure in Caldwell, Reddy and Caldwell, 1984a; on marriage in Caldwell, Reddy and Caldwell, 1983b; and on morbidity and mortality in Caldwell, Reddy and Caldwell, 1983a; Caldwell and Ruzicka, 1985; Caldwell, Reddy and Caldwell, 1986.

2. This work was carried out in two contrasting villages over 100 kilometres to the south by members of the Population Centre staff, Sumitra K. Potnis and P.N. Sushama; in a village area over 100 kilometres to the north-east and in a Tamil Nadu village by ANU Demography Department Ph.D. students, A. Shariff and M. Guruswamy; and in two areas within Bangalore city by Population Centre staff, Sheila Chandra Mauli and Sashikala Kempawadkar. Important supplementary enquiries were also carried out in Bangalore by Revathi N. and Kusum Kumari.

Acknowledgements

This paper draws heavily on a joint research project of the Population Centre, Bangalore, India, and the Department of Demography, Australian National University, funded by the two institutions. Assistance, especially with the analysis, has been provided by the Population Council's Research Awards Program on the Determinants of Fertility in Developing Countries, and the Ford Foundation. Recent mortality analysis has been funded by the Ford Foundation (New Delhi). Assistance has been given in the preparation of this chapter by Wendy Cosford and Sue Sydlarczuk.

Micro-Perspectives on Asian Fertility

3

Focus Group Research on Fertility Decline in Thailand: Methodology and Findings

John Knodel, Anthony Pramualratana, and Napaporn Havanon

Part I: The Methodology: Focus Group Research as a Means of Demographic Inquiry

Of all areas of social scientific inquiry, few have closer association with quantitative data than demographic research. Census, vital statistics and sample surveys, the basic sources of demographic data, provide results that are inherently numerical. As the search for explanation and understanding of demographic phenomena proceeds, however, an increasing number of scholars outside the field of demography proper, as well as demographers themselves, are beginning to question the adequacy of an exclusively quantitative approach based on the conventional data sources and research tools of the discipline.

Probably the most organized, extensive and ambitious efforts to broaden the nature of demographic research are being made by John Caldwell, his associates and their fellow travellers through their advocacy of what is becoming known as the 'micro-approach' to demographic investigation. This anthropological type of approach is eclectic and ambitious, combining ethnographic field research with surveys and even censuses of villages or small areas in an attempt to arrive at a holistic understanding of demographic behaviour and change within a broad historical and sociological perspective.

Less ambitious attempts designed to complement rather than replace the standard quantitative approach of demographic research are also surfacing. One such approach involves what is commonly labelled focus group research. Our aim in the present chapter is to describe this approach, drawing on our experiences in connection with research into the ongoing fertility transition in Thailand, and to present some substantive findings of the investigation.

Our use of the focus group approach was based on a central tenet shared by practitioners of micro-demography, namely that:

> '... most actors involved in major social changes know that something is happening, have some idea of the direction and shape of the changes, and have speculated - at least to themselves - about what is happening and why' (Caldwell *et al.*, 1982a, p.11).

The focus group technique has been widely used in private industry, especially for marketing research. A somewhat natural extension of this tradition has been the use of focus group sessions for aiding in the design and improvement of family planning programs (see the special issue of Studies in Family Planning, December 1981). Their use in basic social research, however, has been quite limited. Our own use of the technique as part of a comprehensive research project on the Thai fertility transition is a recent exception.

What is a Focus Group?

A focus group consists of a small number of participants (usually six to twelve) from a target population who, under the guidance of a moderator, discuss topics of importance to the particular research study. Although the moderator covers topics according to predetermined guidelines, the discussion is essentially open-ended. There is flexibility in the order in which topics are covered and leeway to follow up unanticipated lines of discussion germane to the theme of the session as they arise. In addition, as a study proceeds, guidelines may be modified in response to outcomes of previous sessions. The target populations from which focus groups are drawn are often fairly narrowly defined for a particular study. The process by which specific participants are selected is generally less rigorous than sampling procedures typically used for surveys, although often some attempt is made to keep the process reasonably random. It is standard practice to choose participants for particular sessions so that they are relatively homogeneous with respect to characteristics which might otherwise impede the free flow of discussion. Generally this means that participants of any one session should be of similar social status and not hold sharply conflicting views about sensitive or deeply-felt aspects of the topic under investigation.

Separate sessions with groups selected on the basis of different sets of criteria permit the in-depth exploration of views of persons with quite different characteristics while still preserving the homogeneity of each particular group. The specific criteria serving as a basis on which a group is formed will depend on the nature of the particular research project. There may indeed be situations in which intragroup diversity is desirable but this seems to be an area not yet extensively explored by focus group practitioners. At this point in the development of the methodology, the stress is on intragroup homogeneity.

Sessions should be held in a neutral setting and conducted with a permissive, non-judgemental atmosphere. Within each session, the full discussion is typically tape-recorded. In addition to a moderator and participants, a session should also include a notetaker who later transcribes the complete discussion based on notes and the tapes. These transcripts then serve as the basic data for analysis.

The informal and supportive group situation and the open-ended nature of the questions are intended to encourage participants to elaborate on behaviour and opinions to an extent that might be difficult to obtain in individual interviews or in groups containing persons of opposing views and diverse statuses. Indeed as members of social communities, people do not think in isolation; typically they form opinions and reflect on ideas that agree or disagree with those of others in their social environment. The focus group tries to tap this process. Focus group sessions are not simply group interviews in which each participant is asked a question in turn. Instead, when focus groups work properly, participants stimulate memories and feelings and thus lead to a fuller discussion of the topic at hand. It is this group dynamic that distinguishes focus group sessions from individual in-depth interviews typical of ethnographic research.

The Purposes of Focus Group Research

Given the potential of the focus group approach for yielding qualitative information exposing perceptions, opinions, underlying attitudes, and behaviour patterns, it lends itself to many purposes. It can be helpful in the preparation of a sample survey by familiarizing the researcher with 'consumer language', thereby helping in determining question wording, and in suggesting content areas to be covered by the questionnaire. Focus groups can aid directly in the interpretation of survey results by probing findings from surveys that seem ambiguous or puzzling. More generally, focus group research can serve to generate new hypotheses to be tested by surveys on a broader population base or to investigate topics which do not readily lend themselves to a survey format. Thus the focus group approach is not only useful as part of the survey research process but can be viewed as a mode of inquiry in its own right which complements well the more standard quantitative techniques that currently dominate the study of demographic behaviour.

The focus group approach can be seen as fitting in with the broader research strategy known as grounded theory (Glaser and Strauss, 1967; Glaser, 1978). According to this strategy, hypotheses and concepts emerge during the data collection and analysis process rather than all being determined beforehand. Thus theory is inductively built from data during the course of the research. Quantitative and qualitative methods can be seen as complementary to each other, as mutual verification, and ideally, as different forms of data on the same subject matter which, when compared, generate theory and explanation.

Potential Advantages and Limitations of Focus Group Research

There are a number of advantages of the focus group over standard survey interviews. If participants misunderstand a question in a focus group session, this becomes readily evident to the moderator and can be easily corrected. Comments are typically made within the context of a broader discussion and thus are less likely to be misinterpreted by the analyst. In contrast, one-word or short-phrased answers to standardized questions typical of surveys provide little basis for assurance that the question was understood as intended or that the answer actually means what it appears to mean.

With survey or even in more in-depth individual interviews, the interviewer often comes from a different background and is of higher social, economic and educational status than the respondent. This may lead to a 'courtesy bias' and inhibit frank disclosure of opinions, attitudes and behaviour. In a focus group setting, participants are surrounded by others of their own status, and even if the moderator is better educated and from a higher socioeconomic stratum this may well be a less salient feature of the interaction. Moreover, a group situation may facilitate open discussion of some types of sensitive topics if other participants are perceived as sharing the same perspective. For example, persons deliberately limiting their family size may be more likely to reveal the circumstances and consequences of this decision in the presence of others like themselves than to an individual interviewer whose opinion is not evident. The group structure also provides a sense of anonymity to the individual participant vis-a-vis the moderator in a sense that does not characterize the interviewer-respondent relationship in an individual interview.

As with any research method, the focus group approach has a variety of limitations and potential problems. Clearly, the qualitative nature of the data, the small size of the total sample, and the intentionally purposive manner in which participants are selected make statistical generalizations based on focus group results inappropriate. There is a risk that only one or two participants may dominate the discussion. A group situation can also inhibit discussion if other members are perceived to be unsympathetic to a participant's views. Covert behaviour or opinions which may be disapproved by substantial segments of the community may also be less likely to be revealed in a group than to an individual interviewer, unless they were perceived to be shared by others in the group. Perhaps a more serious risk is that basic values and concerns are not always readily verbalized. Moreover, mechanisms that operate in subtle or indirect ways may be difficult to detect in direct discussions of the behaviour that they influence. Such values and mechanisms may be significant but, just because they are widely shared, may not seem to require overt statements by participants.

Many of the potential problems with group dynamics can be reduced considerably by having a skilled moderator and by careful selection of group participants. Moreover, by conveying a permissive attitude, the moderator can create an atmosphere in which a range of opinions can be expressed and any tendency to simply agree with others for the sake of conformity reduced. Furthermore, in practice individual interviews are frequently conducted in the presence of self-selected onlookers rather than persons of similar status and characteristics. Thus the ability to gain accurate information on matters that would be problematic in a focus group session may not be very high in individual surveys either.

Interpretation of the Data

Given the qualitative nature of the data and the analysis, a considerable amount of subjective judgement is involved in interpreting what was said or even in determining what views appear to be more pervasive among the many opinions expressed. Not all statements can be taken at face value, but rather require interpretation based on the context in which they are made or in light of information available to the researchers from external sources. We have found it useful to have several persons read through all the transcripts and collaborate on the analysis. This reduces the chances that the subjective nature of the analysis process will lead to unwarranted emphasis or invalid conclusions. When transcripts are translated into another language, it is also essential to have at least one member of the team who can continually check on the translation during the analysis stage.

It is useful to keep in mind that the transcripts analyzed in focus group research are the result of a process with several distinct stages and that during each stage there is a risk of error occurring which can affect the accuracy of the final record. In our own project, sessions were tape-recorded (with accompanying notetaking), transcribed and translated into English (and in some cases first into central Thai if sessions were conducted in regional dialects). Thus, it is appropriate to view focus group data as transformed to some degree as a result of the processes through which they have gone. Nevertheless, the analyst is considerably closer to what has actually been said and to the context in which it has been said than is the case with survey analysis. Distinguishing between spontaneous statements and those made only after probing or noting the extent to which a particular topic or question generates discussion, all help the analyst make judgements about the meaning of what is being said in ways that are not possible with the survey approach. Moreover, when the analyst is present at the sessions, as observer, moderator, or notetaker, an additional 'closeness' to the data is gained which should aid in the analysis process.

The use of focus group sessions is clearly a less ambitious approach to collecting qualitative data than a full-fledged anthropological study or the micro-approach to demographic investigation. These latter approaches permit far greater in-depth analysis of linkages between demographic behaviour and socioeconomic and cultural underpinnings in the context of local communities than is possible with a focus group study. However, because the focus group approach does not require long-term residence and extensive participant observation in the communities in which focus groups are conducted, a greater number of communities can be included in a given study and thus broader coverage is attained. Moreover, because transcripts are produced in the course of a focus group study, verification of findings and re-analysis can, in principle, be undertaken by others besides the original investigators. Such an endeavour would be far more difficult with the field notes of an anthropologist or practitioner of the micro-demographic approach.

Some Lessons from Experience

Several aspects of our experience with focus group research in Thailand may be instructive for others who wish to try the procedure. One general lesson we learned fairly quickly was that proper focus group research requires far more time and effort than might originally be anticipated. While there are undoubtedly a number of shortcuts that can be and sometimes are taken, our impression is that they will detract from the value of the final product particularly if the focus group is being used in the more ambitious sense as an aid to explanation and understanding of social behaviour as is being discussed in the present chapter.

We found it essential in our experience to have full transcripts available when analyzing results. An early attempt to rely on summaries of sessions quickly proved unsatisfactory. Moreover, it was important to be able to identify the individal speakers. For example, it was useful to know whether comments of a specific nature were made repetitively by the same participant or by several different participants expressing similar views. Thus it is important to keep in mind from the start of a project that the actual 'data' to be used in the analysis will be the transcripts and to make all reasonable effort to ensure that complete and accurate transcripts result. We found considerable difficulty in correctly identifying participants simply by listening to tapes of the sessions without having accompanying notes. Such notes need not detail everything said but should indicate at least the first few words of each set of comments and identify who the speaker is. Since it is difficult for a moderator to guide the discussion and take notes simultaneously, a separate notetaker is a necessity at each session. Drawing a quick diagram of the constellation of the discussion group at the start and numbering participants sequentially in the diagram can serve as an effective shorthand system for identification purposes. Transcription is also facilitated if the notetaker can act later as transcriber.

Careful preparation of the discussion guidelines and continual modification as the project proceeds were also found to be essential. Especially during the early stages of the project, discussions by the researchers who either observed or served as moderators or notetakers were extremely useful immediately following sessions. By reviewing what had transpired we were able to modify and improve the discussion guidelines and to learn how to conduct subsequent sessions with increasingly better results. In general, we felt it was important for the analyst to be involved at all stages of the research project including planning the discussion guidelines, being present at the focus group sessions, and not just in analyzing the completed transcripts.

When we started the research, we worried that a number of participants who agreed to attend focus group sessions during the screening would not actually appear at the sessions. While this occasionally occurred, uninvited guests, often brought by those who had been initially selected, proved more of a problem. In one of our early sessions, not wishing to offend, we permitted an uninvited but prominent woman in the community to participate. It quickly became evident why persons of contrasting social statuses should not be included in the same focus group session. The uninvited woman rather predictably tried to dominate the discussion, and other members of the group seemed to defer to her. While skilful moderating contained the damage, some concrete strategy to deal with such circumstances was clearly needed. For future sessions we brought along questionnaires from a previous survey which could be used to conduct mock interviews with uninvited guests while the invited participants were attending the actual session. By explaining to the uninvited person that his or her special circumstances made an individual interview desirable, we avoided any potential offence which might have otherwise resulted.

While it may seem tempting to hire a professional marketing firm with experience with focus groups to conduct the actual sessions for a research project, our own experience cautions against this. It is clearly essential that the moderator and monitors of the project fully understand the purpose and background of the research. It is not enough that such expertise be available only at the analysis stage. While the staff of marketing research firms may be quite proficient in the logistics of arranging and conducting focus group sessions, they typically will have little understanding of the basic issues involved in the study of demographic behaviour. This can result in questions being posed in ways that are inadvertently misleading to the participants or in failures to probe where necesary.

While some leeway should be given to the moderator to alter the order in which topics are taken up so as to conform to the spontaneous flow of the discussion, careful thought should be given to the order of topics to be followed in the guidelines in the absence of spontaneous comments. It is important to avoid suggesting answers to subsequent questions by bringing up related topics prematurely. For example, in our own research, we deliberately deferred discussion of birth control until after the discussion of reasons for changing family size, since we wished to determine if availability of birth control methods spontaneously arose as a reason for intergenerational fertility differences. We felt that a prior discussion of the methods of birth control available now and in earlier times could have artificially increased the chance that differences in birth control availability would have been cited as the reason for fertility decline and detract from our ability to determine its true degree of saliency in the views of the participants. Likewise, we found it useful to first ask an open question about reasons for intergenerational fertility differences before probing specific factors that have been suggested in the literature in order to determine which ones were mentioned spontaneously and which were only commented on after the moderator first introduced them. In our discussion of birth control methods available in the past, we followed a similar strategy. An open question about what could be done to prevent birth in earlier times preceded specific queries on withdrawal, abstinence, and abortion.

Conclusions to Part I

The focus qroup technique can be a useful 'addition' to the tools of demographic inquiry. It should not be considered as a total approach or as a substitute for more standard quantitative techniques, in particular, the sample survey. Indeed, we found it to be most valuable when used in conjunction with quantitative approaches. We agree with Calder (1977) that the greatest threat to qualitative research findings is not their lack of generalizability but rather their potential lack of validity and this can best be assessed by comparing results obtained by alternative methods.

Both qualitative research of the focus group variety and quantitative research of the sample survey style have their limitations when used on their own. Together they complement each other quite well. While qualitative research gives investigators considerably more scope for exercising intuition, such intuition can be better grounded when placed in a perspective of a solid knowledge of what the quantitative results show.

We found it quite useful when interpreting results from focus group sessions to draw on our familiarity with past research, including anthropological work as well as surveys, on the general topic of fertility transition. In addition, we usually chose villages in which there was a resident anthropologist who could provide information about the local context. Participants themselves did not always explicitly make the various connections that we read into the discussions. As Part II of this chapter will demonstrate, our own analysis of the focus group sessions we held is not just descriptive but also interpretative, as explanatory attempts must necessarily be. We are reasonably confident that we were able to place the participants' comments in a more meaningful perspective by drawing on our own understanding of the processes at work. To this end, we went beyond the focus group material itself and drew on previous research as well as our own intuition. This is not necessarily less rigorous, and in some respects more justifiable, than the off-the-cuff interpretations that often accompany quantitative analyses.

We view social science in general and demographic inquiry in particular as an ongoing process which aims at a fuller understanding of the phenomena under investigation rather than a final and definitive analysis. In a sense then, demographic inquiry should be a total package, combining not only results from different methods but also familiarity with theoretical arguments and knowledge of previous research efforts. We are optimistic that the incorporation of qualitative techniques into what has been largely a quantitative field will bring us further along towards this goal.

Part II: Substantive Findings: Toward an Understanding of Thailand's Rapid Fertility Decline

The focus group research project described above was prompted by a desire to add a qualitative dimension to the investigation of the remarkable transformation in reproductive behaviour which has been occurring in Thailand. The country has experienced a rapid and pervasive decline in birth rates over the last decade and a half, brought about by a massive increase in the practice of birth control among married couples and accompanied by a substantial reduction in family size preferences. Survey results indicate that within the single decade between 1969 and 1979, marital fertility fell by approximately 40 per cent while contraceptive prevalence among married women in the reproductive ages increased from below 15 per cent to approximately 50 per cent. By 1981, contraceptive prevalence in Thailand had risen further to almost 60 per cent and although information on fertility trends during the last few years is not completely consistent, most evidence points to a continuing decline. At the same time, the mean preferred family size expressed by reproductive-aged married women declined from almost four to under three children. The momentousness of the reproductive revolution taking place is apparent in the contrast between the six to seven live births and five to six living children experienced by the average couple only a generation ago and the two to three child families that, according to recent survey evidence, are almost universally preferred by newly-married women today. Given the widespread use of contraception, the actual fertility of recently married couples in Thailand is likely to conform reasonably closely to these expressed preferences for small families.

In such a situation, where fertility decline has been recent and abrupt and has proceeded rapidly, different generations characterized by sharply contrasting reproductive behaviour coexist side by side, making it possible to probe in a single study the views and perceptions of older and younger generations of married couples regarding the dramatic difference in their fertility patterns. In order to obtain qualitative information on underlying attitudes, opinions and behaviour patterns, the focus group sessions described in Part I above were conducted separately with older and younger men and women in rural villages in all four regions of Thailand and with rural migrant construction workers in Bangkok. Analysis of transcripts of these sessions, when supplemented by other research results, provides the basis for understanding the reasons underlying fertility decline among the large rural majority.

An adequate explanation of the timing, pace, and extent of Thailand's fertility decline involves four major interacting components, as described in the subsequent sections. The first of these is the rapid and fundamental social changes which have been taking place and which have caused couples to increasingly view large numbers of children as an economic burden with which they are neither able nor willing to cope. Second, the Thai cultural setting is one which is relatively conducive to the acceptance of deliberate fertility regulation and limitation of family size as adaptations to changing circumstances. Third, a latent demand for effective and acceptable means to control fertility was present among a sizeable proportion of couples for at least a generation before the fertility transition began. Fourth, organized efforts to provide modern contraceptive methods, especially through the government's national family planning program, resulted in a massive increase in awareness of and accessibility to effective and acceptable means of fertility regulation.

Social Change

Interwoven fundamental social and economic changes that intimately affect both the daily lives of Thai villagers and their future plans for themselves and their children have been under way for some time. They can be seen as responsible in part for the latent demand for fertility control described by the older generation and far more so for the current desire for small families among the younger generation. The net result of these changes has been to increase directly or indirectly the monetary cost of raising children, thus making large families far more of an economic burden than in the past. Both generations agree in their perception that the cost of living in general and the cost of raising children in particular are far greater now than before. The perceived increase in the general cost of living appears to be the result of interrelated processes centring on the spread of the cash economy, mainly through extensive market penetration and the resulting monetization of daily life, and changing consumer aspirations.

Particularly salient for the perceived increase in the cost of raising children is the cost of education, in part because the costs involved in sending a child just for elementary schooling are felt to have increased, but more importantly because of the increasingly felt need to send children for higher levels of education than had been necessary in the past. Increased availability of schooling has facilitated this change. Providing children with more schooling is seen as the primary mechanism through which families can cope with limited land availability and reduced prospects both for themselves but more importantly for their children for making a satisfactory living through agricultural pursuits. It is also perceived as the main vehicle for social mobility and as a prerequisite for more secure and prestigious jobs outside of agriculture.

Changes in what is normally considered appropriate child care and legitimate needs and demands of children have also contributed to the perceived increase in child rearing costs. Rising consumer aspirations, the perceived need for increased education for their children, and changing views on child care have all undoubtedly been reinforced by increasing mass media penetration. At the same time that the perceived cost of raising children has risen, children are generally perceived to be less helpful in doing household chores and contributing to the family's economic activities while they are growing up. This is seen as a result in large part of the increased schooling. To think in terms of monetary costs when contemplating raising children is now considered normal and it has come to be an accepted way of thinking that the more children a couple has, the more costly it will be.

There remain, of course, a variety of both economic and non-economic reasons why couples still want children even if in limited numbers. Among the most important is the persistence of expectations of parent repayment, especially in the form of providing comfort and support during the parents' later years. Some shift towards greater monetization of support is occurring. Many participants viewed a reduction in the amount of support they received as the inevitable but necessary price for avoiding the hardship of raising many children. Others, however, saw little conflict between the amount of parent repayment and reduced family size. Some even felt there was more to be gained from few better-educated children than from many less-educated ones.

The Thai Cultural Setting

In any society, the impact of social and economic change on reproductive behaviour is mediated through the cultural setting. There are a number of important cultural traits characteristic of Thais which can be considered conducive to the adoption of birth control and the limitation of family size as a way to adjust to changing socioeconomic circumstances. Several pronatalist props or barriers to fertility decline thought to characterize many Third World countries are notably absent in Thailand. In particular, reproductive decisions seem to be generally defined as the domain of the couples themselves with only minimal influence exerted by parents and kin. Moreover, the older generation is generally supportive of the lower family size goals of the younger generation. The lack of influence of parents and kin over the reproductive decisions of their children fits in with the prevailing expectation that each conjugal unit will be largely responsible for the support of their own children. Even during the initial period following marriage when the couple is typically co-resident with parents of one of the spouses, usually the wife's, the younger couple may contribute more to the upkeep of the household than the older couple. This contrasts with the situation thought to typify many developing countries whereby co-residence in a joint household results in freeing the younger couple from the direct economic responsibility of rearing children.

In addition, the considerable degree of female autonomy in Thailand has undoubtedly contributed to the extent and pace of fertility decline. Women have considerable influence over birth control practice and family size, enabling them to effectively take into account their own stake as the bearer and rearer of children. Indeed, most birth control methods practised in Thailand depend on women's initiative. Moreover, their autonomy in many other spheres of life exposes them as fully to the forces of social change as men.

Buddhism, as practised in Thailand, also poses no major barriers to the reduction of family size. Although abortion is opposed on religious grounds, there is little opposition to contraception. More generally, Thai Buddhism emphasizes the primacy of individual action and responsibility, thus contributing to the general flexibility and tolerance associated with Thai culture. In such a cultural setting, modern tastes, attitudes, and behaviour, including changing reproductive patterns, can take hold with relative ease. While culture is also subject to change, the traits discussed, at least in their broad outline, show considerable consistency over the last few generations.

Latent Demand for Contraception

According to older generation participants as well as considerable survey evidence, effective means of birth control were neither known nor practised among the vast majority of rural Thais until recently. An exception may be awareness of traditional massage abortion, a potentially effective method but one probably limited to extreme circumstances because of the perceived danger involved and the lack of moral acceptability. Withdrawal and lengthy abstinence are largely alien to Thai culture and, to the limited extent known, considered unsuitable as methods of birth control except among Thai Muslims and some southern Thai Buddhists.

Despite the absence of effective practice of birth control in the past, there appears to have been interest in limiting family size or spacing children, at least for a generation prior to the onset of fertility decline. Evidence of a latent demand for fertility regulation can be deduced from comments made by older generation participants and from their reports of having tried unsuccessfully to control fertility through ineffective means, particularly traditional herbal medicines. These attempts preconditioned couples for the adoption of modern effective methods once such methods became known and accessible. The latent demand for effective birth control arose out of concerns that couples, and particularly women, had about the burdens inherent in childbearing and child rearing as well as from some of the same social forces, although in an incipient stage, that were operating during the more recent period of actual fertility decline.

Provision of Family Planning Services

The existence of considerable latent demand for fertility regulation helps explain why organized efforts to provide contraception to couples throughout the country met with such immediate success. The development of these efforts began during the mid-1960s and by 1972, following implementation of a policy to distribute oral contraceptives and condoms through local level health stations, had more or less penetrated the entire countryside. Moreover, a variety of information dissemination activities was associated with these efforts. The active implementation of the program helped legitimize concern over large numbers of children and reinforced desires for fertility control. Thus the timing of the development of the national family planning program, which is the major supplier of contraceptive methods to rural Thais, helps explain the timing of fertility decline in rural Thailand. It is unlikely that the same massive and rapid increase in awareness and practice of effective means of birth control could have occurred in its absence.

Conclusions to Part II

The two most dynamic components of our explanation for Thailand's fertility transition are the set of fundamental societal changes that have been taking place and the impact of the family planning program. The socioeconomic changes played an essential role in creating the initial and continued receptivity to limitation of births. The organized efforts to promote and provide contraception have facilitated, and in some localities helped initiate, the widespread use of birth control. The effect was often immediate because of the latent demand for effective fertility control methods. In our view, it is the interaction between socioeconomic change and an organized program, both operating within a cultural setting conducive to reproductive change, that has resulted in the rapid and extensive decline of fertility. Under such circumstances, attempts to assign relative importance to family planning programs versus development seem inappropriate.

The forces of socioeconomic change underlying the decline in fertility continue to operate and some may well intensify in future years. For example, the penetration of the countryside by television, undoubtedly the most potent of all the mass media, is still only at an early stage but is proceeding rapidly. Furthermore, the family planning program continues to be active, and access to modern, effective means of birth control is increasing. Travel to existing outlets is easier and new outlets are being created or old ones upgraded to provide a wider variety of methods. Moreover, the almost universal desire for spacing births is only recently being realized to any substantial degree through contraceptive use. Thus there is still sufficient momentum to lead to further decreases in desired family size, increases in contraceptive practice, and reductions in fertility.

Many of the socioeconomic forces discussed in connection with the ongoing fertility transition in Thailand are operating in varying degrees throughout the Third World. Moreover, many countries have also mounted organized efforts to promote and provide contraception. Given these commonalities, it is interesting to consider the extent to which the dynamics of the Thai fertility transition are relevant for understanding reproductive behaviour elsewhere. As already stressed, the factors underlying these dynamics are mediated through a cultural setting unique to Thailand, and latent demand for fertility control may have been unusually far-reaching in Thailand. A challenging task for future research will be to determine more precisely which particular constellations of cultural traits promote and which hinder a fertility response to the combined forces of socioeconomic change and organized efforts to promote fertility control that are increasingly characterizing most of the developing world.

Final Remarks

While there is a considerable amount of quantitative documentation and analysis of the ongoing fertility transition in Thailand based on surveys and official statistics, little qualitative analysis of the changes involved has taken place either from a more abstract institutional perspective or from a micro-level perspective based on the perceptions of the actors responsible for these changes. We believe that with proper scrutiny and interpretation, the information, opinions and attitudes expressed by the actors regarding fertility decline can provide useful and valid insights into the nature and causes of the process which is taking place. The rapidity and magnitude of reproductive change in Thailand means that the information gathered in focus group sessions with older and younger men and women yields rich perspectives on fertility decline from both pre- and post-transition generations.

The information from the focus group discussion has been synthesized with results of past research to construct a plausible interpretation of Thailand's fertility transition. The participants in focus group sessions themselves did not make explicit all the observations we have made concerning the components of demographic change in Thailand; there are obvious differences in the level of abstraction we are seeking in an explanation as social scientists and the level of explanation that seems of direct relevance to the individual participant. Nevertheless, we believe the focus group approach can go a long way toward helping us understand the mechanisms underlying demographic change.

Acknowledgements

This chapter is the amalgamation of two short papers presented at the Micro-Approach Conference in Canberra, Australia. The Thailand research was supported by a grant from the Population

Council's International Research awards Program on the Determinants of Fertility. The Awards Program is supported by USAID funds. Helpful comments on Part I of the paper were provided by E. Helen Berry, Kathy Duke, and Jay and Fern Ingersoll.

4

Combining Research Techniques in the Study of Fertility and Family Planning in Java: Theory and Practice

T.H. Hull, V.J. Hull and M. Singarimbun

The Community Study Method

There has been a long-standing debate about the relative merits of survey and anthropological approaches to fieldwork. Zelditch (1962, p.566) highlighted the distinctions which were being drawn when he wrote of:

> '...a spirited controversy between, on the one hand, those who have sharply criticized field workers for slipshod sampling, for failing to document assertions quantitatively ... and, on the other hand, those who have, sometimes bitterly, been opposed to numbers, to samples, to questionnaires, often on the ground that they destroy the fieldworker's conception of a social system as an organic whole'.

By the 1960s the debate produced an increasing number of calls for a synthesis of approaches. Mitchell (1967) urged anthropologists to develop proficiency in the application of quantitative methods to their data, while Trow (1957) and later Zelditch (1962, p.567) contended that 'a field study is not a single method gathering a single kind of information'. The justification of a combination of methods was not just that it leads to greater variety of data collection, but also, in the words of Pelto (1970, p.145) it 'greatly enhances the credibility of research results'.

In the late 1960s and early 1970s, we carried out community-level research in the Yogyakarta special region to learn something of the social and cultural context of fertility behaviour.[1] The research was undertaken at a time when basic demographic data were largely lacking in Indonesia, and we had to ensure that we had good quantitative information on our communities in which to set behavioural findings. We also wanted information that would be useful to the family planning program that was just being launched in the country, and which would be able to help interpret the macro-level demographic data that eventually was to become available in the mid to late 1970s. For this reason we decided on a research approach which combined a village survey with more intensive methods of data collection.

Both community studies, in Sriharjo (Singarimbun) and Maguwoharjo (Hull and Hull) sought to study demographic issues in the context of a single community, on the assumption that individual behaviour is the product of interacting institutional and cultural influences which transcend the characteristics of individuals as normally measured in surveys. A combination of techniques meant that surveys could gather data on demographic and economic parameters while intensive interviews and observations would help to understand the workings of institutions and the processes of the society. In practice, the techniques were not neatly divisible, and informal interviews were often used to verify survey data, while responses to the survey frequently gave rise to elaborate case studies or encouraged detailed investigations of institutions which had not been recognized as important at the outset of the study.

Organization and Operationalization of the Combined Approach

The first technique brought into use was the field notebook, where the researcher records facts, impressions, events, and any other information which might later prove useful in the analysis of data. At an early stage we also collected background materials such as maps, registration data, local histories, theses from nearby universities and other material which helped in the selection of a study site and to place the micro-study in a macro context.

While field notebooks had an obvious use in the research it soon became clear in Maguwoharjo that the numbers of people being covered would make the task of collating and cross-indexing information extremely large and inflexible. As a result two other data sets were devised. First a series of topical notebooks was developed into which individual team members could copy fieldnotes related to particular issues at the end of each day's work. This was gradually replaced by a system of more focused 'Case Study' cards. The cards were standard 4" x 6" size, with printed formats including the name of informant, date, topic and the survey identification number of the informant to allow easy reference to other files. All members of the research team carried cards with them at all times to ensure that information from interviews, informal discussions, and observation could be recorded immediately.

Surveys in both Sriharjo and Maguwoharjo were carried out in a series of stages. The first stage was a census of the entire village to collect basic information on household structure and characteristics of individuals, and to provide a baseline for observations of changes to the population over the course of a year.

Next an economic survey of the households' wealth, income and productive activities was undertaken in selected hamlets by male interviewers while female interviewers carried out a survey of marital and pregnancy histories of women.

Finally a survey of attitudes toward family planning in particular, and population issues in general was completed in the same selected hamlets. At each stage the interviewers recorded information on changes in household composition, and some questions were included to verify information collected at the previous stage. Survey schedules were checked daily, and any inconsistencies or missing information were referred back to the interviewer who revisited the household for corrections or clarifications.

The major difference between the use of the survey in a community study and a large sample enumeration is that the former allows much greater flexibility in the design and testing of the instruments. Questions can be modified to suit local conditions and take account of local dialects. The compact geography of a community makes a stage approach to the survey feasible, and allows for shorter, more frequent interviews which are less disruptive to respondents, and more akin to the sort of social interactions which prevail in the community (see Appendix for a more detailed description of the methodology of the Maguwoharjo study, and examples of the way in which survey design and implementation drew on knowledge of the community).

Lessons Learned

One justification for a micro-approach is that it provides qualitatively different information than can normally be expected from survey or census data. In part, then, the test of the Yogyakarta field studies is that they produced findings which changed the existing understanding of demographic behaviour in Java. The impact of these studies was to establish facts which were later confirmed by large scale enumerations, such as the existence of a positive relation between socioeconomic status and fertility which was confirmed using data from the 1971 Census. Beyond such early demonstrations, the studies also provided detailed descriptions of the meaning of some common survey measures as they are found to operate in the context of a village. For example, while there had long been discussions of poverty in Java, these tended to be fairly superficial until Singarimbun and Penny (1973, 1976) published studies showing the complex web of factors underlying the extremely low incomes of the majority of people in Sriharjo.

To illustrate some of the differences between the community study and the large scale survey we will review three sets of findings which contributed in different ways to an understanding of demographic processes in Java. First, the discovery in Sriharjo that abstinence was widely practised in the pre-family planning program period is shown as a finding which challenged conventional wisdom. Second, the marriage history and informal interviews conducted in Maguwoharjo found that the rising age at marriage had to be analyzed with reference to the changing patterns of delayed consummation of marriage. Finally, the estimation of ages in the Maguwoharjo surveys was found to be substantially improved through the use of local calenders, reference to official documents held in the village office, and repeated checking of reported birth dates against those for other family members who had some firm evidence of birth date.

Abstinence as a Form of Birth Control

The Sriharjo study was carried out at a time when modern forms of birth control were still relatively unknown in Javanese villages, and it was difficult to obtain contraceptives even in the city. The term 'Keluarga Berencana' (KB or 'Family Planning') was just beginning to be heard on the radio, and there were a few pamphlets appearing which described pills, condoms, IUDs, diaphragms, and sponges as methods of 'KB'. Thus when designing a survey of people's knowledge of methods of preventing conception, Singarimbun had to use general descriptions and specific terms to make himself understood. When asking what people did to prevent getting pregnant if they didn't want more children, some of the older men said that they didn't do anything, that is they just stayed away from their wives. Women described how they would sleep with their children, and in some cases how they would give their husbands money to go to a prostitute rather than submitting to conjugal demands. On closer questioning it became clear that such forms of abstinence were quite common in the past, but appeared to be less acceptable to the younger generation. They were not seen as a form of 'family planning', but rather as normal patterns of marital life, often having as much to do with the relationship between wives and husbands as an overt desire to limit childbearing.

These replies were intriguing. On a visit to the city Singarimbun told the local doctors about the results he was obtaining and asked whether such comments ever came up in clinics. The doctors, all Javanese and many from villages, laughed and said that it was impossible that men would abstain. On returning to the village he was determined to track down the truth, and went to an old man who had proven to be a very knowledgeable informant on many issues. The man listened patiently to the problem and nodded when told of the doctors' reactions, and then proceeded to explain how before the Revolution and the advent of general education it was common for people to observe *pantang* (forms of self-denial) which were dictated by custom. These included abstinence from sex for extended periods following a birth, or close to particular events, or when they were attempting to increase their 'spiritual energy'. If a family could not afford too many children, or if the woman was sick or considered too old to give birth, it was believed that the best thing would be for the couple to abstain from sex completely, but if the man was weak-willed it was accepted that he might go to a prostitute. The younger generation did not follow such customs because they were educated in a new *ilmu* (science which didn't teach self-denial). Doctors were very smart in the new science but ignorant about the old customs.

This explanation made a great deal of sense. It helped to clarify why a custom which was said to be very general could be unknown to many villagers and otherwise knowledgeable people in the city. It also helped to explain why people did not think of abstinence as a family planning method. 'KB' meant the modern devices described in the booklets, and these were meant specifically to avoid having more children.

On return from the field and after some preliminary data processing Singarimbun gave a seminar on the abstinence patterns found in Sriharjo. The reaction of demographers was not much different from that of the Yogyakarta medical doctors, for it was argued that it was impossible for couples to abstain for lengthy periods of time and that the respondents must have been lying. Yet in both Sriharjo and Maguwoharjo it was clear that abstinence was being practised. Confidence in this conclusion comes not only from the logic of birth intervals and fertility levels, but also from detailed case studies, and frank discussions with many people. There has probably always been some variation in abstinence practices, and with modernization there has been an increase of acceptable behavioural options and a decrease in negative sanctions against those who do not abstain for long periods. There remains, however, a certain self-consciousness and even embarrassment among people who are still aware of, but do not adhere to, this traditional norm.

Abstinence has become a particularly bewildering issue for analysts in Indonesia, in part because of a lack of appreciation of the meaning of the Sriharjo results. The World Fertility Survey (WFS) listed it as a method of contraception, and asked people if they intended to use it. The Principal Report indicates that only 13 per cent of women in Java and Bali 'know' of abstinence as a method, which made it less well-known than injection, which was not even available in the government family planning program at that time (WFS, 1978, vol.2, p.75). This indicates complete confusion on the part of both the respondents and the people who designed the survey questionnaire with regard to how abstinence is pratised in village Java, and how its practice is related to fertility. This is particularly unfortunate because as time goes on, and increasing numbers of women follow more modern ways, abstinence will increasingly be an ideal behaviour which is honoured but not practised, and eventually it could effectively disappear as an element of traditional Javanese custom. The WFS missed an opportunity to explore the phenomenon at an early stage of the transition.

Delayed Consummation of Marriage

It used to be nearly universal for parents to arrange the marriages of their children, but in recent years a majority of marriages in the Yogyakarta region arise from the choices of the prospective couples. During informal discussions with women in the village it was obvious that the nature of marriage as an institution had undergone substantial changes related to this alteration in the method of choosing partners. In earlier times, marriages were sometimes arranged for pre-pubertal daughters with the understanding that consummation might not take place for some years. In more recent times, even with the gradual decline in 'child-marriage', delayed consummation was still not uncommon. Thus a young woman could carry out her parents' wishes to marry, but she might still refuse to enter into a 'real' marriage for some months, either out of a desire to remain in the security of the parental home longer, or because of dissatisfaction with the prospective husband. In some cases she might never agree to sexual union with the selected partner, and the marriage would be dissolved without ever being consummated. Of all the unions recorded in the marriage history in Maguwoharjo, 24 per cent of first marriages - and 5 per cent and 7 per cent of second and third marriages, respectively - involved delays in consummation.

A fairly extreme case illustrates how the system might work in practice:

> [Her] first marriage was dissolved without being consummated, because she didn't like her parents' choice of a mate. After her parents arranged a second marriage she again refused to cohabit, but this time on the grounds that her husband had no prospect of getting his own house for several years. The marriage remained unconsummated for nearly three years, by which time the couple was able to get a house alone, cohabitation began, and the marriage was consummated.

The pattern of delayed consummation is clearly related to other demographic variables, since the modal stated reason for divorce (24%) was dislike associated with an unconsummated union. A substantial number of arranged marriages (17%) were followed by delays of consummation of over one year, with the majority of these never being consummated but ending in divorce.

On the basis of these findings it seemed important that any study of trends in the age at marriage in Java should include questions on the method of arrangement of marriage and the timing of the consummation of the union. Women in Maguwoharjo and Sriharjo did not object to such questions and they provided important information. Thus it is strange to find that the World Fertility Survey in Java and Bali failed to include such questions despite advice to this effect. On finding a trend over time toward shorter intervals between marriage and first birth, the WFS Principal Report speculates that the cause is perhaps due 'to understatement of the respondents' current age, or event displacement, or omission of births for the oldest women' (World Fertility Survey, 1978, p.54), but never mentions the possibility that a declining incidence of delays in consummation could offer at least a partial explanation.

Estimation of Ages

One of the reasons analysts commonly turn to age misstatement as an explanation of the patterns they find in data, such as is seen in the quote of the WFS report in the previous paragraph, is that age data are generally poor in societies where little attention is paid to the anniversaries of births. Accurate age determination comes with the spread of bureaucratic demands to record dates of birth, and certify ages for entry into schools, for population registration cards, and for eligibility to receive social welfare benefits. It is also associated with traditions of astrology which rely on dates of birth, and customary celebrations of birthdays. Such things were all absent from most Indonesian cultures and communities until the very recent past, and thus survey researchers have encountered great difficulty in recording accurate estimates of people's ages. The problem used to be thought so great that the colonial government did not even ask a question about age in the census of 1930, except in a few isolated regions with generally high education levels, though in other ways this was the first modern census of the archipelago. Problems of misstatement in the censuses of 1971 and 1980 (Ahmad, 1984) were substantial, but for the most part errors due to rounding off ages have been gradually disappearing as the population grows older and succeeding cohorts are better educated.

At the start of the Maguwoharjo study it was known that the village census would encounter difficulties in determining age. As a result the form was designed with spaces to record the initial statement of age and the relation of each household member to the person providing the age estimates. Then the interviewer asked for a documentary source of the age, and if this was available, the second estimate was recorded so that comparison could be made between the two sources.

Following the census, all of the birth certificates available in the village office and the sub-district centre were copied, while the second stage of the survey, the pregnancy history and economic survey, was being carried out in the field. Respondents to the pregnancy history were questioned in detail about their ages and the dates of birth of their children. Historical event lists, Javanese and Muslim calendars, and questions about sequences and durations of life-course events were all used to try to improve the estimates of age. Where possible the birth certificates of the children were used as the source of the date of birth, and these established points of reference against which other events could be related.

The result of these detailed and time-consuming efforts was the improvement of age estimates for both mothers and children (see analysis of the results in T. Hull, 1975, pp.399-419). Birth certificates were found for over two-thirds of the live births recorded on the pregnancy history. More than one-third of the women provided estimates of their own age in the pregnancy history which involved a shift of five-year age groups, compared to the census estimates which were often provided by other household members. Among women over 35, nearly one in six shifted more than two five-year age categories from the original estimate. Because of the intensive methods used to obtain the later estimates we regard them as being better. Support for this judgement can be found in the reasons for the shifts of estimates. Usually the 'erroneous' estimate was not given by the woman directly, but rather by another householder. In a few cases documentary evidence revealed that women had purposely given incorrect ages to create the impression that they were older or younger than their actual age, in order to conform to some norms relating to appropriate ages to attend school, marry, or bear children.

While there is little doubt that the surveys in Maguwoharjo were improved through the use of intensive techniques to obtain estimates of age, it is less clear that the experience has produced important lessons for those undertaking censuses and sample surveys. Attempts have been made by the Central Bureau of Statistics to use indigenous calendars and event charts, but these are techniques which require lengthy training and great patience on the part of interviewers, both of which are luxuries in surveys done on a national scale. The use of birth certificates can be justified in a community study where everybody is in the sample, but the cost of searching and matching names would rise enormously if certificates were sought on even a small fraction of the children in a large number of villages. Thus, most of the techniques developed in Maguwoharjo and later community studies may be useful to other people undertaking micro-studies, but they do not transfer easily to the large, complex sample survey.

While the techniques may be parochial, one element of the overall strategy may have more general application. That is, just as in the census and the pregnancy history each estimate was recorded with information about the respondent or the documentary source of the information, so in national sample surveys interviewers can be trained to record more details about sources of information to aid later analysis. It is striking that household expenditure, or general demographic surveys, or even censuses in Indonesia do not record information on the name and basic characteristics of the person providing information on the household. Numerous studies have shown that differences in responses of husbands and wives can be significant, and there is every reason to believe that similar differences would occur between responses from people of different generations, or among relatives living together in an extended family. The experience of age reports for women in Maguwoharjo indicates that some respondents can be as much as ten years off in the estimation of ages of relatives in the same household. If national surveys contained more information on the source of information, it would allow analysts to go beyond measures of the degree of error such as Myer's Index and U.N. Index of age misstatement, and into some of the causes of misstatement.

Reflections on Combined Research Methods

A common criticism of community studies is that they make too much of what is happening in a very small place. After undertaking the Sriharjo and Maguwoharjo studies and a number of other investigations, our feeling is quite different. Rather than making too much of the small community studied, we are concerned that we have made too little of the material that was collected. There are many reasons for this feeling, some of which derive from important characteristics of the combined research approach.

First, there is the fact that the combined approaches involve an evolution of methods and directions of inquiry throughout the duration of the research and beyond. The fieldworker is at once data collector, data processor, analyst and critic, and each day brings new insights into the phenomena under investigation, and the opportunity to collect new types of information. Inevitably large amounts of data are gathered which are not later used either because they are found to be invalidly formulated, or merely because the rush of new ideas robs them of relevance. In Maguwoharjo concern with the work schedules of children was overshadowed by the discovery of great differences of fertility and family planning use among different social classes, and the relation of costs of schooling of children to falling ideal family sizes. In Sriharjo an early hypothesis that abortion determined traditional fertility levels was overtaken by the findings on abstinence patterns and the lack of any apparent impact from the limited number of cases of abortion which were discovered. Whereas the designers of sample surveys have to commit themselves to a fixed regime of questions very early in their investigation, and live with the consequences of those decisions, the use of a combined approach allows researchers to try new questions each day, and thus follow intuition in the development of the project.

The second reason community studies amass large amounts of data is that they are inherently interested in the total life of people, including all the gossip, ceremonies, activities and daily routines which are continuously carried on around the researchers. Observation is inevitable, and participation becomes second-nature as the researcher takes on various roles as a resident of the community. At that point the problem is not one of finding data, but rather of developing methods of recording and reviewing information in ways which are efficient, unobtrusive, and permanent.

The third characteristic of a combined approach which leads to massive data collection is the process of hypothesis formation and testing. Whereas the analyst working on an established data set and the fieldworker setting up a laboratory-style survey experiment have formally stated hypotheses to guide and discipline their research, the use of a combined set of approaches fosters the rapid evolution of hypotheses as part of the fieldwork. Without a fixed formal hypothesis to give direction to the data collection the fieldworker must rely on rigorous techniques and mental discipline as well as clear understanding of theory to guide the research. This can be an exhausting process. Each day involves a variety of routine tasks, many of which demand the attention of the principal investigator, but time must still be set aside for informal interviews and review of data already collected, as well as reflection on the meaning of emerging patterns. In the process it is easy to become uncertain about the preliminary results and set out on new lines of enquiry which later prove fruitless. The result is a proliferation of information.

Combining techniques in the study of a community involves more than the accumulation of 'data'; it is much more a matter of establishing a variety of roles and in the process achieving an intuitive understanding - an empathy - concerning the way things work in the community. Singarimbun's insight into poverty in Sriharjo was profoundly affected by seeing an old woman weeping when some pots she was carrying to the market had broken. Though worth only a few coins, they represented her entire trading capital, and she was financially ruined. Another person broke down during an interview when asked how many times a day they ate rice (it being preferred to eat rice three times a day). She cried because she didn't have food for a meal that very evening, and didn't know what she would do. In Maguwoharjo the Hulls found that frequent funerals of children put meaning in the survey results on infant mortality. The mourning, being encouraged to view and touch the corpse, discussing the probable cause of death and later participating in the ritual meal held to seek a return to stability in the community, all served to fix impressions in our mind which helped us to understand why the question 'What is a good thing about having lots of children?' brought the answer 'In case some die'.

The importance of participation goes beyond such issues of empathy to include two related issues of perception and understanding. The first relates to the complexity of institutions. On surveys it is possible to inventory and briefly describe institutions (Freedman, 1974) but it takes a great deal more information to understand how things work in practice. Because institutions are like organic entities, being made of many parts which change and interact over time, the key issue is to see how different people involved in the institution view their own role and the roles of their colleagues. By living for a time in a community the researcher begins to 'feel' the way the bureaucracy works, and developes a sense of the difference between the public and private faces of bureaucrats. Being drawn into conflicts by protagonists anxious to obtain outside support for their positions is an uncomfortable but greatly educational means of understanding the workings of the local government office, the police, a cultural group or the women's organization.

The second advantage of participation is the ability to reach what Jay (1969, pp.20-29) calls lower 'levels of conception'. High levels of conception refer to the standard or automatic answers which people give to questions put by researchers. These are often influenced by social norms, or by habitual responses drawing on clichés, folk sayings, or formal religious and secular teaching. As researchers learn more about the sources of such responses it becomes possible to frame questions which probe deeper, and avoid stock replies. Jay also notes that it is possible to sense the level of a discussion from the posture, expression, vocabulary and general demeanour of the respondent. With growing skill in handling the social and cultural vocabularies, and growing familiarity between themselves and respondents, fieldworkers can eventually reach levels of conception which reveal personal thoughts including doubts and uncertainties which could be very important in explaining behaviour, but would not be revealed either in responses to a survey question or in conversations at more formal levels. Such a process allows for the probing of concepts such as ideal family size, attitudes toward contraceptive methods, concerns about schooling children, and fears concerning illness and death.

Conclusions

We see the Sriharjo and Maguwoharjo studies as coming out of a tradition of anthropological enquiry into population issues, converging with improved techniques of modern survey research. Focus on a single community opens the possibility of interpreting behaviour in a social context, and understanding the complex nature of social institutions. Use of survey and informal interviews leads researchers through different levels of conceptualization, and illuminates behaviour which might otherwise be regarded as inconsistent with answers to simple survey questions. Because hypotheses are not formally set at the beginning of the research, but evolve over time, researchers must pay particular attention to the techniques they are using to discipline their enquiries. The precise combination of techniques will depend on the availability of data from other sources, such as sample surveys, censuses and ethnographies, and the resources available to the researcher. Because personal participation is such an important element in the app oach, the researcher can be faced with an exhausting schedule if the various types of data collected are not carefully planned. Such a problem is, however, more than offset by the exhilaration of being part of a community, and the daily discovery of new insights into the way of life of people who have become friends. The combination of techniques in a community study may be classified as a micro-approach, but like historical studies of villages and genealogical reconstructions, it will yield macro-returns intellectually in the field of population studies.

APPENDIX

Combined Techniques in the Micro-Approach: Examples from Maguwoharjo

Data collection in Maguwoharjo involved the use of journals and fieldnotes; individual 'case studies' or notes on specific topics; and participant observation. Quantitative data included a multistage survey and supplementary information such as village and clinic records. A number of examples of the way in which these field techniques were implemented might serve as a useful record for those pursuing similar studies.

Fieldnotes and Journals

The basic recording tool of the anthropologist, field notebooks, were kept by all members of the Maguwoharjo study team. Early in the research, another set of notebooks on topics of special interest (marriage patterns, pregnancy and childbirth, contraception, and so forth) was kept at the home base so that the assistants could transcribe important fieldnotes for use by others interested in a subject or requiring the information for their *skripsi* (theses). As the study progressed, however, the case study system described below gradually came to replace this central set of fieldnotes. As was expected, some members of the team were more assiduous than others in keeping fieldnotes; those most motivated tended to be the team member with an anthropological background, and those who were writing *skripsi*.

The fieldnotes recorded detailed descriptions of places such as the local market; events such as village meetings and ceremonies; particular incidents such as the death of a neighbour's child, and other aspects of village life. However, in addition the principal investigators kept diaries or journals which recorded the more personal impressions and reactions to scenes, people and experiences. Thus, the death of the neighbour's child was recorded twice - once in fieldnotes complete with description of rituals observed, people who attended the various stages of the funeral, financial and work contributions, discussions of cause of death and comments by family and neighbours, and so on; and for a second time in a journal which dealt with personal observations and reactions, and the role of the outside researcher coming to terms with the event.

As in all such studies, many fieldnotes were not directly incorporated into subsequent written material, and many dealt with areas tangential to the focus of the main research. Nevertheless these notes greatly assisted in observing and absorbing the events recorded, a process which enriched our knowledge of the community.

'Case Studies'

A 'case study' in the Maguwoharjo research was a description of particular incidents or situations which were examples of behaviour patterns and attitudes found in the village. Three main types of information were collected on printed case study cards:

1. Elaborations of information gained during the formal interview.

During the daily checking of interview schedules, we often encountered cases about which we wanted more detail. A case study card was then attached to the interview schedule describing the subject of interest; this would be returned to the interviewer as a possible topic for future conversation, either on a subsequent interview visit, or at a chance encounter. For example, a completed interview schedule might include brief reference to the use of a traditional herbal mixture to assist breastfeeding, which could then be pursued with a request for details of particular ingredients, method of preparation, source of knowledge, cost, and other information.

2. Detailed reports on topics initiated by the field assistants.

This kind of case study was similar to the first in intent, but the topic was chosen by the field assistants. All assistants carried blank case study cards to the field every day (for the last stage of the survey, the card was incorporated into the final page of the interview schedule and was later detached), and they could record information of interest as needed. It was this process that eventually replaced the system of centralized field-notes transcribed by assistants, and to some degree, also replaced the first type of case study described above, as assistants came to anticipate the kinds of topics which we might want pursued through case studies.

3. The case study as a 'mini-survey'.

Through conversation or reading (for the field is an excellent place to read and reread literature about the society), we occasionally encountered something of interest which could not be incorporated into the questionnaire, but which might be important to our research in a broad sense. One example concerned a ceremony called a *ruwatan* that people are meant to conduct if they have only one or two children. When we questioned people informally there appeared to be fundamental variations concerning the conditions under which people are compelled to give the ceremony, about its expense and importance, and we wanted to ask a larger number of people in order to see if a clearer conception could be obtained. Case study cards were filled in with questions about the *ruwatan* and distributed to all interviewers for a week, to be asked of all respondents. While this did not yield the views of everyone in the sample areas, we were able to reach a larger number of people than the few with whom we could personally discuss it. The results indicated that while *ruwatan* may have been a major ceremonial expense at one time, it was currently carried out only in attenuated form if at all.

In the field, case study cards were filed according to the identification number of the individual, so that they were easily found prior to revisits to the respondent, or for clarification of points on subsequent interview schedules. For the analysis stage, however, they were re-arranged according to general topic (for example, marriage patterns, breastfeeding, the various forms of contraception, and so on), and within each topic by identification number. Thus all case studies on topics discussed in the analysis could be referred to easily, while specific individuals could also be located according to their identification number, for further clarification of survey data or fieldnotes.

General Observation

The very fact of living in the community, talking with and observing people first hand, and gradually coming to feel a part - however 'special' - of village life over a year, added immeasurably to the depth of the study. The fieldworker must, however, be prepared for the involvement in terms of work, time and emotions which the approach demands. Simultaneous administration of a survey, which also requires heavy commitment, is a fierce competitor to the more intensive approaches.

In Java, as in most societies, it is expected that neighbours will attend all ceremonies, and these occasions provide excellent opportunities for discussing aspects of local life. It is more difficult, however, to ensure that one takes the time during odd hours of the day to visit, chat, make friends, and observe the daily rhythms of village life as well. It was often found that giving information is a great aid to obtaining it in return, so that the trading of stories about life in Australia and Java yielded new perspectives on both sides. Whether or not meticulous field notes are recorded on each occasion, this experience becomes an invaluable part of the knowledge gained.

The Survey Stages

1. Overview

The survey, done in stages, was improved by knowledge of local conditions in a number of ways, and also included several innovative design features. While the survey approach itself still has basic limitations inherent in the technique, much can be done to improve its quality as a research tool.

2. Schedule design, translation, pre-testing

Although most researchers make some attempt to design surveys appropriate to the culture, the Maguwoharjo survey placed particular emphasis on this aspect. Each stage of the survey was designed only after discussions with local social researchers, village leaders, and village neighbours, and drew upon daily experiences and conversations in the village. Preliminary drafts of each schedule were discussed in detail with the interviewer-assistants. These discussion sessions, which had elements of debate and role playing as well as simple explanation, also ensured that any prejudices or misconceptions on the part of the interviewers could be revealed and corrected. Initial translation of schedules also took place during these sessions: these were then checked by local university contacts.

The schedules were pre-tested in a physically isolated hamlet on the eastern border of the village, with the principal researchers sitting in on initial interviews. The pre-test for each stage was followed by more discussion and revision until the final schedules were agreed upon.

3. Some features of the survey design

An example of one of the innovative features of the survey which aimed at maximizing accuracy was the use of individual marriage and pregnancy cards for each separate event in a woman's history. These were attached to a master form which contained general information and which also summarized data from the individual cards. The card system proved especially valuable for pregnancies, since the interviewer could ask about events using an order of questioning which was simpler for the woman to remember - children still living at home, then those living away, those now deceased, and then pregnancy losses; or whatever order the mother found most logical and easy to remember. The interviewer could then re-arrange the set of cards into chronological order, checking intervals with the woman, relating one event to the other, and finally reading out the entire sequence of events for final confirmation. This was a decided improvement over the chart form of pregnancy history for ease of interviewing, and was also well suited to computer processing.

Another somewhat different feature of the schedule design arose from the fact that interviewing was done in stages, and we were able to use information from earlier schedules to improve the interview situation for subsequent schedules. The final stage, the attitude survey, used this technique extensively in an effort to make the schedule more suited to each individual case. Thus, where eligibility for certain questions varied (for example, those who had been divorced, those who had given birth in the three years preceding the interview, those who were pregnant at the time of the pregnancy history, and so on), eligibility or non-eligibility was noted on the schedule before it was taken to the field. Although in each case the information was briefly confirmed, the approach avoided much of the awkwardness which filter questions often involve. The technique was also used in an effort to help the respondent answer certain sections of the attitude survey. For example, the work history for women was divided into general life cycle stages - the year before marriage, the first year of marriage, the period when the woman had at least one young (under age 6) child, and the period when all the woman's children were aged 6 or older. Before this schedule was taken to the field, pertinent names and/or events were filled in to delineate these stages for the particular woman. Thus she would be questioned on the year before and the year after her marriage to, for example, *Pak Atmo*; then for the period from the birth of *Ponirah* (her first child) to when *Djuminem* (the last child) was about 6 years old, and so on. This process would be less suitable in a situation where respondents were concerned with anonymity or were otherwise threatened by the fact that the interviewer knew the names of their children and other information. However, it was received very well in Maguwoharjo, certainly in part because the interviewers did know most of the respondents quite well by the time of the final stage. The personal approach to the questioning was thus not out of place.

This way of constructing the schedules was also of benefit to us as supervisors of the survey, since we did not do the formal interviewing, yet wanted to have a better grasp of the survey responses. For example, a few days before a woman was to be interviewed for the attitude survey, we read through and coded her pregnancy history (which we had already read as part of the editing process at the time it was collected). Then, using that and the census, we filled in the required information on the pregnancy history follow-up and the attitude survey (the pregnancy interval history, the work history, eligibility for certain questions, and so on). When the attitude survey was completed a few days later, we read through the responses as part of the daily checking routine. By this time the respondent was more familiar, even in cases where we did not know her personally, and we could fit the series of interviews together, questioning the interviewer about any possible inconsistencies. The work involved in a large survey can be overwhelming and it is undoubtedly quite easy to lose touch with the data being collected; this was one means by which valuable contact was maintained.

4. The application of local concepts

Although pre-fieldwork preparations for the study included collecting sample questions from fertility surveys used in many parts of the world, the study aimed at adapting schedules to local conditions. For example, the determination of current marital status considered a wider range of possibilities than the conventional demographic categories, recognizing in addition the situations of women who had had a *kawin gantung* (a marriage ceremony but had not begun sexual relations), *kumpul kebo* (those who were cohabiting without any form of legal marriage), *pisah kebo* (those separated but not legally divorced, deserted wives, and wives of political prisoners). Dates of marriage were often collected according to the Javanese calendar and then converted for use in calculations.

A consideration of local systems of time reckoning is important in schedule design and data collecting, and has particular applicability in Javanese culture. The society's awareness of calendric cycles, frequently marked by rituals, and the overall pervasiveness of the Javanese numerological system can yield much information which enhances the quality of the data collected. Some of the ways in which dates of birth were obtained during the pregnancy history illustrate the variety of these approaches:

a) Women often knew the Javanese month of birth, which could then be converted with the aid of a special almanac. Sometimes the name of a child is a clue to its birth month: the name *Surono*, for example, is derived from the first month of the Javanese year, *Suro*. Javanese months of particular significance are easy to remember when they are birth months, and one respondent related that her marriage month was *Puasa*, (the fasting month), remembering that this necessitated abstinence from intercourse during daylight hours.

b) Another source of dates was discovered on a visit to a house in our hamlet. On one of the main pillars of the house, printed in whitewash, was a number which we were told was the date the house had been built. On further enquiry it was learned that many literate villagers record various important dates on walls, pillars, or doors of their homes, and among these we found several birth dates of children.

c) In instances where it was not possible to obtain an actual date or month, usually for cases of pregnancy loss or children who died soon after birth, an effort was made to relate the event to other events in the pregnancy history. This meant the usual technique of placing the birth of one child relative to the birth or death of another, but in Java it is also sometimes possible to position an event with more precision by utilizing information on *selametan*, (rituals which occur a fixed number of days after births or deaths, and during pregnancy). Thus if one date could be fixed, for example the date of death of one child obtained from village records, we attempted to position a succeeding birth relative to the death *selametan* of the older sibling: before or after the 100-day ritual, the 1000-day ritual, and so on. Deaths of young infants can usually be fixed before or after the ritual held when the child is 5 days old, 35 days old, or 105 days old, and pregnancy losses may be placed relative to pregnancy *selametan*.

d) Also important in the marital and pregnancy histories was the time line of events prepared after consultation with village residents, and which used local events as much as possible.

5. Interviewing, checking, and coding

Training for the survey included a general discussion soon after we all arrived in the village; several sessions specific to each stage of the survey; and spontaneous sessions whenever particular problems arose. Though some assistants had previous interviewing experience, only two had engaged in an intensive project with a community study approach. A great deal of emphasis was placed on our desire for conversational interviews, for the recording (not necessarily at the time of the interview, but soon after) of remarks related to topics on the interview schedule, and for the collection of attitudes and opinions outside the formal interview situation. Assistants were asked to fit into the routine of the village as much as possible, and to learn from the total experience of being part of the community. This was all a valuable part of their training: the formal survey, even though it was at times complex, had its manuals for reference, and had been practised innumerable times. Obtaining information through less structured means, and learning how to establish rapport with respondents, were skills developed during the course of the study. It should be added that although all the assistants had some rural background, many were from elite families and, to varying degrees, at first seemed to lack empathy for the way of life in the village. The year we spent there did much to increase not only their knowledge but their sensitivity in this area.

Interviewing followed a basic daily routine, which included evening sessions between the assistants and ourselves concerning the day's data collection. Also, the procedure of daily inspection and discussion of completed schedules was, in addition to being a check for accuracy, an opportunity to talk about issues arising from the interviews of the day. After reading through each schedule, we could ask an interviewer for more detailed information about responses, and discuss each interview in general. Specific questions or omissions were printed on a question card which was affixed to the interview schedule and given to the assistant to be taken back to the field for clarification.

All coding and check-coding was done in the field by us and by the assistants, using detailed codebooks constructed in consultation with the assistants. During the coding process all cases of responses coded as 'Other' were entered in books with the identification number of the respondent, to assist in the tabulation stage of analysis. Also begun in the field as preparation for analysis was a series of books for editing data, including code ranges and basic consistency checks, which formed the basis for the computer edit program written after returning from Indonesia to Australia.

Notes

1. Some of the substantive findings of the studies, not discussed here, are found in the references by T. Hull, V. Hull, and M. Singarimbun.

5

Micro-Study of Culture and Fertility in Rural Maharashtra

Carol Vlassoff

Background and Objectives

The present paper discusses the advantages of incorporating a micro-approach into larger demographic surveys, using a study conducted by the author in rural India as an illustrative case. The study examined the relationship between cultural factors and fertility and family planning among rural Indian women. The main objectives of the research were to explore the nature and degree of traditionalism among these women, and the extent to which cultural attitudes and values influenced fertility and family planning practice.

The research design was a combination of the micro-study and survey approaches. This strategy was decided upon for several reasons: the greater manageability of the data collection which was done by the author personally; the sensitivity of many of the questions, necessitating trust and acceptance among the villagers; and, most important, the desire to understand the complex phenomena of culture and fertility motivation as comprehensively as possible. While it was anticipated that more traditional women would have higher fertility and lower contraceptive use than more modern women, the accurate identification and measurement of modernity in the village context and the factors responsible for change in traditional attitudes were themselves questions to be resolved. It was felt, therefore, that in-depth acquaintance with local beliefs and practices would not only clarify the meaning of this concept but would also greatly enhance the analysis and interpretation of the survey's findings.

The primary criterion for the selection of a village was that it be, as far as possible, 'typical' of rural Western Maharashtra, an agricultural region where subsistence farming predominated. The community chosen for the study seemed, in most respects, characteristic of the region in terms of economic, social and demographic indicators. The principal cash crops, sugar cane, peanuts and hybrid sorghum, were grown by the wealthier farmers. Subsistence crops were 'local' sorghum, rice, wheat and vegetables. In spite of its largely traditional character, the village had adopted a limited amount of modern agricultural technology, including fertilizers, pesticides and some irrigation. It had a population of 2,100, comprising: 87 per cent of workers engaged primarily in agricultural occupations, and literacy levels were 32 per cent for females and 57 per cent for males. The nearest commercial centre, 14 kilometres away, was easily accessible by road for only 6 months a year. The village had been affected by certain modernizing influences, including a primary and high school; daily newspapers from the district headquarters of Satara posted outside the village council office; considerable out-migration to Bombay, 270 kilometres distant; and a small co-operative seed processing plant, operated by the village on a commercial basis. The area had also been influenced by the national family planning program which had been fairly intensive in Maharashtra for over two decades. Following the failure of a major 1965 campaign promoting the intra-uterine device (IUD), the program concentrated on sterilization, encouraged by mass communication and local leaders. However, legislation for compulsory sterilization was never passed in Maharashtra, and the program was much better organized, more carefully monitored and generally more effective than in northern India at the time.

Methodology

The village study commenced in November 1975, after 9 months of preparatory work in Pune, a large urban centre approximately 100 kilometres from the study village. Preparation included language training, questionnaire design and field trips to select the pre-test and study areas. In general, the villagers were receptive and friendly, expressing a desire for their village to be chosen for the survey. Nonetheless, when the author first moved to the village, the responses of the residents were mixed. Some were hospitable and open, some polite but reserved, others were obviously suspicious. An almost universal reaction, however, was of irrepressible curiosity, about both the study and the researcher. Although the researcher was an expatriate, most village women (and many men) failed to comprehend this fact. A concept of a world consisting of many nations was entirely unknown to them and most people simply assumed that the foreigner came from a distant Indian state such as Assam or Himachal Pradesh.

One soon learned to be as open as possible to the villagers' queries and to gracefully accept their presence during most daily activities. Even routine household chores - cooking, cleaning, laundry, bathing were frequently observed with considerable interest. Gradually, these informal interchanges created an atmosphere of mutual trust and understanding and villagers were delighted to observe the researcher's gradual adoption of local customs and practices. Along with the goodwill came certain hardships and inconveniences - occasional shortages of food and water, isolation during the monsoon, the almost unbearable summer heat and the continual presence of rats and vermin.

Although an effort was made to delay commencing the survey until several weeks had been spent in the community, many villagers were impatient to see the work begin. The survey was therefore initiated earlier than planned (after one month's residence in the community), but at a more leisurely pace. A local assistant, a female high school graduate from the 'backward' or *harijan*[1] caste, was hired to accompany the researcher in all the interviews. The assistant helped to put respondents at ease and, although she spoke only *Marathi*, she repeated the interview questions when necessary and interpreted the more difficult ones for women who failed to understand. While her selection was made on the recommendations of the village leadership, her father being an important political figure in the area, the girl's lowly caste origins sometimes created interesting problems. On the one hand, her presence in the traditional Hindu household was 'polluting', yet her prestigious position as a research assistant and her relatively high salary (equal to an adult male labourer's daily wage) made it difficult to treat her disrespectfully. Thus she was never actually refused entry into any of the houses, but occasional reticence was observed, particularly among the older women.

Several days were spent in mapping the main village, a process which promoted direct contact and familiarization with the residents. A complete census of socioeconomic and demographic characteristics of village households was also carried out. This provided the basis for selection of eligible respondents for the main survey: 349 married women aged 15-49. By the end of these initial steps (lasting approximately 6 weeks) the villagers recognized that the research was having no adverse effects and showed little continuing interest in the nature of the study. This was especially true of women, who found research issues incomprehensible, but never tired of observing and commenting upon the author's personal attributes and activities. In fact, when the researcher returned to the village several months after the study's completion, people had all but forgotten the questionnaires, yet remembered other, seemingly trivial, events which had occurred during the period.

Women were selected as the focus of the investigation because the subjects of most previous research on Third World modernization had been men (Lerner, 1958; Kahl, 1968; Inkeles and Smith, 1974), providing little insight into the cultural values of females. Mothers, moreover, were assumed to be central agents in children's socialization and, as such, in future societal change (Fawcett and Bornstein, 1973). There was also some evidence that wives' opinions were more important than their husbands' in influencing contraceptive practice (Chandrasekaran, 1959; Khalifa, 1973).

In order to allow time to observe and participate in community activities only three or four questionnaires were administered daily, taking about 4 hours in total. Interviews were given at times convenient for the respondents, varying according to the agricultural season. Non-survey time was spent in household tasks, chatting with the villagers and attending special functions such as weddings, naming ceremonies for infants, and religious festivities. Such involvement in local affairs provided rare insights into the women's deeper concerns: frustration over their treatment by household elders; concealed pregnancies and abortions; folk methods of contraception; as well as sexual practices and problems.

Since the survey instruments and results are described elsewhere (Vlassoff, 1978, 1979, 1980, 1982), they are not repeated in detail here. The following sections focus upon selected illustrations of the methodological and substantive insights gained from the micro-approach.

Methodological Contributions of the Micro-Approach

The methodological contributions of the micro-approach to the present investigation can be conveniently grouped into two categories: (i) improvement in data quality and (ii) the development of locally relevant instruments. In this section these insights will be discussed, using concrete examples from the study.

Improvement in Data Quality

The quality of the data was doubtless improved by the micro-approach, firstly because it led to considerable co-operation from a group of shy and largely illiterate women, most of whom were totally unaccustomed to articulating their attitudes and beliefs. Since all important decisions were made by men, women were rarely consulted for their opinions. Hence, many women sought to avoid the interviews altogether, or to seek 'protection' in the presence of friends and relatives.

To circumvent these problems, areas of the village which seemed most receptive to the research were selected first. The interviewing was begun in the *harijan* neighbourhood where the researcher's assistant lived. Within each area the most co-operative women were selected first: neighbours, leaders' wives and women who were openly receptive or inquisitive about the survey. Their example helped to assure more reticent respondents that the interviews were innocuous. The most hesitant or unco-operative women were left until the end of the study, by which time their anxieties had generally disappeared.

Co-operation was also enhanced by scheduling the interview at times which suited the respondents. The researcher's continual presence in the village made such adjustments possible. During peak agricultural periods the interviews were held in the early morning before the women left for work, or late in the day after they returned. In the summer the hot afternoons provided a convenient time, when women generally rested and were in a more receptive mood.

The rapport established by the micro-approach made it possible to obtain complete privacy in the interviews. The personal nature of the questions, especially those concerning husband-wife relations, sexual practices, abortion and contraception, made privacy virtually mandatory. Because it was extremely difficult to obtain privacy in crowded village houses several trial interviews were conducted in the presence of other females and/or children during the pre-test. A multiplicity of problems emerged: some respondents were shy or tongue-tied; some giggled and ran away; others asked their relatives to respond for them (some relatives answered for them without being asked); respondents' answers were generally debated by the audience; and interruptions of all kinds occurred. It was therefore clear that privacy was a *sine-qua-non* of reliable data.

The result of the above procedures was a very high response rate of 98.6 per cent; only five women refused to be interviewed. These women were known for their eccentricity and failure to participate in village affairs more generally. Not all other women were equally co-operative, however, and persuasive efforts had to be made in about one quarter of the cases. For example, women were encouraged to verbalize their doubts or fears which could then be rationally addressed through frank discussion and reassurance. Return visits were also necessary on many occasions. Mothers-in-law frequently objected to their daughters-in-law being interviewed in private. Since the younger woman's status was considerably lower, the mother-in-law could not understand why she was not consulted instead. Sometimes it also seemed that such women feared their daughters-in-law would complain about their ill-treatment, discuss 'indiscreet' topics such as sex or abortion, or divulge family secrets. The intervention and gentle persuasion of male village leaders usually helped to allay such fears.

Although these measures were time-consuming and sometimes troublesome, the results improved the representativeness of the conclusions. During the interviews the reasons for women's hesitancy usually became clear. One, for example, had experienced a tragic succession of infant deaths and felt that the interview would stimulate these painful memories. Another, a daughter-in-law from a relatively prestigious family, had feared detection of her husband's leprosy, something the family had tried to conceal from the community at large. Still others were afraid that the interviews were connected with the sterilization program, and that co-operation would entail eventual enlistment for the operation. Since such doubts and fears were closely related to the aims of the study itself, it was important that such women not be excluded from the analysis.

Development of Locally Relevant Instruments

As mentioned previously, the study aimed at understanding and measuring modernization within the context of rural Maharashtrian women. Many previous studies of the modern-traditional continuum were largely inapplicable because the questions used would have been meaningless to the average respondent. Questions such as 'If ... you could not live in our country, what other country would you choose to live in?' (Lerner, 1958, p.45) were obviously inappropriate for women who could not even name another nation, let alone rank countries in terms of preference. Yet it would have been erroneous to conclude that, relative to rural society at least, there were no 'modern' women.

The case studies summarized below indicate the fallacy of assuming that all village women are equally traditional:

At the age of five Anjeli married her eighteen-year-old husband. She moved to his home when she was eight and hardly remembers her own parents. She still strongly prefers child-marriage. At sixteen she is pregnant but refuses to talk about it. She feels thankful for any number of children God sends. Her coming delivery will be attended only by her sister-in-law at home. She fears and distrusts hospitals and modern medicine.

Ranibai was married when she was thirteen years old and had her first child at sixteen. One of their children, a son, died of dysentery at the age of one. Her youngest child is ten years old and she anticipates no more children. Should she become pregnant she will have to undergo a sterilization operation after her delivery. Ranibai still feels it is too early for her 22-year-old son to marry. Nor will she arrange her daughter's marriage until she has completed secondary school. When her children leave for school each day, Ranibai sits with a slate and copies from a junior textbook, teaching herself to read and write.

Malan, 20 years old, has been married for one year. She is intelligent and friendly but assumes a shy and subordinate manner when her father-in-law is present. Her parents-in-law work in the fields while she manages the household affairs. Having free time she works on her B.A. by correspondence. She hopes to complete it in three years. In her view, this will mainly benefit her children since she does not plan to seek employment herself. Eventually she hopes to join her husband who works in a nearby town and to save enough money to raise a small family. Malan does not want a child for at least three years and will limit her family to two. When her husband is home they use condoms, believing that family planning should not be left to God or fate.

Such cases clearly illustrate significant differences in attitudes and behaviour among village women - in education, age at marriage, fertility and family planning. In order to gauge these differences in more quantifiable terms, indicators were classified into three categories: (i) socioeconomic background indicators; (ii) a cultural attitude scale; and (iii) attitudes related to fertility and family planning. The indicators were selected on the basis of reviews of literature on women in Indian culture, conversations with women of various classes, personal observation of rural and urban females, and testing, revising and re-testing the questions over the study's preparatory period. The intensive village study provided the basis for more adequately testing these variables and interpreting their relationships to the dependent variables, fertility and family planning. For the sake of brevity only those measures which best differentiated women in terms of the independent modernization variables and dependent fertility variables are discussed here.

The socioeconomic background variables included education (or literacy),[2] number of 'modern' household facilities,[3] frequency of travel, husband's occupation,[4] residence in main village or outlying hamlets, age at marriage, family type and caste. Of these indicators education and frequency of travel were consistently strong predictors of fertility and family planning, while husband's occupation, age at marriage and caste were consistently, but more weakly, associated. 'Frequency of travel' was computed from several questions about the number, distance and destination of trips to Satara and beyond. For example, 'frequent' travel, the most 'modern' category, entailed visiting Satara at least four times a year, or visiting Satara twice a year and having visited a larger city once in the respondent's lifetime. The experience of visiting an urban centre seemed to have a significant modernizing effect. Seeing other women walking alone in the streets or eating with their husbands in restaurants, viewing modern Indian and, occasionally, Western movies, exposure to urban markets and the faster pace of city life accelerated the recognition of the existence of different values and lifestyles.

A 20-item additive scale was also developed in an attempt to differentiate modern and traditional women more precisely than was possible by means of background indicators alone. In the search for measures of modernization the 'OM scale' of Inkeles and Smith (1974), intended for cross-cultural application, was carefully examined. It was soon apparent that its relevance to the present study was limited, not only because of its male orientation but also because its questions pre-supposed considerable sophistication on the part of its respondents (factory workers). On the other hand, the categorization of questions into certain themes such as 'active public participation', 'aspirations', 'efficacy' and 'women's rights' (p.320) provided broad guidelines for the initial choice of question types.

The first four items of the scale were concerned with scientific versus non-scientific orientation. For example, an attack of smallpox was traditionally believed to represent the punishment of an angry goddess;[5] hence, someone interpreting smallpox in this way was classified as traditional with respect to this item. Similarly, women who felt that a medical practitioner (whether doctor, nurse, or village midwife[6]) should attend a delivery, rather than a relative or other unqualified person, were classified as 'less traditional'. The remaining sixteen items concerned approval of traditional values and customs (dowry, elders' authority), aspirations for sons versus daughters and attitudes towards women's rights and status.

For the most part cultural attitude scores correlated closely with the background socioeconomic variables. One can therefore ask to what extent the more time-consuming efforts involved in preparing this scale were justified in terms of producing superior measures of cultural traditionalism. The comparative advantages of the scale were not, in fact, conclusively demonstrated by the present study, but there were indications that it provided a more sensitive index than background variables, such as education, alone. For example, there was no statistically significant association between mothers' and daughters' educational attainment, yet more 'modern' mothers, as measured by cultural attitude scores, had significantly more educated daughters. In other words, it seems that modern attitudes on the part of mothers, even though the mothers themselves were relatively uneducated, played an important role in influencing intergenerational change. Generally, daughters were significantly more educated than their mothers: only 10 per cent of the girls had no education compared to 56 per cent of the older women, and 30 per cent of the adolescents had more than 7 years' schooling compared to only 7 per cent of the adult females.

Several attitudinal items related to family size were included in the questionnaire in order to assess fertility motivations and the degree to which they could be captured by the survey approach. The questions related to attitudes towards the economic value of children, fear of infant death, religious constraints and other traditional reasons for increasing or limiting childbearing. These questions proved to be reliable indicators neither of modernization nor of fertility behaviour. Generally, the women found them confusing and, never having thought of the reasons for childbearing in such explicit terms, had considerable difficulty in doing so. Subtle probes, indirect questions, and behavioural observation were required for a more accurate interpretation of fertility motivation in the village context.

In contrast, the questions regarding the dependent variables, fertility and family planning, were easily understood and answered by the respondents. The majority of questions were taken from standard knowledge, attitude and practice (KAP) surveys but were re-phrased in local terminology and carefully introduced. For example, pregnancy histories were gathered in a personal way: the respondent was asked to name each child and encouraged to talk about her/him. This put her at ease for further questions regarding expected and desired fertility which, although potentially difficult, were readily answered. After experimenting with different forms of these questions, it was apparent that a straightforward approach was most appropriate. Women were first asked when they were expecting the next child and, if they indicated that they planned to have another, those with two or fewer children were asked how many they wanted to have in total. Since it was felt that those having more than two might find it difficult to express a desire for fewer than they already had, the question was phrased slightly differently for women with two or more offspring: 'If you could start your life over again how many children would you like to have?'. By this method roughly comparable 'ideals' for the two groups were obtained. While some women still seemed to hesitate to give a lower ideal than the number they had themselves, a fairly sizeable percentage (35 per cent) of those with four to five living children and 42 per cent of those with six or more) said they would prefer a family of three or fewer children in a new life.

Another important question focused on the role of son preference in fertility decision-making: 'If you had only daughters and no sons, how many children would you have to get a son?'. The desire for sons was found to be the major reason for discrepancies between ideal and actual fertility among older women. Most respondents agreed that where there were no sons, it was virtually impossible to stop having children. Further complicating this picture was the feeling that two sons were ideal. Hence, even when a boy was among the first-born, the need for a second son often led couples to have several more children in the interim.

Through daily contact with the villagers, including children, adolescents and older men and women, opportunities were provided for the further investigation of many subjects, both directly related to the study's central theme and somewhat outside the realm of the investigation. Two sub-studies, one on adolescent attitudes (elaborated in Vlassoff, 1980) and one on the condition of village widows, were therefore incorporated into the larger analysis. These are mentioned here only to demonstrate how the flexibility provided by continuous residence in a community allowed for modifications in the study design and the introduction of new elements at a later stage.

Substantive Contributions of the Micro-Approach

The substantive insights acquired through the micro-approach were perhaps even more important than the methodological contributions in the present investigation. Participation in village life yielded rich contextual material on local institutions, beliefs and practices, useful in the interpretation of survey results, and in the development of hypotheses for further investigation. Illustrations of the more significant contributions are given in the following two sections.

Findings and Interpretation

Generally, fertility preferences among village women were relatively low (mean desired number 3.4) indicating the presence of modern values favouring smaller families. The main reason for preferring fewer children was economic: women felt that large families created a financial burden for parents. Of those having fewer than their desired number 83 per cent expected to meet their ideals exactly, sterilization being the chosen means for achieving these ends. Sterilization had therefore come to play an important part in helping women to meet their family size goals.

In spite of fairly low family size preferences, actual fertility often exceeded ideals, especially in the 35-49 age group. The latter cohort had borne, on average, 5.6 children (with 4.5 surviving), the 25-34 age group, 3.8 children (with 3.2 surviving) and the under 25 age cohort, 1.1 children (with 1.0 surviving). The desire to have a son was the most persistent obstacle to family size limitation.

Interestingly, cultural attitudes and the other modernization indicators used in the study were more closely associated with desired or ideal family size than with actual fertility. The expectation that traditional women would have higher fertility was not, in fact, borne out. In fact, in the 25-34 age group, modern women had significantly more living children than traditional respondents, but this was explained by the fact that mortality was higher in the more traditional groups. The anticipated differences between modern and traditional respondents were found, however, with respect to fertility ideals, particularly in the two younger age groups. The need for a son was expressed by all women, but traditional respondents were willing to bear more children in the hope of producing a son than modern women.

Most village women were knowledgeable about family planning, especially sterilization and the IUD, and approval, particularly for terminal methods, was high (90 per cent of non-sterilized couples approved of contraception). Family planning was also fairly widely practised: 29 per cent of respondents (or their husbands) had been sterilized and 7 per cent were using other methods (mainly condom or abstinence). Cultural traditionalism was related to contraceptive knowledge in the expected manner, with modern women knowing the most methods and traditional women, fewest. The relation between attitudes towards and practice of family planning was not as straightforward, and varied according to the contraceptive method examined. Approval and practice of non-permanent methods were consistently and positively associated with modern attitudes. Approval and use of sterilization, however, while positively related to modern attitudes in the 25-34 age group, were negatively related in the oldest cohort. That is, in the latter group, traditional women were more positive towards, and had made greater use of, sterilization than more modern women.

Familiarity with local beliefs and practices provided an explanation for this seemingly unusual finding. Sterilization had a special appeal for traditional women because it was generally undertaken at advanced ages, when reproduction is frowned upon and abstinence frequently practised. Being sterilized at older ages therefore demanded little modernization since no traditional values were called into question. Younger females, on the other hand, required a more modern outlook to adopt a terminal method because they were digressing from traditional roles in their decision to stop childbearing relatively early in life.

Although the study was mainly concerned with fertility, observations were also made of other demographic phenomena, including mortality, migration and nuptiality, which could be applied to future research on these subjects. Mortality, for example, was higher during the rainy season than at other times. This was no doubt partly due to the lack of access to medical facilities and to damp and changeable weather conditions, but an unusual behavioural change was also noted at that time. Whereas the villagers generally obtained their drinking water from wells, they chose to drink from the river during the monsoon because they preferred its taste. Naturally, the river was exceptionally polluted during this period, due to the greater quantities of waste and debris carried from upstream settlements.

Some interesting characteristics of migration were also observed. There was a high level of rural-urban migration, particularly of working-age males. Unexpectedly, Bombay attracted the majority of migrants, in spite of the fact that two large cities, Satara and Pune, were much closer to the village. Such migration was generally temporary, of several months' to many years' duration, and contacts with the village were strongly maintained. In many ways it seemed that urban life was merely an extension of rural conditions: the migrants lived in cramped squatter areas, along with relatives and friends from the village, eating and sleeping in shifts and socializing mainly with former villagers. Migrants' wives joined their husbands for periods of time in order to look after the shopping, cooking and housework for groups of four to twenty men. This was done on an informal rotation basis, with one wife replacing another after 3 to 12 months. In the company of village friends, the researcher visited a few of these migrants, providing interesting glimpses of their urban existence. Such follow-up would not have been possible on the basis of survey data alone, since formal addresses were virtually meaningless in the city's sprawling slums.

Development of New Hypotheses

Although cultural factors were seen to have a significant, independent influence on fertility and contraceptive use, certain community-level variables were observed which may have been even more crucial in determining family planning acceptance. It has been seen that sterilization was in fact utilized by more traditional women, a finding which was interpreted above in terms of cultural acceptability. Other factors, however, including leadership and the strength of the family planning program, were also important determinants. It was therefore hypothesized that community leaders who are both influential and popular can be effective agents in family planning promotion, even in relatively traditional areas. It would be interesting to test this hypothesis in several Indian villages where the strength and popularity of leadership varied, but where other characteristics, such as the degree of official family planning intervention, were similar. Correspondingly, one could investigate the significance of family planning program inputs by comparing communities where such influences differed considerably but where other factors, including leadership, were controlled.

A further hypothesis which emerged from the study was that, in the Indian setting, significant changes can be realized only through the active co-operation of males. This was clearly illustrated when the young research assistant married at the end of the study. She had been exposed to daily interviews and discussions about fertility and family planning, and was well informed about contraceptive methods. She did not want children for 3 or 4 years after marriage and, in fact, hoped to continue her education. Her husband apparently agreed with this plan, but refused to use preventive measures. She therefore became pregnant almost immediately, giving birth to her first child within one year. She later admitted that in her distress she had attempted abortion, using pills her husband procured in Bombay. Curiously, he was willing to subject his young wife to life-threatening risks which could have been avoided with a modicum of co-operation and forethought.

Generally, those areas in which considerable progress among women was evident, such as education, were widely sanctioned by village men. The reason, in the case of education, was primarily economic: the increasingly small size of landholdings (3.9 acres on average) as a result of the subdivision of land among sons after the father's death, made it virtually impossible to employ all one's offspring on the land, and children were therefore kept in school longer. Also, in the case of boys, education was a prerequisite for employment outside the village, and for girls, a few years of schooling were increasingly seen as an asset for marriage negotiations. Other reforms, such as prohibition of dowry, property rights for women, equality in marital and family decision-making and the sharing of household tasks, had not gained much acceptance among village men. Perhaps they viewed such changes as more personally threatening, their adoption requiring too large a shift in customary patterns. Women, adhering to cultural role definitions, were unlikely to support innovations when their husbands failed to do so. While this hypothesis is difficult to operationalize, studies on family-level decision-making patterns may shed some light on the resistance of males to change in certain behavioural domains.

Complementarity of Micro-Approach and Other Strategies

The previous sections of this chapter have concentrated primarily on the contributions of the micro-approach to demographic research. Generally, this approach is not complete in itself and is ideally combined, as in the present study, with other research strategies. In this concluding section, then, a few observations are made concerning the complementarity of the micro- and survey-approaches.

Clearly, the micro-study requires considerably more commitment in terms of time and intensity of observation. Large scale surveys, on the other hand, suffer from the basic problem of 'distancing [the researchers] from the very phenomena they are investigating', and other weaknesses well documented by Caldwell *et al.* (1982a). Thus, as Caldwell and colleagues also note, some compromise between the two approaches is required such as conducting a micro-study, preferably by the principal researchers themselves, before the introduction of the larger survey, or intensive investigation of a sub-sample of the survey population. The former strategy was in fact used to some extent in the present study, although for the most part, the qualitative investigation accompanied, rather than preceded, the survey.

The micro-approach also provides the basis for longitudinal studies, facilitated by previous knowledge about the community and easy identification and familiarity with the respondents. Assuming that the characteristics of the community are similar to those in the surrounding area, the later survey could even be conducted using a larger sample in the same region. Checks of various kinds would, of course, have to be introduced in order to ensure comparability of the new survey population with the old, but this should be possible on the basis of selected community-level indicators gained from the initial study.

Plans for a re-survey of the village discussed here, focusing mainly on fertility and family planning and the effects of interim social and political changes, are, in fact, currently underway. It is expected that re-entry into the community will be relatively smooth and that the original sample can be largely identified because names, maps and other records have been retained. Contacts with the village have also been maintained through letters and occasional visits. Although quantitative data will be collected from selected respondents through interviews, the study will be essentially a micro-level one, in order to strengthen both the new survey findings and the interpretation of the previous analysis.

Notes

1. Previously known as *sudras* or untouchables.

2. Education and literacy were virtually interchangeable, since most women only had sufficient formal education to provide basic literacy skills. Only 28 of the 349 women had more than 7 years' schooling.

3. Articles which were considered modern in the village context, such as bicycles, watches or clocks and radios.

4. Husband's occupation was preferred to respondent's occupation as an indicator of modernization because jobs for rural males were more diversified, and because female employment, consisting mainly of housework or agricultural labour, was not incompatible with child-bearing.

5. The Marathi name for smallpox is literally 'curse of a goddess'.

6. Although such women did not generally have any medical training they were experienced in matters of childbirth and charged a fee for their services.

6

The Use of Genealogies for Reconstructing Social History and Analyzing Fertility Behaviour in a North Indian Village

Monica Das Gupta

Introduction

This chapter experiments with an innovative technique of relating fertility behaviour to its social and economic determinants. Empirical research in this area has shown that conventional cross-sectional analysis has severe limitations, particularly when some of the explanatory variables have inter-temporal dimensions. Therefore successful statistical analysis needs to rely on panel data. Unfortunately, such panel data collected on the basis of repeated surveys over a long period of time are rarely available. In this chapter, an attempt has been made to combine genealogical information with social historical information on the families in the genealogies, in order to test the applicability of some of the widely known theories of fertility behaviour in the context of the experience of successive generations within one village in northern India.

Theories of Fertility Behaviour

In recent years, a great deal of attention has been paid to the problem of why there is persistence of high fertility levels in developing countries. A variety of theories have been put forward to explain how it may be in the interest of an individual couple to have high fertility, even though they, as members of society as a whole, are suffering from the adverse consequences of rapid population growth.

Essentially, these theories fall into two groups, which are in no sense mutually exclusive. The first is that children are desired because they are economically valuable, while the second is that they are desired as security assets against the risks their parents face. The theory of children's economic value has been explored in a variety of ways. Some studies were associated with the school of thought that the contribution of children to household income was sufficient, even at young ages, to give parents an incentive to want a large number of children (see, for example, White, 1976; Nag, Peet and White, 1977; Mamdani, 1972). This was refined further by Cain (1977) who calculated that a son in Bangladesh pays off his own costs as well as those of one female sibling, and becomes a net contributor to the household income before he begins to support his own children. Others, such as Caldwell (1976, 1982) have laid more emphasis on the economic contributions of children over the whole life cycle of the parents and concluded that the incentives for high fertility will remain until the direction of intergenerational flows is reversed.

The theory that children are valued as security assets has fewer variants. This theory has been put forward most forcefully by Cain (1981) and also by Caldwell (1981, 1983b). It has been argued that childbearing is almost the only action which people in high risk environments can take to insure themselves against the variety of contingencies which they face over their life cycle. Even in lower risk environments, children are required to provide old age support in most societies. These considerations may provide an incentive for high fertility, especially if one takes into account the possibilities of some children turning out to be unwilling or unable to provide support, or dying before their parents.

The possibility that parents themselves may come to find high fertility burdensome once child survival rates rise has been raised by a variety of people in differing contexts. It is implied by Heer and Smith's (1968) simulations of the number of children that an average couple would need to bear in order to ensure at least one living son when the father would be 65 years old. It is also implied by Scrimshaw's (1978, 1983) hypothesis that parents with excess children kill them directly or, more often, indirectly through neglect. Recently, Ryder (1983) and McNicoll (1984) have discussed the fact that when parents have a large number of surviving children, they find it difficult to meet their obligations to them, and that this 'imposes a clear strain on traditional systems of intergenerational obligations' (McNicoll, 1984, p.17). In a sense, recognition of this fact is implicit in writings which mention that older siblings pay a good proportion of the costs of younger siblings (see, for example, Mamdani, 1972). However, this has not been perceived as a burden to parents of large numbers of surviving children but rather as a mechanism whereby parents maximize returns from childbearing.

Clearly, each one of the variety of explanations of high fertility are applicable to some societies at the time at which they were studied by the researcher concerned. In anthropological work, to which the micro-studies mentioned above belong, the nature of a theory is strongly influenced by the particular circumstances of the society studied. This is evident to some extent in these theories of fertility behaviour. For example, Caldwell's greater emphasis on the returns from childbearing rather than on its burdens is derived from studying West African societies where land is not a scarce commodity as compared with Asia. Similarly, Cain's stress on risk can be clearly understood when one looks at the extraordinary riskiness of most aspects of life in rural Bangladesh. The predominant considerations influencing childbearing in a given society quite naturally strike the person studying it most sharply.

Of course, the predominant considerations influencing fertility behaviour can and will change in any society as other aspects of its situation change. It would be a useful exercise to map out an overall picture of a society, showing in which kinds of environmental configurations, which sets of childbearing incentives are of primary importance. One tool whereby this can be done is the standard anthropological technique of drawing a genealogy. These can be used to plot out the social and economic history of a number of generations (each with very different experiences) and to understand the main childbearing considerations prevalent for each generation. This paper is based on data collected in Rampur, a village set in the Punjab/Haryana region of India where both mortality and fertility have been declining substantially.

Demographic Rates in the Region

Estimates of the crude birth rate (Registrar General of India, 1982; Preston and Bhat, 1984) and of the total marital fertility rate (Registrar General, 1982; Census of India 1981) vary. However, all the sources mentioned above agree that Haryana's fertility decline has been far more rapid than the Indian average. Dyson and Somawat (1983) concluded that Haryana's decline in the total fertility rate between 1972 and 1978 was the third highest amongst the Indian states.

The Operations Research Group (ORG) 1980 Survey (ORG, 1983, p.113) has presented the figures for Punjab and Haryana combined, and show that the levels of use of contraception are the highest in India except for Kerala state (49.4 per cent current use; 55.6 per cent ever use). Moreover, this survey shows that the increase in use of contraception was higher than in any state except Kerala: levels of current use had risen from 21 per cent to 49.4 per cent between their 1970 and 1980 surveys (ORG, 1983, p.118). Mortality levels have also been declining rapidly. Dyson (1979) estimated from the Sample Registration Scheme data from 1968-71 and the Registrar General's 1972 Fertility Survey, that the infant mortality rate in Haryana was between 71 and 78 per thousand, which was the lowest in the country except for Kerala state.

The Genealogical Method

Anthropologists have used the genealogical method for analyzing patterns of various kinds. For example, some have used it for tracing patterns of mobilization of kinship networks, while others have used it to look for patterns in the genetic transmission of diseases. Here it has been used for examining the patterns of experience of members of successive generations. By doing this, one can develop a picture of the dominant features of the environment within which members of a given generation lived, and can see which sets of considerations predominated in determining societal fertility norms and individual attitudes to family size.

By looking at the experiences of successive generations, it becomes possible also to trace changes in the environment within which childbearing takes place. This is of particular interest in the case of Rampur, because this village and its region has moved in the span of a few generations from a classic pre-transition demographic regime to the third stage of the demographic transition. Thus the genealogies illustrate three totally different demographic regimes and rapidly changing socioeconomic environments, as well as the transitions and lags between these regimes.

The method by which this was done was to draw up a complete genealogy of each constituent patrilineage[1] of the village.[2] Having done this, brief histories of the individuals in the genealogy were collected. This included information on their occupational history, major events in their lives, and other details which demonstrate their successes and failures in maintaining themselves, their kin and their offspring. This was greatly helped by the fact that Oscar Lewis collected life histories of some individuals in 1953. This means that we have first-hand accounts of the life situations of people in the second stage of the demographic transition (in 1953), as well as in the third stage (in the present study). These genealogies were collected for the entire village population and the conclusions presented here are based on the patterns evident in these. However, since it is feasible to present only a few genealogies, an attempt has been made to present two from the landowning group, and another two from the landless.[3]

It needs perhaps to be clarified that this is in no way a variation of a family reconstitution study. It is not possible to build up a picture of changes in fertility and mortality rates from the data in the genealogies, given its retrospective nature (as opposed to the prospective nature of parish records). Fortunately in contemporary India there are a number of sources of data on the demographic parameters of this society. The genealogies are intended solely to provide a visual representation of the social history of the village. In the absence of much written material on the lives of individuals and families in the village, the genealogy forms an excellent framework for collecting and analyzing such information.

The genealogical method has an important advantage over the case study method, in that it provides a complete picture of the experiences of all the branches of a particular lineage over time. This means that there is less danger of obtaining a biased view of the villagers' experiences than is inherent in the selection of isolated case studies.

The genealogical approach has an advantage also in understanding childbearing behaviour in so far as it is possible to see with the benefit of hindsight which childbearing strategies paid off most highly at different times. We are in a position to assess this when all the factors of mortality, quality of children, and children's contributions and parental needs over the parents' life cycles have worked out their effects. After all, societal fertility norms are based on people's experience of the effects of these factors over the life cycle. However, these life cycle considerations remain largely imponderable when studying fertility behaviour at only one point in time.

A Brief Narrative of the Family History of Each Genealogy

The histories of the members of the four genealogies selected here (see Figures 1-4) have been highly condensed in the following sections.

Genealogy 1

Siri Chand's father was one of five brothers and six sisters. The brothers cultivated their land jointly. Being a large family, with twenty acres of land, the family had an air of prosperity. Shortly after Siri Chand's birth around 1900, there was a plague epidemic in which his father died. A few years later he lost his mother and two of his father's brothers' only sons in a cholera epidemic. These events followed upon poor harvests. One of his father's brothers adopted him and brought him up. When he was fourteen, there was a severe famine because of two consecutive crop failures, and another cholera epidemic broke out. The family sold their cow because they could not afford to buy fodder for it. Fortunately, the government started a work centre for famine relief, so Siri Chand's adoptive father was able to earn some money and buy a buffalo. When talking about this epidemic, Siri Chand mentioned that most of the deaths were of women and Untouchables. He explained that when there is a shortage of food, the women are the first to be deprived and suffer from malnutrition, followed by the children. The men are the last to starve.

A few years later, there was a bumper crop and much rejoicing. To celebrate, Siri Chand went on a trip to bathe in the Ganges and to buy a few small items, like a sieve and some sweets for the children, at the fair at the bathing site. When he was twenty, all the crops were destroyed in very heavy rains. Not only was there a shortage of food, but all the fuel became wet, and the dough had to be eaten in the form of half-baked balls. Two years later Siri Chand lost a baby in an epidemic; in all, his wife had nine live births, of which only two girls and one boy grew to adulthood. Nine years after the heavy rains there was another famine, in which the government carried out some relief measures. Siri Chand described how the government distributed food, medicine and blankets to the landless and to the poor Jats, and 'excused them' from paying the revenue that year. Meanwhile, Siri Chand's adoptive father had died, and his two surviving cousins had taken to cultivating their share of the land separately. Feeling unequal to the task of cultivating his land alone, he gave out his land for sharecropping, left his wife and children under the protection of his kinsmen, and travelled around widely in

Figure 6.1 Genealogy of a Jat (Landowning Caste) Lineage, Rampur 1975

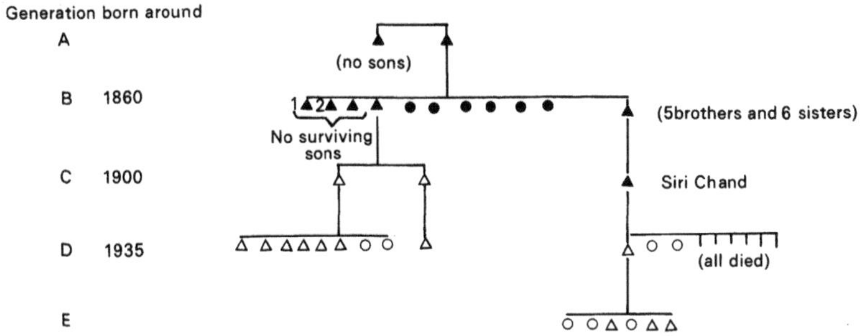

Figure 6.2 Genealogy of a Jat (Landowning Caste) Lineage

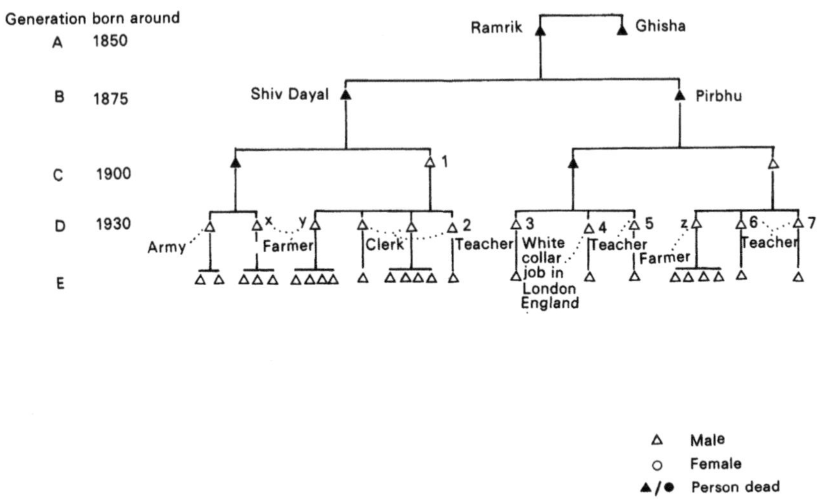

search of employment. He worked for a while as a labourer in a sugar mill, and then in a brick kiln. Finally his cousin, who was working in a school near Rampur, found him a job as an office boy in the same school.

Siri Chand's life provides a stark contrast to that of his son Umed Singh (born around 1935) who completed secondary school and obtained a job as a policeman. He obtains a regular salary of Rs.600 per month, as well as income from his land. He cultivates his land on Sundays, while his wife and elder daughters provide the routine maintenance of the crops and the cattle. He is educating all his daughters and sons as far as they are able to study, and is able to plan on when he will have enough savings for the weddings of each of his children. Despite the secure and well ordered life he leads, Umed Singh remains a rather anxious, worried man, because the uncertainties his father faced left a strong impression on him. His father's account of his life gives the impression that in both fact and in his perception, he had little control over his life, but rather that he made the best of circumstances as he went along. Even when Siri Chand had specific plans, he was vague as to their outcome. For example, when asked in 1953 whether he planned to repair his dilapidated roof, he replied that he was spending all he could on educating his son, and maybe one day he would get a job and mend the roof, who knows, perhaps even during his (Siri Chand's) own lifetime. Siri Chand's experience of losing many members of his household and most of his children, and being for a long time without any other males in the household to provide support, has also affected his son. Umed Singh must have realized how much he meant to his father as his sole surviving son; although he does not need such support, objectively speaking, he himself feels insecure about having no brothers or grown sons, and was worried that the family might die out altogether in the male line. His first two children were girls, and although he subsequently had three more children of whom two were sons, he insisted on having more children. He did not begin to get over his fears of losing all his children until the third son was born.

The second generation of people who lead a secure, ordered life do not experience the anxieties left over from past insecurities. Umed Singh's oldest daughter has completed a course in teacher training and will be married shortly. She says that she has no intention of childbearing in the way that her mother had; three children were the maximum she would have. She is a relaxed, confident woman who is inclined to be a little amused by her father's anxieties on behalf of his family.

Genealogy 2

This is a genealogy of one of the largest landowners in the village. Ramrik and Ghisha (born around 1850) had 100 acres of land. Ramrik had two sons, but Ghisha had none, so he invited his sister's husband with his brothers to settle in the village and to help him cultivate his land, as his heirs. When Ramrik and

Ghisha died, Shiv Dayal and Pirbhu were very young boys. The sister's husband and his brothers attempted to take over the land of the two boys, who were too young to join in a physical fight to defend their property. However, a number of incidents of appropriation of land belonging to the village lineages by members of outside lineages had taken place recently, so the village decided to unite in fighting the intruders and throwing them out of the village. Having large numbers of kinsmen was crucial for physical security; for retaining and cultivating one's land; and also could be used to appropriate others' land. The fact that Shiv Dayal and Pirbhu nearly lost their property because kinsmen had died shows some of the pressures leading to high fertility in those days. The next generation, C, prospered because they had much land and many sons to help them cultivate it. Since the lineage was wealthy, all the members of Generation D were installed in well paid outside jobs with the exception of one son (marked X, Y, and Z) from each of the three of the four branches of the lineage, who were assigned to manage the land. The implications of rapid growth in numbers began to be perceived already by the members of Generation D but it impressed itself on the minds of the lineage members as Generation E came into existence. Since the lineage still had relatively large landholdings and the income from outside employment of the members of Generation D, it was possible to groom all the sons in Generation E for well paid outside jobs without incurring much financial hardship.

However, by this time the lineage members had become acutely conscious of the rapid subdivision of their landholdings. Attitudes to fertility changed dramatically. Earlier, high fertility had been perceived as crucial for physical security and for prosperity. The wife of No.1, for example, had been proud to bear ten children, of whom four boys and one girl reached adulthood. Yet, as she witnessed the burgeoning of her sons' families, she came to change her attitudes to the extent of insisting that her youngest daughter-in-law be sterilized after her third child was born (she bore one boy and two girls, all of whom are alive). Like many of the older women in Rampur today, the mother-in-law herself says that if only she had been more aware of such matters in her time, she would not have had so many children. The wives of Nos. 3, 4, 5, 6, and 7 are also taking steps to keep their family size small.

Genealogy 3

Genealogy 3 is the genealogy of one of the Chamar lineages in Rampur. The fact that X had four surviving sons, while each of his sons had only one who survived to continue the male line shows the effects of uncertainties of mortality in the past. The pyramidal shape of the genealogy reflects the accelerating pace of mortality decline. It is interesting to compare the experiences of the two brothers in Generation E, marked No.1 and No.6. Out of a total of eight children ever-born, No.1 had four sons and one daughter who reached adulthood. All through his

Figure 6.3 Genealogy of a Chamar (Leatherworker and Agricultural Labourer Caste) Lineage, Rampur 1975

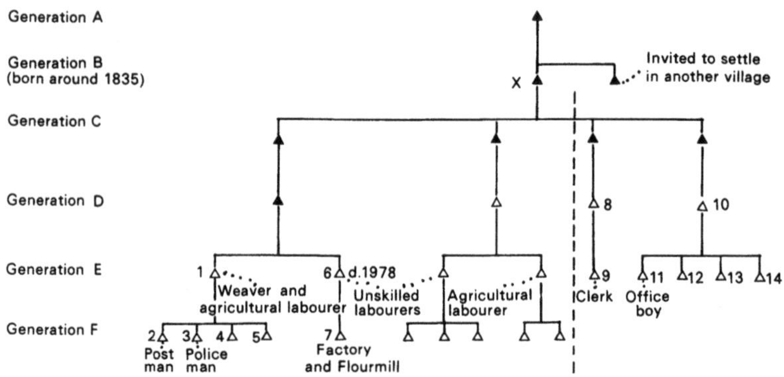

Figure 6.4 Genealogy of the Kumhars of Rampur

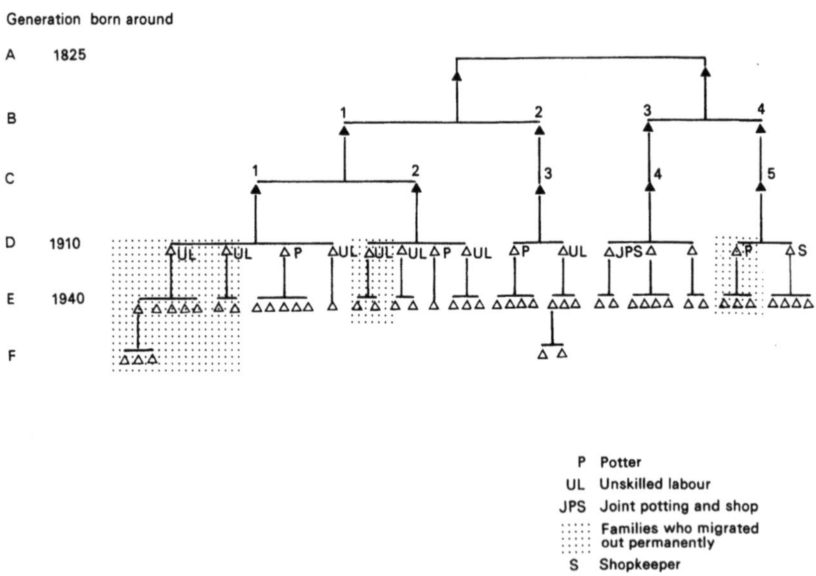

life, he worked hard as an agricultural labourer and as a weaver, and managed to send his sons to school. His children helped with weaving and other labour in their spare time. His oldest son had nine years of schooling and then obtained a job as a postman. He contributed from his earnings to help educate his younger siblings and the second son obtained a job as a policeman. The two younger sons are still being educated and are waiting to find a job. A number of interesting points emerge from their story. Firstly, the sons have done well. The older sons are both in government jobs, which offer high job security, pensions, medical insurance, and many other benefits. However, when they married and began to have children of their own, they found their father's house over-crowded and set up separate households, although they continue to contribute heavily to the parental household income. Since the investments for the two younger brothers' jobs still remain to be completed, while the older brothers are supporting in addition their own wives and children, all the members of the family continue to live extremely thriftily, and all the brothers as well as their aged parents continued to work at ill paid tasks such as spinning and weaving. The old father died in 1978 at the age of 77, having had to continue to struggle financially throughout his life although he had several sons who already or will shortly have good outside employment.

In contrast with this, his brother (No.6) had five children ever-born, of which only one son survived. The father scraped together money working as a labourer, and sent his son to school. The son got a job in a private factory in Delhi, accumulated some savings, and with a loan from his employer, set up an electric flourmill in the village. The mill was a success. The initial loan was repaid and additional machinery bought. The father retired from working many years before he died at the age of 68. The household has financial security and a very prosperous standard of living compared with that of other Chamars. The investment which has brought the family so much status and wealth was only possible because the son did not have numerous siblings to look after. Mortality, of course, was the big risk. If the last child had died, the parents would have had a very hard life. Similarly in the other branch of the lineage, No.8 with only one son gave his son a college education and got him a coveted job as a clerk. The father can now live comfortably while his cousin, No.10 and his sons are struggling to establish their family members in the job market.

Genealogy 4

Genealogy 4 is that of all the potters of Rampur. It illustrates some additional points about the advantages and dis-advantages of having large numbers of children. As in the case of all service castes in the village, each generation had to divide their fathers' hereditary service relationships (their main source of income in the traditional village economy) between themselves.

By looking at the experiences of Generations C and D, it is clear that those who had the larger numbers of surviving sons did not prosper as compared to those with less. This contradicts the expected outcome of the hypothesis of the economic value of high fertility. Instead of prospering, those branches of the lineage with the most surviving sons faced the most problems. Except for C2, none of the members of Generation C were able to maintain more than two sons within the village economy. Given the scope of income earning opportunities available in the village, it was difficult to keep the remaining sons in the village. In Generation D, there was enough work required in the hereditary service relationships to provide an income for only one descendant of each member of Generation C, while the remainder had to earn a livelihood in other ways.

The line of B1 multiplied most rapidly: of his eight surviving grandsons, three left the village permanently to work outside as unskilled labourers, and three more became unskilled labourers within the village. These boys were able to obtain only unskilled labouring jobs because they had poor educational qualifications. Thus even those who migrated out did not earn enough money to be able to send any home after meeting the expenses of their own nuclear families. Thus this branch of the lineage which grew most rapidly had the maximum outmigration and their members in Generation C found it more difficult to prosper than their cousins (C3 - C5) who had fewer surviving sons.

Finally, none of the members of Generation D who have several sons have been able to enjoy the fruits of this during their own lifetimes. Even today, they continue to struggle financially, using all available income earning opportunities. Their consumption levels are low, and instead of being able to feel relaxed and confident at long last when their eldest sons obtain jobs, they continue to be beset by financial and other anxieties on behalf of their other sons.

Discussion

At the beginning of this chapter, a number of theories from the literature regarding childbearing behaviour were outlined. Analysis of Rampur's genealogies helps us to assess the applicability of these different hypotheses to this village today as well as in the past.

The genealogies indicate the overwhelming importance of risk factors in people's lives in the earlier generations, in which situation it would be easy to understand the existence of high fertility norms. The levels of risk were highest around the turn of the century and diminished gradually to more moderate proportions by the 1940s. The primary sources of risk were lawlessness, famines and mortality.

The effects of lawlessness made themselves felt through such possibilities as groups with superior numbers taking others' land by force. This was, for example, the threat faced by Shiv Dayal and Pirbhu in Genealogy 2, because they had few kinsmen to help them protect their land. In their case the other lineages in the village decided to unite to protect them. However, on other similar and larger scale occasions in the mid-nineteenth century, such upholding of private property rights by the village community had not been possible, because the core lineages of the village were weak in numbers as compared with the aggressive intruders.

The effects of famine and epidemics (which often followed on from famines) are most clearly visible in the story of Genealogy 1. The British administrative writings on this region also bring these factors out very vividly:

> 'Nor does famine come only once or twice in a generation. A generation ago Rohtak had three in a decade (1896-1905). "In the first year stores were exhausted; in the second seed would not germinate; in the third there was no money left for a wedding; in the fourth everything went. The fifth started well, but cholera came, and belly and mouth were emptied".' (Darling, 1947, p.83)

The sudden peaks of mortality associated with these famines and epidemics could decimate entire villages. The prosperous household of Generation B in Genealogy 1 was decimated. Siri Chand's uncles lost their sons, he himself lost his parents and was adopted by one of his bereaved uncles. It is difficult for us to imagine the level of uncertainty faced by an individual subsisting on lumps of half-baked dough and wondering whether the following year would bring a bumper crop or worse food shortages and disease. Here again, one has to bear in mind that Siri Chand's family owned much land. The less fortunate would not even have had any half-baked dough.

At a time when immediate kin could be killed overnight, individuals would need to rely on a wide kinship network. Large numbers of kin were required for fighting other groups and to ensure some continuance of the family through mortality peaks: to pick up the threads again and form a new viable unit such as the orphaned Siri Chand and his bereaved uncle. High fertility norms would be expected to prevail in such a society.

By the 1950s, these risk factors had diminished significantly. The administration had already been working for several decades towards more settled conditions in the rural areas of this region. As a consequence, the old stories of arbitrary large scale land-grabbing came to be replaced by more mundane stories of disputes over a particular plot of land being fought in the courts. The need for kin for defence and policing declined gradually, such that today people requiring these services seek help from state law enforcement agencies rather than their kin. The ability to protect one's interests has been disassociated from the question of who is stronger in numbers. In mortality, impressive advances in agricultural productivity have eliminated famines, while public

Table 6.1 Distribution of Dead Children (per thousand ever-born) by Age at Death, Rampur 1975

Age-group of mother	Child's age at death (in years) Below 1	1-2	3+	Age unspecified	Total
20-29	70.35	22.61	10.06	25.13	128.15
30-44	118.23	43.10	19.71	33.25	214.29

Source: M. Das Gupta (1981, p.218)

health measures have eliminated some epidemic diseases and drastically curtailed the fatality from others. The effects of mortality decline are evident from the genealogies, which show a visible burgeoning of population over the past two generations of surviving adults.

However, there was a lag between the decline in mortality and that in fertility. It was only after two generations had experienced declining mortality rates that people in this village began to use contraception on a large scale. The stories told by the genealogies make it possible to understand this lag between mortality decline and fertility decline which has been so widely noticed elsewhere. For example, although Siri Chand's son found that all his own children survived, his own childhood experiences of losing his siblings as well as the memory of his father's experiences prevented him from considering contraception until he had three surviving sons.

The new regime of survival probabilities has to continue for some time before it can provide a credible basis for altering behaviour. Also, mortality has to decline substantially before parents can begin to plan their families with a reasonable degree of confidence in the survival of each child. This situation has been reached in this region. The infant mortality rate for Haryana was presented above; Table 6.1 shows the percentage distribution of child deaths by age at death in Rampur in 1975. These data show that parents in Rampur are now in a position to take sequential decisions about childbearing: waiting until their last desired child is 2 - 3 years old and then terminating childbearing with a good level of confidence in the subsequent survival of their children. The data for Rampur as well as official figures for Haryana show that parents today are reducing their family size quite rapidly.

The hypothesis that children are desired for their economic contribution to the family does not seem to be applicable in any of the generations in the genealogies. While children may have been economically valuable in the generations up to the 1940s, it is difficult to see that this could have been the predominant reason for desiring high fertility. The risk factors seem to have been overwhelmingly important for these generations. In the subsequent generations, for whom the risk factors had diminished, there is little evidence that those with more surviving sons prospered more than others, as we would have expected if children were economically beneficial either during their childhood or at older ages.

On the contrary, it appears that higher levels of child survival were beginning to pose a problem for households in Rampur in the 1950s. Genealogies 3 and 4 reflect the overall experiences of the landless in Rampur. Amongst this group, those with few surviving sons were able to accommodate them within their traditional occupation and in some cases were able to educate them for well paid outside employment. Their counterparts with more surviving sons were unable to accommodate all their sons in the traditional occupation and also found it difficult to invest in their children, with the result that many of their sons had to leave the village to work as low paid labourers. These emigrants found their wages inadequate to support their own wives and children and were unable to remit much money to their parental households. The landed faced the problem of rapid subdivision of holdings, creating holdings which were inadequate for supporting the household. As Genealogy 2 shows, those with fewer surviving sons found it easier to invest in their children to raise their income levels even amongst landed families. The larger landowners faced less of a problem with increased child survivorship than other groups in the village, because they were wealthy enough to support their children - but they do not appear to have benefited financially from having more surviving children than others.

A refinement is sometimes made to the hypothesis of children's economic contribution, *viz.*, that older siblings contribute towards supporting younger ones and that consequently parents do not have to bear all the costs of childbearing while they can benefit from all their children. This does not seem to be borne out by the Rampur genealogies. This argument can be contradicted even on *a priori* grounds: if older children are contributing towards supporting younger ones, resources which would potentially have gone to the parents are being diverted away from them. In other words, when children reach a point at which they can contribute to the household, the beneficiaries are not the parents, but the younger children. Each genealogy brings out vividly the fact that parents with large numbers of children are likely to have continued childbearing until the mother nears age 40 and the father is in his 40s. Consequently, the youngest children will still not be settled (in terms of marriage and employment) when the father is in his 60s.

The stories from the genealogies, for example Genealogy 3, show that even though older siblings help to pay for younger ones, the implication for the parents is that they have to scrape and squeeze throughout their lives in order to settle one child after another. If they had had only the first few children, parents could have had the benefit of having a more relaxed and prosperous old age. This is the case even amongst the larger landowners (see Genealogy 2). The obligations of parents towards their children are as strong if not stronger than that of children towards parents, in South Asia as in many other societies. There is a strong cultural emphasis on the obligation to see all one's children married and 'settled' before one's death. Consequently, having large numbers of surviving children is burdensome for couples, as the younger children are a burden rather than an asset to their aged parents.

The genealogies collected in Rampur have been used as a framework around which to reconstruct the social and economic history of the families in the village. In this chapter, these data have been used for analyzing which strategies of childbearing were the most successful for successive generations of parents over approximately the past century. In the process, insights are obtained into the nature of the institutional changes which form the background against which this village and its region have moved from the first to the third stage of the demographic transition.

Notes

1. The data are presented in the form of patrilineages showing male descendents only, as women marry out of the village and are not remembered for more than one or two generations.

2. By using old informants, it was possible to draw up extensive charts spanning several generations, with each chart covering a large number of the present households in the village. In societies which do not have such strong lineage-based organization, genealogies of a depth of four to five generations can easily be collected (i.e. the old informant can recount the history of his own father up to his own grandchildren). The latter would be adequate for this type of analysis.

3. For more information about the socioeconomic conditions of these groups, see Das Gupta (1981).

7

Structural Change and Fertility Decline in a Northern Thai Community: an Historical Perspective

Christine M. Mougne

Introduction

During the late 1960s, when world-wide efforts were directed towards finding solutions to the potentially disastrous consequences of spiralling birth rates in the developing world, an idea which enjoyed transitory popularity was that the provision of an efficient family planning program alone was sufficient to motivate the impoverished masses to take steps to control their fertility. This naive assumption was quite rapidly eroded by experience, and at the 1974 World Population Conference in Bucharest the consensus of delegates was that in the absence of radical socioeconomic change, family planning programs had little hope of stimulating any significant reduction in birth rates in the Third World.

Cases proving the point abounded. Among the Gurung in Nepal, for example, despite an acknowledgement of the problems of rapid population growth in a context of limited resources, and despite the availability of free contraceptives and the explicit approval of family planning by the most respected village leaders, only a small minority of high parity women showed interest in actually using a method (Macfarlane, 1976, pp.238-44). In 1984, despite an overall slowdown in world population growth - largely due to the successes of fertility control programs in China and a few other countries - the populations of many developing countries continued to grow at very high rates. A recent UNFPA report states a now familiar theme:

> 'Expanding populations and slow income growth in combination with generally inadequate technology is causing over-exploitation of land resources for food and fuel in many developing countries. The result is a deteriorating human and natural environment' (UNFPA, 1984).

A rare and important exception to this rule is found in the case of Thailand. An indication of the extraordinarily high level of motivation of Thai women to control their fertility is seen by the fact that for several years prior to the introduction of the government family planning program in 1970, at a time when public communication or advertising about birth control was still banned by law, tens of thousands of women from all over the country made their way to the nation's first contraceptive clinic in Bangkok

(Rosenfield *et al.*, 1973, p.146). Knowledge of the clinic's existence had spread throughout Thailand simply by word of mouth.

Another much quoted example of Thailand's birth control successes is the village of Ban Pong, 50 miles north of Chiang Mai, which was the first village in the Northern Region to receive a mobile family planning program, early in 1967. Within 2 years, the proportion of eligible women in the village using a method of contraception had increased from 5.4 per cent to 37.1 per cent, while the proportion of children under five had declined from 15.6 per cent of the population in 1967 to 10.7 per cent in 1969, and the proportion of eligible women pregnant had fallen from 15.1 per cent to 8.4 per cent (McDaniel and Pardthaisong, 1973).

Between 1972 and 1974 I conducted anthropological fieldwork in Ban Pong to investigate the circumstances which had led to this exceptional response, and to trace the way in which demographic changes in the community were related to socioeconomic factors. This chapter will concentrate on two main areas of structural change - land and labour, and marriage and residence - and examine the interaction between such changes and the decline of fertility. The analysis will begin at the time of the most recent settlement of Ban Pong one hundred years ago, and will follow the patterns of socioeconomic and demographic change up to the present day. I will also look briefly at the position of women in the community to highlight the significance of this important cultural factor on changing fertility behaviour.

Settlement and Clearance of Ban Pong Valley

After several hundreds of years fighting to retain their autonomy, the Northern Thai states were finally brought under the full control of the Siamese towards the end of the nineteenth century. To a large extent the drive to incorporate the North into the Kingdom of Siam was stimulated by pressures from foreign powers to secure access to the valuable Northern teak forests to supply a growing international market. In order to gain and maintain control of the sparsely populated outlying regions of the North, the Siamese began a program of planned resettlement. The unpopulated valley of Ban Pong (once the site of the small but thriving principality of Mu'ang Kaen) was one such area designated for resettlement. Thus, in the early 1880s, a small group of migrants from the south of Chiang Mai Province, under the leadership of three minor officials, came to the valley and set about the task of clearing the dense forest and undergrowth. The remains of an ancient canal system, a heritage of Mu'ang Kaen, were discovered and restored, and within a few years the first rice harvest was produced.

As the new settlement at Ban Pong gradually became established, more migrants came to clear and lay claim to land in the valley. Land had always been plentiful in the northern valleys, but a farmer's ability to exploit it was limited by the availability of irrigation and labour. Thus the initial clearance of the jungle was a slow and arduous process. By piecing together retrospective data on land cleared, inherited or bought by the parents and grandparents of current residents in Ban Pong, I have been able to make a tentative reconstruction of the rate and scale of land acquisition in the valley from the initial settlement to the present day, tracing the important structural changes which have taken place during this period (Mougne, 1982, pp.291-300).

Most of the initial clearance of land in Ban Pong seems to have occurred during the first 30 to 40 years following settlement. At this time, areas cleared were generally between about 10 and 30 *rai* (1.6 to 4.8 hectares), with a minority of holdings over 30 *rai*. After the early 1920s however, the number of holdings acquired through clearance fell rapidly, since by then most available land had already been claimed. During the 1940s, a small number of new fields were cleared at the margins of the irrigable area by newly arrived migrants, but the total amount of land cleared since 1940 represents only 2 per cent of present day holdings.

Fragmentation and Accumulation

By the second and third decades of this century the primary holdings were being sub-divided, with most heirs inheriting between 5 and 15 *rai* (0.8 to 2.4 hectares). Transfer of land by sale had also begun by this time; again, most of the holdings changing hands were between 5 and 15 *rai*. A considerable number of farmers who had inherited smallholdings during this period had purchased, and in a few cases cleared, additional land to increase their holdings to within the 5 to 15 *rai* range, sufficient to satisfy the basic subsistence needs of an average family.

However, during this same period - the 1920s and 1930s - an important change was taking place, as a small number of farmers were starting to build up large holdings (30 to over 100 *rai*), by purchasing several small to medium sized plots. In a very few cases the farmers involved had been born in Ban Pong and had begun their process of land accumulation with a small inheritance. The majority, however, were recent migrants from the southern part of Chiang Mai Province, who began to buy land within a decade of their settlement in Ban Pong. Although most of these migrants were from landless families, they were quickly able to amass considerable wealth in Ban Pong by gaining a monopoly of the *miang* (fermented tea) trade in the area.

Miang, a wild tea plant which occurs naturally over extensive areas of upland Asia, flourishes in a wild state in the mountainous areas of Northern Thailand. For centuries it has been enjoyed by the Northern Thais, steamed, then stored and allowed to ferment for weeks or months, to produce a chewable substance which is consumed in a way similar to 'betel' among the Central and Northeastern Thai. Picking and processing of *miang* had generally been done on an individual basis by the Northern Thai, though occasionally it was obtained by barter from the Khmu and other minority groups living in the hills. However, as the population in the northern part of Chiang Mai Province began to grow after the turn of the century as new settlers continued to move into the area, the local demand for *miang* also grew, and for the first time its production became commercialized, with people from the lowlands moving into the hills to pick and process *miang* on a full-time basis (Van Roy, 1971).

The economic potential of *miang* production and trade, emerging at a time when markets for other products had not yet developed in this area, was thus of great local significance. Its importance was recognized by a number of commercially-oriented individuals living in Ban Pong, many of whom, as noted above, were recent migrants. In some cases these new entrepreneurs hired landless families from Ban Pong to go into the hills to start production on their behalf, while in others, ambitious and resourceful peasants spent several years in the hills themselves, laying claim to areas of wild tea forest, before returning to the valley, leaving their 'orchards' in the charge of tenant producers. The substantial profits made on the basis of *miang* production provided the capital to build up large irrigated holdings in the valley.

As the process of accumulation of land was taking place among a minority of villagers in Ban Pong, many others were selling their land, usually plots of less than 15 *rai*. Sale of land in the valley in the 1920s and 1930s was apparently on quite a large scale, and many smallholders became landless during this period. The circumstances which led to so many farmers selling their land were no doubt associated with the generalized hardship experienced throughout Thailand during the years immediately prior to and during the Depression (Mougne, 1982, pp.262-4). In addition, it would seem that in many cases, farmers were unable to adjust to the rapidly changing economic conditions, with the spread of the cash economy, availability of credit, and growing commercialization of agriculture. Faced with serious debts (usually acquired as a result of borrowing money to pay for medical treatment or for funeral expenses), smallholders had no alternative but to sell their land, thus paving the way for the accumulation of large holdings by a minority of the population.

During the late 1930s and early 1940s, the pace of land transactions in Ban Pong slowed down considerably, with only a few small to medium-sized holdings bought and sold during this time. However, there was a great deal of sub-division of land through inheritance during this period. In some cases this involved the division of primary holdings cleared two to three decades earlier, into still viable holdings of 5 to 15 *rai*, but others involved the secondary sub-division of plots cleared in the early years of settlement of Ban Pong, thus producing many holdings of less than 5 *rai*. Some of the heirs to these holdings, which had become too small to be economically viable, were able to purchase additional fields. Others began a practice whereby one heir would buy up the shares of his/her siblings to avoid excessive fragmentation. In such cases, the siblings who had sold their shares left the valley to find land elsewhere, or remained as tenants or landless labourers. Some heirs attempted to make a living from their smallholdings, perhaps with the addition of some rented fields, but in many cases such farmers were eventually forced to sell. The situation was exacerbated by an influx of new migrants to the valley in the 1940s, a number of whom arrived with sufficient cash to buy several small plots to create viable holdings of 10 to 25 *rai*.

Throughout the 1950s, 1960s and early 1970s, the process of sub-division of land continued, with many heirs being forced to sell their uneconomic holdings. Various strategies have been developed in an attempt to avoid the total loss of family lands. Apart from the process mentioned above, of one sibling buying the shares of his/her co-inheritors, another mechanism has evolved whereby a group of siblings, in some cases co-residential, and in most cases living in close proximity to one another, have maintained the parental holding intact, still registered in the name of the deceased owner, farming it jointly and sharing the produce.

While the purchase of small to medium sized plots by new migrants has continued on a small scale, more recently a small number of Ban Pong-born farmers, whose parents had been landless or had sold their land, have started to buy land. Typically, such new owners have accumulated capital by working as tenants for many years, producing some cash crops for sale, and engaging in other money-making ventures such as trading and livestock raising. Since this is a comparatively recent development, it is not yet possible to determine the extent to which other landless households in Ban Pong will attempt to follow a similar strategy. However, although structurally there is a potential for upward mobility in Ban Pong, for the large majority of the landless, particularly the landless labourer, acquisition of land is a virtual impossibility in view of the spiralling price of irrigated land in recent years (Mougne, 1982, p.298).

Present-day Patterns of Land Tenure in Ban Pong

In August 1974, there were 460 households in Ban Pong, owning a total of 1,504 *rai* (241 hectares). With a population at that time of 2,090, this would have meant an average of 0.7 *rai* for every man, woman and child, an area barely large enough to provide rice for minimal subsistence needs. However, as we have seen, irrigated land was distributed on a far from equal basis, and the 1,504 *rai* were in fact owned by only 140 households (30.5% of total households). The distribution of areas of land owned by these households is presented in Table 7.1.

Table 7.1 clearly illustrates the considerable disparities in land distribution in Ban Pong, with, at the lower end of the scale, 43 per cent of landowning households owning only 12 per cent of the land, and at the other end, 7 per cent of landowning households owning over 38 per cent of the land.

Table 7.1 Ownership of Irrigated Fields, Ban Pong, 1974

Category of ownership	No. of Households	Total *rai* owned	Prop. of all *rai* owned %	Prop. of land-owning households %	Prop. of all village households %
Landless	320	-	-	-	69.5
Under 5 *rai*	60	182.25	12.0	43.0	13.0
5–9 *rai*	38	239.25	16.0	27.1	8.3
10–14 *rai*	17	194.50	13.0	12.1	3.7
15–19 *rai*	5	91.25	6.1	3.6	1.1
20–29 *rai*	10	217.25	14.4	7.1	2.2
30 & over *rai*	10	579.50	38.5	7.1	2.2
Total	460	1,504.00	100.0	100.0	100.0

Of the 140 landowning households, 91 (65%) had inherited all, or part of their land. Thirty-eight of these households had increased their holdings by buying additional fields, while thirty-nine households (28%) had bought all of their land. Only ten households (7%) had cleared their land. However, although the majority of current landowners had inherited all or part of their land, in 1974 only 35 per cent of all land owned in the village had been acquired in this way. The substantial and continuing impact of migrants on the patterns of land ownership in Ban Pong is illustrated by the fact that in 1974 slightly more than half of all land owned was currently in the hands of people born outside the village. This included 67 per cent of all land bought, 56 per cent of all land cleared, and 26 per cent of all inherited land.

The mode and time of acquisition of land by current householders in Ban Pong are represented in Figure 7.1. The dates are approximate: for example, in the case of inherited fields, the land may have been farmed by the heirs for some years prior to the death of the former owners, and may not have been officially divided until much later; farmers who had bought fields may have done so plot by plot over a long period of time, particularly those with very large holdings, while those who cleared their land are likely to have done so over a number of years. Despite these limitations, Figure 7.1 highlights the enduring dominance of some of the early land accumulators mentioned earlier, with six of the ten current landowners with 30 or more *rai* having begun their

Figure 7.1 Time and Mode of Acquisition of Land, Current Landowners, Ban Pong, 1974

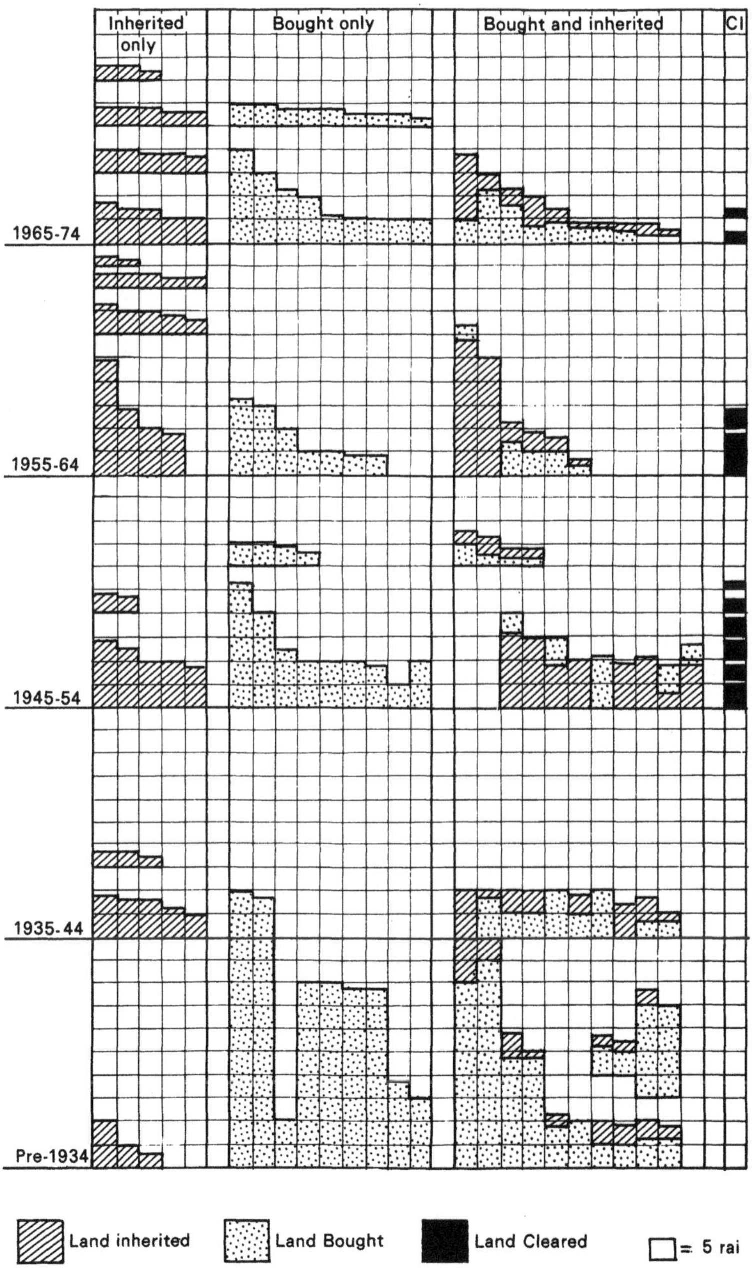

process of land accumulation more than 40 years ago. Figure 7.1 also illustrates graphically the ongoing process of land fragmentation.

Agricultural Labour and Tenancy in Ban Pong

Traditionally, the main source of agricultural labour in Northern Thailand was the reciprocal labour group, which was generally made up of households farming landholdings of a similar size (Tanabe, 1981, pp.432-42). The most important factors in the establishment of labour exchange relationships were kinship (particularly between siblings), cultivation of adjacent or nearby plots, and *kan pen phi nong kan* ('fellowship') (Tanabe, 1981, pp.433-5). With the rise of commercialization of agriculture and the increase in landlessness, reciprocal labour groups are gradually being replaced by daily wage labourers. An important factor in this change is the high cost involved in providing the traditional feast and alcohol required by such exchange arrangements. In Ban Pong in the early 1970s, reciprocal labour groups were found, with very few exceptions, only amongst small owner-cultivators (with less than 15 *rai*) and tenants, with exchanges taking place between households of the same economic status (i.e. owner-cultivator with owner-cultivator, tenant with tenant). However, more than a third of smallholders relied entirely on domestic labour, while a quarter used hired labour, in a few cases to supplement exchange labour.

In the past, tenancy arrangements were generally between kin, and the standard payment was a *beng khru'ng* (half share) of the harvest. More recently, with the increase in large holdings and in land held by absentee landlords, tenancy payments are more likely to be based on a fixed amount of paddy, regardless of annual fluctuations in yield. Together with the increase in use of daily wage labour, this represents a move away from traditional community-based relationships to more impersonal, commercially-based relationships. In 1974, with only two exceptions, all households owning 15 *rai* or more rented out their fields to tenant farmers from the village, most of them on a fixed amount basis.

A total of 133 households in Ban Pong worked as tenants in the early 1970s (30% of total households), in most cases renting holdings of between 5 and 15 *rai*. The large majority of tenants (75%) were landless, and the remainder were owners of small plots under 10 *rai*. Of the 221 landless households without a tenancy arrangement, a minority (20%) were supported by regular salaries of family members working as teachers, a nurse, irrigation officials, and other civil service jobs, or from the income of artisans or full-time traders or shop-keepers. In all, 176 households (38.3% of total households) were dependent entirely on wage labour supplemented by hunting and gathering activities.

Long and short-term migration of family members as a means of alleviating the burden on domestic resources, as well as providing much needed additional cash income, was common among landless households, and to a lesser extent, among small land-owning and tenant households. In 1973-74 for example, 60 per cent of the 87 individuals from Ban Pong who had worked outside the village at some time during the year were from landless households, representing 25 per cent of all landless households in the village. About one-fifth of these temporary migrants had worked in the *miang* orchards owned by fellow villagers. Some of the men had worked as woodcutters for the Royal Forestry Department, several young men and women had worked as 'bus-boys' or conductresses, and the remainder had worked in domestic service, mining, roadbuilding, agricultural or industrial labour.

Members of landless, non-tenant households who remain in the village have to compete for increasingly scarce agricultural labouring opportunities for transplanting and harvesting the rice crop, and for harvesting and sorting of the various cash crops grown in the dry season. These opportunities are, of course, seasonal, and for the rest of the year, such landless households have to struggle to provide even for their basis subsistence needs.

Post-Marital Residence Patterns in Ban Pong

The model for marriage and residence patterns, as presented in the anthropological literature on Northern Thai village society (Davis, 1974; Turton, 1976; Potter, 1976), is one in which a man marries into the village or home of his bride, spending a minimum of one year in her parents' home, working their land with his father-in-law, and then, usually after the birth of the first child (or the marriage of the next sister), setting up a home within the wife's parents' compound, or nearby. As each daughter marries, a new nuclear household is set up close to the parental home, and the parental land is worked jointly, or on the basis of separate tenancy agreements with each daughter's household. On the death of the parents, the last married daughter, usually the youngest, who has remained in the parental home inherits the house and compound. The land is generally divided equally between all sons and daughters, but since, in theory at least, most sons will have married into other villages, the effective heirs are more likely to be daughters who have remained close to the parental home. Clearly these patterns have important implications for the status of women. This aspect will be discussed in the next section.

Although considerable deviations from this traditional model are presented in the literature, the data for Ban Pong suggest that the area is quite atypical in terms of its exceptionally low rate of village exogamy in the past, which has declined still further in recent years. In the case of the older age groups, the low incidence of village exogamy can be accounted for by the fact that on the one hand many couples had already married before moving to Ban Pong, and on the other, that the high proportion of migrants in the community coming from a wide variety of sources provided a much greater range of potential spouses from within the village than in more long-established communities. More recently, the substantial growth of population in Ban Pong has also meant that the range of choice of suitable spouses has been very much greater than in smaller communities.

The rate and period of initial uxorilocal residence following marriage also varies considerably from one part of the North to another according to the anthropological literature. In view of the fact that a number of writers have suggested that the virtual disappearance of initial uxorilocality in Central Thai village society has been a result of economic changes with widespread commercialization of agriculture since the latter part of the nineteenth century (Rajadhon, 1968; Kemp, 1970; Keyes, 1975), it may be that the wide variation of patterns observed in different areas of the North is a result of adaptive modifications made over time within each community.

In the case of Ban Pong, the data indicate that overall, only about 40 per cent of all ever-married men and women interviewed had lived uxorilocally immediately following marriage. What was particularly surprising was that the rate of uxorilocality among ever-married men and women in Ban Pong had 'increased' rather than fallen over time. However, there is evidence to suggest that the actual 'period' of initial uxorilocality has decreased over time (Mougne, 1982, pp.432-3).

Perhaps the most striking feature of post-marital residence patterns in Ban Pong is the high incidence of initial neolocality among the older men and women in the community, a factor probably related to the comparatively recent settlement and hitherto largely migrant nature of its population. Furthermore, it is possible that following the settlement of the village towards the end of last century, economic conditions changed so rapidly and so dramatically, that there was insufficient time for traditional patterns to have become firmly established as in longer settled communities.

To clarify the way in which marriage and residence patterns have been modified over time, it is useful to examine the changes in terms of three broad time periods - from initial settlement to about 1940, from 1940 to 1960, and from 1960 to the present. Inevitably any attempt to relate such changes to demographic or economic factors is a matter of conjecture. Furthermore, in a community with increasing landlessness on the one hand, and a growing monopoly of scarce resources by a minority of households on the other, the patterns described will inevitably mask growing differences between households in the village. Nevertheless, at a fairly general level, it is possible to point to major changes which can account for certain trends evident in the data on marriage and residence.

For example, in the first period, prior to 1940, the majority of the population of the village had moved there from other parts of Chiang Mai Province, or from other Northern Provinces.

Although many couples had moved to the village as families some time after marriage, others had come immediately following marriage, a factor contributing to the high rate of initial neo-locality during this period. Little is known of the evolution of residence patterns in such a recently settled community, but in view of the diversity of origins of migrants to Ban Pong, and their comparatively recent arrival at that time, it could be argued that the traditional residence patterns prevailing in their natal villages had temporarily broken down. The fact that in the second period, when a much larger proportion of individuals marrying were second generation residents of the village, the rate of initial uxorilocality increased quite rapidly, suggests a temporary re-establishment of traditional patterns. Furthermore, it is likely that in most of the first period some of the land in the valley still remained uncleared (even if already laid claim to), and under such conditions, neolocal residence would seem to be the logical choice for a newly married couple. After 1940, however, virtually all land in the valley was under cultivation, and therefore labour requirements would have approached those of longer settled communities. This change may well have contributed to the increase in initial uxorilocal residence of couples marrying at this time.

However, after 1940 the population of Ban Pong had already begun to expand rapidly, not only as a result of a substantial influx of new migrants during the Japanese occupation of Thailand, but also as a result of falling mortality and rising fertility beginning at the end of the decade, and continuing through to the 1950s. Thus by the beginning of the third period, in 1960, the problems associated with rapid population growth were becoming evident, and economic pressures were increasing. Although the problem of landlessness in Ban Pong had been growing since the early decades of this century, this would not have become acute until the population had outgrown the labour requirements of the land available to the community. With growing unemployment and under-employment after 1960, however, some young men in Ban Pong have found it necessary to postpone marriage. With increasing crowding in the residential area of the village, newly married couples have been forced to live with whichever parental family could support them and make best use of their labour, thus leading to a recent increase in the rate of virilocality, hitherto very rare in the community. In this way, economic necessity has taken precedence over traditional values.

Despite the well established sensitivity of age at marriage to changing economic conditions (Coale, 1967), the mean age at first marriage for women in Ban Pong had remained remarkably stable over the 50 years for which data were available, although there appears to have been a slight fall in mean age at marriage for women aged under 35 at the time of my survey. Mean ages at first marriage for men in Ban Pong on the other hand, show much greater variability in age groups over 35, and the fall in mean age at marriage for men under 35 is much steeper than for women. The fact that, in 1973, 14 per cent of men aged 35–39 and 19 per cent of men aged 30-34 were still unmarried, is strongly suggestive of quite considerable postponement of (or non-) marriage among men in recent years, given an overall average age at first marriage for men of about 23, and the fact that in all age groups over 40, at least 95 per cent of men had been married.

It is only when the ages at marriage of women in Ban Pong are looked at 'cumulatively' that some variations emerge. The data indicate that a considerable proportion of women aged 35-49 (in 1973) had married several years later than women in all other age groups (Mougne, 1982, p.498). It is worthy of note that these women would have reached the traditional marriageable age between 1940 and 1960, a period which, as we have seen, was transitional between a situation of relatively plentiful land and scarce labour, and one of scarce land and surplus labour. The impact of these economic changes on fertility patterns will be examined later.

Female Autonomy in Ban Pong

The importance of the degree of female autonomy in a society in determining its ability to respond to demographic pressures has recently been noted by a number of writers (Dyson and Moore, 1983; Safilios-Rothschild, 1982). Dyson and Moore have suggested the following factors as typifying societies in which females have high personal autonomy:

> '... freedom of movement and association of adolescent and adult females; postmarital residence patterns and behavioural norms that do not rupture or severely constrain social intercourse between the bride and her natal kin; the ability of females to inherit or otherwise acquire, retain, and dispose of property; and some independent control by females of their own sexuality ...' (1983, p.45).

As we have seen, the traditional residence pattern in Northern Thailand is uxorilocal, thus enabling groups of female kin to remain in close contact with each other throughout their lives. This pattern also has implications for land tenure, since, as noted earlier, although inheritance is generally bilateral, with all siblings, male and female, receiving equal shares, sisters are more likely to retain their inherited holdings than brothers. Thus for many men, who are expected to leave the natal village to find a wife elsewhere, access to land after marriage is gained through their wives. Although to a large extent such traditional patterns of post-marital residence and inheritance have broken down in Ban Pong, the strength of female kin groups has remained intact. In many households, these groups are supported and given supernatural sanction by the existence of female-based spirit cults, from which men are generally excluded. The cults are also significant here in terms of their role in controlling the sexuality of women in the group. The major, and often the only, ritual required to legitimate marriage is an offering of food to the group spirits, paid for in cash by the bridegroom to his new mother-in-law.

A further critical factor which enhances the autonomy of women in Northern Thailand is their economical role. Women throughout the region play an extremely active part in the economic sphere, both in agriculture and in trade. All agricultural tasks (with the possible exception of ploughing) can be, and are, performed as much by women as by men. Furthermore with the increase in use of daily wage labourers in agriculture in recent years, many landowners and tenants prefer to employ women because they can be paid a slightly lower rate than men for the same job. In addition, women have long dominated the local trading networks, both within and outside the village. Nowadays, with the majority of households in Ban Pong landless, the importance of trading as a major source of domestic income has strengthened. Male landless labourers, in fierce competition for limited seasonal agricultural work, have to seek non-agricultural work, often on a day-to-day basis for most of the year, and commonly outside the village. Consequently, a man's contribution to the domestic budget is often less reliable than that of his wife.

The main factor which can inhibit a woman from pursuing her economic goals is pregnancy. A pregnant woman is said by the Northern Thai to be an unwelcome trading partner since she is likely to be 'greedy', and is thus liable to demand excessively high prices. The physical constraints of late pregnency, as well as those imposed during the postpartum period (Mougne, 1978), also serve to limit a woman's participation in trade and other economic pursuits. Thus the availability of contraception enables women to involve themselves in the economic sphere to an even greater degree.

Another important factor relating to the status of women in this context is that although initially motherhood 'does' enhance a woman's status, prestige does 'not' increase with additional births, as it does in many other societies. Most women in Ban Pong expressed the opinion that nowadays two, or at the very most three, children were sufficient, and that any more would be an impossible economic burden. Furthermore, most women said that they found adherence to customs associated wih pregnancy and the postpartum period to be tiresome, boring and a dreadful nuisance. The freedom to travel around, visiting the city markets, more or less at whim, was said by the large majority of women to be much more *sanuk* (fun) than producing numerous children.

In turn, this freedom to travel outside the village brings women into contact with new ideas and technologies. An example of the responsiveness of Ban Pong women to new ideas was the introduction, in early 1974, at McCormick Hospital in Chiang Mai, of a new method of female sterilization. This *per vagina* technique appealed to women who had been reluctant to have the abdominal incision normally required for sterilization. Within two months of first hearing of the new technique, five young women from Ban Pong had been to Chiang Mai for the operation, and many others followed suit later that year. An indication of the particular suitability of this technique for women in this part of Thailand is the way in which it quickly became dùbbed *tham haeng* (literally, to be dried), incorporating the traditional concept of 'drying' the womb to prevent pregnancy (see below), instead of the more formal term used for all other methods of sterilization, *tham man* (to make sterile).

A final point of importance here is that although women in Ban Pong are able to - and do - make decisions and take action independently of men, in almost every case when talking about their use of contraception or their decision to be sterilized, they would comment that they had discussed it with their husbands, and that their husbands had supported their decision. However, very few of the husbands were prepared even to consider the idea of taking the responsibility for birth control themselves by using condoms or having a vasectomy. Family planning is very much the affair of women in Ban Pong.

Patterns of Demographic Change in Ban Pong[1]

In the first few decades of this century, it is likely that the major factor influencing population growth in Ban Pong was continuing in-migration, as a slow, but steady stream of migrants, coming mostly as families from more densely populated areas further south, moved into the village. The disruptive effects of the Second World War and the Japanese occupation of Thailand in the early 1940s, however, had a significant impact on the demography of Ban Pong. As the Japanese reached the south of Chiengmai Province, a flood of migrants moved northwards, contributing to a sudden increase in the rate of in-migration to Ban Pong valley. With deteriorating conditions and this surge of population movement, a number of epidemics broke out in the village, and infant mortality rates soared.

As the situation became more settled in the late 1940s, and preventative and curative medical services became more accessible to the rural population, infant mortality rates began to decline precipitously. In Ban Pong, deaths in the first year of life fell from 293 per 1,000 between 1944-1946, to 105 per 1,000 a decade later. Fertility rates, meanwhile, having fallen slightly during the mid-1940s, started to increase rapidly, reaching a peak in the mid-1950s. Analysis of the age-specific fertility rates of ever-married women in Ban Pong indicates that, to a large extent, this surge in fertility was the result of 'delayed fertility' of women in their mid-to-late thirties at that time. Mean pregnancies per eligible woman rose from 0.57 between 1944-1946 to 1.01 between 1956-1958. With in-migration continuing on a moderate scale, the population of Ban Pong increased rapidly during the 1950s.

By the turn of the decade however, fertility rates had already begun to fall, slowly at first, and then very quickly after the introduction of the family planning program in 1967. By 1968-1970, the mean number of pregnancies per eligible woman had dropped to 0.41. Although registration data for Ban Pong were severely limited, the estimated crude birth rate for this period clearly reflects the pattern presented by my survey data, falling from 40.3 per 1,000 in 1965, to 32 per 1,000 in 1967, to 15.5 per 1,000 in 1969. An examination of the age-specific fertility rates of women in Ban Pong in the 1960s shows clearly that this decline was achieved not only by an overall reduction in the number of births, but also by women in successive cohorts gradually cutting back their age of peak fertility.

Mortality patterns in Ban Pong do not appear to have changed significantly since the late 1950s, with both the crude death rate and the infant mortality rate fluctuating slightly from year to year, but remaining comparatively low overall. Patterns of migration on the other hand, have changed substantially in the last two or three decades, with the rate of out-migration now greatly exceeding that of in-migration. During the seven years (from 1965-1971) for which registration data on movement in and out of Ban Pong were available, there was a net loss of migrants in all but one year. The mean migration ratio for the 7 years was 67; in other words, 33 per cent more people had moved out of Ban Pong during this period than had moved in. Again the registration data supported my own survey data on movement in and out of the village between 1973 and 1975. The mean migration ratio for these 2 years was 54. Since the method by which population movements are registered in Thailand is unlikely to create a bias towards under-reporting in one direction rather than the other, the latter figure probably reflects a greater than average outward movement from Ban Pong between 1973 and 1975. In fact there are very clear economic reasons to explain this, since the rice harvest of 1973 was devastated on three successive occasions as a result of unusually erratic and heavy rainfall. The entire population of Ban Pong valley suffered as a result of this severe loss, with a harvest well under 50 per cent, and in some cases under 25 per cent of average annual yield.

An important feature of recent patterns of migration in Ban Pong is the age of migrants involved. Mean age-specific turnover figures for men and women aged between 20 and 29 were 205 per 1,000 and 250 per 1,000 respectively during 1973-1975. Although this age group constituted only 12 per cent of the total village population in 1973, the volume of movement was so great that it artificially raised the mean turnover for the whole village to 88, although the figure for most other age groups was much lower. The migration ratios showed a net loss of males and females in all age groups under 30, while those aged over 30 were comparatively balanced in terms of inward and outward movements.

The growing numbers of people leaving Ban Pong in recent years fall into three main groups. The first, predominantly young females, had moved to Bangkok to find work in the bars, brothels or in domestic service. The second group, including young families and young single people of both sexes, had moved to the *miang* orchards to work as tenants and labourers. The third group, mostly young families, had moved to the sparsely populated and politically insecure districts in the far north of the

Province, near the border with Burma, to open up new lands or to seek work as tenants or labourers.

Family Planning and Fertility Decline in Ban Pong

As we have seen, the fertility decline in Ban Pong had begun almost a decade before the introduction of the family planning program in 1967. In a survey of elderly women in the village (conducted in 1973), a number of questions were asked about traditional methods of contraception. Only a small minority of informants knew of a method, and it appears that such methods were very rarely used. Although most women knew about abortion, this had been practised, in the past at least, only under exceptional circumstances. The most common method of abortion mentioned in the survey was *bip* or *rip tong* (to squeeze or press the belly), which involved strenuous manipulation of the uterus to dislodge the foetus. Although this method was known to be extremely painful, dangerous, and occasionally fatal, it was generally considered to be more reliable than herbal methods.

In many pre-contraceptive societies, fertility was controlled to an extent by extended postpartum abstinence, prolonged lactation and less frequently, by withdrawal (Nag 1968; Caldwell *et al.* 1982b, p.694). In Ban Pong, however, postpartum abstinence was observed for little more than 2-3 months, and was obligatory for only one month, while breastfeeding rarely continued for more than a year. The idea of withdrawal was viewed by informants with amused disbelief (see also Knodel *et al.*, 1983, pp.15-17). Furthermore, couples in Ban Pong generally continued to be sexually active up to menopause (and beyond), with about 80 per cent of post-menopausal women having had their last pregnancy after the age of 35 (Mougne, 1982, p.96). Although about one in five first marriages in the community end in divorce, remarriage is very common, and the period between successive marriages is short. It would appear therefore, that there were very few traditional constraints on fertility in Ban Pong. Nevertheless, there is evidence to suggest that a widespread desire to space births had existed for generations, in view of one of the explicit, and major functions of various postpartum customs, which are believed to 'dry out the womb', a process thought to delay further pregnancies. Such customs were observed by the large majority of women in the past, and are generally still adhered to by village women today (Mougne, 1978).

A critical change in this rather casual attitude to fertility control among women in Ban Pong took place during the 1950s, at a time when fertility rates had reached an unprecedented peak. According to a number of informants, the practice of induced abortion increased suddenly at this time. Although cultural constraints to admitting to the practice of abortion limited my efforts to obtain data on its incidence among village women, fertility histories did yield some evidence to support the popular view of its increased frequency after the mid-1950s. The reported incidence of 'foetal losses' was exceptionally high among women aged between 40 and 59 in 1973, the majority of whom were in the middle to late stages of their reproductive lives between the mid-1950s and mid-1960s (Mougne, 1982, p.111).

Although modern methods of contraception had been available in Chiang Mai city clinics since 1963, by the time the family planning program began in Ban Pong in 1967, only 14 of the 258 eligible women in the village were using a method. It is important to note, however, that despite the total ban on advertising of birth control services, and the distance of Ban Pong from the city clinics, these women had been sufficiently motivated to control their fertility to overcome these barriers. Inevitably, these 14 women were by no means the only rural women prepared to travel to the city to seek family planning services in the 1960s, and the organizers of the clinic at McCormick Hospital in Chiang Mai soon became aware of the increasing demand for birth control methods among the rural population.

In late 1966 therefore, Dr McDaniel, Director of the McCormick Hospital family planning program, decided to conduct a pilot project to assess the potential for mobile family planning services in the rural areas of Chiang Mai Province. Ban Pong was chosen for this project, and between December 1966 and February 1967 a small survey team conducted a census of the 382 households in the village, and a detailed 'K.A.P.' (knowledge, attitude and practice) study of the 258 eligible women. The survey indicated that there was indeed a widespread desire amongst village women both for information about family planning, and for the provision of services. Thus on completion of the survey, Dr McDaniel conducted an educational program about birth control in the village and then made contraceptive pills and the injectable, Depo-Provera, available to the women of Ban Pong. Women requiring IUD insertion or sterilization could obtain these at the hospital in Chiang Mai.

As noted earlier, a follow-up survey conducted in Ban Pong two years later indicated a very high rate of acceptance of contraception which, in this short space of time, had already begun to influence the birth rate significantly (McDaniel and Pardthaisong, 1973). In March 1973, I conducted a further follow-up survey of eligible women in Ban Pong to investigate the patterns of contraceptive practice in the community during the 6 years since the beginning of the program. In 1973 there were 278 eligible women, 170 of whom had used a method of contraception by this time (61%), with 111 of them currently using contraception at the time of the survey (40%). Analysis of continuation rates indicated that 77 per cent of the women had used a method for at least one year, 64 per cent for 2 years, 45 per cent for 3 years, and 26 per cent for 6 years or more. It should be noted here that the downward trend in these figures does not simply reflect a decline in usage over time, since not all women had started a method at the same time. In fact, of the 66 women who had accepted family planning in the first year of the program, nearly 60 per cent had used a method without interruption for 6 years.

Table 7.2 Acceptance of Family Planning by Economic Category: Women Aged 25-39 Eligible in 1967 and 1973

(% by economic category)

Economic Category	N	Accepted Between 1967-1969 %	Accepted By 1973 %
Landless Labourers	46	28.3	41.3
Landless Tenants	54	74.1	78.0
Landowners Less than 10 *rai*	43	67.4	80.0
Landowners 10 *rai* or more	17	58.8	100.0
Other	10	60.0	75.0

Early studies of family planning acceptance in Thailand tended to emphasize the importance of urban residence and high education as significant factors in the acceptance of contraception (Knodel and Pitaktepsombati, 1973; Knodel and Debavalya, 1978). Pardthaisong, however, in his study in Chiang Mai Province in the early 1970s, found that the majority of contraceptive acceptors were wives of agricultural workers with only primary school education (1974, pp.20-1). In Ban Pong in 1973, the large majority of eligible women had completed only 4 years' schooling or less (in common with most rural Thai women and men), and thus the education variable could not provide enough differentiation to study its influence on family planning acceptance. Variations in economic status, on the other hand, 'were' significant and 'did' appear to be correlated with acceptance rates. When rates of contraceptive acceptance were analyzed according to five broad economic categories (see Table 7.2), the rate amongst women from landless labouring households was found to be substantially lower than for women in all other categories. This difference was particularly striking in the first 2 years of the family planning program, and although the rate of acceptance of contraception by such women had increased considerably by 1973, the difference remained (Mougne, 1982, pp.231-3). In view of variations in the age distribution of eligible women in the different economic categories, the data presented in Table 7.2 are restricted to women aged between 25 and 39.

The consistently low levels of contraceptive acceptance amongst women from landless labouring households, even for those women in the age groups normally most highly motivated to control their fertility, reflected the commonly observed phenomenon that for most impoverished members of society, children continue to provide the only means by which a family can hope to improve its economic standing, as well as being a vital source of support for parents in their old age (Mamdani, 1972; van Rensalaar, 1974).

For landless tenants on the other hand, the hope of improving one's economic position by hard work, careful housekeeping, and minimizing financial outlay by limiting family size can, and in a few cases in Ban Pong has, become a reality. Households owning small plots of land can strive in a similar way to increase, or at least retain, their holdings. In such cases family planning is an extremely important factor in realizing these ambitions. For landowners with medium to large holdings, the desire to retain a privileged economic position in the community, and to preserve it for the next generation, means that limiting family size is of critical importance.

Apart from such economic considerations, another major and explicit factor motivating people in Ban Pong to limit the size of their families is education. In recent years, education has increasingly been recognized as a means to social and economic mobility by rich and poor alike. In the mid-1970s the minimum period of schooling was increased from 4 to 6 years, and thus the cost of educating each child has also risen. The significance of rising educational aspirations as an incentive for parents to use birth control has been noted for Thailand generally (Knodel *et al.*, 1983, pp.41-6) and in other developing countries (Caldwell *et at.*, 1982b, p.699). The following extracts from interviews with women in Ban Pong illustrate the factors involved in their decision to use family planning. The first respondent is a 31-year-old woman (T) with two daughters, who was one of the few women who had used contraception before the beginning of the family planning program in Ban Pong:

> (Anthropologist): Don't you want another child? Wouldn't you like to have a son?
>
> (T): Certainly not! Two children are enough. Having children is so exhausting ... you get so tired having a lot of children. In the countryside these days it is so difficult to make a living. It's impossible to bring up a big family, you just can't do it. And this education business, they keep on increasing the school leaving age and if you have a lot of children you could never afford to send them all to school.
>
> (A): What does your husband say about family planning?
>
> (T): He agrees with me. Two children, that's enough.

The second informant (B), is aged 39 with a son and a daughter. She was one of the five women sterilized by the new *per vagina* method early in 1973.

(A): How were you able to make such a quick decision about the operation?

(B): It wasn't difficult because I knew sterilisation was good for me. My husband supported me. You see our family has very little to hand on, and if we had any more children there would be nothing to give them. We were both afraid that the children would not receive a proper education.

Conclusions

In the Introduction to this chapter it was noted that Thailand is one of a small number of countries in the Third World in which modern methods of birth control have been accepted readily by a predominantly peasant population. In view of the fact that women throughout Thailand had been taking steps to obtain contraceptive services on a private basis for several years 'before' the government introduced its family planning program in 1970, the initial response at least can in no way be attributed to national program effectiveness. It seems clear that in the case of Ban Pong, and probably in Thailand as a whole, a 'latent demand' (Knodel *et al.*, 1983, p.63) for birth control had existed long before the government was prepared to take steps to satisfy it. The apparent increase in the practice of induced abortion in Ban Pong in the late 1950s supports this view. In addition, I would suggest on the basis of evidence from Ban Pong that there was a 'cultural predisposition' to the acceptance of family planning in the population, given the traditional motivation to space births made explicit in postpartum customs.

Perhaps the most important factor in terms of converting this cultural predisposition into action has been the radical change which has occurred in the relationship between human and land resources in Ban Pong, as in most other parts of Thailand during the course of this century. As we have seen in the case of Ban Pong since its settlement one hundred yeas ago, a combination of economic and demographic changes has resulted in a transformation from a situation of plentiful land and scarce labour, to one in which there is considerable unemployment and underemployment while land has become the scarce resource. This transformation is demonstrated by the changing patterns of land tenure in Ban Pong discussed above, and is reflected in the breakdown of traditional residence patterns. It is further illustrated by the change in the migration pattern in the community from one in which Ban Pong provided a focus for immigrants from more densely populated areas in the past, to the current situation of increasing net emigration.

However, such major structural changes are common to many parts of the developing world and have by no means inevitably resulted in widespread acceptance of family planning. A factor which is of crucial importance in Thailand's exceptional responsiveness to the concept of fertility limitation is the comparatively high status of women. As we have seen, women in Ban Pong enjoy a considerable degree of autonomy, which is largely the result of traditional patterns of residence, inheritance and economic activity. This autonomy has been reinforced and enhanced by the substantial economic changes occurring in the region in recent decades. As Dyson and Moore have noted, it is particularly in the context of an organized family planning program that the significance of the degree of female autonomy in a society can be recognized in terms of the timing and speed of the demographic response (1983, p.57, note 41).

The full effects of the acceptance of family planning in Ban Pong will not be seen for some time to come, until the children born after the beginning of the program have reached maturity. Nevertheless, the significant changes which have occurred in the age structure of the population since the 1960s will inevitably have long term implications for educational, employment and marriage patterns. Furthermore, it is likely that the continued use of contraception by the majority of fertile women in Ban Pong will not only serve to enhance current trends in social and economic behaviour, but may also lead to structural changes made possible only by the effective control of fertility. Such changes might include, for example, a gradual reduction in the extreme economic polarization which has developed in the community since the first decades of this century by slowing down the pace of land fragmentation and providing the landpoor and landless tenants with the possibility of improving their economic position through limiting family size, while improved educational opportunities for children of small families may lead to rising expectations and increased movement away from the rural areas into the cities. I would suggest that the social, economic, and demographic consequences of high rates of acceptance of family planning will be among the most important factors shaping the face of Thailand as it approaches the twenty-first century.

Notes

1. The detailed demographic data in this section are drawn from Mougne, 1982.

The Family and Fertility in Africa

8

Investigating the Timing of Additional Children in Non-Contracepting Societies

Lawrence A. Adeokun

Introduction

Interest in the mechanism of the timing of additional children at the level of individual couples with no knowledge or practice of modern contraception, is derived from the larger concern with pragmatic and intellectual issues relating to the role of high fertility in rapid population growth and to the lack of understanding by demographers of the role of disaggregated decision-making in the formation of aggregate demographic patterns. An understanding of the considerations upon which fertility decisions are based will not only assist the interpretation of data on determinants of fertility but should assist the design of programs of intervention for the changing of fertility behaviour and reduction of rapid population growth through lowered fertility.

In the pursuit of this interest, it was apparent from the first that a focus on disaggregated data, as opposed to the macro-level focus of formal demography would create some problems:

1. The potential contribution of the disaggregated approach to improved understanding of relevant aspects of family formation and fertility decision-making had to be determined.

2. The inadequacy of aggregated data on child spacing for the understanding of the considerations that influence the timing of additional children under natural fertility conditions had to be explained.

3. The concepts and the operational definitions relevant to the study of child rearing, caring and spacing practices had to be selected and adapted from cognate disciplines and made to serve the purpose of subjecting social, economic and biological behaviour of reproductive adults to coherent analysis that enhanced formal demographic analysis of fertility patterns and determinants.

4. The appropriate methods of investigating the various aspects and actors in the fertility decision-making framework had to be developed and applied.

5. The new theoretical framework within which the new materials gathered are to be interpreted had to be formulated with

careful attention to existing theories and their inadequacies for the study of disaggregated fertility behaviour.

6. The new material also had to be gathered and analyzed in such a way as to assure the validity and reliability of findings and the adequacy of such materials for testing the appropriate hypotheses emanating from the theoretical framework.

7. The success of materials and methods in achieving the objective of greater understanding of the basis of individual couples' decisions on the timing of the next child had to be evaluated in terms of the general applicability of the findings from the studies to a wider population context other than the one in which it was developed.

8. The adoption of this disaggregated/anthropological approach to some of the aspects of the study did not have to result in the rejection of the formal demographic emphasis on empiricism. Instead it had to be complementary to the clarification and the understanding of mechanisms, thereby enhancing the ability of formal demography to present a coherent description and explanation of phenomena.

It is the description of the process of working out these problems and of some of the successes and failures of attempting to marry the empirical and the qualitative evidence produced, that forms the primary aim of this essay. A regrouping of the various problems identified above into the theoretical and conceptual, the methodological and the analytical form the basis of the three sections of the chapter.

SECTION I

Theories, Concepts and Intuition on Child Spacing

The starting point for this examination of the theories and concepts concerning child spacing and fertility is the concept of natural fertility. This was defined by Louis Henry as the fertility level prevailing in populations where there were no deliberate steps to limit the size of family. In such societies there had to be no practice of modern birth control methods and abortion. Thus the probability of a child of parity 'n' was independent of the number of children a family already had or desired. In effect, the fertility of such a society was largely determined by the biological factors of fecundability and the social context in which reproduction took place. Such social factors include the timing of marriage and the first birth (in the absence of sub-fertility and infertility problems); the continuity of marriage and the consequent exposure to the risk of pregnancy; and the absence of any wish to regulate or limit family size. Fertility within such a given society will also be influenced by cultural factors relating to the rearing and caring for children. Such cultural factors include the presence or absence of extended lactation and the presence or absence of a sexual prohibition associated with lactation (lactation taboo).

The concept of natural fertility has, of course, been subjected to extensive elaboration by Henry and by subsequent writers on the issue (Leridon and Menken, 1979). But the abstraction above contains the main elements related to the immediate purpose at hand, that of setting the boundaries of the theoretical framework in which the issue of child spacing can be viewed. Specifically, although the natural fertility concept did not include a direct specification of child spacing conforming with a natural fertility schedule, some indirect inferences can be made from the operating factors:

1. A combination of early marriage and universality of marriage will produce extended marital duration and the continuity of exposure to the risk of pregnancy;

2. Since there is no deliberate effort to limit births the relationship between fertility and child spacing will be inverse - short birth intervals will produce high fertility;

3. Within any single inter-birth interval, the contribution of modern contraception and abortion must be ruled out; non-susceptibility should therefore be the outcome of the interplay of breastfeeding and the duration of the postpartum amenorrhoea as well as a function of socially acceptable behaviour which has the effect of making the timing of the additional child a product of a consistent sequence of events.

Given the last condition, if biological factors are operating with regularity and social factors are also operating within a narrow range of options set by ethnic homogeneity in beliefs and norms, then fertility levels will be predictably regular and natural fertility will be determined within a narrow range of levels. The absence of such regularity was in fact recognized by the original formulation. Louis Henry did relate the various elements of natural fertility in such a way as to open the way for recognizing the basis of variations in the levels of natural fertility from society to society. But such variation was a product of inter-societal differences in such factors as the duration of lactation and abstinence as well as differences in social factors such as the preferred inter-birth interval. The possibility of intra-society variation in natural fertility as a response to some factors of change can also be taken for granted. Read against the background of demographic transition theory, social changes should produce changes in the fertility regime and such changes can reduce the rigorous applicability of aspects of natural fertility.

It is at this point that the efforts at explaining the observed differences in fertility through the interpretation of the impact of biosocial factors can be introduced as a further theoretical clarification of the determination of fertility.

Attempts at the explanation of the basis of differences in the fertility of given populations at different levels of development goes back to the pioneering efforts of Davis and Blake (1956) who provided the framework for the interpretation of the impact of various societal, biological and individual factors on fertility aspirations and behaviour. But by far the most rewarding line of investigation of the determinants of fertility was that which focused on the variables which directly influenced the fertility prospect. A distinction was thus made between the primary and the secondary links between biosocial variables and fertility. In addition greater sophistication was achieved in the quantification of the impact of the various 'proximate' determinants (Bongaarts, 1978, 1982). The most relevant of these variables were (i) the proportion married among females; (ii) contraceptive use and effectiveness; (iii) prevalence of induced abortion; and (iv) duration of postpartum infecundity resulting from breast-feeding patterns, postpartum abstinence and related practices which determined the pattern of the non-susceptible period. These are the variables which collectively account for the marital fertility of traditional as well as other societies falling far below the theoretical maximum. And it is the relative impact of each that determines the ultimate level of fertility in any one population.

By combining group indices with some individually determined variables of child spacing, the Bongaarts analytical framework opened the way for the quantitative analysis of fertility not only at the group level but with attention to the contribution of variance of individual variables to fertility differences. But it was not so much the quantification of variables which facilitated the investigation of the decision-making process as much as the clarity of the framework. This clarity allowed the presentation of the combinations and permutations of determinants from population to population and for sub-groups of any one population. The internal consistency of the various equations developed for the framework allowed a rigorous analysis of the implications of uniformity in fertility-inhibiting effects of the social and cultural factors pertaining to breastfeeding and marital sexual behaviour within family formation.

It was the extension and application of the framework and its implications for the variations in fertility among Yoruba sub-groups that reinforced the intuitive approach to the analysis of sub-ethnic variation in determinants of fertility first in the Next Child Project (Adeokun, 1981) and subsequently in the expanded program of investigating the sub-ethnic variations in specific proximate determinants of Yoruba fertility and child spacing practices. But before providing a short description of each of these projects and the associated methodological innovations in Section II, some unresolved problems of theories and concepts relating to the analysis of individual decision-making will be discussed.

One problem that could not be resolved by the attention to individual level variables within the aggregated analysis still implied in the Bongaarts framework is the uncertainties about the mechanism through which individual circumstances affect the timing of the individual child. Such mechanical detail was, of course, not the objective of the aggregated analysis but it was essential to the ability of the analyst to understand how individual decisions can be free whilst operating within a norm prescribed by the group. It was also essential information for the planning of change in fertility behaviour at the individual family level. In effect, the determination of the components of fertility was quite distinct from the identification of the strategy adopted by the individual couple to achieve a given pattern of family formation.

For example, the application of the Bongaarts equations to data collected from the Next Child Project allowed a demonstration that although the fertility levels of two Yoruba groups were similar there were significant differences in one of the major components of the non-susceptible period within the inter-birth interval. Specifically, the postpartum sexual taboo played no part in one of the groups (Adeokun, 1982). To compensate for this, estimates based on the Bongaarts equations imply that the contracepting effort, albeit within the traditional birth control options, accounts for the equivalent of 39 per cent of the mothers practising modern contraception. The actual reported level of contraceptive use was only four per cent (Adeokun, 1983b).

Once the possibility of adopting alternate sexual strategies for the attainment of child spacing had been recognized, the conceptual problem was focused on the basis on which child spacing decisions were made. If there was a uniform strategy, then the mode of decision could hardly be a matter for serious concern or study. The argument of the sexual taboo and long inter-birth interval being mutually reinforcing would hardly be a matter for controversy. But if convergence of child spacing derived from alternative sexual behaviour within marriage then child spacing could be disengaged from sexual habit and its basis located elsewhere.

The Anthropological Evidence

The possibility of locating the rationale of child spacing and timing of family formation events in non-sexually related phenomena has long been known. Even on the basis of everyday observation of child caring and rearing, it is possible to argue that child spacing in non-contracepting communities can be explained in terms of a mechanical model of decision-making. Such a model will specify the degree of physical and social maturity of a preceding child that is consistent with the decision of parents to start a next child at a stage when the preceding child can be said to have been satisfactorily integrated into the pattern of domestic and economic activities of the mother. Such intuitive use of common knowledge formed the basis of the Next Child Project. But before one could make sense of the mechanical model of decision-making, attention had to be paid to the existing anthropological insight into the nature of child rearing and its feedback into the productive and reproductive activities of mothers.

Long ago, Fortes (1954) had observed that young children constitute considerable constraints on Ashanti adults performing economic activities. He also observed that the prevailing child spacing practices were influenced by the extent of that constraint. More recently, another anthropologist, Sudarkasa (1973) in a study of Yoruba women in the market place and in the home identified the main elements of family organization aimed at relieving productive mothers of some of the tedium of child rearing.

However, it was Lee (1979) in a comprehensive and truly multidisciplinary study of the !Kung San of the Kalahari Desert who provided a quantitative assessment of the mother's physical input into child caring and rearing of San children under the foraging existence of the community. As a result of very careful observation and recording of mother/child interactions, detailed information was published on various aspects of subsistence production and reproduction. Weights of San children from birth to 8 years, workload of mothers of children of various ages and the effect of birth interval on the work effort of mothers were made available (Lee and DeVore, 1978). Such information reinforced the argument that a mechanical basis existed for the decision on child spacing in that society as parents lived in a state of critical balance in a rather precarious environment. The information also encouraged the pursuit of formulating a mechanical model of child spacing for the Yoruba even though they were living in an agricultural rather than foraging setting.

Mechanical Model of Fertility Decision-Making

Encouraged by the empirical evidence provided by the !Kung San study and the observations in the other sources, one felt that the validity of the mechanical model will rest on the convincing demonstration of a link between child rearing and child spacing, 'irrespective of the economic basis of the society'. However, much more than the anthropological insights sketched above and much more than commonsense knowledge of child rearing and spacing was required for the formulation of the model. Additional information was needed on the determinants of children's physical and social maturation in different environments and socioeconomic groupings so that the culture-specific elements of the model could be reduced.

Stated briefly, the specifications of the mechanical model of fertility decision-making contain the following elements:

1. In nearly all democratic societies, and especially in traditional societies, early childhood (up to age 6) is situated in the family system and influenced by the organization of the family.

2. In nearly all such societies, child rearing is primarily the mother's duty and the role of mother is played in conjunction with other roles ascribed to the mother in the society.

3. The two dominant features of child rearing in such societies are the minimization of the risk of infant and childhood mortality (against substantial odds) and thus maximizing fertility; and the maximization of econmic/productive output by all adults, especially the women.

4. Unless the preceding child is adequately integrated into the productive lifestyle of the mother before the arrival of the next child, the rhythm of the productive lifestyle of the mother will be disturbed and this will be detrimental to the efficient performance of both productive and reproductive roles.

5. Changes in the physical (motor) and social maturity of the preceding child will determine the degree of reduction in its dependence on the mother and the degree of the involvement of others (surrogates) in its care.

6. Changes in the maturity of the preceding child will be related to the probability of a next child pregnancy and the arrival of the next child.

7. Arising from condition number 4, inadequate child spacing will be associated with higher infant and childhood mortality whilst adequate child spacing will be associated with improved mortality.

8. The provision of child rearing support systems which reduce the direct involvement of the mother in child care will permit the shortening of the inter-birth interval without the predicted reproductive and productive disruption.

9. Variations in early child development from child to child, from mother to mother, and from group to group will be related to variations in child spacing, that is, 'irrespective of the marital sexual conventions of the individual couple' or of the group.

There are, of course, other elaborations of the mechanical model which can be developed from the main propositions above. But such elaborations will, for the purpose of simplicity be ignored the better to illustrate the major problems that have been encountered in the application of the model. Such problems span the initiation of the Next Child Project, the problems of data collection, the selection of appropriate materials and analytical techniques and the validity of the conclusions reached so far.

SECTION II

The Next Child Project: Methods and Materials

The Project

Once the emphasis has shifted to the proximate determinants of fertility, from the aggregated analysis of data on fertility levels, attention was now focused on the determination of inter-birth intervals and on the conditions which decided the shortening or lengthening of the interval, that is, irrespective of the desired family size. Such a concentration on child spacing strategy to the exclusion of the relationship between birth intervals and fertility level, allowed the distorting effect of family size ideals to be side-stepped. And, in any case, the conditions of natural fertility prevailing made the assumption of high fertility aspirations realistic.

The Next Child Project took the position that as Bongaarts has clearly shown, the determinants of the inter-birth interval were (i) the duration of the postpartum amenorrhoeic period, (ii) the extension of non-susceptibility by the prevailing breastfeeding and lactational taboo beliefs, (iii) the trial period for a next pregnancy and (iv) the gestation period. But noting the variance of the first three components from society to society the Next Child Project tried to establish which factors accounted for the observed variance. Specifically, an assumption of ethnic homogeneity in breastfeeding and marital sexual taboo was questioned on the simple ethnographic principle that such a homogeneity would be strange in an apparently heterogeneous society such as the Yoruba. It was also questioned on the commonsense knowledge of differences in marital sexual attitudes as well as some anthropological evidence of the existence of some departure from the popularized model of Yoruba marital sexual behaviour (Ward, 1937).

Discussing Marital Sexual Behaviour

When it came to the selection of appropriate variables to study, the first major consideration was to tackle the issue of marital sexual behaviour which the typical KAP-type fertility survey barely touched upon beyond the question on the duration of postpartum abstinence. It was generally believed that discussion of marital sexuality was too delicate for the large scale interview method. Here again, methodology was guided by the dictates of commonsense knowledge of substantial discussion of marital sexual activities among females at the quasi-social gatherings such as attendance at maternal and child health clinics, when the progress of the youngest child and the implications for family formation are on interested public display. Marital sexual practices are also exuberantly discussed at ritualized occasions such as at annual harvest festivals, during which the more *risqué* aspects of sexuality could be openly discussed without giving offence. If, therefore, the question of sexuality could be approached not from the point of view of curiosity but from the dimension of essential information for the understanding of vital phenomena, then the validity of assumptions of universal observance of taboos could be established.

Besides, marital sexual behaviour was the variable of interest in effecting changes in family formation and fertility levels. It was also the major ultimate act that could indicate the timing of the decision on a next child. Furthermore, it was the act which could be manipulated to shorten or lengthen the inter-birth interval not only through action or inaction but by combining the sexual act with pregnancy prevention strategies which, whilst not constituting deliberate effort at limiting family size could be evidence of intention or lack of intention to have a next child.

The selection of an appropriate method of study of marital sexuality was intricate. If its avoidance was because of the delicacy of the subject, the Next Child Project would not ignore the fundamental wisdom of that position. Consequently, the close association of the topic with the issue of child spacing had to be invoked as the basis for its study. Since the sexual activity was dyadic, the couple had to be brought together somehow in the discussion or questioning. Such is the nature of lovers, that the editing of versions of the same story by either partner elicits some conventional response in the other. Such response can be observed and interpreted by the trained or initiated observer. There was a distinction, however, between the stylized questions on postpartum marital sexual experiences for all live births contained on the questionnaire and the more flexible discussion of sexuality contained in the recorded interview of a panel of the respondents. Whilst the questionnaires were administered separately to the wife and the husband, the recorded discussions were jointly held.

This distinction in the form of questions and the appropriate method of administering the questions is also based on the distinction between quantification and qualitative insight into phenomena. The short questions of quantitative estimates of postpartum abstinence were more suitable for the derivation of child-specific child rearing practices. In contrast, the recorded discussion was not on the specific details of abstinence but was aimed at drawing out the couple in discussion so as to appreciate how they perceive the intent of the lactational taboo. That the recorded interviews go beyond the mere reporting of attitudes and practices relating to marital sexual patterns to the subtle purposes of various actions or inactions can be gathered even from the translated transcription of such taped discussions (Adeokun, 1981).

Deciding on the appropriateness of each of the approaches to the discussion of marital sexual behaviour benefited from the pilot test of the questionnaire containing these unusual details under a contrived environment. Women attending a maternal and child welfare clinic were administered the interview within the framework of the routine record keeping activities of the clinic.

Whilst this approach may have eliminated any hostility to probing, it did not stop the discovery of inappropriate details which were dropped or made conditional questions in the final questionnaire.

Implications of Early Child Development

The next consideration in the conceptualization and the operationalization of the mechanical model of child spacing was how to link early child development to the socioeconomic and demographic aspects of production and reproduction and how to obtain the necessary information for its study. Early child development could benefit from the longitudinal and in-depth approach of the anthropologist, observational methods could illustrate, for specific children, the linkages between the mother's activities and the extent of the child dependence on the mother at different stages. So would the selective observations of a panel of children at work and at play throw light on the constraints that children of different stages of growth and development constitute on adult activities.

But in order to demonstrate the consistency of the mechanisms and linkages proposed in the mechanical model, empirical evidence was also required that would set the timetable of development and of child dependence. It was on such evidence and its analysis that the replication of the study and the validity of the model and its implications would rest. This was the most trying of the tasks of formulating the Next Child Project, and it has taken the detailed analysis of the Project information and further re-thinking of the data collection strategy in the current study of sub-ethnic variation in breastfeeding, marital sexuality and fertility among five main Yoruba sub-groups to reach the stage of realization of the objectives.

Two complementary approaches were adopted to the study of early child development. The first derived from the extensive phychological and medical literature on early child development and the orderliness of such development information which had hitherto been marginal to demographic consideration (Breckenridge and Murphy, 1969; McCall, 1980; Morley, 1976). From these sources and from the increasing awareness of the role of physical and social development in the welfare of a child it was possible to start with the idea of establishing a number of culturally relevant 'milestones' of growth and development to which traditional women could relate without compromising the universal application of the findings.

The method of selecting the milestones consisted of reviewing some six varieties of developmental milestones from the sources and shortlisting those on which information of a precise age estimate could be obtained, whilst adding a couple that were of relevance to the family organization of traditional societies. Subject, of course, to the risk of recall error attached to the methodological ploy of asking mothers to make child-specific recall of the timing of each event. Information was gathered from about a thousand women living in two sub-ethnic groups (Ekitis and Ikales). The following milestones were canvassed:

1. Sitting unsupported.
2. Cutting first tooth.
3. Introduce first solid food.
4. Walk unsupported.
5. Stop breastfeeding.
6. Say short phrases.
7. Stay at home with others.
8. Stop being carried on the back.

To offset the greater problem of fathers recalling the timing of children in whose care they played a lesser role, ideal types were presented to fathers to respond to. They were asked to provide estimates of the time it took their fastest child, their slowest child, a male child and a female child, to attain the various milestones.

Realizing that there could be problems with the quantitative data, coming as it is from non-clinical sources, it was essential to make certain of the reasonableness of the estimates, in comparison with clinical data. Consequently, the analytical approach adopted required that the highly successful age/height/weight method of monitoring child growth and social development (Morley, 1976) be adapted to the analysis of the data.

The second approach to the study of child development required that the translation of child growth and development to socially relevant actions that (i) permitted others to take part in their rearing; (ii) reduced reliance of the child on its mother; (iii) encouraged the mother to pursue productive activities; and (iv) was regular from situation to situation, should be observed. It was obvious that since some of these actions were initiated by the children, and since it was not possible to 'interview' the children on the quantitative lines of the parents, a mixture of observation and systematic recording of events was required.

Again for the purpose of assuring complete coverage of the relevant population (infants and children under age 4, when the reduction of reliance would have been complete) an apparently quantitative approach to the recording of observation was developed and is now being tested in the Breastfeeding, Marital Sexuality and Fertility (BMSF) Project. A list of activities which children can carry out was drawn up, the list benefiting from the fieldwork experiences of Cain (1977) in analyzing the economic activities of children in Bangladesh. The questionnaire required that at three 6-monthly visits to each household, the children aged 4 and below should be observed and their ability to perform or not perform a number of tasks should be recorded. This quantification of observation allowed the fixing, in time, of the stage at which each child attained some level of growth and development and provided an improvement on the earlier recall of a much more restricted list of milestones. The extended list also allowed the documentation of the enabling actions which can lead to the reduction of the child's dependence on its mother. This is more reliable than the use of inferences for the explanation of changes in the degree of the child's reliance, as was the case with the earlier Next Child Project data.

Decision-Making Processes

The rationality of decisions as to the timing of the next child depends on the perception of the respondents as to the intended outcome of actions as well as on demonstrating the validity of the proffered mechanism through which early child development affects child spacing. In investigating this aspect of the next child decision, the procedure was to start from (i) the assumptions of the model; followed by (ii) the identification of the normative basis of child rearing practices; and (iii) the collection of appropriate data to test the validity of the line of reasoning, as expanded on below:

1. The assumptions of the model touching on the decision-making process and its rationality are (i) that mothers will exploit family organizational forms to achieve the needed reduction in their own efforts in child care; (ii) that acceptable child rearing practices will include the range of social and cultural options which are not detrimental to the well-being of the child; and (iii) that the pattern of early child development will determine the regularity or otherwise of parents' responses.

2. The normative bases of behaviour are located in the practices which are condoned or accepted for the convenience of both the child and its mother. The place of confinement, domicile in the postnatal period, and the use of grandparents in child rearing and minding are some of the features of postpartum practices which depend on the acceptable behaviour in any given society. The prevailing marital sexual behaviour is as much a function of norms as it is a factor in deriving new norms. Consequently, the investigation of beliefs and practices surrounding marital sexual behaviour serves the purpose of distinguishing between the normative values and the innovative behaviour.

3. Investigation of reasons for any given pattern of postpartum practice should then reveal the consistency of expectation with the actual benefit derived in terms of the reduction of child dependency.

In the Next Child Project, these three aspects of the decision-making process were the subject of a series of questions aimed at establishing what couples actually do, as opposed to what they think is expected of them. The assumption that the extended family allowed child rearing support to be readily obtained was investigated by asking to what extent confinement and the post-natal period was spent with grandparents rather than in marital homes. The motive of any duration of postpartum abstinence was investigated in terms of the desire for a next child pregnancy, the intention of resumption of the marital sexual relationship and the consistency of practices after each live birth. So also was the involvement of relevant others in the details of child rearing investigated.

The extent to which the various methodological devices succeeded either in the collection of appropriate information and in facilitating analysis, form the substance of the following section.

SECTION III

Illustrative Findings

In this section some selected aspects of the mechanical model of decisions on the timing of the next child are presented. The aim is to illustrate the extent to which the methodological problems raised were resolved either in the data collection or in the analytical procedures adopted. The aspects are: the extent to which measurement of early child development from cross-sectional, non-clinical information succeeded in revealing a pattern of growth and development in Yoruba children which could form the basis of inferring changes in the degree of dependence of the child on its mother; and the extent to which the pattern of growth and development is consistent with the observed pattern of child spacing so that some hypotheses relating to the mechanical model of child spacing could be tested.

Pattern of Early Child Development

The clinical methods and use of growth monitoring are very well known (Tremlett *et al.*, 1983). For effective use, age, height and weight of children have to be regularly measured and carefully recorded in clinic contacts with health personnel. Besides the quantity and precision of the information so gathered, there is some controversy surrounding the use of a 'standard' which more often than not is derived from a group of children from the industrial/middle class societies of the West. Figure 8.1 shows the elements of a typical age/weight chart. On the chart is marked the progress of the 10th, 50th and 90th percentile of the standard against which the progress of an individual child is assessed.

In the case of the Next Child Project the one available piece of information was the estimated age at which the children ever born to a group of about a thousand Yoruba women attained eight selected milestones. Although some recall error was to be expected, especially for the older children, the effect was not significant enough to vitiate the use of the data as the basis for deriving some form of index of 'normal' timing of such milestones among these Yoruba children. By averaging all the estimates the average ages for the attainment of the milestone was constituted

Figure 8.1 Typical Weight for Age Chart

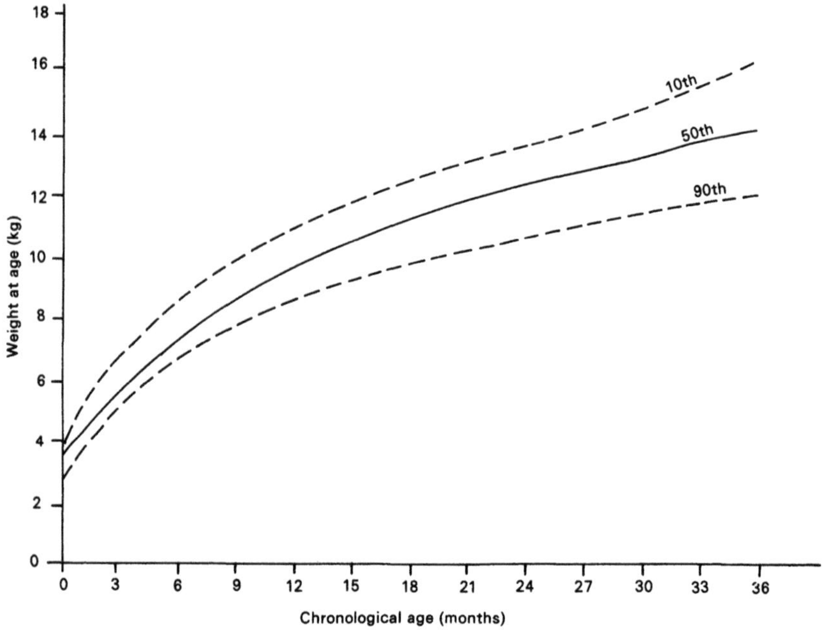

Figure 8.2 Two Hypothetical Chronological Age for Norm Age Paths

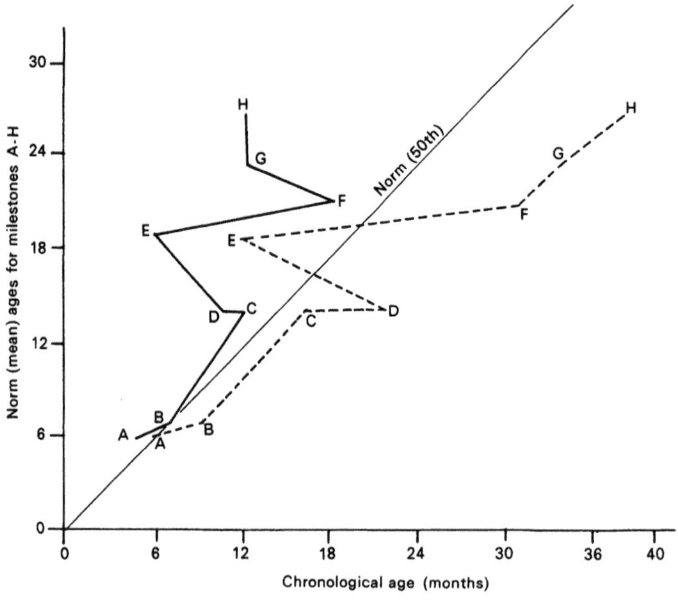

Table 8.1 Average Ages at the Attainment of 8 Milestones by Rural Yoruba Children (in months)

Event		Average age for all children born alive (months)
Stage I:	Sit up	6.0
	Cut first tooth	6.8
Stage II:	Introduce solid food	14.0
	Walk unaided	14.0
Stage III:	Stop breastfeeding	18.5
	Talk simple words	21.4
Stage IV:	Stay at home with others	23.8
	Stop being carried on back	26.6

Source: Author's analysis of NCP data.

into a 'local rural Yoruba standard', shown in Table 8.1. The standard will represent the progress of the 50th percentile. Other percentile growth paths can be derived from raw data or can be transposed from similar growth charts (Adeokun, 1984).

By adopting a set of ages at which the average rural Yoruba child should attain the milestones, it was then possible to take the chronological ages at which given social and other groupings of children actually achieve those milestones. Where the chronological age is less than the norm, a child is making rapid progress and vice versa. Figure 8.2 shows the effect of converting the growth chart from one relating age to weight as an indicator of health status, to a chart relating the chronological age to the norm or local standard of attainment. Figure 8.2 can thus form the basis of assessing the rate of development of different groups of children or of the individual child. It will be observed from the two hypothetical growth patterns shown on Figure 8.2 that some children make rapid progress on the social developments whilst others make slow progress in the biosocial milestones. The social and economic factors which can influence the pattern of growth and development will consequently have some impact on the reduction of dependency of the child on its mother. The details of such factors are contained elsewhere (Adeokun, 1983a, 1984).

Child Development and Reduction of Dependence

An inspection of Table 8.1 shows approximately 6-monthly shifts in the attainment of the pairs of milestones that have been grouped into four stages. It is from this pattern that inferences have been made as to the effect of stages of growth and development on the reduction in the dependency of infants and young children on their mothers and the increase in the opportunity for other adults to take part in their care (Adeokun, 1981). The main changes envisaged are:

Stage 1: The time span covers the first 7 months of life. Except for when the child is asleep or in the physical care of another individual, the child is in close contact with the mother. Sudarkasa (1973, p.136) estimated that at this stage, a child spends up to 8 hours daily on the mother's back during the itinerant trading activities of the mother.

Stage II: These two milestones - the introduction of solid food and the ability to walk unaided - show significant variation by the socioeconomic status of mothers. Such variations have been shown to have implications for the survival chances of children, especially at the weaning age. The ability to move around in the domestic situation can confer some freedom of action on the mother. The existence of others with whom the child can interact and on whom the mother can rely for the child's safety make the reduction in dependency at this stage a possibility for women engaged in the non-formal sector.

Stage III: By this stage, there has been an improvement in the physical as well as the social development of the child. The termination of breastfeeding removes a major demand of the child on the mother's caring. The ability to talk also opens up channels for the participation of others in its care.

Stage IV: By the final stage, two major social developments with direct relevance to the degree of dependency take place. To stay at home with others implies that the child has given up the company of the mother partly out of economic necessity and partly out of the social maturity of the child. That the child is no longer being carried on the back implies partly that it is competent to cope with the efforts needed in participation in the activities of the mother outside the home. It is also an indication that the mother is unable to accommodate the substantial weight of the child at this stage. A third possibility bearing directly on the timing of the next child is that the mother is no longer available to carry a preceding child along with the pregnancy of the next child.

The Timing of the Next Child Pregnancies

Although information on pregnancy histories obtained in illiterate societies suffers from poor dating of events, one of the advantages of longitudinal studies of the type embarked upon in the BMSF Project is the improvement which can be gained by monitoring the reproductive behaviour of women over a 12-month period. The cross-sectional data from the Next Child Project was

Table 8.2 Duration in Months of Birth Interval of a Group of 588 West African Mothers Expressed as Percentiles

Percentile of next child	5%	10%	25%	50%	75%	90%	95%
Duration (months)	27	29	31	34	38	45	50
At conception	18	20	22	25	29	36	41

Source: Morley, 1976, p.309.

Table 8.3 Proportion of Next Child Pregnancies which have Occurred by the Norm Ages for the 8 Milestones by the Proportion of Pregnancies

Event		Norm ages (Table 8.1) (in months)	Proportion of pregnancies
			%
Stage I:	Sitting unsupported	6.0	0.0
	Cut first tooth	6.8	0.0
Stage II:	Introduce solid food	14.0	1.6
	Walk unsupported	14.0	1.0
Stage III:	Stop breastfeeding	18.5	6.3
	Say short phrases	21.4	20.5
Stage IV:	Stay at home with others	23.8	40.0
	Stop being carried on back	26.6	60.0

Sources: Norm ages from NCP (see Table 8.1) and proportions estimated from Morley, 1976, pp.306–9.

not an adequate basis for investigating the timing of the next child pregnancy. This does not preclude the tentative testing of the expected association between the stages of development of a preceding child and the next child pregnancy if 'reliable proxy data' could be found.

Table 8.2 shows the duration in months of elapsed time since the birth of the preceding children born to a cohort of 588 West African mothers and the percentile distribution of the pregnancies which have occurred at various durations. The elapsed times at the conception of the next pregnancy are also shown. For example at the 18th month of the birth interval only 5 per cent of the mothers were pregnant with the next child, which then arrived at the 27th month.

In Table 8.3 the proportion of the next child pregnancies which have occurred by the norm ages for the selected milestones are shown. The association shown forms the basis of the following observations:

a) At the end of Stage I, no mother had already conceived.

b) Only 1.6 per cent of mothers were carrying their next pregnancy by the attainment of Stage II milestones.

c) It is at the end of Stage II that about a fifth of mothers were carrying the next pregnancy.

d) More than half of the next pregnancies actually occurred within and after Stage IV.

It is clear from this pattern of association between the stages of growth and the timing of the next pregnancy that the first two stages of growth and development are incompatible with the next child decision. The association also lends some support to the mechanical modelling of child development, mother's productive activities and reproductive pattern.

Conclusion

From the discussions of methodological features of the Next Child Project so far, the view must be gained that focusing attention on the primary level of demographic behaviour may not imply a substitution of qualitative evidence for the conventional emphasis on empirical data. It is hoped that the chapter did demonstrate the possibility of combining the quantification of phenomena and the detailed recording of observations with the qualitative knowledge of the inner workings of family organization and the mechanism of decision-making within the family.

It is also our experience that the methodological innovations of a study cannot be restricted to the data collection only, but must extend to the analysis of the material thus collected. This is an area where the adoption of a micro-demographic perspective must imply freedom from the narrow data base of the conventional demographic approach. The multi-disciplinary implications of micro-demography will required more than rhetoric and include some risky but worthwhile involvement of skills and expertise from cognate disciplines.

As a result of the central place of early child development in the fertility decision-making studies (Next Child Project and BMSF), some unusual applications of growth monitoring techniques have emerged. The problems of comprehension of the concepts of weight and height in the assessment of health status can be expanded by the dimension of varying growth patterns based on chronological and norm ages for attainment of milestones. It could also serve as an early evidence of disability in children which mothers can pick up in largely non-numerate societies such as Nigeria's. Such inter-disciplinary contacts will enhance the detailed study of the child and its role in the process of child spacing.

9

The Seven Roles Framework: Focused Biographies and Family Size in Ghana

Christine Oppong and Katharine Abu

Introduction

This chapter addresses a common conceptual and methodological problem encountered in demographic studies: how changes in the roles of women may be indexed, documented, and linked to lower desired family size and contraceptive innovation. A framework for data collection and analysis is outlined and one micro-technique, the focused biography described. The remainder of the chapter examines some of the empirical evidence from a Ghanaian study using this framework and technique to demonstrate how changes or differences in aspects of women's roles are related to new family size desires and associated practices. Given that the focus of interest is procreation, the discussion centres upon childbirth and child care and the ways in which shifts away from traditional values and practices are linked to changing maternal norms, values and beliefs, as well as changes in other roles. The discussion thus addresses two sets of hypotheses, one which attempts to link increasing expenditure of time and money on children and desires for 'higher quality' offspring with smaller family size desires and adoption of more effective birth control, and the other set which tries to associate the latter changes with conflicts of time and interest between occupational, community and individual roles and motherhood.

The Seven Roles Framework

In the study discussed here, a conceptual framework of seven roles of women was adopted (Oppong, 1980), a framework which has been used elsewhere to systematize the findings of a wide range of work (Oppong, 1983b).

The design was such that information collected would pertain to seven roles women play during their lives including: (i) maternal; (ii) occupational; (iii) conjugal; (iv) domestic; (v) kin; (vi) community; and (vii) individual. Information to be collected relevant to these several roles included activities associated with a particular role and the time, money and energy spent on it; expectations of that role, including norms, values and beliefs; its importance to the women concerned and the economic, social and political status rewards accruing from it; and the satisfaction or otherwise gained. Also taken into account were the ways in which decisions appear to be taken with regard to the associated activities and the knowledge upon which these decisions are based; the set of people *vis-à-vis* whom the woman plays the role; and the content of their relationships with her. It was intended that the collection of these sets of data would make possible multi-dimensional insights into the lives of the women concerned, as well as providing appropriate data for the generation and possible testing of a range of hypotheses. The central focus of attention was women's maternal roles and effects of their other role activities and expectations as workers, wives, and members of particular cultural and social environments.

The Case of Ghana: Fertility Contrasts and Changes

The data were collected in Ghana, where family size ideals and achievements remain among the highest in the world. Numerous now classic ethnographic studies of agricultural communities and households in different ethnic areas have documented in great detail the traditional, cultural and socioeconomic contexts of such high fertility (for example, Fortes, 1949, 1950, 1954; E. Goody, 1973; J. Goody, 1956; Nukunya, 1969). They have indicated the high demand for agricultural and domestic labour in subsistence economies with primitive production techniques. They have described the general availability of land for farming in a relatively sparsely populated country and the high levels of infant and child mortality and general vulnerability to tropical diseases in communities with limited access to modern medical care. All of these factors have facilitated and encouraged repeated and prolonged childbearing and begetting, as has been described for West Africa as a whole (Ware, 1983). In addition the proximity and solidarity of kin and practices of fostering have traditionally assured the availability of multiple parental figures, who may both share the responsibilities of child care and enjoy the benefits of child company and labour (E. Goody, 1978, 1982).

During the past two decades, however, demographic inquiries in Ghana have noted increasing contrasts in fertility between different categories of the population by employment status, ethnicity, income level, educational standard and size of community of residence (for example, Caldwell, 1968). While certain contrasts are clearly apparent in the wider population, for example farmers tend to have higher fertility and the highly educated to have relatively fewer children, when more refined analyses are undertaken and several factors are taken simultaneously into consideration, differences between particular categories by education, employment, residence, and so forth are not always in the expected direction. Ghanaian demographers have openly admitted the difficulties involved in providing explanations for such differences (Addo, Gaisie and Nabila, 1978). Simple one-factor explanations of differences are recognized as inadequate, moreover they tell nothing about the causes, processes and consequences of change.

Diversity and change in the reproductive behaviour of the educated and employed, mainly in urban settings, has been the focus of concern in a series of micro-demographic studies spread through the past decade and a half using a variety of populations and types of materials for analysis (reviewed in Oppong, 1985). Data on both role expectations and behaviour have supported the contention that increases in individual parental costs lead to reduced family size desires (for example, Oppong, 1983a). These increased costs may be in terms of time or material goods, and can be caused by decreasing delegation of costs to kin and others, spouses not sharing costs, higher demands in terms of children's education, and other changes. At the same time role conflicts caused by separation of work and home, in contexts where it was difficult to delegate child care, were also associated with maternal and paternal role strain and reduced demand for children.

These studies concentrated upon occupational and familial roles, however, and little data pertinent to community roles and individual leisure and pleasure pursuits were systematically collected, even though changes in these roles have been demonstrated to be relevant to fertility and have been well documented in parallel studies (for example, Dinan, 1983). It was therefore decided to build upon and expand this earlier work using similar concepts and hypotheses but expanding the roles considered to seven as outlined above, and to simultaneously collect more detailed data which would give more insight into changing values and role priorities affecting motherhood, especially those affecting perceived costs and opportunity costs of children. It was intended in particular to increase the sophistication of measurement of role strain and conflicts between different roles and also to look at the issues of values, satisfaction and gratification in relation to the array of potential and observed role rewards or status benefits. It was also the intention to examine an urban educated segment of the population and try to find out how and why some remained more traditional than others with regard to procreation and child rearing.

The Biographical Approach to the Study of Social Change

To provide material sufficiently multifaceted and rich to fulfil the above objectives, the focused biography mode of data collection was chosen. The biographical approach to the documentation of human behaviour has long been recognized as offering a valuable method for scholars of many disciplines. Levine (1982) and Young (1983) are among those who have recently shown how female biographies can be used to enhance understanding of how social, psychological and cultural systems, as well as economic constraints and political pressures, shape women's roles as wives, kin, mothers and workers. Recently the biographical or life history approach has reassumed a prominence which it earlier enjoyed in the work of sociologists; increasing numbers have become disenchanted with the efficacy of rigidly structured questionnaires and surveys as major means of data collection (for example, Bertaux, 1981)[1]. Life histories have been viewed as structured self-images or 'identities' in construction. The individual represents those aspects of the past which are relevant to the present in terms of the intentions by which present actions are oriented (Kohl, 1981, p.65).

Among the critical aspects of social change for which life histories have proved effective modes of documentation are the ways in which former systems of ideas, representations and values may persist among migrants in new contexts and in very different material circumstances (Catani, 1981). They have also been used to illustrate ways in which a sense of present relative deprivation may exist in relation to the image maintained of the past (Hankiss, 1981). A number of other advantages of the method have been emphasized, including the capacity to present images of social relations in action (Bertaux-Wiamé, 1981) and to reintroduce the dimension of time into sociological inquiry (Thompson, 1981). Certainly an important asset of the method is its flexibility, the possibility of developing questions and approaches during the course of a study and as it seems appropriate to do so. Thus Thompson (1981, p.294) for example has argued that it can become part of a more powerful methodology, a continuous process of testing and reformulating hypotheses, helping to develop new theories and new questions, leading to more theoretical vigour and a more substantial grounding in social reality.

Three other points relevant to the use of the life history approach are very pertinent to our concerns here. The first is increasing realization that a high proportion of individual decisions are as likely to be made by women as men, in their capacities as workers or migrants, as well as parents and spouses. It was realization of the need for more research at the level of the individual woman, her activities, expectations, resources, decisions, knowledge and relationships that promoted the design of the present study.[2] The second is that economic and family life are interdependent (Thompson, 1981, pp.299-300). The third is that the separation of sociological and historical analysis and the relegation of the family to a purely subsidiary function is not a productive research approach (Thompson, 1981). It was precisely with a view to demonstrating the interdependence of individuals' roles in the workplace and in the home, and the centrality of the latter for any study of fertility change, that a conceptual framework was developed for data collection, using the focused biography method, which would take account of each of the roles that women assume.

Data Collection: Focused Interviewing

The main method used for the collection of data was focused interviewing, particularly valuable because of the qualities of non-direction, specifity, range, depth and personal content. On the topics selected, women were encouraged to give retrospective accounts of their past activities, feelings and attitudes and to discuss their current situations as well as expectations for the future. At the same time the interviews ranged widely enough to allow women a chance to report unanticipated items relevant to the inquiry, thus permitting further probing of attitudes to their several life roles. The very technique of encouraging people to talk freely or branch off into subjects that held their interest or were of personal concern was advantageous. It gave women some psychic rewards from the interview sessions, for they were not so much 'victims' as co-operators and collaborators in the exercise. Each woman had some control of the interview and could discourse on topics she felt important. Given the fact that each woman appeared interested in what she wanted to talk about, they were generally helpful when asked to be specific on certain key fertility-related areas.

An interview guide was used, based on the categories of data in the seven roles framework described above, listing the topics to be explored in the course of the interviews (Oppong and Abu, 1985).

In order to collect this type of data over extended periods of time, the investigator needed to establish and maintain excellent rapport with each woman. The actual time involved in the interviewing process varied - depending upon the rapport established, the woman's age and complexity of her life events - between a minimum of 3 or 4 hours in one case to other instances in which continuing social relations were formed. Supporting data were also collected from the women's kin, colleagues and neighbours. The context of their situations was further documented by genealogical and household census data, and participant and non-participant observation.

A short and relatively simple method for categorizing and coding the focused biographical data was devised for both role activities and expectations of various kinds (Oppong and Abu, 1985, 1986). A number of categories were used for comparing critical role attributes such as 'role strain', 'salience', 'satisfaction', feelings of 'relative deprivation', 'conflicts', and 'social, economic and political rewards' (status benefits).[3] These have been hypothesized in one way or another in various models of change, as being connected with changing fertility desires and achievements. Elsewhere the ways in which the individual texts were analyzed has been described in detail (Oppong and Abu, 1985).

The Sample

Education, urbanization and migration have all been linked to reproductive innovation. It was thus decided to study urban, educated women, both locals and migrants, in two towns - the capital city of Accra and the northern town of Tamale. Six women from the Ga and Dagomba ethnic groups were purposively selected from three age groups at different stages of the reproductive span (18-24 years; 25-34 years and 35-50 years).[4] Thus there were twelve sample categories (by location, ethnicity, age group and migration status) and five women in each category. Individuals were contacted in a variety of ways. Several key women to whom

Table 9.1 Role Profiles: Priority, Satisfaction and Status (mean scores)

	Priority	Satisfaction	Economic rewards	Social rewards
1. Parental	2.9	2.5	.07	1.8
2. Occupational	2.5	2.4	2.1	2.1
3. Conjugal	2.7	2.3	1.9	1.8
4. Domestic	1.6	1.7	.05	.3
5. Kin	2.4	2.5	1.0	1.4
6. Community	1.5	1.9	0.0	.7
7. Individual	1.9	2.4	.2	.7

Source: Oppong and Abu (1986, p.78).

Role priority: the salience of each role to the respondent was categorized by the researcher as (1) low; (2) medium or (3) high.

Role satisfaction: similarly each role was classified according to the extent to which the respondent appeared to derive satisfaction from it - (1) very little; (2) some; (3) quite a lot; (4) a lot.

Economic rewards: material rewards accruing from a role were designated (0) nil; (1) a little; (2) some; (3) a lot.

Social rewards: the extent to which a role provided prestige, deference, influence was similarly classified.

Examples of coding for these and other indicators are given in Oppong and Abu (1985).

the project was explained were instrumental in contacting their friends, relatives, colleagues and acquaintances. Only two women out of those contacted were reluctant to co-operate. Some were dropped from the sample because they did not fit the necessary criteria. The sample was thus 'analytical', selected for theoretical and methodological purposes and not to represent all urban or all educated women in Ghana. The primary aims of the study were to enhance the understanding of recent demographic and economic change processes at the micro-level and to introduce greater sophistication, from the points of view of both theory and method, into the collection and analysis of micro-level data on women's roles and statuses in relation to changing educational and employment practices and opportunities on the one hand and

Table 9.2 Role Strain, Relative Deprivation and Desire for Change (mean scores)

	Role Strain[1]				Relative[2] depri- vation	Desire[3] for change
	Overall	Time	Money	Relation- ships		
1. Parental	4.1	1.6	1.9	1.5	1.6	.5
2. Occupational	3.8	1.7	1.0	1.1	1.6	.5
3. Conjugal	4.3	1.2	1.1	2.0	1.9	.5
4. Domestic	5.3	2.0	1.9	1.4	1.5	.3
5. Kin	4.0	1.1	1.4	1.5	1.2	.06
6. Community	3.3	1.3	1.0	1.0	1.1	.05
7. Individual	4.4	1.4	1.9	1.1	1.3	.1

Source: Oppong and Abu (1986, p.78).

1: Role strain: the extent to which fulfilment of the responsibilities attached to a role constituted a strain was classified in terms of time, money and interpersonal relationships as (0) no strain; (1) a little; (3) some; (4) a lot.

2: Relative deprivation: the extent to which women felt a sense of relative deprivation with regard to role rewards (i.e. a perceived gap between expectations and reality) was categorized as (1) not at all; (2) somewhat; (3) very much.

3: Desire for change was categorized in terms of efforts to exert pressure for change in terms of (0) none; (1) some; (2) a lot.

reproductive expectations and behaviour on the other. The study was not meant to be simply descriptive or to focus on a typical or representative set of women. A survey of the urban educated provided economic and demographic information from such people, collected more than a decade previously (Caldwell, 1968).

One of the most striking impressions gained from talking with these women, ranging in educational level from elementary school leavers to university graduates, was the clarity of their aims in life and the ease with which they were prepared to express them. This included their reproductive goals: they knew what sort of family size they wanted, whether few or many children. In addition they were quite sure about what kinds of marriage and conjugal relationships and career situations they wanted to accompany their child-raising. Most of them were also ready to

Table 9.3 Occupational Role Attributes by Ethnicity, Age and Migration Status

		Ga (N=30)							Dagomba (N=30)						
		mean hours per day worked away from home	priority of occup. role	satis-faction from occup. role	econ. status from occup. role	occup. time strain	occup. depri-vation	occup. conflict	mean hours per day worked away from home	priority of occup. role	satis-faction from occup. role	econ. status from occup. role	occup. time strain	occup. depri-vation	occup. conflict
Young	Static	5.6	2.4	2.4	1.4	1.8	1.6	.2	3.6	2.2	2.2	1.2	3.0	1.6	.6
	Migrant	4.2	2.4	2.0	1.6	1.2	2.0	.8	3.6	2.4	2.4	2.0	1.0	1.4	.4
	Total	4.9	2.4	2.2	1.5	1.5	1.8	.5	3.6	2.3	2.3	1.6	1.8	1.5	.5
Middle aged	Static	4.0	2.8	2.4	2.4	1.4	1.6	.2	5.8	2.6	3.0	2.8	1.6	1.2	.8
	Migrant	3.2	2.4	2.2	1.6	1.8	2.2	.4	5.2	2.6	2.4	2.2	2.8	1.4	1.2
	Total	3.6	2.6	2.3	2.0	1.6	1.9	.3	5.5	2.6	2.7	2.5	2.2	1.3	1.0
Older	Static	6.0	2.6	2.4	2.2	2.7	1.6	.6	6.4	2.6	3.0	2.6	1.0	1.4	.6
	Migrant	5.6	2.0	2.4	2.2	1.6	1.8	1.6	5.6	3.0	2.6	2.8	1.4	1.0	.8
	Total	5.7	2.3	2.4	2.2	2.1	1.7	1.1	6.0	2.8	2.8	2.7	1.2	1.2	.7
		4.7	2.4	2.3	1.9	1.7	1.8	.6	5.0	2.5	2.6	2.2	1.7	1.3	.7

Source: Oppong and Abu (1986, p.79).

Indicators were calculated as in Tables 9.1 and 9.2.

admit it when they failed to achieve the sort of family situation desired and when they had been compelled to compromise.

Women's Roles: Income-Earning and Childbearing

The need for brevity prevents us here from describing in detail aspects of the seven roles of the women studied (see Oppong and Abu, 1986). However Table 9.1 gives some numerical indices of the relative priority given to different roles by the women themselves, their comparative satisfaction derived and the observed economic and social status benefits enjoyed. Occupation ranks only after parenthood and marriage in priority and after parenthood and kinship as a source of satisfaction (see Table 9.1) and occupational activities, not ties of kinship or marriage are increasingly likely to be an educated woman's major source of maintenance and security and social status. At the same time they are, however, a focus of time strain (see Table 9.2), as is domestic work and child care, given the necessity for many to work away from home for varying periods of time and the general impossibility of combining child care with occupational activities. Among relationships it is the conjugal tie which is the main focus of strain and feelings of relative deprivation.

Table 9.3 shows some of the variations in occupational role attributes among women of the sample, according to ethnicity, migration, and age. At the time of the study only three women were unemployed. They were all housewives, monogamously married, who wanted to work but were prevented from doing so - two by their domestic circumstances, and one by her husband who did not want her to work. Two women in the study were students; three were skilled and unskilled manual workers; six were in sales and service jobs; sixteen were clerical workers; twelve were lower professionals and eight were higher professionals or administrators; six were trading and one was an independent manufacturer. The majority were working for government institutions (60%). One in six was self-employed, two were paid family workers, and the rest were working in private firms.

Nearly a third of the women, and nearly half of those in government employment, had former or current subsidiary income generating activities. It has long been common in Ghana for salaried workers to supplement their income with some form of private enterprise. These sidelines ranged from substantial businesses to petty trade. Two women owned commercial vehicles and one was a licensed lotto receiver. Sewing and baking were popular income-earning activities because they could be done at home outside office hours, and many girls with a medium or high level of education had also learned baking or sewing skills from a kinswoman.

Hours of employment or income-earning activity spent outside the home ranged from 0 to 8 hours per day. The mode was 6 hours, and the mean 4.8 hours. More than half worked 6 or more hours outside the home (see Table 9.3). There were marked differences by age with the oldest women working the longest hours away from home. This is related to the fact that the majority of the older women were salary earners with fixed hours of work outside the home, as compared with less than three-quarters of the middle age group, and fewer than half of the younger group.

Women in their home towns worked longer hours away from home than migrants, and there were also differences according to marital status. More than half (32) of the women felt no strain in fulfilling their ocupational role in terms of time, though a small minority (5) did experience a lot of time strain. A majority of women experienced strain regarding the low level of their incomes in relation to rising costs of living. The older ones described how they used to be able to save regularly out of their salaries and now they cannot. Several women also had a sense of occupational deprivation regarding slowness or unfairness in promotions or the inability to get a job.

The majority of women gave their maternal roles a higher priority than any other. As a source of personal satisfaction the maternal role shared top position with the kin role. Motherhood is also perceived as an important source of social status, especially by older women, though not as much as the occupational role.[5] Slight, but possibly significant, differences are noticeable in maternal role satisfaction between locals and migrants.

Without doubt the maternal role is still given the pride of place among all roles in spite of its lack of economic rewards (unless for the elderly) and in spite of its being a cause of varying levels of financial and time strain in terms of fulfilling children's needs for care, clothes, schooling, living space, food, and so forth. It is also a focus of deeply felt ambition and goals and of considerable desire and pressure for innovation and change in terms of child care values and practices which are radically altering the costs and outcomes of child care, as we shall see.

The average age at birth of the first child was 23.6 years for the Ga and 21.3 years for the Dagomba. Most women, and especially among the Ga, deliberately postpone their first birth until they have reached their desired level of education. However, the pressure upon Dagomba women to marry at a young age is intense. Thus it is interesting to note that the seven Dagomba women who bore their first child outside their home area had an average age of 23.2 years at the birth of their first child, as compared with 19.6 years (N=19) for those who had their first child in the home area. The latter are likely to have been subjected to more intense pressures by their kin, peers, and community to marry and bring forth at an early age.

The mean number of births preferred is lower than four; two-thirds perceive themselves as still in the process of achieving their desired family size. A few admit that they already have more than they would have liked. In addition to their own children, most Dagomba women have step-children (mean 2.6), as do a few Ga women (1.3).

Some differences in family size achievements and preferences are apparent by educational level, wealth, migration status and size of family of origin. The migrants of both ethnic groups and all ages have on average fewer children than the non-migrants although they do not necessarily want fewer children. There are fairly wide differences in the expected direction between family size desires of women of higher education (mean 3.5 desired) and lower education (mean 4.1 desired). Such a difference is, however, even more sharply accentuated among those few women who are relatively wealthy. Fourteen women were assessed as well-off and among these the eight with higher education desired a mean family size of 3.1; the three with medium levels of education 4.7 and the three with low levels, 5.0.

Having stated certain important numerical norms and averages and instances of deviance regarding work and childbearing, we shall now go on to look in more detail at child care and birth control in the light of differences and changes in non-maternal roles.

Child Care: Tradition and Innovation

In the past Ghanaian households have commonly relied upon children in agricultural and domestic production and the processing and transportation of needed resources such as fuel and water and petty trade. This still continues. Households find such assistance, even when there are no children of suitable age born to adult members or none available because of school attendance, through fostering children of kin and obtaining children from the rural poor. Fostering of children is a traditionally valued and accepted practice (see Oppong, 1973, on the Dagomba). Furthermore, customary emphases during child care and training upon the values of respect, obedience and service to elders, have ensured that many children remain oriented towards working diligently for the adults in their households.[6] Since in Ghana today transfers of children with a view to providing services usually take place from poorer to wealthier homes, the educated women studied were observed to be often recipients of others' children, sent either to help in the home, to attend school, or both. Women were also frequently separated from their own children, especially when their further training or work demanded it.

Being educated at least to some extent and being on the whole wealthier than most people, they usually had the ability and the desire to assume the main responsibility for raising their own children, either alone or jointly with a husband. The majority did, however, always have some kind of assistance available with small children and the rest had help part of the time.

There were, meanwhile, notable differences among the women according to ethnicity and migration status. This was apparent both in the extent to which they were ready to approve of fostering and the extent to which they had in fact lived separately from their own children. It is the Dagomba in Tamale, among whom fostering continues to be a culturally sanctioned practice, that separation is most common. It is also more common among separated, divorced and polygynously married women, who are less likely to disapprove of the practice.

The participation by fathers in care of young children is limited to those living with the mother. Most of the polygynous fathers thus have little to do with the young children of the women studied since they are rarely found in co-residential polygynous situations. Only one out of eleven polygynous fathers contributed even a little to child care, whereas in monogamous marriages about a fifth participated a lot and a further third participated a little.

Differences in expectations and activities regarding child rearing were estimated from what women said and, where possible, from observations of parent-child interactions. Two aspects of expectations for the parental role were compared: first, the extent to which conscious thought was given to child rearing; and second, the extent to which ideas on child rearing were innovative in relation to culturally prescribed norms. These two dimensions of maternal role consciousness and innovation were closely linked. Moreover, innovation was closely associated with reluctance either to foster children or to delegate their care.

The greater concern of the more highly educated and innovative mothers to care for their children themselves and to do it in their own way indicates a growing individualism in parenthood. The idea that children belong exclusively to their parents who are the best people to bring them up is new in West Africa, where the transfer of children to kin or fostering is traditionally widespread.

Associated with individualism in parenthood and also a widespread characteristic of the parent with education is the desire for children who will do as well if not better than the parent in school and at work. Children with comparatively large investments of personal parental care and education are costly to raise in terms of money and in terms of the mother's time and the child services forgone.

Innovation in child care is also more common among mothers with late, monogamous marriage in church or registry to co-resident professional husbands with whom the relationship tends to have salience and to be unusually joint and participatory. Their husbands are more likely to share in leisure pursuits and child care and wives more apt to perceive their conjugal relationships as important, both for economic status and personal happiness and companionship (see Table 9.4). Mothers who innovate in caring for their children are also more likely to feel their domestic roles are more important. In addition they have far better material resources in terms of accommodation, consumer durables and transport. They consequently feel more social prestige from their

Table 9.4 Correlates of Maternal Innovation

	Innovation		
	X^2	Kendall's Tau	Pearson's R
Maternal innovation and child-care			
Approve less of fostering and child-care delegation	.001	.0004	.0007
Maternal innovation and marriage			
Husband's participation in child-care	-	.02	-
Perception of marriage as important for companionship	.009	.002	.003
Level of priority given to conjugal relationship	-	.05	.05
Amount of joint leisure	-	.02	-
Extent to which husband is co-resident	-	.04	-
Amount of economic support from husband	-	.03	.03
Age at marriage	-	.04	.04
Type of marriage	.003	.04	-
Husband's level of occupation	-	.04	.05
Maternal innovation and associated domestic role attributes			
Level of accommodation	.008	.002	.001
Number of consumer durables	.0001	.0001	.0003
Priority of domestic role	-	.05	.05
Amount of social status gained	.008	.001	.001
Level of domestic role satisfaction	-	.05	.05
Level of strain in domestic relations	.001	.0004	.0002
Maternal role innovation and associated occupational role attributes			
Priority given to the occupational role	.03	.009	.008
Satisfaction gained	-	.03	.03
Status accruing	-	.01	.009
Maternal role innovation and community role attributes			
Level of priority given to the community role	.02	.005	.004
Extent of participation in community activities	-	.02	.01
Amount of strain perceived in finding time for community participation	-	.03	.03

domestic positions given that their levels of living are conspicuously higher, and they thus tend to feel more satisfied. Being mainly highly educated, half of the innovators are women in professional and clerical occupations and innovators place greater stress on their occupations than the rest. They also gain more satisfaction and feel a greater sense of social status accruing from it. They are in addition more active than the other women in community affairs, giving such activities greater priority, feeling a sense of satisfaction and prestige from their participation but at the same time feeling some element of strain in terms of lack of time to do all that they would like to do. These findings do not apply to individual leisure pursuits.

Significantly, family size preferences are also linked to consciousness and innovation in child rearing. Desired quality

Table 9.5 Family Size Preference According to Consciousness and Innovation in Child-Rearing

	Mean family size preference	N
Very little thought given to child-rearing (no innovation)	4.0	(27)
Some thought given to child-rearing (some innovation)	3.6	(16)
A lot of thought given to child-rearing (some innovation)	3.3	(9)
A lot of thought and high innovation in child-rearing	3.1	(8)

Notes: The correlation between level of maternal consciousness and number of birth preferences is statistically significant. (X^2 sig. = .03, Kendall's Tau sig. = .01, Pearson's R sig. = .01) as is the correlation with maternal innovation (X^2 sig. = .003, Kendall's Tau sig. = .004, Pearson's R. Sig. = .005).

of children in terms of conscious individual inputs of the mother's time are associated with number of children preferred, although the differences are small, ranging only from three to four children (see Table 9.5).[7]

Thus alterations in maternal expectations and behaviour involving greater stress on modern approaches to child care and child quality are demonstrated to be associated with a number of elements in other roles, including greater flexibility and emotional salience in marriage; higher levels of living within the home; greater concern for community participation; involvement in status-enhancing jobs; and a desire for fewer than average children.

Role Conflicts and Strains

Half of the women throughout adulthood have combined child-bearing and care with income-earning and nearly all the rest had done so for much of the time. Thus it is not surprising that many women showed indications of role conflict and a third evidence of time strain, even though as noted, there is considerable delegation of care responsibilities. The occupational role is in greatest conflict with the parental. The two roles most supportive of the parental and harmonious with it were the kin and domestic roles. Significantly, it was migrants living away from their home towns and at a distance from most of their relatives who experienced most conflict between their parental and occupational role activities (see above, Table 9.3). The extent to which potential conflict and strain were minimized or avoided by delegation of child care to relatives and maids appeared an important factor differentiating the women.

Monogamously married women were more apt to complain of time strain. Those who felt time strain least were the Dagomba in Tamale, as they were more likely to have enough domestic assistance from relatives, children and others. Among both Dagomba and Ga women perceptions of lack of time increased with age. Lack of time appeared less important than lack of money in rearing children. The latter was a problem for those who neither had salaries perceived as adequate nor sufficient material support for their children from their husbands or the fathers of their children (see above, Table 9.2). Such financial strain was particularly in evidence among women in Tamale in polygynous marriages and the older age group.

The continuity of some of the customary expectations and behaviour which spread the responsibilities for children among a group of relatives and reduced the time required of mothers has been noted. In these ways the potential conflicts and strains involved in simultaneous motherhood and occupations outside the home are reduced. New elements in child care have also been identified. These include more consciousness, innovation, individualism and ambition, which lead to child-rearing practices requiring more of mothers' time. In addition there are new occupational demands for some which entail longer physical separation from infants and children and thus involve increasing role conflict and strain.

Birth Control

Two important changes which have taken place in Ghana during the childbearing years of these women are the arrival of widely available family planning facilities, at least in urban areas, and the steady decline in living standards and economic prospects for most educated Ghanaians. The first occurred in the early 1960s, and so the older women have been fertile during a period of change in the conditions for the control of reproduction. The second took place from the late 1960s to the present time. Real wages have fallen steadily and the costs of maintaining and educating children have accordingly risen sharply (Bequele, 1980).

Nearly all of the older women who have had five or more children cite four as being the ideal family size. Frequent reference to the cost of living is made when discussing family size: for example, 'If I had known how hard things were going to be, I would only have had four' (mother of nine).

The patterns of birth control practices vary considerably. Over three-quarters have used some form of modern contraceptive

Table 9.6 Role Correlates of More Systematic Contraceptive Use

	Significance levels	
	Kendall's Tau	Pearson's R
Occupational		
1. Work more often located away from home	.05	.07
2. Work longer hours	.01	.01
3. Amount of conflict experienced between occupational and domestic roles	.01	.01
Maternal		
Less approval of child-care delegation	.03	.07
Less separation from children	.04	.05
More harmony of maternal/conjugal roles	.05	.06
Fewer births preferred	.03	-
Less child-care assistance	.05	.03
Perception of lack of time for child-care	.01	.008
Conjugal		
Husband's level of occupation	.01	.02
Perception of marriage	.02	.02
Domestic		
Type of accommodation	.01	.01
Fewer co-resident relatives	.03	.03
Higher social status from domestic role	.001	.001
Individual		
More social status as individual (friendship, etc.)	.001	.001

but less than one in three are systematic users. Contraception was slightly more frequently used by Ga women than Dagomba and was more prevalent among residents of the capital Accra than Tamale, thus including more Ga non-migrants and Dagomba migrants. There were, however, no significant differences in use by marital status or religious affiliation.

Abortion is also a commonly used method of birth control. Seventeen women admitted that they had terminated one or more pregnancies by inducing abortion (one claimed six times). Fifteen of these were women who used contraception only erratically, though the remaining two claimed to be systematic users.

Significant differences are observable between women who systematically have used contraception and others in terms of several related role behaviours and expectations. The role expectations and activities most in conflict with maternal responsibilities are those associated with an occupation. However, there is some variation in the amount of such conflict experienced by women, depending upon the degree of separation of work and home and the availability of kin and others to whom child care and domestic tasks can be satisfactorily delegated (see Table 9.6). Thus, as has been frequently hypothesized, women whose work is located at a distance from the home and who work longer hours and thus feel more under pressure and who experience more time strain and conflict between occupational and domestic activities and responsibilities are those most likely to be systematic contraceptive users. It is not employment *per se* or income earning which appears to be related to birth control, but the type of work and how it affects resources in time available for other activities in the home. Thus while only one out of eleven paid family workers or self-employed workers is a systematic user of contraception, 16 women out of 41 employed in large private firms or government services are systematic users.

There are also statistically significant differences in the child care activities, resources and expectations between women who more systematically contracept and the rest. Of women who are highly conscious of maternal care, 41 per cent are systematic contraceptors, of those partially conscious 31 per cent and only 25 per cent among those who do not appear to consciously think about child rearing. Contraceptors also desire and practise more personal supervision of their children, approving less of child care delegation, having less assistance from relatives and others, being separate from their children less often and accordingly they feel somewhat more under strain and experience lack of time for child care. They also desire smaller family sizes.

Women who more systematically control conception also differ from other women with regard to their marriages. They have husbands with higher levels of professional status and also a tendency to stress more the companionate aspect of their relationship (cf. Richard and El Awad Galal el Din, 1982, pp.35-6). They also live in better accommodation, with fewer co-resident relatives and enjoy a higher level of social status from their domestic situation. At the same time they enjoy more opportunities for friendship and leisure pursuits.

Conclusions

The evidence thus supports a number of hypotheses linking more costly child care and greater occupational/maternal role conflicts with lowering of family size and more careful control of births. The ways in which children may become more costly of parental time have been indicated, and we have described the particular aspects of occupations which are likely to be linked to greater strain and conflict and thus propensity to contracept, as well as the aspects of kin roles, domestic situations and community and peer involvements which affect maternal role behaviour.

The scope of this short essay precluded a presentation of the actual texts of the cases of the women. It was, however, possible to indicate the potential cumulative effects of these individual women's life pressures for change, in particular, their widespread desire to bear fewer children than their mothers before them and their methods of achieving this goal and the changing values, relaxing of traditional norms and sanctions, and resource constraints, which spur or permit them to innovate in this way. As Thompson (1981, p.298) remarked with regard to demographic and economic changes in Western Europe and North America in the past fifty or more years, the rise in economic productivity and the reduction in the number of births, both depended to a large extent on individual decisions and actions of parents, women and men and they remain scarcely understood, unpredictable and unknowable. These Ghanaian cases were collected to help show how the small decisions and actions occur which can ultimately have such aggregate and overall demographic effects in the contexts of two West African towns.[8]

Many models of economic/demographic change forget the individual parents involved. This study and its methods of data collection and analysis are one more attempt not only to focus on the individual within a particular cultural, social and economic context and to help uncover the spurs to demographic change, but to point the way to more systematic incorporation of role theory and more systematic collection and analysis of biographical data to enable such micro-methods to be used in truly cross-cultural comparative studies.

Acknowledgements

The project from which this study originates was funded by a Ford Rockefeller Population Studies Award (Oppong, *et al.*, 1977). The fieldwork on which this paper is based was carried out by K. Abu. A report of findings on impacts of education, migration and employment has appeared, as well as a handbook on the methods used (Oppong and Abu, 1985, 1986).

Notes

1. Life histories and biographies have been used to explore experiences of social change over several decades (Gagnon, 1981, in Quebec); orientation to parental and occupation roles (Bolte, 1980, in Germany); for purposes of historical demography (Synge, 1981, in Ontario); to study mobility and urbanization (Karpati, 1981, in Hungary); to study industries (Denzin, 1981, liquor in the United States; Bertaux and Bertaux-Wiamé, 1981, baking in France); to examine political elites (Camargo, 1981, in Brazil); and to explore differences between female and male migrants (Bertaux-Wiamé, 1981, in France).

2. This realization developed well before the commencement of the 'women's decade' and in reaction to the shortcomings of the demographic surveys and KAP inquiries of the earlier decade carried out in Ghana.

3. 'Role strain': the extent to which the individual feels unable to cope with the demands of a particular role - in terms of time/energy, financial or material resources needed and interpersonal relations is estimated and approximately indicated on a continuum from none to a lot. It is used to serve as a potential pointer to desired areas of change.

   'Role salience': the extent to which a particular role is of high priority to a woman, who stresses its importance, strives to carry out the attached activities and fulfil the expectation of others, as well as enjoying in various ways the benefits accruing from the role. A highly salient role is likely to be involved in the pursuit and achievement of a woman's major life goals. Levine (1978) in discussing the concept of life course has noted that it is the individual's goals rather than roles that organize career activity and an individual's stress upon certain roles may only be comprehensible in terms of career paths towards long range goals. Describing the case of Gusii of Kenya, for example, he has emphasized how pervasive is procreative achievement as the *sine quo non* for goal achievement throughout life and in death. On the number of offspring depends building and maintaining a home, the number of descendants, the size of a funeral. Thus relaxation is only found among the old who have many descendants. As he remarks, evidence of the salience of the fertility goal is provided by the urgency with which individuals pursue it, the personal sacrifices they will undergo and the importance of this pursuit in contrast to others.

   'Role satisfaction': the extent to which a woman gains a sense of gratification or pleasure from the performance of role activities or enjoyment of attached status rewards. Levine (1978) notes in the case of the Gusii that the main source of pleasure is counting progeny on the land. Affliction is caused by any interruption of the sequence of births and family building.

'Role deprivation': the extent to which a woman feels a sense of relative deprivation with regard to her role status benefits - the gap between her expectations of reward (material and non-material) and the actual outcomes. Again as Levine (1978) has noted with regard to Gusii roles and life course goals, the relevant achievements at various stages of the life course are compared consciously or subconsciously with the cultural beliefs and values, which provide standards against which individuals may evaluate their own performance. Thus the individual's self-evaluation in relation to age norms and career goals plays an important part in building up the personal sense of worth. At the same time a sense of achievement or deprivation develops according to the relative achievements and rewards observed of significant others, class mates, age mates, neighbours, siblings, and others.

'Tension and change': an important concern in this study is dynamic aspects of roles - the extent to which individuals are being constrained or desire to alter their behaviour and expectations attached to different roles and the pressures or incentives linked to those constraints or desires. Thus for each role an estimate is made of the extent to which a woman is trying to exert pressure for change.

'Role rewards': we have carefully separated out the different potential rewards for each role into two categories: (i) economic - indicating by numerical codes the extent to which each role is a source of material rewards; and (ii) intangible - the extent to which each role is a source of prestige, deference and influence.

'Role ranking': roles are also ranked in terms of those from which most satisfaction is derived and those which are perceived as causing the greatest problems in life.

'Role conflicts': the extent to which roles appear or are reported to be in harmony or conflict is also documented, through scoring the latent or manifest conflict observed between any two roles. This scoring procedure facilitates the calculation, estimation and comparison of levels of conflict overall for individuals and between one key role and all others (e.g. parental role, conflict scores and occupation conflict scores).

4. Descriptions of the towns and traditional social systems from which these women were chosen can be found in Oppong and Abu (1986); also Azu (1974); Dinan (1983); Field (1940); Kilson (1974); Oppong (1973); Robertson (1974, 1977); Sanjek (1983); Sanjek and Sanjek (1976); Staniland (1975). See also Oppong (1983c, 1986).

5. It should be noted that the scores for satisfaction and social status rewards associated with the maternal role are negatively affected by a few infertile or sub-fertile women, as well as young women who have not yet started childbearing.

6. Cf. Levine (1984, p.2) who notes that 'The behaviour of mothers in a particular setting reflects the prevailing parental investment strategy as interpreted in local cultural tradition'.

7. Cf. Levine (1978), whose hypothesis after comparing infant care among the Gusii of Kenya and a Mayan community in Yucatan and American babies is that Gusii mothers will not begin to deliberately limit births until they develop new ideas of what is involved in raising children, in terms of both ends and means.

8. An earlier study of Akan couples demonstrated in a similar way how changes in kinship and marriage were occurring among educated urban dwellers (Oppong, 1982).

10

Birth Expectations in Bobo-Dioulasso

Francine van de Walle

A multi-round survey of infant and child mortality was undertaken in Bobo-Dioulasso, a medium sized city in Burkina-Faso (formerly Upper Volta), under the sponsorship of the Sahel Institute. Eight thousand births were recorded between 1 April 1981 and 31 March 1982, and the infants were followed up for 2 years. Although the purpose of the study was to measure infant and child mortality and analyze mortality determinants, periodic interviews with women for 24 months after delivery made it possible to investigate some proximate determinants of birth intervals at the same time.[1] The fertility study was restricted to the 6,000 women whose child survived and who were followed for the full two years. These women represent a biased sample of the population of the town in that they had a child in that particular year (the survey thus selects for high fertility) and that the child was alive after 2 years (thus selecting for low mortality).

As part of the fertility project, a qualitative survey of a small subsample of women was included. This exercise had several objectives: (i) checking on the quality of the main survey; (ii) shedding light on some of the concepts used in the survey; and (iii) investigating individual attitudes and motivations which could not reasonably be covered in the Multi-Round Survey.

The Qualitative Survey

The Sample

We selected women from two ethnic groups, the Bobo, autochthones of the region who gave their name to the city and the Mossi, the largest group of the Voltaic family. Among these we took two groups of women, those who had reported being aged between 20 and 24 years at the time of the birth of their child (the young women) and those who had reported being over 35 years of age (the older women). In Africa age declaration does not attain great precision, nonetheless our two groups broadly reflect the beginning and the end of the reproductive experience. The women were interviewed in their own homes; they were accustomed to the survey and to the fact of being questioned on their post-partum experiences. They had been visited seven times during the preceding 2 years and little explanation needed to be given to tell them that this was an addendum to the 'survey' and that this time we would tape a conversation instead of writing down their answers. They were invited to ask us any questions they wished.

Two female Bobo interviewers talked to the women in their mother tongue, *Bwamu* or, if they preferred, in the exchange language of Bobo-Dioulasso, *Dioula*, which is a Manding dialect. The two Mossi interviewers conversed with the Mossi women in *Moré*. The great majority of Mossis, who came from the central plateaus of Burkina-Faso continue to speak *Moré* in Bobo-Dioulasso. Using the vernacular in such in-depth interviews is of primary importance. First, people express themselves more easily and more freely in their mother tongue, and the rather personal matters which were discussed demanded this freedom of expression. In addition, many *Moré*, *Bwamu* or *Dioula* concepts may have no precise equivalent in another language. Finally, being taped in a familiar language is more reassuring.

We chose women who had had a child during the months of May or June 1981, using the main survey as sample frame, and the micro-survey took place in Bobo-Dioulasso during the months of July and August 1983. Political events (a military coup in Ouagadougou) slowed down the work during the month of August and this made it impossible to interview all the Mossi women. The survey was only completed in January 1984 using another sample of women whose child was born during the months of November or December 1981. Therefore all the women in the qualitative survey were interviewed when their child was approximately 25 to 27 months old.

The Questionnaire

A questionnaire or, more accurately, a set of guidelines for the interviewers, was designed at the Sahel Institute in Bamako and circulated around the Socio-Economic and Demographic Research Unit for comments. It began with a description of the survey we were planning to do and of the advantages of this type of interview. Such in-depth surveys have rarely been conducted in French-speaking Africa by demographers, who tend to be trained statisticians. Most demographers seem very skeptical about their functions; they are even more puzzled about the kind of results these surveys can yield and about the methods with which to analyze them.

The questionnaire listed the following main points:

1. Age of the mother.
2. Existing norms on breastfeeding.
3. Knowledge of the relation between breastfeeding and fertility.
4. Knowledge of the relation between amenorrhoea and breast-feeding and between amenorrhoea and fecundity.
5. Knowledge of the women's menstrual cycle.
6. Existing norms on abstinence.
7. Existing reasons to avoid conception.
8. Knowledge of methods to avoid pregnancy.
9. Desire for and decisions about the next child and family building.

In sum, we wanted to know about the norms and customs related to fertility behaviour; to what degree and under what circumstances did women follow these norms; how these norms were evolving (Were changes taking place? Why and where were they happening?); and what knowledge women had on the subject of fecundity.

The questionnaire itself was short. It contained a list of possible questions on each of the topics cited above; these questions were to serve as a basis for the conversation between the women and the interviewer. The interviewers were instructed never to suggest the answer and always to ask open-ended questions. During the course of the survey the questions and the subjects evolved; we eliminated some questions and added others as we got deeper into the core of our research and gained experience. For example, after a while we became convinced that all the women in Bobo-Dioulasso breastfed on demand day and night. They laughed when we asked some basic questions on breastfeeding and exclaimed '... the questions of white people!'. Thereafter we eliminated a number of questions on breastfeeding, and added instead some questions on relations and communication between spouses which appeared to be important.

The Interviewers

Neither the selection, the training nor the actual job of the interviewers was easy. To direct and animate a conversation which must lead to scientific results is not a small task. We wanted female interviewers (the larger Infant Mortality Survey had been conducted by women). Among many applicants we selected two Bobo women: a 23 year-old single student at the university of Ouagadougou who was on vacation and a 38 year-old mother of eight children who had completed Catholic primary school. The first one specialized in the interviews of the 'young women' and the latter of the 'older women'. The first one was very intelligent, quick, literate, and an excellent translator. The second one was mature, full of experience, and had superb contact with the women. Her interviews often lasted 2 hours, and ended up in sharing the family meal. We had selected two Mossi, but the second did not appear because of the political situation. The one Mossi interviewer was 23 years old and about to get married. She had completed secondary school and had participated in a survey on health in rural areas. She was a typical Mossi who had immigrated to Bobo-Dioulasso for schooling purposes and spoke only the *Moré* language. She turned out to be very dynamic and well organized. The three of them, even though very different, showed themselves to be excellent interviewers.

The four of us worked very closely during the entire period. The first week was spent getting acquainted with each other and learning about qualitative small scale surveys. This kind of survey was completely alien to them. We went through the questionnaire several times, outlining the kinds of topics we were focusing on. We practised interviewing each other. They learned fast, and at the same time taught me many local customs and concepts. While they were studying qualitative demography I was learning about the cultural setting of the survey. I took many notes and we compiled a glossary. During the span of the survey we met every day at 7.30 a.m. and spent mornings discussing the fieldwork, the interviews, the translations and the findings. We also took time to solve the problems of the day.

Fieldwork and Methodology

Fieldwork is rarely without problems. It is tiring to walk long distances in the sun or in the rain. It is often difficult to locate the women in the sample, as there are no street addresses and in an urban area people do not know their neighbours. The interviewers had a sketch of the woman's address taken from the Infant Mortality Survey questionnaire, but this was usually vague or ambiguous. When they found the house, the woman was often at the market or visiting with a friend. During the rainy season some women were absent because they were cultivating millet on the outskirts of the city and had left for the day. Others were back in the village for a few weeks. Further, some women were travelling, and some had moved away. When the interviewer found the house and the woman was not at home she would leave a message and make a date with her.

The interviews usually went smoothly. We started by chatting with the woman and making her feel comfortable and secure. After introducing ourselves and explaining the reason for our presence we showed her the tiny tape recorder and asked for her permission to tape the interview. This was always granted without hesitation, and the recording did not seem to interfere with the conversation.

It is a difficult task to cover every subject in an open-ended discussion. The interviewer must listen and follow up with new questions in accordance with the answers received, even when the woman jumps from one subject to another. Often there is no order in the conversation and the interviewer misses some important questions. Such interviews are thus not appropriate for quantitative analysis, but rather accumulate a rich interchange of opinions and thoughts that cannot exist in quantitative data. As much as I could, I accompanied the interviewers. With my little knowledge of the vernacular I was able to follow some of the conversation and I was very interested in first-hand observation. For example, I better understood the trauma that accompanies weaning while observing a 27-month-old boy playing with his siblings and suddenly rushing into the arms of his mother, whom we were interviewing. I watched him, the little wheedling tyrant, hiding his head under her dress, grasping her breast with his two hands, drinking greedily, grasping the other breast, devouring it, playing with the two breasts and falling asleep happily while his mother was dandling him. She told us later that the next morning she was going to put hot pepper on her breasts; it was time for him to be weaned and to join his brothers and go and sleep with them.

Even though we had planned to interview 120 women, sixty Bobo and sixty Mossi, we ended up with eighty women, forty Bobo and forty Mossi. These were equally distributed between 'young women' and 'older women'. We were satisfied with this number and with the experience we had gained. Moreover the time devoted to the fieldwork had already exceeded what we had expected. Qualitative surveys should end before the stage of diminishing returns, when the questions become mere routine and the team loses its enthusiasm.

The tapes were translated into French by the interviewers themselves shortly after the interview and discussed while the memories were still fresh. One out of four interviews were selected randomly for a second translation done by a university student whose mother tongue was also the one used in the interview. The translations were then read by the interviewer and myself, and comparison and reconciliation with the first translation were undertaken. The problems were mostly missing sentences and inaudible passages due to noisy children. The two translations were reconciled in consultation with the interviewer and the outside translator. Both were instructed to keep as closely as possible to the original, to preserve the local terminology and images used by the women and to keep alive the dominant tone of the interview.

The Analysis

After they had been translated into French, the interviews were edited. Again we tried to keep the cultural setting intact in a more literary French. Over 500 pages were entered in the microcomputer and a Bobo and a Mossi manuscript were prepared. The women are now identified by a number and a letter('B' for Bobo and 'M' for Mossi). The text can be printed easily, and moreover the files lend themselves to indexing and searches on the machine. One of the advantages of the editor software used (EDIX) is that it is easy to 'cut and paste' to make new files and re-order the text by subject, while retaining the original. To facilitate the analysis we set up files by topic, and now have sixteen files. For example, the file 'contraception' includes everything that has been said relating to this subject. This is invaluable at the stage of analysis.

Qualitative Versus Quantitative

Aims of the Qualitative Survey

Qualitative surveys have their drawbacks. A small sample may be easily biased. The interpretation, translation and analysis of the interviews may be subjective. It cannot yield any numbers. It only reflects the views expressed by the women and their behaviour under specific conditions. It is a tool to better understand how they live, what they think, what they know about different subjects. In our case, the survey was meant to complement an existing Infant Mortality Survey. But a logical step in the preparation of any large scale survey would be to have a free-form qualitative pilot that would guide in the selection and phrasing of the survey questions.

This micro-study, as noted earlier, was to serve several objectives. The first one was to check on the quality of the quantitative survey responses. Before starting the discussion the interviewer was instructed to ask the woman's age and fertility history. She carried with her the information given in the main survey approximately 26 months earlier. She was instructed to crosscheck the two sources with any official papers the woman had in her possession, such as birth and marriage certificates, hospital or health booklets. In the absence of these, a last resort was observation and careful probing to assess as accurately as possible age and fertility history. In any case, it was felt that information is easier to collect during a friendly conversation with the women than with formal questions.

A second aim of the qualitative survey was to investigate the respondents' understanding of some of the concepts used in the quantitative survey. We suspected for example that the women would not distinguish sharply between miscarriage, a stillbirth, and a neonatal death. We were also interested in probing their views on the physiology of reproduction, and the justifications they gave for their use of certain child spacing practices.

All too often, even the best large scale surveys do not make the effort to adapt their vocabulary to the people they interview. The interviewees find themselves faced with ready-made concepts and definitions which are alien to them and they have to answer within these limits. Defective questions lead to confused answers and misleading interpretations. An illustration of this is the practice of classifying breastfeeding and abstinence as contraceptive methods. For example, in the Ife and in the Ngwa Iglo Village Surveys (Ukaegbu, 1977) the interviewers enumerated a series of folk methods (coitus interruptus, rhythm, abstinence, breastfeeding, and so forth...) and asked whether the women had been using any of those to avoid childbearing. Not surprisingly many women reported using breastfeeding and abstinence. The conclusion was that traditional methods of contraception were widespread in the population. The survey takers assumed that the population was aware of the contraceptive effect of breastfeeding and used it for that purpose. In the qualitative survey, we systematically asked whether nursing affected the return of menses or the date of the next conception. There was no one who reported that breastfeeding had any impact.

Similarly, survey takers have assumed that the purpose of abstinence is always to avoid or to space the next birth. In the Senegal Fertility Survey, which used the sophisticated methodology of the World Fertility Survey, a large proportion of women are said to use folk methods of contraception, on the basis of their response to a probe as to whether they were resorting to abstinence. An insight gained from studies in a different cultural area (the Caldwells' investigations among the Yoruba in Caldwell and Caldwell, 1981) was converted into the assumption that abstinence, including the Muslim ritual proscription of 40 days which is widely practised in Senegal and sometimes also in Burkina-Faso, must always have a contraceptive intent. In Bobo-Dioulasso, the qualitative survey indicates that extended abstinence is often closely associated with breastfeeding: it is believed that the suckling child might get sick if its mother has sexual relations. Even when the purpose of abstinence is to space births for health reasons, limiting ultimate family size is not a concern.

The third objective of the qualitative survey in Bobo-Dioulasso was to investigate motivations and patterned modes of behaviour which are not easy to summarize in one or two lines of quantitative questionnaire. We would like here to deal with some points which focus particularly on the process of decision-making in the context of what it is convenient to call 'natural fertility'. This particular topic is chosen because it allows us to compare the approach followed in the main survey, with its disregard for the subtlety of motivation and behaviour, and the non-directive recording of conversations where the respondents are free to present issues in their own terms.

A Specific Comparison of the Two Approaches

Two questions concerning the desire for another child were asked in the Infant Mortality Survey. These were asked of the women seven times during the 2 years succeeding the birth of their child. The questions were the following:

'Do you want another child?
Yes____ No____ Indeterminate____'
'If yes: When?'
'If no: Why not?'

Table 10.1 gives the responses to the questions. The results are based on about one-fourth of the sample (the first 3 months of births), the survey results available at the time of writing. Over 85 per cent of the women answered 'yes' to the first question. In those instances, the outcome of the second question was almost invariably 'in 2 years' or 'in 3 years', independently of the amount of time elapsed since the birth of their child. Still, there were a few exceptions. For example, the 'in 3 years' answer was sometimes radically reduced to as little as 'in 2 months' by the next visit. In those instances the woman was pregnant and was expressing less a wish than a state of resignation. Other women answered: 'Yes, when God sends it'. This could reflect an assessment of probable outcome. Are the women who say 'in 2 years' or 'in 3 years' ultimately so different, or are they also expressing an expectation rather than a desire? Because a 2 to 3 year birth interval is indeed the one which prevails most often, the respondents may simply be conforming to a pattern sanctioned by their society. The fact that the proportion of women who answer '2 years' or '3 years' changes very

Table 10.1 Desire for Another Child and Number of Women Pregnant at Each Visit. Infant Mortality Survey.

Answer	Round 1 1 mth.	Round 2 4 mths.	Round 3 8 mths.	Round 4 12 mths.	Round 5 16 mths.	Round 6 20 mths.	Round 7 24 mths.
Indeterminate	90	67	50	96	106	131	97
Percent	7.4	5.4	4.1	7.8	8.5	10.5	7.7
Yes	1037	1068	1080	1029	1006	827	605
Percent	84.9	86.6	87.6	83.6	81.1	66.5	48.3
No	94	96	98	94	79	73	62
Percent	7.7	7.8	7.9	7.6	6.4	5.9	4.9
Pregnant	-	2	5	12	50	212	489
Percent	0.0	0.2	0.4	1.0	4.0	17.1	39.0
TOTAL	1221	1233	1233	1231	1241	1243	1253

little over time, even after 2 years have elapsed since the birth (see Table 10.2) tends to confirm the strong normative content of the answer.

It will be noted that there was a small number of women who responded that they did not want another child. This number increases with age, from 3.6 per cent among women aged 15 to 29 to 19 per cent for women aged 30 and over (not shown). To the question 'Why not?', some replied: 'Because I am not married', meaning 'Not now' and implicitly reserving their wishes to have more children when they would be married. Even the most frequent negative reason, 'Because I am tired' may not always have referred to the desire never to have another child, but rather to the widely held preference for spacing and 'resting'.

It is clear *a posteriori* that the semantic content of the question in the quantitative survey was not well determined, and the interviewer's rephrasing of the French questionnaire in the language of communication may not have made things less confusing. Were the questions clearly referring to stopping rather than spacing behaviour? Were they implying the possibility of making

Table 10.2 Desire for Another Child and Reasons for Wanting One and For Not Wanting One. Percent of Women at Risk. Infant Mortality Survey.

Answer	Round 1 1 mth.	Round 2 4 mths.	Round 3 8 mths.	Round 4 12 mths.	Round 5 16 mths.	Round 6 20 mths.	Round 7 24 mths.
Indeterminate	7.4	5.4	4.1	7.9	8.4	12.7	12.7
Yes	84.9	86.8	87.9	84.4	84.5	80.2	79.2
No date	1.1	8.1	11.4	6.2	6.5	5.7	5.9
In 1 yr	.9	2.9	1.1	1.6	3.8	4.2	9.3
In 2 yrs	47.4	40.2	35.0	36.5	36.0	37.9	35.8
In 3 yrs	28.1	24.5	25.4	25.2	21.1	17.2	9.7
God's will	1.3	4.3	8.2	9.4	8.5	9.3	13.1
Other date	6.1	6.8	6.8	5.7	8.6	5.9	5.4
No	7.7	7.8	8.0	7.7	6.6	7.1	8.1
No reason	.2	.2	.2	.5	.6	.6	.6
Enough	2.3	2.5	3.7	2.7	2.9	2.8	2.9
Tired	4.1	2.9	2.6	3.2	2.0	2.7	2.9
Other	1.1	2.2	1.5	1.3	1.1	1.0	1.7
TOTAL	1221	1231	1228	1219	1191	1031	764

Note: The total excludes the absentees and the women who have acknowledged a pregnancy.

a fertility decision, or reflecting passive acceptance of the inevitable? Because of the unresolved ambiguities, tables such as Table 10.1 and Table 10.2, despite their profusion of details, remain fundamentally unsatisfactory.

The qualitative survey followed a slightly different approach, and its results are therefore not strictly comparable. Rather than asking systematically 'Do you want another child?' we asked a variety of questions according to the flow of the conversation and to the fertility status of the women. For example, if the woman was pregnant, we asked her if she was happy, if it had been a surprise for her, if her pregnancy was the result of a personal or a joint husband-wife decision. To the older women, we asked sometimes: 'How many children do you think your daughter should have?' In a number of instances, we asked a question comparable to that in the quantitative survey. For example:

'Int. Do you want another child?
B7. No, no, I don't want anything more...I pray God to give me a daughter-in-law now. If God gives me that, it will make me very happy.
Int. Ten children, do you think it is enough?
B7. Eh, yes.
Int. Now you say you don't want any more children. How are you going to do it?
B7. Guia! (laugh) Truly I don't know...(laugh) If God does not give it to me, it will really make me happy.
Int. And if He gives you some more?
B7. Eh! This will not make me happy, but if it is God's will I cannot refuse. If God does not give me any more, let Him give it to my daughter-in-law. This would really please me. This would please me more than having one myself.
Int. If God thinks that you have not borne enough, you will have many more!
B7. That is so, it is true!'

It will be seen that it would be difficult to classify this question in a quantitative survey as either a 'no' or an 'up to God' response.

To the majority of women, however, we asked the standard KAP question: 'How many children do you want altogether?'. We had been intrigued by the assumption of the Easterlin framework (1975) that women in high fertility regimes have implicit family size objectives which cannot be attained under existing conditions of 'supply' (i.e., prevailing fertility, infant and child mortality). This seemed an unwarranted assumption under a natural fertility regime such as Bobo-Dioulasso, and it was indeed difficult to extract numerical answers to the question. It is partly because the notion of an ideal or desired number of children does not fit in the local culture that the answer to the question 'How many children do you want altogether?' is invariably in the order of 'Eh...is it not God's decision?' or 'The number that God will send me'. The question seems even perverse to most women who explain that it would be wrong to set a number when one has no way to influence the outcome. 'A woman cannot say how many children she wants. If you say a number and if you don't reach it, where are you? And if you say a small number and you have many more, what do you do?'

According to Caldwell this 'up to God answer' is

> '...neither an evasive nor a superstitious reply and such respondents are perfectly happy to discuss what they mean, which is really that these are matters over which they have little control and to attempt more control would probably achieve little while bordering on the impious' (1982, p.21).

In Bobo-Dioulasso, women do not yet control their fertility. Giving birth is part of being a woman; it is her role to have children and for her it is the only way she might gain credit *vis à vis* her husband and the entire community. Women do not argue about that; but does this mean that they are yearning to have 'as many children as God will send' as a blessing or as a stroke of luck? One should analyze in detail the concept of 'God's will' because it is open to at least two divergent connotations, that of a God-Fatalism and that of a God-Providence. Does it mean 'We accept everything God sends us because we do not know what else to do' or 'We want as many children as possible, as part of God's bounty'?

Conversations with the women give the impression that it is often the 'God-Fatalism' who gives the numerous children in Bobo-Dioulasso. The 'God-Providence' is not completely absent and one hears from older women: 'If we gain a lot of children, we are really happy. We Africans, we love many children. Eh, yes, many children' (B33). On the other hand, a number of women seem to deplore the successive deliveries. Many older women whom we asked whether they wanted more children would answer in the same way as B29:

> 'Ah! Is it not God's business? It is God who shares the children. If God tells you to take a baby, you cannot say "Oh! I don't want it". Can a person say so? It is God who gives the children. If He gives you many, you are pleased. If He takes pity on you, you may stop delivering...But a person can never say that she is going to refuse the child that God gives her.'

M5, 39 years old, who is pregnant for the eleventh time, is also not very enthusiastic:

'Int. Did you want this pregnancy?
M5. It is God who gave it to me.
Int. How long would you have liked to wait?
M5. God brings it at any time.
Int. After this child would you like another one?
M5. To tell the truth man cannot contradict God, otherwise I would stop.'

This can be translated like this: everything is conditioned by God, you always accept God's gifts, but you are tired of giving birth and you are fatalistic. This state of mind is typical of women over 30 years old and with high parity. Among them some go further and put it bluntly like M4, 38 years old, ten children:

'Int. Are you happy about not being pregnant?
M4. Ah! I am happy. I don't want any more belly; when you have ten children you don't wish even one more.
Int. Do you know something to stop?
M4. No, I don't know anything.
Int. Would you like to know something?
M4. I don't want to know.
Int. Then, you are not interested to know something to stop a belly?

M4. Ah!...If I could find that...I would be pleased not to ever take a belly anymore. I don't want to be pregnant anymore, not even one child...'.

The question on the number of children is not relevant for the women who do not know that they are responsible for their fertility. They are perplexed and they answer vaguely, they give a conformist answer. We found that in Bobo-Dioulasso in our interviews there was not one woman who proclaimed at the beginning that she wanted no more children. But in the conversation, slowly they admitted that they wanted to stop childbearing altogether. It is remarkable that some young women who had four or five children also showed some sign of wanting to stop:

B17, 27 years old, has five children:

'Int. Do you want more children?
B17. I don't want any more.
Int. Then five is enough for you?
B17. Yes.
Int. What are you going to do not to have any more children?
B17. I don't know.
Int. Does your husband agree for you to stop like that?
B17. (laugh) I don't know.'

These women seem to be in a stage of confusion. Do they want to space the next birth or do they want to stop altogether? We suspect that they do not know themselves; being tired because of successive pregnancies and overwhelmed with work, they wish to rest. There is not yet real determination on their part, but they are in a more advanced stage than those who endure repeated pregnancies as sent from heaven.

The third stage is the one in which some young women have a more precise notion of the dimension of the ideal family size. This is perhaps a consequence of the influence of cultural patterns of western origin; or perhaps the notion of the ideal size appears at the same time as the means to obtain it. B27, 22 years old and with two children, illustrates this category:

'Int. How many children would you like altogether?
B27. Ye! If I gain two more, I will be happy. (laugh)
Int. If you gain two more, you will stop?
B27. Yes.
Int. And your husband, does he agree?
B27. Ah, no. It rests entirely with me.
Int. What are you going to do to stop at four?
B27. For the time being, I don't know what I will do.
Int. Don't you know anything to stop a belly?
B27. I hear people talking, but I don't know anything myself.
Int. What do people say?
B27. Some say that there are shots, others say there are pills.'

This is a textbook case of family limitation according to Henry (1961): a woman who waits to have the number of children she does not want to exceed before she resorts to control. It may be, of course, that she will fall in the category of the women described by Easterlin (1975), where the offer exceeds the demand because they do not master contraceptive methods. At any rate, some of the younger women have a different attitude towards childbearing, and already in their twenties show some concern about an ideal number.

Conclusion

This detailed comparison of one specific question demonstrates the strengths and weaknesses of the two approaches. The quantitative survey gives quantifiable and systematic answers, but their precision is illusory and they often add no new knowledge. The categories on the questionnaire are sure to be filled, but any item that is truly specific to the people surveyed is likely to be left out.

The net of the qualitative survey brings back many strange creatures and concepts, some of which do not conveniently fit into a mould. The format of the conversation between an interviewer and a respondent leads in unexpected directions, and it is hard to ask systematically the same questions of everyone. Many answers are inconsistent and contradictory. Analysis is difficult, as the reader tends to highlight particular points of view that fit his or her own preconceptions. The role of the interviewer is critical; but the transcript at least reveals prompts and biases of the survey-taker that would remain hidden with closed answers. Finally, the qualitative survey is unlikely to be representative of the population; it must deal with small numbers and in doing so, it gives privilege to articulate spokespersons.

One thing seems certain. In the past, too many surveys have been attempted on large samples, using untested questionnaires with often poorly phrased questions. Much of social science has been aimed at a residue of questions with universal validity and comparability. The qualitative survey of the type discussed here provides a needed antidote for the western-trained demographer, and it has its place as a companion of the larger surveys, preferably one whose lessons are integrated in the design and phrasing of the main questionnaire.

Notes

1. The study on fertility and proximate determinants was funded by an award under the Population Council's International Research Awards Program on the Determinants of Fertility, a program supported by USAID funding to the Population Council. Principal investigators were Nassour Ouaidou and Francine van de Walle.

A Micro-Approach to the Study of Breastfeeding Patterns in Rural Kivu (Zaire)

Michel Caraël

Introduction

It is well-established that breastfeeding is a main determinant of birth intervals through its effect on the duration of postpartum amenorrhoea, especially in societies with natural fertility and where strong traditions of prolonged postpartum abstinence do not exist (Bongaarts and Potter, 1983; Page and Lesthaeghe, 1981).

This is the existing situation in Central Africa - Kivu (Zaire), Rwanda, Burundi, and part of Uganda - where sexual relations resume one week after delivery, but where an average breastfeeding duration of 2 years favours birth spacing of 33 to 39 months (Vis *et al.*, 1975).

The only widespread norm concerning breastfeeding is that of nursing the last child until the next pregnancy. This implies that weaning is mainly determined by the return of menses. The strong relationship observed between the long durations of breastfeeding and amenorrhoea is probably due to the correlation between the intensity of breastfeeding and the resulting duration of amenorrhoea.

While the mechanisms by which lactation inhibits ovulation are still only poorly understood, frequent nipple stimulation, hyperprolactinemia and amenorrhoea appear to be strongly associated (Tyson and Perez, 1978; Howie and McNeilly, 1982). But many questions remain to be answered. How frequent and intense does suckling have to be to maintain anovulation, and for how long? It has been suggested by McNeilly *et al.* (1983) and by Delvoye *et al.* (1977) for nursing mothers from the urban area (Bukavu) of Kivu that a threshold of five to six sucklings per day is enough to maintain high prolactin levels during the first year postpartum. As a previous study has shown (Caraël 1981), important regional variations occur in Kivu with respect to breastfeeding and amenorrhoea durations and the length of birth intervals. It is important to investigate whether these differences are related to differences in breastfeeding patterns and intensity.

Central Africa, with a population density of more than 100 persons per square kilometre, forms a densely populated area, rare in Africa. This high density combined with a crude birth rate of 50 to 53 per thousand and an annual growth rate of 2.5 to 3 per thousand accentuates rapid deterioration of the environment and food supply (Wils *et al*. 1978).

The detection of changes in breastfeeding patterns in such a situation is therefore of considerable importance for the society in terms of the health of the mother and child. To compare patterns of breastfeeding and amenorrhoea durations in Kivu sub-populations, a micro-approach will be used, first to detect recent changes in birth intervals, then to explore how to collect suckling frequency data in order to compare it to probabilities of resumption of menstruation. The discussion of preliminary results will focus on the existence of particular breastfeeding patterns depending on environmental factors and social behaviour, and on the difficulties of adequately measuring the frequency of breastfeeding.

Background of the Study

A previous study (Caraël, 1981) has shown important regional differences in the duration of birth intervals in Kivu (Table 11.1). Three regions are compared: (i) the rural area of the Havu ethnic group, highly traditional and isolated; (ii) the rural Shi area, more oriented towards a market economy (50 per cent are hired farm labourers), with a higher population density of 200 to 300 people per square kilometre and with the highest protein-calorie malnutrition and infant mortality (Vis *et al*., 1975); and (iii) the urban area of Bukavu, the regional capital, with approximately 200,000 inhabitants.

The results of this past study shown in Table 11.1 display a mean birth interval about 10 months shorter in the urban centre than in the most traditional area of the Havu. The Shi interval centre length occupies an intermediate position. The short mean waiting time to conception in all three areas points to a similarity in terms of fecundability and an almost total absence of some form of contraception as a method of child spacing. The differences in birth interval lengths stem almost entirely from differences in postpartum amenorrohea. The correlation between the durations of breastfeeding and amenorrhoea is relatively striking.

Changes in breastfeeding patterns and shortening of the post-partum non-susceptible period are known to be associated with several factors - education, occupation, income. 'Modernization' and acculturation has been linked to shorter birth intervals through disruption of traditional breastfeeding practices (Nag, 1979; Romaniuk, 1980). In the following sections, we will concentrate on data from the Shi and from the Havu. The Shi area, more than the Havu, appears to be moving towards a market economy. Do these factors contribute to the breakdown of traditional breastfeeding patterns?

Table 11.1 Birth Interval Components and Mean Birth Interval in Two Rural Areas and One Urban Area of Kivu (1975).

	Rural Havu	Rural Shi	Urban
Mean duration of breastfeeding, in months (i)*	21.9	17.2	14.9
Mean duration of postpartum amenorrhoea, in months (ii)*	18.7	14.4	9.6
Mean waiting time to conception, in months (iii)*	7.7	7.3	6.6
Mean length of birth interval estimated from components (ii) and (iii), in months**	36.8	31.7	26.1

* Birth interval components are derived from retrospective surveys of 300 women in each area.

** For method of calculation see Potter (1963).

Source: Caraël, 1981.

Birth Intervals in the Past: Rural Shi

A retrospective evaluation of the evolution of birth intervals in the Shi region is possible due to the Catholic parish registers of Walungu, a church which was started in the 1920s. The data are based on all marriages with completed fertility: families having six or more children in which the wife is at least 35 years old and without marital disruption. The means of successive birth intervals have been computed for each completed family size, according to the period of marriage (Leridon, 1977).

Table 11.2 presents some of the findings. For marriages formed during years 1935–1939 the means of birth intervals show a shortening by each successive birth order after birth order six, instead of the characteristic increase expected at the end of the reproductive period in a non-Malthusian population. The lengthening of the birth interval with parity appears progessively for families after 1945, where stablizing of the mean birth intervals is observed around 31-32 months. A comparison of the interval between the second and third births, and third and fourth, according to the year of marriage clearly indicates a decrease of mean birth interval between 1935–1939 and 1945–1949 of the order of 2.8–3.7 months, and stability in the decades that follow.

Table 11.2 Mean Length of Birth Interval by Interval Order for Non-Contracepting Families Having Six or More Children (all final sizes), by Date of Marriage. Rural Shi.

Date of marriage (years)	number of families	mean age at first marriage Man (years)	mean age at first marriage Woman (years)	interval order -1* (months)	-2	-3	-4	-5	-6	-7	-8	-9	-10	mean length (months)
1935–39	85	21.3	18.5	17.0	33.9	35.3	35.2	34.0	32.4	32.8	32.3	31.5	30.4	33.6
1945–49	160	20.6	19.3	18.7	31.1	31.6	32.0	31.8	32.8	31.6	32.3	33.7	33.3	31.9
1950–54	105	20.3	18.8	15.0	31.2	30.2	31.1	31.2	33.0	32.7	35.6	33.6	33.6	32.0
1955–59	110	20.3	19.3	14.5	29.9	31.6	31.7	32.8	33.2	34.3	32.1	37.4	32.7	31.7
1970–74**	77	20.9	19.5	12.9	29.9	31.6	31.5							

* Interval between marriage and first birth.

** Families having 4 or more children.

Source: Leridon, 1977.

The average age at first marriage among the Shi is relatively stable. The decrease in the 'marriage - first birth' interval in Table 11.2 suggests that the difference noted above may be due to a shortening of the waiting time to conception. This could be explained by the increased time that men spend at home, following the gradual disappearance of their traditional activities such as tending cattle, service to local traditional authorities, or clearing new land. After 1945-1949, birth intervals show no evidence of a progessive decrease which could be traced to changes in breastfeeding patterns associated with 'modernization' even though this was a period of extreme socio-cultural changes in the region, with the introduction of mass education, health services, and salaried employment. If this is true, are the differences in length of postpartum amenorrhoea between the Shi and Havu women in fact due to differences in breastfeeding patterns?

Breastfeeding Patterns of Shi and Havu Women

Data

In a medical survey of 562 women in a Shi hill (community) and in a household survey of 240 families in a Havu hill, 342 Shi and 166 Havu breastfeeding mothers who had had at least one live birth were asked to provide information on menstrual status, frequency of feedings, supplementation and general breastfeeding behaviour. The two surveys were not conducted under the same conditions; however, comparisons with previous surveys allow us to assume that the two samples are representative of the populations being studied. From the Havu sample, a sub-sample of 42 breastfeeding women chosen according to the age of the nursing child evenly distributed between 1 and 30 months, was observed during 12 hours, from dawn to dusk. The recorded observations included duration of feeding, the factor which provoked it, the duration and number of supplementary feedings and the length of physical contact between mother, child and family. Each mother-child dyad was observed only once, during the dry season (May-June 1984). A similar study is presently taking place among the Shi women.

Results

1. Amenorrohea duration

The life-table method permits us to compare proportions of Shi and Havu women still amenorrhoeic, according to months elapsed since delivery (Figure 11.1). The median durations of postpartum amenorrhoea for Shi and Havu women are 13-14 months and 18-19 months respectively. These values are basically in accordance with the average values observed in Table 11.1. The first and third quartiles are 7-8 and 24-25 months for Shi women and 12-13 and 26-27 months for Havu women. According to the shapes of their distributions, the conditional probabilities of resuming menstruation are much higher for Havu women after 15 months.

Figure 11.1 Proportions of Havu (o) and Shi (•) Breastfeeding Women Still Amenorrheic by Months Elapsed Since the Birth

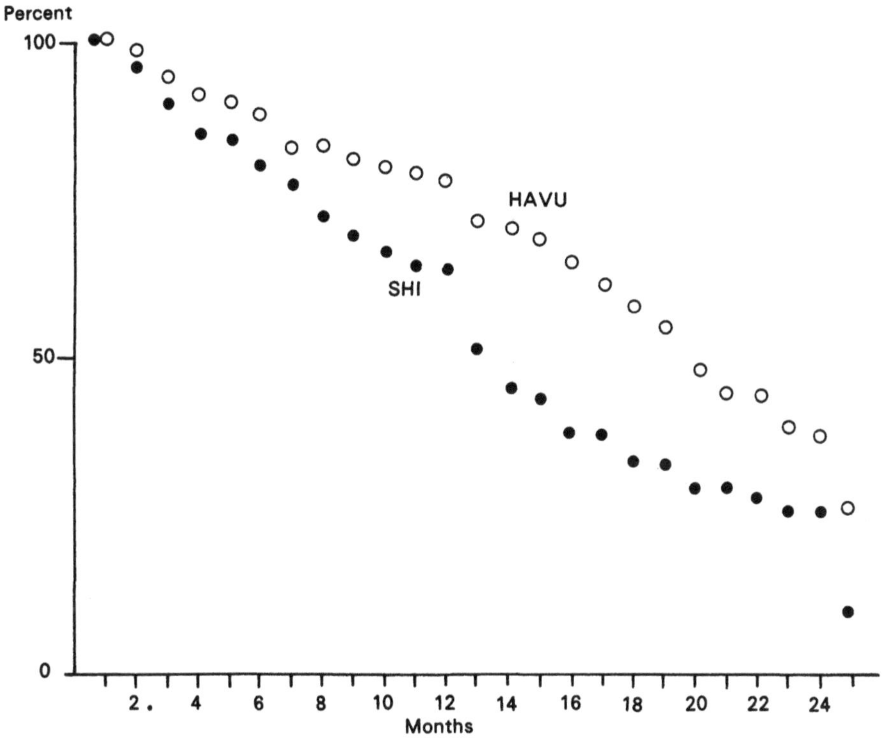

2. Breastfeeding practices

For the question 'How many times has your child suckled during the preceding day and night?' the averages were 4.1 ± 1.7 times in the day and 3.3 ± 1.3 times in the night for the Shi. For the Havu, comparative figures were 7.2 ± 1.8 times in the day and 4.1 ± 1.5 times in the night. Thus there was a difference in frequency of about four sucklings in 24 hours between the two groups, the 24-hour means being 7.4 ± 2.3 versus 11.3 ± 3.1, largely due to the difference in the daytime frequency of nursing. These two frequencies gradually decline after 12 months.

During the questioning it became apparent, in both areas, that the mothers underestimated the frequency of suckling in a proportion difficult to establish. The majority counted only the 'large' suckles; those times that corresponded to when they intended to feed the child. These 'nutritive' sucklings often took place at precise times of the day and were remembered, such as when the child awoke or when the mothers returned from the field. This was not the case for the 'little' suckles, those given 'on demand', where the frequency day and night were neither counted nor remembered.

Supplementary food is begun at a median child age of 1-2 months in the Shi area, with the third quartile around 4-5 months; in rural Havu the median is 2-3 months with the third quartile at 5-6 months. These early supplements were of poor nutritional quality, usually consisting of sorghum porridge or mashed bananas. Hot supplementary foods are initiated around 6-7 months.

According to the mothers, the major factor influencing the number and length of sucklings is the age of the child. The second factor is the mother's diet and activity in the fields. The beginning of the rainy season (October-December) is a period of reduced protein intake and intense sowing activities. The feedings are more numerous because the child is hungry and cold but shorter as the mother has little breastmilk or time. Among the factors that reduce sharply the number of feedings, the most often mentioned is illness of mother and child, particularly due to malaria, measles, bronchitis and tonsillitis.

The survey of the Shi mothers brought to light the custom of the *busire*, an enclosure of the newborn which affects the frequency of suckling. At one week of age the child is put in an enclosure which he or she does not leave until an average age of 5.5 months. The mother works in the fields several hours a day or more depending on the season, leaving the infant in the care of a paternal family member or a guardian. The length of seclusion is fixed by the *mulaguzi* (diviner) according to several criteria, one of which is the survival of previous children. The higher the incidence of infant mortality in the family, the longer the period of seclusion as it is believed to protect the child from the hostile environment.

Historically, the competition to acquire land and livestock, the sources of riches and power, was stronger in Bushi than elsewhere in Kivu (Colle, 1937). Cattle were numerous and rules of neighbourhood guaranteed all nursing women *entonda y omwana*, (milk for the child); the Shi women who like the Havu woman does most of the work in the fields, could partially liberate herself from maternal duties without endangering the child, who could be left with a guardian who could feed the infant cows' milk and sorghum porridge. By encouraging early weaning, the *busire* also permitted mothers to attain the ideal of high fertility to which the women of Kivu aspire. With population growth and higher densities, and with the disappearance of pasture and cattle, cows' milk has become rare, being replaced by water, but the *busire* remains and is in fact reinforced by the increasing infant mortality rate.

In the rural Havu area, the custom of *busire* is unknown; mother and child do not separate. The child is taken to the field up to an average age of 18-20 months. The practice of breastfeeding is not altered, as confirmed by micro-observation.

Figure 11.2 Average Nursing Frequency (o), Average Total Sucking Time (x) (min) and Mean Length of Intervals Between Nursing Bouts (●) (min) During 30 Postpartum Months. Rural Havu Area. Each Point Representing the Mean ± SD of 3 Observations

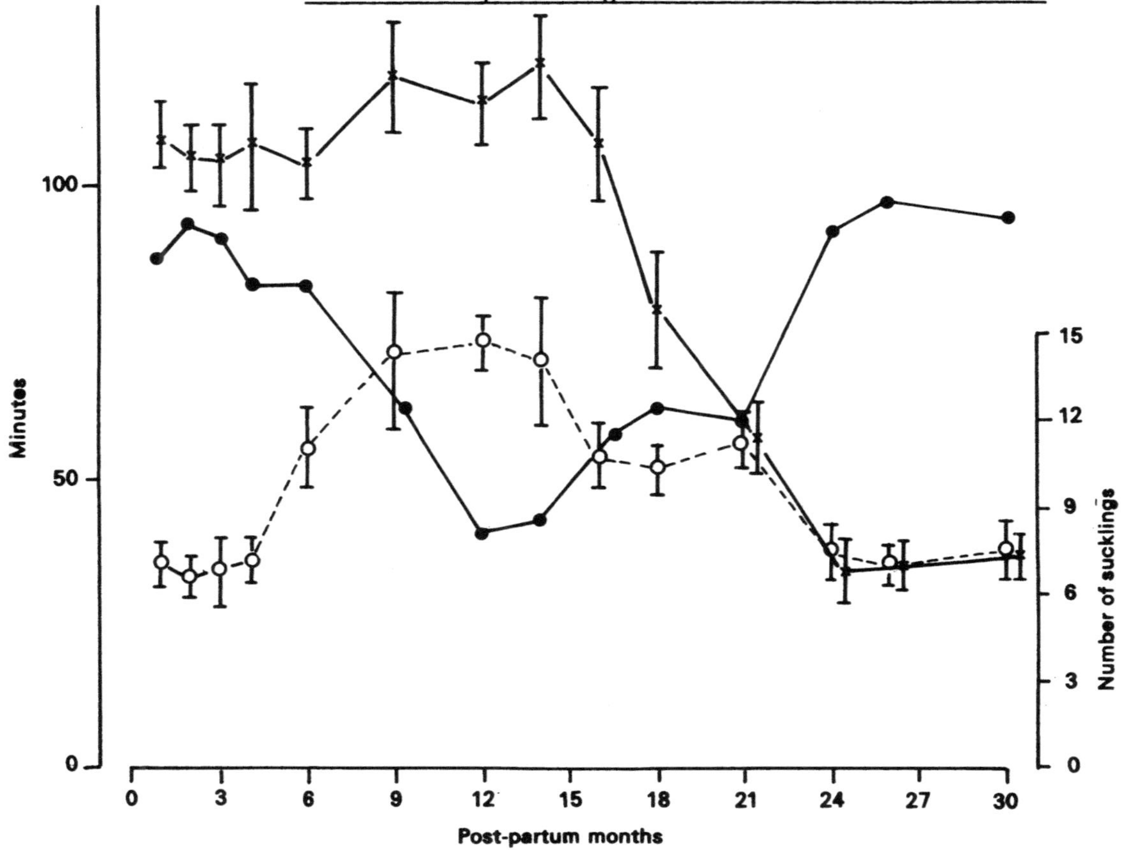

To complement the survey, which resulted in an underestimation of the number of feedings per day, 12 hours continuous daytime observations were conducted with 42 breastfeeding Havu women. Due to the small sample size it is not our intention to quantify the observed variables but rather to present their relationships schematically (Figure 11.2).

2 a). Nursing frequency

Sucklings increase from 6–7 during the first postpartum months to a maximum of 14–15 between 9–14 months. They then decrease irregularly until 24 months, when their number stabilizes at around 7.

2 b). Total feeding time

Relatively stable during the first 6 months, the feeding time increases to a maximum of about 110 minutes between 10 and 14 months. The time then decreases rapidly due to the combined effect of decreased frequency and duration of suckling. Sucklings lasting longer than 10 minutes represent 32 per cent of all sucklings. Frequent during the first 6 months, these long sucklings become rare after 12 months. Sucklings of 5–9 minutes are more frequent (39 per cent). They are distributed regularly according to the postpartum months. Sucklings of 1–4 minutes form 29 per cent of the total but occur principally from 7–17 post-partum months.

2 c). Intervals between nursing bouts

The interval is high during the first weeks following birth, reaches a minimum of 40–45 minutes between 12 and 14 months, and then lengthens, at the same time the average nursing frequency decreases to stabilize around 90–100 minutes between 24 and 26 months.

2 d). Supplementary foods

Beginning with a frequency of 3–4 times during the first 6 months, supplementation increases in subsequent months. The day-time becomes for the child one long series of 'nibbles', tasting a variety of foods, and short sucklings between 9 and 16 months. Suckling is mostly given on demand during this period and 'emotional' sucklings are in the majority. At around 18 months, the nibbling becomes spaced and the child begins to be integrated into adult eating habits.

2 e). Physical contact with mother, child and family

There are an average of 229 ± 86 minutes of physical contact per 12 hours between mother and child, not counting contact during breastfeeding. Thus a Havu child spends an average of 40 to 45 per cent of the day in direct contact with his or her mother. This contact is longest at the age of 2-4 months: the child spends almost 60 per cent of the day in bodily contact with the mother at this time, which is the period when breastmilk is beginning to be supplemented with other food. Physical contacts with family members average 153 ± 98 minutes. In all, bodily contact represents half of a nursing child day until the age of 13-15 months. Havu children seem to be cut off from exploring their physical environment; when not nursing, they are carried on their mothers' backs where their movements are restricted, or they are held on someone's lap. This relationship of strict physical dependence may be one of the factors explaining the observed increase of 'emotional' sucklings between 9 and 14 months.

Discussion

A specific pattern of breastfeeding amongst rural Shi that does not occur among Havu women appears to explain, at least partially and at the population level, the shorter length of the birth interval and of the postpartum non-susceptible period. The median duration of postpartum amenorrhoea of 13-14 months for Shi women versus 18-19 months for Havu women corresponds to a decreased suckling frequency of about four feeds per 24 hours and to longer intervals between nursing bouts. This difference is supported by the Shi custom of *busire* which creates a daily separation of mother and child and hinders demand feeding.

In the rural Shi area where acculturation seems more regionally discernible, a retrospective analysis showed a greater stability in the mean length of birth interval since 1945-50. The associated variables of 'modernization' - education, employment, income, have not seemed to alter traditional breastfeeding patterns in rural areas. Further studies are nonetheless necessary to confirm the results. Before embarking on an investigation between women's background characteristics and breastfeeding practices, however, we have to consider the adequacy of the research methods used. It is necessary to know the pattern of suckling by month of breastfeeding in order to compare it to probabilities of resuming menstruation.

In comparing the two methods of estimating breastfeeding frequency, the 12-hour micro-observation suggests that survey data considerably underestimate the number of feedings. Better estimates result in a significant change in the curve of the evolution of nursing frequency according to child age. This curve agrees well, as a working hypothesis, with the increasing rate of resuming menstruation after 15 months for Havu women. Studies in Kivu have shown that prolactin levels are highly correlated with the frequency of suckling rather than the duration or the total suckling time (Delvoye *et al.*, 1977; Hennart, 1983). Thus all sucklings are important, even those of short duration. The 'emotional' sucklings are not necesssarily shorter or less intense than 'nutritive' sucklings, and even a short suckling can be nutritive because 80 per cent of the milk yield is taken by the child in the first two minutes of a suckling (Lucas *et al.*, 1979).

It is interesting to compare our observations with the results of a serum prolactin study of 160 Havu breastfeeding women (Hennart *et al.*, 1981). The average rate of serum prolactin stayed at more than 1000 mu/litre until 12-15 months and then declined rapidly to a threshold of 500 mu/litre (the level considered normal for non-pregnant and non-breastfeeding women) between 15-18 months. This drop occurs at the time in which the nursing frequency decreases, as we saw in Figure 11.2. In addition to serum prolactin level measures, the previous authors recorded the number of feeding episodes during a 24-hour period in a health centre where mothers and children were under observation to collect information on mother's milk volume by infant test-weighing. By this laboratory method of observation, the frequency was 8-10 feedings during the first 20 postpartum months, and did not decrease until older ages.

The survey method used to establish nursing frequency appears to be helpful in the interpretation of overall results and perhaps for a better understanding of the relationship between breastfeeding patterns and the length of postpartum amenorrhoea. The 12-hour continuous observation of nursing mothers, on the other hand, could be one of the best methods for clarifying the different variables associated with breastfeeding patterns.

To confirm this assumption it is our intention to make further surveys with the same method and larger samples in order to establish a median curve and percentiles of the evolution of the number of feedings according to child age. These data, in parallel with that of median postpartum amenorrhoea duration, would permit some valuable comparisons. It would be useful to undertake surveys during the dry and the rainy seasons in order to take into account seasonal variations in breastfeeding practices and in the onset of postpartum menses (Chen *et al.*, 1974; Whitehead *et al.*, 1978; Huffman *et al.*, 1980). Possible variations in breastfeeding patterns among subpopulations should also be investigated.

Acknowledgement

I am grateful to R. Schoenmaeckers and E. Coussaert for their advice and comments.

12

Households, Women's Roles and Prestige as Factors Determining Nuptiality and Fertility Differentials in Mali

Duncan Fulton and Sara Randall

Introduction

Micro-approaches to demography can essentially cover three domains. First, studies of small populations or groups which are restricted because the population itself as a meaningful entity is limited, such as island populations or small ethnic groups. These studies follow traditional demographic procedures in that they aim to measure population indices, although they may incidentally involve more personal contact and intimate knowledge of the subjects simply because of the scale of the study. Second, studies of the small units constituting larger populations: for example, of the dynamics of households, examining the effects of single demographic events or of large scale events such as migration or political change. The third micro-demographic approach remains closer to traditional demographic data and population level measures but uses supplementary data and approaches to interpret these results, taking a small sample of the population for study through flexible, non-questionnaire based investigation. This type of study follows up problems and anomalies in the higher level data; it focuses on values, attitudes and expectations and their effects on decisions made at the level of individuals, couples or households, and on the social processes which combine to create the population level effects.

It is this third domain which is reported on here.[1] Through a comparison of two populations we explore the determination of different fertility patterns. In particular this paper aims to address the separation of those constraints which operate on the population as a whole from those which affect the decisions and actions of smaller units and individuals.

The Study Populations

The paper deals with two rural populations, both with very low levels of technological development. Single round demographic surveys (samples of 10,000 and 6,000 individuals) showed that the two groups had very different fertility and mortality profiles, although for both modern contraception is unknown, durations of breastfeeding and lactational amenorrhoea are similar and long, and postpartum abstinence is limited to 40 days for most women.

Table 12.1 Estimated Total Fertility and Total Marital Fertility

	Bambara	Kel Tamasheq
Total fertility (estimated by P/F ratio method)	8.1	6.6
Total marital fertility	8.9	10.1

Source: 1981 Demographic Surveys - Household Data.

The Bambara, a sedentary, village-based population of millet farmers, live in large extended households based on patrilineal descent. Their estimated total fertility is 8.1.

The Kel Tamasheq are nomadic pastoralists. Those in this study herd their cattle, goats and sheep in the Inner Niger delta during the dry season, and never cultivate. Tamasheq society is highly stratified, with five main social classes, of which the three high status classes (here referred to as nobles) still have access to the labour of an ex-slave dependent class (here referred to as Bella).[2,3] Kel Tamasheq estimated total fertility is 6.6.

Quantitative analysis indicates that controlling for the marriage pattern leads to the disappearance, even to the reversal, of these fertility differences (Table 12.1).

'Micro-Demographic' Intensive Study

From the survey data on marriage, it is possible to identify population level differences and similarities in marital behaviour between the two populations, but not to answer questions about why these marriage patterns prevail, how they are maintained, and the relationships between marriage and fertility at the level of the individual, the couple, the household or the group. Although one can say that differences in marriage patterns are responsible for the variations in fertility, the quantitative data do not allow one to say whether and in what way this may result from conscious or unconscious strategies and manipulation of fertility.

These were the questions which were the subject of a 'micro-demographic' approach. A 3-month intensive study of the Kel Tamasheq focused on marriage through case histories of marital careers and interviews about marriage and divorce, supplemented by observations of day-to-day behaviour and reactions to marriage-related events. This study was undertaken in a large camp of about 180 individuals representing four of the five Tamasheq social classes. For Bambara the data on marriage were obtained as part of an 18-month social and economic study centred on two villages (population 800), both of which were included in the demographic survey.

Theoretical Background

Two current theoretical approaches informed these inquiries; although different, both related the explanation of fertility to the economics, more or less broadly defined, of child bearing and rearing and of patterns of labour use.

In the literature on pastoral populations there is frequent mention of the lower fertility of pastoral nomads compared with that of sedentary populations in general, and of sedentarized members of the same ethnic group (Henin, 1968, 1969; Swift, 1975; Bernus, 1981). A variety of explanations has been offered for this presumed lower fertility (often expressed in crude birth rates). Some share with the explanations offered at the level of folklore a measure of ethnic stereotyping, such as a belief that pastoral nomads are riddled with veneral disease, or an assumption that malnutrition resulting from the pastoral way of life is responsible for their lower fertility. A leading type of explanation, however, argues that lower fertility is the result of a need to balance resources, that is herd growth rates, with the growth of population.

This type of explanation does not stand up well to examination either *a priori* or in the light of facts about the actual constraints governing pastoral production, and the social responses to them, in an area such as the Sahel. The explanation raises more questions than it answers; like many functionalist arguments of its kind, it suggests that because things are the way they are, that is the way they are intended to be, without elucidating the actual mechanisms involved.

It does not explain how a strategy at the level of the population as a whole could be created out of the potentially contradictory strategies pursued at the level of individuals and households. An overall balance of animals and people at the population level does not entail an equal distribution of both at a lower level. In fact pastoralists in an environment like the Sahel are not faced with a steady though slow rate of reproduction of their herds, but rather with the random, sudden and severe effects of animal disease and drought. What they need are flexible short-term responses to these fluctuations. These responses do exist, but are completely unrelated to fertility and its possible manipulation; they generally operate at the level of the household and consist of loans or gifts of animals, or the short term alteration of the human-animal balance through migration - in the case of the Kel Tamasheq through the shedding of surplus Bella labour.

Economic factors are of course important in the determination of these household and individual strategies, and clearly at the societal level, economy and fertility have a constraining effect on each other. The second main theory of fertility which was relevant to this research offers what seems to be a more satisfactory account of the differences between the two populations studied.

Caldwell's hypothesis (Caldwell, 1977) of the relationship between fertility and the value of children measured by intergenerational wealth flows appears to be helpful in bridging the gap between measuring population level fertility differences and understanding the processes which cause and maintain them.

The Problems

Bambara economy and society in the area studied provide at first sight a classic case of a high-fertility/high-utility-children regime. Land is still plentiful and is exploited by households using labour-intensive methods; this labour is recruited almost entirely through marriage and reproduction. A structure of large, extended, polygynous households means that the peaks and troughs in dependency (consumer/worker) ratios are flattened out. An extra child is not a burden, and both boys and girls start to contribute labour, in farming and in a multiplicity of other activities, from a very early age. They are members of the family workforce, the only providers of security for the old age of their parents' generation, and, through their marriages, are the medium of important political and economic exchanges with other families. Wealth flows unequivocally from the junior to the senior generation. This fact, and the fact that other social, political and emotional benefits also accrue to parents from having many children are openly acknowledged by Bambara and by their language itself, whose terms for 'power' include the idea of 'wealth', seen as control over things and over people, principally in the form of descendants. The struggle for power in this agricultural society consists largely in demographic competition between opposing lineages. High fertility is to be expected, and does in fact prevail.

By contrast the Tamasheq case seems to fit less well into the frame of this hypothesis. Livestock production is relatively insensitive to labour input, so that there is a point beyond which increased household size tends to reduce the income of individual members; and reproduction within households is not the primary means of recruitment of labour. Labour for nobles is provided by their Bella (ex-slave) population, while for Bella themselves increased reproduction does not increase their own source of labour, but rather that of the noble. So the flows of wealth between generations are cut across by the divisions of class, and for neither class alone is there a high economic value of children. Nor are children the sufficient or even the necessary source of status, since the system of social classes determines the status of individuals at birth, and there is no mobility between these classes.

Logically, then, and in terms of the hypothesis, one might expect Tamasheq fertility to be even lower than it is. In fact, although lower than the (very high) Bambara fertility, it is still high when compared with post-demographic transition populations. Of course it is not that children are not desired by the Kel Tamasheq. Apart from the emotional satisfaction derived from parenthood, nobles do need children for political as well as economic reasons, to be the inheritors of their status and of their cattle and slave labour; and they do express concern about this aspect of their reproduction, regarding themselves as menaced by their inferior demographic performance compared with the Bella. (This is in fact due to class differences in mortality rather than in fertility: see Hilderbrand *et al.*, 1985; Hill *et al.*, 1983 and Hill and Randall, 1984). As Muslims, all classes regard children as an important aim in life, and all have some interest in having children as a measure of security for old age, though not necessarily in having the maximum number possible.

So a simple economic determinism, based on returns to productive labour, cannot explain the differing patterns of fertility. Measures of net flows of wealth between generations are complicated by factors of power and social structure; in the case of the Kel Tamasheq by the existence of a system of social classes, and even in the Bambara case, where the exploitation of the junior by the senior generation is admittedly a foundation of political economy, by the different interests of men and women in reproduction and by inequalities within and between households. In both cases the questions which need to be asked concern how fertility is managed and controlled, and by whom.

We argue that an examination of roles, interests and decisions involved in marriage and reproduction in the two societies concerned suggests that while differences in marriage patterns are responsible for the observed differences in fertility, it does not follow that fertility strategies are determining marriage. Because in contracepting populations fertility is largely a product of a decision-making process, there is a tendency, in looking at a non-contracepting population where the principal fertility differentiating mechanism is social, to explain this too by a conscious fertility strategy. A closer look at the pattern of marriage, and at the roles and marital careers of men and women in Tamasheq society suggests that Tamasheq marriage can plausibly be regarded as a relationship between a man and a woman, subject to certain social constraints, and that children are almost a by-product of a relationship which happens to include legitimized sexual relations. Looking at Bambara marriage with this point of view, one sees that although the incentives for high fertility are such that the marriage pattern for women maximizes reproduction, other factors influencing the system of marriage are equally important.

Entering Marriage

The survey data showed differences and similarities between the two populations in entry into marriage, and marriage duration and

Table 12.2 Measures of Entry into Marriage

	Bambara		Kel Tamasheq		
	male	female	male	female	
Median age at first marriage	28.3	17.5	26.3	18.2	yrs
Percentage never marrying	0.0	0.0	1.1	5.5	%
Speed of marriage (number of years for per cent never married to drop from 75 per cent to 25 per cent of the population)	6.1	2.5	5.7	5.9	yrs

Source: 1981 Demographic Surveys - Household Data.

remarriage. Table 12.2 shows measures of the three main components of entry into marriage, and Figure 12.1 gives a graphical illustration of the variation between the two populations caused by differences in marital duration and remarriage. The median age of women at first marriage differs little between the two populations, but Tamasheq women marry over a wider age span than Bambara women. The small percentage of Tamasheq women who remain unmarried is not sufficient to account for the fertility differences. Figure 12.1 provides the most striking indication of where the populations do differ. All Bambara women are more or less continuously married throughout their child bearing years, whereas at all ages a substantial proportion of Tamasheq women are widowed or divorced. It is these long periods between marriages that do most to reduce Tamasheq total fertility.

This in itself is evidence against the existence of simple and direct control over fertility effected through a control of marriage. If this were so, one would expect control to be exerted at entry to first marriage, where change of status is greatest and individuals are youngest and easiest to manipulate by social or economic means. The fact that the differences in marriage pattern only become evident for the already married suggests that different mechanisms may be involved, and leads us to look at the roles of women in and out of marriage; at support for women out of marriage; at the interests of the various categories of individuals and groups involved in marriage and marriage stability; and at the roles of children and the economic and social factors which regulate the marriage market.

Important differences in the marriage systems of the two populations relate to the availability of potential spouses.

Figure 12.1 Proportions of Women Currently Single, Married, Divorced and Widowed by Age and Ethnic Group

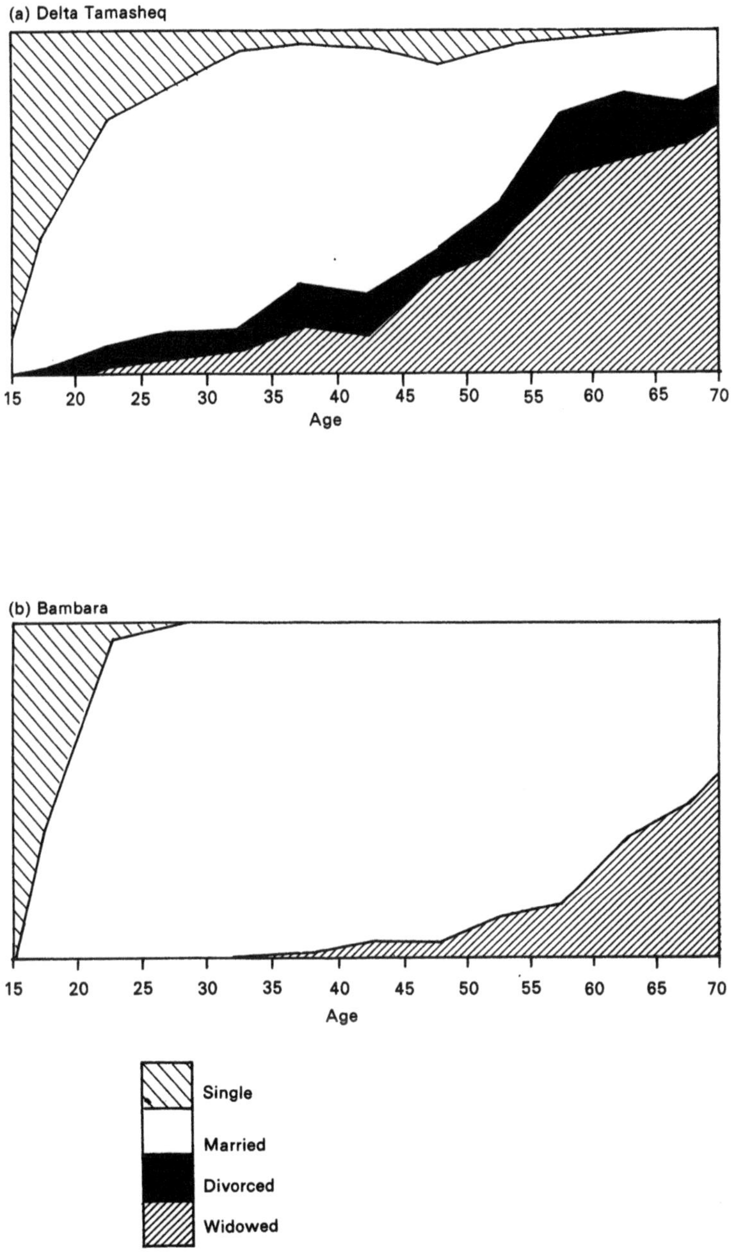

Source: 1981 Demographic Surveys - Household Data.

Bambara are polygynous, practise the levirate and have exogamous lineages. Preferred marriages are those with women of lineages with existing marital ties. Bridewealth is distributed amongst relatives of the bride, but the expenses of the marriage celebration, which are paid by the groom's family, are consumed on the spot.

By contrast, the five classes in Tamasheq society are all endogamous. Kel Tamasheq are monogamous in practice, with preferred close kin marriages; all types of first cousin are very desirable spouses. Tamasheq bridewealth is high, but becomes an indirect dowry (Goody and Tambiah, 1973) which, depending on the wealth and status of the bride, is either converted into the prerequisites for marriage such as a tent or household utensils, or remains as a cattle holding which continues to be the property of the woman. In the case of divorce or widowhood she retains these cattle, which represent security for her and her children. The rules of residence mean that whereas a Bambara man continues to live with his father or brothers after marriage and his wife thus comes to join an already existing household, Tamasheq marriage entails the creation of a new household.

Clearly these rules contribute to the observed marriage, and hence fertility, patterns. For Bambara, polygyny ensures that there is never a shortage of potential husbands, and the levirate that widows are immediately remarried. Tamasheq monogamy entails more individuals outside marriage at any given moment, because those recently widowed or divorced have not yet found a new spouse. Supplementary Islamic rules that a divorcee must wait 3 months and a widow 5 months before remarrying compound the numbers of women outside marriage; men need not wait to remarry.

But these rules do not explain all the differences between the two populations. They are themselves in need of explanation and are the result of negotiation. For example, Tamasheq monogamy is not the result of a rule as such; as a Muslim the Tamasheq man is entitled to have up to four wives, provided that he can afford to keep them and that he treats all of them equally. In practice, the wives of any men who have tried to have more than one at a time have always refused to accept this, and have succeeded in obtaining divorces on the grounds of unequal treatment. This suggests that we need to consider the real constraints governing marriage and its outcome by looking at the interests of the various parties in marriage and in fertility within marriage.

Bambara Marriage

Interests at Stake

A Bambara man has an interest in marrying as early as possible which is separate from any desire or need that he may have for children. In the short term, apart from a sanctioned sexual partner, he gains a personal cook and domestic attendant (main meals are cooked and eaten communally in Bambara households, but private and occasional food is also provided by wives for their own husbands and children in nuclear family units within the larger extended structure). Most importantly, by marrying he becomes a senior rather than a junior, a member of adult society. Becoming a father is part of the full achievement of this status; the control over children brings the possibility of both wealth and power, and having descendants enables religious as well as political fulfilment. But it is not his immediate aim in getting married. Entry into marriage is determined by a process of choice on the part of a group of male relatives, within the framework of opportunities and constraints as they see them; it is made possible by their effective control over and disposal of females.

In so far as he forms part of a patrilineal household which is successfully reproducing itself, he can be protected from the disastrous economic consequences of childlessness. Through the levirate he may become the social father of a deceased elder brother's children. He wants control over sons, whether his own or those he may inherit with a wife, because the distribution of power within households, just as between them, is largely dependent on demographic competition - in this case between brothers. Those who have no sons to contribute to the work force have less authority, and have no option of becoming independent households in case of a threatened split in the larger unit. They have to submit to the authority of those who are more fortunate and successful reproducers. In fact it is the logic of a system of production and reproduction organized in the largest possible household units which in this case imposes choices on individuals. Several men in the village were either explicitly unwilling to marry a second wife, or found it very difficult to manage polygamous unions in political or emotional terms. (The only wives motivated to accept or encourage it were those in the smallest households, where an extra woman relieved them significantly of domestic work.) The levirate is a part of this logic, giving the different sub-units of sets of brothers making up an extended household an interest in continuing to collaborate in production and in investment in wives.

Control of Entry to Marriage

From the point of view of the Bambara household group, or rather of the senior men who control it, there is obviously an interest in the reproduction of the labour force which will support them in their retirement. But at the same time the control of juniors' labour by seniors is largely exercised and assured by their control over the marriage system. Apart from their provision of agricultural labour, young men before their first marriage go on dry season labour migration to earn the cash needed to pay taxes and, indeed, to finance their own marriages. Their elders have an interest in keeping them at this cash earning as long as possible, but they also have to make sure that they do return each year to farm. The young men do so because on the whole the village structures of production and reproduction offer them greater security than those they can find elsewhere or in towns. They have an interest in keeping up their subscriptions to these institutions, even though they themselves hardly benefit from them at the moment; they are off again at the next harvest, leaving the millet they have grown to be eaten or exchanged by those who stay behind. But at some point they will want to be provided for in their turn, to have their chance to control surplus production and any inherited wealth, and to avoid being dependent on the market for food. And this applies also to the marriage market. Bridewealth is a great deal higher in towns, and where long-established networks of marriage alliance cannot be exploited; furthermore although a young man could theoretically pay the bridewealth to get himself a wife in his home area, he cannot actually get married without the support and therefore the accord of his elders. They provide the grain so that the marriage can be celebrated, but they also control the political apparatus which has to be used for the marriage to be arranged. A man who marries through these proper channels gets a wife who is vouched for by his and her families; both will ensure that she fulfils the duties expected of her, and make it hard for her to run away from him.

The basis of the political economy is the appropriation of the surplus labour of the young by their elders. This in turn is made possible by the control of women by men. Surplus is reinvested in the provision of wives for young men, by which means they eventually attain the status of elders themselves. The control of this circulation of wealth flows is in the hands of the senior generation, who are able to delay the marriages of young men; the women who are their equals in age are assigned to older, possibly polygynous husbands. Thus the control of fertility, so far as this is related to the entry into marriage, is exercised not by the potential reproducers themselves but by their fathers.

Women as Exchange and Investment

Wives represent other important values besides their role as reproducers of labour. Bambara women work in the fields of their fathers before marriage, and of their husbands and fathers-in-law or brothers-in-law after it, and are a direct addition to the household agricultural labour force. They also have small fields and gardens of their own, which are an important form of extra production. Their role as cooks is vital; a household is not a viable unit without a woman. But the exchange of women as brides also represents in itself a key element in the political and economic structure of Bambara society.

The network of marriage alliances of an exogamous lineage or descent group is both an economic resource and a field of political action. Redistribution of grain passes along the so-called 'marriage roads' which link lineages and whole villages with their partners in marriage exchanges. Women go to villages and families with which they can claim a link through marriage, or when married, back to those with which they have links of descent, to earn grain for work in harvesting and winnowing millet; daughters and sisters are expected to apply to their fathers and brothers whenever difficulty or hardship faces them in their family of marriage. The rights that they retain in their natal families are expressed in the fact that men are obliged to give a portion of their millet harvest to their sisters after these have married and live, work and eat elsewhere. Women do receive a quantity of grain for themselves from their husbands' fields, but this is conceived of as a payment for the work they have done weeding, harvesting and winnowing these men's millet. Some of their own fathers' and brothers' millet belongs to them by right of descent, even though they have done no work in producing it. At the ceremony when a daughter leaves her father's house to go to be married, and again when she is received at her new husband's and in-law's house, a speech is made by one of the men of her family, listing all the other women of the family who are married elsewhere, and the various villages where they live. These are all places for her to go, in case of abuse or distress, and signify to her husband's family her potential support and influence. Descent through women is a principle of economic and political structure, although residence and production are organized on patrilineal principles; and the women who by successful reproductive careers are the pivots of the system are respected and remembered as individuals.

In an environment of uncertain rainfall and high agricultural risk, links through women to producers elsewhere, even over quite a short distance, provide potentially crucial insurance. Wife-givers are also in a strong position to get help from in-laws, and may be able to extract large amounts of labour from the future husband and his family or age-mates.

Women therefore represent an investment in themselves, apart from their value as reproducers, and their inheritance through the levirate by the whole group of patrilineal investors relates to this as well as to their role as mothers of children who represent the common future of the group. This value is shown most clearly by the fact that even post-menopausal women are desired as wives. All Bambara women, except the very oldest who have outlived all the members of their own generation, have husbands; where there is no younger 'brother' of the deceased husband to inherit them, they attract an impressive number of suitors. These marriages between retired man and women are uxorilocal; the woman does not move house but remains with her children, if any, and is visited by her husband. For him and his household she does not represent labour or potential descendants, but she is of an age when she has acquired a certain economic independence. Old women who have retired from the work of cultivating in the field of the household (the men's field) have time to devote to their own private farming and to a little private commerce. They are often the major proprietors of small stock, especially of sheep. By marrying such a wife the husband acquires companionship and access to some of the comforts and luxuries of life.

The case of one such middle-aged bride illustrates the point. J. is a woman now in her late fifties, who was pursued by a number of men on the death of her husband. She was left a widow 8-10 years ago by her first husband, and remarried to a man who died soon after. On his death, there was considerable competition for her, despite the fact that by this time she was beyond child-bearing age. Life for J. became impossible, with medicines and charms being left about her house by the agents and supporters of one contender or another, and she decided to leave the village with her son, who was then in his late teens, and go to the neighbouring hamlet from which her first husband's family had originated. She has since been married by one of the older men of that hamlet's founding lineage.

Fertility - Male and Female Motivation

From the male point of view, although the role of women as reproducers is obvious, and everything is arranged so that their fertility is maximized, there is much more to marriage than the maximization of fertility. At the level of households and individuals, this may not necessarily always be the priority. Unlike some neighbouring West African cultivating societies, Bambara rarely integrate those children born to women before marriage into their legitimate descendancy. Among the Samo of Upper Volta, for instance, it is reported by Heritier (1968) that it is quite normal for a woman to bring her first child with her to her husband's house, and that this may indeed be regarded as a proof of fertility. The husband almost always acknowledges the child as his, even where it is known not to be so. By contrast Bambara strongly disapprove of such births. A woman will almost always leave such a child behind when she goes to be married, to be brought up in her own father's household. But here too the child is not welcomed unequivocally as a member of the workforce or as an agent in the reproduction of the family. Illegitimate girls can be married off, usually to illegitimate husbands, but boys are required to move out of their mothers' natal households as soon as they are old enough to become independent.

Looking at marriage from the woman's point of view also helps to explain how the Bambara regime of high fertility is maintained. The basic fact is the political ideological and economic domination of women by men. This means that a woman is constrained to perform her role as object of exchange and reproducer of labour when and where her father and brothers decide. And it is only through fulfilling this role that she can aspire to a fully adult and civil status. She is obliged to marry because there is no such thing as an unmarried adult Bambara woman, and she is strongly motivated to have children because a childless woman is unfulfilled and is, besides, dangerously anomalous. Even a woman who has had children but has lost them all by death is regarded with as much fear as pity, since childless women are held to be potentially responsible, whether consciously or unconsciously, for the deaths of other children.

On the positive side a woman is motivated to have children, and to have as many and as quickly as possible, by the consideration that she thus gains not only prestige in general but a degree of economic independence through her control and influence over people. She can get her daughters to help her with cooking, water-carrying and wood-collecting, and her sons with the cultivation of her personal fields and gardens. But in order to qualify for the fullest economic autonomy she needs to acquire a daughter-in-law, on whose entry into the household she is entitled to retire from work in the family field and from the cooking rota, and to devote herself to her private commercial, agricultural and animal-husbandry concerns. For both men and women, then, daughters are valuable and desirable; as labour in themselves, and as a means to acquiring daughters-in-law. They bring in income as brides which helps to speed up the acquisition of wives for sons. Personal satisfaction and sense of worth and autonomy are plain to see in Bambara women in the final phase of successful demographic careers, when influence over descendants has begun to counterbalance the official subservience to husbands and to men in general.

Marriage Stability

Within the Bambara marriage system, everything conspires to create and reinforce stability of marriage. Divorces are in fact extremely rare, and are only likely to occur before the birth of children.

The fact that marriages follow the lines of a network of alliances between patrilineages means that more is at stake in the breakdown of marriage than a single union, and that relatives on both sides are mobilized to prevent this from happening by conciliation and coercion. The whole of Bambara theory and practice of marriage, both in the selection of partners and in the rules and expectations of behaviour within marriage, involves the assumption that conflict between spouses is inevitable, and includes ways of preventing it from leading to a breakdown which would threaten a whole structure of exchanges.

Direct exchange of women (the exchange of women of the same generation as brides between two lineage groups) is not favoured. This is because it is thought that an outbreak of trouble in one marriage would inevitably lead to reciprocal separation in the other. What is preferred is cross-cousin marriage in alternate generations, in which a man marries his (real or classificatory) mother's brother's or father's sister's daughter. The immediate implications of this for marriage stability are that the partners have enjoyed a joking relationship as cross-cousins before their marriage. Although this does not survive the marriage, giving way to the public formality and respect expected of spouses, it can come into play in easing the inevitable tensions which arise, by turning potential insults into jokes. For the new Bambara wife, the fact that she is married into a household where her mother-in-law is also an aunt with whom she has had a close and indulgent relationship before her marriage also eases the difficulty of her separation from her natal family.

Here too male power over women is essential to make the system work. We discussed earlier the motivation of young men to acquiesce in the control of their marriages by their elders. In the case of women the same lack of alternatives compels them into accepting their role as instruments in the overall marriage and reproduction policy of their fathers. The protection offered to them against ill-treatment is minimal; even in a case where a woman had been badly beaten by her husband, the desire on the part of both families to prevent a politically disastrous break in relations was strong enough for her family to send her back to him, on the understanding that his elders would remonstrate with him. But even this is better than no support; which is the lot of women who marry outside the approved channels or leave their husbands against the wishes of their fathers and brothers. The fact that bridewealth cannot be returned means that such backing is most unlikely to be forthcoming, unless the father does not care what happens to his future relationship with his in-laws. A., the father of a young bride who had run away from her husband almost immediately after the marriage, and who had threatened and browbeaten her into going back, admitted that because modern Malian law forbids the marriage of women against their will, he had no legal right to do this, and that if she had been older she might not have allowed him to convince her. But his field had already been cultivated by the entire age-grade workforce of his son-in-law, and he could not afford to do other than enforce his side of the bargain. Although Bambara wives may be protected to some degree against disrespect and abuse by bringing a dowry of gold or animals with them - and their mothers make efforts to save for their marriage with this in mind - their best insurance is through marrying and having children.

Bambara society, in this region of Mali and at this stage, thus displays a convergence of interests in high fertility on the part of individuals and groups up to the level of the household and the lineage. Extremely high levels of infant and child mortality make it rational to continue to have children even when one might appear already to have more than enough on any economic basis of calculation, and even when - in the case of women especially - desire to do so has ceased. But this result is produced by the acceptance of the expected or prescribed patterns of behaviour in marriage rather than by a conscious fertility decision. In general, though the rationale for high fertility is clear at the level of the group, the desire and need for children at individual or couple level is only one of the factors which leads to the existence and maintenance of a pattern of marriage which maximizes fertility.

Tamasheq Marriage

Social and Residential Groups

Bambara marriage strategies and marital relationships contrast strongly with the Tamasheq situation where marriage does not create or perpetuate links between lineages but is a contract between two individuals, with neither alliance nor children being necesary motives. Endogamous social classes and the preference for close kin marriage with any kind of cousin inhibit the development of corporate lineages; a marriage is between two individuals already linked by kinship in several different ways. As these links exist prior to and despite her marriage, the Tamasheq bride never plays the role of an emissary creating or consolidating an alliance. In times of need, loans, aid and political favours may be requested from people apparently related by marriage, but it is the pre-existing kinship ties that are cited as justification and not the marital relationship.

Households as production and consumption units are hard to define for the Kel Tamasheq because both the interdependence of nobles and Bella (ex-slaves) and physical mobility and flexibility of living arrangements inhibit the creation of permanent units that can be pinpointed through time as households. The residential units, tents, may be independent households for some purpose and at certain times of the year, but usually a combination of a Bella tent with a noble one is the production and consumption unit. The Bella tent's degree of autonomy varies. Ideally (from the noble viewpoint) a Bella man herds the noble's animals and his wife does domestic work for the noble woman; in return the Bella receive milk and grain which the woman cooks for the inhabitants of both tents, though they eat separately. In practice, several tents' herds may be kept together though milked separately; the female servant may be a young woman living in the noble's tent; and the Bella tent may have a substantial extra income from mats made for the market, work on village harvests and even supplementary paid work for other noble families in the camp.

Both noble and Bella tents as residential units are created on marriage, and are either dissolved or lose much of their autonomy when the marriage ends. Hence the newly-married Tamasheq couple is in a different economic position from the Bambara, because they have to be a potentially viable unit, either by owning animals (the nobles) or having a noble family to work for (the Bella). The newly-married man immediately becomes a head of household with certain responsibilities of provision for his wife. These are particularly constraining for the noble class whose women do little or no work, and, being unproductive, have to be supported; this produces a situation where incentives for a man to marry are less prevalent than among the Bambara. A wife is expensive in terms of the bridewealth which has to be found (though it is often provided largely through gifts from friends and kin) and also the means for supporting her to a certain standard - especially because in order to conform to Tamasheq ideals of beauty and prestige, noble women like to force-feed themselves and be very fat. Since marriage is obviously an expensive business which reduces a man's income and freedom, one is led to ask what drives him to it?

Motives for Marriage

For the noble man there are three main motives. Marriages may be arranged entirely by the parents of both partners; on the man's side this is usually part of a strategy to make him settle down and lead a less dissipated and expensive life. A young man cannot disobey his father in such matters whereas direct control by his father over his behaviour is less easy to enforce. Most marriages, however, are entered into willingly with two recognized motives: love for a particular woman or a desire for children. In love marriages neither economics nor children are important, and an actual loss of prestige may even result if an offence to public opinion is involved. One case of such a marriage was an incestuous union between M. and the former wife of his uncle. M. was so infatuated that he suffered the ridicule of the whole community as well as the enormous economic demands that his potential father-in-law laid upon him just to be able to marry this particular woman.

Marriages for children are generally undertaken by older men who have not been married for one of the other two motives. The desire for marriage and children is partly a fulfilment of Islamic prescriptions and partly emotive. A man wants children to inherit his animals; also Tamasheq men generally like and enjoy the company of children. Children are not desired to increase his status nor to herd his animals; the former is assured by his birth and character, the latter by his Bella. Admittedly it is expected that a man or a woman will have children but this expectation is really just a statement of biological fact. A man does not have to have children to achieve the status of a full adult; although a young bachelor is not taken very seriously, this is purely a function of age. Young married men are taken no more seriously. Bella men, conversely, are never full adults in this sense because of their inherent inferior status. Marriage for the Bella man is his one way of achieving a modicum of independence and power, even if only on the domestic front. That marriage is more desirable for Bella than for noble men is reflected in their younger age at first marriage. (Median age at first marriage is 26.0 years for Bella and 29.2 years for nobles.)

Ideals and Reality

The structural independence of Tamasheq marriage is crucial to an understanding of the role of fertility in marriage. Essentially a marriage, whether of nobles or Bella, is a contract between two individuals; it is subject to the constraints and relationships which apply to those two individuals, who may, or may not, have chosen their partner themselves. The constraints within which this marriage operates are at first dictated by various rules such as class endogamy and the economic arrangements for marriage such as the payment of bridewealth and the acquisition by the woman of a tent and its furnishings. Thereafter the constraints are determined by the interplay of expectations of marriage and of prescribed behaviour within marriage.

There is a large disparity between the Tamasheq ideals and expectations of marriage and reality. Ideally marriage consists of love and respect on both sides and is very harmonious. However, the newly-married couple's expectations of concord are confronted by the social and personal expectations of male superiority and power. For a Tamasheq man it is very shameful if he is not seen, in public at least, to control his wife and make all the decisions; for a noble man to quarrel openly with his wife would be exceedingly degrading. All this is far removed from the premarital situation where a young girl or woman is sanctioned to flirt, court and pet with one or several suitors, and where it is she who manipulates the emotions and behaviour of the men. After marriage she is suddenly more restricted. Jealousy may lead her husband to ban her from visiting other camps and even other tents; this does not conform either to her expectations of concord nor to her previous experience of liberty in her own camp. Divorce is a likely consequence of any disobedience on the woman's part, because through the male prerogative to divorce, the husband can publicly reassert superiority and power and restore his prestige. B. provided a good example of his. He was a rather poor, young, noble man with extravagant tastes and a desire to impress people. He left his pregnant wife in his camp and went off travelling for several months visiting friends and kin in other camps. His wife wanted to return to her parents to give birth, and since B. was absent she went home without asking his permission. When he found out he was furious and divorced her *in absentia*. His kin and friends all deplored the divorce but for B. it was the only way he could publicly reassert his authority.

After divorce a woman returns to her kin, usually to her father's or brother's camp, and leads a less constrained life than while married. There is no real shame in being divorced and certainly no stigma attached to a divorcee. On her return to her father's camp there is a big welcoming feast to show her, and the world, that her kin accept her and are happy to have her back with them. This feast does not take place if she herself has run away from her husband, a shameful situation from which her parents will try to extricate her by sending her back, although this usually fails. It is in these cases that the contractual aspect of Tamasheq marriage emerges. If a woman who has run away from her husband cannot get him to divorce her or really wants no more to do with him, she sometimes returns all the bridewealth (which in the case of a real divorce belongs to her) and so annul the marriage. Although an undesirable situation, this does occur, and provides women with a *de facto* means for getting themselves out of a situation where legally they have no powers of divorce. It is undesired because not only does it break the rules, but it also overturns male supremacy. But, unlike the Bambara situation, alliances and relationships are not contingent upon the maintenance of the marriage, and so this strategem is usually ultimately successful, and the woman returns to her kin.

The reason that both divorce and a small pool of never-married women can exist is that a single, divorced or widowed woman is always supported by her kin to the best of their ability; such kinship obligations can never be ignored. In this state, she has more liberty to behave as she wants, to go visiting and meet people, since, when she is with her kin she is not part of the image that someone else (her husband) has to present to the world. An unmarried woman does not have lower status than a married one, although if she is past her twenties and has never been married, she may be pitied. The currently unmarried woman may participate in more social events than her married counterpart; she may be economically independent through her own inherited cattle, gifts and the remainder of her bridewealth; and she does not need to work, because her natal family will also have Bella. The older a woman, the more say she has in her own destiny, and older women frequently veto proposed marriages.

A curious anomaly in Tamasheq marriage further confirms that prestige and status are more important than economic considerations or fertility in marriage. Like Bambara men, Tamasheq men have to invest heavily in a wife. For all social classes the bridewealth is high, and although it is not consumed at the marriage, it is not recuperable afterwards. This would seem to be an economic sanction against divorce. The fact that it fails as a sanction indicates the importance of maintaining prestige and acknowledged dominance on the part of the man. The social importance of behaving according to his status is more crucial than the potential loss of a wife and animals. This is indicative of the fact that Kel Tamasheq marriage and fertility are less directly related to economic factors and more related to the complex patterns of class, prestige and status than is the case for the Bambara. It is one reason why Kel Tamasheq fail to conform to purely economic models of fertility.

Bella

Only about half this Tamasheq population is noble and thus obliged to maintain an appropriate public image. Bella are low in status, have no prestige, and no possibilities of acquiring any; yet Bella women's marriage patterns are very similar to those of the nobles. There are fewer young widows because there are fewer marriages between young girls and old men, but divorce is just as frequent. Bella divorce is provoked less by disapproval of wifely behaviour - there are no sanctions against men and women disagreeing publicly, and vociferous quarrels are quite common - and more because one of the spouses, usually the man, has found another partner. Unlike the noble woman who returns to her kin at the end of a marriage, the Bella woman returns to her master or mistress, with whom she can generally find work, support and security. The economic role of Bella women is related to the maintenance of a pool of currently unmarried women, since as single women they are economically independent and have no need to remarry. When married they are at the bottom of the Tamasheq status scale, being both Bella and women. They often choose the relative independence of working for their master in preference to being subject to a husband. Extramarital sexual relations and illegitimate births are acceptable for Bella, though less common in this zone than elsewhere (Randall and Winter, 1985). These standards are again related to the all-pervasive system of status. Bella women have no chance of climbing the social hierarchy; lax sexual behaviour is not only permitted, but, for the nobles, offers confirmation of the justice of the low status of the Bella.

The relationship between Bella labour and noble marriage emerges on a different level through a tendency for 'arranged' Bella marriages. At the creation of the noble residential unit after marriage the noble couple need Bella labour both for the herds and for domestic purposes. For nobles, a problem arising from virilocal Bella marriage is that female labour is lost when a Bella woman marries. This can be resolved by arranging a marriage between Bella belonging to each of the couple, which may be encouraged by noble contributions towards the Bella bridewealth. Such was the case of nobles E. and F. who were going to marry. E. owned a Bella man and F. had a Bella women whose labour would be necessary to the new household. E. took his Bella to F.'s camp, introduced him to the Bella woman and suggested that they marry. The Bella courted the woman briefly, discussed marriage with her parents and it was all settled. E. contributed a bull towards the bridewealth. Such a situation is also advantageous for the Bella man because he retains control over his children who otherwise would go to work for their own master. (Bella are owned by the noble who owns their mother, and virilocal marriage means that they are rarely brought up in their owner's camp). Such marriages resolve some of the conflicts inherent in a situation where labour is neither recruited on an open market nor through reproduction.

Marriage and Recruitment

Marriage is related to most aspects of social life including the political, economic and religious. This is because of its two important functions as an organizational institution creating relationships between lineages and manipulating household structure, and its role as a recruiting institution essentially for children but also for women (see Reyna, 1975). For the Bambara both these aspects of marriage are equally important and one cannot be understood without the other. For the Kel Tamasheq the recruiting component of marriage is much reduced. Even for the individual man a wife is not being recruited for her productive labour; noble women are unproductive and Bella women rarely produce for their husbands, although they do provide domestic labour. A wealthy woman does have more suitors than a poor one, but she is as likely to be divorced as her poor counterpart, and the women who never marry are not the poor, but the ugly, the deformed or those with very aggressive and domineering characters.

Evidence for the lack of emphasis on marriage as an institution for recruiting children among the Tamasheq comes from two sources. Sterile Tamasheq women, or women whose children all die, have no more precarious marital histories than women who are more successful reproducers. There is no automatic divorce of sterile women, and in a monogamous society this effectively means that neither partner will have any children whilst the marriage continues. That men do not seek a wife ostensibly for her reproductive powers is also shown by the frequency of marriages with pre-pubertal girls. This could be understood in a situation of great scarcity of marriageable women or where a great premium was placed on virginity, neither of which is the case among the Tamasheq. There are two main reasons for these precocious marriages: firstly the husband is more certain of being able to control and dominate his wife and secondly, it is easiest to force-feed women when they are very young, and a very fat wife augments a husband's prestige in the community.

If there were a high value on fertility in marriage one would expect that young widows or divorcees who already had one or two children would be pursued and remarried quickly, but it is precisely these women who spend long periods between marriages. This is of course partly because they themselves see no great advantage in remarrying, and are able to veto marriages. Tamasheq women may stop marrying long before the end of their reproductive years, because they no longer want a husband or more children, but also because they are less sought after, bringing no economic advantages with them, unlike older Bambara women. Older Tamasheq women have more power to do what they want and are far less likely to submit to the passive role expected of a wife.

Conclusion

The comparison of these two populations, using intensive qualitative study in the light of population-level data, suggested three ways in which those data could be better understood by being dismantled and subjected to a 'micro' level inspection.

First, there was the evident fact that completely different patterns and explanations were revealed for two populations which are geographically so close that they would have been obscured in average levels derived from national or even regional analysis.

Second, in exploring the rationality of levels of fertility and of decisions and institutions related to them, it emerged that it was necessary to look at them separately at the level of the individuals and groups concerned, and at the structure of constraints and opportunities within which choices and strategies were determined. In both populations one could start by distinguishing between the interests and options of men and of women concerning fertility, to ask to what extent the female fertility levels were the outcome of male strategies of reproduction. For the Kel Tamasheq, the system of stratification into distinct social classes is the fundamental factor in the determination and maintenance of the fertility regime. Although women's marriage patterns are the same for the two main classes, the rationale is different in each case. For the Bambara, age is the basis of social hierarchy, and the key relationships for understanding how the fertility pattern worked are those between the individual and the group based on descent and marriage. In both cases fertility resulting from a particular pattern of marriage is not in itself the outcome of a strategy, but an aspect of the organized way in which society as a whole reproduces itself. The pastoral economy does not determine the Tamasheq fertility, with the population adapting itself to its environment in some unexplained way. Rather those conditions permit a particular social, political and economic structure to exist, and of this the marriage system and its resultant fertility patterns is a part. In the Bambara case too, what needs to be explained is not so much the correspondence of high fertility and high returns to labour as the social determinants of this particular example of a high fertility regime.

Finally, returning to the various possible micro-demographic approaches distinguished at the beginning, we would argue that the one adopted here does not represent anything methodologically new in demography itself, but is simply a *rapprochement* of demographic and anthropological techniques brought to bear on a set of problems. The next step in this kind of micro-demographic approach would involve moving inside the sketches of static general outlines which we have tried to draw here for comparative purposes, and using the same methods to explore processes of change in detail - household and group dynamics, the control of marriage and fertility as part of structures of inequality, and the demographic components of social and economic change.

Notes

1. The Tamasheq field research by Randall was supported by an award under the Population Council International Research Awards Program on the Determinants of Fertility. The Awards Program is supported by USAID funding to the Population Council. Other support was provided by a studentship from the Social Science Research Council. The International Livestock Centre for Africa commissioned and supported much of the demographic survey work on Bambara and Tamasheq. Research on Bambara society and economy was done by Fulton with Camilla Toulmin. It was part of the work of the socioeconomic section of the International Livestock Centre's Programme des Zones Arides et Semi-Arides in Mali. They were supported by the International Service of the United Nations Association.

2. The quantitative Bella data presented in this chapter include the small class of blacksmiths (total population = 254). Although distinct in terms of status we considered them to be most like the Bella.

3. Although theoretically slavery has been abolished in Mali, and practically they are no longer captured, bought or sold, many nobles and Bella still behave and speak in terms of the past *status quo* of owners and slaves.

Institutions and Inter-Generational Transfers

Transactional Analysis and the Measurement of Institutional Determinants of Fertility: A Comparison of Communities in Present-Day Bangladesh and Pre-Industrial England

R.M. Smith

Introduction

In the still limited literature concerning the 'institutional' determinants of demographic behaviour there has been some discussion of the differing forms of such behaviour associated with, on the one hand, societies in which institutions work to spread the effects of personal actions by individuals over politically constituted 'communities' and, on the other, those in which kinship, or patronage-clientage provides the mediating influence in the linkages between an individual and the wider society (McNicoll, 1980a; Potter, 1983; Smith, 1981). Investigation of these issues implies the need for the empirical testing of specified hypotheses at societal levels higher than those of the individual, household or family. Such research, as has been recently noted in the context of fertility analysis, concerns the 'empirical investigation of how social, economic, political, administrative and cultural structures create fertility incentives or disincentives and otherwise impinge on reproduction' (Population Council, 1981). This paper presents data, methods and some of the analytical and conceptual difficulties associated with research that concentrates upon 'local' institutional settings which might supply some of the 'mediation' between global and individual levels of analysis.

The focus of this paper is influenced, indeed largely determined, by the work that Mead Cain has recently undertaken on 'institutional determinants' of fertility in village-focused research in Bangladesh and India (Cain *et al.*, 1979; Cain, 1981, 1982, 1983b). My own research relates to village-focused economic and demographic analysis of certain pre-industrial English communities. Although our individual interests may seem to be poles apart within time and space, we have for the most part been dealing with societies linked by one common fundamental demographic characteristic. Both display 'natural fertility', for in neither situation is there much evidence to suggest significant amounts of parity-dependent fertility control. Nonetheless, total fertility levels in the two contexts are very different - a difference determined very largely by the age and incidence of marriage (Smith, 1980, 1983a; Poos and Smith, 1984). It is a consideration of the institutional forms that relate to certain of these differences which forms the focus of this chapter.

At this stage in my research I am, like Cain and McNicoll, inclined to accept a rather loose definition of institutions as 'rules that govern social interaction' (Cain, 1983a, p.18), or structures within which social and economic intercourse occur. For that reason communities considered as local, territorially-defined groupings are 'potentially' (never invariably) 'significant entities in influencing individual behaviour to the extent they are "institutionalized" and whose members share certain commonalities in exposure to a "local" environment' (McNicoll, 1983, p.7).

Cain, as he puts it, had 'used a variety of kinds of data' (with varying degrees of success) in trying to flesh out institutional structures in rural Bangladesh (and India) although to date his work has displayed a striking commitment to measuring what might be termed 'objective' institutional environments in which individuals find themselves rather than specifying the 'cognitive' environment from the point of view of the individual decision-maker (Cain, 1983a, pp.18-28). This measurement process is concerned therefore primarily with charting how things actually work, rather than with the local populace's perception of how they work, insofar as rules or customs may be ideals rather than actualities. Nevertheless in an optimal research situation one would hope to take account of both sides of this particular coin. For the demographic and family historian whose sole evidence is that of the documentary record, a one-dimensional approach is generally inevitable, if not wholly desirable. Nonetheless, for the field-based participant observer the apparent luxury of the perception of institutions from the actor's standpoint is not without manifold interpretational difficulties. Attention has already been drawn to the great difficulties stemming from the fact that individuals are often incapable of verbal depiction of these institutional structures which only become apparent to the observer with sufficient clarity through the observation of roles, for as Cain cogently writes 'a respondent will be very knowledgeable about roles he has played...much less familiar with those he has not played' (Cain, 1983a, p.18). Likewise, the institutional image gained from the participant's perception of the environment will most likely reflect modal behaviour rather than its variance, something the historical approach if undertaken over decades rather than months or years is more likely to unearth. As such, historical data will reveal much about institutional flexibility or the lack thereof in times of flux or in circumstances of great variability and uncertainty.

Some Issues in Studying Objective Environments of Risk

Cain (1981) has used information relating to transactions of various kinds and partners in these transactions as a measurement device in his attempts to identify the institutional structures that both determine and reflect so-called 'environments of risk' believed to have some bearing upon the perceived value of kin, and especially children, as a means of insuring against personal misfortune. Environments of risk therefore refer both to events whose origins are external to the society, for example, weather extremes, and those that are to a great extent socially determined, for example widowhood in societies where remarriage is proscribed, and which are capable of threatening normal consumption streams of families and individuals.

In two studies Cain (1981, 1982) has relied in part on the identification of so-called 'distress sales of land' which he defines as the 'sale of land for the purpose of satisfying basic consumption needs' (Cain, 1981, p.436) such as the purchase of food, to provide payments for medical treatment, and so forth, as a means of establishing *ad hoc* quantitative dimensions of the effectiveness of risk insurance. The plausible assumption made by Cain was that such sales in fundamentally agrarian societies can be interpreted as indicating a failure or absence of adequate insurance mechanisms, especially when they can be shown to expand rapidly during periods of political or climatic instability. The effectiveness of this argument is increased when Cain is able to show that such assumed vulnerability to risk in the Bangladesh village of Char Gopalpur is not evident in the land transactional evidence concerning two villages from Maharashtra and one from Andhra Pradesh. Cain was able to collect data on land transfers from a random sample of 114 households in Char Gopalpur for comparison with information from a sample of 119 households from the Indian communities. Data on current 'ownership' holdings were collected on the means of acquisition (for example, whether inherited or purchased), the date of acquisition, the partner in transaction, and the circumstances of the transaction. Additional data were collected on land to which title had been lost, either through sale or otherwise, between the times that the current head of household inherited land and the present (that is, the date of interview, 1976 in Char Gopalpur and 1980 in the Indian villages).

The evidence indicated that the frequency of land sales in the Bangladesh village had been highly responsive to natural and man-made disasters. Furthermore, a stratification of landholders into ownership categories showed that all 'classes' were vulnerable to distress sales. In fact, Cain estimates that of all land transactions that were recorded in the village, 80 per cent could be classified as distress sales for such purposes as purchasing food and medicine. Nonetheless after 1944 the frequency of sale transactions never exceeded that of purchases in the large owner category of landholders, while the 'medium' and 'small' categories have undertaken many more sales than purchases in the most recent two time periods.

In marked contrast, the Indian villages showed low frequency of sale transactions and a notable constancy in their numbers over time and no signs of the sharp peaks that characterize the experience of the sample households of Char Gopalpur. Furthermore, sales to meet the immediate costs of consumption and medical treatment accounted for only 18 per cent of all transactions and this was more characteristic of the largest land-owner category whose motives for such activities, Cain feels, are more appropriately to do with a form of conspicuous or status consumption. Cain is of course, impressed by this difference and provides interesting evidence and arguments to show why he believes a combination of more advantageous forms of credit and a far-sighted set of public relief and works programs in the Indian village of Maharashtra have done much to reduce the hazards of risk. He proceeds to suggest that it is more than a coincidence that Maharashtra has one of the lowest rates of fertility among all states in India; that in both Maharashtra and Andhra Pradesh fertility has fallen in recent years as the diffusion of risk has increased the relative cost of children, who now no longer provide a source of risk insurance. This is in sharp contrast to their role in rural Bangladesh, where one of the highest and most unyielding fertility rates in all of South Asia can be found.

Research into harvest-induced economic difficulties in pre-industrial England has tended to conclude that for a number of reasons, some of which will be considered here, the population, at least after the 1540s, was not subject to the traumas of famines and problems of food supply crises that have affected rural populations such as those of Bangladesh at periodic intervals (Appleby, 1979; Wrigley and Schofield, 1981; Schofield, 1983). There appears to be no consistent evidence of a positive relationship between grain price movements and mortality. There does, however, appear to have been an inverse relationship between grain prices and fertility which may in fact include the effect of foetal deaths (Schofield, 1983, p.283) whose occurrences as 'births forgone' is not detectable because of the nature of the data upon which this research is based, that is, parish registers relating to infant baptisms. It would be very difficult to obtain from the period after 1500 reasonably comprehensive evidence on land transactions for a defined group of farmers and smallholders in any one community, parallel to the data that Cain and his field assistants obtained in India and Bangladesh.

I have therefore been drawn to data that can be collected from the proceedings of English manorial courts for rural communities of the later thirteenth, fourteenth and fifteenth centuries. These data relate specifically either to customary tenants (serfs or villeins) who existed in a dependent relationship to a landlord, or to customary land, that is, land that carried with it rent (either in cash or kind) or labour service obligations to a landlord. The manorial court existed as a tribunal in which transfers, *post-mortem* and *inter-vivos*, of such customary land were recorded. In addition, they provided a forum for litigation surrounding the terms under which such land was held and the resolution of disputes relating to its tenurial status. In theory, the land was held conditionally and not in a fee-simple manner. However, in practice land could be transferred between partners as if it were 'alienation' in the sense of freehold tenure, provided that the transaction was done in public and the entry fines (cf. key money) paid by the new 'owner' or tenant were collected and recorded in the manorial tribunal. Clearly, given that charges were placed on such transactions, some evasions must have occurred, as witnessed by a scattering of cases in which manorial officials fine individuals or confiscate their land for failing to abide by the proper procedures. Nonetheless, the importance of the court as a forum in which rights and claims to land were settled and the frequency with which the written records (especially after 1250) were scrutinized as a basis for settling conflicting claims to land suggest that it was in the interests of landholders to have such transactions publicly displayed and properly entered in the curial record (Smith, 1983b).

The later thirteenth and early fourteenth centuries constitute an interesting period in which to observe the patterns formed by land transactions among the customary tenantry for we have very considerable evidence to suggest that at this point (as was the case throughout Europe) populations were precariously balanced in relation to agricultural resources and that the quality of harvests was highly sensitive to climatic variability (Duby, 1968). In the eastern counties of England we know that there existed a land market possibly more volatile than that which characterized the rural communities of Bangladesh (Smith, 1984a).

These are the features that characterize the manor of Coltishall in northeast Norfolk and that of Redgrave in extreme northeast Suffolk. The manor of Hakeford Hall in Coltishall, a township just 7 miles north of Norwich in the valley of the River Bure, was territorially small. Its demesne amounted to less than 111 acres and it is unlikely that there were more than 200 acres of land in the hands of the customary tenants. In the year 1348 the male tenants numbered 168 when the median holding size was only one acre (Smith, 1984a, p.96). In Redgrave, a much larger manor of 704 acres of demesne land and 1,317 acres of customary tenant land, in the year 1289 there were 347 tenants, 42.4 per cent of whom had holdings less than 2 acres in size (Smith, 1984a, p.143). In both communities holdings were small in size but quite intensively worked within the constraints of the climatic conditions of a Northwest European cool temperate climate. Both communities practised a system of partible inheritance in which land was inherited in equal amounts by all male offspring and in equal amounts by females in the absence of males. This custom had doubtlessly been a factor that had contributed to the fragmentation of property units. Although less anciently settled than some parts of England the cultivated area had by the time of our investigations long since reached its limit. In the Norfolk manor, although a feature not characteristic of the Suffolk community, output per acre had been raised by the adoption of extremely intensive methods of husbandry, which required massive labour inputs (Campbell, 1983). A considerable quantity of non-agricultural work was undertaken in such industries as saltmaking, textile manufacture and tanning that absorbed labour that was surplus to agriculture's needs. Redgrave's economic base was further diversified by the presence of a periodic market in which many of the local farmers had stalls and shops from which they sold basic foodstuffs such as bread and ale.

The records of the Coltishall manor court survive for 335 sessions for the period 1276–1405, although our focus will be on the period prior to the Black Death, 1349. Although court sessions exist for Redgrave from the middle of the thirteenth until the twentieth century our analysis will be restricted to the courts surviving for the period 1260 to 1320. In both these data sources the transacting of land looms large and these transactions suggest that as much, frequently more, land was redistributed by *inter-vivos* means than by inheritance. Acknowledging that court records which would most likely change the absolute totals deriving from this study have gone astray, it appears that between 1260 and 1348 land devolving by inheritance accounted for just over 13 per cent of the transactions and a little over 50 per cent of the area of customary land transferred in Coltishall (Smith, 1984a, p.125). Quite evidently *inter-vivos* transfers concerned very small parcels or slivers of land, often less than half an acre in area. Yet it is to be expected in an area with the majority of customary holdings containing no more than 2 acres that transactions would involve parcels of small size. Nonetheless in the quarter century before the plague struck this community, far more land was transferred by *pre-mortem* than by *post-mortem* exchanges.

In the adjacent county in the manor of Redgrave between 1295 and 1319 only 171 out of 1,979 transactions (8.7 per cent) recorded in the manor court proceedings concerned inheritances (Smith, 1984b, p.157). However, as with Coltishall, the size of properties devolved through inheritance was considerably larger than those transferred by *inter-vivos* exchange. Between 1305 and 1319, when court roll evidence is very complete, both in the quantity of courts surviving and as to the aerial measurements of properties recorded, it appears that 42 per cent of tenant land was redistributed subsequent to deaths. *Pre-mortem* transfers in both these East Anglian communities were therefore very important, both in their absolute quantity and in the total area of land involved.

In Coltishall between 1260 and 1348 at least 787 acres of land exchanged hands - a minimum figure as not all the *pre-mortem* transactions have left a record of the plot size. This represents a very high land turnover rate as there were only 200 acres of customary land 'at risk' to be transferred. In Redgrave, 1,756 *inter-vivos* transfers of customary land between 1260 and 1319 totalled 1,304.75 acres, a figure which must be seen in relation to the total customary land of 1,317.5 acres on the manor. This figure also represents a minimum sum, as 652 transfers were without their dimensions in the court records.

The high level of land exchange did not in either community remain at a constant pitch throughout the periods under examination

Table 13.1 Coltishall, Norfolk: Correlation Coefficients of Number of Land Transactions per Court against the Norwich Average Annual Price of Barley

Period	Actual yearly values	Actual yearly values with a 12 month lag	3 year moving average	3 year moving average with a 12 month lag	5 year moving average	5 year moving average with a 12 month lag
1287-1300	0.5653	0.6014	0.7563	0.6221	0.8969	0.8039
1301-1312	-0.2514	0.0940	-0.5211	-0.4569	-0.0491	-0.1396
1313-1332	0.0365	0.5908	0.3298	0.7278	0.1282	0.5708
1333-1342	-0.6108	-0.1277	-0.6258	-0.2545	-0.8133	-0.5633
1343-1352	0.0763	-0.4227	-0.2980	-0.5646	-0.4999	-0.6716

but waxed and waned in a noteworthy fashion. Indeed in Coltishall the market in land was characterized by a succession of short-term fluctuations in the turnover of land; until the middle of the fourteenth century there was a strong correlation (mostly positive but at times negative) between the number of land transactions and the price of grain (and by implication therefore, the quality of the harvest) (see Table 13.1). The Coltishall land market was clearly 'harvest-sensitive'. As evidenced by the grain price information from the Norwich market the period between 1280 and 1320 was one of steady inflation followed by a period stretching to 1348 of mild deflation. Superimposed upon this general trend were a number of short-term fluctuations, the result of exceptionally good or bad harvests: 1293-4, 1314, 1321-2, 1346-7, were dear years, and 1287-8, 1299-1300, 1312, 1318, 1326, and 1334-41 were cheap.

Of these periods of dearth and glut, worst on the criterion of price change were the 'famine' years of 1314-17; the best were those of 1334-41 (see Figures 13.1 and 13.2). It was these two periods which apparently elicited the greatest response from the land market. During the Great Famine there was a threefold increase in the number of land transactions recorded in Coltishall's court rolls.

A remarkably similar pattern in the relationship between Norwich grain prices and land transactions is to be found in the Suffolk community of Redgrave in the period up to 1319 where the

Figure 13.1 Land Transactions and Barley Prices: Coltishall 1280-1348

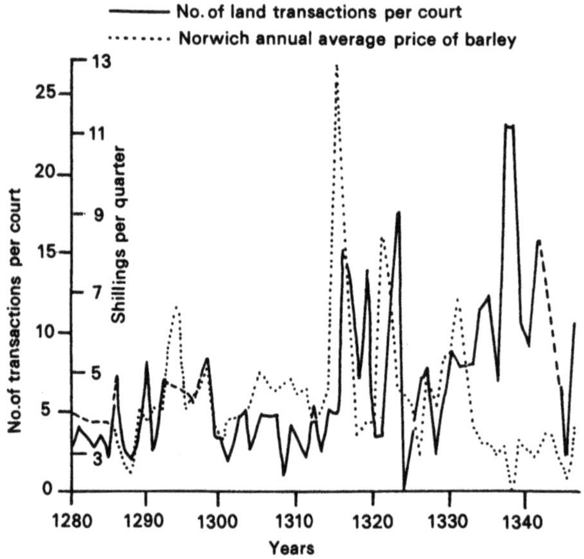

Figure 13.2 Land Transactions and Barley Prices (5-yr moving averages): Coltishall 1280-1348

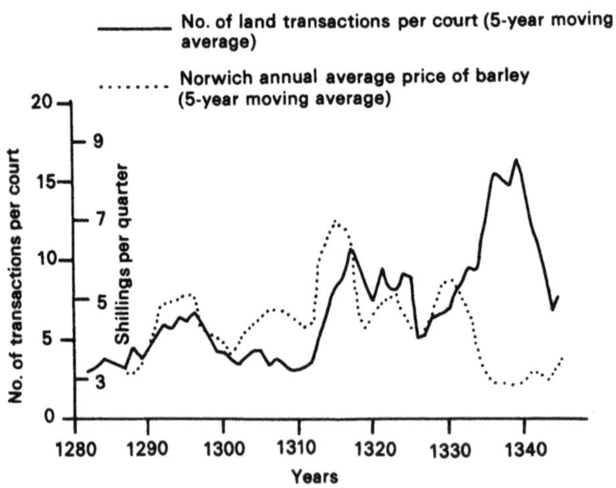

Figure 13.3 Land Transactions and Barley Prices: Redgrave 1260-1319

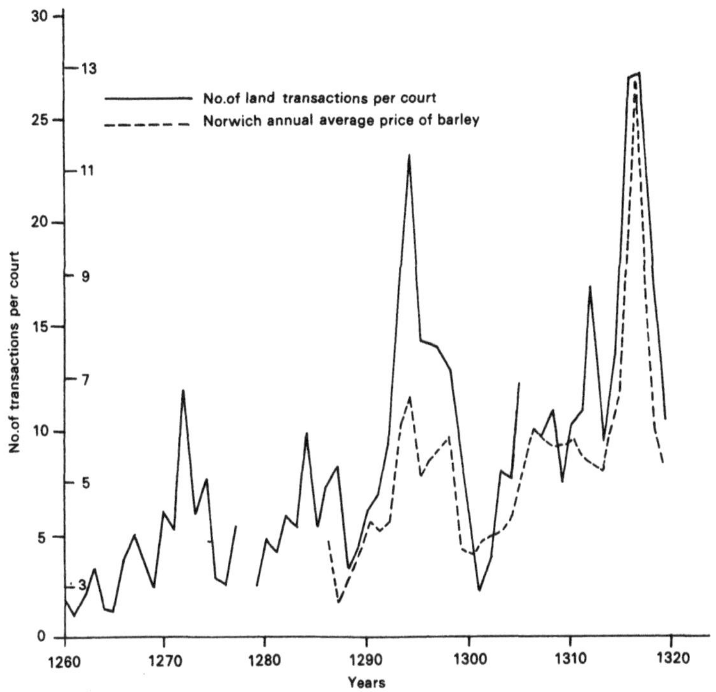

evidence suggests that inadequate harvests were associated with considerable surges in both the quantities of land sold and the number of sales (see Figure 13.3). The years including and immediately following the harvest difficulties of 1272 seem to have witnessed considerable increases in the quantity of transactions, as did the year 1277 and the year following the poor harvest of 1283. The 1290s as a whole reflect the almost ever-present economic difficulties, with 54 surviving court sessions recording 571 transactions, compared with the 455 transactions registered in the 78 courts of the 1280s. A burst of activity is also to be found in the early years of the second decade of the fourteenth century, after the poor harvests of 1311, and the infamously bad spell of years stretching from 1314 to 1317 saw a two to threefold increase in land transactions.

In both Coltishall and Redgrave the relationship between grain prices and land transactions is most clearly manifest during the closing decades of the thirteenth century: abundant harvests and low prices of 1287-8 and 1299-1301 encapsulated a period of high prices and mounting rural crisis during which harvest failures

Figure 13.4 Ratio of Buyers to Sellers (5-yr moving averages) and Barley Prices: Coltishall 1280–1348

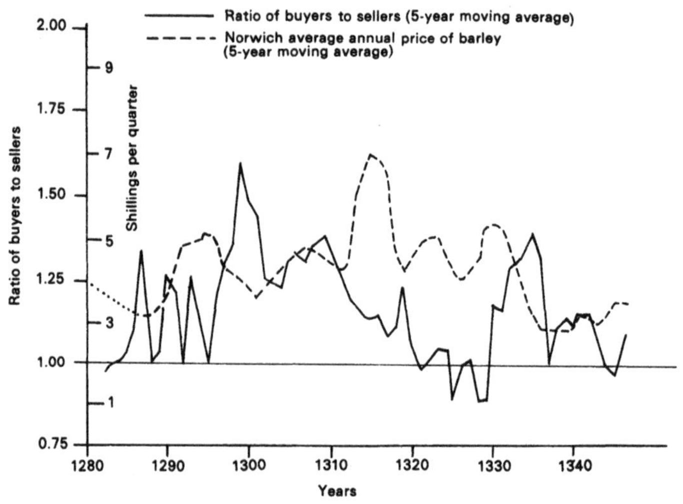

Figure 13.5 Ratio of Land Buyers to Sellers (25-yr moving averages) and Barley Prices: Coltishall 1280–1319

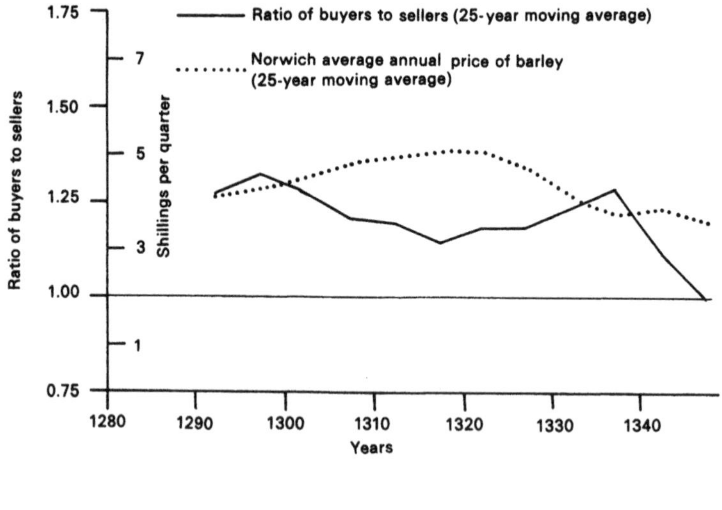

Figure 13.6 Ratio of Land Buyers to Sellers and Barley Prices: Redgrave 1260–1319

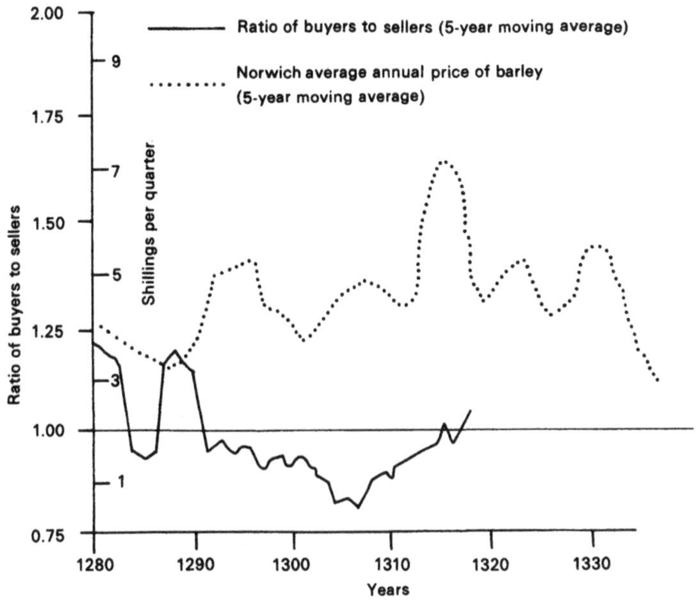

thrice (in 1293, 1294 and 1297) narrowly approached famine proportions. In Coltishall this period shows there was a consistently high positive correlation, higher than any other period, between the price of grain and the number of land transactions.

There were nonetheless some differences between the communities: the rural society of Coltishall has the appearance of showing a greater resilience in the face of harvest deficiencies than did that of Redgrave. For instance, in Coltishall there was an immediacy with which the supply of land contracted as soon as the bad harvests of the 1290s had passed; this is indicated in the sudden improvement in the ratio of buyers to sellers at the turn of the century as individuals apparently endeavoured to make good their losses and to protect themselves from renewed harvest failure (see Figures 13.4 and 13.5). In Redgrave, although there was a noteworthy improvement in the ratio of buyers to sellers after the dramatic drop in that ratio during and subsequent to the harvest failure of 1283, no such recovery characterized the years after the 1290s (see Figure 13.6) (however the 25 years running average reflects a not dissimilar long-term deterioration in that ratio to 1320 at Coltishall). In Redgrave an excess of sellers over buyers is to be found for almost every year from 1290 to 1317 whereas in the preceding 3 decades only 5 years had been so fated. Of course, a valid comparison is currently thwarted by the absence of a detailed analysis of the Redgrave land market for the period after 1320.

What is evident in Coltishall is that after the extraordinary run of adverse years that characterized the earlier period, the years from 1334 marked a succession of unusually good harvests during which the activity of the land market was transformed. During this period for the first time in at least half a century a strong inverse relationship existed between the price of grain and the number of land transactions (see Table 13.1). At the same time there was a marked improvement in the ratio of buyers to sellers (see Figures 13.4 and 13.5). It seems evident that bountiful harvests had at long last presented the peasantry with an opportunity to make good some of the losses they had sustained during the preceding decades.

It would seem therefore that while there was a striking propensity to part with land in these communities during periods of economic hardship there is a notable indication of recovery during periods of improved economic well-being. Such evidence suggests the presence of a strongly evident 'upside' counterpart to catastrophes, or at least more symmetry in the processes of gain and loss than can be discerned in Char Gopalpur (Cain, 1981, p.457). Nonetheless, it cannot be denied that we have some indications of 'distress sales' with many representing foreclosures on mortgages (Smith, 1983, p.118), and, in the case of Redgrave responsible for a relatively short-lived phase in an increasingly socially differentiated tenant population (Smith, 1984b, pp.165-9).

Even allowing for the indications of recovery, at least for the longer term, in the wake of environmentally-induced disasters, it would still seem that there are notable similarities between the Asian and Northwestern European societies insofar as the sale of land might be thought a desperate act to remedy liquidity problems in the short term rather than resort to capital markets as a means of evening out consumption streams in periods of adversity. Superficially, further support for this view might be gained if other features of the Suffolk village are compared with those from Char Gopalpur.

Extended Family Networks and Risk Insurance

Cain suggested that in the absence of effective institutional means of minimizing risk the extended family might be expected to provide an alternative context of support (Cain, 1982, p.172). He rightly notes that there is no reason why a high incidence of distress sales of land will not occur even though the family purports to perform this role of an insurance network. Such sales are especially likely, Cain argues, if the impact of an economic hardship such as harvest failure acts upon all co-insurers simultaneously, or if destitution is widespread across the whole kin group. He would not, however, expect to find a large number of such transactions taking place between close kin and especially brothers if the fraternal joint family or agnatic relationships between males were of great functional significance in an individual's personal welfare. As Cain notes, 'a brother with enough cash to purchase land is also in a position to lend his brother the same amount or give it to him outright if he so chooses' (Cain, 1982, p.172).

On finding that 40 per cent of transactions undertaken by the sample households in Char Gopalpur were between close kin (18 per cent with brothers and 22 per cent with father's brothers or father's brother's sons), Cain concluded that the extended family functioned inadequately as a source of insurance for its members. Of course, the basis of this interpretation is Cain's assumption that the 'true measure of a kinship network's effectiveness as a source of insurance is its success in preventing loss among members' (Cain, 1982, p.173) and its capacity to prevent economic differentiation within sibling groups (especially in circumstances where all males retained equal shares in their inheritance of the patrimonial estate).

If all kin categories are considered it would appear that a clear minority of land transfers (42 per cent) in Char Gopalpur involved parties who were unrelated through blood or marriage (Cain, 1982, p.172). A striking feature of the medieval East Anglian evidence concerns the high proportion of *inter-vivos* transactions in Coltishall and Redgrave between unrelated parties. Only one-third of *inter-vivos* transactions in Coltishall concerned related persons (Smith, 1984a, p.121); and in Redgrave only 20 per cent of the transactions involved kin. In fact, in the latter community kin dealings in land accounted for only 15 per cent of the volume transacted between living persons in the period 1305-19 (Smith, 1984a, p.157). These figures must nonetheless be seen as representing minimum values because of our inability to identify with greater accuracy possible affines who may have been related through marriage that are absent from the court proceedings. Although of limited significance for its influence upon the overall incidence of transactions between kin, the category '? Relation' in Table 13.2 accounts for 20 per cent of all such transactions. These are presumed relationships in so far as the transactions concern persons (principally males) bearing the same surname. Some of the latter in fact, were most likely unrelated. Others, however, may have been agnates - a factor that should be borne in mind in the following discussion.

The data in Table 13.2 are notable in identifying the predominance of lateral transfers between siblings (both male and female) over any other kin relationship in the matter of *inter-vivos* transactions between kin. In fact, if we include transfers between uncles, aunts, nephews and nieces, the lateral component accounts for almost 43 per cent and parent-to-child transfers for only 34 per cent of the intra-familial exchanges. However, the average value disguises notable volatility in the data and certainly does not expose the great growth in later transfers, especially between brothers during the decades that we have

Table 13.2 Types of Intra-Familial Dealings in Property, Redgrave 1260–1319

	1260–69		1270–79		1280–89		1290–99		1300–09		1310–19		Total	
Intra-familial land transfers	No.	%	No.	%	No.	%	No.	%	No.	%	No.	%	No.	%
Vertical Parent to child	15	71.4	36	48.0	30	35.7	38	33.6	42	48.8	23	13.7	184	33.6
Vertical Child to parent			1	1.3			2	1.8	2	2.3	2	1.2	7	1.3
Lateral Brother to brother	2	9.5	16	21.3	19	22.6	37	32.7	16	18.6	78	46.4	168	30.7
Sister to sister	1	4.8	6	7.8	13	15.5	6	5.3	5	5.8	5	2.9	36	6.6
Lateral Husband to wife Wife to husband			3	3.9			7	6.2	1	1.2	1	0.6	12	2.2
Vertical*/Lateral			1	1.3	2	2.4	5	4.5	4	4.7	16	9.5	28	5.1
Vertical/Lateral (Young to old)			1	1.3							1	0.6	2	0.4
? Relation	3	14.3	11	15.1	20	23.8	18	15.9	16	18.6	42	25.1	110	20.1
Total (A)	21		75		84		113		86		168		547	
All land transfers Total (B)	164		348		455		571		368		850		2,756	
A/B %	12.8		21.6		18.5		19.8		23.4		19.8		19.8	

Note: * Uncles to nephews and nieces
Aunts to nephews and nieces

earlier identified as producing large quantities of distress sales of land, that is 1290-99 and 1310-19. During this period, more than 40 per cent and sometimes over 50 per cent of *inter-vivos* transfers between family members concerned male siblings as both parties, even though intra-familial transfers did not increase their share in the overall hyperactive land market.

The equating of the patterns exhibited by lateral kin in medieval Redgrave with those of Char Gopalpur should be done with caution, for the intra-sibling group component in the land market involving all *inter-vivos* transfers was only a little over 6 per cent in the East Anglian community. Although it rose to almost 9 per cent of all *inter-vivos* exchanges in the decade 1310-19, which included the disasterous famine years of 1315-17, the proportional significance of such kin-based transfers was five times greater in Char Gopalpur. We should note, furthermore, that Cain undertook his analysis of land transactional patterns in Char Gopalpur as a means of testing Caldwell's conception of the family as a unit embodying a set of 'mutual obligations' (Caldwell, 1976, p.329), and in particular the view that in extended family systems a man's orientation is towards the larger group rather than the immediate nuclear family (Caldwell, 1978). In this context a man's economic and emotional commitment, it is assumed, would be greater to brothers and uncles than to children and wives, precluding therefore heavy emotional investment in offspring and encouraging a flow of wealth from children to parents. Essentially, the argument is that high fertility would be sustained by kinship relations that diffused both the costs of child rearing and the economic gains of children's work and welfare activities widely over the kin group.

Cain would argue that these Caldwellian theories need very careful empirical specification and testing in so far as it is important to distinguish between immediate lateral kin (brothers, cousins, uncles) and immediate lineal kin (father, son and perhaps grandson). Cain treats the relationship an individual might have with his kin categories in 'mutually exclusive' terms - 'the weaker the lateral bonds of obligation and economic co-operation, the more an individual must depend upon lineal kin', and ventures the hypothesis that '*ceteris paribus* the greater the reliability of extended and lateral kin networks, the less important children will be as a source of insurance...' (Cain, 1982, p.173). What seem to be highly convincing arguments are proposed by Cain to support his hypothesis when he presents contrasting patterns between the Bangladesh village and the Indian villages in Maharashtra and Andhra Pradesh. Almost two-thirds of the brothers in the Indian villages persisted in joint production for long periods after their father's death, with a median period of such continuation of 10 years. This was in sharp contrast to the great rarity, indeed almost total absence, of such practices in Bangladesh. Cain is uncertain of an explanation for these differences but implies that the effect is to permit a greater diffusion of risk in the Indian setting (Cain, 1982, p.174).

As in discussions of land transactions patterns over time and between kin, it might be supposed that the evidence on male sibling behaviour in medieval East Anglia is very close to that exhibited by fraternal groups in Char Gopalpur. Like brothers in rural Bangladesh, males in Redgrave shared their inheritance equally - a factor highly influential in producing a distinctive tenurial pattern. For instance, a survey of tenant holdings drawn up in 1289 shows that there were fifty male sibling sets (identifiable either through stated relationships or from further evidence provided in the contemporary manorial court proceedings) containing in all 116 individuals who constituted approximately one-third of the 345 male tenants. Of the fifty male sibling sets, thirty-three (accounting for seventy-seven individuals) held land jointly, accounting for approximately 20 per cent of the total tenant land area, and by definition in equal amounts, in the same *tenementum*. These latter were tenurial units to which rents and services for the manorial demesne farms were generally affixed rather than to individual holdings. The majority of tenants (marginally under 60 per cent) held all of their land within one *tenementum*, 34 per cent held their parcels in two to five *tenementa* and 6 per cent held this land in six or more units. In fact, the co-parceners within each tenemental unit had certain collective responsibilities as the failure of these groups to fulfil their obligations is reflected in amercements in the court rolls of groups of co-parceners in omitting to pay rents or to perform labour services attached to particular holdings.

To this area of land we would need to add that made up of other holdings described in the survey as in the possession of the 'heirs of A or B' and a further 215 acres which siblings held individually, but in common *tenementa*. These categories of land would *in toto* produce an area that might well be interpreted as an absolute maximum proportion of the customary land held by the laterally extended family, as detected through sibling relationships. The maximum proportion of the land so held was somewhere between 24 and 40 per cent. However, only five sibling groups displayed absolute equality of amount in each *tenementum*. For example, the sons of Richard Mercator appear as joint holders of their father's land scattered over Redgrave village (see Table 13.3). More typical were the sibling sets in which siblings held land in unequal amounts in the *tenementa* such as Robert, Adam and Walter Wulstan. It is significant that only five (10 per cent) of the sibling groups who held land in one *tenementum* displayed absolute equality in the area of their holdings and that in four of these five cases the inheritance had taken place in the 5 years prior to the survey's construction in 1289 - a fact that might help to explain why such symmetry was maintained undisturbed by disruptive forces during this short interval. We should note too, that as a whole the holdings of the 116 members of the fifty identifiable sibling groups possessed a size distribution that differed significantly from that relating to the remainder of the tenant population. Only 13 per cent of the siblings had individual shares that were under 2 acres in size, compared with 44 per cent in such a size class for the whole tenant population

Table 13.3 The Holdings (in rods) of Radulphus and Walter Mercator in the Manor of Redgrave 1289

	Radulphus Mercator	Walter Mercator
Tenementum (name of former co-holder)		
Hubert son of Hugh	5½	5½
Walter of Smalebusc	2½	2½
Robert Goldwyne	1	1
Wydon Skyl	½	½
Peter Kypping	2½	2½
Simon Pikerel	2	2
John Wodecock	½	½
Folcard de Stigulo	1	1
Robert son of Agnes	4	4
Sickle Olon	1	1
Eustace Blome	½	½
William Sket	4½	4½
Matilda Spore	3½	3½
Total	29 rods = 7 ac. 1 rod	29 rods = 7 ac. 1 rod

The Holdings (in rods) of Walter Wulstan, Robert Wulstan and Adam Wulstan in the Manor of Redgrave 1289

	Walter Wulstan	Robert Wulstan	Adam Wulstan
Tenementum (name of former co-holder)			
Sickle Olon	2	–	–
Eustace Blome	2	–	–
Hubert son of Wulstan	16	16	16
Beatrix Burs	–	11	1
Warin Gossyng	–	4	4
William Sket	4	–	2
Alfrich Buntyng	6	–	–
William Ketel	3	–	–
Matilda Spore	1	–	–
Total	34 rods = 8 ac. 2 rods	31 rods = 7 ac. 3 rods	23 rods = 5 ac. 3 rods

Table 13.4 The Distribution of Holding Sizes: Redgrave 1289

	Sizes (acres)						
	< 2	2-6	6¼-10	10¼-14	14¼-18	18	Total
Customary tenants (land in one sub-region only)	133	87	17	7	4	2	250
Customary tenants (land in more than one sub-region)	6	18	17	7	1	1	50
Customary tenants (with minority of free land)	4	9	8	1	1	3	26
Sub-Total	143	114	42	15	6	6	326
Free tenants (with minority of customary land)	4	7	3	3	-	4	21
Free tenants	30	13	3	2	2	4	54
Sub-Total	34	20	6	5	2	8	75
Grand Total (Percentages)	177 (44.1)	134 (33.4)	48 (11.9)	20 (5.0)	8 (2.0)	14 (3.6)	401 (100)

Holding Sizes of Individuals in Male Sibling Groups; Redgrave 1289

Acres	< 2	2-6	6¼-10	10¼-14	14¼-18	18
Number	15	70	17	10	2	2
Per cent	13.0	60.3	14.7	0.6	1.7	1.7

(see Table 13.4). Does this pattern suggest that joint tenure may have been a means by which individuals were able to resist the processes that had led to or were leading to the fragmentation of properties in the remaining population? Indeed had the laterally extended family shown itself successful in fending off the erosive influences through its capacity in Cain's words 'to permit a greater diffusion of risk' (Cain, 1982, p.174) in an inherently high risk economic environment?

To investigate this proposition requires us to consider the relationship between the inheritance practices and *inter-vivos* transfers in more detail. We are obligated to review the evidence bearing upon the degree to which the siblings prior to, at and after inheritance displayed a marked tendency to act together in 'jointly' owned and operated enterprises. Of the fifty sibling groups identified on the 1289 survey and traced in the subsequent 30 years only thirteen showed an overall gain in their land resources, whereas twenty-seven saw their patrimonial holding shrink. Indeed, even among five of these groups that gained, one or more of the siblings suffered a personal deficit in his transactions. This pattern appears to mirror that presented in a different set of evidence of forty-one sets of sons who are identifiable in the manorial court proceedings between 1260 and 1289 as having inherited partible holdings. Of these forty-one sets of sons thirty-three are known to have included at least one sibling who transacted land with persons outside the immediate family. Twenty-five of these sets were in absolute deficit with respect to their dealings, seven in surplus and only one with no gains or losses. These thirty-three sets contained 104 individuals, fifty-two of whom were individually in net deficit in their extra-familial dealings, nineteen in surplus and thirty-three showing no evidence whatsoever of entering the land market.

Clearly it would seem that there were more sons subsequent to inheriting property who could be seen to sell land to persons outside their families than there were sons who proceeded to acquire land, behaviour inevitably leading to fragmentation of family holdings and a reduction over time in the holding size of co-heirs; such processes help to explain the discrepancy we noted earlier between the holding sizes of sibling groups as identified in the 1289 survey and those of the remainder of the tenantry.

Furthermore, fathers with sons and daughters as potential heirs or heiresses, especially among the precariously situated tenants in the lowest quartile of landholders, frequently sold land outside the confines of their immediate family, sometimes while making no *pre-mortem* provision for their offspring or doing so inadequately in combination with, or as a consequence of, their extra-familial sales. The two brothers John and Walter Moyse appear in 1289 sharing a holding of 6 acres. They apparently proceeded to divide most of their inheritance, selling off approximately half of it to persons outside their family. When John died in 1318 his son, Eustace, received marginally over half an acre as his inheritance. Walter, although marrying in 1276, may

Table 13.5 *Post-Mortem* Family Transfers, Redgrave 1295-1319

Date	Father-son(s)	Lateral siblings	Other familial	Total
	%	%	%	
1295-99	14 (50.0)	7 (25.0)	5 (17.9)	26 (2)
1300-04	9 (40.9)	5 (22.7)	7 (31.8)	21 (1)
1305-09	14 (58.3)	8 (33.3)	1 (4.2)	23 (1)
1310-14	17 (48.5)	11 (31.4)	5 (14.3)	33 (2)
1315-19	31 (49.2)	11 (17.5)	10 (15.9)	52 (11)
1295-1319	85 (49.4)	42 (24.4)	28 (16.3)	155 (17)

have been widowed without surviving offspring, for in the years before his brother's death he passed the residue of his holding (which had also been eroded after 1289 by sales) to Matilda, daughter of Simon Hicche, with reversion to him for the remainder of his life.

Internal adjustments of property within the sibling group have left another distinctive pattern of behaviour in the manor court proceedings. In fact, among twenty-nine of the fifty sibling groups identifiable in a survey drawn up of the manor in 1289, there is clear evidence of these adjustments taking place in one or a combination of two ways: by an *inter-vivos* sale of his or their portion of the holding, by one or more brothers to another brother; by a *post-mortem* transfer involving a brother dying without direct heirs and his holding consequently reverting to the remaining brother or brothers.

In 1297 William Walter, who in 1289 held part of a messuage and 7.75 acres, died and his land was inherited by his sons, William, John and Eustace. Eustace appears to have been the oldest of the siblings, holding 1.5 acres himself, which had evidently been obtained with his father's assistance, judging from the pledging support he gave his son. Although he sold three-quarters of an acre in the courts in the second decade of the fourteenth century, he managed to increase his holding size overall. Likewise, his brother John (apart from the sale or gift of half an acre to his sister Matilda), acquired almost 1.5 acres from extra-familial purchases. However, John also purchased an acre of land from his brother William who died in 1317, holding only one cottage and three rods, having sold a quarter of an acre to persons outside the family. Since William had no heirs, apparently dying a bachelor, his property was shared by his brothers, Eustace and

Table 13.6 Group Participants in Redgrave Land Market, 1260–1319

	Buyers						Sellers						Total	
Group type	All (N)	Column %	Row %	Intra-familial (N)	Column %	Row %	All (N)	Column %	Row %	Intra-familial (N)	Column %	Row %	N	%
Siblings (male)	47	17.1	29.0	13	25.0	34.2	115	28.4	71.0	25	43.9	65.8	162	23.8
Siblings (female)	40	14.5	59.7	21	40.3	63.6	27	6.7	40.3	11	19.3	26.4	67	9.9
Siblings (mixed)	4	1.5	66.7	-	-	-	2	0.4	33.3	-	-	-	6	0.8
Father and child(ren)	23	8.4	71.9	5	9.6	100.0	9	2.2	28.1	-	-	-	32	4.7
Mother and child(ren)	31	11.2	72.1	3	5.8	74.0	12	2.4	27.9	1	1.8	26.0	43	6.3
Parents and child(ren)	4	1.5	100.0	-	-	-	-	-	-	-	-	-	4	0.7
Husband and wife	105	38.2	31.4	10	19.3	33.3	229	57.7	68.6	20	35.0	66.7	334	49.1
Other kin	17	6.1	63.0	-	-	-	10	2.0	37.0	-	-	-	27	4.0
Others unrelated	4	1.5	80.0	-	-	-	1	0.2	20.0	-	-	-	5	0.7
Total	275	100.0	40.4	52	100.0	47.7	405	100.0	59.6	57	100.0	52.3	680	100.0

John. In Redgrave between 1295 and 1319 approximately one in four deaths involved inheritances by brothers from celibate or childless siblings (see Table 13.5). In fact, father-son inheritances involved slightly fewer than one in two deaths. The implications of these inheritance patterns for marital incidence within possibly inheriting male sibling groups appear to have been quite considerable.

We have little reason to believe that laterally extended kin-groups provided an efficient means of protecting their members against the threat of property loss in Redgrave. All the evidence we have considered suggests that the net effect of the inheritance system in conjunction with an intensive *inter-vivos* system of land exchange was to insure the fragmentation of holdings in ways that produced a degree of economic differentiation within sibling groups. The transfer of property via inheritance remained of subordinate importance to *inter-vivos* transactions that were clearly sensitive, in their frequency, to harvest-determined economic conditions.

Indeed if the laterally-bonded joint family was functionally highly significant in Redgrave one would expect to detect evidence of it in action, perhaps as it added to the collectively managed patrimonial estate. The 2,756 *inter-vivos* transactions of which the record has survived in the court rolls involved 6,115 'parties'. Of these parties 680 involved 'groups', the composition of which is set out in Table 13.6. It is clearly evident from these data that group participants were much more likely to have been selling or disposing of land than accumulating it - a characteristic that is most marked among male sibling groups than any other type. Furthermore the group-type most frequently found, whether as buyer or seller, was the conjugal pair (which accounts for one half of the recorded instances) and not the group founded upon the sibling bond. This latter feature is significant as in many 'classic' joint-family systems the husband-wife relationship most certainly takes a subordinate position relative to those kin relationships that link the males related by blood.

In the discussion so far we have given considerable emphasis to the laterally extended kin group as an economic unit and little has been said of its social and political functions. The nature of the data prohibits a wider ranging treatment of this matter although what evidence survives in the manorial court proceedings is highly suggestive.

We know that partible inheritance had the effect of increasing the residential and tenurial propinquity of male heirs, at least for a particular phase in their life cycle. Considerable residential adjustment was made in the internal arrangements of the patrimonial household. For instance, 38 per cent of all dealings in residential property involved kin as both parties - a much higher figure than for all other classes of property. Tenurial propinquity was also very high for male siblings. The 116 brothers (the fifty sibling groups) held 538 acres of land of which 518 (90 per cent) were located within a single sub-region of the manor. The comparable proportion for the remaining tenants as a whole was only 71 per cent.

It was also possible to consider sixty-five sibling groups who had a total of 1,359 recorded contacts with those outside their kin group between 1260 and 1293. For example, Simon, Henry and Hugh Seward in 1289 held land in three *tenementa*: of their ninety-nine recorded relationships in the court proceedings, fifty-three were with fellow co-parceners. In fact, at least two of the three brothers were involved with sixteen of the thirty-six persons with whom they came into contact as a group. Most of the reciprocal sureties (pledges) were undertaken with the families of Walter Thede, Geoffrey Goding, Ademyn Sutor and the Redings, who were also their co-parceners. The brothers also show signs of joint litigational activities in court. For example, Simon and Henry were jointly involved in selling a small outbuilding to John de Bosco in 1275 and together acted as surety for their brother Hugh. In the same year Simon and Hugh settled a land dispute out of court in exchange for a rod of land, although there are no instances of their purchasing land together. Being jointly fined was not a rare experience for these siblings: in 1275 Simon and Henry were fined for failing to fulfil their responsibilities as sureties to Robert de Bosco and with their co-parcener, Walter Thede, were fined for damage to part of the *tenementum* formerly under the charge of Ademyn Sutor. In 1271 Henry and Hugh had been jointly amerced for illegally raising the hue and cry against Geoffrey Goding, whose wife Henry later assaulted, as did Hugh's son in 1276, the same year his father was fined for trespass in Geoffrey Goding's corn. It cannot be stressed too greatly that these patterns of close sibling contact were for the most part only characteristic of the period following their inheritance of the patrimony. In most such cases we observe the sibling group, in union with a widowed mother, pressing claims for, or defending claims against them, to disputed property, frequently following their father's death, or fined for failing to perform services owed to the manorial demesne. Of the sixty-five sibling groups, twenty-seven were jointly fined and of these twenty-one (78 per cent) received their amercements within 10 years of the inheritance.

We may indeed in these activities be observing patterns highly specific to a particular phase of the sibling group's life cycle, for these years were as likely to display inter-sibling strife as support. Between 1260 and 1293 we have evidence of 141 individuals from fifty-two families appearing in court as litigants in disputes with other family members (see Table 13.7). Highly significant is the evidence bearing upon the principal category of kin relationship that gave rise to intra-familial discord. Over 57 per cent of recorded disputes were between brothers. Of the sixty-five sibling groups to which we have already referred, thirty-six showed signs of conflict on at least one occasion, although these were in thirty-two cases confined to the decade following entry into their inheritances.

Table 13.7 The Kin Relationship of Litigants in Intra-Familial Disputes, Redgrave 1260–1293

Kin Relationship	Number	%
Brother/Brother	80	57.2
Father/Son	15	10.7
Mother/Son	11	7.9
Brother/Sister	8	5.8
Brother/Sister-in-law	8	5.7
Sister/Sister	3	2.1
Father/Son-in-law	5	3.6
Brother/Brother-in-law	3	2.1
Cousin/Cousin	3	2.1
Uncle/Nephew	2	1.4
Father/Daughter	1	0.7
Husband/Wife	1	0.7
Total	140	100.0

For example, Walter Oligrant appeared in court in 1269 to inform an inquisition jury by what authority he had entered into the holding of his brother Ralph (an action perhaps induced by Ralph's failure to fulfil services owed by the holdings over the previous 2 years). In a later court that same year Ralph charged that on two occasions Walter had entered his house (implying separate residences for the two brothers), beaten him with a stave and in so doing had drawn blood. The jury found Walter guilty, fining him heavily and forcing him to pay Ralph damages of 40 shillings. However, as was so characteristic of the events involving siblings, subsequent to their father's death Ralph sold out his share in the original holding to Walter and may have left the community, for we find no further references to him in the records.

We have identified both in the previous and the current section of this paper some noteworthy comparisons that can be made between certain transactional patterns susceptible to measurement in the rural communities of medieval East Anglia and present-day Bangladesh in behaviour associated with property by peasant families in periods of economic and social instability. In particular we have noted the apparent willingness with which individuals in both societies sold land as an expedient in the securing of basic needs during periods in which basic consumption streams were severely disturbed. We find furthermore, considerable evidence to suggest that in neither society did the laterally extended family provide a very effective means of reducing an individual's vulnerability to the risks of property loss. For unlike the Indian villages that Cain has studied, in Redgrave and Char Gopalpur it would be hard to argue that the divisions and readjustments that took place in the internal disposition of patrimonial land were necessarily associated with the acquisition of full adult status on the part of each of the male siblings. The acts of division through both intra- and extra-familial alienations of property were linked with movement of the majority of the siblings into the ranks of the landless or the near-landless, rather than to a position heading a freshly created labour farm.

I am reluctant, however, to pursue or press these similarities much further because there were also certain differences that need careful specification. Firstly, we noted that in the medium to longer-term evidence, especially that relating to the Norfolk manor Coltishall, that there was, during periods of good harvest conditions, a strongly evident 'upside' counterpart to catastrophes or at least more symmetry in the processes of gain and loss than can be detected in Char Gopalpur. It could perhaps even be argued that at Coltishall the intense market in land, overwhelmingly involving unrelated individuals or neighbours, itself provided a kind of security against risk, enabling peasants to raise cash or credit at little notice and thereby weather periods of often acute economic hardship.

Secondly, intra-familial purchase and sale of land was never as prominent (20 per cent in Redgrave compared with 60 per cent in Char Gopalpur) in the total land exchange systems of the English village as they were in rural Bangladesh. Furthermore, while the fraternal bond appears as weak when contrasted with joint-family systems of the kind that Cain describes for Maharashtra and Andhra Pradesh, sibling relationships were not wholly inconsequential, at least for certain phases of the male life cycle. What is perhaps more striking is that in the absence of strong or resilient lateral kinship bonds there seem not to be prominent indications of Cain's converse, namely an emphasis in Redgrave on lineal kin in the economic sphere. In fact, on investigating the process of holding fragmentation in Redgrave in the post-inheritance phase we noted that for an important minority of male siblings (fifty-eight out of 178 surviving inheritance records) there were possible important demographic consequences, for when no direct heirs were available to inherit a brother or brothers inherited, this suggesting that for many marriage had been forgone.

Some Concluding Comments

There is much evidence from these interactional patterns to suggest a number of institutional contexts outside of the kin group within which social and economic relations were conducted in Redgrave. It should be noted too, that the manorial court itself provided an important arena in which relations were formally recorded and in which some considerable degree of certainty was brought to personal behaviour. The actual records themselves were used and consulted constantly to obtain precedents and to establish the existence of prior transactions and agreements both by court officials and the village and/or manorial juries that presented judgments on many disputes. Furthermore, this court was part of a complex set of hierarchically-organized legal institutions that linked villages and their local governments to the national centre embodied in Parliament and the King's courts within which the common law operated (Smith, 1984b).

There is no space in this discussion to add to our consideration of institutional organizations that could be identified and subject to some form of measurement within the detailed localized case study approach that has dominated this chapter. We could, however, have looked at the evidence bearing upon the involvement of women in the manorial court; such courts brought security to widows whose personal property rights were secured either by reversionary arrangements made by their husbands that transferred the holding to the wife for the remainder of her lifetime or through maintenance agreements negotiated with kin or unrelated persons. Her capacity to lease, to sell or to manage this land is reflected in the fact that females constituted marginally over 20 per cent of the landholders on the manorial survey of 1289. Indeed, female participants in the landmarket, although in a clear minority, were present in significant numbers, accounting for 28 per cent of the participants. What is more, 65 per cent of these women appeared in net surplus in their dealings compared with only 45 per cent of the men. Although almost one third of these transactions were intra-familial and many concerned premarital gifts (dowries) or purchases by daughters, widows figured prominently among the purchasers as well. In this sense we could observe through the manorial court records if we considered the economic involvement of women of all marital status categories in the village and extra-village economy, a set of institutional environments that differed markedly from that described by Cain in Char Gopalpur.

It would of course, be a gross distortion to suggest that Cain had argued that his findings regarding the prominence of distress sales of land in periods of economic and political upheaval, and the failure of the lateral kin group to show evidence of protecting individuals against property loss, could serve as an empirically observable pattern that was ubiquitously encountered in situations in peasant societies in which children or more specifically lineal kin were valued in limitless quantities. What is evident in the medieval English community which we have investigated and where some similarities of behaviour pattern can be observed with the landholders of Char Gopalpur is that although the nuclear family is economically isolated from the lateral kin group, kinship seemed of low overall significance in the matter of social and political organization as preserved for us in the proceedings of the manorial court. The significance of this fact for the society's nuptiality patterns and total fertility pattern, not a question considered directly in this chapter, was most likely very considerable.

Glossary

co-parceners: tenants who held land in a *tenementum* and who collectively owed rents and services to a manorial lord.

customary tenant: a tenant who was regarded as unfree.

demesne land: land on a manor not held by free or customary tenants but directly cultivated for the lord by an agent.

entry fine: payment by a tenant as a condition for admission to a holding.

inter-vivos land transaction: a land transaction involving two parties; both of whom are alive at the time of its occurrence.

messuage: a dwelling with its adjoining lands or yards and outbuildings.

pledge: an act whereby a surety or guarantee is offered by one person of another. It can also refer to the person providing such a service.

post-mortem land transaction: a land transaction involving two parties, one of whom is dead at the time of its occurrence.

tenementum (plural *tenementa*): an area/unit of land which could be made up of parcels, not necessarily contiguous, that owed rents and services to a manorial lord.

14

Demographic Transition in a Punjab Village*

Moni Nag and Neeraj Kak

Manupur, one of the more than a half-million villages of India, has acquired a special place in the field of population. Mahmood Mamdani's 1972 book, *The Myth of Population Control*, based on a micro-demographic study of this village in the early 1970s, has had a strong influence on thinking about population policy in India as well as internationally. It expressed forcefully the fashionable view of the early 1970s that family planning programs are of little use to the villagers of developing countries.

Mamdani interviewed Manupur men of all castes and occupational classes and quotes their views copiously in the book. All, rich and poor, landholder and landless alike, conveyed the same message: because children, particularly sons, are economically valuable as a source of household and paid labour, as insurance against various risks and old-age disability, and as providers of remittances from outside the village, Manupur villagers want as many children as possible, and, hence, family planning does not make sense to them. Using data collected in 1982 from the same village, this chapter shows that the family planning attitudes and behaviour of villagers are now significantly different from those documented by Mamdani, and seeks to relate these differences to socioeconomic changes that have occurred in the village.

Manupur is located in Punjab, which was the pioneer and most successful among Indian states in implementing the agricultural technology of the green revolution. At the time of Mamdani's investigation, Manupur farmers, all of whom are Jat by caste,[1] were already benefiting from improved varieties of wheat and mechanization of some agricultural activities. Mamdani found, however, that benefits actually increased the demand for agricultural labour - and, consequently, the labour value of children - among both landholders and landless labourers. He also cited examples to show that introduction of new technology - for example, the sewing machine - deprived many artisans of their traditional occupations and made them more dependent than before on the labour inputs of large families.

* Reprinted with the permission of the Population Council, from Moni Nag and Neeraj Kak, 'Demographic transition in a Punjab village', *Population and Development Review* 10, no.4 (December 1984), pp.661-78.

Table 14.1 Population of Manupur by Caste/Religious Group, 1970 and 1982

Caste/ religious group*	Traditional occupation	1970		1982	
		No.	%	No.	%
Jat	Farmer	1,122	59.5	1,351	57.2
Brahmin	Priest, moneylender, traditional physician	81	4.3	99	4.2
Harijan**	Leather worker, sweeper, weaver	445	23.6	585	24.7
Other service castes*** and Muslim	Shopkeeper, blacksmith, carpenter, barber, tailor, potter, water carrier, drummer, etc.	238	12.7	329	13.8
All groups		1,886	100.0	2.364	100.0

Note: Percentages may not add to 100 due to rounding.

* The term 'caste/religious group' is used in the absence of a more apt designation. All the Jat living in Manupur are Sikh, many of whom do not consider themselves a caste or section among the Hindu. Most of the other residents, except Brahmin, Khatri, Sonar, and Muslim, are Sikh. The migrant labourers (mostly from Uttar Pradesh in the early 1970s and from Bihar in the early 1980s) who come to the village for temporary periods are not included in population figures. It is difficult to estimate their number, but the number was much higher in 1982 than in 1970. During the last quarter of 1982 it was around 150.

** Harijan refers to what Mamdani designates as Achuta (outcastes) and includes Chamar, Majbi, and Julaha castes.

*** Other service castes include Khatri, Sonar, Lohar-Tarkhan, Nai, Marasi, Gujjar, Jheevar, Darzi, and Ghumar. The word 'other' is used since the Brahmin is also regarded as a service caste.

Source: For 1970, Mamdani (1972, note 1, p.71); for 1982, records from the Primary Health Centre of Manupur.

Manupur Revisited

In 1982, 12 years after Mamdani's investigation, we carried out a field investigation in the same village.[2] The main objective was to assess the economic and social changes, particularly in contraceptive behaviour and attitudes toward family size, in the pattern of labour force participation among various castes, and in the economic value of children. We carried out informal discussions with key informants and administered a questionnaire to 266 currently married women aged 15-44 years. The total number of women in the village belonging to this category was 310. The remaining 44 women, representing all caste/religious groups, were either unavailable or unwilling to provide information. Some information for all 470 family units in the village was available in the records of Manupur's primary health centre. Data on ownership of land and a few other items were collected from a random sample of 180 families stratified on the basis of caste. We also made a special effort to locate and have informal discussions with individuals who are referred to or quoted in *The Myth of Population Control*.

The total population in Manupur increased from 1,886 in 1970 to 2,364 in 1982 - a growth rate of 24.8 per cent, similar to that for India as a whole. Its caste and religous composition hardly changed during the period (Table 14.1). The proportion of the Jat, the dominant caste group, in the total population declined from 59.5 per cent in 1970 to 57.2 per cent in 1982, as the increased income from agriculture allowed some Jat to buy land in other states where land prices are cheaper and emigrate from the village. In the decades prior to 1970, the Brahmin population in the village had decreased significantly, as their economic and social power declined in relation to the Jats (p.119), but their proportion remained almost the same during 1970-82. Both birth and death rates have declined steadily in Punjab State as well as in India as a whole since the 1960s. The birth rate in Punjab declined from 35.1 per thousand per year in 1961-71 to 31.7 in 1971-81, and the death rates from 14.5 in 1961-71 to 12.0 in 1977-79 (Bhat *et al.*, 1984, pp.1-8). All-India birth and death rates in these years were each about five points above those of Punjab, a difference probably attributable to the state's greater economic development and better health infrastructure than the Indian average. It could be expected, however, that vital rates would fall sooner and faster in Manupur than in rural Punjab in general on two grounds: (i) an Intensive Agricultural Development Program (IADP) was introduced in 1960 in seven 'model' districts of India including Ludhiana, to which Manupur belongs; and (ii) an action-cum-research project on family planning, the Khanna Study, was carried out in eight villages around the town of Khanna during 1954-60 and Manupur was one of these villages.

The Khanna Study, undertaken by the Harvard University School of Public Health in collaboration with the Governments of India and Punjab State, was a pioneering field trial of a contraceptive program to distribute foam tablets and condoms along with adequate educational and follow-up service by trained staff. Reports indicated appreciable progress in contraceptive acceptance in the project villages from year to year. The findings of an evaluation study in 1969, however, were not very encouraging. The study concluded:

> 'Apparently the chief accomplishment of the programs for family planning had been to induce between one-quarter to one-half of the couples previously practicing birth control to switch to modern methods, easier to use and more effective. The striking change in age at marriage is more important' (Wyon and Gordon, 1971, p.298).

Use of Modern Contraceptives

In his critique of the Khanna Study, Mamdani traced the rise in age at marriage to socioeconomic changes but asserted that the contraceptive program was a total failure. He attributed the failure not to the 'ignorance' or 'misunderstanding' of the villagers (as most of the project personnel alleged) nor to the limitations of the contraceptive methods offered, but to the fact that the material condition of most villagers was such that 'they want "larger" families' and, 'more important, they want them because they "need" them' (p.43). A government birth control clinic was opened in Manupur in 1963 but apparently had very little impact in the village up to 1970. By 1982, however, family planning acceptance was not uncommon in the village, as shown in Table 14.2.

About 50 per cent of Manupur couples with women of reproductive age were using a contraceptive method in 1982 - a proportion considerably higher than the 33 per cent in Punjab and 26 per cent in India for the same year. Although Mamdani does not provide an estimate of contraceptive prevalence in Manupur in 1970, the rate in 1982 was much higher than his case studies and descriptive statements would lead one to expect. His case studies include a few Jat, none of whom seems to have been using any contraceptive in 1970. Among the 154 Jat couples we surveyed in 1982, 60 per cent were using a contraceptive method. (We found, however, that three tubectomies out of 35 among the Jat had been performed prior to Mamdani's investigation.) The contraceptive prevalence rate among the Jat in 1982 was on a par with that of the Brahmin rate (derived, however, from a very small sample), the sole caste identified by Mamdani as favourable to family planning in 1970. The 1982 prevalence rates among the other two caste/religious groups in Manupur were lower than those of the Jat and Brahmin, but higher than the average Punjab and all-India rates.

Sterilization, particularly tubectomy, is currently the most popular method in Manupur, as in India, but it accounted for only 47 per cent of all methods in Manupur in 1982, compared with 67 per cent in Punjab and 82 per cent in India. The proportions of couples using condoms and IUDs in Manupur, while not high, are significantly higher than in Punjab or India as a whole, perhaps

Table 14.2 Married Women of Reproductive Age (15-44) Reporting Use of Contraceptive Methods: Caste/Religious Groups, Manupur, 1982

Method	Jat	Brahmin	Harijan*	Other service castes** and Muslims	All groups
Number					
Tubectomy	35	1	15	5	56
Vasectomy	2	0	3	2	7
IUD	18	2	1	1	22
Condom	35	3	4	4	46
Rhythm	3	0	0	0	3
Total using a method	93	6	23	12	134
No method used	61	4	45	22	132
All married women	154	10	68	34	266
Percent					
Total using a method	60	60	34	35	50
No method used	40	40	66	65	50
All married women	100	100	100	100	100

* See Table 14.1, note **.

** See Table 14.1, note ***.

reflecting the longer history of family planning programs in Manupur than in other areas.

New Attitudes Toward Family Size

Apparently, attitudes toward family size and family planning have changed markedly among all castes in Manupur since 1970. Before attempting to analyze the socioeconomic factors underlying the change, we relate below what we learned about the change from our in-depth interviews in 1982 with five men residing in the village. Four of them were interviewed by Mamdani in 1970, as was the father of the fifth. Our interviews with four other men also indicate attitudinal change. The selection of case studies cited below has been made with a view to represent varieties of castes.

D.C. (Brahmin)

D.C.'s grandfather, a rich man, was a moneylender. He was also a *Hakim* (traditional physician) with a large clientele in the villages around Manupur. In postindependence years, as the prosperity of the Brahmin aristocracy declined, many with adequate money and/or with good educational qualifications emigrated from Manupur. When Mamdani talked with D.C. in 1970, he, like other not-so-well-educated Brahmin who were left behind, was struggling to maintain a semblance of his customary status, privilege, and income (p.121). D.C. spent 4 years after high school learning the profession of the *Hakim*, but his practice had declined considerably because many villagers had started using the government-operated free medical facilities at Khanna, a town 4 miles from Manupur. He supplemented his income by running a small shop and working as the village postmaster.

D.C.'s total monthly income of about 300 Rupees (US$1 = about 10 Rupees) was hardly sufficient to support his wife, three sons, and three daughters. He told Mamdani that he was lucky to have three sons who were working outside Manupur. They sent him part of their salaries, which covered the family's ceremonial and emergency expenses. D.C. explained to Mamdani why he and many other villagers had accepted foam tablets from the Khanna project staff but without intent that their wives would use them:

> 'But they were so nice, you know. And they come from distant land to be with us. Couldn't we even do this much for them? Just take a few tablets?... If they are happy writing my name, let them do it. Why should it worry me?' (p.23).

Mamdani reported that 2 years after the birth of his sixth child, a daughter, D.C. decided to practise abstinence as a birth control measure and has done so ever since. He gave two reasons: (i) even if the seventh child were a boy, he would not begin earning until D.C. was too old or dead; (ii) he could not take the chance of having another daughter.

When we talked with D.C. in 1982, his income appeared to be lower than in 1970. He was still working as village postmaster, but his earnings as a shopkeeper and *Hakim* appeared negligible to us. His three sons were still working outside Manupur, but they only occasionally sent remittances. Two of them were married and not living in the village. Interestingly, both went for vasectomies at the initiative of D.C. - one after having two sons and two daughters, the other after having one son and one daughter. D.C.'s youngest son, unmarried, lived at home and commuted daily to work in an industrial town about 10 miles away. An unmarried daughter lived at home with D.C. D.C. told us that it was good to have one son for security in old age, but it was too expensive these days to have a large family.

G.S. (Jat)

On retiring from his military job in 1966, G.S. returned to Manupur and established himself as a farmer, owning 11 acres of land, an electric tubewell, and an electric chaff-cutter (p.81). After having two sons and a daughter, the couple were unable to have more children. At the time of Mamdani's visit in 1970, G.S.'s oldest son, aged 21, his wife, and their daughter were living with G.S., and his younger son, aged 19, was in the military. Since there was a shortage of family labour for farming, G.S. had to hire about 540 man-days of labour per year at such a high cost that, according to Mamdani's report of his family budget, had G.S. not been the recipient of a military pension, his total earnings would have fallen short of his minimal expenses. He told Mamdani that 'if he had more sons, his labour costs would be significantly reduced and his household maintenance costs would only marginally increase'. He also 'expressed the hope that his second son would soon be married and that his two daughters-in-law would bear him many grandsons so that in the near future they could accumulate enough savings to buy more land' (p.85).

When we saw G.S. in 1982, his prospects had greatly improved. By this time the family owned a tractor and was hiring immigrant labour from Bihar for a major part of the agricultural activities. Their annual income from agriculture had increased from Rs.3,000 in 1969-70 to Rs.30,000 in 1981-82 (in current Rupees). G.S. was amused to hear what Mamdani had written about him. While he still agreed with most of it, he added that things had changed radically and that he was wrong about his expectations concerning benefits from children. He told us:

> 'Children are of no use any more in old age of parents. They also do not do any work while going to school. My son in the military does not keep any connection with me. My son living with me has two sons and one daughter. I have advised him to get a vasectomy'.

The son living with G.S. told us later that he was considering a vasectomy. He wanted all of his children to be well educated and thought that it was better to use Bihari labourers for most farming activities than family or local labour.

M.S. (Nai)

Although traditionally low in the caste hierarchy, the *Nai* (barber) along with the *Darzi* (tailor) are relatively prosperous among service castes in the village. Since modernization has eroded the need for traditional services provided by members of both castes, they are struggling to adjust to a new life by educating their sons. According to Mamdani, some *Nai* and *Darzi*, including M.S., go 'against another widely accepted "truth" among family planners: that families who want education, and particularly higher education, for their children will limit their families because higher education is expensive and, therefore, to have many children is expensive' (p.113). He got the impression from M.S. and other members of his caste that since they earned too little to finance advanced education for any children, the only solution open to them was to have enough sons so that one could finish high school by spending a part of his afternoon working for a farmer and then go to college, while the others worked to save and pay his fees. Once his college education was completed, he would use his increased earnings to finance his brothers' education.

Mamdani reports that M.S. succeeded in following the above strategy with his five sons. The three eldest sons have college degrees. At the time of Mamdani's visit, two of them were school-teachers and another was a civil servant. The fourth was in college, and the youngest was in school. The third son remained unmarried at 30 in order to put his younger brother through college.

During our visit M.S. was not available, but we spoke with his second son (whom we shall call M.S., Jr.), a teacher in the local school. M.S., Jr. is the only person we encountered in the village who has read Mamdani's book. He was very critical of it because, according to him, it ignored the views of a portion of villagers, albeit a minority, who favoured family planning. M.S., Jr. agreed that he and his brothers helped one another in attaining higher education, but all of the family members had to endure such prolonged hardship that he did not find it worthwhile. He thought that one reason for such hardship was the large size of their family - five sons and two daughters. His thinking about the advantages of a smaller family was already formed at the time of Mamdani's visit, but Mamdani did not interview him. When asked why he himself has five children, M.S., Jr. explained that he had two by his first wife, who had died, and his second wife wanted at least one son of her own.

H.S. (Lohar-Tarkhan)

Given the change in agricultural technology, the demand for the traditional skills of the *Lohar-Tarkhan* (blacksmith-carpenter) has decreased sharply in Manupur. Since their numbers have increased, Mamdani argued they might be expected to be receptive to family planning (p.112). In reality he found them reasoning in a different way. H.S., who was barely earning a subsistence living, serving only five farmers where his father used to serve 50, felt the solution to his financial troubles was not to reduce the size of his family, but to increase it:

> 'Unless I am to leave this village, I must teach my sons to repair the new machines and maybe even get some machinery (tools) myself. The problem is I have no money, and the Cooperative Society only loans to farmers. So there is only one way out. And that is to have enough sons. Don't smile. If I have sons, they will work outside, labour even as animals

> do, but save. While the rest work, one son will learn the new skills. And maybe we will even be able to get some machinery with the savings of the other sons... A rich man invests in his machines. We must invest in our children. It's that simple' (p.113).

When we met H.S., his two sons were working outside Manupur as mechanics and had families of their own. His only daughter was also married and had left his household. He told us:

> 'There is plenty of work for me to do. New technology has not made me useless. Of course, I have to work very hard at this old age. My sons don't help me. These days very few do. It is better to have a small family.'

T.S. (Jheevar)

The members of the *Jheevar* (water carrier) caste lost their traditional job to the water pump. Since they had no skills in farm labour, the Jat employed them mostly to perform menial and time-consuming tasks, such as sending messages to other villages or collecting manure for the farmer or tending his cattle. When Mamdani spoke with T.S., the latter mistook Mamdani for a Khanna Project worker who had returned for the summer and said:

> 'You were trying to convince me in 1960 that I shouldn't have any more sons. Now, you see, I have six sons and two daughters and I sit at home in leisure. They are grown up and they bring me money. One even works outside the village as a laborer. You told me I was a poor man and couldn't support a large family. Now, you see, because of my large family, I am a rich man' (p.109).

When we saw T.S. he still depended on his sons for survival, but he felt that the labour situation had changed drastically during the last decade. His sons were no longer satisfied being menial agricultural labourers, working for the Jat. They had to compete with immigrant labourers from Bihar and Uttar Pradesh who were willing to work at a lower wage rate. Local labourers wanted their children to be sufficiently educated to qualify for industrial, commercial, or government sector jobs. At the end of our discussion with T.S., he remarked: 'These days one shouldn't have more than two sons.'

One gets the impression from Mamdani's book that in 1970 parents of all caste/religious groups except the Brahmin still preferred to have as many sons as possible. In our 1982 survey, only 16 per cent of Jat males and 10 per cent of Harijan males mentioned three or more when asked what they considered the ideal number of sons. Most Manupur residents, however, still want to have at least two surviving sons. This is reflected both in their verbal responses and in their contraceptive practice. Out of 63 couples who had undergone sterilization in our sample, 56 (89 per cent) had at least two surviving sons. Still, it is notable that among the Jat, six couples out of 37 who had undergone sterilization (16 per cent) had only one son. In view of the Mamdani's depiction of Manupur Jats' craving for large numbers of sons and their firm resistance to birth control, a major change in their attitudes toward family size seems to have taken place.

The data collected from both interviews and questionnaire surveys show that attitudes toward family size and contraceptive behaviour have changed considerably among all Manupur residents during recent years. The change in contraceptive behaviour may be attributed at least in part to utilization of the government's family planning program. More contraceptive methods are available, and delivery of services is more efficient. The change in attitude toward family size can be linked mainly to a change in the economic value of children - actual as well as perceived by parents. The economic value of children in Manupur is manifested in their labour value and their value as a source of old-age support and risk insurance.

Change in the Labour Value of Children

A decline in the labour value of children has been hypothesized to be associated with the emergence of motivation for small families and the lowering of fertility levels (Cain, 1977; Kasarda, 1971; Nag *et al.*, 1978). Let us see what the children in Manupur currently do and how the pattern of their activities has changed during recent years.

From our interviews and observations, we learned that children of all castes in Manupur still do plenty of work for their own households. Tending the household livestock is a primary responsibility of both boys and girls. Most Jat and Harijan households own cattle, as do the majority of the service caste households. Children gather fodder for the cattle in the fields and cut it with a chaff-cutter to make it suitable for cattle feed. Children also help their parents in milking and washing the cattle. On holidays, Jat boys help their parents in agricultural activities, often working 7 or 8 hours a day. Boys of Harijan and poor service castes spend hours collecting firewood over long distances. From an early age, girls of all castes help their mothers in a variety of household tasks - processing and cooking food, washing clothes, cleaning utensils, making cow dung cakes for fuel, carrying water from the pump or well, sewing. They spend more time caring for younger siblings than boys do and spend considerable time weaving colourful mats that are sold or used as dowries.

We could, however, identify three changes in the labour value of children during the period between Mamdani's investigation and ours: a reduction in remunerative work by children; a reduction in children's work time due to changes in the nature of agricultural and household activities as well as to higher enrolment of both boys and girls in school.

Mamdani's case studies show that the children of the Harijan and service castes often performed agricultural work for which they were paid as well as given free meals and clothes. During our investigation we could not find any child working as a paid labourer. Our inquiries revealed that children participate in paid work only when their families get contracts to harvest wheat for Jat farmers. The *Jajmani* system (the traditional exchange of services and goods among castes) has been almost totally replaced by wage labour and a system of crop-sharing in which an entire family contracts to harvest a piece of land. The latter arrangement, according to Mamdani (p.94), has led to an increase in the labour participation of children, since not only boys but also girls now work side-by-side with their parents, and the payment to the family relates to the amount of work performed. We too found that many Harijan and service caste families had contractual arrangements with Jat farmers for harvesting wheat, but the number of days per year in which they engaged in this work was so small (usually 4 or 5 days) that parents did not perceive their children's participation as an economic contribution of any significance.

Changes in the nature of agricultural and household activities reduced or eliminated tasks previously performed by children. Increasing use of fallow land for agriculture and the growing practice of multiple cropping have led to a virtual disappearance of grazing land in the village and, with it, of the age-old custom of boys grazing cattle in the fields. The disappearance of grazing has also reduced the time spent in another job typically done by children - collection of cow dung for use as fuel and manure. The increasing use of chemical weedkillers by Manupur farmers has largely diminished the need for children to perform weeding. The introduction of rice cultivation in Manupur (and in Punjab as a whole) during the 1970s, replacing more labour-intensive crops such as cotton, maize, and other vegetables, has also diminished the need for child labour.

Old-Age Support and Risk Insurance

Economic theories of fertility recognize that one main reason for high fertility in developing countries is parents' expectation of support from their surviving children, especially sons, in their old age. The decline in the need for such support is presumed to be one of the ways in which growth in income reduces fertility (Leibenstein, 1957). Parents in developing countries may also view children as a source of insurance in times of crisis, brought on by drought, flood, illness, death of spouse, or loss of job (Cain, 1981). Almost all the case studies cited by Mamdani indicate that parents' dependence on sons for old-age support and in times of crisis is an important reason for wanting many sons. (Daughters are not regarded as a source of security since they are not income earners, and, moreover, they leave the parental home upon marriage. To the contrary, parents are worried about the amount of money - in view of an increasing trend toward payment of dowries - that they have to pay on daughters' marriages.) Mamdani observed three kinds of crises in which sons are of great help to Manupur parents: loss of job, natural disaster, and violent conflict.

During our field investigations in 1982, we found that Manupur parents still valued sons as a source of old-age security and risk insurance, but not to the extent observed by Mamdani. Almost all of the men of various castes whom we interviewed complained that sons are not as dependable these days as they used to be. A few reported that they had almost no contact with their sons, who had families of their own and were living outside the village.

About agricultural labourers Mamdani reported that the seasonality of employment and farmers' power over them were sources of job insecurity for many. And while the non-agricultural labour market in the town of Khanna had begun to expand by 1970, job security for unskilled labourers in Khanna was even less than in the village agricultural sector. Only households with large numbers of adult males could afford the risk of sending a son to Khanna to seek wage labour (p.95). During our investigation we observed that the bargaining power of agricultural labourers has increased and, along with it, their job security. The numbers of villagers working in industrial, commercial, and government sectors, in which job security is greater than in the agricultural sector, have also increased. The proportion of Manupur workers in skilled and unskilled services in these sectors increased from 8 per cent in 1970 to 29 per cent in 1982.

One type of natural disaster that, according to Mamdani, affected the lives of villagers seriously was the destruction of their *kutcha* (dried mud) houses due to flooding during the monsoon season. Because the owners of these houses were usually poor, they could not afford to hire labourers to rebuild them; so the presence of a few able-bodied sons was of great help in such emergencies. Manupur villagers still suffer from various types of natural disasters, but the destruction of houses due to flooding affects few households these days. During 1970–82, *pukka* (brick and cement) houses have largely replaced *kutcha* houses. We found that almost all of the houses belonging to the Jat, Brahmin, and other service castes, and more than half of the Harijan houses were *pukka*.

Mamdani found that although most intercaste conflicts in Manupur were settled through arbitration by the village *Panchayat*, serious intracaste conflicts, usually between farmers, were often solved through the use of force (p.134). Since numbers are a source of strength on such occasions, parents favoured large families. We learned from Manupur residents that inter- and intracaste conflicts still occur in the village, perhaps as frequently as before, but the use of physical force to resolve them has declined and reliance on the village *Panchayat* and police station at Khanna has increased. Communication between Manupur and Khanna improved significantly when the entire 4 miles of road connecting them was made fit for year-round vehicular traffic by 1980.

These findings suggest that both the labour value of children and their value as a source of old-age support and risk insurance declined considerably among all caste groups of Manupur between 1970 and 1982. The decline is associated with various kinds of economic and social change. Three factors seem to have played especially important roles: (i) the introduction of modern agricultural technology; (ii) institutional innovations and changes; and (iii) expansion of formal education, particularly for girls. We now explore each of these in turn.

Introduction of New Technology

As we noted earlier, Punjab was the first state in India to experience the green revolution, and also the state to benefit most from it. The district of Ludhiana, to which Manupur belongs, has fared even better than most other districts in Punjab, mainly because innovations in agricultural technology were introduced in Ludhiana in the early 1960s, through the Intensive Agricultural Development Program. One of the most important changes in Manupur was in the method of irrigation. Tubewells run by oil engines quickly replaced the Persian wheel and the drilled well. In 1964 the village was electrified, and by 1970 of 127 tubewells 35 had electric motors. Some of the chaff-cutters were by then also operated by electric motors. A new variety of wheat called *Kalyan* (prosperity) was introduced in 1967, and as a result wheat yields trebled in good years (p.51). Chemical fertilizers and weed-killers were being used by most Manupur farmers by the late 1960s.

Mamdani observed that although by 1970 the state-owned Land Mortgage Bank was giving loans to buy tractors, the price of a tractor was so high that only the prosperous farmers could afford to buy them and repay the loans. Only 6.6 per cent of Manupur farmers owned tractors in 1970 (p.85). Farm incomes, however, have increased so rapidly since 1970 and the tractor has become such an important implement that at the time of our visit, despite a steep rise in tractor prices, about 39 per cent of farmers owned a tractor; a few even owned two.

The increase in tractor ownership in Manupur as well as elsewhere in Punjab is largely explained by a rapid increase in rice cultivation since 1975. Ploughing land for rice cultivation with the help of bullocks is much more arduous than doing so for wheat; hence a tractor is more useful for production of rice than for wheat. Wheat is the staple cereal food for the residents of Punjab. Prior to the green revolution, Punjab farmers grew very little rice. However, the heavy demand for rice in other parts of India and the innovations in the technology for its production encouraged Punjab farmers to cultivate rice as one of their multiple crops. The area under rice production in Ludhiana district rose from 3,000 hectares in 1966-67 to 91,000 hectares in 1979-80. The amount of rice produced per hectare increased from 1,500 kg in 1960-61 to 3,443 kg in 1979-80 (Government of Punjab, 1982).

Table 14.3 Ownership of Land Among the Jat: Manupur, 1970 and 1982

Size of holding	1970 No. of house-holds	1970 % of house-holds	1970 % of land held	1982 No. of house-holds	1982 % of house-holds	1982 % of land held
Up to 5 acres	49	37	15	24	33	11
6 to 16 acres	68	51	56	38	53	54
17 acres or more	14	11	30	10	14	35
Total	131	100	100	72	100	100

Note: Percentages may not add to 100 due to rounding.

Source: For 1970, Mamdani (1972, note 1, p.71); for 1982, data from our field investigation.

Mamdani conjectured that because of the high price of tractors 'the pattern of landownership had to be changed if agriculture in Manupur was to be mechanized further' (p.87). We found, however, that in the intervening 12 years, mechanization of agriculture progressed and productivity increased quite significantly, while the pattern of landownership remained nearly unchanged, as seen in Table 14.3. The modest change in landownership that did occur in Manupur was toward further concentration of land in the hands of prosperous farmers rather than toward a more equal distribution. Thus, the percentage of households owning 17 acres or more increased from 11 in 1970 to 14 in 1982, and the percentage of total land held by them increased from 30 in 1970 to 35 in 1982.

The main reasons why many more farmers owning medium-sized plots could own tractors in 1982 are that the income of all farmers increased considerably since 1970 and so did the number of credit facilities. The use of tractors is no longer confined to their owners. Unforeseen by Mamdani in 1970, a number of farmers with small and medium-sized holdings in Manupur rent tractors from their owners, often for less than it would cost to maintain bullocks. Our survey data show that 37 per cent of farmers not owning tractors used rented tractors only, 37 per cent used both rented tractors and bull-ploughs, and 27 per cent used bull-ploughs only.

In sum, the introduction of new technology and the success of the green revolution in Manupur have reduced the need for child labour in a number of ways. Because the fallow and waste land have been made cultivable for one or another crop almost year-round, cattle-grazing and collecting cow dung from the fields - jobs previously done by children - hardly occur these days. Previously children participated in weeding and fertilizing; they do not take part in the application of chemical weedkillers and fertilizers. Manupur children do not participate in any activity related to the production of rice. Neither do children operate tractors or any electrical machinery. The introduction of new agricultural technology has, however, made all Manupur parents conscious of the need for their children to learn more about it and, hence, to be educated in schools and colleges. It has also improved the economic condition of many villagers so that they have to depend less on children as a source of security in old age and against various types of risk.

Institutional Innovations

One reason why Manupur farmers - even those who were not prosperous - could take advantage of advanced agricultural technology is the institutional innovations that have occurred during the last few decades in Manupur and in India as a whole. The principal innovations that encouraged, directly or indirectly, the increased use of more advanced agricultural technology, as well as the emergence of preferences favouring smaller family size, are: (i) an increase in credit facilities through co-operative societies and banks, (ii) a shift from the *Jajmani* system to a market economy, and (iii) institutional mechanisms for uplifting 'Scheduled' and 'Backward' castes.

Until about mid-century, Jat farmers were totally dependent on Brahmin moneylenders for credit. Agricultural production was so subject to the vicissitudes of nature that too much or too little rain was enough to plunge the farmer into debt. Gradually an increasing number of farmers had their land mortgaged to money-lenders. The farmers had little motivation for increasing agri-cultural output, since the moneylender would demand a larger share of the produce. A law passed by the Punjab government in 1937 cancelled any debts where total interest payments had at least doubled the principal. While the law helped most Manupur farmers temporarily, the failure of a single harvest was sufficient to drive them back into debt.

A breakthrough in institutional credit facilities for Manupur farmers came with the establishment in 1960 of the Cooperative Society as a component of the Intensive Agricultural Development Program. It has two branches - the Primary Society and the Land Mortgage Bank - both of which make loans for agricultural purposes. By 1970, 98 per cent of Manupur farmers were eligible for low-interest loans from the Primary Society, the only require-ments being to own land and pay the necessary modest dues. The Land Mortgage Bank makes larger loans (e.g. for buying a tractor) by taking land as a pledge and claiming part of its yearly yield as interest. In the 1960s not many farmers could take advantage of the Land Mortgage Bank, but with gradually increasing productivity of land in the 1970s, the number of clients increased much more rapidly than Mamdani seems to have anticipated.

Until recently, however, the Cooperative Society extended its credit facilities only to farmers, so that the members of the service castes (e.g. blacksmiths) who suffered economically with the introduction of new technology could not take advantage of them. After major Indian banks were nationalized in the 1970s, their credit policies toward rural farmers and other rural occupational groups allowed some members of Manupur service castes to obtain loans from the newly established bank branches in Khanna. The extension of credit facilities to Manupur villagers contributed to the decline of the labour and risk insurance value of children.

As we mentioned earlier, Mamdani observed that the shift from the *Jajmani* system of exchange of goods and services among castes to the contractual system of payment between the Jat farmers and other castes led to an increase in child labour among the latter (p.94). Our observations in 1982 about the shift lead to a different conclusion. The Jat farmers' contractual arrangements with Harijan and service caste families for harvesting wheat still exist, but these involve children's labour participation for only 4 to 5 days of the year. Under the *Jajmani* system the Harijan and service castes were obliged to serve the Jat throughout the year in lieu of a share of crops. Since the terms of this exchange were far from equitable and were not based on payment for specific services rendered, the demand for services from the lower caste involved not only their adult males but also adult females and children. The wage system of payment is a reflection of the shift from a semi-feudal economy to a market economy. Its net effect in Manupur, as elsewhere, has been a reduction in the prevalence of child labour.

Immediately after India's independence from British rule in 1947, laws were passed and institutions established for the uplift of 'Scheduled' and 'Backward' castes. Provisions were made to give special privileges in education and employment to these disadvantaged groups. The traditional economic and social structure of rural India, however, was so unfavourable to members of these castes that very few could take advantage of these opportunities until political and technological forces altered the traditional structure. The green revolution in Punjab, along with industrial and commercial development, seems to have opened up opportunites for the Harijan and a few other service castes in Manupur since the late 1960s. They have taken advantage of the expanded scope of employment in non-agricultural sectors in Manupur as well as in neighbouring towns. For example, Mamdani found only 7 per cent of the Chamar and Majbi (Harijan castes) working in non-agricultural sectors (p.93); during our investigation in 1982, 41 per cent were doing so. The feasibility of occupational mobility and free education for Harijan children drastically changed perceptions regarding the economic value of children.

Expansion of Formal Education

The enrolment of boys and girls in both primary school (grades 1-5) and secondary school (grades 6-10) increased from 1970 to 1982 among all castes in Manupur. The increase, however, was proportionately higher among girls than boys. For example, the enrolment of school-age boys (roughly 10-14 years) in secondary school among the Jat increased from 63 per cent in 1970 to 81 per cent in 1982, while the enrolment of girls in the same age group increased from 29 per cent to 63 per cent. Mamdani observed that the introduction of new agricultural technology, increased contact with the commercial world, and the institution of a modern credit system had meant a growing feeling among Jat farmers that a secondary school education was necessary for boys (p.100). There was less recognition of a need for girls' education, but at least some parents felt that educated boys wanted to marry educated girls and that the amount of dowry demanded by future in-laws would be less if girls were educated.

During our visit in 1982, we observed that the aspiration to educate both boys and girls was quite high among all castes. Many Brahmin and Jat parents wanted their sons and daughters to attend college because higher education could qualify the children for white collar jobs outside Manupur. Jat parents wanted at least one of their sons to have a white collar job, so that the family would not be entirely dependent on agriculture. The success stories of relatives or friends who were remitting money regularly from the Middle East, Great Britain, the United States, and Canada encouraged such aspirations. Harijan and other service caste parents wanted their children to have at least secondary education and to seek jobs in non-agricultural sectors outside Manupur.

Mamdani observed that even though children were in school for about 6 hours a day, they could find considerable time to do household and agricultural tasks. The workload of children of all castes seems to have declined during the 1970s. Children now commonly do school homework or play after school hours. Parents want their children to be good students.

The expansion of formal education in Manupur has undoubtedly increased the cost to parents of raising children. Although Harijan children do not have to pay any school fees and the fees for other children are moderate, the clothing and textbooks necessary for school attendance are significant expenses for poor parents. Parents also have to sacrifice a part of their comfort and leisure when their children go to school instead of doing household work. Some parents have to sacrifice income their children could have earned if they did not go to school. Despite the rise in the cost of children and the decline in their labour value, school enrolment in Manupur is likely to continue to increase.

Discussion

The use of modern contraceptives increased considerably in Manupur between Mamdani's field investigation in 1970 and our study in 1982. The contraceptive prevalence rate in the village was 50 per cent in 1982, compared with 33 per cent in Punjab and 26 per cent in India in the same year. Although sterilization, particularly tubectomy, is currently the most popular method in Manupur, as in Punjab and India, the use of temporary methods (mostly the condom and the IUD) is proportionately higher in Manupur. The change in contraceptive practice of Manupur residents is partly attributable to the availability of more effective methods in the 1970s than in earlier decades, but seems largely to be a reflection of changes in attitudes that are themselves reflections of social and economic change.

It is extremely difficult to pinpoint the specific factors that have caused a decline in the economic value of children. However, the data collected during our investigation, coupled with a study of the socioeconomic history of Manupur and Punjab, as documented by Mamdani and others, enable us to conjecture that the following three interrelated aspects of development have played crucial roles: (i) the introduction of modern agricultural technology, (ii) institutional innovations, and (iii) expansion of formal education, particularly among girls.

Das Gupta has described remarkably similar technological and socioeconomic changes causing a decline in the economic value of children in another Indian village near Delhi (Das Gupta, 1978). She found that by the late 1950s, tractors, tubewells, and electric pumps, owned by richer and bigger landowners and often rented by other farmers, reduced considerably the demand for agricultural labour. There was also a significant rise in the parents' aspiration for schooling for the children because of the expanding opportunities for employment of village youths in jobs that require education. This was a greater factor in the village Das Gupta studied than in Manupur because the former is situated within commuting distance of the Delhi metropolis.

In analyzing the fertility decline in nine Karnataka villages situated 125 kilometres from Bangalore city, Caldwell and his colleagues identified three factors critical to reducing the economic value and increasing the economic costs of children: (i) fragmentation of agricultural land due to population growth and the success of land reform legislation; (ii) increased availability of non-farm employment, particularly that requiring at least functional literacy and minimal arithmetic calculations; (iii) recent increase in educational facilities in all nine villages, especially the smaller ones that previously had very few. The second and third factors above are operative in Manupur and in the village studied by Das Gupta, but increasing fragmentation of land has not been found to be an important factor in the decline of children's economic value in Manupur, as it was in the other two studies. Change in agricultural technology seems to have had greater influence in the villages of Punjab and Delhi than in Karnataka. Instituional change, particularly pertaining to credit facilities, has perhaps occurred more in Manupur than in the villages studied by Das Gupta and Caldwell *et al.*

Although the relative roles of different factors in causing a reduction in the economic value of children and a consequent decline in parents' desire for large families differed among the villages studied by Das Gupta, Caldwell, and ourselves, taken together they seem to represent a consistent pattern of change in the rural areas experiencing the green revolution (Caldwell, 1983a; Caldwell *et al.*, 1982b). If so, the rapid changes in contraceptive practice and desired family size we found are a hopeful sign that the still incomplete demographic transition will continue - indeed, accelerate - in the future. Our experience also suggests that countries that have not yet begun the transition cannot hope to emulate the Indian experience by focusing on one factor - say, the pattern of landownership - to the exclusion of other factors we have identified here.

Notes

1. Mamdani refers to the Jat as a Hindu caste, but in recent years many Jats claim that they belong to the Sikh religion, which, they contend, is not a sect of the Hindu religion.

2. The field survey in the village of Manupur, Punjab, on which this article draws was carried out by Neeraj Kak during October-December 1982 with the assistance of local female health personnel. Moni Nag visited the village twice and conducted in-depth interviews with some of the men quoted by Mahmood Mamdani in his book. The authors are grateful to Sardar Joginder Singh, headman of the village *Panchayat* (council), and to all the inhabitants of Manupur for the hospitality and co-operation they extended to us.

Studying Mortality and Morbidity

15

Micro-Approaches to the Study of Childhood Mortality in Rural Bangladesh

Lincoln C. Chen

The term 'micro-demography' is more difficult to define than the more established term 'demography'. By the latter, we imply research approaches employing quantitative methods for the study of large populations and demographic processes - births, deaths, and migrations. Demography as a discipline possesses close affinity to the quantitative sciences of statistics and epidemiology. Micro-demography, in contrast, implies the use of in-depth observation or detailed measurements in field research that typically involve (very) small sample populations often clustered in contiguous geographic areas. The disciplinary tools associated with micro-demographic studies therefore usually involve anthropological methods as well as other research tools that are suited to the study of small populations.

The purpose of this paper is to advance the proposition that our understanding of the determinants of childhood mortality in developing countries would be strengthened by the application of micro-demographic methods to complement traditional demographic approaches. There are several reasons for this proposition. Firstly, certain parameters of research significance can only be undertaken through micro-level, field measurement techniques. Under most circumstances, for example, time budget studies require objective observation rather than superficial questionnaires. Likewise, anthropological, interactive, or participating methodologies in the study of human behaviour - not simply the quantitative outcome of such behaviour - are essential to further understanding of the complexities inherent in social relationships. Certain types of health, nutrition, and disease data also require meticulous, intensive fieldwork or biological specimens obtained through invasive techniques. All of these present constraints in terms of validity, social constraints, cost, and logistics to research in large, widely-scattered populations.

A second role of micro-approaches is to validate findings from large scale demographic studies. Rarely have large scale demographic and micro-methods both been applied to address the same hypothesis in the same population over the same time period. Consistency of the findings from both approaches would lend reassurance to the validity of results obtained from each alone. Thirdly, micro-approaches are essential to facilitate the application of knowledge to policy formulation. An example is the widely observed relationship between female education and childhood survival. Should the policy prescription be female education, or does the schooling of women imply social processes with which education is associated, or which education endows, that may be influenced powerfully by policies other than the education of women *per se*. Finally, this chapter argues that micro-approaches deal fundamentally with different types of research hypotheses than those addressed by the quantitative demographic sciences. Demographic analyses usually deal with the 'what' questions: the level, pattern, and trends of population processes. Through indirect analytical techniques, demographic research may also draw inferences regarding the determinants of these processes. Micro-methods, in comparison, address questions related to the 'why' or 'how' of particular demographic phenomena.

This chapter illustrates these comparative uses of micro-demographic techniques in the study of childhood mortality in one rural region of Bangladesh. The two case studies selected illustrate simultaneous demographic and micro-studies of mortality determinants in the same population over similar time periods. By comparing the findings generated from two different approaches, the comparative roles and advantages of large scale quantitative versus smaller scale but in-depth micro methods are highlighted.

Methods

All of the data cited in this chapter were obtained in Matlab Thana, Bangladesh at the rural field research station of the International Centre for Diarrheal Disease Research, Bangladesh (ICDDRB, formerly Cholera Research Laboratory). The Matlab economy is primarily agricultural. The population is 88 per cent Muslim and 12 per cent Hindu. The average household consists of six persons, and households of patrilineally-related families are grouped in residential clusters called *baris*, having a common courtyard. Landholding patterns are skewed, with 18 per cent of the households owning 47 per cent of the land. About 40 per cent of males and 16 per cent of females over age 15 years have completed at least 4 years of schooling. Per capita income is low, near the Bangladesh average of about US$100 annually.

Since 1963 the ICDDRB has operated a demographic surveillance system and has provided diarrhoeal treatment services to a 1974 study population of 263,000. Details of the population's demographic and socioeconomic characteristics, field data collection procedures, and diarrhoeal treatment services have been reported in many previous publications (see, for example, Ruzicka and Chowdhury, 1978; Sheik *et al.*, 1979). For this chapter, the demographic data on births and deaths over the period 1974-77 are employed.

Complementing the quantitative demographic analyses generated from the large scale surveillance system have been several micro-research studies on specific topics related to health, nutrition, and diarrhoeal diseases (Chowdhury and Chen, 1977; D'Souza and Chen, 1980; Chen *et al.*, 1981; D'Souza and Bhuiya, 1982).

Table 15.1 Mid-Year Population and Vital Events in Matlab, Bangladesh, 1974-77

	1974	1975	1976	1977	Total 1974-77
Mid-year population	263,807	259,194	260,381	268,894	1,052,276*
Births	11,316	7,622	11,265	12,485	42,688
Deaths	4,362	5,393	3,856	3,644	17,255
Crude rate per 1,000					
Natural increase	26.4	8.6	28.5	32.8	24.2
Births	42.9	29.4	43.3	46.4	40.6
Deaths					
Both sexes	16.5	20.8	14.8	13.6	16.4
Male	15.5	21.0	14.7	13.3	16.1
Female	17.6	20.6	14.9	13.8	16.7

* Person-years

Source: D'Souza and Chen, 1980.

Relevant to this chapter are two in-depth studies addressing the sociobiological processes responsible for sex differentials of childhood mortality and for the role of female education in determining child survival.

In-depth data related to gender-based child care behaviour were obtained from the Matlab Food and Nutrition Study, which aimed to elucidate and quantify the nutritional effects of household socio-economic variables, incidence of infections, food availability, and dietary practices, including food distribution within the family (Chen *et al.*, 1981). A baseline survey was conducted in February-March 1978 amongst all 882 pre-school aged children residing in six villages. This was followed by a one-year longitudinal study of 130 families containing 207 children under 5 years of age. Beginning in June 1978, the longitudinal phase included the following measurements: initial baseline asset survey; income-expenditure survey, bimonthly; 24-hour measurement of household and individual food intake, bimonthly; anthropometry (weight, height, mid-upper left arm circumference and left triceps skinfold thickness) of mothers and children monthly, and for all other household members, trimonthly; and morbidity surveillance, weekly.

Table 15.2 Number and Adjusted Rate (per 1,000) of Deaths Among Children Under Age 5 Years According to Cause in Matlab, Bangladesh 1975-77

	Mortality (Infants)		Mortality (Ages 1-4)		Mortality*	
Causes of Death	No.	Rate	No.	Rate	No.	Proportion dying to age 5
1. Diarrhoea	613	19.6	1,486	15.1	2,099	67.3
Watery	(526)	(16.8)	(732)	(7.4)	(1,258)	(40.3)
Dysentery	(87)	(2.8)	(754)	(7.6)	(841)	(27.0)
2. Tetanus	1,174	37.4	59	0.6	1,233	39.3
3. Measles	96	3.1	440	4.5	536	17.3
4. Fever	230	7.3	290	2.9	520	16.5
5. Respiratory	328	10.4	160	1.6	488	15.5
6. Drowning	20	0.6	217	2.2	237	7.6
7. Skin	61	1.9	38	0.4	99	3.2
8. Others	1,953	62.2	693	7.0	2,644	84.3
All	4,475	142.6	3,383	34.3	7,858	250.9

* The death rate 0-4 was estimated by multiplying the 1-4 year death rate by a factor of 3.16 and adding the infant mortality rate.

Source: Chen *et al.*, 1980.

The micro field research on the role of female education in promoting child survival was undertaken during February-May 1983. An anthropologist who had conducted field research in Matlab during 1963-66, again established residence in one Matlab village. Daily observations and probings were undertaken to illuminate the social significance of female education and the possible mechanisms through which female education might operate to exert its effect on child survival (Lindenbaum, 1983).

Results

Demographic Analysis

Tables 15.1 and 15.2 summarize the demographic situation in the Matlab surveillance population during four study years 1974-77.

Table 15.3 Mortality Rates (per 1,000) at Ages 1-4 for Children of Both Sexes According to Socioeconomic Status in Matlab, Bangladesh, 1974-77

Socioeconomic Status	Child Morbidity (1974-77)
Occupation	
Agricultural worker	42.9
Owner/worker	27.5
Land owner	15.9
Dwelling size	
< 169 sq. ft	39.0
170 - 242 sq. ft.	31.5
243+ sq. ft.	22.7
Cows owned	
0	34.4
1 - 2	27.2
3+	19.9
Use of fixed latrines	
No	35.6
Yes	28.1
All	29.4

Source: D'Souza and Bhuiya, 1982.

For the period as a whole, the average size of the study population is 263,000. Birth and death rates average 40.6 and 16.4 per thousand population per year, respectively. Annual fluctuations of these rates are notable, particularly during and after the 1974-75 food shortage and famine.

The levels of infant (under one year) and child (one to four years) mortality and the medical causes of these deaths are summarized in Table 15.2. The infant mortality rate is moderately high, averaging 142.6 per thousand live births. So too is the child mortality rate at 34.3 per thousand. The most common medical causes of death are tetanus and other perinatal causes

Table 15.4 Mortality Rates (per 1,000) at Ages 1-4 for Children of Both Sexes According to Education in Matlab, Bangladesh

Education	Education of Household Head (1974-77)	Highest Educational Attainment in Family (1974-77)	Mother's Education* (1975-77)	Mother's Education** (1980)
None	34.5	41.9	33.3	24.6
1 - 6	25.8	28.9	20.2	13.2
7+	18.1	18.5	6.3	0.0
All	29.4	29.4	29.2	21.0
Ratio***	1.9	2.2	5.3	∞

* Only for children and deaths between ages 1 - 3 years.

** Child mortality rates relate to 1,522 mothers in five Matlab villages.

*** Ratio of mortality rates of those without education in comparison to those with 7 or more years of education.

Source: D'Souza and Bhuiya, 1982.

among infants, and diarrhoea, measles, respiratory diseases, and unknown fevers among children one to four years of age.

Table 15.3 summarizes the relationship between child mortality and selected background variables. Four socioeconomic variables (occupation of head of household, dwelling size, ownership of cows, and possession of fixed latrines) all correlate inversely with child mortality.

The relationship between education and child mortality also conforms to the expected pattern (Table 15.4). For all indicators of educational attainment (head of household, highest level attained within the family, and mother's) the level of child mortality shows an inverse relationship with education. This relationship is most marked with mother's education.

Sex differentials of childhood mortality are shown in Table 15.5 and Figure 15.1. Table 15.5 presents infant (neonatal and postneonatal) and child mortality rates by sex. Although the sex differential of the overall infant mortality rates does not appear striking, a breakdown of infant mortality into neonatal and

Figure 15.1 Ratio of Female to Male Mortality Rates for Children Under Five Years in Matlab, Bangladesh, 1974-77

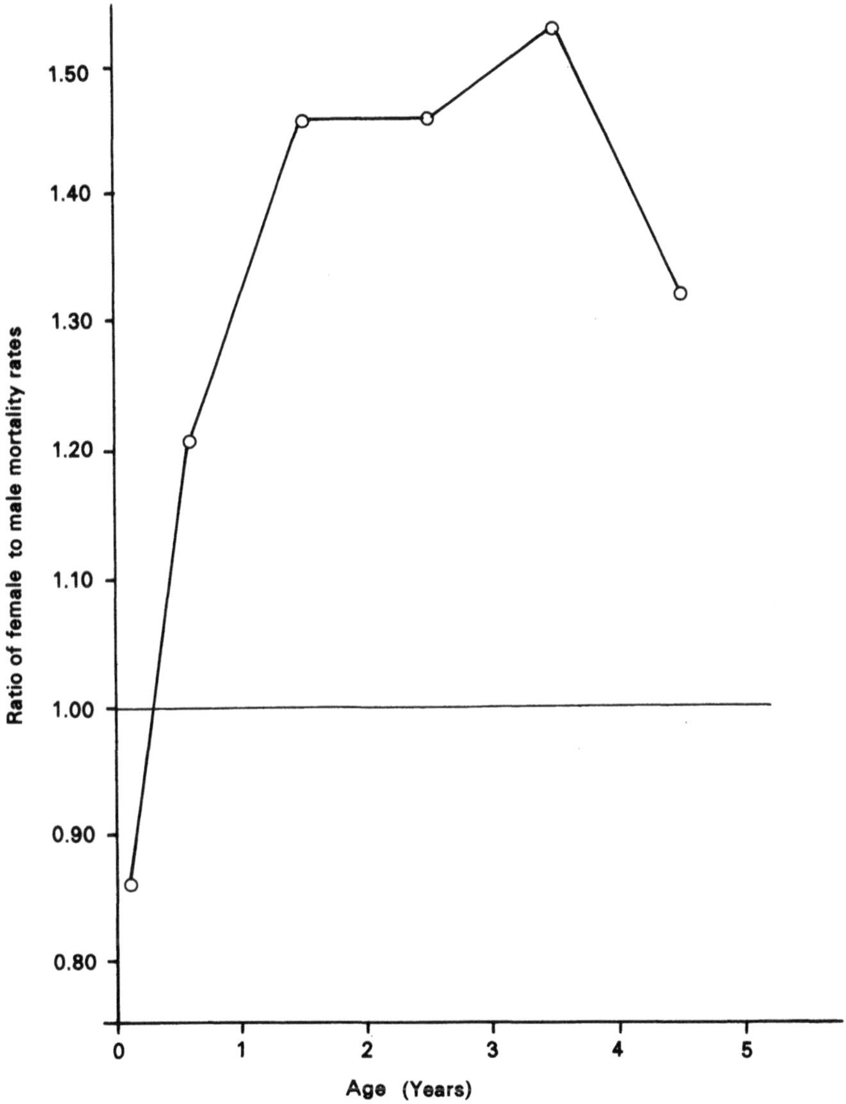

Source: D'Souza and Chen, 1980.

Table 15.5 Infant and Child (1-4) Years Mortality Rates (per 1,000) by Year and Sex in Matlab, Bangladesh, 1974-77

Mortality Measure	1974	1975	1976	1977	1974-77
Infant mortality rate (all infants)					
Both sexes	137.9	191.8	102.9	113.7	131.2
Male	142.5	165.1	113.6	113.3	130.9
Female	132.9	184.1	110.3	114.2	131.5
Neonatal mortality rate (infants less than one month)					
Both sexes	78.1	79.9	65.3	71.3	73.0
Male	87.9	81.6	72.0	73.1	78.2
Female	67.8	78.1	58.1	69.4	67.6
Postneonatal mortality rate (infants 1-11 months)					
Both sexes	59.8	111.9	37.6	42.4	58.2
Male	54.6	98.4	33.3	40.2	52.6
Female	65.1	126.3	42.1	44.8	63.9
Child mortality rate (1-4 years)					
Both sexes	25.4	24.9	29.6	19.6	28.43
Male	18.3	28.8	25.5	14.5	23.27
Female	32.9	41.3	33.9	25.2	33.89

Source: D'Souza and Chen, 1980.

postneonatal components (i.e., for infants up to one month and for infants aged one to twelve months) presents a very different picture. Neonatal rates for males are significantly higher than those for females. Conversely, female postneonatal rates are significantly higher than male rates. Sex differentials of infant mortality therefore undergo a reversal from the neonatal to the postneonatal periods. The pattern in Bangladesh clearly does not conform to the pattern in most societies, where male mortality predominates during both the neonatal and postneonatal periods. In fact, the female predominance of mortality during the post-neonatal period is further accentuated during the one to four year age group.

Figure 15.1 depicts the direction and magnitude of sex differentials in mortality for children under age 5 years. The ratios of female to male mortality at specific ages are plotted.

Figure 15.2 Framework of Health and Nutritional Determinants of Child Mortality

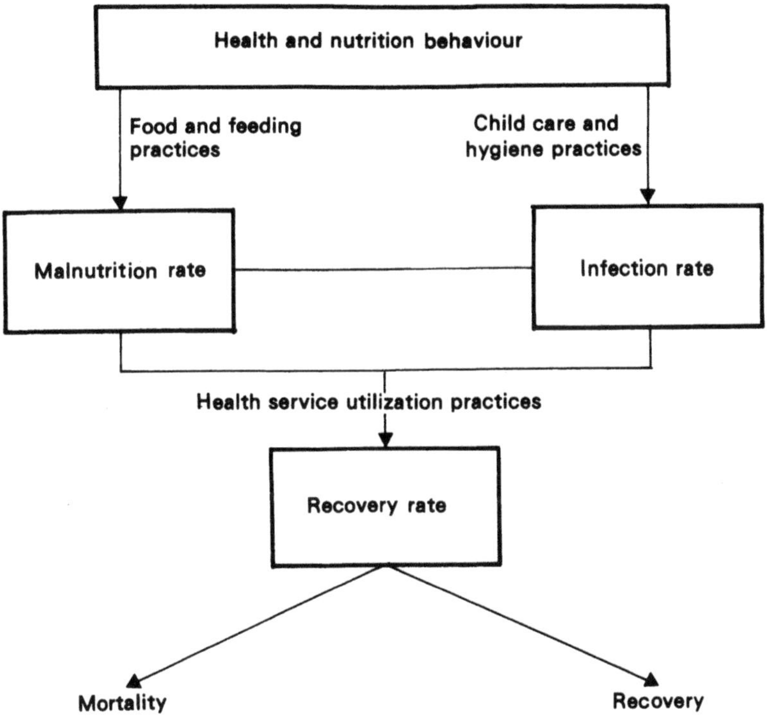

Source: Chen *et al.*, 1981.

Male mortality exceeds female mortality only during the neonatal period. Thereafter, female mortality exceeds male mortality by increasing amounts up to age 3 years, where female death rates are 46 to 53 per cent higher than the corresponding male rate. The ratio declines in the fourth year and falls further for ages beyond 5 years, but the predominance of female mortality is retained until the end of the reproductive years (not shown).

Micro-studies

1. Sex differentials of mortality

To examine whether behavioural variables account for sex differentials of childhood mortality, a framework conceptualizing the hypothetical mechanisms by which sex-biased health and nutritional behaviour might produce the observed mortality differentials in children was developed (Figure 15.2). The major forms of illness among children in developing countries are protein-calorie malnutrition and the common childhood infections, such as diarrhoea, measles, respiratory diseases, and infections of the skin, eyes, and ears.

Protein-calorie malnutrition is basically determined by two factors: food intake (including breastfeeding) and infections. Food consumption is obviously fundamental to nutritional well-being, but infections too are critically important in determining nutritional status because, through a series of biological mechanisms, infections cause loss of appetite, malabsorption of ingested nutrients, and biologic wastage of available nutrients (Chen and Scrimshaw, 1983). Infections, in turn, are determined by two factors: host susceptibility and exposure to disease transmission. The capacity of the host to defend itself against infection is known to be at least in part determined by nutritional status. Exposure to disease transmission is believed to be affected by the quality of the physical (water, sanitation, housing) and personal (child care, hygiene) environment. There are thus both separate and mutually reinforcing determinants of nutritional status and infections. Malnutrition and infections have been postulated to be 'synergistic', a bi-directional causal relationship in which malnutrition and infection each predisposes and exacerbates the other, resulting in a combined effect that is more deleterious than either alone.

In addition to nutritional status and infections, child mortality would also be expected to be influenced by health care practices in response to illness. The burden of morbidity is known to be many times that of mortality. Thus, the recovery rate from individaul episodes of illness is normally high. Given the power of modern curative services, such as antibiotics for common childhood diseases and oral rehydration and feeding rehabilitation for malnutrition, however, very much higher recovery rates are possible. Improved recovery would be dependent in part upon the nutritional status of the host and upon the utilization of available, appropriate, and effective curative health services.

Table 15.6 Daily Intake of Calories and Protein by Age and Sex in Matlab, Bangladesh, June-August 1978

	Calories (number)			Protein (grams)		
Age group	Male	Female	Ratio M/F	Male	Female	Ratio M/F
0 - 4	809	694	1.16	23.0	20.2	1.14
5 - 14	1,590	1,430	1.11	50.9	41.6	1.22
15 - 44	2,700	2,099	1.29	73.6	58.8	1.25
45+	2,630	1,634	1.61	71.8	46.9	1.53
All ages	1,927	1,599	1.20	55.0	45.5	1.21

Source: Chen *et al.*, 1981.

Simplified for the sake of clarification, this framework permits us to identify several health and nutrition behavioural and outcome variables that sex-biased attitudes would necessarily have to operate through in order to affect mortality. Rates of malnutrition, infection, and recovery are three such variables. These, in turn, would be expected to be influenced by 'behavioural patterns' related to food intake, child care, and health service utilization, respectively.

The in-depth Matlab Food and Nutrition study systematically examined the gender-bias of these three behavioural variables depicted in the analytical framework (Chen *et al.*, 1981). Field anthropometry confirmed that females had higher proportions of severely malnourished children than corresponding males, even after weights and heights were compared to sex-specific standards of well-nourished populations. More laborious and time-demanding dietary measurements examined intra-family food distribution and also individual nutrient intake. Table 15.6 showing the average daily intake of nutrients by age and sex confirmed that male caloric and protein consumption exceeded female intake in all age groups. These gender differences of food intake persisted, or were further accentuated, when intake was adjusted for the sex-specific requirements of men and women.

A similar sex-bias was noted in the utilization of health care services. Although in-depth field surveillance showed that the illness or morbidity rate was similar for children of both sexes in the field, the use of ICDDRB diarrhoeal treatment services in Matlab was much more frequent for male children; in fact infant male child hospital utilization rates exceeded female child use by a startling 66 per cent. This difference existed even though the diarrhoeal treatment services were free, and travel to and from the facility was provided without fee in jeeps and speedboat ambulances. Thus, despite free services (involving, of course, social, time, and other indirect costs), male children were brought to the treatment facility by their guardians far more frequently than were female children.

2. Education and childhood mortality

In an anthropological exploration of the social processes responsible for the inverse correlation between female education and child survival, Lindenbaum (1983) noted the universality of the phenomenon reported in the demographic literature. While it seems firmly established, many hypotheses have been advanced to explain the relationship as cause-and-effect. These include, among others, that female education (i) produces psycho-social changes in the mother affecting favourably her attitude and behaviour toward her children (Levine, 1980); (ii) changes the intra-familial power structure so that family resource allocation of food, time, and child care are shifted toward children (Caldwell, 1979); (iii) generates a 'synergy' of both biological and social factors affecting child mortality risk (Mosley, 1983); and/or (iv) is associated with subtle income differentials which are not detected by large scale quantitatively-oriented economic surveys.

Lindenbaum's in-depth field investigation was not able to confirm or refute conclusively the relative merits of the various hypotheses. The hypotheses, in any case, are not mutually exclusive. Rather, her use of anthropological techniques enriched our understanding of female education as a component of social change and generated many novel insights. She noted, for example, that female education may affect intra-familial power relationships. As female education is a recent phenomenon in Bangladesh, as in most Third World countries, the decision-making process of those households containing educated daughters-in-law and uneducated mothers-in-law could be presumed to differ from households wherein both daughter-in-law and mother-in-law are uneducated.

This assumption seemed warranted since education appeared to exert a profound psychological impact on the young mother. The community perceived education as a key element of a woman's 'social identity'. In fact, all villagers could reliably report on the educational attainment of most women in the village. Educated women were reported to be more self-sufficient and assertive, and better able to cope with stress and to use external resources (e.g. health care services). Education conferred a sense of the 'social geography' beyond the household in a society where *purdah* customarily confines women to their homestead. The social value of education was reflected by its desirability in a marriage partner (lower dowry for educated women), and educated women consistently tended to marry men with equal or higher levels of educational attainment.

In addition to these psycho-social and intra-familial power effects, Lindenbaum noted that disguised demographic and economic factors could also be playing an explanatory role. Educated women tended to marry later than their uneducated counterparts. Delayed marriage would postpone childbearing to the lower mortality risk ages of the 20s, rather than customary childbearing in the teens. Moreover, divorce was less common among educated women. Both later marriage and fewer divorces would exert favourable biological and social forces in child survival. Also, because educated women have better prospects of attracting a more economically advanced spouse, one would also expect higher incomes among the households of educated women. Some of these income effects, however, may be disguised, because the preference in Matlab is not for higher income of the male spouse *per se*, but rather for security and stability of income (locally termed *chakri*).

Counter to intuition, Lindenbaum found no difference in beliefs and theories of disease causation (germ theory) between educated and uneducated women. Rather, all tended to share common traditional beliefs on illness causation and attitudes toward appropriateness of various medical interventions. How then were educated women able to achieve better child survival? Lindenbaum postulated that education facilitated an earlier and more effective use of allopathic health services in response to child illness. Education also fostered 'upward social mobility' behaviour - which included cleaner homes, neatness, and better personal hygiene. These behavioural patterns served the dual purposes of conveying higher social status as well as generating indirectly beneficial health effects.

Discussion

The set of analyses presented in this chapter, taken as a whole, lends powerful support to the proposition of sex-related and education-related differentials in childhood mortality in rural Bangladesh. The Matlab demographic surveillance system generated an unusually reliable data base which, when analyzed, demonstrated marked differences in the mortality risk of female versus male children and amongst children of educated verses non-educated mothers. The quantitative analysis was able to confirm conclusively these demographic phenomena. It was also able to facilitate indirect analyses of possible causes and processes responsible for the observed differentials. Thus, in addition to simple measurement of events (e.g. births and deaths), straightforward characteristics of the population (e.g. sex and education) could also be reliably and easily generated by large scale demographic research.

Micro-approaches were not able to draw such firm conclusions for an entire population. Rather, their results complemented the results of quantitative demographic analysis. In the case of sex-differentials of childhood mortality, the micro-study assessed various intermediate health and nutrition variables which are believed to influence mortality. Consistency in the sex differentials of these intermediate variables lent assurance to the validity of mortality analysis alone. The anthropological study of female education's relationship to child survival examined beliefs, attitudes, and social processes associated with the educational process among young women to derive hypotheses regarding both the social changes engendered as well as their link to improved child survival.

Micro-approaches have been characterized as distinctive in four ways: small scale, intensity, continuity, and variety of methods. The Matlab cases illustrate several of these characteristics. The food and nutrition study and the anthropological field investigation both dealt with small, circumscribed populations. In the latter case, the intensity of measurement required the full-time residence of the principal investigator in Matlab villages, while in the former, several of the measurements required intensive field work. Not all of the measurements in the former case were undertaken by the investigator himself, however. The methods employed in these two studies were extremely diverse - ranging from the weighing of food, to weekly morbidity reporting, to observational techniques. Finally, both maintained continuous data gathering with the results reflecting changes over time or historical perspectives.

Despite these consistencies with features prescribed for micro-approach research, the Matlab experience nevertheless suggests that these characteristics are 'insufficient' to describe fully the relative uses of micro-approaches versus macro-approaches. Demographic methods also may be limited in scale, depending upon the event frequency and the statistical confidence limit desired. Intensity too may be high, particularly with complex instruments such as recall of pregnancy history or income-expenditure surveys. The range of methods - direct and indirect - is numerous in the quantitative sciences, and continuity need not be unique to micro-studies. The Matlab surveillance system, for example, had maintained continuous monitoring of the study population for over 20 years.

What then characterizes micro-approaches in contrast to demographic studies? The Matlab experience suggests two common features. The first relates to the nature of the research hypothesis itself. As the examples illustrate, demographic data are superior for identifying the patterns, levels, trends, and socio-economic correlates of demographic processes. Analytical techniques also can generate useful insights into the determinants responsible for the observed outcomes. These require the study of intermediate health and nutrition variables, such as morbidity, diet, time allocation, beliefs, behaviour, and social relationships.

A second issue relates to the process of research instrument selection and design in addressing specific hypotheses. Among others, research instruments must be assessed on the basis of validity, reliability, cost, logistical requirements, skill endowment of field workers, social constraints, and ethical considerations. Several of these retain primacy, such as ethical considerations, but rarely does any single criterion overwhelm the others entirely. Rather, there are 'trade-offs' between them. In the female education study example, the quantitative relationship between female education and childhood mortality had already been well-established in the literature and in Matlab itself. The major research agenda had shifted from documenting the phenomenon towards an understanding of the processes responsible for the differential. Thus, an anthropological investigation was most appropriate given the nature of questions being posed. In the case of sex-differentials of mortality, the micro-studies were undertaken as part of an overall study of the determinants of childhood mortality. Again, quantitative data confirmed the sex differentials. But much more intensive, logistically-taxing, and skill-demanding measures were required to elucidate the 'antecedents' to the observed mortality pattern. Ethical considerations played a central role in the study design. The Matlab diarrhoea treatment unit which provided free services and paraprofessional field staff who obtained morbidity reports weekly provided curative health services for all treatable illnesses; all of the study children received simple treatment for illnesses and no mortality was observed during the study period. The morbidity data also involved stool and occasionally blood specimens to confirm disease diagnosis. Such intrusive and invasive demands obviously posed important logistical and social constraints. Intra-familial food distribution measurements were particularly challenging since client-reporting methodologies were suspect for this purpose. Instead, a weightment/volumetric method was especially developed for the study, involving quantitative measurements and observations. Even then, study-induced biases could not be eliminated entirely. The time budget study too placed heavy demands on field staff. Pre-tests found recall methods entirely unreliable, and objective observations (every 30 minutes) over the course of a full waking day were required. All of these methods were specifically selected and developed because they each suited the hypothesis being addressed while at the same time were affordable and feasibly managed. For each method other alternatives were possible but discarded because of inappropriateness.

The nature of the research hypothesis and trade-offs of characteristics associated with the research instruments are thus the common features of micro-research approaches employed in Matlab. Such micro-approaches provide an invaluable complement to demographic techniques. Taken together, both demographic and micro-methods permit a 'triangulation' of research findings, facilitating the confirmation, refutation, or elaboration of specific hypotheses from several different research approaches, thereby lending assurance to the final results obtained.

16

Observing the Unexpected: Nutrition and Child Mortality in Guinea-Bissau

Peter Aaby

Introduction

The popular image of science suggests that research is a process of exploring the unknown. In most instances, however, methodology is mainly concerned with reproducible ways of observing an anticipated reality. This is clearly the case for the social-life sciences such as demography, epidemiology and nutrition which form the focus of this chapter. No matter whether the primary objective is data gathering or hypothesis testing, reality is analyzed in terms of predetermined categories and relations between these categories. The essential types of causal relations and range of outcomes are pre-ordained in the planning of the research project. The only unknowns are the specific values of variables and the relative strength of the association between variables. This type of research is highly reproducible. In disciplines using intensive studies and participant observation, on the other hand, prior expectations play a smaller (but still very important) role. For example, much anthropological fieldwork can be seen as an attempt to understand unexpected or new experiences. As a consequence, the degree of replicability may be quite low in much anthropological research.

Science seems to be most fruitful when it is confronted with new or contradictory observations. When basic assumptions are refuted by observations, possibilities are created for imagining alternative causes which might account for both new and old observations. However, little has been written of how to observe the unexpected and what to do when it occurs. In a methodologically ideal approach, the unexpected becomes merely an opportunity to formulate new hypotheses to be tested in controlled studies. In practice, however, the unexpected is frequently the result of extensive data collection and intensive analysis. For example, a study of infant and child mortality in rural Mali (Hill *et al.*, 1983) found that relative mortality risks for different ethnic groups were directly contradictory to initial expectations.

Presumably the unexpected is frequently unobserved or neglected because there is no way to revise the initial research design. In this sense, there seems to be good reason to discuss the methodological problems in observing something new or contradictory and how to allow for its occurrence in planning the research. These issues will be discussed using the example of a nutrition and child health survey in Guinea-Bissau. Our starting point was that, contrary to common assumptions, the research found no relation between state of nutrition and child mortality from measles infection.

Nutrition and Child Mortality in Guinea-Bissau

Background and Objectives

With a child mortality of about 500 per thousand for children under 5 years of age, Guinea-Bissau is typical of several parts of West Africa (Morley, 1963; Billewicz and McGregor, 1981). In 1978, 4 years after the liberation of Guinea-Bissau from Portuguese colonialism, an interdisciplinary study (nutrition, medicine, and anthropology) was undertaken to provide baseline data on the children in the country and to find the major causes of malnutrition. A basic assumption was that improving the nutritional situation of the children would reduce child mortality.

The study consisted of general surveys of children under 6 years of age in one urban and five rural areas (Aaby *et al.*, 1981b). The areas were chosen to represent Guinea-Bissau's major ethnic groups and the different ecological zones. The total child population involved was 4,000. The surveys included anthropometric and clinical examinations of the children as well as information on feeding practices, maternal, sociocultural, and socioeconomic background factors. Re-examinations were made after one year and non-attending children were identified, so it was possible to obtain accurate assessments of mortality levels in the different areas. The anthropologists in the study team made short field visits among the different ethnic groups to obtain more detailed sociocultural background data, as well as information on food production and child feeding patterns. Observations and interviews focused on division of labour, food production, control over resources, food security, food preparation and distribution, breastfeeding and weaning patterns. Some information was also sought on morbidity and on disease perception. Neonatal tetanus was assumed to be a major cause of high mortality rates during the first month of life, and interviews therefore emphasized hygiene in connection with birth practices.

The point of the more intensive interviews was to discover different productive and feeding patterns which could be related to differences in the nutritional situation of the children. We thought it most effective to try to find local positive variation and reinforce the connected practices rather than trying to introduce new types of food or feeding patterns. At the same time, the anthropological studies tried to identify possible obstacles in terms of cultural beliefs, traditions, production patterns or division of labour which might hinder efforts to improve the health of the children. Although we did study hygiene surrounding birth practices, overall more emphasis was placed on nutritional practices rather than morbidity patterns, and little systematic morbidity data were collected. However, we happened to be present during part of a severe measles epidemic in the urban district of Bandim, and we organized home visits to treat sick children during this period.

Preliminary Results

Child mortality below 5 years of age turned out to be between 400 to 500 per thousand in all the areas examined (Aaby *et al.*, 1981b). The growth pattern was in accordance with international standards during the first 6 months of life, but in the following 9 to 12 months growth was insufficient, and an increasing proportion of the children had a weight-for-age below 80 per cent of standard. There were no clinical signs of protein or vitamin deficiencies. Around the age of 18 months, the frequency of malnourished children more or less stabilizes, though at a sub-optimal level. With respect to mean weight-for-age, the different communities in Guinea-Bissau stabilized between 90 per cent and 80 per cent of international standard.

Preliminary analysis of the nutritional data was frustrating. There was no indication that nutritional practices such as time of introduction of supplementary feeding, length of breastfeeding, number of meals, consumption of palm oil, or availability of staple food (rice) had any impact on the growth pattern of the children. Nor was there any correlation between the state of nutrition and socioeconomic background factors. Quality of house, education of father or mother, religion, work situation, type of child care, co-residence with mother or other relative, birth order, age of mother, or proportion of dead children of mother did not have a clear association with nutritional status.

Malnutrition and Measles Mortality

However, a surprising observation turned up in the analysis. The Bandim measles epidemic killed as many as 7.6 per cent (52 out of 682) of all children under 3 years of age (Aaby *et al.*, 1983a). Among the cases seen during the epidemic and treated in the home, the case fatality rate was as high as 25 per cent for children under 3 years of age (12 out of 48). Most surprising, however, was the fact that the children who died were not particularly malnourished. The 60 children reported to have died of measles between the first survey and the re-examination did not differ in weight-for-age, height-for-age, and weight-for-height from the total population in the district (see Table 16.1). Furthermore, for the 98 persons we had actually examined with measles and treated during the epidemic, there was no difference in state of nutrition between fatal cases and survivors.

This was surprising inasmuch as high mortality in many infectious diseases in the developing world is generally assumed to be caused by the high degree of malnutrition in these countries. During the Bandim epidemic we arranged popular meetings to inform and discuss the treatment of measles and where

Table 16.1 Nutritional Status of Children Aged 0-2 Years Who Died of Measles and the Total Population. Bandim, Guinea-Bissau, 1979.

	Died of measles (N=52)	Total population (N=682)
	%	%
Weight-for-age	92.2	93.1
Height-for-age	97.1	97.4
Weight-for-height	96.5	97.3

Source: Aaby *et al.*, 1983a.

we particularly emphasized the importance of nutrition. The presumed causal link between malnutrition and severe disease has been particularly stressed for measles infection (*Lancet*, 1968; The Kasongo Project Team, 1983). For example, it has been suggested that malnourished children may have several hundred times the risk of dying of measles than well-nourished children (Walsh, 1983, p.330). The WHO manual on *The Assessment of the Nutritional Status of the Community* goes so far as to suggest that data on measles mortality provides approximate indices of the nutritional status of the child population (Jelliffe, 1966, p.105). Malnutrition is assumed to have been the cause of the high case fatality rate encountered in measles infection among poor people in industrialized countries 100 years ago (*Lancet*, 1983).

Replicability

Assuming for the moment that there is no apparent technical or methodological problem with the observation, the first concern after something unexpected has occurred is whether the observation is replicable. In a laboratory situation where a new phenomenon has been observed, this condition is easily met since it merely implies the repetition of the experiment. However, in a real-life situation many considerations, including ethical ones, may prevent one from repeating the conditions of observation. For example, in an area with a 25 per cent case fatality rate in measles, it would seem of questionable ethical value to set up a study to examine the relation between state of nutrition and measles mortality without vaccinating simultaneously. This would, of course, make the study pointless. (That we did not vaccinate in the first survey is due to the fact that measles vaccine was not generally available in Bissau and we did not know measles to be so severe.) Under such conditions, it may be more feasible to test a new observation/hypothesis through some of its implications, as will be discussed later on. However, in a situation where something is unexpected not because it is new but because it contradicts what is commonly believed to be true, the first requirement is to show that there is no foundation, or only disputable evidence, for the commonly accepted beliefs. Reinterpretation of previous studies therefore becomes necessary.

Previous studies

Evidence for the assumed connection between malnutrition and high mortality in measles has come mainly from hospital studies showing that weight-for-age at admission is correlated with outcome of infection (Morley *et al.*, 1967; Savage, 1967). However, children already lose weight during the incubation period of measles infection (Meunier, 1898) and children of low weight-for-age who subsequently die may be the most severely affected before admission; for example they may be more dehydrated (Savage, 1967). Such studies, therefore, do not prove that state of nutrition determines outcome of measles infection. It should also be noted that some hospital studies have failed to find an association between state of nutrition and measles mortality (Manshamde and Vuylsteke, 1981; Aaby *et al.*, 1983a).

However, a number of community studies also suggest some relation between state of nutrition and mortality risk from measles infection. One study from Guatemala (Scrimshaw *et al.*, 1966) has often been quoted as showing the importance of nutrition for measles mortality (Dover *et al.*, 1975; Walsh, 1983). In this study, measles mortality was 6.8 per cent (eight deaths) among pre-school children in a control village as opposed to 4.3 per cent (two deaths) in a village having a feeding program. It should be noted that one more death in the feeding program village would make the rates identical. More importantly, the epidemiological patterns in the two villages were totally different. In the control village, there were two outbreaks with an average of 103 cases in the 5 years of study. In the feeding program village with closer contact with a trade centre, there were five outbreaks with an average of twenty cases per outbreak. Since it is well established that mortality is usually higher during major epidemics, the difference in epidemic pattern could easily account for the small difference in mortality between the two villages.

Two community studies from Africa have claimed to find support for the importance of state of nutrition as a determinant of measles mortality. In Senegal, a study of measles outbreaks in three Serer and three Wolof villages found that the case fatality rate was higher in villages where the state of nutrition had been low prior to the epidemic (Debroise *et al.*, 1967). The Serer suffered both high malnutrition and a high case fatality rate in measles compared with the Wolof. By not showing that within the same ethnic group, it was the children with low weight-for-age who died of measles, however, the Senegal study did not prove that state of nutrition determined the case fatality rate. It is possible that both high mortality and low state of nutrition are caused by the same factors. Another study of two epidemics in Kenya found support for the malnutrition hypothesis: children who died had significantly smaller arm-circumferences than those who survived (Muller *et al.*, 1977). However, the difference of 4 per cent (6mm) in arm-circumference is not very significant. Moreover, the result may have been influenced by the combination of cases from two epidemics, where the states of nutrition had been significantly different. As further support of the importance of the state of nutrition, it was pointed out that the nutritional status was significantly better in the last epidemic when the case fatality rate was low then in the first epidemic when the case fatality rate was high. However, the malnutrition hypothesis is still not strongly supported in this example. This is because non-measles mortality during the second period was higher than during the first, suggesting a direct, rather than the expected inverse, relation between state of nutrition and mortality in other infections.

One 2-year study from Bangladesh (Chen *et al.*, 1980) showed a a 2.3 times higher risk of dying of measles for malnourished children below 65 per cent of weight-for-age (11 out of 742) compared with children above 65 per cent of weight-for-age (8 out of 1277) ($0.05 < p < 0.10$, chi-square). This may, however, be the result more of differences in incidence than of differences in case fatality rate, since state of nutrition is lower and the incidence of measles higher in large families (Aaby *et al.*, 1984b). Most noteworthy in the study from Bangladesh was the fact that no difference in mortality risk could be found for normal, mildly and moderately malnourished children (Chen *et al.*, 1980). To complete the picture, a few studies have suggested the opposite tendencies of those to be expected from the malnutrition hypothesis; namely, low case fatality rate among severely malnourished children (Sinha, 1977) and high mortality among relatively well-nourished children (Black *et al.*, 1979; Cox, 1973; Heyworth, 1973).

Thus the existing literature fails to provide clear proof of an association between state of nutrition and measles mortality. Furthermore, there appears to have been no consideration of the possibility that a covariation between low state of nutrition and high measles mortality may not necessarily indicate a causal relation between state of nutrition and mortality. In Guinea-Bissau, for example, measles mortality was high and the state of nutrition lower in polygamous families, but the state of nutrition of children who died in polygamous families did not differ in nutritional status from other children in these families (Aaby *et al.*, 1983a). From this perspective, our unexpected observation from the epidemic in Bandim is not an isolated contrary case. Even if further studies should show a somewhat higher case fatality rate for the most malnourished children, as suggested by some studies (Chen *et al.*, 1980), it can clearly only account for a very small part of the excessive mortality in measles. In Bandim, there were no severely malnourished (i.e. weight-for-age below 60 per cent of standard) among the children who died of measles. This empirical refutation of a common belief should be sufficient to suggest a search for other determinants of measles mortality.

Alternative Observations and Hypotheses

In a situation where common assumptions have failed, there is a strong inducement to formulate alternative hypotheses. Even before the replicability of the observation on state of nutrition and measles mortality became clear, we looked for other determinants of high case fatality in measles. Comparing the case fatality in measles as the dependent variable with socioeconomic background factors yielded no significant correlation. There was no relation between nutritional parameters, including breast-feeding (Aaby *et al.*, 1981b), housing conditions, age and education of parents, work situation of the mother, or adoption and the case fatality rate. However, the case fatality rate was somewhat higher in polygamous families. This suggested that the clustering of many children in a family could be a health problem. Consistent with this, there was a high case fatality rate among the Mancanhas, the ethnic group with the highest rate of polygamy and the largest families; whereas the Balantas, an ethnic group with a relatively high rate of polygamy but small families due to long spacing, had a lower case fatality rate (Aaby *et al.*, 1983a; 1983b). Yet these tendencies were not very marked, and we imagined that an explanation of increased case fatality would have to be sought in a multitude of different factors, including higher rates of complications and improper treatment of the ill, e.g. withholding of water. However, while coding the re-examination list from a rural area where there had also been a measles epidemic (Aaby *et al.*, 1984d), it appeared that deaths had adjacent numbers on the list of children. This suggested that deaths often belonged to the same families; in other words, that disease became more severe when several children were sick simultaneously.

We tried to test this by dividing cases according to whether there was only a single case or multiple cases in the household. This procedure required a re-organization of the material. In the intitial organization, the individual child was assumed to be influenced by nutritional practices and morbidity; the influence of its household membership was defined through such variables as parental education and work and quality of housing. For the individual child there was no information on its siblings or household mates. It was therefore necessary to reclassify the material according to the co-occurence of cases. This procedure was only possible because the children could be identified by household membership, and because a census of the total population in Bandim had been carried out just prior to the first survey.

Regrouping the material by household membership showed a clear tendency toward a higher measles case fatality rate in households where there was more than one case. As this was not a result of the lower state of nutrition in households with several cases, we hypothesized that measles somehow got more severe when several children became sick simultaneously. It therefore seemed a reasonable hypothesis that 'secondary' cases, i.e., those infected after prolonged contact within the home, were more severe than the 'index' cases who had caught the infection outside the home. While the low number of cases precluded definite corroboration, our hypothesis was supported by the record from the home visits during the epidemic, where we registered a higher mortality among the later cases in the house (Aaby *et al.*, 1984b).

The observation of high mortality among both multiple cases and secondary cases suggested different mechanisms of severe infection. However, these observations also revealed a number of gaps in our data. These gaps were caused by the fact that we had not initially planned to study the epidemiology of measles. Because data on measles attack in the population had been obtained only during the general re-examination, measles data were lacking for the 34 per cent of the children who did not attend the re-examination because they had died, moved or were temporarily absent. There could also be doubt about the reliability of the measles diagnosis in cases where information on measles infection had been provided not by the mother but by a neighbour or older sibling bringing the child for examination. Furthermore we had no information on measles among children above 5 years of age in the general population in Bandim. Home visits during the epidemic had suggested that 15 to 20 per cent of the measles cases belonged to this older age group. This lack of information clearly affected the validity of the classification of patients as single or multiple cases. Finally, we had no information on exposure as index or secondary cases for those cases not seen during the epidemic.

In terms of textbook methodology, the proper thing to do would have been to organize better data collection and wait for the next measles epidemic. Apart from the technical and financial problems involved in setting up a new study, however, it was also ethically impossible. If data collection were to be organized, vaccinations would also have to be given, which would eliminate the point of the study.

Instead, we decided to make a retrospective study of the epidemic in Bandim. A re-census was made and interviews were carried out in all houses where measles had been reported, in order to check on the co-occurrence of cases and on the sequence of infection in the house. This study could only be made because there existed a census from the time of the epidemic which made it possible to check when all members had had measles. The results, which have been reported in detail elsewhere (Aaby *et al.*, 1984b) showed quite clearly that mortality had been much higher in houses with multiple cases. In the age group 6 to 35 months, where measles is most severe, multiple cases had a mortality of 34.7 per cent (34 out of 98), whereas the rate was

Table 16.2 Rate of Low Height-for-Age (below 95% of standard) According to Age and Clustering of Cases. Bandim, Guinea-Bissau, 1979.

Age (months)	Single cases Below 95%/Total	Rate	Multiple cases Below 95%/Total	Rate
		%		%
0 - 11	2/13	15.4	8/40	20.0
12 - 35	3/16	18.8	32/65	49.2
36 - 71	3/7	42.9	37/74	50.0
Total	8/36	22.2	77/179	43.0

only 9.4 per cent (3 out of 32) in houses with only a single case. Likewise, the case fatality rate was three times higher for secondary cases than index cases (Aaby *et al.*, 1984b).

Given this background, it may be more understandable why there could be a covariation between state of nutrition and high mortality without implying a causal relation between the two. In households with many cases of measles, significantly more children aged one-to-two years had low height-for-age than in households with only a single case (Table 16.2; $p < 0.05$; chi-square).

The case fatality rate in measles was higher in those households with several cases. However, within the families with several cases, the case fatality rate was not higher for those children with a low height-for-age (see Table 16.3). This type of covariation may explain some of the minor tendencies toward higher mortality among children with low state of nutrition revealed by some studies (Chen *et al.*, 1980). The example clearly illustrates the danger of interpreting associations (malnutrition and severe measles) as indicating causal relations since they may depend on a common determinant, overcrowding.

These observations also raised the question of why severe disease is associated with overcrowding of cases and intensive exposure. We have suggested that this could be due to a higher dose of infection or a higher rate of intercurrent infections where several children are sick simultaneously (Aaby *et al.*, 1984b). It is possible that the index cases transmit a number of other infections besides measles and therefore aggravate the condition of secondary cases. Another possibility is that the

Table 16.3 Case Fatality Rate in Measles According to Age and Height-for-Age. Only Households with Multiple Cases. Bandim, Guinea-Bissau, 1979.

Age (months)	Below 95% of standard height Deaths/cases	Rate	95% and above of standard height Deaths/cases	Rate
		%		%
0 - 11	1/8	12.5	14/32	43.8
12 - 35	11/32	34.4	10/33	30.3
36 - 71	3/37	8.1	4/37	10.8
Total	15/77	19.5	28/102	27.5

intensive exposure of secondary cases causes them to receive a higher dose of measles virus. Animal studies show a clear link between high dose of infection, short period of incubation, and high mortality. While the importance of dose of viral infection in humans has not been studied systematically, there exist many suggestions that dosage influences the period of incubation and that short incubation periods are associated with severe course of infection (Aaby *et al.*, 1984c). Since the preventive consequences are much the same, we shall not go into a detailed discussion of the different mechanisms and their relative importance.

Test of an Argument: Consistency, Generality, and Deductions

Before making a retrospective study, we had tried other ways of testing the usefulness of the observations. This was done by controlling for:

1. the consistency with known variation in severity of measles infection;
2. the generality, i.e. the applicability of the argument to similar infections; and
3. the possibility of making deductions which corresponded to the observations.

1. Consistency

To be tenable, an alternative observation/hypothesis should be compatible with the known distribution of data. Apart from the severe form encountered in present-day developing countries, measles is known to have been very severe in the industrialized world at the turn of the century, having a reported case fatality rate of 10 to 15 per cent (Drinkwater, 1885; Chalmers, 1930). There is good evidence that mortality increased with crowding, being higher in small apartments (Chalmers, 1930) and where there were many persons per room (Wright and Wright, 1942). Mortality was also particularly high in institutions or situations where many persons were grouped together; for example, children's homes, military camps, emigrant ships, and refugee camps (Aaby *et al.*, 1984b). To mention only a few examples: during the siege of Paris in 1871, the case fatality rate in measles infection was as high as 40 per cent (86 out of 215) in the Garde Mobile (Hirsch, 1883, p.168). In children's institutions in New York, mortality was 24 per cent in the period 1916–18 (Godfrey, 1928).

An interesting feature of such epidemics is that measles was often described as initially relatively mild only to become more severe later on (Picken, 1921; Hirsch, 1883). For example, in an epidemic in 1914-15 in the Scottish Highland army division in Bedford, the case fatality rate was 2.3 per cent (2 out of 87) during the first month but increased to 14.3 per cent (63 out of 442) during the subsequent 2 to 3 months, suggesting that secondary cases are more severe than index cases.

Virgin-soil epidemics have also been characterized by increased severity. In these epidemics no one had prior immunity and virtually everyone came down with measles simultaneously. For example, 20,000 Fijians, around one quarter of the total population, died when measles was first introduced on the island (Squire, 1877). Likewise, there have been very high case fatality rates in measles among American Indians (Black *et al.*, 1979). While the older literature demonstrating high case fatality rates among poor people in the industrialized world made it reasonable to speculate that nutrition could be of importance, there is no indication that the Indians were malnourished (Black *et al.*, 1979). It therefore seems reasonable to see clustering of many cases as a common feature of these epidemics with high case fatality rates. This may partly explain the increased severity found in virgin-soil epidemics (Aaby, 1984).

2. Generality

We also tried to test the generality of the observations by looking for variation in severity in other infections having a similar mode of transmission. A study of chickenpox (varicella) tested the severity of index and secondary cases and found the secondary cases to be more severe (Ross, 1962). There are also epidemiological indications that paralytic cases of polio virus infection are secondary to index cases with an inapparent infection (Aycock and Eaton, 1925).

3. Deductions

In pursuing the implications of the unexpected observations, the attempts to test for consistency and generality were supportive as was the fact that not so long ago some doctors thought that 'chief among the causes of high mortality (in measles) are overcrowding and insufficient ventilation' (Williams, 1897). However, due to the quality of data it is often difficult to make precise tests of consistency and generality. It is therefore most important to generate alternative hypotheses which can be subject to verification. We made several deductions, but we shall discuss only the most important here.

Measles Vaccination and Survival

It has often been suggested that measles vaccination may have a limited effect on survival because malnourished children saved from dying of measles by vaccination are likely to die of something else instead (Hendrickse, 1975). The argument has been expressed by Mosley (1983, p.44) as follows:

> '...even when a child is successfully immunized, the protection is only against one specific agent. The child remains at risk to all other causes of death, and, *all things being equal*, a certain proportion will go on to die of these "competing" causes... But, all things are not equal. Specifically, the children whose deaths might be prevented by measles vaccine are at risk of dying not because of the severity of measles *per se*, but because they are on the "road to death", and their nutritional status is so poor that they are more likely to die of any infectious disease. Thus preventing a measles death among these children may not necessarily save a life, but only change the cause of death'.

No one has actually substantiated this notion by showing that general mortality either remains the same or decreases only minimally for children who receive measles vaccination in comparison with children who have not received the vaccine.

Based on the alternative notion of overcrowding being a major determinant of measles mortality, we deduced that measles vaccination should have a very marked effect on survival rates. We had introduced measles vaccination in Bandim in December 1979 as a consequence of our experience with the severe epidemic. Since the local registration continued in the community, it was possible to test in a preliminary fashion the hypothesis about the survival consequences of measles vaccination. The result far exceeded our expectations. In 1979, mortality during one year of follow-up for children aged 6 to 35 months had been 12.7 per cent (77 out of 605). During 1980, despite a fall in the state of nutrition in the community, mortality was only 1.9 per cent (7 out of 361) for the children in the same age group who had received a measles vaccination at the end of 1979. More important, among children not vaccinated at the end of 1979 because they were not present, mortality continued to be as high as 14.3 per cent (10 out of 70). We have no indication that children not attending examinations are generally worse off; it is mainly a question of them being absent from the community (Aaby *et al.*, 1984a). While this was not a controlled experiment, our data thus suggested a very strong difference in mortality following the introduction of measles vaccination.

In a sense, these data suggested another unexpected observation. The difference in mortality exceeded the percentage of mortality usually attributed to measles (deaths within one month of a measles attack). It is therefore possible that measles not only kills many children but may also weaken some children, leading to delayed excess mortality when comparison is made with children who have not had measles. This was supported by our data from Bandim. Children with measles in 1979 had subsequent excess mortality when compared with children who had not had measles (Aaby *et al.*, 1984a).

Since the observation was unplanned, a controlled experiment would have been desirable to test the reproducibility of the observation. However, for reasons outlined earlier, a new experiment was not possible. While we were contemplating how to document the unexpected connections, a controlled study from Zaire was published (The Kasongo Project Team, 1981). This was a study of general mortality in an urban district where measles vaccination had only been given to one group. For the children initially aged 8 months, general mortality during the first 15 months of follow-up was 3.4 to 4.7 times higher in the three unvaccinated groups than in the vaccinated population. In the second period of follow-up, there was some diminution in the difference in mortality between the groups. This was interpreted as supporting the malnutrition hypothesis, that is, children spared measles due to vaccination were seen as more likely to die later on (The Kasongo Project Team, 1981). It was concluded that measles vaccination was not a priority. However, this conclusion was based on erroneous statistics (Aaby *et al.*, 1981a); at the age of 3 years, when virtually all child deaths have already occurred, the three unvaccinated groups had 1.8 to 2.4 times higher mortality than the vaccinated group. This would correspond to a 44 to 58 per cent reduction in child mortality in the 7 to 35 months age group. The data from Zaire therefore strongly support our observation of a markedly higher mortality among unvaccinated children.

Thus, an emphasis on overcrowding and intensive exposure raised new questions and provided new insights, probably the best support any hypothesis can get.

Undernutrition or Overinfection?

We started out by assuming that malnutrition was the major determinant of high child mortality and that changing this pattern would have a beneficial effect on mortality. Much to our distress, we found very little evidence that nutritional status was strongly related to the variation in nutritional practices conceived in our survey approach. Moreover, there seemed to be little relation between state of nutrition and mortality risk, particularly in measles. If this was true, we could not expect initiatives having a beneficial impact on the state of nutrition to necessarily reduce child mortality.

Observations made during the measles epidemic and the analysis of measles mortality provided us with a different perspective. There seemed to be more reason to emphasize the morbidity pattern and its determinants. For example, when the data on nutritional status was analyzed from this perspective, it was evident that children said to have had frequent diarrhoea had poorer nutritional status than other children (Aaby *et al.*, 1981b). There was also a clear preventive lesson in the analysis. It has often been argued that improving the resistence of the host should determine the choice of preventive strategy since this would increase defence capacity in relation to several different infections (Mosley, 1983). While we initially placed little emphasis on vaccinations, our data strongly suggested that the first strategy should be to reduce morbidity. This was particularly true for measles, where vaccination was apparently associated with at least a 50 per cent reduction in mortality. Similar arguments can be made for polio, tetanus and probably for whooping cough vaccination, though these vaccines will have much less impact on mortality.

The emphasis on morbidity rather than feeding patterns pointed towards a different set of background factors as detrimental to child health and survival. Those social institutions and cultural patterns which lead to clustering of small children tend to increase the health risks due to earlier infection, children becoming ill simultaneously, and greater possibilities of being intensively exposed. For example, children in polygamous and large families had a lower state of nutrition and higher mortality (Tables 16.2, 16.3). Hence, family and marriage arrangements, spacing patterns and housing traditions acquire a new meaning because they influence the age and risk of intensive exposure to infection. Variation in the crowding patterns could therefore be important in understanding historical, regional, or ethnic variations in mortality. One thing which had initially puzzled us was the fact that the largest and socio-politically strongest ethnic group in Guinea-Bassau, the Balantas, had a lower birth rate but seems to have maintained their relative share of the national population. Seen from this alternative perspective, it made sense because they had longer spacing and smaller families than other ethnic groups (Aaby *et al.*, 1983b). During the epidemic in Bandim, the Balantas showed a lower risk of dying of measles. Thus the difference in crowding may provide part of the explanation for the Balantas' ability to hold their own in the demographic 'competition' with other groups.

This perspective also had implications for the understanding of other health problems, for example high infant mortality. The high mortality of infants in the post-neonatal period and the high case fatality of infants in many infections have usually been attributed to immunological immaturity or to the high prevalence of malnutrition in this age group (*Lancet*, 1983). Our studies as well as others' have found that there are often many well-nourished infants who die of measles (Manshande and Vuylsteke, 1981). The emphasis on crowding and intensive exposure suggested a different approach. The particular severity in this age group could be a result of a higher risk of intensive exposure for infants. This hypothesis was supported by the data from the epidemic in Bandim. Among infants, 68 per cent of the total number of cases were secondary, as compared to 49 per cent secondary cases among children aged 3 to 4 years. Several studies support the same tendency for both measles (Picken, 1921) and varicella (Ross, 1962). In a social situation where infants are not attending nurseries, infection during the first year of life is most likely to come from an older sibling. To the extent that secondary cases are more severe, increased severity among infants might be related to the transmission pattern. One study recently examining this problem found that infants do not have diminished immune reactivity in relation to measles when comparison is made with other children. It was concluded that intensive exposure was a probable cause of the high mortality among infants (Coovadia *et al.*, 1984). From this perspective, having siblings could be a risk factor for an infant. For example, Bandim children born in 1979 in households without siblings under 6 years of age had a post-neonatal mortality of 1.6 per cent (one out of 64) during 1979, compared with 7.2 per cent (20 out of 276) for infants with siblings in the age group under 6 years ($p = 0.11$, Fisher's exact test).

Reproducible Observations

We started out by focusing on undernutrition-feeding patterns but ended by emphasizing overinfection. This was the result of a series of unplanned, but logically connected observations:

1. lack of correlation between state of nutrition of the individual and mortality risk in measles infection;

2. high measles mortality in homes with several cases;

3. high case fatality rate for secondary cases of measles;

4. strong reduction in mortality associated with the introduction of measles vaccination;

5. delayed excess mortality among former measles patients.

Practical as well as ethical considerations precluded further studies to confirm the new observations when they were first suggested by our data from Guinea-Bissau. Nonetheless, several of these observations were in fact being tested by studies carried out elsewhere at the same time or could be tested by re-analyzing studies already made. For example, a community study from Bangladesh showed that mean weight-for-height ratio of 33 children who died of measles did not significantly differ from that of control subjects without a history of measles during the period of observation. A major study from Zaire has likewise indicated that there was no major difference in nutritional status of children who died of measles compared with the general population (The Kasongo Project Team, 1983). Finally, in one of the rural areas in Guinea-Bissau there had been several minor outbreaks of measles before regular vaccinations had been initiated. Once again the result was much the same: little or no difference in weight-for-age for fatal cases of measles and survivors (Aaby *et al.*, 1984c). In this rural epidemic, we also found a clear tendency for case fatality to be much higher in houses with several cases. One epidemic of measles in Gambia has been re-analyzed to test the importance of clustering of cases. Multiple cases had a five times higher risk than single cases of dying of acute measles (within one month) and during a follow-up period of 9 months (Hull, 1983). Re-analysis of an old description of a severe measles epidemic with a 10 per cent case fatality rate for children under 3 years of age in Sunderland (England) in 1885 has also shown that (i) multiple cases had a four times higher mortality risk than single cases, and (ii) that secondary cases were more severe (Aaby *et al.*, 1984c). As mentioned above, the study from Zaire showed a marked reduction in mortality for children vaccinated against measles (The Kasongo Project Team, 1981). A recent study from the Gambia has also shown a very strong excessive mortality among former measles patients during a 9 months period of follow-up compared with children who had no measles in the period (Hull *et al.*, 1983).

It is obviously too early to know the extent to which these observations are reproducible. The fact that some comparable results have been obtained seems to support our argument, though future studies may well introduce modifications in the interpretation. However, the further problem to be discussed here is not the validity of these observations nor their implications. Rather, using this study in Guinea-Bissau as an example, we shall discuss how to allow for the unexpected in research design and how to analyze it when it occurs.

Observing the Unexpected: A Methodological Note

The unexpected resists being observed. More precisely, we are likely to overlook or disregard unexpected occurrences (Dover *et al.*, 1975). In our case, we disregarded several hints before realizing that something was wrong. Our initial anthropometric survey in Bandim had clearly shown the nutritional status to be relatively good in the community; mean weight-for-age being 92 per cent and mean height-for-age being 97 per cent of international standards (Aaby *et al.*, 1983a). When we made in-depth interviews on maternity history and disease perception it became quite evident that measles was the disease mothers feared the most. The experience during the epidemic taught us that the mothers were right; child mortality was as high as 25 per cent, even among those who had received treatment in the home. Yet we continued to entertain the possibility that the children visited in the home could comprise a particular subgroup. Only minor changes were made in the data collection to gather more precise information on the epidemiology of measles. It was not until one-and-a-half years after the epidemic when we had all information in the computer, that it became definitely clear that there was something fundamentally wrong.

While observing the unexpected can obviously not be planned, it is still worth pointing out some features which may facilitate the recognition of anomalies. In interdisciplinary research, basic assumptions are probably more easily questioned. Both the intensive interviews and the specific curative work during the epidemic in Bandim were instrumental in making us aware of contradictions to commonly-accepted ideas. Still, without the general survey in the community we probably would have interpreted our personal experiences as accidental occurrences. On the other hand, had we had only survey data and no in-depth knowledge, we might not have noticed the problems, or might have doubted the quality of the data, for example the diagnosis of measles. The combination of more intensive personal experiences which can raise doubts, and material from a larger survey on which to test these doubts, may be the best data collection strategy. It allows for both the 'experiences' and 'recognition' of the unexpected.

The same considerations may apply to the question of how to find and test alternative interpretations; a combination of personal experiences and more general survey data seems most important. To test the idea of clustering, it was necessary to reorganize data at a different level of aggregation, from an individual to a household level. The shift in level of analysis was possible only because we had a census by which we could determine co-residency. Had we only examined a sample of individual children, rather than houses, as originally planned, or had we been without a census, we would not have been able to retrace our analysis and further test our hypotheses.

To test alternative hypotheses generated from data of a long-term research project, new well-planned prospective studies are desirable. However, there are several problems connected with this approach. Such studies are time-consuming, expensive, and may be difficult to fund. In the epidemiological field, such follow-up studies may be unethical. Before undertaking a new project, it may also be desirable to have better knowledge of the phenomenon than that provided by unexpected and possibly incomplete data from one's own material. It is therefore important to find different ways to ensure that observations are reproducible, and to make sure that one is on the right track. We used several different methods to achieve these goals: re-analysis of other studies, correspondence with known regional/historical variation, applicability to other structurally similar phenomena, retrospective studies and deductions.

If relevant data exist, one of the best ways to reach certainty about controversial observations is to re-analyze other people's material or have others re-analyze their own data; this would ensure that the result is not an accidental occurrence or a result of one's own biases. The drawback, of course, is that other people's information will often not be sufficiently complete or systematically collected to enable re-analysis from the point of view of a new observation (Aaby *et al.*, 1984c).

Retrospective studies may also be a valuable method. If the observation is unplanned, some information is likely to be missing; in our case, we needed information on measles infection among guests and children older then 5 years, so as to make a more definite assessment of the difference in mortality for single and multiple cases. Such a retrospective study will usually be far cheaper than a new prospective study because much data is already available and the phenomenon of interest, e.g. an epidemic, is known to have occurred. Despite these advantages there seem to be surprisingly few such retrospective studies. Perhaps it is considered 'bad manners' to report unplanned observations in the scientific literature since they may be statistical artefacts. However, that risk would seem minimal if other ways of substantiating the observations have been marshalled in support.

The kind of retrospective studies or hypothesis-testing which can be made naturally depend on the existing data base. To facilitate retrospective studies and the testing of hypotheses, it would seem indispensable to have a minimum of baseline information such as age, sex, residence, kinship relations, and socio-economic position on all individuals in at least some part of the population studied. A sample chosen from one set of assumptions is likely not to have information on those social groups or categories of individuals who might become relevant from a different perspective. It is therefore important to have the possibility of going back and reorganizing data at a different level. Furthermore, to enhance the reliability of retrospective studies, it is essential to have at least some registration of part of the population from the beginning of the study. For the group which has been registered, it is also essential to have some follow-up data on survival, fertility, migration, and other relevant parameters. The social questions which interest us are usually chronological; it is therefore easier to make relevant retrospective studies or testing of hypothetical deductions if there is some follow-up data in addition to the survey information.

To sum up our experience from Guinea-Bassau, the most fruitful structure of data collection with respect to demographic questions appears to be a combination of longitudinal surveys and more open-ended interviews/participant observation. The essential feature of the research process is the pursuit of all contradictions. This is best done by using different levels of observation and data collection. The combination of different sets of data and approaches facilitates the recognition of contradictions and the analysis of the unexpected.

Acknowledgement

Data presented in this publication were collected in a study jointly organized by the Ministry of Health, Guinea-Bissau, and the Swedish Agency for Research Co-operation with Developing Countries. The last part of the study was supported by funds from the Council for Development Research, Denmark.

17

Age Patterns of Mortality in Eastern Senegal: A Comparison of Micro and Survey Approaches

Gilles Pison and André Langaney

Introduction

Improvement in the quality of demographic data in developing countries is hindered by two problems: firstly, progress in the field of vital registration is very slow, or in many cases, non-existent; and secondly, estimates based on large scale surveys - censuses or national surveys - are not always reliable because of poor data quality, and also because the estimates often employ models with assumptions that cannot be verified.

In the medium term, one means of improving the situation may be micro-level data collection. In small scale surveys, the size of the population observed permits the collection of individual data of better quality, and more diversified, than is possible with large scale surveys. The primary aim of small scale surveys is often a detailed study of behaviour patterns; but the quality of the data collected may also mean improved population estimates, particularly in developing countries.

A small scale population survey conducted in the Bandafassi area of Eastern Senegal will be used here to illustrate this secondary role. A presentation of the Bandafassi study is followed by a description of several new data collection techniques which were used on this occasion and which are specific to small scale surveys. Then the age-specific mortality estimates obtained in Bandafassi with these new techniques are compared with those obtained through traditional survey methods, and the improvements discussed.

The Bandafassi Study

The area chosen for the study is located in the departément of Kedougou in Eastern Senegal, near the triple border between Senegal, Mali and Guinea. The population of the area comprises three ethnic groups. In order of the time of settlement in the area, they are: the Bedik (1,829 inhabitants on 1 March 1983), the Niokholonko (1,075) and the Fula Bandé (4,002). The Fula Bandé are Muslims, while the other two populations are mainly animists.

The main survey components in Bandafassi were the census, followed by a multi-round survey. The interval between two successive visits was one year. The duration of the multi-round survey varies from 3 years in the case of the Bedik to 13 years for the Niokholonko, and 8 years for the Fula Bandé. During the first census, information about marriages was collected for each adult and about all live births for each woman. The nominative list of the population was checked at each round, and all demographic events - births, deaths, marriages and migrations - occurring since the previous round, and all current pregnancies, were registered. The months of events are determined using cultural and lunar calendars. The respondent in this survey is in most cases the head of the compound (the compound is the living unit, grouping an average of 14 members).

Apart from the multi-round survey, other surveys were also conducted in Bandafassi. Two of them, an 'age survey' and a 'genealogical survey', will be discussed in detail in the second part of this chapter. The data collected in the first census on children ever-born to women indicate a high rate of under-reporting of dead children. Detailed 'fertility surveys' were thus conducted with more care in order to register the children who were originally omitted. The periods covered by the multi-round surveys were of different length because the study was initiated in each population at different times, the last being the Fula Bandé. Moreover, the study of the Bedik was not conducted in the same manner as those of the two other populations. A few rounds were performed after the first census in 1964, but only the data of the 1970 round are available to us. After March 1980, a follow-up survey with one year intervals was started, using the list of the population in January 1970. Dates of events which occurred between January 1970 and March 1980 were registered retrospectively, and are inaccurate. No retrospective fertility survey was conducted for the Fula Bandé.

New Methods of Data Collection Used in Small Scale Surveys

With small scale surveys, data collection can be considerably improved by modifying traditional survey methods or devising new ones. Two such new techniques - chronological classification of vital events, and collection of genealogical data - are presented here in order to show the differences with traditional survey methods, and the gain in data quality.

Chronological Classification of Vital Events

1. Principle

Since the first population studies in developing countries, the methods used for dating vital events have varied little. They consist of asking practically the same questions as in developed countries, for instance: 'In what year were you born?' or 'How old are you?' or 'How old were you when you married?'. The answers to such questions are unreliable in societies where a calendar system and written registration of events does not exist.

Human memory does, however, mentally register events: if it cannot be trusted as far as dates are concerned, it often retains the order of events. This fact is exploited with the historical calendar method, which consists of placing an event of unknown date within a chronological sequence of dated events, providing it with an approximate date. This method, which is currently used in almost all surveys in developing countries, often yields disappointing results. This is partly due to the fact that the events drawn from administrative records for the historical calendar are all (apart from a few rare exceptions such as war, famine) the type of events people tend to forget, or have difficulty relating to their own family events.

The chronological classification method, while based on the same principle as the historical calendar one (comparing several past events to reconstitute their sequence), differs from it in the following ways:

a) the events classified are all closely associated with the individual interviewed, his or her family or village;

b) the events are often of one type: only births, only deaths, etc.;

c) they are numerous - several tens or sometimes hundreds - and are mostly undated. This has a practical consequence: it necessitates a card system where each vital event is represented by a card, these being of a size which can be easily handled and shuffled about, like playing cards.

The classification of these cards will be described below. When completed, the result is a relative chronology. This may become absolute if several of the events can be dated: in this case, the dates of the others can be estimated by interpolation.

2. Application to age-estimation in Bandafassi

This card-based chronological classification is still at the experimental stage, and has been used as far as we know by only a few authors: Gubry (1975); Howell (1979); Langaney, Dallier and Pison (1979) and Pison (1980, 1982a) for estimating age; Hull *et al.*, for pregnancy histories in their 1972 Java study (see Hull, Hull and Singarimbun, chapter 4 in this volume); and Ferry (1976) for dating several events constituting female biographies: marriages, births, migration, etc.

The method may be applied in different ways, according to the type of events, the survey and the population. For age-estimation in Bandafassi (Langaney, Dallier and Pison, 1979; Pison 1980, 1982a), the process was briefly as follows:

a) a card was filled in for each individual, with the information enabling him or her to be identified without any ambiguity: first name, nickname, family name, parents' names, identity of spouse(s), village of birth, address, etc.;

b) the cards were grouped by village of birth; then, for each village, by broad age group: children, youths, adults and the aged;

c) the cards for each village were then classified by birth rank, following the answers given by one or several aged villagers. For this stage, the method is as follows:

   (i) the cards are stacked at random (it is supposed that no information on age is known at the outset);

   (ii) taking the first two cards in the pile, we ask the informant(s) who is the elder of the two individuals;

   (iii) taking a third card, we compare it with each of the first two, asking the same question. If, according to the informant(s), this third individual is older than the elder of the first two, younger than the younger of the first two, or aged in between, his/her card will be placed beneath, on top of, or in between the first two cards;

   (iv) this operation is repeated with the next card, and so on until all the cards have been presented.

The number of two-card comparisons increases rapidly with the number of cards already classed. However, certain methods used in automatic classification reduce these comparisons to a minimum. The classification may be further accelerated if information from another source enables an approximate pre-classification to be made. This is the case for the example observed here, where individuals were previously classed by broad age groups.

a) Then the age of each circumcised adult was estimated indirectly, taking, into account:

   (i) his rank within his circumcision group (group circumcisions are performed in each village every 3, 4, or 5 years);

   (ii) the date of his circumcision, according to a circumcision calendar established by applying the chronological classification method to the circumcision ceremonies in the whole region under study;

   (iii) the estimated mean age at circumcision.

b) Finally, female ages were estimated by interpolation between ages of males; and a process based on a stable population model was used for estimating the ages of non-circumcised children.

The double utilization of chronological classification improved age estimation in this study. Several sources of bias affecting

Table 17.1 Distribution of the First Marriages of Fula Bandé Women During the Period 1975–1980 by Age at Marriage and Marriage Date (before or after 1 January 1978)

(The women of the first group (marriage before 1 January 1978) were married when their birth date was estimated; the women of the second group were single at that time)

Age at marriage (age in completed years)	Number of first marriages during the period 1975–1977	1978–1980	Total
10	1	4	5
11	5	6	11
12	6	5	11
13	17	11	28
14	31	17	48
15	22	15	37
16	9	9	18
17	5	5	10
18	2	6	8
19	2	1	3
20	1	0	1
21	0	0	0
22	2	0	2
Whole	103	79	182
Mean age at first marriage (exact age)	15.0	14.8	14.9
Standard deviation	2.0	2.1	2.1

almost all African surveys were eliminated here. One example concerns the influence of marital status and parity on age determination of females. In most African surveys, women of about 15 years old are assigned older ages if they are married and younger ages if they are not. The age of women of high parity has a greater chance of being overstated and those of low parity, understated (Gendreau and Nadot, 1967; Ewbank, 1981). Table 17.1 gives the age distribution at first marriage of Fula Bandé females in

1975–1980. The women were divided into two groups: those who married prior to the age survey, who were therefore married at the time of the survey, and those who married after the survey, who were therefore single at that time. Age at marriage was computed from estimated dates of birth and from dates of marriage known to a month from the multi-round survey. No noticeable difference in age at first marriage is to be observed between the two groups; in other words, there is no bias in age-estimates of females due to marital status. Similarly, no bias is produced by the number of children.

Collection of Genealogical Data

Genealogical data are not generally considered of interest to demographers, as in most cases they do not offer a reliable reconstitution of past populations. They are often restricted to small populations and moreover, in many cases, sub-groups or minority groups which are not representative of broader populations. Finally, genealogical data are not always reliable. They are, however, essential for studying family correlations and have been used for constructing social history, including demographic behaviour (see Das Gupta, chapter 6 in this volume). They may also be used for improving the quality of demographic data collected through traditional methods. This is what will be discussed here.

After presenting the method used for collecting genealogical data in Bandafassi, we will examine two cases where these improved the quality of data obtained elsewhere: on one hand, concerning the population reported at the census, and on the other, information on the survival of parents.

1. The method of collection

During the census, the filiation of each living individual was noted as follows: family name and first name of both father and mother, their survival status (dead or alive) and their address if they are still alive.

Subsequently, a genealogical survey was conducted independently of the census in each compound; genealogical data on the head of the compound and each woman member were collected. These consisted of the names of all ascendants and collaterals according to the ascendant genealogy method, and the survival status (dead or alive) and address (for the latter) of the relatives thus noted.

2. Improvement of demographic data

The matching of data from different sources on the same individuals or the same events always reveals certain inconsistencies. A comparison of a population census and a genealogical survey provides a good example. The collection of genealogical data as described above involves noting the living collaterals of

Table 17.2 Distribution of Omissions in the Fula Bandé 1975 Census by Category of Omission and by Survey Which Detected the Omission (the size of the population is 3,654, after correction of the omissions)

	Category of omission		Survey which detected the omission: genealogical survey	multi-round survey 1975–1980	Total
1	Whole compound		32	22	54
2	Part of compound		40	10	50
3	Adult male		1	9	10
4	Adult female with children		7	4	11
5	Aged remarried female living in a different compound from her husband		27	4	31
6	Adult female living in the same compound as her husband		5	2	7
7	Unmarried child	both parents dead	15	8	23
8	Unmarried child	mother alive, father dead or divorced; the child lives with his mother	12	17	29
9	Unmarried child	father alive, mother dead or divorced; the child lives with his father	6	13	19
10	Unmarried child	both parents alive and still in union. The child lives with them.	-	41	41
	Total		145	130	275

each individual. Certain of these also live in the study zone. When we attempted to find their names on the census schedules corresponding to the addresses given in the genealogical survey, certain names could not be matched. After verifying the addresses given in the genealogical survey, we concluded that these were census omissions. The inverse may also occur, although this does not necussarily mean an error: an individual reported at the census may be named by no-one in the genealogical survey, if for instance he/she is an immigrant.

The 1975 Fula Bandé census, like any census, involved certain omissions, 275 of which were detected during various post-censal surveys (Pison, 1982b). These omissions represent almost 7 per cent of the total census population. Table 17.2, which presents these omissions distributed according to the post-censal survey which revealed them and the group of persons concerned, shows that most of the omissions were detected by the genealogical survey: 145, or almost 4 per cent of the total census population. These omissions often concern individuals with a special status of some kind: beside whole families (types 1 and 2 in Table 17.2), we find many aged females, in particular widows or remarried divorcees who do not live with their new husbands (type 5), and also many orphans,[1] in particular motherless children (types 7 and 8).

A high rate of omissions in certain of these groups may cause strong biases in demographic measures. Indirect estimates of adult mortality, for instance, may be based on the proportion of orphans (Henry, 1960; Brass and Hill, 1973); the under-registration of this group during a population census therefore causes under-estimation of mortality. Another possible course of bias exists with this method of estimating mortality: incorrect answers to questions on survival of parents (Blacker, 1977). Here again, as we shall see, the study of genealogies may avoid errors, or permit their correction.

The most common method of collecting data on survival of parents consists of noting the answers to the following questions: 'Is your father (mother) dead or alive?' Sometimes the father (mother) is reported to be alive when he (she) is in fact dead. Such errors, which are fairly frequent in certain regions, particularly in Africa, stem from confusion where these terms are used to refer to a wider circle of kin.

For the Fula Bandé, the matching of the 1975 census data with the post-censal genealogical survey data revealed errors concerning survival of parents which could thus be corrected. Table 17.3 gives the proportions of fatherless orphans for different age groups in 1975, obtained with crude data and with corrected data. For the 10 to 14 age group, for instance, almost a third of the fatherless orphans revealed by the genealogical survey were wrongly reported at the census as having their fathers alive.

Table 17.3 Errors in Orphanhood Data by Age-Group,* Fatherless Orphans,** Fula Bandé First Census (1975)

Age group of individuals in years	Number of individuals	Number of true fatherless orphans			Proportion orphaned	
		reported orphan	reported non orphan	all	rough	corrected
			male			
0 - 4	275	4	3	7	0.015	0.025
5 - 9	239	14	6	20	0.059	0.084
10 - 14	260	36	20	56	0.138	0.215
15 - 19	157	35	12	47	0.223	0.299
20 - 24	126	52	6	58	0.413	0.460
25 - 29	125	58	8	66	0.464	0.528
30 - 34	139	94	4	98	0.676	0.705
35 - 39	83	57	5	62	0.687	0.747
40 - 44	78	61	0	61	0.782	0.782
45 - 49	79	68	0	68	0.861	0.861
			female			
0 - 4	310	8	5	13	0.026	0.042
5 - 9	262	29	6	35	0.111	0.134
10 - 14	194	26	14	40	0.134	0.206
15 - 19	212	60	5	80	0.283	0.307
20 - 24	136	64	1	80	0.471	0.478
25 - 29	129	71	5	76	0.550	0.589
30 - 34	120	87	2	89	0.725	0.742
35 - 39	98	80	4	69	0.663	0.704
40 - 45	106	91	1	92	0.858	0.868
45 - 49	109	99	1	100	0.908	0.917

* Non-orphaned individuals mis-reported as orphaned are very rare, and this kind of error is not examined.

** Motherless orphans, when they are registered in the first census, are almost never mis-reported as having their mother alive.

Characteristics Specific to the New Methods of Data Collection

The two examples of collection techniques presented above have certain aspects in common which set them apart from the methods traditionally employed in demographic surveys:

1. They do not always use a standard questionnaire. This does not mean that the interviews are non-directive; on the contrary, they follow a certain sequence of questioning which, if it cannot be defined in advance for each informant, must nonetheless be strictly observed.

2. The collection process is a long one, compared with the interviews of traditional surveys.

3. The absence of a questionnaire means that the interviewers are required to have a high educational status and be very well trained. For checking the quality of the data, it is moreover preferable to reduce the number of interviewers to an absolute minimum. Ideally, when the size of the population studied makes this possible, it is best for the principal investigator to do the work.

These collection techniques are adapted from methods used in social anthropology. The descriptions of traditional populations made by ethnologists often give the impression that they lack numerical precision and give exaggerated importance to certain aspects of behaviour. In borrowing certain techniques from this field of study, it might be thought that we risk taking certain of its faults at the same time. On the contrary, as we have shown, the adaptation of these techniques can result in a definite improvement in the collection of demographic data. This improvement is naturally reflected in the findings when these data are analyzed; to illustrate this, we now present a study of age-specific mortality in Bandafassi.

The Age-Pattern of Mortality in Bandafassi

Direct Estimation of Life Tables

The demographic data we collected provide accurate information on the age and sex distributions of the population, and on the events which occurred during the observation period in each ethnic group. Estimates of age-specific mortality rates can be derived directly as if dealing with conventional data. We examine here the results of this computation and then compare them with results obtained when applying indirect methods of estimating mortality to the same population and to the same data.

The death rates were calculated by sex and age, as the ratio of the number of deaths registered in the category during the follow-up period to the number of person-years lived in the category during that period. The death rates were then transformed into probabilities of dying between exact ages.

Table 17.4 Bandafassi Life Table Computed from Multi-Round Survey Data

(The data for the different ethnic groups are combined though they correspond to different periods: 1970–83 for the Niokholonko, 1975–83 for the Fula Bandé and 1980–83 for the Bedik. For ages over 10, the Bedik data correspond to the period 1970–83)

Data			Life table					
			Probability of dying within the interval		Survivors at the beginning of the interval	Deaths within the interval	Life-expectancy at the beginning of the interval	
Interval exact age in years	Number of deaths	Number of person-years	q*	σ**	ℓ	d	e***	σ****
0 - 1	479	-*	0.209	0.008	1.000	0.209	31.4	0.6
1 - 2	207	1,768	0.111	0.007	0.791	0.088	38.5	0.7
2 - 3	159	1,568	0.097	0.007	0.704	0.068	42.2	0.7
3 - 4	83	1,437	0.056	0.006	0.636	0.036	45.7	0.7
4 - 5	49	1,346	0.036	0.005	0.600	0.021	47.4	0.7
5 - 10	89	6,144	0.070	0.007	0.579	0.040	48.1	0.6
10 - 15	40	8,023	0.025	0.004	0.538	0.013	46.6	0.6
15 - 20	47	6,847	0.034	0.005	0.525	0.018	42.7	0.6
20 - 25	35	5,448	0.032	0.005	0.507	0.016	39.1	0.6
25 - 30	43	4,515	0.047	0.007	0.491	0.023	35.3	0.5
30 - 35	44	4,257	0.050	0.007	0.468	0.024	31.9	0.5
35 - 40	39	3,941	0.048	0.008	0.445	0.021	28.5	0.5
40 - 45	46	3,501	0.064	0.009	0.423	0.027	24.8	0.5
45 - 50	79	3,172	0.117	0.012	0.396	0.046	21.3	0.5
50 - 55	65	2,645	0.116	0.014	0.350	0.041	18.8	0.5
55 - 60	77	2,116	0.167	0.017	0.309	0.052	15.9	0.5
60 - 65	65	1,601	0.184	0.021	0.258	0.048	13.6	0.5
65 - 70	52	1,044	0.221	0.027	0.210	0.047	11.2	0.5
70 - 75	53	541	0.393	0.042	0.164	0.064	8.6	0.5
75 - 80	25	290	0.355	0.057	0.099	0.035	7.7	0.5
80 - 85	16	112	0.526	0.091	0.064	0.034	5.5	0.5

* $_1q_0$ is a cohort measure for the generations born after the first census, $_nq_x$ when x > 0 is a cross-sectional measure, derived from death rates.

** Standard deviation of q.

*** The life expectancy at age 85, the end of the last closed interval has been assumed to be 4 years.

**** Standard deviation of the life expectancy.

Source: Pison and Langaney, 1985, p.392.

Comparisons between results for each ethnic group show that the differences are small, and not significant at nearly any age when dealing with probabilities of dying within a 5-year age interval (Pison and Langaney, 1985). The data for the different ethnic groups are combined here.

Table 17.4 shows the life table directly estimated from the multiround survey data. Standard errors for the probabilities of death and for the life expectancies were computed with the formulae proposed by Chiang (1968) and Keyfitz (1977). We focus first on the mortality estimates from birth to age 5.

1. The high mortality level in late infancy and early childhood

The high value of the infant mortality rate (IMR) in Bandafassi (${}_{1}q_{0}$ = 0.209 for both sexes) is not surprising considering the results of studies of other rural populations from tropical regions with few medical services. The high values of the probability of death from age one to five (${}_{4}q_{1}$ = 0.268), and especially from age one to three (${}_{2}q_{1}$ = 0.196) are more unusual. This pattern of infant and child mortality can be compared with similar patterns observed by Cantrelle (1969) and Billewicz and McGregor (1981), and reviewed by Garenne (1982) in Ngayokheme (Senegal) and Keneba (Gambia).

The Ngayokheme and Keneba areas are around 500 kilometres from the Bandafassi area, and have a much drier climate. In these conditions, the observation of a similar age pattern of infant and child mortality reinforces the suggestion that the pattern described in nearly all the model life tables developed until now may not be the right pattern for a large number of West African rural populations with a still high level of mortality. The collection of accurate demographic data in other regions could help to define the geographical and ecological distribution of this pattern, and to describe its determinants.

2. The adult mortality pattern

The directly estimated life-tables for each sex, for ages above 10 years, are presented in Figure 17.1 (the data are in Table 17.4, including ${}_{5}q_{5}$, not illustrated in the Figure). In the Figure, we adopt a length of 10 years for the intervals so as to reduce the random variations of the estimates.

No clear difference appears here between sexes, although surprisingly, ${}_{10}q_{20}$ is significantly higher for males than for females. This allows us to group the data and retain only the estimates for both sexes together. Random variations in ${}_{5}q_{x}$ remain. But if we consider only life expectancy, the approximate 95 per cent confidence intervals are 30.1 to 32.7 for life expectancy at birth, and 45.4 to 48.0 for life expectancy at age 10 (using the approximate standard deviations equal to 0.65 years in each case). Such precision is quite encouraging.

Figure 17.1 Bandafassi Age Pattern of Adult Mortality for Each Sex (direct estimates)

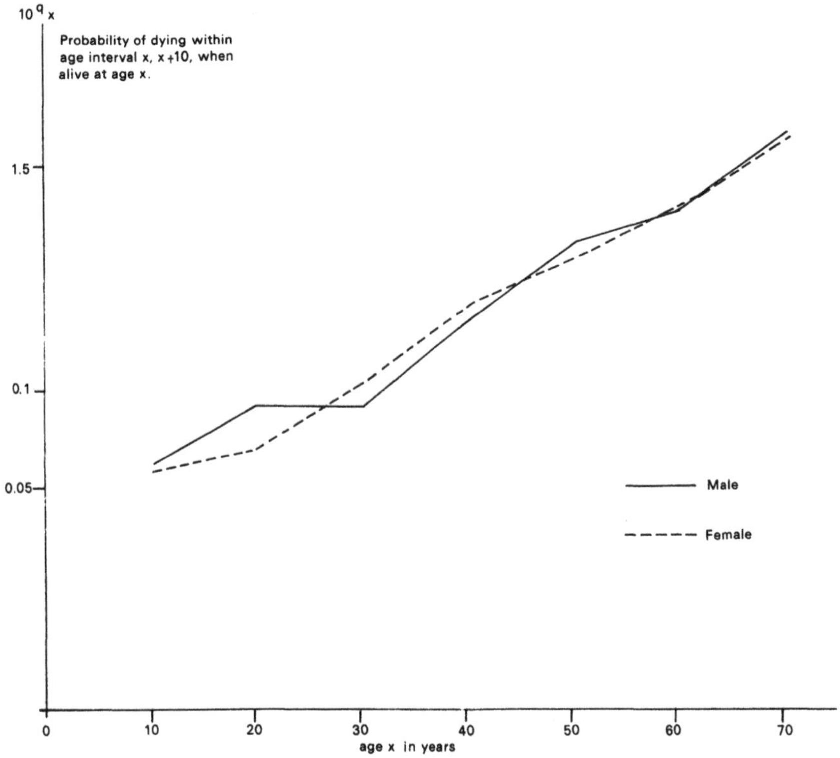

3. Comparison with other life tables

The comparison with model life tables will be limited here to a graphic examination of differences between our adult mortality estimates and two model life tables. Figure 17.2 shows a surprisingly good fit with the West pattern of the Coale and Demeny life table with a life expectancy at age 10 for both sexes equal to 46.7 years (level 10), identical to that observed in Bandafassi. A good fit also exists with the Brass standard life table (e_{10} = 47.4), without any prior adjustment.

We shall not discuss differences for young ages, before age 10, since the inadequacy of nearly all the model life tables when considering West African mortality, has already been demonstrated in detail. It is well illustrated here by the fact that the observed adult mortality corresponds approximately to the model

Figure 17.2 Comparison Between Bandafassi Life Table and Model Life Tables for Adult Ages (over 10)

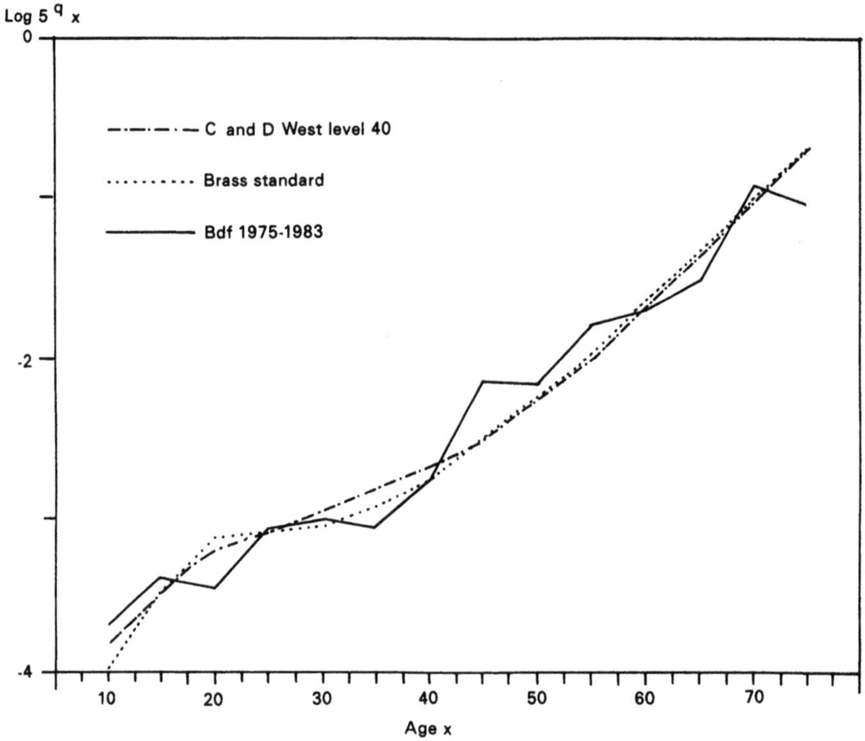

life tables with life expectancy at birth equal to 41.1 (Coale and Demeny) and 43.6 (Brass African standard), although the observed life expectancy at birth is 31.4 years. The balance between child mortality and adult mortality in Bandafassi, and in a few other areas, is quite different from that proposed by models until now.

4. Conclusions relating to direct estimation

Another paper (Pison and Langaney, 1985) gives more detailed results on mortality in Bandafassi. Though our estimates for this area must not be extended without caution, they provide answers to several questions about West African mortality patterns:

a) The very high level of child mortality between age 6 months and 3 years, already described for a few West African rural areas, has once again been identified.

b) The seasonality of child mortality is characterized by two periods of higher risk: the rainy season, and the second part of the dry season. The first period is associated with a high level of malaria transmission, and the second, with periods of measles outbreaks.

c) The age pattern of adult mortality does not differ from the age pattern described by the model life tables, which relies mainly on the experience of traditional European populations of the past.

d) There are no perceptible sex differences at any age for the population and for the period of the study.

Comparison with Results Using the Indirect Methods of Mortality Estimation

We will deal here with the two indirect methods of mortality estimation commonly used: the first, usually called the Brass method, provides estimates of child mortality; the other, called the orphanhood method, gives estimates of adult mortality.

1. Evaluation of the Brass method of estimating child mortality

We decided to limit our evaluation study of the indirect child mortality estimation methods to the data almost unaffected by under-registration of dead children. We shall consider only the women whose children's births were all registered by the prospective survey, that is to say the women resident at the first census and less than 25 years old in 1983 in the Fula Bandé case, less than 30 years old in 1983 in the Niokholonko case.

The successive modifications in the original Brass method of estimating child mortality led to slightly different results. We decided to apply two versions of the method: the original approach, first proposed by Brass and Coale (1968), and the more recent Trussell version (U.N., 1982), so as to check whether the assumed improvement in the method is effective when applied to the Bandafassi populations. We added a third version, where the models of fertility and mortality correspond to the direct estimates derived from the prospective data.

The results of the indirect estimation of child mortality using these three versions of the Brass method are presented in Table 17.5. $\hat{q}^I(j)$, the indirect estimate of the probability of dying from birth to exact age j, which is not shown here, can be calculated from the estimates of the multiplier $\hat{K}(i) = \hat{q}^I(j)/\hat{D}(i)$ and $\hat{D}(i)$. The estimates of the multipliers, $\hat{K}(i)$, identical to the ratio $\hat{q}^I(j)/\hat{D}(i)$, are compared to the observed ratios $\hat{q}^D(j)/\hat{D}(i)$ (last column of Table 17.5), with $\hat{q}^D(j)$, the direct estimate.

For i = 1, i.e. for the age group of women 15 to 19 years, the differences between $\hat{K}(i)$ and the observed ratio $\hat{q}^D(j)/\hat{D}(i)$, whatever version of the Brass method is considered, are dramatic for the Fula Bandé: q(1) would be overestimated by approximately

Table 17.5 Results of the Application of the Brass Method to Estimate Child Mortality: Comparisons with Direct Estimates.

Name of the method				Brass	Brass	United Nations			Simulation	Observed
model	fertility parameters			m	m	P1/P2 and P2/P3			fertility	ratio
	mortality model pattern			Brass General Standard	Brass African Standard	Coale and Demeny North	South	West	and mortality as direct estimates	
Population	Age group of women	i	j	multiplier R(i) (= $\hat{q}I(j)/D(i)$)						$\hat{q}D(j)/D(i)$
Fula Bandé	15 - 19	1	1	0.933	0.945	0.995	0.960	1.020	0.843	0.669
(1983)	20 - 24	2	2	1.013	0.988	0.895	0.938	0.954	0.843	0.795
Niokholonko	15 - 19	1	1	0.996	0.964	1.213	1.183	1.224	0.902	1.053
(1983)	20 - 24	2	2	1.020	0.997	1.022	1.061	1.062	0.946	0.790
	25 - 29	3	3	0.999	0.968	0.932	0.993	0.980	0.972	0.988

m = mean age of the fertility schedule.

P1, P2, P3 = average parities of women in age-groups 1, 2, 3 (15 - 19, 20 - 24, 25 - 29).

$\hat{q}I(j)$ = indirect estimate of the probability of dying from birth to exact age j.

$\hat{q}D(j)$ = direct estimate of the probability of dying from birth to exact age j.

D(i) = observed proportion dead among the children ever-born to women in age group i.

50 per cent. On the contrary, there are only slight differences for the Niokholonko. But in their case, the estimate of D(1), based on only nine children born to forty-five women (to be compared to 107 children born to 189 women for the Fula Bandé), is unreliable. q(2) would also be overestimated (by approximately 20 per cent for the Fula Bandé, and approximately 30 per cent for the Niokholonko). Only the indirect estimate of q(3) for the Niokholonko would be reasonably close to the direct estimate.

This first examination of the results of the application of the indirect child mortality estimation techniques to the Bandafassi data show an important mis-estimation of the infant and child mortality pattern. The differences from one version of the method to the other seem negligible in comparison.

Evaluation studies show evidence that in general the estimate of q(1) is unreliable, though the errors are commonly smaller than observed here. As a consequence, we ignore this value and rely only on the estimates of q(2), q(3) and q(5). But even the estimate of q(2) here is quite unreliable.

These inconsistencies are not produced by errors in the data since we have restricted the evaluation study to the age groups of women whose data on children ever-born and children surviving are reliable. They can only result from deviations from the assumptions in the model.

The distortion of the proportion of dead children among children ever-born from one group of women to the other, compared with what would be expected under a stable model, is mainly the result of a combination of a birth order effect and a mortality fluctuation effect (Pison, 1985). We shall not attempt to separate them here.

To evaluate the indirect estimation method in an ideal situation where these effects do not exist, we applied the Brass method to the expected values of D(i) under the stable population model. Other effects, such as those caused by the age distribution of the women, in general different from the stable one, or by random variations, are also suppressed at the same time. The effects which remain are only those produced by the differences between the model and the actual age patterns of fertility and mortality. The indirect estimates in such an ideal situation are not too far from the real age pattern, the differences being less than 10 per cent, with the exception of q(1) in the Fula Bandé case (Pison, 1985). The clear underestimation of q(1) for them would be for a large part a consequence of the very early fertility pattern, compared to the range of patterns considered for establishing the regression equations. Niokholonko fertility starts later, and the errors in the indirect estimates of mortality would be caused principally by the inadequate pattern of mortality applied in their case. The comparison between the results with different mortality models does not provide a definite conclusion about which one is to be used: of the three

Figure 17.3 Observed and Model Proportions Orphaned by Age-Group: Both Sexes

The observed proportions orphaned are computed from corrected data on survival of mother or father.

The model proportions orphaned correspond to the stable population with mortality and fertility equal to cross-sectional direct estimates for each population.

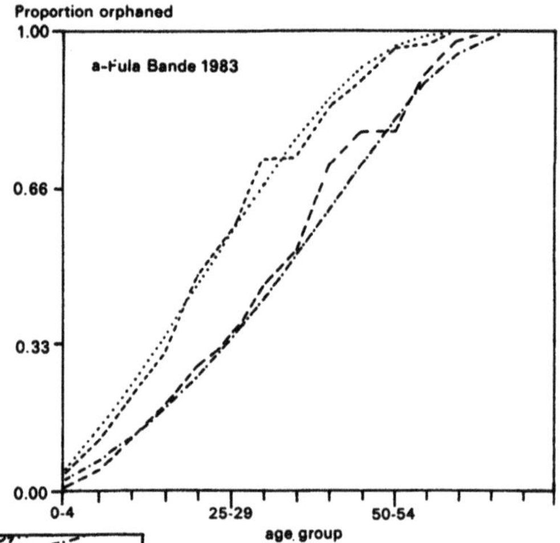

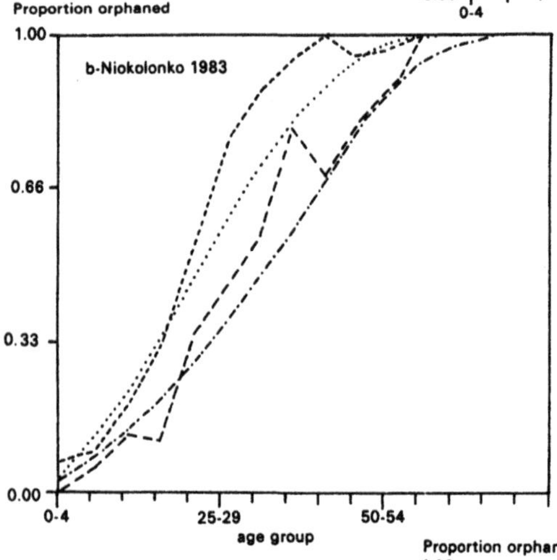

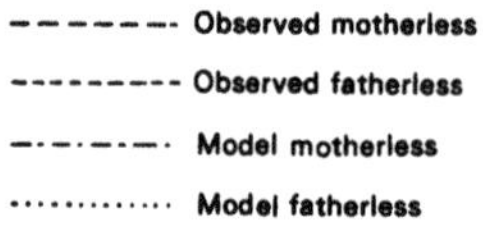

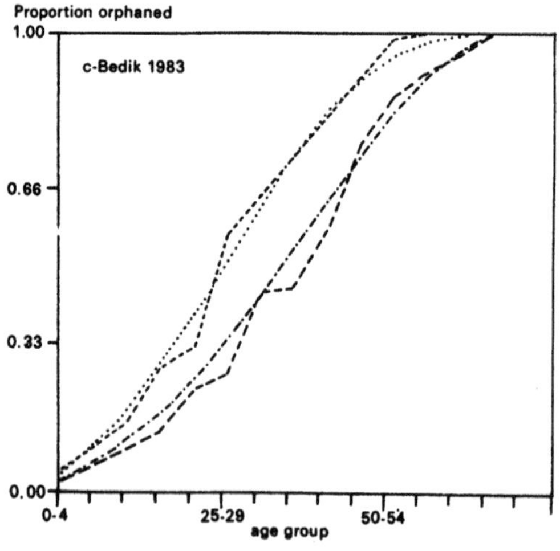

Table 17.6 Adult Mortality. Comparison Between Indirect Estimates Using the Orphanhood Method and Direct Estimates.

	Indirect estimate			Direct estimate
	Fula Bandé	Niokholonko	Bedik	All populations
$_{20}q_{35}$ female	0.316	0.420	0.258	0.298
$_{35}q_{35}$ female	0.556	-	0.625	0.632
$_{20}q_{50}$ male	0.588	0.793	0.550	0.535

that we have tried here, the North model seems to be the best one for the Fula Bandé, and the worst for the Niokholonko.

2. Evaluation of the orphanhood method of estimating adult mortality

Information on survival of father and survival of mother classified by age group of respondent can be used to derive estimates of adult male and female mortality (Henry, 1960; Brass and Hill, 1973). The available orphanhood data for Bandafassi are not conventional ones. The original orphanhood information - identification and survival of each parent - collected at the first census, was subsequently corrected; its quality after correction is exceptional, if compared with classical orphanhood data.

The observed proportions orphaned by age group, computed from the corrected data, are compared with model ones in Figure 17.3. The model assumes that mortality and fertility patterns are constant over time and equal to cross-sectional direct measures for each population. The differences between observed and model proportions are small, except for the Niokholonko. The good concordance in the case of the Fula Bandé and the Bedik may be explained by the quality of the corrected data and the absence of strong mortality and fertility change during the recent past. In the case of the Niokholonko, we cannot determine here which of these assumptions is false.

These good conditions suggest that indirect mortality estimates applying the orphanhood method (Brass and Hill, 1973) to the corrected data should not be too far from direct estimates. The results are presented in Figure 17.4 (values of M, the mean age of women, or men, at the birth of their children, are estimated from the births which occurred during the observation period; M

Figure 17.4 Comparison Between Direct and Indirect Estimate of Adult Mortality

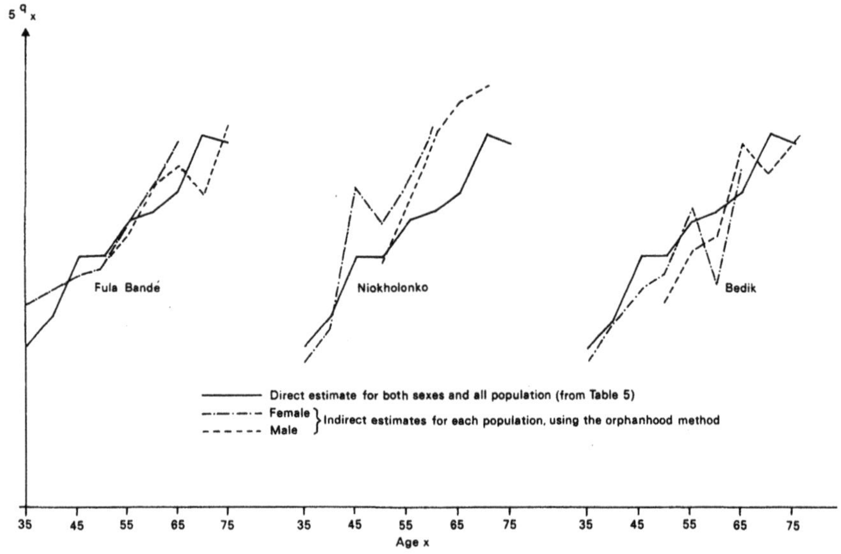

is around 26 years for women and 39 years for men). We compare the indirect estimates of $_5q_x$ for each population and each sex the direct estimates for both sexes and all populations (from Table 17.4). As expected, the Niokholonko orphanhood data result in much higher mortality estimates than the multi-round survey data. In the case of the Fula Bandé and the Bedik, the impression is that there is a relatively good fit between both estimates. If we combine the indirect $_5q_x$ estimates, we obtain death measures over large age intervals, less dependent upon random variations or biases. The results are presented in Table 17.6. The correspondence between direct and indirect estimates is quite good in the case of the Fula Bandé and the Bedik. This is the result of the high quality of the data and of the probable quasi-absence of changes in vital rates in the recent past.

3. Conclusions relating to indirect estimation

Two main conclusions are to be drawn from this evaluation study of two indirect methods of mortality estimation:

a) The method using the data on the proportion of children dead may be less robust than usually thought. Even with good data, deviations from several assumptions of the model may result in important errors in the estimates;

b) the method using the data on the survival of the parents, on the contrary, gives valuable rough estimates of adult mortality. The model seems robust and the quality of the estimates depends critically on the quality of the data.

These conclusions are related to the fact that infant and child mortality patterns from one population to another may vary much more than adult mortality patterns.

Conclusion

Our aim in this chapter is to provide some arguments on the applications of small scale and intensive surveys for future improvement of demographic measures in developing countries.

The Bandafassi study in Eastern Senegal is presented as an example of a multi-round survey using new techniques of data collection. This kind of survey provides excellent measures for the area studied. Such measures can be used to correct the biases of large scale surveys. Follow-up studies may feasibly be pursued over long periods of time, and even transformed into permanent population observatories. A few of these already exist, and it would be useful to multiply them in the future.

In the case of the single-round small scale surveys, our results show the benefit to be drawn from an association between intensive methods of data collection and indirect techniques of estimation. The indirect methods of demographic estimation are rapidly being developed. They use information on the informant's relatives - their survival or their residence - to estimate mortality or migration. The Bandafassi example shows that the collection of genealogical data considerably improves information on relatives. We recommend that future small scale studies using single-round surveys utilize a combination of genealogy collection with indirect techniques of demographic estimation.

Notes

1. 'Orphan' here is defined as a child who has lost either or both parents.

Marriage, Household Formation and Fertility

18

When Did You Last See Your Mother? Aspects of Female Autonomy in Rural North India

Patricia Jeffery, Roger Jeffery and Andrew Lyon

Introductory Remarks

Female autonomy, or a woman's ability to influence matters which directly affect her, is a subject of potentially crucial significance. It is obviously important to women themselves, but beyond that, demographers have suggested that it is the best predictor of changes in fertility and child mortality (Anker *et al.*, 1981). More 'autonomous' women have smaller families and fewer of their children die. However, most discussions of female autonomy are limited to indicators which are presumed to be a good guide to autonomy - most notably, female versus male educational attainment, female employment, age at marriage, differential mortality rates by sex, and so on. In this chapter, we want to look at indicators of female autonomy which are closer to being defined as such by the women involved. We take some ethnographic material from our research in 1982-3 in Uttar Pradesh, North India, where women, by the commonly employed indicators, would appear to have very low autonomy. In general, our focus was on married women in the childbearing years and on various aspects of pregnancy, childbirth and the postpartum period, among them, the influence that a woman has on the conditions in which she experiences childbearing. Here, we particularly concentrate on how aspects of kinship organization and domestic politics impinge on a woman's contacts with her natal kin.

A paper by Dyson and Moore (1983), 'Kinship Structure, Female Autonomy and Demographic Behavior in India', which appeared after we returned from fieldwork, is one of our starting points in this chapter. The central aim of their analysis is to relate different kinship structures through differential female autonomy to the contrasting 'demographic regimes' of North and South India. They argue that the North Indian kinship system is such that women's autonomy there is lower than in the south, and that these differences can be linked to the generally higher fertility and infant/child mortality in the north, as well as to North India's higher sex ratio (males per 100 females).

Dyson and Moore argue that in agrarian societies, access to scarce social resources is largely obtained through kinship ties, the very nature of which may limit women's ability to exploit their kin networks. Women's autonomy is enhanced by freedom of movement and association; by their access to property; by some independent control over their own sexuality; and by post-marital residence patterns and 'behavioural norms' which do not rupture or constrain women's contacts with their natal kin. In all these respects, there are significant contrasts between South and North India. In North India, women rarely inherit productive property such as land; at the time of her marriage, and throughout the rest of her life, a woman's parents must give substantial presents and dowry payments to her husband and his family. Women generally marry distantly from their natal village (both geographically and genealogically), and seldom support their parents in old age; the new bride is under the tutelage of her husband's older female kin; bride-givers are inferior to bride-takers; and women's sexuality is controlled through *purdah* practices and the segregation of the sexes to a much greater degree than in the South. It is these patterns, Dyson and Moore postulate, which relate to lower female autonomy in the North, in turn linked to the different demographic regimes outlined above.

Dyson and Moore's account in fact covers a wide range of commonly-used indicators of female autonomy such as access to economic resources and level of education, but they added another item, 'marriage distance', or how far from her parents a woman moves when she is married. They presume that this relates directly to the contacts a woman can retain with her natal kin, and thus can be taken as a plausible indicator of her autonomy. Their reference to a woman's contacts with her natal kin is particularly innovative, and we aim to unravel some implications of their comment: 'cultural practices - such as those of the north Indian system - that tend to constrain or erode the personal links between a married woman and her natal kin directly diminish a woman's autonomy' (p.46). In their view, women in this kind of structural position are 'left socially almost powerless' (p.46).

While we are wholly sympathetic to Dyson and Moore's attempt to relate marriage and household organization to women's autonomy, we have found their framework inadequate in some respects. Our own thinking on this topic was guided by several basic questions. What are female informant's views of their situation, and what categories might correspond with our idea of autonomy? How do women feel they can attain autonomy and what affects their access to it? The Hindi word *azaadi* can be reasonably translated as 'independence', 'freedom', or 'autonomy'. Young married women distinguish sharply between *sasural* (their lives in the husband's village) and the *piheer* or *mainka* (their situation when they return to their natal village for a visit). The natal village is portrayed as the place where they are loved and experience warm supportive relationships with other women, where their movements and activities are not so controlled or overseen by others, and where they obtain freedoms which are unavailable in their affinal village. In fact there were a few examples of women obtaining intra-uterine contraceptive devices and other contraception, as well as abortions, during visits to their natal kin and without informing their affinal kin. By contrast, the woman in her husband's village is bound by *zimmidaari* (responsibilities), her movements and her work are subject to surveillance by her husband and his mother, and she must seek their permission for what she does. She is expected to fulfil her obligations and any sign of slacking will be met with criticism from other women and possibly a beating from her husband.

From these contrasts between women's natal and affinal villages, we derive a basic assumption: that is, for almost every woman, the relationship with the mother is primal and, given a choice, a woman would opt to see her mother often. Failure to do so, then, could indicate barriers to her freedom of movement and thus be a measure of her level of autonomy.

Our interest in this topic originally arose from earlier work among Muslims in Hazrat Nizamuddin in Delhi (Jeffery, 1979). Women there consider that marriage within their own village has considerable benefits. In the case of village endogamy, the woman probably moves into a household of people she already knows; she may be able to maintain substantial contact with her mother and sisters and rely on her father and brothers for various forms of support. Among North Indian Muslims, marriage within the village is a common, though not universal, practice; among Hindus in North India, it is almost universally disapproved. Hindu brides are liable to be married somewhat distantly from their natal kin, possibly into a household of total strangers. The idea of exploring women's support networks in a locality with both Hindu and Muslim populations was crucial to our decision to locate our 1982-83 fieldwork in Bijnor District in Western Uttar Pradesh, where the rural population is about 30 per cent Muslim.

Dyson and Moore's analysis presumes that cultural systems which permit 'close marriage' will also tend to enhance women's contacts with their natal kin. By comparing Hindus and Muslims in one locality, we wish to investigate this, and begin to explore what affects a young woman's contacts with her natal kin. We cannot here go on to consider in detail the relationship between contacts with natal kin (as one indicator of autonomy) and demographic behaviour, which is what Dyson and Moore try to do. We wish to demonstrate that there are enough complexities and problems in assessing levels of 'autonomy' in the first instance.

North Indian Kinship Organization

Our Hindu and Muslim informants alike conform to most of the general parameters of North Indian kinship organization laid out by Dyson and Moore. A married woman normally retains only fragile and fleeting contacts with her natal kin (especially female kin). These contacts, indeed, are often mediated by men.

A married woman has to negotiate the permission of her husband and older affinal kin for absences from her affinal village. Often they will resist her requests to visit her natal village, largely because they worry about who will do her work while she is away. Women's work is time-consuming and consists mainly of numerous necessary daily tasks, and finding a substitute to do this work is often difficult. Moreover, a woman rarely goes to her natal village unless she is accompanied by a man from her affinal village (husband, husband's brother, or husband's father) or unless she is 'called' by her own male natal kin. Thus, her visits to her natal village depend on obtaining permission, on finding someone to do her work, and on having a man with enough time to act as her chaperon.

The few visits received 'from' a woman's natal kin also highlight the erosion of a woman's ties, especially with her mother and sisters. A woman's unmarried sisters past puberty are unlikely to be permitted to go visiting; links between affinally-related households are largely maintained by men visiting, which are influenced by considerations surrounding hypergamy. Generally, those who have 'given a daughter' should receive nothing from their daughter's in-laws, for example food, without making at least a nominal payment for it; and the 'shame' experienced by a woman's father when he visits his daughter in the place where she is in her sexual role of wife means that he normally leaves his sons to visit their married sisters. Since men often visit their wives' parents, without taking their wives with them, a married woman's contacts with her female kin are often mediated by her brothers or her husband. Thus the transfer of 'news' is constrained, for some topics are not suitable subjects for discussion in mixed company.

Furthermore, in Bijnor, women virtually never give birth in their own natal village. In other parts of North India (see, for example Gideon, 1962) women almost always return for the birth of their first child, and frequently for subsequent deliveries, but in Western Uttar Pradesh women say they would be deeply embarrassed to give birth in the village of their fathers and brothers. Some women who live in their natal village go to their marital village to give birth; those who are married in the same village as they were born into have to stress symbolic barriers which minimize their contacts with their own kin during late pregnancy and at the time of delivery.

In other words, a woman usually only makes direct contact with her mother and sisters when she herself visits her natal village. Married sisters often meet in their natal village only after several years have elapsed, for instance if they have been 'called' to attend some function, such as a brother's wedding or the birth of a brother's child. Clearly, this does not provide the best of foundations for a supportive sisterhood - and there could hardly be a starker contrast to the day-to-day relationships experienced by married men with their male kin.

Briefly, then, married women (Hindu and Muslim alike) become effectively rooted in their affinal villages. They are subject to controls over their mobility, are rarely visited by their female natal kin, and are substantially cut off from their early roots.

Marriage Distance

However, these Hindu/Muslim parallels co-exist with some differences. Almost all Hindu marriages (including Harijan) are arranged at a much greater distance then Muslim marriages. Close kin marriage and village endogamy are permitted among Muslims but they are by no means the dominant form of marriage. However, some of the Muslim caste groups do arrange their marriages within a cluster of neighbouring villages. In the light of Dyson and Moore's discussion, we are prompted to ask what (if any) is the effect of marriage distance on women's ability to maintain contacts with their natal kin?

On the face of it, 'marriage distance' seems a straightforward and easily quantifiable variable. We asked women where they were born and located their natal villages on 1:50,000 maps. However, for distances too long to be covered by foot, the availability and cost of transport, the direction of roadways and the availability of male drivers and chaperons suggest that any simple measurement of distance as the crow flies would be inappropriate. In our tabulation, we distinguished between distances a woman can walk in a round trip in one day (less than 5 kilometers), distances over 10 kilometers requiring transport, and an intermediate category. However these distinctions should not be treated as clear-cut; for example, the distance a woman can walk in one day may be affected by the season or the number of small children who hamper her progress.

Table 18.1 summarizes our material from the women interviewed in our survey. Almost all these marriages took place within Bijnor District. The overall picture is that wealthy Muslims, particularly those from 'high' caste groups, generally marry closer than poorer Muslims. By contrast, Hindus (including Harijans) marry more distantly and there is little variation in marriage distance by caste or landownership. Thus, our material demonstrates intra-district variations in marriage distance, variations which could not be exposed by Dyson and Moore, since they used district level estimates based on the 1961 Census in which, moreover, no data are available on religion. Perhaps, then, we have proceeded rather further than they could in measuring 'marriage distance'.

However, geographical and social distances are not necessarily equivalent. What are the implications of different marriage distances for women's contacts with their natal kin? Some contrasts do emerge between Hindu and Muslim informants. Women themselves argue that a woman married close to her natal village is less cut off: she can receive instant news of *marney-jeeney* (dying-living) and of *dukh-sukh* (sadness-happiness). Muslim women often see this as an advantage of being married nearby while Hindu women and Muslim women married somewhat distantly often regret that important life-events can occur in their natal villages without the news reaching them immediately.

Table 18.1 Marriage Distance by Caste, Landholding and Religion: Survey and Base Villages

	Marriage Distances							
	< 5 kms		5 - < 10 kms		> 10 kms		(N)	
Caste	SV	BV	SV	BV	SV	BV	SV	BV
	Percentages							
	Landless Hindus							
Landed	20	0	0	0	80	100	(5)	(7)
Service	6	10	0	0	85	90	(16)	(10)
Harijan	3	100	16	0	70	0	(30)	(2)
Other	0	100	14	0	85	0	(7)	(4)
Total	5	30	10	0	85	70	(58)	(23)
	Landowning Hindus							
Landed	10	0	12	0	78	100	(90)	(8)
Service	8	2	4	6	90	92	(25)	(50)
Harijan	8	9	4	9	78	82	(21)	(45)
Other	0	25	40	0	60	75	(7)	(4)
Total	9	6	11	6	80	88	(143)	(107)
	Landless Muslims							
Landed	42	25	21	25	36	50	(33)	(4)
Service	31	0	0	0	69	100	(13)	(12)
Total	39	6	15	6	46	88	(46)	(16)
	Landowning Muslims							
Landed	58	55	6	20	36	24	(36)	(49)
Service	33	17	0	42	66	42	(6)	(12)
Total	55	47	5	25	40	28	(42)	(61)

Notes: SV = Survey Villages and covers only women who had given birth during a defined year (1.7.81 - 30.6.82). BV = Base Villages and covers all married women resident in the village.

Hindu castes are divided as follows: landed castes include Jat, Rajput; service castes are miscellaneous groups who are not traditional landholders, such as Sahnis and Dhimars; Harijan includes all ex-Untouchable castes; and Other includes Brahman and Nepali. For the Muslim caste-like groups, Sheikhs and Rangars are the main Landed castes, with Julahas, Telis etc. in the Service caste category.

Visiting patterns also suggest that marriage distance has some impact on the time a woman spends in her natal village. Muslim women married within easy walking distance distinguish between *milna* (going to their natal village to meet) or *rehna* (to stay). They may hurry to finish their day's work, go to visit their parents for a few hours and return to their affinal village to prepare the evening meal. Such visits do not necessarily involve a male chaperon; women may go with their children and/or with other women from their natal village married into the same village. Some Muslim women also visit their sisters married in nearby villages. In addition, they may be 'called' to their natal village to 'stay' for a while. Hindu and Muslim women who are married more distantly rarely go just to 'meet' their parents. They go when they are 'called' or when their husband takes them, and they go to 'stay'. Hardly any had ever gone to their natal village without a male chaperon.

The significance of these contrasts is hard to assess and perhaps easy to exaggerate. Muslim women married close to their natal village potentially can make short visits there; in our base village this was by no means a daily occurrence, though it does seem to have been common for about a third of the Muslim women covered in the survey who lived in large Muslim villages.

If, however, we examine two contrasting situations in which married women are living in their natal village, we can see that matters are much more complex than a consideration of 'marriage distance' alone would indicate. Here we discuss the situation of *gaon-ki-gaon* marriage (marriage within the village) and that of the *ghar-jamai* (living-in son-in-law). Numerically these cases are insignificant, but they can shed interesting light on informants' views about the appropriate contact between married women and their natal kin.

Gaon-ki-Gaon Marriage

In practice, marriage within the village is relevant only for Muslims. Our female informants (Hindu and Muslim alike) stress some of the benefits to them of being married close to their natal village, but we were surprised by the vehement disapproval with which many Muslim women (and men) opposed marriage in which partners are from the same village. Their reasoning emphasizes the significance of the distinction between the congenial natal and harsh affinal village, highlighting the following points: that a woman cannot effectively retreat to her parents' house for a visit, as she can be too easily called back by her mother-in-law; that a woman cannot maintain the necesssary distinction between her male natal kin and her male affines (e.g. in avoidance behaviour); that a pregnant woman cannot conceal her condition from her natal kin when she lives in the same village as they do; and that her natal kin will be needlessly grieved by news of her marital problems and rows with her mother-in-law, while marriage at some distance protects them from knowledge of problems in which they should not (in any case) meddle. In many important ways, then, 'zero marriage distance' can be problematic rather than beneficial for women.

Ghar Jamai

In these unusual cases, the woman marries a man from elsewhere, and then returns with him to her natal village. This, too, is a situation which most men consider should be avoided. The *ghar jamai* himself is likely to be in a weak position and the butt of ridicule in his wife's home - while his wife can avoid the norms of deference and constraint which would restrict her in her husband's village. She also has greater access to her mother and sisters than she could normally attain in her affinal village. In other words, perhaps it is not 'proximity to natal kin' so much as 'distance from affines' which is beneficial to women. We shall return to this point later.

The position of married women living in their natal village highlights the problem of concentrating on marriage distance in the spatial sense alone. The meanings which are attached to the distinction between affinal and natal village are crucial, for geographical distance alone cannot tell us a great deal. In Bijnor, notions of the appropriate social distance between a woman and her natal kin generally override the potential for greater contact that small 'marriage distances' might seem to provide. This suggests that the use of 'marriage distance' as a proxy for 'contacts with natal kin' is of limited value.

But matters are a good deal more complex than even this suggests. While we cannot argue that a woman's contacts with her natal kin are directly related to 'marriage distance', neither can we say that women's contacts with their natal kin are uniformly eroded. Such contacts are indeed varied, and our informants' ability to maintain them can be seriously limited by aspects of the economic position of their affinal household and by its demographic composition. The following case provides one example of the kinds of economic and demographic factors which are considered in subsequent sections:

> 'Shamima is a Muslim woman, married into our Muslim base village from another village about 2 kilometres distant. She has three small children. She is also the only adult woman in a landed, livestock-owning household. Her mother-in-law and the two women married to her husband's two brothers all live in separate hearths and they do no work co-operatively. Her brother visits her occasionally, but never her father or mother. She herself had not been to her natal village during the 2 years up to the end of our fieldwork'.

Economic Position of the Affinal Household

Women in rural Bijnor do not normally own land and they cannot enhance their autonomy through independent earning power. Our interest in economic variables, then, is not in differential economic power among our informants, but in how households' different class locations can generate major differences in the workloads of young married women. Women with more responsibilities get no more credit for their work than other women, but they do experience greater problems in absenting themselves from their affinal village.

The consequences for women of different land-holding patterns are by no means straightforward. All the women cook and clean and deal with the needs of small children. There are few opportunities for regular earning for women, either outside the house or in craft work at home, and this means that aside from basic household maintenance, the workloads of poorer women tend to be lower than those of their more affluent neighbours. Women in wealthier households may have animals to service, crops to clean and store after harvest, or (more rarely) work to perform in the fields. However, in the wealthiest households, women's workloads may be alleviated (sometimes irregularly, sometimes seasonally) by paid assistance.

The servicing of animals has daily implications for a household's workload. Only landowners or those sharecropping land own draught animals but some landless households do own milk animals and goats. Generally, female animals are more likely to be women's responsibility though all the work involved cannot unequivocally be regarded as 'women's work'. However, the collection of dung from male and female animals is never done by men, and entails, during the dry seasons, around 2 to 3 hours a day in making and stacking *oopley* (dung cakes used for fuel). During the monsoon, cattle dung is merely thrown into the midden and used later for fertilizer, rather than dried for fuel. Moreover, the seasonal demands of tasks such as cleaning and drying crops mean that some women's workloads wax and wane accordingly.

These variations generate widely different claims on women's time, so that their workloads are affected in quite complex ways by both class differences and seasonal factors. Negotiating an absence from the affinal village, therefore, poses different problems for different women and even for each woman at different times in the agricultural cycle.

In addition to these overriding influences, class differences also affect women's visits to their natal kin in rather more direct ways. When a woman returns to her natal village to 'stay' for a while (though not when she just goes to 'meet' her kin) she is expected to return to her affines with gifts of food and clothing. This does seem to inhibit poorer people from 'calling' their married daughters for frequent visits.

Demographic Composition of the Affinal Household

Perhaps the significance of women's workloads would be less if women were equally well-placed to find substitutes prepared to do their work for them. The demographic composition of a woman's household, including also the dynamic element of life-cycle changes, must be considered in this regard. Particularly relevant is the presence or absence of the mother-in-law and the number, age and sex of a woman's own children.

Who may or may not act as a substitute? Firstly, it is very rare indeed for a woman's work to be taken over by a man (such as her husband). Secondly, a woman's natal kin will never take over her work in her affinal village when she is absent (and they very rarely do so when she is present).

A woman's most likely substitute is her mother-in-law. Women generally begin their married lives in the same 'hearth' as their mother-in-law. But the interests of the daughter-in-law are subordinated to those of her mother-in-law, who expects to control the workloads and mobility of her daughters-in-law. A woman living with her mother-in-law finds that 'it does not look nice for a daughter-in-law to rest while her mother-in-law works'. The maintenance of a hearth in which two brothers and their wives live together is rare, but when it happens it probably indicates that the women work well together and they may be able to arrange to visit their respective natal kin regularly.

However, quarrelling among women is often given as a reason by women themselves for the separation of hearths. When acrimonious splits occur it is difficult, if not impossible, for a woman wanting to visit her natal kin to call on help from her husband's brothers' wives and possibly even her mother-in-law living in separate hearths. The woman alone in her hearth finds her mobility constrained by the workload for which she alone is responsible, while the woman living with her mother-in-law is restricted by the demands placed on her by her mother-in-law.

The other demographic factor affecting a woman's ability to visit her natal kin is the stage in her own maternity career. In the early years after her marriage she may spend more time with her mother than with her mother-in-law, but once she has children her visits tail off. Later on, when her own daughters are old enough to take over from her, she may be freer to travel; though if anything, our material suggests that women later in their childbearing careers spend less time in their natal village than younger married women.

Summary

On the basis of our fieldwork, would we say that demographers ought to include questions about 'marriage distance', 'close kin marriage', and 'when the woman last saw her mother' in studies designed to assess levels of female autonomy?

The commonly used indicators of autonomy such as ownership of productive resources, access to education, and so forth could be applied to our case material, but they do not give much leverage for trying to comprehend variations among our informants. The issue of 'marriage distance' and women's contacts with their natal kin seemed to provide us with a promising opening in the Bijnor context, in which some facets of Hindu and Muslim marriage arrangements differ. However potentially useful and plausible an approach this might seem, we hope we have demonstrated how difficult it is to generate useful indicators of female autonomy from these phenomena.

Firstly, there are problems in measuring 'marriage distance' at all. The complexities thrown up by our own micro-level data are concealed by the macro-level data which demographers such as Dyson and Moore generally use. Our individual level data perhaps provide rather better measures of 'marriage distance'. However, we remain far from convinced that simply measuring distances is a meaningful exercise, even though we have been able to highlight some interesting ethnic differences.

We need to go further than this. What can 'marriage distance', however measured, tell us about married women's contacts with their natal kin? Our material indicates no necessity for co-hesiveness between 'marriage distance' and the norms which pertain to women's contacts with their natal kin, because such contact is affected by economic and micro-demographic considerations which vary for each woman over time, as well as norms which set the parameters within which women operate. The contact which women can maintain with their natal kin is the outcome of several factors, not just how far away they were married.

Here we have been concerned solely with 'contacts with the natal kin' as a possible indicator of women's autonomy. Others could certainly be considered, such as the extent to which a woman is freed from some contraints within her affinal village following her mother-in-law's death. Several informants claim that having no mother-in-law has several benefits, even if it probably means a heavier workload. The young daughter-in-law is expected to defer to her mother-in-law and patiently wait until she herself is a mother-in-law. But what of the young married woman whose mother-in-law is already dead or who has a separated household? Such a woman has responsibilities which may reduce her contacts with her natal kin, but she may have a more congenial daily round. Could not the structure of a woman's household and the question of hierarchical relationships among women itself be another aspect of young married women's autonomy? This certainly seems to be perceived as such by our informants themselves. But if this is so, another problem arises, as illustrated in the following case:

> 'Khurshida was born near Lucknow (some 400 kilometres away). Since her second marriage in Bijnor she has never once visited her natal village because of threats to her life from her first husband. She has only been visited in her second husband's village by his sister's husband, a truck driver from her natal village who acted as go-between in arranging her second marriage'.

Khurshida is an outstanding case of 'low autonomy' as assessed by her contacts with her natal kin. However, she herself presents a very positive picture of her life, due (she considers) to the fact that her mother-in-law had died before she even arrived in the village. She detailed occasions when she had been able to buy fruit in Bijnor with her husband when she was pregnant, something she claimed would have been impossible if his mother had still been alive. This opinion echoes many comments made by our informants about the mother-in-law's significance, not just in controlling work and mobility but also in relation to access to food and even direct physical abuse, as in reported cases where the mother-in-law encourages her son to beat his wife by telling tales about her daughter-in-law.

This case indicates that different yet still plausible indicators of female autonomy do not necessarily cohere neatly with one another. A lack of contacts with the natal kin may co-exist with a lack of control by the mother-in-law. Briefly, then, the closer we look at 'female autonomy' the harder it is to grasp it.

We are thus rather unwilling to attempt to link 'female autonomy' to differences in demographic behaviour, as attempted in Dyson and Moore's analysis. In any case, our own material does not really permit the sort of statistical analysis which would shed light on the 'demographic regime' in North India. Nevertheless, a brief comment here can add further weight to our general conclusions: that is, that the neatness of Dyson and Moore's model begins to disintegrate the closer we go to the grass roots. Their 'demographic regime' of North India is characterized by rates of infant and child mortality and of fertility which are higher than in the South, and by higher sex ratios than in the South. Uttar Pradesh state level data on fertility and mortality and district level data on the sex ratio fit Dyson and Moore's picture fairly well - until we insert ethnic variation into the equation.

The puzzle is this. Contrary to what we would expect if 'marriage distance' has any influence on women's autonomy, Muslim rural fertility rates in Uttar Pradesh are significantly higher than Hindu fertility rates (and our own data concur with this). Child mortality data are too suspect to be useful - and they present no consistent pattern of ethnic difference. However, to muddy the waters still further, the sex ratio is (and has been for as long as records have existed) higher among Hindus than Muslims. Dyson and Moore's 'demographic regime' seems rather elusive.

This discussion is something of a cautionary tale. Dyson and Moore's paper has a convincing ring about it on first reading, but we have faced tremendous problems in trying to fit our own data into their framework. The use of aggregate data provides Dyson and Moore with a much neater picture than emerges from detailed micro-research. This raises the general problem of how useful models based on aggregate data can be for the interpretation of local level and even individual data such as our own. Dyson and

Moore themselves comment that the 'untidiness of reality cannot concern us too much here' (p.43), and they produce a very tidy model indeed. In trying to employ their framework to make sense of our material, we have not allowed ourselves the luxury of ignoring the 'untidiness of reality' - with the result that our material leaves open far more questions that it answers.

19

The Structure of Households Amongst the Malian Fulani:[1] Linking Form and Process

Allan G. Hill and Adam S. Thiam

Introduction

The structure of families or households, the basic residential units forming the building blocks of every society, should be a valuable clue to the nature of their formative processes. There is, however, a surprising uniformity, at least in the size of households, in a variety of contemporary and historical populations despite their contrasting demographic regimes and diverse rules on household formation and deformation (see Hajnal, 1982; Laslett and Wall, 1972; and Garenne, 1981). The problem when dealing with such an elastic unit as the family or the household is a more complex version of the problem familiar to demographers in another form - trying to deduce mortality, fertility and migration rates from data on the proportional composition of a population by age. In both cases, the core of the problem is that the same structure can be the outcome of several different sets of processes. The solution is of course to have only one unknown in the equation. This is the goal towards which some studies of the demography of families and households are moving (for a recent summary, see CICRED, 1984 and Bongaarts *et al.*, in press). For the moment, the task ahead is the description of the processes affecting household structure in a variety of cultural settings with different demographic regimes. This chapter forms a part of this larger descriptive effort.

Principles

In a much simplified form, we can see from Figure 19.1 that the size and structure of households represent the outcome of the prevailing fertility and mortality regimes mitigated by the set of rules or recommendations on the splitting of existing households or the formation of new ones. These rules and the accompanying demographic schedules are not independent of each other, which is one reason why the systematic study of the size and shape of families and households is difficult. Figure 19.1 does at least suggest that one fruitful form of analysis may be the examination of household structure within sub-populations to which the same rules on household formation and deformation apply. If these sub-populations also have contrasting demographic regimes, as they will have in most circumstances, then the chances of drawing some definite conclusions on the importance of the mortality and fertility in determining household structure greatly

Figure 19.1 Schematic Diagram of the Principal Factors Affecting the Size and Composition of Households

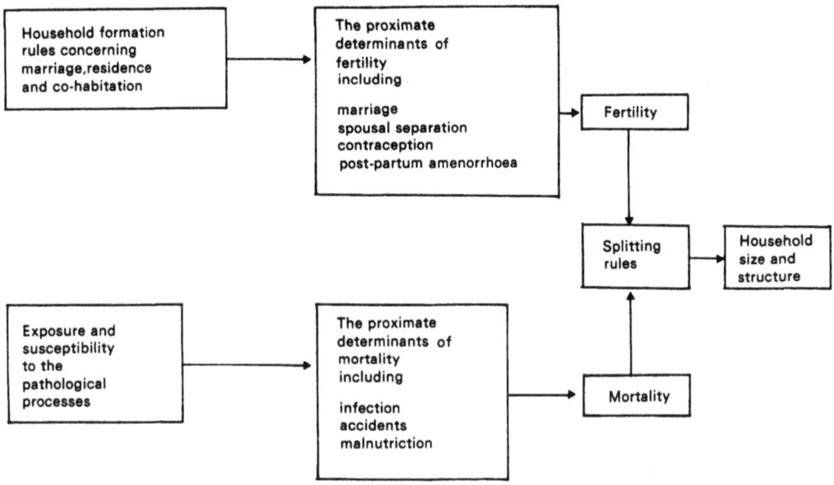

increase. An alternative form of research design could involve the comparison of populations with broadly similar demographic characteristics but with different rules on household formation and deformation. This latter approach seems less attractive since, in a particular region, there is probably greater diversity in the household formation rules than in the demographic regimes.

The Malian Fulani

The basic statistical data presented here come from a single-round demographic survey conducted in 1982 by Hill and van den Eerenbeemt amongst a sample of the Fulani agro-pastoral population in central Mali in two contrasting geographical zones. The survey was then supplemented by other more detailed work on nutrition, health, and socioeconomic aspects of production in a few small, selected communities. Details of the survey and the basic demographic results are available elsewhere (see Hill, 1984; Hill, Randall and Sullivan, 1982; and Hill, Randall and van den Eerenbeemt, 1983). The summary in Table 19.1 shows that in both zones, the Masina or inner flood zone or 'delta' of the river Niger, and the semi-arid Seno-Mango, the population suffers from heavy adult and child mortality, and has a moderately high level of fertility which is entirely 'natural' (that is, with no evidence of deliberate control of fertility). There are striking differences in the mortality levels of the two zones and smaller differences in fertility. More interesting are the differences between the two 'status groups' or 'social classes'.

Table 19.1 Population-Level Measures of Mortality and Fertility Amongst the Fulani of Central Mali

Measure	Population Group				
	Masina		Seno-Mango		All
	Fulbe	Rimaibe	Fulbe	Rimaibe	
Mortality					
1000 $_1q_0$	217	227	152	151	193
ℓ_5	.531	.478	.695	.623	.589
e_{15} males	40	39	46	42	42
e_{15} females	44	42	48	47	45
Fertility					
Total fertility rate	7.9	6.4	6.9	5.7	6.8
Crude birth rate (000)	60	52	47	40	50
Rate of natural increase (%)	1.8	1.0	2.5	1.5	1.7

Source: Hill, Randall and van den Eerenbeemt (1983).

In Mali, Fulani society is organized vertically into clans, each with a distinctive patronym, and horizontally into endogamous social status groups, here called social classes for simplicity. The terms in use in central Mali are shown in Table 19.2. In pratical terms, the most important distinction is between the *Rimbe* (freemen or nobles) and the *Rimaibe* (non-nobles or serfs). The Rimbe largely comprise the *Fulbe*, the cattle-owning part of the Fulfulde-speaking population, whereas the Rimaibe are an amalgam of different ethnic groups dependent on the Fulbe and settled by them in *saare* (cultivation hamlets) to produce cereals. These distinctions between the semi-transhumant Fulbe herders and the settled agricultural Rimaibe have become more blurred since Malian independence in 1960, but in social and economic relations, the Fulbe-Rimaibe distinction remains important (see Hess *et al*., 1984; and Hilderbrand, 1984 for details).

Table 19.2 Summary of Social Stratification Amongst the Masina and Seno-Mango Fulani, Central Mali

Social Class		Status	Profession
1.	Rimbe	Nobles	Herders or land owners, using manual labourers
2.	Jawanbe	Free, but of lower status than the Rimbe	Merchants, courtiers, couriers in the service of the Rimbe
3.	Nieyeebe	Free, but of lower status than the Jawanbe	
a)	Wailube		a) blacksmiths
b)	Maabube		b) weavers
c)	Awlube		c) traditional historians
d)	Sakeebe		d) shoemakers
4.	Rimaibe or Maccube	'Non-nobles': captives and therefore not free	Serfs in the service of the Rimbe

Note: In the demographic surveys, classes 1, 2 and 3 were grouped together and are referred to as 'Fulbe'. *Rimbe* and *Rimaibe* together, the community of Fulfulde-speakers, are here called 'Fulani'.

In Fulfulde, there is no direct translation of the word for 'family', nuclear or otherwise. Instead, the Fulbe have a unit called either *wuro* (Seno-Mango) or *galle* (Masina) which translates as 'village' but in fact can vary in size from a single married couple and their children to an extensive group of kin comprising perhaps two or three generations related patrilineally to a common male ancestor. This *wuro* or *galle* is also a unit for the purposes of pastoral and agricultural production. It served as the basic unit of enumeration during the demographic surveys in central Mali in 1981-82 and the subsequent socioeconomic research in sub-samples of these populations. There is a larger unit called a *suduu baba* (literally, grandfather's shelter) which incorporates several of these *wuro* or *galle* but except when major issues arise (for example, conflicting inheritance claims), the *suudu baba* is not important on a day-to-day basis. The word *suudu* (shelter) is used to describe the structure itself and the residents of a single hut but this unit has little economic and social importance relative to the *wuro* or *galle*, not least because it changes in composition according to the season (Thiam, 1984). Amongst the Rimaibe, the system of social organization is quite similar except that the name *wuro* is usually replaced by the word *saare*.

Table 19.3 The Composition of Fulani Households (*Galle*) by Number of Residents

No. of Residents in Galle	% of Population MF	SF	MR	SR		% Living in Nuclear Families MF	SF	MR	SR
1	0	0	0	0		100	100	100	100
2	2	1	1	0		86	98	86	100
3	3	3	3	2		89	91	87	80
4	7	3	5	4		83	88	86	89
5	10	5	7	4		86	84	82	87
6 - 10	41	32	33	31		75	79	75	75
11 - 15	21	17	21	16		63	59	21	60
16 - 20	12	12	16	9		57	56	55	52
21+	4	27	14	35		32	16	43	41
Mean:	10.0	18.4	13.3	19.2	All:	71	63	67	60
All:	5.9	16.9	10.0	15.1					

Notes: (1) Social class abbreviations are:

MF - Masina Fulbe SF - Seno-Mango Fulbe

MR - Masina Rimaibe SR - Seno-Mango Rimaibe

(2) 'Nuclear' here means the household head with his wife or wives and their children (codes 10 to 20 on Figure 19.2).

The Composition of Households (*Galle* or *Wuro*)

The description of the composition of Fulani households or indeed any households would be greatly enhanced if we had a satisfactory model to generate the expected structures for comparison with the structures observed. This model has yet to be developed even though there appears to be some progress with the statistical description of the age patterns of departures from the parental home, ages at first birth and so on (Bongaarts *et al.*, in press). In any detailed study, often the most striking feature is the diversity of domestic living arrangements and the complexity of the economic and other relationships between households not related by blood or marriage. In the Sahel, the existence of dependent groups, 'slaves' in the case of the Tamasheq, 'serfs' in the case of the Fulani, complicates the study of households in isolation still further since the continued

Table 19.4 Proportional Distribution (%) of the Fulani Population Surveyed in Central Mali by Relationship to Household Head, Area, Class and Sex

I - MALES

Relationship (see Figure 19.2 for codes)	Codes	Masina Fulbe	Masina Rimaibe	Seno-Mango Fulbe	Seno-Mango Rimaibe
Parents etc. of HH	(0+5)	*	*	*	*
HH	(10)	25	23	20	18
Others gen. 1	(15)	13	17	12	15
Children of HH	(20)	36	32	35	30
Others gen. 2	(25)	14	19	16	20
Grandchildren	(30)	5	4	7	7
Others gen. 3	(35)	2	4	4	7
Gen. 4	(40+45)	0	*	1	*
Other rel.	(66)	1	1	0	0
Not rel.	(55)	3	1	3	2
Total		100	100	100	100
N		1,381	1,868	2,117	786

II - FEMALES

Relationship (see Figure 19.2 for codes)	Codes	Masina Fulbe	Masina Rimaibe	Seno-Mango Fulbe	Seno-Mango Rimaibe
Parents etc. of HH	(0+5)	6	5	5	4
Wives of HH	(11-14)	27	25	21	20
Others gen. 1	(15)	13	17	14	15
Children of HH	(20)	27	21	23	18
Spouses	(21)	4	5	7	8
Others gen. 2	(25)	12	16	16	19
Grandchildren	(30)	3	3	8	8
Others gen. 3	(35)	1	3	4	6
Gen. 4	(40+45)	*	*	*	*
Other rel.	(66)	1	1	*	*
Not rel.	(55)	3	2	2	*
Total		100	100	100	100
N		1,298	1,872	2,019	735

Notes: (1) * = less than 1 per cent.
(2) For a fuller explanation of the relationship codes, see Figure 19.2.

Figure 19.2 Schematic Diagram of the Coding System Used to Describe Relationship to the Head of Each *Galle* in the Fulani Survey, Central Mali, 1982

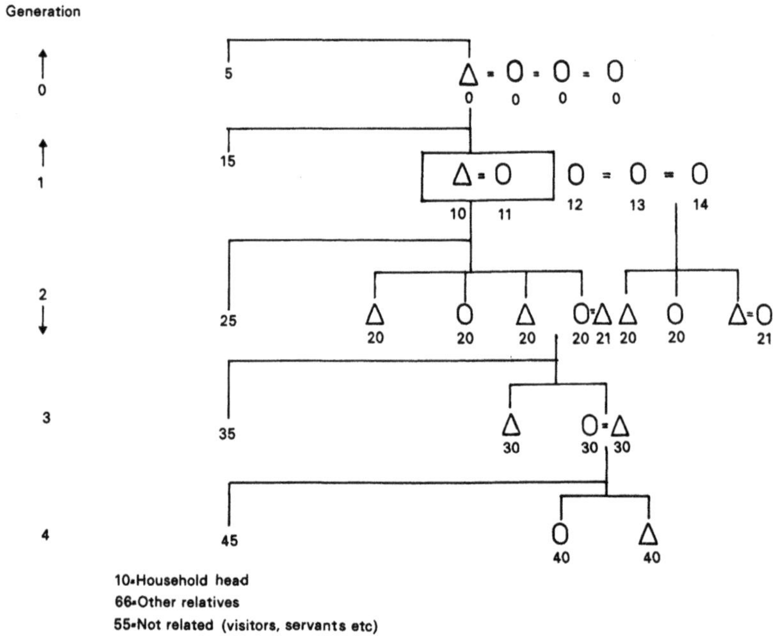

survival of the 'noble' household may be to a large extent dependent on tributary or reciprocal ties with members of the dependent class.

In a general way, we know that labour needs are greater in agricultural societies than in pastoral or hunter-gatherer communities. On this rather loose generalization is founded the idea that fertility amongst agricultural societies will also be higher, and therefore the residential units will be larger. This rather naively ignores the importance of household formation and deformation rules, not to mention consideration of marriage and inheritance. Indeed, if we look at marital fertility, itself full of contradictions in many African societies, we see in Mali almost no difference between the marital fertility of the agricultural Bambara and that of the agro-pastoral Fulani or the truly pastoral Tamasheq (Hill, 1984). Nonetheless, the idea that farming populations have higher overall fertility and live in larger residential units consisting more commonly of joint families is a useful Aunt Sally for our examination of the Fulani survey data.

The first test of the accuracy of our predictions about household size is the data in Table 19.3. There it is shown that the

Table 19.5 Malian Fulani 1982: Relationship Between Entry into Marriage and into Headship (males) by Class* and Region

Age Group	Percentage of All Males who are:											
	Ever-Married				Heads of Household				Ever-Married Heads of Household			
	MF	SF	MR	SR	MF	SF	MR	SR	MF	SF	MR	SR
18-22	7	33	4	18	6	3	3	0	1	2	0	0
23-27	26	77	29	56	14	10	14	5	3	8	6	5
28-32	63	91	60	90	25	27	14	14	20	25	11	12
33-37	87	97	89	100	40	39	23	23	37	39	22	23
38-42	95	98	94	100	45	40	26	28	44	39	26	28
43-47	100	98	99	100	63	50	51	53	63	49	50	35
48-52	100	99	100	100	67	70	89	45	67	69	47	45
53-57	100	100	100	100	82	75	67	56	82	75	67	56
58-62	100	100	100	100	86	70	89	74	86	70	88	74
N	720	954	990	394	720	954	990	392	720	954	990	392

* Social class abbreviations are:

MF - Masina Fulbe SF - Seno-Mango Fulbe

MR - Masina Rimaibe SR - Seno-Mango Rimaibe

highest proportion (60 per cent) living in households of eleven or more people is found among the agricultural Seno Rimaibe. The pastoral Fulbe of the Seno-Mango are not far behind on this measure (56 per cent), but the major departure is the Masina Rimaibe with just over half of their members in households of eleven or more people. The data on nuclear families in the same table are also not at all decisive in distinguishing the agro-pastoral or agricultural groups from the groups more dependent on livestock rearing.

An alternative way of presenting these data on relationships is to look at the proportions of the population in the separate relationship categories. From Table 19.4, it does seem that headship rates amongst males are slightly higher, implying smaller households, in the Masina than in the Seno-Mango but the differences by social class within each zone are much less pronounced. Broadly the same is true of the female population amongst whom the proportions who are wives of the household head are higher for both groups of the Masina than in those of the Seno-Mango.

Some data on headship rates and entry into marriage, tabulated in the same way chosen by Hajnal (1982), are helpful in identifying one of the factors distinguishing the two zones (Table 19.5). Whilst the age at entry into marriage for men is earlier in the Seno-Mango than in the Masina, by about age forty no bachelors remain in either population (Fulbe or Rimaibe) in both zones. In Table 19.5, the columns showing proportions of all men who are ever-married heads of households indicate much more clearly a distinction which may reflect contrasting marriage and inheritance rules between the zones rather than differences linked to economic organization (pastoral production amongst the Fulbe, agriculture amongst the Rimaibe). Can our micro-level observations on marriage and inheritance help us explain these surprising differences?

Marriage and Inheritance Rules

The Fulbe and the Rimaibe of both zones have patrilocal systems of residence and patrilineal ways of tracing descent. The Masina Fulani, however, often marry outside their clan (hence there are different patronyms amongst spouses) whilst in the Seno-Mango, marriages are more frequent amongst closer kin. Marriage with parallel cousins is preferred in both zones although marriage with cross-cousins also occurs. Unions with matrilateral parallel and cross-cousins are avoided: contact with in-laws is shameful, especially in the Seno-Mango, and the mother's brother has a special position with reference to his nephews and nieces.

Amongst the Fulbe of the Seno-Mango, cattle are pre-inherited and a couple must own enough livestock in order to form a separate *suudu* or *galle* at marriage. Broadly the same applies to the Masina Fulbe but in a society with a greater stress on agriculture, transfers of tenure rights in land are of greater importance. This tends to limit the prevalence of pre-inheritance. For the Rimaibe of both the Seno-Mango and the Masina, rights in land are of supreme importance although in the less densely settled Seno-Mango, access to new land is not such a problem as in the more populous Masina. The marriage system for all involves a transfer of animals, goods and money from the family of the bridegroom to the bride's family who then endow her with a portion of these gifts (indirect dowry). This dowry is intended for the wife and her offspring. In the Masina, however, inheritance is more common than pre-inheritance so that the wife is more dependent on her husband's support there than in the Seno-Mango. There 'her' animals are placed in the family's pre-inherited herd, in contrast to the custom in the Masina where the beasts remain in the bride's kin's herd. In general in the Masina, transactions in goods and cash are more common than in the Seno-Mango. The *farrila* (dowry) in the Masina can amount to about £60 plus additional gifts of clothing. At the marriage ceremony itself, the bridegroom may spend *sufande* (another £5 to £10 in cash on the bride's family) quite apart from the *fute* (the gift of a heifer or a young bull to his wife). The Rimaibe, being 'non-noble', are forbidden by religious custom to make this last payment.

Table 19.6 Percentages of Ever-Married Male Household Heads Married More Than Once by Age-Group: Masina and Seno-Mango Fulani

Age Group	Masina		Seno-Mango	
	Fulbe	Rimaibe	Fulbe	Rimaibe
25 - 29	12	8	40	-
30 - 34	5	22	38	33
35 - 39	14	19	47	45
40 - 44	41	37	49	64
45 - 49	46	50	58	75
50 - 54	58	45	77	73
55 - 59	60	49	71	68
60+	51	53	69	76
All	43	44	60	58
N	328	399	418	139

Note: (-) = zero or less than five cases.

A major difference between the Seno-Mango and the Masina is the stability of marriage and the frequency of polygynous unions. Table 19.6 shows that the proportions of ever-married household heads married more than once are much higher in the Seno-Mango than in the Masina for both Fulbe and Rimaibe. Complementing this, Table 19.7 shows that the proportions of currently married men with more than one surviving wife are also higher in the Masina than in the Seno-Mango. In brief, in the Masina, monogamous marriages are the norm although a substantial proportion - nearly a third overall - take another wife, while always retaining the first. This compares with the very different situation in the Seno-Mango where frequent divorce and remarriage produces a kind of 'serial monogamy'. Several factors may account for this difference. They include the greater degree of administrative control exercised in the Masina since the days of the religious empires of Shaikh Ahmadu in 1818-46 and al-Hajj Umar Tall and his successors in 1862-93 (see Gallais, 1984; and Clarke, 1982 for details). Another possible factor is the closer contact of the Masina Fulani with other ethnic groups. Some of these, like the Bambara, practise the levirate, and the Masina Fulani have been able to follow suit in some cases because of their system of exogamous clan marriage (for Bambara marriage, see Randall, 1984).

Table 19.7 Polygyny Amongst Malian Fulani: Ratio of First Wives to Second and Subsequent Wives by Class and Region

Age Group	Masina		Seno-Mango	
	Fulbe	Rimaibe	Fulbe	Rimaibe
20 - 24	4.2	5.0	3.4	2.2
25 - 29	6.6	5.0	5.6	0.0
30 - 34	4.3	3.5	4.9	2.1
35 - 39	5.3	5.6	6.2	5.7
40 - 44	11.0	4.5	6.7	4.4
45 - 49	7.2	3.1	0.0	6.0
50 - 54	3.7	5.4	14.5	4.0
55 - 59	22.0	4.8	4.7	3.4
60+	20.0	2.9	9.1	6.3
All	6.4	4.2	6.5	3.9
N	327	432	422	173

Note: The frequency of polygyny is probably understated in the figures above because some second and third wives live in different *galle* from those of their husbands, and their relationship to the head of that *galle* misrecorded.

Interpretation

In the data presented above, the major surprise is the discovery that household structure is not strikingly different either between the two geographical zones, the Masina and the Seno-Mango, or between the two social class groups, Fulbe and Rimaibe. Whilst fertility, especially marital fertility, is quite similar in all four sub-groups, child mortality is very much higher in the Masina than in the Seno-Mango. This factor alone might be expected to produce noticeable differences in the composition of households, but this is not the case. Instead, the factors responsible for the differences in household composition which do exist between the two zones and to some extent between the two social classes within a single zone are connected with the processes of marriage and inheritance. The absence of very marked differences between the Fulbe and the Rimaibe within a single zone suggests that economic factors linked to production at the household level are not the most important determinant of the shape of the residential and the production units. Instead, it seems from intensive study that more complex reciprocal ties between households, some related by kinship, others not, allow the households to combine flexibly for the purposes of production. An additional complication in Central Mali are the residual ties of dependency between the social classes dating from the pre-colonial period. In this way, an element of specialization is introduced into traditional society. Our conclusion is that the more detailed work carried out in the wake of the demographic surveys has been essential in highlighting the emptiness of further analysis of the demography and the demographic structure of households such as the Fulani without more knowledge of these links. An essential improvement in any analysis could be the development of some predictive models which could be used as more rigorous testing of some current ideas in demography and economic anthropology. What our current studies seem to be suggesting is that in the rural subsistence economies of the Sahel, the links between demographic and economic behaviour are still very tenuous, possibly because of the enormous amount of risk and uncertainty associated with every vital event and every new season.

Notes

1. 'Fulani' is used to refer to the whole community of Fulfulde speakers, comprising both *Fulbe* or *Peul* (freemen), and *Rimaibe* (their ex-dependants).

Migration and Urbanization

20

Population Movement Studied at Micro-Scale: Experience and Extrapolation*

Murray Chapman

> 'If we had had two eyes of different sizes, we might have evolved a faculty for combining the points of view of the mammoth and the microbe' (Eddington, 1935).

> 'Clearly one good case can illuminate the working of a social system in a way that a series of morphological statements cannot achieve' (Gluckman, 1961, p.9).

In a paper stimulating for its range and depth, Mitchell (1983) argues that the nature of generalization about aspects of social reality depends on the quality of understanding rather than on how many cases have been subject to examination. By thus unhitching the prospect of broader conclusions from the inevitability of them being based on statistical extrapolation, he has confronted one of the most persistent misconceptions with which the social sciences have been bedevilled for the past 25 years. In one critical sense, there is no difference in drawing inferences from a statistical sample or from the idiosyncratic mix of elements or events that constitute a case study. For both, the process depends on the power of theoretical reasoning and logical extension. As a quantitative sociologist, Mitchell's key contribution has been to emphasize that extrapolation from a statistical sample to a wider universe is grounded in probability mathematics and depends on typicality, whereas neither of these two conditions applies to the case study nor affects the quality of generalizations drawn on the basis of theoretical connections or compelling logic.

This chapter is concerned with methodological aspects of four different studies of population mobility at micro-scale, undertaken between 1965 and 1977 in the Solomon Islands and Northwest Thailand. Despite the persistent stereotype, detailed research of village communities in places such as these does not seek to replicate the undisciplined eclecticism of the Renaissance scholar nor the vicarious journeys made by eighteenth century wanderers to unknown domains. As demanded by Mitchell's criteria for generalization from the particular case, each of these field projects was articulated within a conceptual frame of reference,

* This chapter was first published in *GeoJournal*, vol.15, no.4, (December 1987).

Figure 20.1 Solomon Islands, Guadalcanal, The Weather Coast and Study Villages

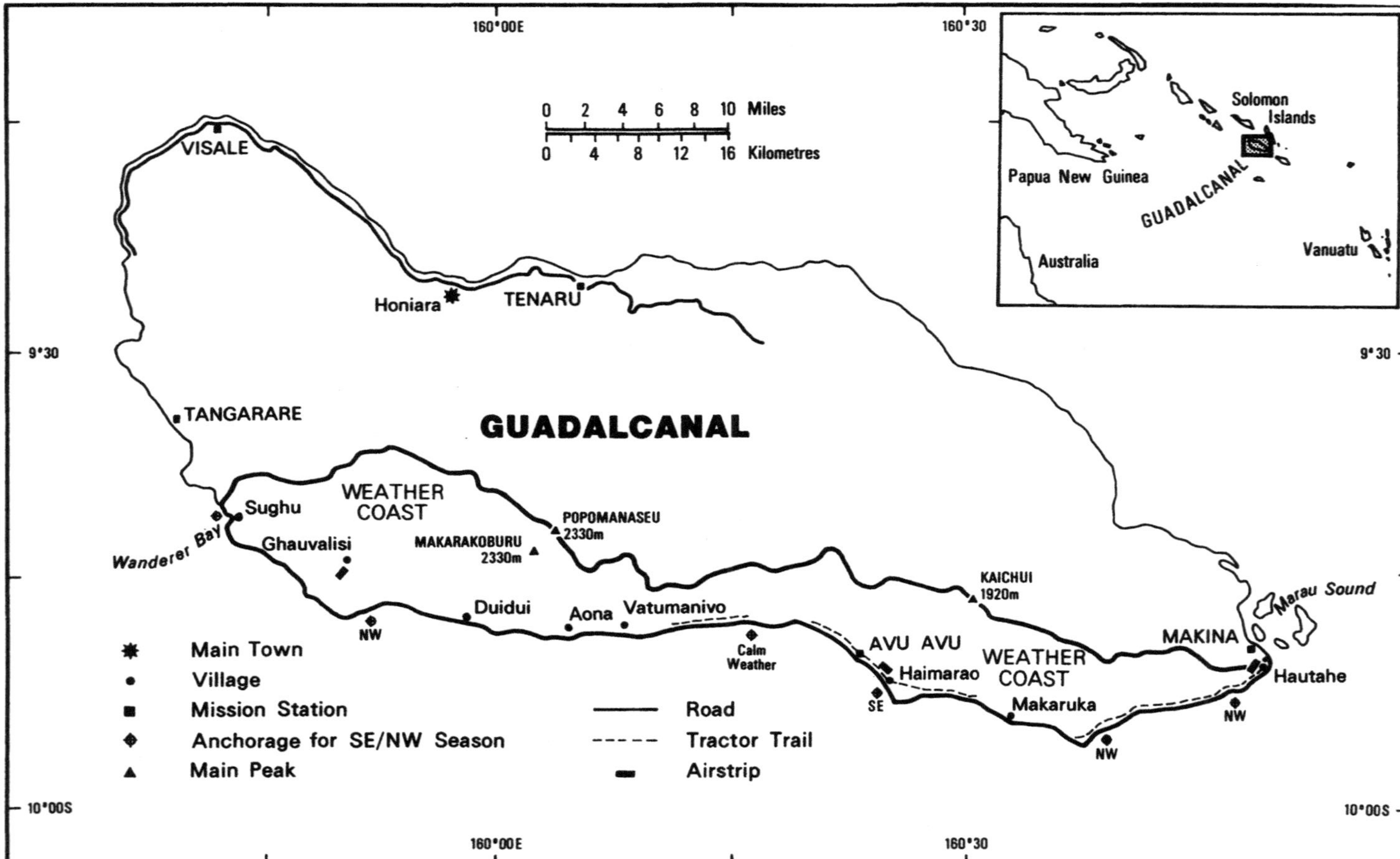

proceeded with due regard for disciplinary history, and was rooted in scepticism about the transferability of conventions evolved from vastly different contexts. Collectively, these local studies sought to inform academics and policy makers about the human condition in Third World societies.

Two Community Studies - South Guadalcanal, 1965-67

Between October 1965 and February 1967, a detailed investigation was made of a coast and inland 'bush' village on the Weather (south) Coast of Guadalcanal, in what today is an independent Solomon Islands (Figure 20.1). The specific focus of this field research was the reasons that underlay the people's considerable mobility and, more particularly, the interplay of social and economic factors. It was designed to test the notion that considerations other than economic were far more significant than had often been recognized in movement research, especially in Third World societies; and that, in a process as complex and dynamic as a people's mobility, single-factor explanations were simplistic distortions of reality. On 1 March 1966, the coastal community of Duidui had a *de jure* population of 221 spread throughout 40 households; on 1 October 1966; the bush community of Pichahila contained 110 persons in 18 households.

Although the research design, underlying rationale, and detailed results of this study have appeared elsewhere (Chapman, 1969, 1970, 1971, 1975, 1976, 1985), certain features require brief summary. First, mobility was viewed in all its ongoing complexity from the standpoint of the village and was defined as any absence of 24 hours or more. In turn, this reflected a deliberate attempt to derive definitions that were locally meaningful rather than predetermined by external conventions or alien contexts (Chapman, 1975, pp.130-3). Second, the field instruments were carefully chosen to yield both cross-sectional and longitudinal data, so that information about presence and absence obtained through a village census for one moment in time was augmented by continuous records that spanned varying periods. Namely, a mobility register maintained for ten of the months between December 1965 and November 1966, a 2-year record of absences of more than 4 weeks for wage labour (1965-66), conjugal histories for all married or formerly married persons, a handful of migrant life histories, and oral accounts from senior men about the relocation of village communities since the turn of the century (Chapman, 1971, pp.10-20). This range of instruments underlined a third and more technical aim: to test the complementary use of demographic procedures with those that are more customarily geographic (settlement mapping, cartographic analysis) and anthropological (participant observation, collection of individual or family histories).

In defining 'population movement' and 'mobility' as any kind of territorial displacement from 24-hour journeys to the relocation of entire villages, this research abandoned the prevailing conventions of migration study in favour of that broader area

Goodman (1961) aptly terms the 'mover-stayer' problem. Of several field instruments deployed over 16 months, greatest attention will be paid here to the establishment of a prospective mobility register among a nonliterate population - an effort that is still sufficiently novel a generation later to be summarized in recent treatments about collecting movement data (for example, Goldstein and Goldstein, 1981, p.42; Findley, 1982, pp.18, 55).

In both communities of Duidui and Pichahila, a daily register was kept for 5 months - for the former, from 1 December 1965 until 31 May 1966, but excluding the month of April; in the latter, between 1 July and 30 November 1966. Into this register was recorded any individual who either left or came into the village for 24 hours or more. This time span was chosen because it entailed an overnight stop and, consequently, a conscious decision. It also meant checking one's supply of tobacco, betel nut and lime, taking a change of *calico* (clothing) and, sometimes, even carrying a bedroll. For every entry, information was obtained on the date of the inward and outward shifts, the name of those involved, their origin or destination, by what means (foot, canoe, ship, aeroplane) and with whom the move was made over what time period, and for what reasons, for example, entry from mobility register, Pichahila, 12 August 1966, inward move:

name	origin/destination	method of move
Jim (see 10 August)	Buturua-Pichahila	Walk with Paura about 9 hours, because went slowly; hunted opossum in *bush* (secondary forest); stopped half-way at garden house (Nakoga). Arrived 6 p.m. Slept in single men's house.

Reasons for move

Returned from unsuccessfully trying to catch pig with Michael, Hesikibo, Mario (see 10 August entry) for feast for John's father who died in February at Palulu. Did not return with others for was raining then and did not want to catch cold (Length of absence: 2½ days).

The mobility register began on 25 November 1965 for the coastal village of Duidui, 6 days after arrival. Viewed in retrospect, this seems an astonishing display of aggressive efficiency, but recourse to field notes reveals that such a peremptory start reflected a deliberate strategy of enforced familiarization. Having to observe movement required knowing the layout of the settlement and its boundaries; identifying which of the palm-leaf structures housed family members as distinct from stone ovens, visitors, drying copra, canoes, worshippers, or pigs; and learning as many of the people's names as quickly as possible.

'Most of the villagers were understandably nervous of me at the beginning. So that they would quickly become more used to me, I walked around the village many times, learned as many of the people's names as possible, sat down with the men in the late afternoons when they were watching fishing, and attempted to talk to those who could understand simple English. By about the second or third week, the prevailing attitude was one of reserved acceptance which in turn, and particularly following a large meeting at the end of the third week, was translated to one of full acceptance' (Chapman, 1966, p.3).

At the outset, the register was very time consuming and took up to half of each day to complete. Apart from insufficient knowledge about the village population and an initial period without any interpreter, the magnitude of the task partly reflected the considerable amount of mobility during December, as children returned from boarding schools for their annual vacation, relatives visited kin before Christmas, and nearby villagers attended a special feast on 25 December. Whereas in these first few weeks such moves often were recorded several days after they had occurred, one month later potential entries became apparent the moment a group of women walked by with bedrolls on their heads or men were seen resting on the stone wall outside the visitors' house.

With the first month of inquiries deliberately conducted single-handedly, the time had come to choose an interpreter and research aid. Aged 19, Sandy Jonathon had just finished 5 years of primary schooling which, for Weather Coast society of the mid-1960s, meant that in formal terms he was a highly educated person. The mobility register provided a simple but effective means to train him in research techniques - first, to observe movement as it occurred; next, to record pertinent details and to anticipate the physical act of departure or arrival from locally suggestive cues; later, to go beyond the basic details of movement and capture its variable contexts; and finally, by early February 1966, to take complete control of the daily record. Each week, at the Eurocentric time of Monday forenoon, we compared our independent entries to the mobility register, discussed omissions and differences, noted emergent patterns, and raised queries for further investigations - many of them to be conducted by Jonathon himself. Perhaps the most instructive experience from maintaining this daily register was that very rarely, for a total of 10 months in two communities, did a village member and an outside observer enter the same number of moves into the weekly record.

For both Duidui and Pichahila, during 10 selected months between December 1965 and November 1966, entries to the mobility register totalled 1,478, ranged from 83 to 243 per month, and in only two instances were less than one hundred. About two-fifths and one-fifth of these moves were undertaken by persons not *de jure* members of Duidui and Pichahila or were directly or indirectly influenced by the fieldworker and his family (Table 20.1). As the ebb and flow of people literally unfolded

Table 20.1 Moves* for Selected Months 1965–6, Duidui and Pichahila

	Duidui	Pichahila
Total moves	746	732
Village members	416 (55.8%)	582 (79.5%)
Outsiders	321 (43.0%)	103 (14.1%)
Influenced by fieldworkers	9 (1.2%)	47 (6.4%)

* For 24 hours or more.

Source: Chapman (1975, p.132).

before our eyes, perturbations in the daily record identified unknown sequences of events or raised questions that often linked with information contained in the village census, wage-labour histories, or field diaries. On 17 February 1966, for example, thirteen men left for wage work, followed by another six on 23 February. Urgent inquiries revealed that this exodus followed a meeting of members of the Melanesian Mission (now Church of Melanesia), at which it was decided to build a European-style church and to levy each adult to pay for nails, sawn timber, cement, and roofing iron. In total, the men departing from Duidui accounted for 46 per cent of those aged between 21 and 54 but, lacking available cash, had to seek paid employment beyond the village. The collective response within the community, observed over several weeks, was for the 3 to 6 year-olds, the elderly, and the infirm to be utilized more and more to carry water from the river, prepare vegetables, supervise infants, and keep the village swept and weeded.

Being aware, from the village census, that for seventeen out of eighteen households it was the married male who had left, details were collected about domestic arrangements. In eight households some reorganization was necessary and for the remainder there were clear reasons why this did not occur (Appendix 20.1). Wives with one or more dependent children to nurse and no independent children as helpers secured assistance for domestic tasks and food cultivation, frequently with the active support of their husband. Such arrangements were crucial for two widowers who, in a reversal of custom, still maintained their own domestic unit. The most recently widowed, unable to pay his local head tax, was forced to ask his brother and wife whether they would be prepared to house, feed, and supervise four children aged 1 to 12 years so that 'I can go away and earn money' (Appendix 20.1: household H). Females assisting other women were, in order of preference, related by blood, by marriage, or by descent group, with the last named a member of the wife's sub-clan if at all possible.

Households to which additional kin were not recruited or that were temporarily shuttered and barricaded had access to teenage daughters, elderly mothers, or age mates who could be pressed into additional service (Appendix 20.1: households I to Q). In every case, all such assistance was rewarded upon the husband's return, often by a 'fathom of calico' (6' length of cloth) and all in careful proportion to the amount of effort expended. This same adjustment also was observed during 1966 among the Tadhimboko of northeast Guadalcanal (Figure 20.1), for whom 'sojourn at places of work does not necessarily cause excessive strains on the functioning of the village. Men who go away unaccompanied on paid work for brief periods can and do make arrangements for the welfare of their families. Their cash remittances are often used to hire labour to perform essential services' (Lasaqa, 1972, p.268).

As previously noted, a *de jure* census of the two village populations provided cross-sectional anchor to the longitudinal records being compiled both prospectively and retrospectively. One of the unanticipated results from this field census was the relocation of entire communities revealed by the question on place of birth. Fifty-two per cent (114 out of 221) of those belonging to Duidui and 64 per cent (70 out of 110) of people of Pichahila were born elsewhere. Between one-quarter (Duidui) and one-half (Pichahila) came from inland settlements that no longer existed, thus documenting the 'bush' origin of these and most Weather Coast communities. Congruent policies by a colonial administration and proselytizing missionary groups to concentrate villagers in coastal and near-coastal areas undoubtedly were influential in this continuing process. 'We moved because (Guadalcanal) Council told us to' (Pichahila); 'Government and missionaries invite us to come' (Duidui); 'The (Guadalcanal) Council told the people who live in small villages to come and live in a big village' (Pichahila). Other frequent reasons were: natural hazards, such as the 1931 'big earthquake' and the recurrent flooding of some sites; idiosyncratic events like the burning of several dwellings by a teenage girl; and for earlier shifts, the persistence of hit-and-run raiding between antagonistic 'bush' communities.

This fascinating dimension of a people's mobility behaviour was not part of the original research design, if only because the aim was to establish a baseline from which future studies might proceed rather than to attempt historical reconstruction. But with the field census completed, 4 weeks of unplanned discussions were held with several old men, partly because the reasons for community relocation appeared different from those that led individuals and families to be so peripatetic; partly because the census question on birthplace had raised many issues about customary forms of physical transfer (cf. Bathgate, 1985). Pichahila, established at the direction of a district headman in 1953 by amalgamating four 'big villages', represents the most

Figure 20.2 Duidui: Village Shifts 1900–1966

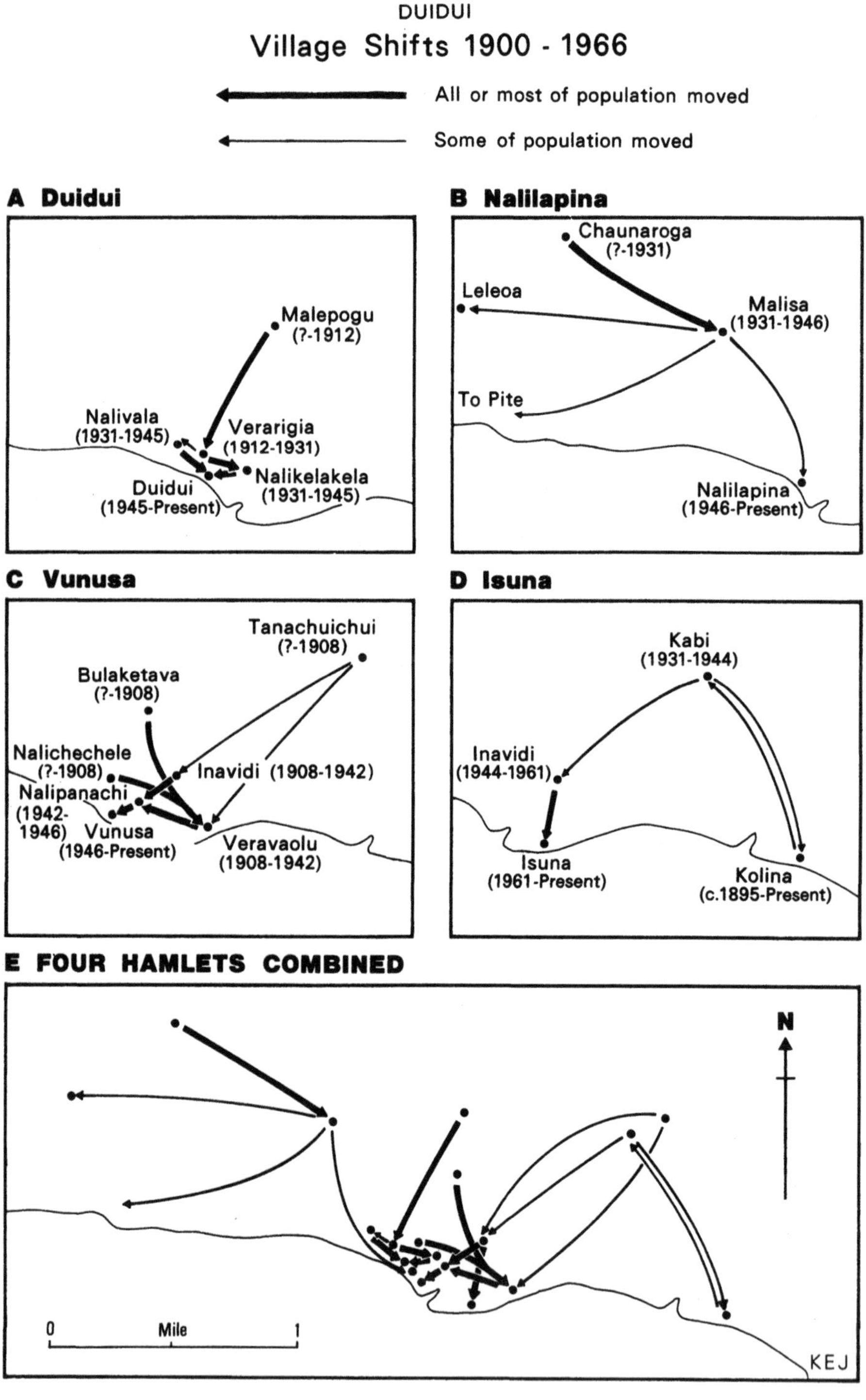

coastward settlement of Alualu people since 1900 and probably for all time. In each of Duidui's four hamlets (Duidui, Nalilapina, Vunusa, Isuna), men aged more than forty-five could remember at least two inland antecedents to the present site, the first of which was abandoned in 1908 (Figure 20.2). In every case the most recent transfer had occurred since 1945 (Duidui 1945; Nalilapina and Vunusa 1946; Isuna 1961).

Taken overall, the people of both Duidui and Pichahila were found to be far more mobile than might have been predicted on the basis of stereotypes then prevalent in the social sciences. Field inquiries over 16 months revealed three clusters of population movement:

1. Shifts in village locations, generally though not inevitably from the interior to the coast: a customary practice in response to natural hazards, epidemics, land exhaustion, warfare, and sorcery that, since about 1900, had been reinforced by administration and mission efforts to consolidate settlement on the coasts or in the river valleys.

2. Moves by younger persons, and predominantly of adult males, that were of at least 10 days' duration but seldom for more than one year: to earn money in the main town, at district centres, on European-owned plantations, or from Solomon Island entrepreneurs; to visit Honiara, district headquarters, and mission stations for retail, educational, medical, and administrative services; to leave for other villages to go to school, or because of a serious dispute.

3. Short-term, mainly familial moves of a highly spontaneous nature that usually involved absences of less than 8 days are rarely extended beyond the language boundary (Poleo for Duidui and Birao for Pichahila): to 'go walkabout' to other villages and visit kin, discuss lineage and church business, attend a feast; to live temporarily in the garden shelter; to hunt wild pig or trap fish; to quit the community briefly out of shame or by way of protest.

In terms of field instruments, the village census and the settlement histories yielded the first pattern; the census, marriage and wage-labour histories, and the daily record of shifts of more than 24 hours' duration the second; and the mobility register the third. Each of these was augmented by intensive interviewing, group discussions, village meetings, the observation of daily events and, not least, simply by becoming as much part of the communities of Duidui and Pichahila as was possible for an outsider. To have ignored any of these field strategies would have been to miss many of the interwoven threads comprising the fabric of a people's mobility.

Reconstructions Through Oral History - Solomon Islands 1972 and 1976

The experience of reconstructing the antecedents of Duidui and Pichahila not only emphasized the need for a more codified approach but also how deeply rooted was the practice of relocating hamlets and villages. Was it possible, using the methods of oral history, to comprehend more precisely the magnitude and persistence of collective transfers? Could a system of inquiry be initiated that would yield information over two or three generations for South Guadalcanal in general rather than for particular communities like Duidui and Pichahila?

Some answers to such questions became possible when patterns of land utilization throughout South Guadalcanal were examined by a multidisciplinary team that included a trained historian (Judith Bennett) along with agricultural economists, geographers, political scientists, and public health specialists. Undertaken for 5 months during 1972, this project owed its origin to the administration of the British Solomon Islands Protectorate and to a concern that population growth was beginning to exert pressure on a region whose rapidly changing terrain was by local standards quite densely occupied (Chapman and Pirie, 1974). Given the 1965-67 experience with settlement histories, the challenge for Bennett was to reconstruct changes in population distribution since 1870 and, more specifically, to chart the relocation of entire communities from ridge crests to valley floors and coastal fringe. This was a daunting prospect, for it meant having to contact elderly persons resident in 211 settlements that, even along the coastal perimeter, were spread over 135 kilometres and often could only be reached on foot. On the other hand, initiating these inquiries was helped by being one of a team whose members were located at eight village sites (Figure 20.1), each of them indicative of the ecological and cultural niches that comprise Weather Coast society and polity (Chapman and Bennett, 1980, pp.53-6).

To assist with identifying older people who might subsequently be interviewed, each team member was given a check list of questions that could be integrated with their own inquiries. Since the previous field materials for Duidui and Pichahila complemented the documentary evidence in suggesting two broad patterns in village relocation, these questions focused on both the actual transfers made by a particular community and the sequence of movement for every lineage found in an existing settlement (Appendix 20.2). Often the resultant information was anecdotal and fragmentary, but collectively it provided an invaluable context for subsequent interviews and for the overall inquiry to be far more codified and tied to particular localities.

Working with African societies, Vansina has systematized techniques for recording, analyzing, and evaluating oral traditions that 'consist of all verbal testimonies which are reported statements concerning the past' (Vansina, 1965, p.19).

For the Weather Coast of Guadalcanal, the facts of relocation were not sought before 1860-70, which meant that most personal testimony fell within Vansina's category of eye-witness accounts rather then oral tradition passed down through several generations (see Miller, 1980, for the Solomons in general). Apart from some details obtained about the movement of lineages, the chain of transmission was short - from actual observer to person being interviewed to recording historian. Consequently the susceptibility of error or distortion was far less than if the concern had been with much broader spans of time. To many historians, such heavy reliance on oral sources is conditioned by the lack of documentary evidence about past transfers made by specific communities or by gaps in the written record - as in the absence for South Guadalcanal of any detailed patrol reports written by colonial officers during the 1920s (Bennett, 1974a, p.x). But there was an even more basic reason for eliciting oral testimony. Philosophically, it represented a deliberate attempt to obtain the people's perspective on a customary practice of such visibility and antiquity that it had entered the literature in several European languages (for example, Woodford, 1980; Nerdrum, 1901-2; Bertin, 1928; Paravicini, 1931).

From October until late December 1972, Bennett and her associates interviewed 106 men and women living in 98 different hamlets or villages. Most were aged between 60 and 80, many of them brought forward by kin as being particularly conversant with the past. Interviews usually took from 1 to 2 hours and ranged from 30 minutes, for a few particularly unobservant folk, to 6 hours for certain wise communicators of local history. An especially skilled interpreter with command of many Weather Coast dialects, himself a 'big man', was present at all times but many interviews were conducted by Bennett herself in the *lingua franca* of Solomons Pidjin. All were taped for later transcription on a portable cassette recorder - a potentially inhibiting technique in the opinion of many field workers, but sufficiently novel to pique the curiosity of South Guadalcanal people, who made numerous requests for the tape to be replayed.

In general, interviews occurred at the natal place. As with the 1966 censuses of Duidui and Pichahila, family members were often present and encircled by a fluctuating group of curious observers, who provided both sporadic information and important verification. To establish the internal consistency of parallel accounts, a key requirement for oral testimony, between three and ten persons were questioned from any one locality. Not surprisingly, the level of accuracy was extremely high when able to be compared with documentary evidence from as early as 1870, since Weather Coast people esteem their ancestry and a 'leader or "big man" traditionally was expected to be conversant with a body of tribal or lineage knowledge, among which was the story of the origin of villages and the migration of their people' (Bennett, 1974a, p.xix). The tape recording of information was in itself a serious matter and opinion was repeatedly distinguished from fact and eye witness from hearsay with the expression: '*No gud me bullshit long paper belong yu*' (It is not good for me to give you incorrect information for you to record).

Of all items of information to be established onsite, at times in challenging circumstances, to date the year of relocation was the most basic. Although demographers usually associate the historical calendar with estimation of age (for example, Scott and Sabagh, 1970), in fact this technique can be used to fix the chronology of any sequence of events to the Gregorian calendar. Potential difficulties exist where several generations are the period of reference and in whether locally important events can be dated, but these served only to underscore the disciplinary contribution of the historian to the wider project. In the 1966 community censuses of Duidui and Pichahila, an age table was constructed by updating the one for Guadalcanal used in the 1959 sample census of the Solomon Islands (McArthur, 1961, p.92), supplemented for the south coast by events recorded in district administration files, village diaries, and family Bibles (Appendix 20.3, top panel). With this document as baseline, Bennett worked through records held in the former Western Pacific High Commission (Suva, Fiji), administrative files in the main town of Honiara, and mission archives, as well as through lists of events assembled by long-standing residents (for example, Marriott n.d., c1969). She also talked with Weather Coast residents, such as teachers and elected councillors, who were both literate and informed. The result was a research document in itself: a calendar of locally-specific events for virtually every year between 1894 and 1970 (Appendix 20.3, bottom panel).

With the answers obtained from old people somewhat codified through following the the check list (Appendix 20.2), a great wealth of detail had to be transcribed, collapsed, and analyzed to decipher its essential meaning about the patterns and processes of relocation by clans and communities. Reconnaisance maps revised in 1971 by the World Health Organization malaria eradication campaign were used as a base to plot both previous and current locations of Weather Coast communities. Although information gleaned from villagers, archival documents, field observations, and secondary literature added historical depth to these contemporary maps, it proved impossible to establish the exact position of many former sites. Five composite maps constructed for the region as a whole depict which of the many settlements were inhabited in December 1972 and also whether they occupied a 'foundation site' from which other hamlets or villages originated (see Figure 20.3 for one example). On each of these base maps, it was possible to link named settlements and chart the direction taken by collective relocation; to use the transcribed interviews for estimating the ratio of community populations involved (all, some, few); and by reference to the calendar of local events to fix the likely dates of transfer (Figure 20.4). A humanist by inclination and by training, Bennett's reaction to this exercise was emphatic:

> 'By concentrating upon spatial representation, the full implication of trends in population movement since 1870 became

Figure 20.3 Villages of Wanderer Bay: Location of Foundation and Present Sites

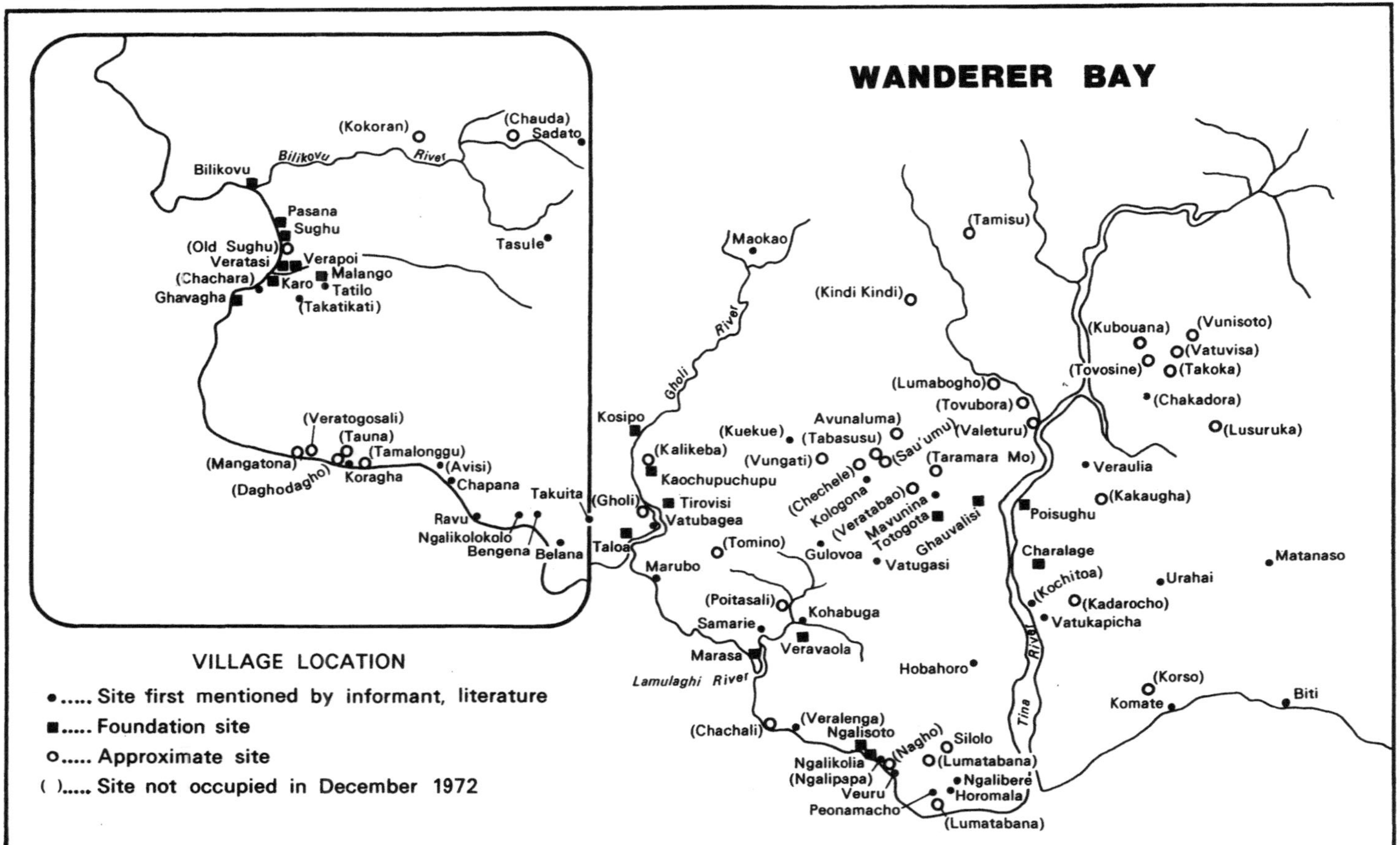

Figure 20.4 Wanderer Bay: Relocation of Village Populations, c1860–1972

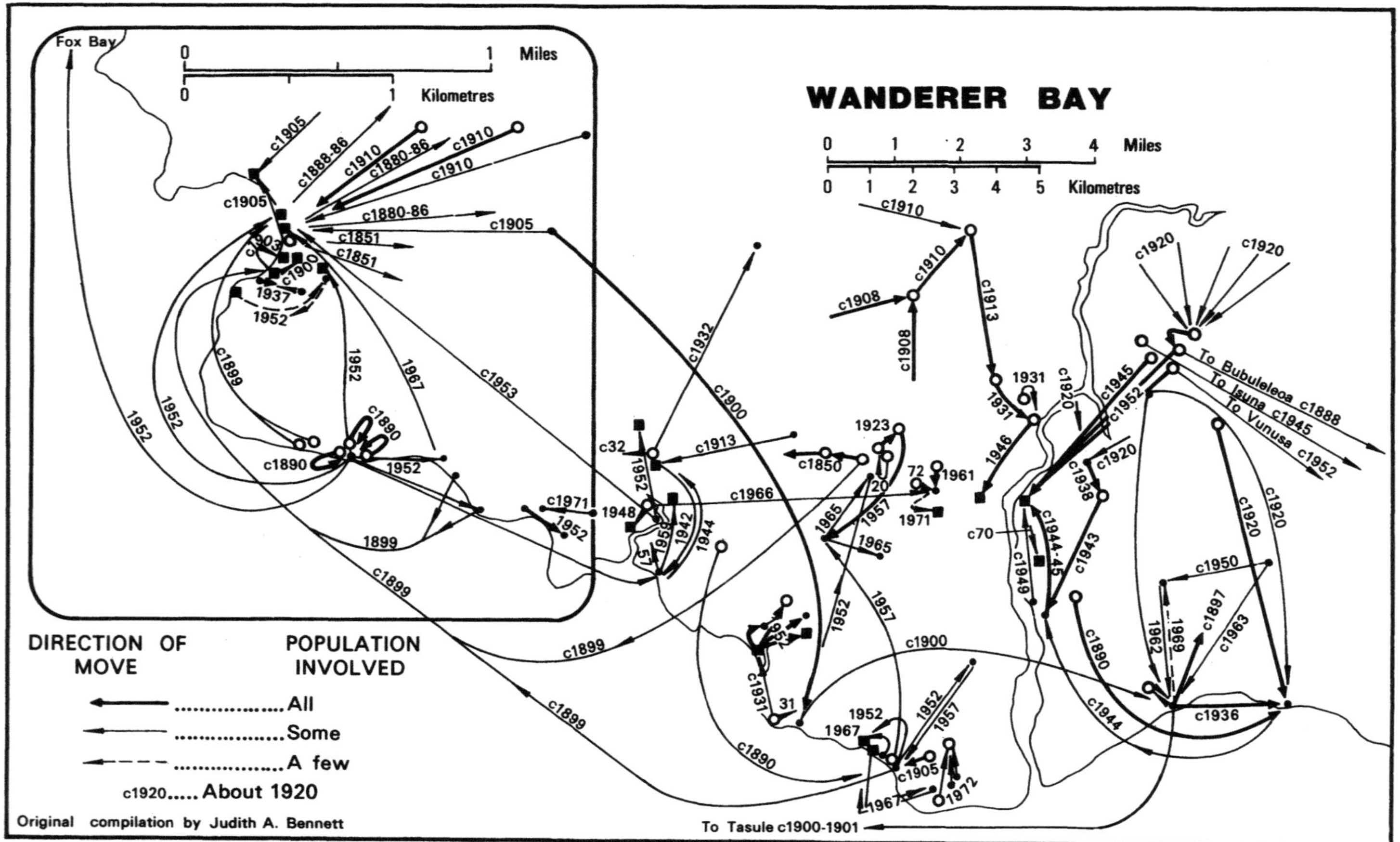

Figure 20.5 South Guadalcanal: Movement of Village Populations, 1850–1972

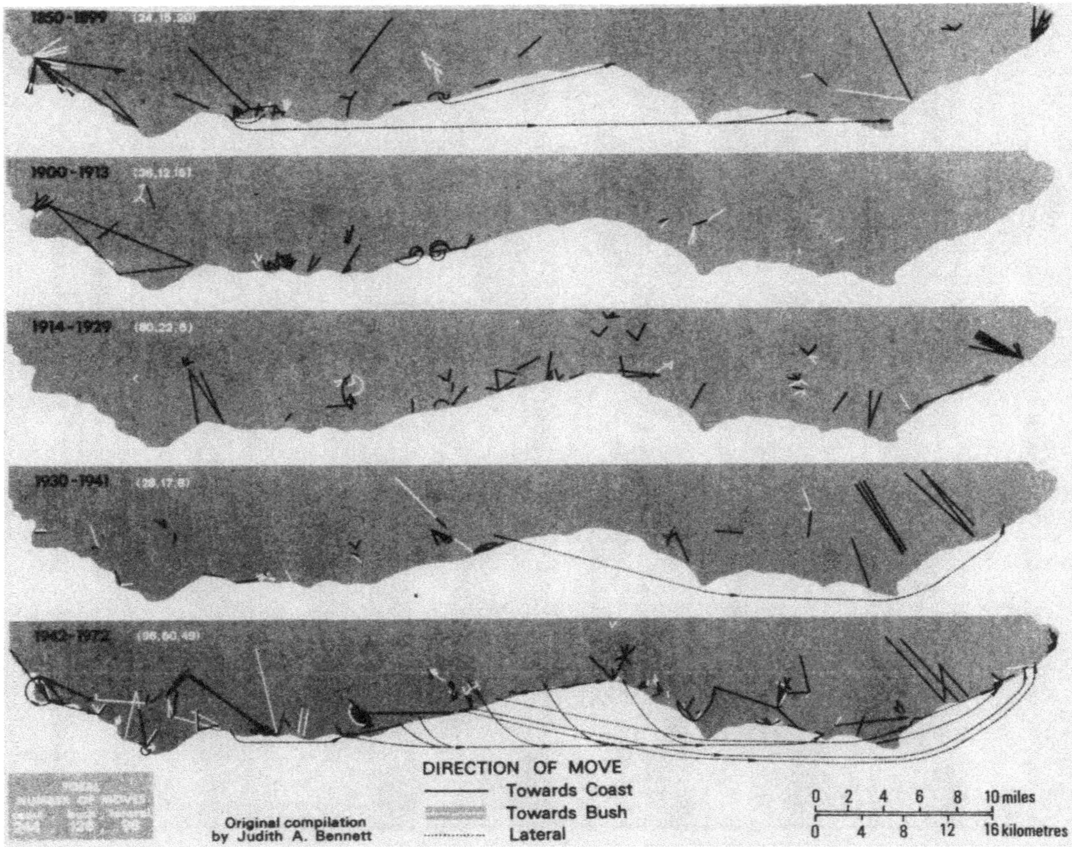

Figure 20.6 South Guadalcanal: Primary Reasons for Village Relocation, 1950–1972

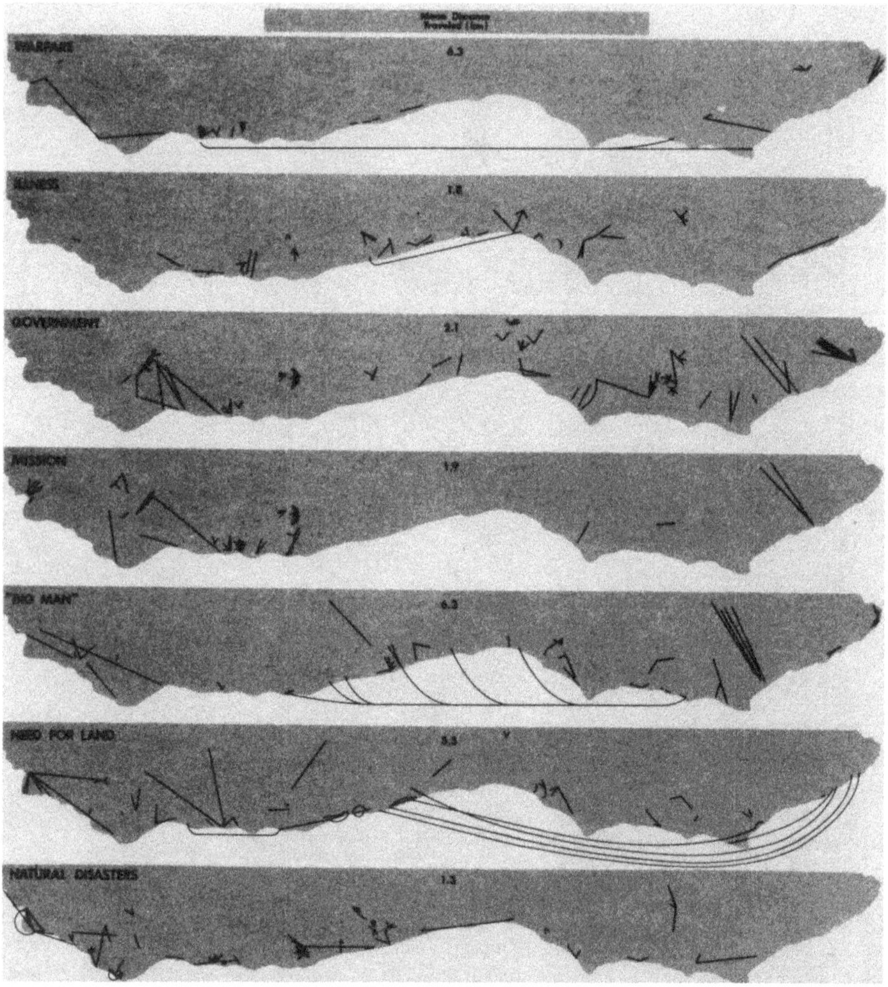

0 2 4 6 8 10 Miles

Original compilation by Judith A. Bennett. 0 4 8 12 16 Kilometres

far clearer than by using conceptual and textual analysis alone. What had begun as an excercise in plotting field data emerged as an integral part of my analysis of population history' (Chapman and Bennett, 1980, p.62).

From these composite maps, it became possible to group and categorize information about village relocation on the same principle that single years of age from any population census are combined into cohorts. Thus all transfers that occurred between 1850 and 1972 could be differentiated by direction - coastward (244), inland (126), lateral (98) - and summarized in five time periods that were defined in locally meaningful terms and consequently were of varying length (Figure 20.5). More sophisticated links in the field record could be abstracted through a careful index of details contained in transcribed interviews, on which basis the mean distance and standard deviations of 438 out of 468 village relocations were related to the five primary reasons why they occurred between 1850 and 1972. All results were expressed in both graphic and tabular format (Table 20.2; cf. Figure 20.6). Given the original concern with processes of collective resettlement in Weather Coast society, this summary table documents that factors either pre-dating (warfare) or post-dating (government, mission) European contact are far less important than those that have persisted over 70 years (173 as against 265). In short, it is continuities rather more than the discontinuities of experience that are the more powerful influence in village relocation during the past three generations. Over time, 'mediation of kin and customary purchase has persisted and demonstrates a cultural constant' (Bennett, 1974b, pp. 2, 67).

Conceptually, these same procedures of oral history may be used when the focus lies more with individuals and small groups in movement than with entire communities and if the analytic goals are more numeric than graphic. This was precisely the situation when, in 1976, Bennett returned to the Solomon Islands for a further 10 months and conducted a more macroscopic inquiry into the impact of trading and the plantation economy on village society between 1800 and 1945 (Bennett, 1979, 1987).

For the period between the two World Wars, for instance, extant returns of the annual number of wage labourers list only those newly recruited or already working under indenture (Bennett, 1981, p.44). Eliciting oral testimony, following precisely the same methods already described, was consequently the only way to calculate the incidence of labour mobility, including the total time spent in paid employment away from the natal community and the range of jobs held outside the plantation economy. When aggregated, tables constructed from the transcripts of 109 interviews with former wage labourers (Table 20.3) reveal marked regional differences in the kind of employers, the degree of dependence on institutionalized work, and the ratio of a man's lifetime spent in locations away from village and family. The employment patterns for workers from four major source areas - San Cristobel, Malaita, Guadalcanal, and the Shortland Islands (Figure 20.7) - can be viewed both comparatively and in terms of the

Table 20.2 Frequency and Distance of Village Relocation, by Primary Reason, South Guadalcanal, 1850–1972

Primary Reason	Number of Moves	Mean Distance Travelled (km)	Standard Deviation (km)
Warfare	28	6.3	15.0
Need for land	62	5.3	11.6
Natural disasters	92	1.3	1.4
"Big man"	63	6.3	10.9
Illness	48	1.8	2.4
Government	94	2.1	1.8
Mission	51	1.9	1.9
Total	438		

Source: Bennett (1974b, p.2.14).

Table 20.3 Work History of Wage Labourer, 1915–42

Job	Place	Duration	Interval at Home
Brushing and catching beetles	Baunani plantation	2 years	6 months
Drove cart	Yandina plantation	2 years	
Crewman, later in engine room	*Royal Endeavour*	8 years	1 year
Head crew	*Mindaro* (Burns Philp)	1 year	10 years
Head crew	*Namunini* (Chinese)	6 months	Short
Village storeman	Ghaliatu (home)	1½ years	Short

Summary: 15 out of 27 years spent in wage employment. Of these, 13½ years were away from village.

Source: Based on Bennett (1981, p.55).

Figure 20.7 Employment Patterns of Male Wage-Earners from San Cristobal, Malaita, Guadalcanal, and the Shortland Islands

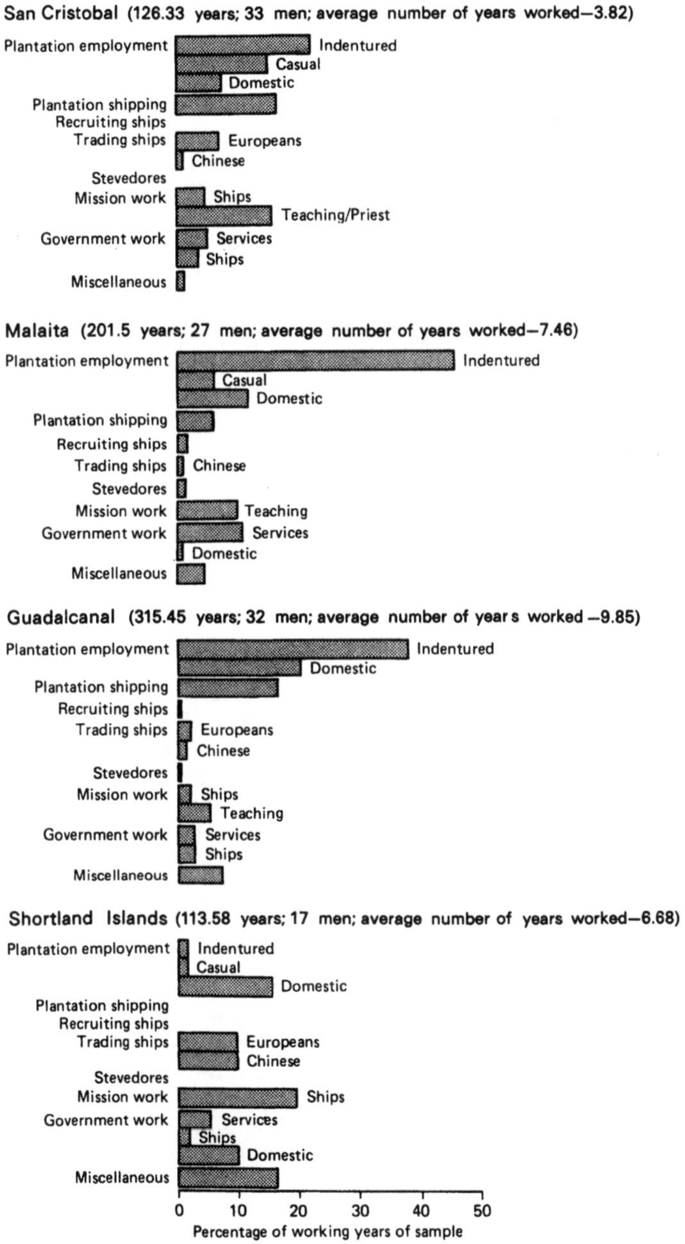

Source: Bennett (1981, Fig.3).

social, economic, and ecological factors that constituted their context. In general, if Solomon Island settlements were located in places where copra was made or other sources of cash were available, then able-bodied males tended to seek local work rather than go away and sell their labour to the manager of some distant commercial plantation.

An Integrated Field Design and Broader Implications

Experiences common to these three field projects in the Solomon Islands only emphasize that to locate population research within the village or larger corporate group of Third World societies demands a range of techniques drawn from a number of disciplines. At first glance, Bennett's obvious concern with oral testimonies and with distilling a people's perspective on relocation seems less reliant on a variety of approaches, but in fact as much research time was spent in combing the documentary record so that these two sets of evidence might be integrated for a more comprehensive understanding of community-level processes. Also common to these three inquiries was their focus on mobility behaviour as it unfolds over time, on identifying the kaleidoscopic contexts within which it occurs, and on searching for ways to capture the fluidity and ambiguity that is so much an inherent part of people's movement on the ground.

Further progress towards more sensitive and more incisive field research will come from tightly integrated designs, for which a theoretical concern with changes over time constitutes a key dimension. During the past decade, there has been renewed interest in longitudinal approaches to mobility behaviour, about which a more recent field project in Northwest Thailand provides both illustration and the basis for concluding comments. Desiring, as a person of *khon muang* (Northern Thailand), to investigate how local concepts of mobility are embedded in culture and language, the geographer Anchalee Singhanetra-Renard lived for 8 months in a village 13 kilometres north of the provincial capital of Chiang Mai. Of greatest concern was the means and the criteria by which the Northern Thai conceive of their mobility and of how far the interchange of people expressed the complementary nature of different places (Singhanetra-Renard, 1982). Fieldwork in both urban centre and hinterland village extended from February 1976 until April 1977.

Mapping and sketching, questionnaire surveys, formal interviews, participant observation, genealogical reconstruction, and informal discussion were used to collect different levels of information about Mae Sa village (Appendix 20.4), whose *de jure* population on 1 October 1976 totalled 1,039 individuals distributed amongst 226 households. An understanding of communal lifeways and of how history has influenced people's thinking was one product of village residence, while being participant observer enabled Singhanetra-Renard to be included in family discussions about movement and gradually become aware of their conceptions of it. A household census and economic survey (Appendix 20.4:

stage 5) served as cross-sectional baseline for a prospective mobility register and retrospective life-history matrix (stages 4 and 9). For 8 months, two local assistants recorded every exit from or entrance into Mae Sa that involved a period of at least 6 hours. During early morning and late afternoon, each was stationed at one of the settlement's two entrances to document the great amount of commuting.

Changes in the character of movement over generations were deciphered from a life-history matrix, by which free ranging conversation about a person's life course focused on critical events of birth, education, marriage, and work that were subsequently linked to moves made between various places at different times (Lauro, 1979). Vivid memories of village events quite unrelated to mobility thus drew out forgotten details of those that were. To provide both context and internal cross check, this basic information about families, economy, and mobility was supplemented by a checklist of movement over three generations, by observing agricultural practices, by collecting genealogies, and by plotting land holdings and their ownership (Appendix 20.4: stages 6-8, 10). Since Chiang Mai is the key urban destination for Mae Sa movement, selected studies were made of minibus drivers, of the major employers, and of workers in formal establishments during the 4 months before village inquiries began (stages 1-3).

In the quest for broader generalization, two experienced *khon muang* spent April 1977 comparing preliminary results about Mae Sa mobility since before the Second World War with those of sixty other communities in six different districts (stage 12). This is a novel and powerful strategy that undoubtedly enhanced the substantive range of Singhanetra-Renard's results. Rarely, however, do field workers have the funds, time, and stamina to set a case study within its variable contexts by instigating still further case studies whose objectives are far more limited. Rarely can the results of a particular field study be extrapolated by enlarging both breadth 'and' depth of treatment through a multitude of comparable cases.

Integrated field designs that focus on a particular case have the advantage over more removed and more determinant approaches to mobility research, since inquiries can proceed simultaneously at several levels: from the individual and the family to larger groupings or aggregates. As Singhanetra-Renard (1982, p.33) notes, such a design enhances the 'ability to utilize a range of approaches and to shift instantly to the particular technique most appropriate to a given situation'. For the two community studies of Guadalcanal, this involved an unexpected change from the prospective mobility register to the open-ended interviewing of men about to leave for wage labour and, once they had gone, to observing how households reorganized themselves by way of collective response. Thus information collected from monitoring the actions of individuals often leads to the broader structural contexts - of environment, culture, society, economy, and polity

- within which those actions are embedded and by which they are constrained (cf. Chapman, 1985, pp.437-41).

On a more conceptual plane, research designs that combine field instruments to collect intersecting primary data admit the prospect of establishing internal consistency, of deciphering the logic of given situations, and of apprehending the ambiguities, the paradoxes, and the contradictions contained in different dimensions of the field record. Based on careful study of the history of Solomon Islands settlement, Miller (1980) argues that whereas oral testimony reveals a high degree of mobility from village to village, archaeological reconstruction documents the continued occupation of particular sites for successive generations. For the Weather Coast of Guadalcanal, detailed mapping and the conjunction of oral and documentary evidence achieved by Bennett suggests that these contradictions might be more apparent than real (compare Figures 20.3 and 20.4). Both processes are at work, for the relocation of several extended families or entire communities over long swings of time is anchored to and circulates around certain key 'foundation sites' that are central to the lineage, its ancestry and identity (Chapman, 1976, pp.128-31; Bathgate, 1985, pp.97-106).

Miller himself reaches a similar conclusion by observing that inherent discrepancies in the oral traditions about ancient sites often reflect differences between the structure and the content of those traditions. Consequently, both Bennett and Miller converge on the fundamental issue. Miller states:

> 'Complex patterns (of movement and settlement) may stem from the internal logic of people's categorisation of their world, whether expressed in the types of site, the oral histories of these sites, or the identification with objects as symbols which differentiate one group from another. These are considerations that derive from very different epistemological foundations from the current positivism' (1980, pp.464-5).

A recurrent philosophical problem in the study of population movement is how to combine information about individuals and small groups with that documenting their variable contexts. One solution proposed by Morrison (1983, p.14) is to construct alternative scenarios that 'rely on qualitative specifications of relationships in areas where quantification is impracticable'. Yet the temptation, even the congenital reflex in the social and behavioural sciences is to proceed on the basis that more cases inevitably result in more powerful understanding. It has been left to Mitchell to clarify the epistemological fallacy in such reasoning. For, as he reminds us, wider conclusions about villages, market centres, or urban neighbourhoods do not necessarily depend on a greater number of examples nor on larger and larger frames of territorial reference. 'Generalization from the case study', he wrote in a paper that preceded the one with which we began, 'is premissed upon the universality of the theoretical propositions relating relevant aspects of the case to one another, not upon its "representativeness" of some universe of "cases"' (Mitchell, 1985, pp.52-3). In this logic lies a resolution of Sir Arthur Eddington's problems with combining the mammoth and the microbe; in this manner of reasoning, when applied to Third World peoples, lies some prospect for a population science that is a little less culture bound.

Acknowledgements

My appreciative thanks go to Judith Bennett (Department of History, University of Otago, New Zealand) and Anchalee Singhanetra-Renard (Department of Geography, Chiang Mai University, Thailand) for permission to use original field materials that are far more theirs than they are mine. Helpful comments on an earlier version were made by Judith Bennett, Ian Frazer, Shekhar Mukherji, and Nancy Pollock.

Appendix 20.1 Domestic Reorganisation Through Departure of Married Men for Wage Labour, February-March 1966

Household	Absent Male	Domestic Reorganization
		Departure Involved Reorganization (8 households)
A	Aged 30:* two sons, two daughters**	Soon after departure, pregnant wife (aged 29) went to rural maternity clinic with youngest son (aged 1). Remaining son (aged 4) at home cared for by wife's mother.***
B	Widower aged 46: two daughters live in brother's houses, one adopted by lineage relative.	Second daughter (6) accompanied father to workplace, village 3 hours' walk to west.
C	Aged 35: two daughters	Wife (20) and daughters (2, 0) leave house in one hamlet to stay with wife's father (60) in another. Sporadically visit own house during the day.
D	Widower aged 45: one son, two daughters	House shuttered. Only daughter (13) in village goes to house of brother's unmarried daughter (21).
E	Aged 33: two sons	Before departure husband invited lineage relative to visit from own village, 2 hours' walk to west. Presence of relative to look after two young children (3, 0) permits wife (23) to go to food gardens each morning.
F	Aged 38: one son, two daughters	Wife (39) and only daughter (10) at home sleep in wife's brother's (54) house, in another hamlet, but return daily to own dwelling to go to gardens and cook food. Also periodically visit birthplace, 3 hours' walk to west.
G	Aged 48: two sons, three daughters	Before departure, husband asked single female (16), a lineage relative, to live with wife (35) during absence. Relative supervises two youngest children (3, 0); also helps in food gardens and with household tasks.
H	Recent widower aged 42: five sons, one daughter	House closed and barricaded. Four children (12, 9, 4, 1) transferred to brother's (37) neighbouring house; one son (13) to woman (42) in another hamlet, a lineage relative whose husband also away at wage work.
		No Domestic Reorganization (9 households)
I	Aged 53: three sons, two daughters	As usual, eldest son (9) assisted wife (36) with two younger sons (5, 0). On 2 March, however, that son left for school for first time and wife subsequently received intermittent help from kinswomen.
J	Aged 40: no children	Married only 6 months and lives with widowed mother (62). Wife (28) walked with husband for first 3 hours as far as her sister's village, where stayed whilst spouse at work.
K	Aged 50: one son	Teenage daughter (14) of wife's (48) former marriage always available to look after young son (2).
L	Aged 33: one son	When time for wife (19) to go to food gardens, son (1) is supervised by wife's older but unmarried lineage relative (25).
M	Aged 32: one son, one daughter	Where necessary, wife (20) takes young children (3, 0) to husband's partly-blind mother (58), who lives with her younger son (25) in adjacent hamlet.
N	Aged 54: six sons, two daughters	Mature but unmarried daughter (18) constantly shares with wife (38) duties in household, food gardens, and supervision of younger children not at school (13, 8, 4, 2, 0).
O	Aged 42: polygynous household. Two sons, three daughters from first wife; one son, one daughter from second wife.	Two eldest daughters (15, 13) of first wife (42) always available to look after her younger children (6, 2) and those of second wife (36) that are of identical age.
P	Aged 24: two daughters	Whenever wife (21) needs assistance, daughters (3, 1) are taken to house of husband's widowed mother (61) in same hamlet.
Q	Aged 38: four daughters	Widowed mother (71) lives in household and is therefore available to supervise children (8, 5, 1, 0) for wife (27).

Total households from which male absent for wage labour: 17.

* As at census date, 1 March 1966. Children aged less than one are recorded as 0.

** Dependent and independent children who normally eat with household. Married children with separate domestic units not included.

*** Absent male is the referent for all relationships noted, unless context clearly indicates otherwise.

Source: Chapman (1970, Table 29).

Appendix 20.2 Site Checklist, Village Relocation

1. Has this village always been at this present site?

   If no, follow with questions 2A-12A.
   If yes, follow with questions 2B-6B.

2A. Where was it situated before? ('Saltwater' or 'bush'? River bank or hill top? Get landmarks and area names).

3A. Why was the village moved from its other site to this one? (As well as reasons, try to find out if any individuals led this move and a little of their background, especially in terms of travel beyond the Weather Coast and education).

4A. About when did this move occur? (Use Gaudalcanal calendar of events*).

5A. In the past, did groups of people come from other villages to live with the people already here?

6A. If so, from what villages did they come?

7A. Why did they leave their own villages?

8A. About when?

9A. In the past, did groups of people leave this village to live elsewhere?

10A. To what villages did they go?

11A. Why did they leave?

12A. About when?

oooooooooooooooooooooooooooooooooooooooooooooooooooooooooooooooooooooooo

2B. What are the 'lines' (lineages) in your village? (Note: there should be three or four; for example, Garavu, Garavuvatale, Manukiki, Manulava).

   [To be asked of the leaders of each lineage]

3B. What is the story of your 'line's' coming to this village? Mention each village/place the 'line' stopped or lives at on its journey here. (Note: be sure to get the area each village is/was in and whether one still exists there.)

4B. What were the reasons for the 'line's' leaving each of these villages or places?

5B. Who were the leaders in each move? (Sex as well as name).

6B. Try to ascertain the approximate time of the most recent moves. (Use Guadalcanal calendar of events*). For example: Was it before or after coming of the white man? Were guns and/or other Western artifacts in use at the time of the move? It is particularly important to do this for the last 1-3 moves).

* See Appendix 20.3.

Appendix 20.3 Excerpts from Calendar of Important Events on Guadalcanal

Duidui-Pichahila Study 1965-67 (Chapman)		
Year	Age in 1966	Event
1907-1911	55-59	1911: Survey of HMS Sealark begins. 1909: Frank Bollen, Melanesian Mission, died at Maravovo. 1908: Mr Sprott, Melanesian Mission, at Tasimboko

Population-Resources Study of Weather Coast 1972 (Bennett)		
Year	Age in 1972	Event
1911	61	First news sheet, Turupatu, in Ghari language, published by Roman Catholic Mission at Rua Sura. Survey by HMS Sealark. Fr. Rinaldo Pavese arrived at Tangarare Mission and stayed (except for 1922-28) until 1933; well remembered and acknowledged as a Ghari expert.
1910	62	Recruiting of wage labour for Fiji stopped. Roman Catholic mission at Visale opened; Resident Commissioner Woodford present. The sacrificial site of the great Tindalo Puraka, at Visale Peak, fell into the sea. First Chinese came to work as boat-builders and carpenters for Burns Philp. Burns Philp opened trading stations at Makambo (Tulagi), Faisi (Shortlands) and Gizo.
1909	63	Frank Bollen, Melanesian missionary at Maravovo, died.
1908	64	Missionary Sprott at Tasimboko (Melanesian Mission). Henry Welshman, missionary on Santa Isabel, died.
1907	65	Fr. Jean Boudard first arrived at Avu Avu Roman Catholic mission and stayed until 1942.

Sources: Chapman (1971, p.34); Chapman and Pirie (1974, Appendix D7).

Appendix 20.4 Types of Field Data Collected February 1976 - April 1977

Stage	Place	Date Administered	Type of Instrument	Respondents	Information Collected
1	Chiang Mai city	March 1976	Mini-bus survey	40 mini-bus drivers from 8 queues plying between Chiang Mai and 18 districts.	Mini-bus routes, kinds of rural passengers, the villages of origin, reasons for coming into the city. Information concerning the drivers: age, sex, education, their previous occupations, when started driving mini-bus.
2	Chiang Mai city	April 1976	Employer survey	40 owner/managers representing major enterprises and industries in the city.	Nature of work/qualification of employees, number and place of origin of employees, method of recruitment, benefit and welfare of employees, fluctuation in demand and supply of employees, reasons for employees working, absence, or quitting the job.
3	Chiang Mai city	May-June 1976	Employee survey	2% (161) of employees in formal establishments.	Type of job, age, sex, marital status, education family economic background, occupational history, mobility history, method of acquiring the job, place of origin, type of accommodation, transportation, frequency of home visit, amount of remittance, attitude toward the city.
4	Mae Sa village	September 1976 to April 1977	Mobility register (8 months longitudinal mobility data)	All 1,039 Mae Sa *de jure* residents who move in or out of the village involving 6 hours or more.	Date of move, destination(s), distance, objectives, duration of absence, means of transportation, kind of move locally viewed.
				Any visitors who were present in Mae Sa 6 hours or more.	Date present, sex, place of origin, distance from Mae Sa, objectives, duration of stay, means of transportation, relationship with Mae Sa people.
5	Mae Sa village	October 1976	Household census, combination of *de jure*/ *de facto*	226 household heads	Basic characteristics of all household members, including those temporarily away from the village (*de jure*), and visitors in the households at census date, 1 October 1976 (*de facto*). Information includes: name, age, sex, education, birthplace, marital status, occupation(s), present or not at date of census. For those born outside: reason and date for move into Mae Sa; for those absent: reasons for being away and date left for that particular reason.
			Household economic survey	226 household heads	Type of crops cultivated in what amount of land, land tenure status for each type of land operated: lowland rice-field river bars, foothill areas. Sources of family rice supply and cash income, livestock, housing conditions: materials, household material possessions, lighting, amount of donation for village temple reconstructions.
6	Mae Sa village	November 1976	Checklist	Selected group of informants from 3 different generations	Change and mobility patterns in relation to the following activities: religion, trade and commerce, public affairs, education, and work.
7	Mae Sa village	December 1976	Agricultural survey	Agricultural household heads (150)	For each major type of crop grown: amount of land, type of land, tenure status, yields. Agricultural calendar of each crop, number of labourers used for stage in agricultural cycle, name and number of exchanged or hired labourers.
8	Mae Sa village	February 1976	Genealogical survey	Senior couples in each household	Number of marriage partners, their place of residence/origin. Number of children ever born, their place of residence and their marriage partner's place of origin.
9	Mae Sa village	March 1977	Life history matrix survey (retrospect-longitudinal mobility data)	Selected sample of 3 Mae Sa generations, 50 each	Detailed information by year from birth till 1976 includes: life cycle and reproductive history, occupational history and mobility history, which focuses on where and when and how long each event took place.
10	Mae Sa village	April 1977	Land ownership survey	Household heads (226)	Type and size of land owned, rented, shared. Method of acquiring them, from whom and since when.
11	Chiang Mai city, *maing* villages, foothill settlements	April 1977	Places of destination survey	Mae Sa residents and migrants at destination places	Their objectives at destination places, when moved there, how. Type of economic, social, and cultural participation at destination and at Mae Sa. Their remittance, frequency of return, and attitude toward destination place.
12	Districts bordering Chiang Mai city	April 1977	Circular mobility survey	60 *kamnan* (sub-district headman) for 6 districts	Based on Mae Sa experiences, comparing circular mobility patterns in those districts for the 3 periods: pre-WW II, post-WW II, and contemporary.

Source: Singhanetra-Renard (1981, pp.140-41).

21

Micro-Approaches to the Study of Population Movement: An Indonesian Case Study

Graeme Hugo

Introduction

There has been a tremendous increase in the scale, complexity and significance of population mobility in developing countries in recent years. However, demographic study of the phenomenon has changed little during that period. We have very limited understanding of its fundamental causes, impacts, its interactions with other elements of demographic change and its interrelations with the complex processes of social change and economic development. This is not surprising given that the field has been characterized by a slavish reliance upon conventional census and large scale migration surveys. These sources are often based upon inappropriate Euro-American models which do not always detect the most significant forms of population mobility let alone shed light upon their causes and implications.

This chapter demonstrates that the micro-approach to demographic research has much to offer the student of migration, and argues that this approach can yield greater understanding of population mobility and its complex two-way relation with socio-economic change, as well as with other demographic processes. These issues are exemplified through a detailed study of fourteen villages in West Java, Indonesia.

Some Conceptual Problems in the Study of Migration

The demographer studying migration is confronted with a number of conceptual difficulties which do not bedevil the researcher concerned with fertility or mortality. The first of these relates to measurement. Birth and death are infrequent events in households and hence amenable to total measurement, but mobility of members of those households can be constant, so that all moves cannot be measured. While fertility and mortality data in many Third World contexts are certainly not perfect, there is at least universality and agreement on what constitutes birth and death. The demographic measurement of migration, however, will always involve the detection of only a sub-set of all population movement. To qualify for measurement a movement will generally have to exceed some arbitrarily set time and space criteria rather than a theoretically meaningful threshold. In the Indonesian census definition of migration, for example, a person has to cross a provincial boundary to qualify as a migrant, yet intra-provincial migrants have been shown to outnumber inter-provincial movers by a ratio of six to one (Hugo, 1982a, p.35). In addition, only persons who have made a permanent shift in their place of residence qualify as migrants, yet it has been demonstrated that non-permanent residents are more numerous and have considerable significance for social change and economic development (Hugo, 1982b). If the main purpose of demography is to seek explanations of population change, students of migration have problems not only in identifying and examining relevant independent variables (in common with their colleagues studying mortality and fertility) but also in identifying and defining the dependent variable.

Generally the more macro-scale a set of migration data, the more restrictive the set of time and space criteria used to define migration and the greater the number of truly mobile people who are defined as non-migrants. The problem in Third World migration studies has been that the cut-off point used to define population movement is usually fixed without reference to the social and economic system in which it is occurring. The common approach is to take definitions and concepts developed and used in Euro-American censuses or surveys and presume that they are of universal relevance. The writer's research in West Java illustrates many ways in which the indiscriminate transfer of these concepts and definitions can produce misleading results. My original proposal was to study the causes and effects of rural to urban conventionally-defined migration between West Java and the national capital of Jakarta (Hugo, 1976). Once my village-based fieldwork began, however, I was dismayed to find in region after region a lack of this form of migration. For example, after walking around a village some 300 miles from Jakarta, in which scarcely a male person between 15 and 35 could be seen in the fields or in the central cluster of houses and gardens, I asked the *lurah* (village head) and some other village leaders about *pindah* (migration) out of the village. The spontaneous reply was that *pindah* was insignificant; it was only after some detailed discussion that it emerged that *merantau* (temporary movement) to Jakarta was particularly important in the village. Although both terms are defined similarly in the dictionary (Echols and Shadily, 1970) - the former as 'to move' and the latter as 'to leave one's home area' - they have come, in West Java at least, to denote important differences in the mover's intended duration of absence. As fieldwork proceeded, this pattern was repeated in many villages throughout West Java, leading to a complete recasting of the survey design and the drafts of questionnaires which had been formulated after several months' intensive reading of the migration literature and extended discussion with city-based officials and academics in Indonesia. If a conventional Western-derived migration questionnaire would have been used in the study it would not only have ignored many of the forces shaping population mobility in West Java but it would have systematically excluded much of the mobility (which is non-permanent) itself and characterized as non-migrants individuals and families who were in fact extremely mobile.

Micro-level studies of migration can potentially assist in overcoming the measurement problem in two ways. First of all, the greater intensity of effort that is possible in micro-studies allows a greater number of types of moves to be detected than is the case in more macro-level studies. The space and time thresholds adopted to define movement can be reduced so that more non-permanent and short distance moves can be encompassed. The most intensive of micro-studies have maintained prospective mobility registers which record virtually all moves out of and into the study village (Chapman, 1969, 1971; Mantra, 1981). Mantra's study of two Central Javan hamlets with 345 and 393 residents recorded 8,179 and 9,028 outmovements during the 9 months over which a mobility register was maintained, of which only twenty-eight and thirty moves respectively were incomplete in that the mover did not return to the village. This gives a totally different impression of the mobility of Javanese from that presented by writers such as McNicoll (1968); Bryant (1973) and Naim (1974) who base their observations on the immobility of Javanese on conventional definitions of migration.

While studies which maintain meticulous records of population movements are an important antidote to studies based on much more restrictive definitions of migration, there is no way that the mobility register methodologies can be applied on a large scale, and in any case the contribution of micro-studies should go beyond the mere counting of movers. Mobility *per se* is of little significance; it is the social and economic implications of the movement that are of importance. Detailed micro-studies can assist in identifying what types of mobility are of some significance and deserving of close study, thus assisting and focusing large scale attempts at more detailed measurement over a wider area. By close examination of the full gamut of mobility at the micro-level, informed recommendations about what types of movement should and could be detected in large scale sample surveys and censuses can be made.

It is apparent then that micro-studies of migration should be an essential preliminary to any large scale survey or census to establish precisely how migration should be defined and measured in those larger data collection exercises. Beyond this, however, the fundamental concern of demographers should be with 'explanation' of demographic change. Micro-level analysis is important in the identification and specification of independent variables which explain the patterns, levels, types and impacts of movement and changes in those patterns over time. Micro-level studies should address themselves to how hypotheses derived from theory and studies in other areas can be operationalized in particular social, economic and cultural contexts.

Population movement involves individuals and families making decisions in a social and economic environment, and hence is profoundly influenced by the specific context in which the decisions are made as well as the subjective perceptions, attitudes, and values of those individuals. The sheer size, scale and breadth of subjects covered in censuses and large scale surveys constrain their ability to probe these decision-making processes and the contextual factors which affect them. To approach a comprehensive understanding of population mobility processes in a region as was the aim of the West Java study, census data had to be supplemented by detailed questioning of persons involved in those processes and observation of the context in which those decisions are made. At any single point in time, however, persons involved in any of the types of population mobility outlined earlier will be at one or other of a sequence of stages in relation to that mobility. Moreover progress from one stage to another may involve a change in an individual's location so that persons at different stages of the same process have different locations. Thus in all forms of village-to-city population mobility, individual villagers or families can be identified to be in at least six contexts:

1. rural residents who have not yet ever thought about moving to the city;

2. rural residents who have thought of moving to the city but rejected it;

3. rural residents who have intentions of moving to the city but have not yet departed;

4. persons who are in the actual physical process of moving to the city from the village;

5. persons who have moved out of a rural area and into the city;

6. persons who have moved to the city and since returned to their rural home.

In seeking an understanding of the entire process of movement one should thus question the same individual passing through each of these stages. Such an approach has obvious procedural difficulties and would be extremely costly in both time and money. A more viable approach would be to study different individuals with similar backgrounds at various stages of the process (see, for example, Appleyard, 1964) although there are disadvantages due to inevitable differences between the individuals studied at the respective stages and the fact that they enter those stages in different absolute time contexts. This approach is also expensive of time and money because it involves interviewing at several locations. A third approach which makes less logistic demands is to survey individuals in one of the three spatial contexts which are implicit in the various stages of the process - rural, *en route* or urban. Then, in order to gain an understanding of all stages of the process, respondents are asked to reconstitute their migration experience. A decision of absolutely crucial importance is thus which of these contexts shall be the 'breaking-in point' of the study. The bulk of research attention has tended to focus on migrants at the 'urban end' of the migration process, a smaller but growing body of work has been carried out in rural districts of origin while virtually no studies have concerned themselves with movers who are *en route* from rural to urban areas.

Several authors have convincingly demonstrated that an approach to the study of rural-to-urban population movement from the rural pole is theoretically justifiable since the important decisions about migration must occur at the rural end of the process (Caldwell, 1969, p.15; Connell *et al.*, 1976). In addition, individuals actually passing through four of the six stages outlined above can be detected in villages, whereas only one such stage is covered by the other approaches. Moreover, in the West Java context, persons engaged in circulation rather than migration are very difficult to locate in the city since they are not registered with local officials and have no permanent residence in the city. Hence they are rarely detected in surveys based on population registers or household listings. A further advantage of rural-based surveys is that they allow rural-to-urban movements to be placed in the correct perspective by providing information on rural-to-rural movers and non-movers (Conning, 1972, p.148). Although current outmigrants are not interviewed, some important information on the *en route* and urban stages of the process can be collected from retrospective accounts of villagers who have returned after spending a period in the city. The prevalance of circular forms of rural-urban mobility in West Java is established elsewhere (Hugo, 1975, 1978) but it is apparent also that many of the more permanent migrants eventually return to their village. Wander (1965, p.115) for example, found that gross migration (entries + exits) in Jakarta was about five times as large as the net gain of migrants. McNicoll's (1968) analysis of the Indonesian National Social and Economic Survey 1964-65 indicates that only half the migrants to urban areas in Java remain longer than 5 years in the city. This high volume of return movement of migrants to the city, together with the large amount of circulation between village and city, meant that in West Java much of the information concerning the experience of migrants in cities was obtained first-hand from the migrants themselves back in the rural area.

The most important difficulty with the rural-end research strategy is that people who have moved to the city and not returned at the time of survey cannot be interviewed. However if the household is taken as the basic unit of study rather than the individual it is possible to use a technique similar to the 'family reconstitution' procedures widely used in historical demography (Wrigley, 1966; Krier, 1969). Caldwell (1969, p.209) shows how the technique allows one to take a kind of population census which encompasses all living persons 'ever' born into a household and thus permits the tracing of all persons who have moved from the household. The fact that much mobility is short term, together with the very strong family, kinship, and local ties of the Sundanese (Palmer, 1959; Harsojo, 1971) means that close links are invariably maintained between movers and their village-based families, and persons in their former households can usually report on their migration experience. The accuracy of such reports is of course open to question but the frequent contact maintained between city and village by movers means that relatives in the village are constantly supplied with information about the mover's life in the city. There is no doubt that this information is occasionally coloured to heighten images of the success of the migrant or to conceal failure, but field experience suggests that in West Java the impact of such exaggeration is minimal.

The most important objection to this approach is that it does not detect entire families who have moved. In West Java, checks of population registers and interviews with village leaders suggested that there were few extended families who moved in their entirety from the survey villages. In his study of rural-urban migration in Ghana, Caldwell (1969, p.209) maintained that the shortcomings of the rural-based 'family reconstitution' method did not obscure the general picture of migrant movements and the part they play in rural society. This was also the case in the present study of West Javan villages. The methodology of that study is outlined in the following section.

The West Java Population Mobility Survey

In West Java the basic administrative unit is the village or *desa*. The *desa* is a territorial community but it does have the authority to excercise both legislative and executive power in internal affairs (Hofsteede, 1971) and a village administration to carry this out. Moreover, although West Javans' primary loyalties are to family it is difficult to unravel village, community and family loyalties and it is clear that most village inhabitants do identify with their *desa* of origin (Hugo, 1981, p.195). At the time of the study there were 3,709 non-urban *desa* in the province of West Java and they had a mean population of 5,640 persons in 1980, although there was wide variation around this mean.[1] Much store is placed in demographic research upon obtaining a random sample of communities' families or individuals so that a representative picture of the particular phenomena being studied can be derived. In the West Java case the task of carrying out surveys of a random sample of these villages within acceptable levels of sampling error was well beyond the resources of the project. In addition, there was no sampling frame which would enable the universe of villages to be stratified by their level of migration for a sample of outmigration villages to be taken. Moreover, the writer's aim to gain an appreciation of the interactions of a large number of variables with mobility required close involvement in each village survey, and hence severely limited the number of communities that could be studied. In order to gain maximum benefit from the resources available, it was decided to sacrifice quantitative precision in the selection of villages 'for the greater depth attainable by more intensive methods of attack' (Moser and Kalton, 1970, p.3), in striving toward an understanding of the causes and impact of population movement.

Accordingly, a purposive selection of fourteen villages was made which aimed at including the main source areas of movers from rural West Java to the cities of Jakarta and Bandung. The selection was made in two stages and was based on 4 months' intensive field reconnaissance, analysis of local population change statistics and discussion with local informants. Firstly, the major source areas of migrants were delimited. Secondly, lists of outmigration villages in each of these regions were assembled. These lists were the bases of selection of one village (or more, where more than one mobility pattern appeared to be important) which, after examination of village records and discussions with officials, appeared to have population movement patterns representative of the region.

The aim of the survey was to probe the dimensions of the process of population movement, not to estimate the overall scale of movement. The results cannot be interpreted as being representative of all West Javan villages. They are, however, illustrative of patterns of population movement between village and city which intensive field investigation in the province indicated are widespread and significant over substantial areas.

After the fourteen villages for close study had been selected, permission to carry out the survey was sought and obtained from the relevant officials in each case. Then a village questionnaire was constructed and pilot tested and field assistants were recruited and trained. Eight field assistants were recruited to assist on a full-time basis in the interviewing, coding and check-coding stages of the fieldwork. They were selected by the writer from some thirty interviewed applicants and were male, had at least 5 years' university or teachers college training, were fluent in Sundanese, and had worked on surveys in West Javan villages and urban areas. Perhaps most importantly they were all from first generation rural-urban migrant families and were in effect one type of participant in the process being studied. From the beginning, the interviewers showed enthusiasm for the project, quickly appreciated its relevance and were keen to learn the survey techniques used for possible adaptation to their own research work.

The researcher spent some time in reconnaissance in each of the villages before and after they had been selected. This was to conduct discussions with village heads and other officials, examine village records and make logistic arrangements for the interviewing phase. It was also arranged with the village head that a meeting of village household heads be called on the first evening the research team arrived in the village. The team, comprising the researcher and his wife and the interviewers, were billeted with families in the village. All members of the team shared the same work and living conditions and a strong spirit of camaraderie quickly developed within the group. My colleagues' local knowledge and sensitivity to the correct social forms was an invaluable aid, and helped neutralize at least some of the biases emanating from working in a culture very different from my own.

The meetings held on the day of arrival were invariably attended not only by leaders but by a sizeable number of other villagers as well. The meetings proved extremely valuable in establishing rapport, allaying suspicion and gaining background knowledge of patterns of population movement in the village. The writer and one of the interviewers addressed the meeting (in Indonesian and Sundanese, respectively), explaining the aims of the survey and the methods to be employed. The meetings generally began in a formal manner but later developed into an informal and relaxed discussion of the village, its structure and the patterns of population movement that characterized it. By the following day all villagers, even those not at the meeting, had been told details of the project and little difficulty was experienced in obtaining interviews. In fact, there was only one outright refusal in more than 1,400 formal interviews.

One of the advantages of the relatively small scale of the survey was that the writer could absorb considerable local knowledge and gain a 'feel' for the data as well as carry out field supervision personally. I conducted 5 per cent of all interviews and each night I closely edited all interview schedules which had been completed during the day. Any irregularities, inconsistencies and omissions detected resulted in the interviewer having to return to the respondent to correct the schedule. In each village the writer sat in on several of the interviews conducted, and also visited at least two respondents of each interviewer to verify questions taken at random from the completed schedule. This not only kept a close check on the quality of interviewing but allowed interesting issues and points arising out of particular interviews to be identified and followed up in the field. Wherever an interesting pattern arose in an interview schedule I would follow it up the next day by visiting the particular household and discussing informally that issue, and this invariably led to a lengthy and detailed conversation which often turned up details and relationships which I had not hitherto recognized.

One cannot stress enough the important insights into the process of population mobility and its complex interrelationships with social and economic change in the village which arose from the chief researcher living in the village during the period of data collection and conducting a significant proportion of the formal interviews personally. The simple fact of living in the village was an unexpected rich source of information and understanding not only through direct observation of day-to-day village life, but through informal (though focused) discussion with community members from a wide range of backgrounds. Caldwell, Reddy and Caldwell (1982a) have discussed in some detail this approach in which 'The major instrument for studying change turns out to be the long, discursive, semi-structured conversation which may go on for hours'. My experience in Indonesia duplicates theirs in that the voluminous field notes taken as a result of such conversations were at least as important as knowledge gained from the migration literature and migration theory in informing my interpretation of the data collected in the more formal survey phase of the study.

The village investigations were based largely around an interview schedule which was designed to collect information about sampled households[2] and individuals within those households. All questions in the schedules were asked by the interviewer. The original interview schedule was extensively changed as a result of field experience, in-depth non-structured interviews and discussions with government officials, academic colleagues, village leaders and other people with a wide knowledge of West Java, during the several months of the reconnaissance phase of the fieldwork. The schedule was translated into the Indonesian language by the writer and then back into English by an Indonesian colleague who had no professional background in migration studies. This revealed several ambiguities which were then removed. Versions of the schedule were then prepared in Sundanese and Javanese (the two main local languages represented in West Java) and translated back into Indonesian by a different person to remove translation errors. The schedule on which information was entered was in the Indonesian language but the interviewers all carried a version in Sundanese. The interviewers who were fluent in Javanese had a Javanese version of the schedule and were assigned to conduct all interviews in households where only Javanese was spoken.

Due to the small scale of the survey close supervision of all interviewers could be maintained and a comparatively complex interview schedule was able to be employed in the survey. The schedule consisted of seven separate sections, with the first two asked of the heads of each sampled household and the remaining sections being registers seeking information of different types of population movement for each eligible individual in the household. Where possible answers were sought from the individuals themselves but if they were absent from the village the answers were given on their behalf by other members of the household. A final section was completed by the interviewer and included details of the interview situation, the language used and his estimate of the accuracy of interviewee responses.

The content of each of the sections of the schedule and the eligibility criteria of persons to whom they were applied are outlined in Table 21.1. At first glance the schedule may appear unwieldy but in many households all sections did not have to be used and the interviewers, after some initial difficulties, quickly became adept at administering the questionnaire.

An additional 'community' questionnaire was constructed to collect aggregate demographic, social and economic data for each of the sampled villages. This questionnaire was usually completed by the *juru tulis* (secretary) of each village in consultation with other leaders. The questionnaire was assembled in the light of knowledge of the nature of village records available gained during the fieldwork reconaissance, and experience with it is detailed elsewhere (Hugo, 1985a).

Table 21.1 Summary of Content of Household Schedule Applied in Survey Villages

No.	Section Title	Eligible Persons	Information Sought
I	HOUSEHOLD INFORMATION	Each Sampled Household Head.	Identification of past and present members of the household, their basic demographic characteristics and where they fit into various movement classifications. Determination of which of registers III, IV, V and VI have to be applied to which members of the household. Estimation of the income and economic status of the household.
II	KNOWLEDGE OF, AND ATTITUDES TO, CITIES AND POPULATION MOVEMENT TO CITIES	Each Sampled Household Head.	Identification of demographic, economic and social characteristics of household head. His/her attitude towards city and village life. His/her knowledge of city life. His/her attitude toward rural to urban population movement. His/her level of participation in modern and traditional life. His/her intentions of moving. His/her patterns of circulation.
III	MARRIAGE AND DIVORCE HISTORY	All ever-married persons currently resident in the household or who have lived in the household at some time during the last 10 years.	Dates of marriages and divorces and details of population movements associated with them.
IV	MIGRATION HISTORY	All persons aged 10 or above at present residing in the household or who lived in the household at some time during the last 10 years and have spent a continuous period of 6 months or longer outside of the village.	All communities in which the individual has lived continuously for 6 months or longer recorded consecutively together with his/her age, occupation, level of education and marital status at the time of each move. Reasons for leaving each point of origin and selecting each destination.
V	FIRST PERMANENT RURAL TO URBAN MIGRATION	All persons from Section IV who had spent a continuous period of 6 months or longer in a city.	Details of knowledge of city destination. Costs and method of travelling to destination. Aims of migration. Experience in the city. Nature and strength of links maintained with village while in the city.
VI	CIRCULATION OUTSIDE OF THE VILLAGE (EXCLUDING SOCIAL AND SHOPPING VISITS)	All persons aged 10 or above at present residing in the household or who lived in the household at some time during the last 10 years who spent continuous periods of less than 6 months outside of the village to earn a living or attend an educational institution.	Details of the destination. Length of time spent at destination. Mode and cost of travel to destination. Reasons for leaving village and selecting destination. Details of activities and remuneration at destination. Details of housing and costs at destination. Nature and strength of links maintained with village while at destination. Future plans concerning mobility.
VII	INTERVIEWER ASSESSMENT		Circumstances of interview. Assessment of accuracy of responses.

In selecting the village households to be interviewed it was decided that the precision of the study would be improved if the intra-village samples were stratified on the following bases:

Firstly the village population was divided into two groups - leaders and the general population. The existence of a small group of leaders who have a strong influence on the decision-making of the population at large is an important feature of West Java villages (Hofsteede, 1971). In his study of three Sundanese villages, Jackson (1971, p.226) found that five or six men 'controlled the heights of the pyramid' and were the 'chief source of authoritative messages in the village communicative system'. Accordingly in each village approximately ten of the most influential formal and informal community leaders were interviewed. Because they were not selected randomly however, their responses are not aggregated with those of the randomly selected households in the analysis of the data. The leaders' interviews were almost always successful in obtaining a large amount of valuable additional background detail concerning population mobility in the village. Thus in each village a first step was to assemble a list of ten major formal and informal leaders in consultation with the head of the village and other members of the village administration. Later discussion with other villagers and personal observation in village meetings confirmed that the nominated leaders were invariably the most highly respected and influential men in the village. Moreover the major formal and informal leaders do represent a clearly recognizable group.

Secondly, since the study was concerned with all stages of the moving process outlined earlier, both persons who have already moved and those who have not yet moved need to be adequately represented in the survey. It was considered that an examination of the process of population movement should not only ask why some people move, but also why others do not move. So that mover/stayer comparisons could be made it was thus necessary to stratify the sample so that it contained adequate numbers of both reconstituted households containing movers and those containing only stayers.

The time-consuming procedure of actually selecting the sample (Hugo, 1975) was necessary because of the lack of an accurate, readily usable sampling frame. Much care was taken in drawing up the sample and there were few cases in which sampled households proved to be wrongly classified.

The disadvantages of the small size and unrepresentativeness of the fourteen-village survey were offset by the depth and detail of the information collected and by the tight control that could be exercised over the accuracy of the data, an aspect lacking in many large scale surveys in Indonesia. The low non-response rate and the willingness of respondents to co-operate all contribute to the writer's conviction of the essential accuracy of the information as a generally faithful reflection of the respondents' behaviour and opinions.

Testing Migration Hypotheses in Micro-Studies

The approach adopted in the West Java study described above is obviously somewhat specific to that particular context and the scale of study undertaken. However, it is our conviction that the broad methodological approach outlined is highly suited to the testing of some important hypotheses regarding the causes and consequences of population mobility which are not readily tested with census or large scale survey data. Here we seek to demonstrate this by advancing a number of propositions regarding the occurrence, causes and impacts of population mobility in contemporary Java for which the micro-approach outlined above appears to be a most appropriate *modus operandi*. In particular these propositions relate to the relationship between changing patterns of population mobility and the sweeping structural, social and economic changes in rural Java which were evident to some degree at the time of the 1973 survey but which have gained much greater momentum in the subsequent decade (Hugo, 1985b).

The propositions refer to the following three aspects of the population mobility/modernization interface which have considerable policy relevance:

1. the nature and incidence of population mobility between village and city;

2. the relationship between decisions to move and agricultural modernization, commercialization and rural social change;

3. the impact which this mobility has in turn on economic, social and demographic change in both the city and the village.

Given the meagre amount of research concerned with population mobility (as opposed to more or less permanent migration) and modernization in Indonesia, it is difficult to formulate specific, relevant and testable research hypotheses. Instead we put forward tentative propositions which could be effectively tested using micro-level approaches.

With respect to the first broad area concerning the nature of population mobility between village and city, the following propositions could be tested:

1. in several cultural contexts in Indonesia rural dwellers are aware of, and adopt, a range of rural-urban mobility strategies which vary in their degree of permanence. Significant numbers opt for a strategy of circulating between village and city rather than staying permanently in village or city;

2. the incidence of non-permanent rural-urban mobility has increased at a faster rate than permanent migration from village to city over the last 5 years;

3. the majority of circular migrants have a long-term commitment to the village and do not see this form of mobility as a phase of adjustment leading to eventual settlement in the city;

4. the degree of permanence of movement is largely determined by the level of education of the mover and, related to this, the nature of his/her employment in the city, the distance between village and city, and village norms;

5. permanent migration, as opposed to circular migration, is less selective of males and more selective of young adults and family of procreation groups;

6. most rural-urban mobility is a form of 'chain' movement.

These propositions predominantly relate to the specification of what actually constitutes population mobility in this particular context. In addition to obtaining appropriate definitions of mobility and achieving meaningful separation of the mover and non-mover populations, micro-approaches make it possible to establish significant differences between types of mobility and the characteristics of movers and non-movers.

Investigation of these issues is a necessary preliminary for exploring the second, more important set of propositions which relate to how modernization in rural areas (especially in agriculture) affects population mobility. The agricultural development policies executed under the Indonesian National Development Plans have led not only to the widespread use of new agricultural inputs and techniques but also to some changes in the ways in which agricultural tasks are organized (Collier, 1981). The last decade has seen unprecedented levels of structural and institutional change in the economies of village societies in many Third World countries. In rural communities in Java, for example, this decade saw the rapid spread of the green revolution technology in rice agriculture, increased mechanization of much farm-related activity, increased commercialization of agriculture, changing of traditional land tenure and agricultural labour arrangements, increased penetration of manufactured consumer goods and mass media, a virtual revolution in the availability of transportation, and changing local power relationships - all of which had major implications for population mobility out of villages (Hugo, 1985b). There is evidence that these changes have resulted in substitution of labour inputs in agriculture and other rural-based activity so that job opportunities in some areas have declined. It also seems that, in addition to changes in the total number of job opportunities available, access to these opportunities has varied between different socioeconomic strata in the village. *Prima facie* outmigration on a permanent or temporary basis would appear to be a logical adjustment to a reduction in the number or availability of income-earning opportunities in the village. However, policy-makers have no research findings to draw upon which indicate the extent to which this adjustment strategy is adopted, by what specific conditions might it be triggered, what forms the outmovement takes, what types of people migrate and what is its impact. The patterns of population mobility associated with agricultural modernization are highly complex and variable from one region to another. The present writer, for example, has observed contrasting situations between a village in West Java, where changes in agriculture led to circular outmovement of the landless and lower to middle income groups, and a village in South Sulawesi, where modernization resulted in many relatively wealthy landowners making their land available to share-croppers and moving to the city.

Many of these structural and institutional changes and their effects are difficult if not impossible to investigate using census or large scale survey approaches and their influence can often be more clearly analyzed from a community based micro-level perspective. Given the importance of economic factors and structural change within village economies in shaping migration, much of the emphasis here will be upon propositions relating population mobility to changing patterns of availability of economic opportunities. The methodology outlined earlier would appear appropriate to examine the complexities of these recent social, economic and political changes on the one hand and changing patterns of mobility on the other.

Given the widespread impact of agricultural development programs in Indonesia, there is an obvious pressing need for more information concerning the relationship between modernization in rural areas and population mobility. Accordingly, the following propositions for testing in rural contexts in Indonesia are put forward:

1. agricultural modernization and commercialization has released significant numbers of rural dwellers from permanent residence in villages;

2. whether or not people move away from the village and if so, what form that mobility takes, is determined largely by:

   a) one or more of the following 'community level' variables:

      - the degree and nature of agricultural modernization;
      - the traditional patterns of land ownership/operation and organization of agricultural tasks;
      - community and/or *sukubangsa* (ethno-linguistic group), *adat* (customary law), and mobility norms;
      - the nature and strength of existing links with urban areas;

   b) one or more of the following 'individual' or 'household level' variables:

      - land ownership status;
      - level of education;

- socioeconomic status;
- position in community power structure;

3. improvements in the rural public transport system have facilitated 'increased' outmovement from the village, especially movements of a circular, non-permanent nature.

The above hypotheses are necessarily very broad, as a result of the dearth of existing 'relevant' theory linking agricultural modernization and mobility in such Third World contexts as Indonesia, and the lack of suitable empirical studies from which specific hypotheses could be generated.

The third set of propositions related to the impact which the population mobility identified has on economic, social and demographic change in both the city and village contexts as well as on the movers themselves and their families. An important area of focus is on the impact of the mobility in rural areas, a particularly neglected area in rural-urban mobility studies in Indonesia. The impact of population mobility on village communities can be conceptualized as being of two types:

> 'Firstly there must be some adjustment to the *passive* impact of the permanent or temporary absence of some of its former inhabitants. Secondly, outmigration may have an *active* impact through the migrants establishing ties between city and village along which they transmit newly acquired money, goods, ideas, attitudes and innovations from their destination' (Hugo, 1978, p.249).

Some propositions which could productively be investigated using the micro-level approach outlined earlier are as follows:

1. there are consistent and significant differences in the nature of the 'commitments' to the village maintained by permanent and circular outmigrants;

2. there are substantial and consistent differences in the 'type' and 'intensity' of the impact of permanent and circular migrants on both village and city;

3. the impact of circular migrants on economic and social change in the village is greater than for permanent migrants;

4. remittances from movers to urban areas make substantial contributions to the incomes of village-based families;

5. movers are significant agents of social and cultural change in the village;

6. circular migrants will be predominantly employed in the informal sector of the urban economy while permanent migrants will be predominantly employed in the formal sector.

In sum the micro-approach to studying population mobility as described here allows the complex two-way interactions between movement and economic and social change to be more readily tackled than is possible in large scale surveys or census data. This is largely because the approach allows individuals, households and communities to be studied in 'context', where it is possible to examine in some detail the complex economic and social forces which impinge upon them. It is often difficult to identify these forces in large scale surveys. For example the labour displacements within Javan rural communities referred to above are the result of the penetration into village communities of a number of macro-structural forces associated with the capitalist mode of production; the spread of commercialization and consumerism and the greater integration of the village economy into the national market economy; as well as the rapid spread of education and mass media into villages. The effects of such changes upon population movement out of communities are considerable but we know little of how precisely they impinge upon the population mobility of individuals and households. Which groups are affected most by these changes, how do their mobility patterns change and what effects does it have on distribution of wealth and social change? These are questions to which the available macro-data can give us only very partial answers at best.

The above discussion leads us to another important issue in the investigation of interaction between population movement and economic and social change. This is that the approach described here can be used not only to collect and analyze cross-sectional information to allow the relevant variables and population movement to be considered between communities at one point in time, but also to collect time series information in single communities. Since our main interest is in a dynamic process, namely demographic change, it is imperative that a historical perspective be adopted in examining population mobility and that information be sought regarding changes in important structural variables. My experience has been that the approach outlined earlier lends itself to the reconstruction of change, certainly for the decade or so prior to the study.

There has long been a polarization in migration research between a concern with large scale structural forces which have an overriding influence in shaping the aggregate pattern of population movement, and those forces which impinge at a micro-level upon individuals and families. However, both approaches only provide a partial and incomplete understanding of the causes and consequences of population movement. Pryor (1975, p.37) has pointed out that sooner or later we must deal with the problem of linking knowledge regarding motives at the micro-level with inferred causal mechanisms at the macro-level. There is a growing feeling among migration researchers that this gap may be bridged at least in part by approaching the study of population mobility from a wider range of levels of investigation. It has been suggested that the community-based approach offers a possible means whereby we can link two groups of causal factors (as identified by Gardner, 1981, p.71): firstly, those which individuals and families can perceive, feel, articulate, relate to and evaluate as pertinent to themselves and their goals; and secondly those less proximate, more basic structural factors beyond the consideration and often even the awareness of individuals but which nevertheless shape migration. Bilsborrow (1981, p.10), for example, states that

> 'It is important to have information about both the individual and community variables to investigate the factors that influence migration decisions. Thus the exclusion of community variables in empirical studies of individual behaviour generally results in statistically misspecified models'.

It would seem that the community offers a meaningful and manageable unit in which both micro and macro influences on migration can be considered together. However, the inclusion of community level variables and contextual considerations into the analysis of migration (and fertility) decision-making raises a number of difficulties. Not the least of these is the problem of separation of individual and community effects. The body of studies which explicitly considers both individual and community level variables in attempting to explain migration behaviour is limited. Moreover in many of these studies the community level variables considered are more a function of what data are available from central data collection agencies than the result of any careful development of explanatory hypotheses via detailed community studies. As McNicoll (1980b) has said in reviewing a study of community effects on reproductive behaviour in South Korea which found that such effects were minor,

> 'In the tradition of multivariate studies, however, only cursory attention is given to the theoretical justification for the particular independent variables selected - another can always be added - giving a high ratio of tables of beta coefficients to pages of interpretive text'.

Obviously the inclusion of particular variables, as with any independent variables, is only justifiable in the analysis of demographic change if there are good theoretical reasons to suggest that there is an explanatory relationship between that variable and demographic behaviour.

There is a need for us to be much more careful in our identification and specification of these variables and also to be less constrained by model questionnaires developed in different contexts. This necessitates more micro-level work to supplement and in fact guide the actual type of individual, household or community-level data collected in larger scale studies. My experience in Java has been that even short periods spent in the field are of basic importance in modifying, operationalizing and indeed totally reshaping hypotheses derived from theory. The mixture of participant observation, long discursive semi-structured interviews, discussion with key respondents and following up of leads which invariably arise during visits to villages may appear somewhat messy to the statistical purist but it can be tremendously rewarding in terms of gaining insights into complex interrelationships and clarifying cause and sequence.

Links With Sample Surveys

At several points in this chapter reference has been made to ways in which the micro-level type of analysis focused upon here can be integrated with large scale sample surveys. It is argued that this integration is not only possible but highly desirable. Despite the limitations of large scale surveys described by Caldwell, Reddy and Caldwell (1982a, pp.2-10) they obviously have an important role in investigating demographic change and its causes and effects. In my own work in Indonesia I have constantly encountered difficulty in convincing policy makers and planners of the significance of short term mobility and its effects because I could only point to case study evidence in support. Large scale surveys are needed to establish the degree of representativeness of particular demographic phenomena. Appropriate preliminary micro-studies can greatly inform and improve the design and execution of such large surveys. Several communities should be studied in detail in the planning stages of such studies before the survey instrument is finalized.

Bilsborrow (1981, p.10) has suggested that community questionnaires are likely to remain the major element in collection of information about most of the community structural-institutional factors that influence migration in large scale surveys. However, it is also important to consider the possibility of supplementing this with more detailed community level micro-studies. These should not only be of the 'pilot survey' nature indicated earlier, but it has been argued (Hugo, 1982c, p.211) that many additional insights into the causes and impacts of population mobility upon welfare, development and inequality would be gained if large scale sample surveys were supplemented by detailed community case studies. These studies should be of a 'linked, follow-up' nature in that the communities selected as case studies should be a subsample of sampling units from the large scale survey. The case study communities could perhaps be selected on a stratified basis (by type of mobility, etc.), based on data collected in the larger survey. If this strategy is adopted it will be possible to link the findings of the detailed case studies to those of the more representative wider survey (albeit not in a strictly statistically respectable way) and give them a wider relevance than would otherwise be the case. The advantages of linked data sets are fairly obvious and have been spelled out elsewhere (e.g., see Khoo *et al.*, 1980).

The community level detailed case studies could be especially selected to test specific hypotheses. For example, an area which has undergone substantial rural development could be closely studied to test the hypothesis that such programs retard rural-urban migration. Another consideration could be to select study areas which represent a range of communities according to the time period over which migration has been a significant influence. From individual and household questionnaires it is not possible to discover whether mobility influencing communities is long-standing or recent and it is clear that adjustments to the movement and the nature and degree of impact on the community will vary over time. Such a stratification will make it possible to differentiate between short-term and long-term development and welfare impacts of particular mobility patterns. A further major consideration in the case studies is that there is a need to look closely at the structural causes and impacts of population mobility. This would involve collecting time series information relating to patterns of agriculture, income levels and distribution, institutional changes, access to local employment, investment in productive activity, and other phenomena and investigating whether or not these can be related to migration. In areas of inmigration the impacts on service provision, pressure on housing, job opportunities and other effects can all be investigated in some depth, but always with a linkage to the findings of the wider survey being possible. The case studies will allow a more detailed and explicit assessment to be made of the development impact of migration in specific areas where it is needed. It may also be possible to incorporate more specialized examinations within this framework; these could include the impact of temporary labour migration on fertility levels and the influence of mobility on health (e.g. that of temporary workers who often have to live in very crowded or unsanitary conditions).

A community based micro-study approach could be taken to enable greater insights to be obtained into the distributional impacts of population mobility. By taking this perspective, an assessment can be made of the influence of movement on increasing, decreasing or conserving the amount of income inequality or social stratification, and on equality of access to the means of production, job opportunities, services, etc. within social units. Moreover, special interviewing would allow some time perspective to be given to this analysis by reconstructing changes in these aspects of life over time.

A community case study approach would allow more detailed investigation to be made into the influence of mobility on 'modernity', the breakdown of traditional authority and traditional ways of carrying out day-to-day activities. Similarly in the examination of the impact upon political participation and political change, observation of patterns in the community and discussion with key respondents in the case studies will almost certainly be more productive of insights than the questionnaire survey.

Analysis of aspects such as the causes of movement or non-movement will be best undertaken in full knowledge of the structural historical and contextual forces which impinge upon and shape mobility. Such forces as agricultural change, increased capital penetration, land tenure changes, increased commercialization, transport penetration, and greater emphasis on individualism over traditional co-operative relations can often be more readily discerned and examined in community-level questionnaires. In all, the case studies used as a supplement to the larger survey will allow a much more detailed assessment of the net costs and benefits occurring to individuals, families, communities and nations as a result of various patterns and levels of mobility. Large scale migration surveys provide many insights into population mobility but their value could be enhanced by the addition of another role - that of a framework for more detailed micro-level studies.

Conclusion

This chapter indicates some of the possibilities of adopting a micro-level community approach in the exploration of the causes and effects of changing patterns of population movement in Third World situations. It is argued that the 'context' of demographic decision-making exerts a significant influence in shaping that behaviour. In many developing world situations the community constitutes a valid and manageable unit within which to analyze contextual effects in conjunction with individual and household variables studied using a range of observations and structural and semi-structural interview techniques. The neglect of contextual factors in analysis of demographic behaviour has resulted from a preoccupation with the individual as a unit of study, especially in large scale studies. It is virtually impossible to gain an adequate view of the context of decision-making using such strategies in research design and analysis. Nevertheless it has been possible here to advance a number of, albeit tentative, propositions linking changing migration behaviour to contextual effects. These are indicative of the fruitfulness of incorporation of micro-level considerations of community in studies of population mobility. However, the adoption of this perspective must be carefully conceived and fully integrated into the research design. There are still problems, daunting in number, scale and complexity, in collecting and analyzing such data, not to mention integrating it with that collected at other levels. However, the results thus far achieved are encouraging and suggest strongly that this approach offers one avenue in which our understanding of demographic change can be significantly improved.

Notes

1. In the fourteen villages selected for close study, for example, the resident populations ranged from 2,219 to 11,576.

2. A household was defined as a group sharing the same hearth.

22

UNDOING MIGRATION MYTHS IN MELANESIA: APPLICATION OF A DIALECTIC MIGRATION ANALYSIS

Gerald Haberkorn

Information on regional population growth during the 1970s shows that of all developed and developing areas throughout the world, Melanesia had by far the highest annual 'urban' growth rates, with 8.8 per cent (UN, 1976). Although its levels of urbanization are much lower and of lesser political importance than in most developing countries of Asia, Africa and Latin America, the 'rapid' growth rate of urban populations throughout the Melanesian region is of considerable significance. Macro-level data suggest that these phenomenal urban growth rates are not mainly the result of the natural increase of already established urban populations as Preston (1979) would argue, but must be interpreted in the context of changing internal migration patterns. While intercensus comparisons allow for the detection of new trends such as those indicated by changing sex ratios, age distributions and choices concerning main destination areas, they cannot provide evidence on the dynamics underlying such changing mobility patterns, nor on implications for their future development. Given the limited format and static nature of a census, we cannot determine to what extent rapid growth in female migration and increasing preference for urban over rural destinations, for example, will lead to new movement patterns, such as a change away from predominantly short-term and circular migration giving way to long(er) term rural absenteeism. To pursue such issues in a more meaningful way, another research methodology is required, in the form of specific village, island and urban-based research. If we consider migration as an 'ongoing dialectic process' between an individual, his or her family and the local community on one hand and the larger political economy on the other (Swindell, 1979, p.225), we should logically analyze migration 'in a dialectic manner' as well.

Levels of Analysis and Problems of Data Collection

My own research on changing mobility patterns in Vanuatu is based on such a strategy (Haberkorn, 1985, 1987). My conceptual framework for mobility analysis follows Mitchell's (1985) emphasis on the need to differentiate between two separate yet interrelated phenomena: the setting and the social situation. The 'setting' of migration refers to the 'overall general features of the social system within which the acts of movement of individuals are located' (p.38); the analysis of objective economic conditions is as important at this stage as the examination of general political and social structural features (p.35). Issues such as available agricultural land in rural areas, wages paid in destination areas, and the cost of living, to name just a few, are as valid features on this level of analysis as existing legal frameworks more directly interfering with the process of migration. Yet to what extent and which people respond to these conditions cannot be specified at such a general level of abstraction. What is needed at this stage, according to Mitchell, is an examination of the social 'situation' 'represented by the particular set of circumstances in which migrants actual or potential find themselves' (p.35). Phenomena such as kinship obligations and roles migrants play in their rural home areas exemplify this level of analysis.

Despite certain role requirements in their rural home areas, people perceive, interpret and evaluate such roles (and implicitly the norms and sanctions connected with them) quite differently, which again will account for varied responses. In other words, although the analysis of social situations is of primary importance in order to clarify specific aspects of our setting analysis as postulated by Mitchell, analytically it is not quite sufficient.[1] We need additional information on yet another level of abstraction to account for variations on the 'situational' level. This level of analysis may be referred to as the 'phenomenology of migration', emphasizing the subjective perceptions and interpretations of (potential) migrants and stayers of such realities as the setting and the situation of migration.

Irrespective of what theoretical emphasis to which we submit in our historical and setting analysis, our recognition of the need to include other, more 'concrete levels of manifestation' (and hence explanation) indicates the necessity for empirical migration research. The obvious question then arises as to what particular strategy, or method(s) of inquiry should be adopted. Acknowledgement of the dynamism implicit in the interrelation between levels of manifestation of migration, and adherence to a dialectic migration analysis, imply that our process of data collection has to proceed accordingly, involving continuing shifts between different analytical levels of inquiry. Considering the planning and execution of empirical migration research, there are three interrelated implications:

1. specific methods should develop for a specific problem to be studied, rather than have the adoption of any particular method dictated to us by mere availability (and/or alleged 'efficiency' in other research situations);

2. recognizing a need for different levels of analysis implies that we cannot submit to any one single methodology, method or technique;

3. we are dealing with social processes where, unlike in natural sciences, outcomes cannot be determined in advance. This implies that our methods of field investigation ought to be flexible enough to accommodate the unforeseen, and allow for its systematic exploration.

Referring to the first problem, we know that migration research in Melanesia and elsewhere has for many years relied on one predominant methodology: the survey approach. Irrespective of the idiosyncratic nature of migration studies, large scale questionnaires based on sample surveys or more localized interview studies were the rule rather than the exception. Analytically, the predominant concern was with migration *per se*, and research was largely taxonomical, focusing on migrant characteristics, migration differentials and the development of typologies. With a more structural analysis not in vogue for some time, the general social, cultural, economic and political context out of which migration originates, was often either ignored in the sense of being 'controlled for', or described to give the reader a 'feel' for the place. To what extent the widespread reliance on a survey approach was the cause or result of such a situation cannot be speculated upon in the present context.

To criticize survey research on the basis of conceptual and technical inadequacies is quite legitimate, but to equate technical inefficiency (for example, bad survey design and/or implementation) with methodological inadequacy, implying that surveys in general are 'bad', is conceptually not only a different issue, but superficial and distracting from more important matters. It is unfortunate that much of the debate between macro- and micro-researchers has focused on just this issue. The more significant methodological issue affecting migration research is not so much the question of whether or not a survey approach *per se* is inadequate and qualitative research strategies are better, but to delineate the very conditions[2] under which any particular technique serves the purpose of our research best, in the sense of bringing us closer to understanding the phenomenon under study. If, for example, we require information on the contemporary incidence of out-migration from one particular area to place our case study village in a proper context (asserting for example that the latter's out-migration rate is typical of the area rather than location-specific), a quick visit to all villages concerned and conducting a brief census-type survey will produce the desired information quite efficiently. If, on the other hand, we need to obtain information on land or urban-to-rural remittances, the adoption of a survey-type strategy is unlikely to yield very accurate or trustworthy results, since most people, at least in Vanuatu, are only willing to part with such information after a certain amount of trust and credibility have been established.

With regard to our second point, acknowledging the complexity of a social process like migration and the sensitive nature of some of its dimensions, it is obvious that relevant empirical data cannot be obtained by relying on one single research method. Most migration researchers in Melanesia throughout the late 1960s and 1970s combined local censuses and specific surveys with some more qualitative approaches such as direct and/or participant observation, unstructured or semi-structured interviews, group discussions, and the collection of oral histories, to name just a few.[3] Despite obvious and at times very considerable methodological improvements, stretching from the initial widening of one's analytical perspective to quite sophisticated multi-method research strategies, many 'survey ills' were nevertheless repeated. One aspect derives from a lack of time. Concerned with the scientific goal of generalization to as wide a universe as possible and/or due to an analytical necessity to engage in comparative research, a good number of migration researchers (myself included) have spread their inquiries over several villages, across different districts and at times various islands. Living at the place of one's investigation together with the population we are working with has the invaluable advantage of allowing us to observe rather than merely listen, to talk and discuss with people rather than stereotypically ask questions and record answers. But to spend just a few weeks or a couple of months at a time in each location will not suffice to engage properly in both quantitative and qualitative research. Time is often too short to allow for villagers and researchers to 'check each other out', to establish mutual feelings of some warmth, respect and trust, all essential pre-conditions for any type of qualitative research to eventuate and be effective. With time itself such a crucial factor, a lack thereof will mean that qualitative methods are primarily used to supplement information gained via larger surveys or interview schedules rather than as instruments in their own right. One of the more problematic implications is that both methods often measure different aspects. Caldwell (1985, p.5) in comparing the efficiency of what he terms the 'quasi-anthropological method' with formal surveys states that in employing the former:

> '...we have found a near consensus... but surveys on the same matters (conducted by the same people) find a range of answers;...in most cases the explanation is that a complex matter can be explained only at length and some people start with some aspect of the problem and others at a different place even though they eventually lay similar stresses'.

Furthermore, a lack of local knowledge and understanding has the additional and unfortunate implication that a selective reliance on some qualitative techniques often obscures rather than clarifies available survey information.

Another fundamental problem associated with the 'ills' of the survey method is the construction of elaborate and often voluminous survey questionnaires 'prior to the actual field research', in order to gather a vast amount of empirical data for more formal hypothesis testing. While such a procedure is widely regarded to be quite 'normal' if one's goal is to 'verify' theory, and is also considered to produce 'scientific results'[4] - though lacking a substantive theoretical body from which such hypotheses could be deducted, more attention should be given to the generation and subsequent continuous testing of hypotheses and ultimately theory. Most survey practitioners would see no problem in the use of their method for such a purpose. Yet the sheer volume of many survey questionnaires points to some awkward distortions of empirical induction:[5]

'...a most unfortunate tendency in the preparation of surveys ...is the writing down of scores or hundreds of 'hypotheses' mostly in terms of permutations and combinations, using the volume and coverage of all the suggestions to justify the lack of knowledge possessed of the society and implying that investigations of all these hypotheses will eventually sort the plausible from the ridiculous' (Caldwell *et al.*, 1982a, pp. 7-8).

While Caldwell's critique is undoubtedly justified concerning this practice of empirical induction, implications of this procedure point to a far more distorting exercise, when applied to the process of 'verifying' theory. Glaser and Strauss (1967) in their discussion of discovery made through quantitative data, emphasize this problem in the following way:

'Typically, discovery made through quantitative data is treated only as a byproduct of the 'main work' - making accurate descriptions and verifications. When discovery forces itself on the analyst, he then writes his induced hypotheses as if they had been thought up before the data were collected, so that they will seem to satisfy the logical requirements of verification' (p.185).

Referring to our third point, another problem implicit in a survey approach is the danger of misrepresenting reality due to certain 'preconceptions'. One obvious preconception refers to the fact that migration survey questionnaires, particularly those containing several options, give the impression of knowing all likely outcomes in advance. Besides submitting to deterministic models based on some economic and social 'laws', supposed to determine forms of social action such as migration, they additionally presume to know exactly how to go about 'measuring' these phenomena. Even considering hypothesis testing and irrespective of whether such hypotheses have been deducted from substantive or grounded theory, our exclusive analytical reliance on their translation into survey questions precludes the acquisition of real knowledge; neither in the case of 'verification' nor falsification are we sure about the underlying theoretical dynamic. While instances of falsification (if we are fortunate enough to read about them) may lead to a scrambling for contextual explanations often transcending the original theoretical and methodological framework, an apparent 'verification' of hypotheses, interestingly enough, does not seem to warrant such additional contextual validation. Suffice to say, that if our concern is primarily with the acquisition of knowledge, for example via generating new hypotheses, we cannot afford to cling to preconceived concepts, categories, and sequences; but must allow for context-specific and systematic exploration, as in the case of lengthy and probing discussions, multiple cross-checking of the same information with others and cross-checking the validity of a phenomenon with the same person by discussing its salience on different dimensions. Limiting one's perception not only to the spoken reality by excluding observation from our inquiry, but due to highly pre-structured methods also to 'the unknown', this standardization (the implicit strength of a survey) undermines the very basic nature of research in preventing us from experiencing 'new realities'.

Contemporary Migration in Vanuatu - Application of a Dialectic Migration Analysis

Acknowledging the complexity of a social process such as migration, my research of contemporary Vanuatu migration focused on the following four levels of analysis:

1. the historical setting and development of mobility patterns;

2. the contemporary social, political and economic setting of mobility;

3. the situation of mobility;

4. the phenomenology of mobility.

Evaluating context-specific strengths and weaknesses of quantitative and qualitative methods of data collection, I opted for a 'comparative case study approach', combining the collection of migration histories, structured and unstructured interviews and group discussions (on such issues as general motivation for migration out of this area, perception of mobility change over the years, collection of oral histories), with specific population and agricultural censuses and some small scale surveys (for example on income and expenditure, to collect network data). Archival data were also included, such as log-books of recruiting ships during the last century, colonial government gazettes, and registers of trading companies involved in inter-island copra transport. Village co-operative society accounts also provided a valuable source of information on income (sale of copra to the co-op) and expenditure, and allowed for a cross-validation of income-expenditure survey data. Needless to say, such an inquiry cannot be pursued within a survey-type framework, both regarding methods used and time involved. The rationale behind opting for a case-study approach involving six rural settlements on two islands, was to allow for some comparative analysis on phenomena considered to be of crucial analytical importance: time and 'type' of European contact (impact of missionaries and colonial economy); social organization (for example societies where rank and status are achieved by merit rather than 'closed' systems where they are inherited, patrilineal versus matrilineal descent groups); and the availability of land. Furthermore, including a sample of urban migrants originating from the six rural communities provided two major advantages: from a 'substantive-theoretical' point of view and considering the dialectic nature of our framework, it allows for the analysis of rural-urban linkages and their development over time. A most welcome 'methodological improvement of such a design is the possibility of cross-validating empirical information obtained at either the rural or urban end. Throughout

Melanesia, economic linkages between migration source and destination areas are of a two-way nature: urban-to-rural transfers of money, food and goods is generally paralleled by rural-to-urban supplies of island foodstuffs, in the form of yams, taro and 'island cabbage' for example.[6] Yet many studies analyzing the importance of remittance flows often concentrate exclusively on either urban-to-rural remittances or the reverse, and/or with research being carried out in only one location. Inconsistent findings throughout the literature on the incidence and magnitude of such flows, as well as regarding the proportion of senders and recipients, may be more a reflection of the adopted research design than actual remittance practices. By adopting a case study approach focusing simultaneously on rural-to-urban and urban-to-rural remittance flows at both urban and rural ends, we obtain more reliable information.

How such empirical migration research has to proceed out of a dialectic between sometimes more than two different levels of analysis, will be discussed by considering the following illustration. As point of analytical entry I shall choose the rural setting from which migration not only originates, but which also may contribute to the particularities of specific mobility patterns. Mobility research throughout developing countries often states that one of the major reasons underlying rapid urban population growth and the fast pace of urbanization can be seen in landless peasants being driven out of rural areas and leaving for town in search of a 'better' life. While such observations may undoubtedly be accurate for many areas where feudal systems play(ed) a significant role, it is a known fact in Melanesia that most urban migrants still have access to land in their home areas.[7] That is, we cannot assume a mono-causal relationship between the lack of land as such and the propensity to migrate. Despite access to land, many rural out-migrants in Melanesia find it difficult or impossible to rely on their land to meet an ever-growing demand for cash. In the case of Vanuatu, minimal expenses today affecting all adults are any combination of the following: school fees for children and/or younger siblings (even for primary school), head tax and Church fees, clothing and foodstuffs. That is, land as such becomes of secondary importance at this point of our analysis, calling for a conceptual shift within our analysis of the rural setting; if people, despite access to land, continue to migrate, emphasis has to be placed on examining the meanings, function, and value of land, which brings us to a situational and phenomenological level of inquiry.

In one rural area, people may not be able to use their land for cash-cropping; widespread land fragmentation due to a fast growing population visible in 100 square feet patches here and there, does not make it the most viable enterprise. Elsewhere we encounter 'functional landlessness' (Howlett, 1980, p.195), that is, people who, despite access to vast areas of land, are economically disadvantaged because environmental or locational constraints prevent them from earning a cash income. We also find a variation of this 'functional landlessness' generally affecting young married men, who do have access to land, as well as numerous ideas of how to make money from it. But as in many instances they do not (yet) own their land, having only received usage rights from fathers or uncles, it is the latter who indirectly determine what is planted, which in most cases excludes even seasonal cash-crops.[8]

These examples highlight the analytical inaccuracies we would face by treating access to land on only one level of analysis; they also point to the need to consider other setting variables (again, even if they have been looked at previously in other contexts) such as forms of agricultural production, social organization of (agricultural) activities, changes in these phenomena over time, alternative sources of cash income, social values attributed to agricultural employment, to name just a few. These examples also indicate that if landlessness is a primary cause for rural out-migration, we might find quite different forms of population movements. While long-term rural absenteeism would logically be quite compatible with the situation of real or 'functional' landlessness (that is, a situation not expected to change dramatically over time), short-term movements may be more predominant amongst people who by virtue of their social status have not yet acquired control over their means of production.

While different forms of mobility to some extent reflect structural phenomena in rural areas like the one just mentioned, an examination of the economic setting in destination areas would be appropriate at this stage of our proceedings, specifically an analysis of the labour market to assess its capacity of absorbing long-term or short-term movers, or for that matter, any new job-seeker at all. To only consider setting variables such as the lack of economic opportunities in rural areas, available employment elsewhere, and such demographic features as age, sex, education and job qualifications, may be justifiable in terms of economic theory (testing), but often proves to be quite inadequate considering Melanesian reality, where we find many urban migrants who cannot find a job, but would not consider returning home or working on a plantation.

In all fairness to models implicitly acknowledging a phenomenological level of analysis by considering, for example, that prospective migrants assess the probability of getting a job in town before they eventually move, we still face the reality of rural-to-urban migrants who 'know' in real terms that their chances to get a job in town are close to zero. Not having any other information to rely on at this stage, why should we even expect that 'knowledge' about urban unemployment would deter people from leaving their rural areas and come to town? The knowledge that someone already established in town will feel obliged (by custom) to help could make such moves into urban employment uncertainties a lot more bearable as Ryan (1985) suggests; while rural-urban kinship networks and local organizations in town provide the social setting for our examination, a situational and phenomenological analysis is required to evaluate both the specific placement of each (prospective) migrant, with regard to acceptance into or membership of such organizations, as well as their own interpretations and evaluations of the meaning and importance of such groups.

Ward's (1971, p.101) argument that 'underused' labour in town would most probably still be underused in their home village is an idea worth further exploration. Concerning our analysis of the rural setting, we need to direct our attention to the social and economic organization of a village, examine the roles and obligations of specific groups of people to understand their importance or dispensability regarding the social and economic functioning of the village. Considering the situational level of our analysis, we need to assess how specific individuals fit in this context, and how people themselves perceive and evaluate such roles and obligations. To what extent this 'underused labour' in town might also be 'underused' on a plantation also deserves further inspection. Economic hypothesizing would suggest that, *ceteris paribus*, without economic opportunities in rural areas, no prospects of securing a job in town but the certainty of plantation wage-employment, plantation migration to be the obvious alternative. Yet unemployment amongst rural-to-urban migrants as mentioned previously indicates that such assumptions are only partially accurate. To understand such an apparent inconsistency, we need to expand our analysis and examine such objective realities as the nature of plantation employment, working and living conditions and wages paid, as well as their evaluation in comparison with perceived realities associated with urban unemployment.

Not everyone without economic opportunities in their rural home areas (other phenomena being 'controlled for') considers out-migration. Recalling Mitchell's view of migration as an 'epiphenomenon' should serve as a timely reminder to view the rural setting of out-migration as a whole. This implies that we should place as much analytical emphasis on those who remain in a particular area, as on out-migrants. Needless to say, such a recognition in our analytical framework should go beyond treating these people as statistical control groups for out-migrants, as is often the sad reality in migration research. Some may be 'stayers' while others are 'non-migrants',[9] representing far too much complexity to be ascribed the non-status of a control group. Some engage in business activities such as running a store, a taxi-boat or bakery, but given our entry point of a widespread lack of economic opportunities in a particular area, who could be expected to afford such services, that is, allow such business to function? With regard to those who have no stake in their rural area, how do they manage to survive economically, socially and psychologically?

A straightforward setting analysis would indicate that a lack of local cash-income opportunities cannot be equated with a large-scale unavailability of cash itself. Remittances from urban or rural wage earners are of major importance, calling for yet another examination of existing networks between migration source and destination areas, their role and meaning in the perception of migrants and remittance receivers. While rural, non-agricultural self-employment such as the running of a taxi-boat or store does provide some economic alternatives to rural out-migration,[10] it not only applies to just a small minority of villagers, but its very success and survival ultimately depends on the mobility of others!

Considering the economic viability of rural business endeavours as alternatives to out-migration also requires an examination of the meaning and values attributed to owning and running such an enterprise. Throughout Melanesia we find that small scale rural business activities do not primarily thrive for economic, but for social (prestige conferred to it by a group) and psychological (actual prestige experienced by operator) reasons. Actual business 'ownership' is often seen as equally or even more important than profits, that is, business success does not necessarily reflect western economic logic, which provides an important analytical feedback to what has been said earlier about the control over land.

The attraction of such a method of inquiry and analysis is that it allows for more realistic social research to take place; coming across a particular reality (for example business management) and recognizing its contextual similarity to another phenomenon encountered previously (for example, control over land), allows for the immediate elaboration and checking of new hypotheses, and what is more, these hypotheses are actually grounded in reality.[11] To those readers more accustomed to linear social research,[12] this ongoing process of shifting between levels of analysis may give the impression of highly anarchic or plainly unorganized research. 'Unorganized' it is meant to be, to the extent of allowing a dialectic research process to unfold.

Yet such a dialectic procedure extends beyond ongoing shifts between different levels of analysis, and plays a central role in the interviewing process itself. Descriptions and interpretations regarding such phenomena as for example causes and consequences of rural out-migration, and their change over time, are never accepted at face value. Via a continuous process of antithetic feedback through the interviewer, it becomes obvious after some time that the most salient and prominent features figuring in an interview situation are theoretically not necessarily the most important ones. This particular procedure extends beyond the traditional probing in interviews, where the primary objective is to extract more information regarding the same general direction. By confronting interviewees with continuing 'antitheses', also in the context of different levels of analysis, we avoid superficiality and the 'obvious', since interviewees continuously re-evaluate their own opinions and interpretations.

General questions such as 'why do people from this area move?' are used as 'starters', yet this approach does not stop at the mere recording of the obvious. An answer like:

> 'People leave because they don't have enough land here to grow enough food and cash crops to properly look after their families',

will elicit the following response from the interviewer:

> 'I see, this means if I understand you correctly, that those people remaining here have plenty of land, or at least enough to look after their families?'

The respondent has basically two options: to agree with this statement, or to deny it. In the case of an agreement with such an antithesis, we then confront our respondent with some contradictory information obtained in a previous local agricultural census, that many people remaining in this particular area have little or no land, while many out-migrants have access to considerable land areas. It is at this stage that a more formal interview situation gives way to discussion, and where our causal analysis may begin. Perceptions of reasons (focus on individual) are gradually replaced by an emphasis on causes (focus on structure), that is, the desire to earn money and the wish to look after one's family become of secondary importance, while references to control over land, changing inheritance laws and marriage exchange networks become more salient. In case of a denial of the antithesis, most interviewees themselves would re-evaluate their first statement, to the extent that 'this only applies to some people'. Our next step then tries to uncover why people without land could possibly remain in the village, and how this situation differs from those without land who have migrated elsewhere.

The comparative advantage of such a dialectic method of inquiry over traditional survey techniques is its generation of more complex information. By extending our scope beyond the obvious and a strict individual level of concern, trying to understand the underlying structures responsible for such individual 'decisions', we obtain a more realistic picture and potentially more policy relevant information. While a standardized survey-based approach may lead to agricultural development projects suitable to small landholdings, such as the growing of pepper, they will not succeed in providing an economic alternative for out-migration, unless they are matched by some structural reforms, such as those identified above. Not that such information will always lead to realistic policy formulations; the comparative advantage of such a data gathering process is that 'wrong' policies based on only superficial facts can, ideally speaking, be avoided.

Abstracting from Case Studies

From our discussion so far it becomes quite clear that given our specific research emphasis, a strict adherence to either a survey approach or pure qualitative research methods is doomed to analytical failure. Furthermore we realized that to engage in a more truly interactive or dialectic process of field research requires a case study approach rather than a large scale sample design. Irrespective of whether we work with total populations as in the case of entire villages, or rely on samples, when the sheer size of a particular locality does not allow for total coverage, we face the question of to what extent we have the 'right' to extrapolate from one particular instance or case to other places and times. Such expressions of concern are often voiced by critics of case studies, and somewhat unimaginatively refer to the 'smallness' of a sample or its uniqueness, which does not allow for 'generalizations', all of which reveals some interesting misconceptions about the analytical value of this methodology. Most textbooks on social research methods emphasize the need for large samples if we want to collect 'systematic' data to engage in solid empirical generalizations,[13] insinuating that large scale surveys are the only way to collect systematic data, and that empirical generalizations are somehow the ultimate goal of empirical research.

To review in brief what has been discussed earlier, survey research based on large samples can provide us with systematic data, if we are primarily concerned with 'product' rather than 'process' information, and if we view 'systematic' data exclusively in the form of answers to standardized questions. While objective statements about contacts of villagers in town ('product' information) can be readily obtained via standardized questions, using that approach to elicit information on remittances might prove much more difficult. Qualitative research techniques, in the form of semi-structured interviews and with the benefit of long-term residence in the field, will provide systematic data to the extent of making sure that all people involved understand the meaning of the questions, and only then are capable of producing systematic data.

While many migration researchers who persist with a survey approach involving a large sample are quite content with establishing statistical associations to generalize to other populations across time and space, others regard the understanding of the underlying structure and dimensions of mobility patterns as their primary scientific task. The latter's concern is less with empirical generalizations of their data, and more with conceptual and theoretical extrapolations, with uncovering generic forms of population mobility for example, which can vary in empirical content. Mitchell (1983) addresses this issue of inference and extrapolation from case studies. Discussing the validity of inferences with regard to quantitative procedures, he criticizes the tendency:

> '...to elide logical inferences with the logic of statistical inference: that the postulated *logical* connection among features in a sample may be assumed to exist in some parent population simply because the features may be inferred to "coexist" in that population' (p.200).

If we discover a relationship between two phenomena, or characteristics or variables in our sample, Mitchell continues, our inference to a parent population is:

> '...simply about the concomitant variation of two characteristics. The analysis must go beyond the sample and resort to theoretical thinking to link those characteristics together' (p.198)

The obvious implications concerning our discussion about the validity of extrapolating from one case study to other situations is that our:

> '...inference about the 'logical' relationship between two characteristics is not based upon the representatives of the sample and therefore upon its typicality, but rather upon the plausibility or upon the logicality of the nexus between the two characteristics' (p.198).

To ignore or outrightly dismiss potential analytical contributions based on a case study such as the one discussed in this paper, solely on grounds that what actually happens on two specific islands does not precisely reflect what goes on in other places in Vanuatu, elsewhere in Melanesia or in the Pacific Islands, sadly misses the point. Of course we could observe possible variations in the empirical 'content' of mobility, especially since we deal with people, different cultural systems and geographies. But if our analysis is 'right', within the context of a specific theoretical framework, we should expect to find the same 'form' regarding mobility. The obvious implication then, considering the analytical value of case studies as a basis for generalizations, is, to paraphrase Mitchell, that we have to move beyond fairly low levels of abstraction which somehow stress the uniqueness of a case, and place our analysis in a coherent theoretical framework. The geographic setting for our migration analysis then becomes less relevant and somehow loses the stereotypic label of 'a case'.

Notes

1. Mitchell emphasizes that his differentiation between setting and situation is essentially expediential and a matter of perspective rather than substance.

2. Specify the exact nature of the problem to be analyzed; the social and cultural context for this research to take place; the geographic setting.

3. See for example Bedford (1971, 1973, 1985); Bastin (1985); Bathgate (1975, 1985); Bonnemaison (1976, 1977); Chapman (1969, 1975, 1976); Connell (1985); Curtain (1980a, 1980b); Frazer (1981, 1985); Friesen (1983); Ryan (1985); Young (1977, 1985).

4. Bertaux (1981, p.33) regards such scientific contributions as not more than 'adding stones to the mythical monument (of one's discipline)'.

5. Defined here as discovery made through quantitative data. I am not in this context distinguishing between enumerative and analytical induction (see Mitchell, 1983).

6. I noted a widespread practice amongst rural residents of modifying 'traditional exchange patterns': rather than wait to acknowledge the receipt of urban remittances with a shipment of island food, as it has been a 'custom' since inter-island labour migration evolved in Vanuatu towards the end of last century, there is an increasing tendency of sporadically remitting food to town in order to deliberately instigate a 'customary' return flow of urban goods.

7. See, for example, Curtain (1980a, 1980b), Young (1977, 1985), Garnaut *et al.* (1977), Howlett (1980) for Papua New Guinea; Chapman (1970), Bathgate (1975), Frazer (1981) for the Solomon Islands; Bedford (1971, 1973), Tonkinson (1968), Bonnemaison (1976, 1977), Bastin (1985) for Vanuatu.

8. Most younger men interviewed in Vanuatu view 'jealousy' as the main reason for older men preventing them from planting cash crops, while older men give the impression of a more straightforward, although patronizing concern with securing enough land for subsistence food production, as the following quotations illustrate (Haberkorn, 1987):

   'They are too lazy to work hard themselves. They are jealous of us if we make money. We have plenty good ideas to make business with our land. But they don't give us our land' (31-year-old man).

   'You can see for yourself that we are too many people here. Now, if all young men want to plant their own coconuts, kava or pineapples to sell, where do they plant food? They only think about making money, so we have to block them so they have ground to plant food' (53-year-old man).

9. 'Stayers' are here defined as people who remain in their home areas out of their own free will. 'Non-migrants' instead remain at home because of external circumstances: no jobs available for them, or the decision not to migrate has been made for them by others, like fathers, chiefs, or other elders.

10. Being able to remain on their home island and running a business there involved for most of these people considerable migration in the past, in order to obtain the necessary starting capital (Haberkorn, 1987).

11. For theoretical elaborations see Glaser and Strauss (1967).

12. Gradual progression from hypothesis formulation, to data gathering and hypothesis-testing, to analysis, to conclusion and to report writing.

13. See, for example, Williamson *et al.* (1977) and Bailey (1978).

23

Social and Supernatural Control in a Mayan Demographic Regime

Philip Kreager

Historical Setting

For more than half a century anthropologists have been conducting field studies of the Mayan Indians, who live chiefly in upland areas of Guatemala and the Mexican state of Chiapas, and in the great hinterland of the Yucatan peninsula. Some four million Maya, speaking ten varieties of the Mayan language, comprise just over half the population of Guatemala, and one of the most important Indian groups in Mexico. The demographic implications of Mayan social organization are a major theme of their anthropological and related literatures; this is not surprising, as processes of population composition and decomposition are fundamental to the mystery which the Maya have presented in almost every period. Their archaeological puzzle is perhaps the best known (Coe, 1966). Contemporary Indians are direct descendants of a sophisticated classical civilization of the third to ninth centuries A.D., which appears to have been abandoned abruptly for unknown reasons. While a continuity may be traced in some major aspects of their cosmological and social organization down to the present day, the population movements that must have been a major consequence, if not cause, of the dispersal of such a large and complex social system remain a matter of speculation.

We would like to know more, too, about how Mayan culture and peoples withstood the demographic dislocations of the colonial period (Trens, 1957). Conquest introduced forced labour and movement of the population to areas permitting greater control. The best lands were taken over by Spanish colonists and remain to this day the territory of *Ladinos* (those of dominant, national, Spanish-speaking culture). The colonial period brought epidemic diseases which decimated most indigenous populations of the western hemisphere, and from which the Mayan recovered only in the nineteenth century. At that time a pattern of periodic migration and poorly paid labour in lowland *fincas* (plantations) was established, and remains an important feature of Indian and regional economy.

The economy and social structure of contemporary Indian communities have thus been shaped by four centuries of colonial and national domination. The Spanish policy of indirect rule has continued in the national period, and today in Chiapas and highland Guatemala, Indian elected officials form the lowest tier of the provincial administrative and judicial system. Local autonomy has enabled Indian communities to develop and maintain their own political and economic organization, centering upon a hierarchy of religious office. These hierarchies are the basis of an accommodation at once religious and economic. On the one hand, they are a fusion of indigenous cosmology, ritual, and belief with Catholicism. On the other, individual and collective improvement are defined in terms of personal advancement in a hierarchy, at least in the highland Chiapas communities with which this chapter is concerned.

The priority given to the internal religious and political economy has made Mayan society dependent upon the national economies, to the advantage of Ladinos. The small scale of individual Indian landholdings, together with the absence of administrative and economic organization higher than the local township level, have generally restricted their ability to compete successfully in regional and national markets. Basically, community economy is one of subsistence agriculture in which consistent short-falls in production, together with the capital needed to run the hierarchies, is made up by wage labour on Ladino *fincas*. The Mayans' wider role in the economy has remained predominantly that of a cheap supply of unskilled labour, and a growing market for certain consumer goods. Economic and political disadvantage have with time become synonymous with Indian cultural identity, and this has helped to sustain the prejudice, dating to early Spanish influence, that Indians are innately and racially inferior. Under the circumstances, it is not surprising that the long history of Maya-Ladino relations has been one of hostility and violence. Current conflict in Guatemala has important historical precedents (Bricker, 1981).

Diminishing Returns?

The broad implications of this history for an understanding of population processes in contemporary Mayan communities may be summarized in two observations. One is that it is difficult to know anything very precise about Indian population statistics. Labour migration, the isolation of many communities, the complexity of Mayan linguistic variation (including bilingualism), and the fact that the census is, after all, an agency of external, Ladino bureaucracy - all combine to limit the accuracy of the usual data sources. According to Early (1974), misclassification and underestimation of Indian populations in the Guatemalan census of 1964 was of the order of 17.4 per cent. No comparable reanalysis of the 1973 census has been carried out; the census scheduled for the early 1980s could not be completed in the Indian areas. The total Guatemalan population has been projected at 6,237,000 for 1976, and is expected to double by the end of the century (IPPF, n.d.). Sample surveys of two Indian areas in 1978 showed that women of a mean age between 30 and 34.5 had on average 4.6 to 5.7 pregnancies, with surviving children averaging 3.3 to 4.7 (Bertrand *et al.*, 1979).

The picture for highland Chiapas is even less complete. The 1979 Mexican National Prevalence Survey selected its Chiapas sites in such a way that the Mayan populations are scarcely represented. The last census to publish data on ethnicity (1960) was so arranged that no cross-tabulation with respect to particular Indian groups is possible, even for basic measures of marriage age or infant mortality. Province level returns are not yet available for the 1981 census. The results of the Prevalence Survey for the Southern Region (including the Yucatan as well as Chiapas and Oaxaca) give at least an indication which is consistent with ethnographic reports coming from the Mayan area (Manautou, 1982, pp.276–96). Most women marry young (74.3 per cent before age twenty), the marital fertility rate is 7.2, and contraceptive use is the lowest of any region. However, the area also records the most prolonged lactation, and consideration is also needed of the influence on fertility of ceremonial abstinence, divorce, nutritional deficiency, and absence of husbands due to labour migration. As the average figures for surviving children cited earlier suggest, however, the level of fertility is quite sufficient to sustain population growth.

The second consequence of the troubled history of the Maya may be traced in the current and precarious balance of their population and resources. The situation is in important respects similar to the process of 'involution' in Java described some years ago by Geertz (1963). As in Java, the labour pattern established in the colonial period encouraged population growth; the 'solution' to the competing requirements of plantation labour, their own subsistence, and their elaborate ceremonial system appears to have been to increase numbers and intensity of labour. Of course, *finca* labour is no longer forced, but the relative disadvantage of Mayans as peasants in the regional marketplace, and the considerable expense of their hierarchies, have been exploited by Ladino merchants and landowners, and produced a chronic indebtedness which has been called 'debt slavery' (Crump, 1976, p.154).

The crucial difference from the Javanese case is that the shifting or 'slash and burn' cultivation of maize is not as benign an agricultural system upon which to base population expansion as is rice cultivation. Confined by previous history to highland areas varying from 3,000 to 8,000 feet, the Mayans of Chiapas have with time and increased numbers exploited ever more marginal lands. Distressing conditions of deforestation, over-use, erosion and deterioration are described by several authors (Colby and van den Berghe, 1969; Collier, 1975; Smith, 1977). In effect, environmental limits and economic disadvantage appear to act as a syndrome, producing an ever greater reliance on external sources of income. For over 20 years townships such as Chamula and Zinacantan in Chiapas have derived of the order of 4/5 of their subsistence from income other than their traditional farmlands (Cancian, 1972). There is some evidence that those communities most dependent on selling their labour have come to have larger and more dense populations than the townships surrounding them (Collier, 1975; Crump, 1976).

The Mayan response to this situation can hardly be described as passive. They have participated actively in the general economic improvement in the region, epitomized by the gradually expanding network of roads. Indeed, the road network has been built in many areas with Indian labour, and has thus provided an important new source of income. There has been an expansion of opportunities for Indians to market their own maize; the land shortage has been countered to some extent in some townships by renting tracts of land in the lowlands, devoted largely to commercial production (Cancian, 1972). Mayan townships have formed co-operatives to buy their own lorries for commercial purposes, and there has also been an expansion of local Indian monopolies, of which the production and sale of bootleg alcohol is a considerable industry (Crump, 1976; Nash, 1970). Greater attention and power accrues to those families which serve as brokers between Indian communities and agencies of the Mexican government (Collier, 1975).

Crump (1976, pp.117-8) has called attention to the similarity of Indian credit and money systems to mercantilism, the commercial system of Europe in the sixteenth and seventeenth centuries. The township of Chamula maintains what are, in effect, two systems of circulating value, one open to trade with outside markets (the net imbalance of which works to their detriment) and an internal system of mutual indebtedness (which works to the benefit of the most successful local merchant families). It may be added that the Mayans appear to have essentially mercantilist attitudes to population, insofar as their livelihood and economic expansion are built on the backs of readily available manpower.

Finca labour in the course of over 100 years has given the Maya much experience of Ladino customs, and many Indians 'pass' for a time as Ladino by the expedient of adopting Ladino dress and speaking Spanish while away from their home communities. Those who choose to remain in Ladino society, however, are a small minority, while those who return to their highland villages see their earnings and knowledge of the Ladino world in terms accessory to Mayan language and culture. Becoming Ladino is disdained as such, and a common object of ridicule and humour; though this does not keep many individual traits and aspects of the material culture from being adopted. In sum, sustained contact and even intermingling of Indian and Ladino populations, rather than signalling an end to Mayan identity has become an aspect of a complex boundary mechanism defining the two groups (Bricker, 1973; Haviland, 1977; Colby, 1965; Siverts, 1969).

These general considerations help to clear away two stereotypes that might otherwise be projected upon Mayan communities. A simple trajectory of Indian modernization by exposure to western technology and values is rejected by most commentators: agricultural and medical technology, for instance, enter Indian communities via Ladino society, and must therefore be understood as an aspect of historical relations of these two peoples. Although the long history of Mayan disadvantage might suggest, in maximizing economic rationality, that the best individual course of action would be rapid assimilation to Ladino society, the material facts of environment, production and population consequent upon the historical relation of Maya and Ladino rule out any radical, across-the-board improvement in the standard of living of the mass of people. Even as Ladinos, the Maya would remain for the most part agricultural small-holders and substantially under-employed, at least in the forseeable future. The main effect of 'Ladino-ization' would very likely be a greatly increased migration to regional centres, and to Mexico City. The Maya have in this respect arguably shown greater realism in their ability to adapt while remaining Indian.

Historical relations based to a large degree on exploitation of Mayan labour make possible a second economic formula, a Marxist critique of economic development. In this view Indian population growth and the deterioration of their environment are secondary and historically predictable concomitants of class relations. The Mayans are trapped in a syndrome in which Ladino control of land, government, markets and relations of production ensure that wages remain low, opportunities for capital accumulation are limited, and population tends to increase, as more hands mean more wage income. The considerable expense of holding religious offices exacerbates poverty, and explains why Ladinos have tolerated a considerable degree of Indian self-government. Indian 'ethnic consciousness' and social organization are archaisms, lingering forms of colonial relation, which provide the Indians with alternate sources of satisfaction and power, without threatening Ladino dominance.

There is little disagreement over basic trends of advantage and disadvantage which characterize Ladino-Maya relations, or whether this political economy has historical analogues in Europe and elsewhere. Writers who forcefully argue the Marxist position, notably Stavenhagen (1975), and ethnographers who find in the Indian economy an independent development of mercantilism, notably Crump (1976), may both without difficulty refer to the Maya as a rural proletariat. The distinction made between 'class' and 'colonial' relationship, or between 'class' and 'ethnic consciousness' is, as Stavenhagen remarks, purely analytic; the analytical value being that it enables the description of class relations to be formulated (1975, p.211). Stavenhagen accepts that the Ladino and Maya are not simply social classes, as class relations 'are not yet totally formed because "colonial" relationships still determine the social structure at different levels' (p.205). The way in which Mayan identity and attitudes to Ladino society 'contribute to the concealment of objective relationships between classes' represents, in Stavenhagen's opinion, 'an interesting field of research' (p.206). If we wish to understand the Indian experience of history, and the criteria upon which their actions continue to be based, it is the processes underlying the maintenance of their identity we must study.

Thus, the contemporary puzzle which the Maya present is one of an historically conditioned pattern of adjustment via demographic and cultural means to wider economic and social forces, which in the last three decades has come, in the opinion of a number of researchers and theorists of differing persuasions, increasingly to suggest an application of the law of diminishing returns. The Maya are a classic case of a society that appears to be experiencing a mounting pressure of population upon resources, but which is inclined, precisely by the reasons of history which have produced the pressure, to resolve this problem by continuing a long-standing pattern of demographic expansion. Their long history of adjustment to radical displacements suggests not only that they are likely to be able to resolve current constraints, but that the means adopted will be in essential respects demographic, and will be designed to ensure the continuity of Mayan identity.

Reasons of space unfortunately confine this paper to consideration of a single Chiapan township, but more extended consideration of comparative issues raised in Mayan ethnography may be found elsewhere (Kreager, 1983).

Chanula Political Economy

Mayan townships in the Chiapas highlands, of which Chamula is both the most populous and the highest in altitude, consist of numerous dispersed settlements, each usually numbering less than 1,500 persons. Family organization is nuclear, and residence upon marriage is patrilocal. Families tend to be grouped in a settlement around successful office-holders or elders; this informal association comprises a patrilineage, which performs the main domestic, agricultural and life crisis rituals, and is the basic land-holding and working unit. The patrilineage, possibly together with some poorer unrelated families, forms the labour force and retinue which is the office holder's power base. Without children and a network of kin, little social and spiritual advancement is possible.

Children are considered to have a natural debt to their parents for the assistance and protection they receive when young. In the case of infants, this protection is in important respects spiritual, and may involve considerable ritual expenses. Later on, sons depend on parents and kin to help in the cost of the lengthy and expensive courtship which is, in effect, a bride-price paid in ritual and labour over the course of 2 or 3 years. Considerable importance is attached to inheriting land, and access may be delayed as long as parents find possible. The importance of owning land does not appear to be linked to particular pieces of property, as fields may be alienated and, in any case, are likely to provide only 2 to 3 months of an average family's annual needs. A large family does not imply a hardship, since labour outside the community on lowland *fincas*, for Indians of other townships, and in construction and related jobs, is a primary support of group economy.

Settlements are related to each other by co-participation in a hierarchy of religious and civil offices. The chief responsibility of the religious hierarchy is to perform the ritual which sustains the goodwill of the gods and saints, and determines individual and collective destiny. Its activities focus on a ritual calendar of some thirty saints days and fiestas. The hierarchy consists of four levels, the two highest having six offices, the lower levels having more positions. Although the hierarchy is unified throughout Chamula, each of the three *barrios* in the township maintains its own full set of offices, so that the total number is nearly 150. Most offices are held for one year, and those of the upper two tiers are full-time positions. Each office holder must finance his own contribution, which may on occasion entail providing food and drink for one hundred or more persons. Since holding office means, in addition to these considerable costs, that a man takes himself away from his own affairs to a large extent, the aspiration to serve the community in this way requires preparation and financial backing. The cost of the highest offices is in the range of 20 to 55 thousand pesos (1,600 to 4,400 U.S. dollars, *circa* 1970), in an economy in which an average individual's income is in the hundreds of pesos (Linn, 1977, p.58). The great value attached to the offices and the nature of the planning they require is indicated by the waiting list for higher positions, for which office holders are appointed some 15 years in advance. They are the most prestigious community service, as they sustain Chamula spiritual identity and reputation.

The expense of the rituals and related festivities in food, drink, fireworks, costume and the like, involves the office holder in a complex set of financial and social obligations, binding people to him as well as himself to others. The successful holder of high office uses it to establish his own reputation as a man of great 'heat' by visibly building himself a following. There are a variety of paths through the hierarchy, which confer correspondingly different prestige. Members of larger, propertied kin groups may hold offices at varying levels in the course of their lives, depending on the availability of offices and finance. The highest offices tend to rotate amongst a few very wealthy men, who tend to monopolize both the higher reaches of the religious hierarchy and to appoint themselves and their allies to the parallel set of civil offices which, while less prestigious, carry advantages in dealing with the Mexican authorities.

As Crump remarks (1976, pp.126-205) the hierarchy is effectively a bureacratic and corporate body. The corporate character of the hierarchy is evident in the complex credit system necessary to finance office at each level. Less expensive offices may consume the better part of a man's annual income; the office holder relies on his family's crops and *finca* labour, together with what he can borrow from an extended kin network which includes members of his patriline, affines and *compadres* (his own or his children's godparents). Of course he undertakes office knowing that previous office holders in this network are already indebted to him; in effect, he spends half his year in office calling in the credit he has established in the past, and the second half accumulating new debts that he will, in turn, have to pay off. However, where financial need outstrips this rotating system, the holder is likely to borrow from wealthier Chamula, possibly mortgaging his land in the process at high rates of interest. Credit is a critical underpinning to a man's following, insofar as it is often politic for the creditor not to call in a debt, but to maintain the debtor's sense of obligation.

The higher offices require more income than can be generated by a system of rotating credit alone. These offices tend to go to wealthier Chamula, whose accumulated credit over time has cast them in the role of local bankers. Their returns have been invested in various enterprises, including land, lorries, shops, and - most important - in the monopoly production of bootleg liquor (referred to locally as *pox*), necessary for all ritual. Distilling, transport, commercial agriculture and shopkeeping involve their own expenses, and require purchases from Ladinos which remove capital from the community. The greatest part of income is likely to be expended on ritual. The system as a whole is an expensive one, and Crump has argued that the oligarchy depends for its continuing cash surplus on its banking activities, which rest in turn on the income from *finca* labour generated by the mass of poorer Chamula (Crump, 1976, p.236).

In sum, the performance of ritual, the grounds of personal identity, and decision-making entail three material elements: a credit system that keeps members locked into the hierarchy at all levels; a surplus generated by labour outside the community; and a centralized administrative structure. These rest, in turn, on the way in which young people are recruited into the system of religious politics, in virtue of their obligations by socialization, marriage, and labour in local descent groups.

The argument to this point suggests that the Chamula could well be modelled as an example of a 'rationality of high fertility', in which political and domestic economy, and norms of elder and parental authority, are principal supports. Such a 'model rationality' remains, of course, a reflection of demographers' interests, since it singles out fertility as the central variable. The Chamula, however, have constructd a system in which the primary issue of conscious control over human numbers refers to access to office, or relative position and opportunity in a hierarchy. If we wish to understand the significance of changes in fertility in Chamula, then fertility must first be understood as a function of aggregate priorities and properties of Chamula institutions. Two sets of measures would clarify this matter: household demography, including the arrangement of labour migration; and the demography of the office system. Neither set of measures can be modelled without reference to institutional recruitment at levels higher than the domestic group.

The aggregate properties of the hierarchy of offices may be expected to comprise a distinctive formal demography, which would give evidence of trends in social organization, and of fundamental properties of Chamula social structure. The parameters of this system would have to be decided by the nature of the data, but may be expected to include measures of: the age structure of office holders; durations in and out of office; the changing number of incomplete careers; the changing lengths of the waiting lists; characteristics of the holders of respective offices; the tendency to move upward or downward in the relative prestige of offices held; the relations between careers in the civil and religious lists; the relation of office to mortality, age at marriage, divorce, numbers of offspring; the changing distribution of offices between different local descent groups; and so forth. The waiting lists (were access available to them) would provide an interesting source of recent local history, not only as a numerical record of the offices, but as a document in which the continuous revision of social position is actually carried out. Such data would lend themselves to comparison of the religious and economic organizations of different Mayan communities, and would be especially useful regarding differences of anthropological opinion.

Four related problems call for measures of a more familiar kind, all of which pertain to households and patrilineages. One is the study of domestic group formation, which would address differentials in the followings of particular officeholders, such as: numbers of sons and daughters; their ages at marriage; inheritance and purchase of property and the units within which labour and capital are shared. Studies of neighbouring Mayan townships suggest that particular attention might well be given to the problem of divorce, since female labour and the continuity of marriage are critical to office, and are often precariously balanced, given patterns of domestic quarrels (Collier, 1974). A study of proximate determinants of fertility would be useful, distinguishing the relative influence of breastfeeding, young age at marriage, infant mortality and foetal loss, divorce and separation, and the patterns of sexual abstinence required of office holders or consequent upon absence due to labour migration. A good study of the migration and work patterns of Chamulas is needed. Cancian (1972) developed a number of parameters in his study of Zinacanteco labourers and farmers who work outside of their own township, including, for example, the size and age composition of work groups, travel time and transport costs, wages and work locations, and moves per farmer.

Fertility, Heat and Cold

A set of institutions and measures, such as just described, effectively outlines a society's population structure, seen as the recruitment component of social structure. In the case of Chamula, at least, this approach has already taken us much further in understanding community life than would a set of standard variables. The strategies described to this point, however, such as competitive advancement to office, the husbanding of limited resources in land, and the deployment of youthful manpower, are all idealized and schematic. They may tend to reduce Chamula to a local application of laws of supply and demand. Indeed, they could still perhaps suggest some single-minded strategy of maximizing utility. They may also, insofar as Chamula is typed a 'traditional' society, suggest a kind of 'steady-state' system, prior to 'development', 'transition', and the like.

We remain substantively outside of a society as long as we accept any of these stereotypes. As it turns out, both of the extreme positions have been dealt with already for the highlands of Chiapas. Cancain uses his study of Indian agriculture to develop a critique of maximization (1972, pp.189-99); the strategies he describes resemble the idea of 'satisficing' recently put forward as a general framework by McNicoll (1980a). Crump, in his analysis of Chamula credit systems, is adamant that the Chamula do not see their economy as static, especially in its relation to opportunities in the surrounding Mexican economy (1976, pp.167-8).

The reduction to supply and demand is more difficult to counter, however, than the hypotheses of perfect utility and torpor; the translation of cultures is always vulnerable to the naive assumption that, because western common sense applies in part, it will suffice to represent the whole. Competition, debt and credit, self-serving oligarchic power - these are, surely, powerful motivating forces in Chamula. They account for many of the very real differences in Chamula society, but with the effect of making other essential differences seem, frankly, bizarre. Why, for example, do the Chamula go to great lengths to maintain even small local land holdings, when these lands produce a relatively minor part of their income? Why, given that a larger income, upon which they are already dependent, is consistently available outside the township, do they with only occasional exception always return to Chamula? Why do men accumulate debts on such a grand scale, when it is clear that the highest positions are effectively confined to a minority? It may be noted that an account of local political economy can proceed quite far, without ever inquiring into the purposes that ritual - upon which the greatest time, effort, and income are expended - actually accomplishes for the Chamula. The facts of life may be ancillary to an economic *quid pro quo*, but does this get to the root of, for example, the implications of being male or female in Chamula society? The study of recruitment and political economy gives, in short, a pattern of local incentives and disincentives, but it does not tell why people are willing to live with them, and what changes they are willing and able to make.

A model of local institutions and recruitment cannot, therefore, stand in lieu of inquiry into peoples' value structures. Both are needed for the former is subject to two sorts of imbalance. First, emphasis on the rigour implied by a given political economy causes analysis to miss the elasticity with which societies ordinarily function. Second, institutions are ordered by value no less than their aggregate propensities of wealth and reproduction. Local religious and political organization co-exists, in some instances uneasily, with the economic differentials to which the system gives rise, but remains the conventional frame of reference in which decisions are made. Gossen's study (1974) of the cosmological basis of this framework, and the order which it gives to daily life in Chamula, is corroborated by studies in Zinacantan and elsewhere, and provides the natural starting point for any discussion of the structure and value of the facts of life in these communities.

The medical anthropology of rural communities in Latin America abounds with reference to a classificatory principle distinguishing hot and cold states of being (Adams and Rubel, 1967; Wisdom, 1952; Logan, 1977). It is uncertain whether the principle was derived chiefly from sixteenth-century humoral pathology introduced by the Spanish, or indigenous belief, but by now it is characteristic of both Indian and Ladino populations, albeit in differing forms. The principle may be described roundly for Chamula and many Indian communities as follows. Every person is born with an innate balance of hot and cold propensities. 'Hotter' people tend to be stronger and more capable, while for 'colder' persons the reverse is true. The primary issue is usually one of obtaining the proper balance of these propensities, relative to persons, objectives and conditions in question. Not only persons, but time, space, diet, parts of the human body, medicine, speech and sacred substances (incense, rum, candles, tobacco, etc.) are described in this idiom. Evidently 'heat' and 'cold' do not refer simply to physical temperature; the balance described is an admixture of moral and spiritual states.

Improper behaviour, divine displeasure, and the ill-will of others (notably, witchcraft) are interpreted as the cause or possibly as the result of imbalance, or excess heat or cold. Cumulative social and economic success or failure thus carry potentially wider and deeper implications. The toll this takes on the individual, physically and psychologically, is recognized by the Chamula: the characteristic manifestation of imbalance is illness, expressed variously as 'punishment', 'sadness of heart', 'soul loss', and 'death'. This helps to explain why ritual is so essential, and why it is a part of every important undertaking. It is necessary to petition the ancestral gods and saints to keep vital force in harmony, to support collective activities of the township, to obtain forgiveness for moral failings, to uncover witchcraft, and so forth.

Gossen (1975) cites four general implications of this principle, at least as applied to decision-making in Chamula. First, it may be taken as given that not everyone is equal, and that differences are an aspect of divine intention. This applies not only to an individual's power to do good, but also, evil. Second, individuals are not altogether in control of their own nature. Indeed, from birth they are faced with the interesting question of identifying what that nature is.

The third feature of this principle is that it is applied as a kind of continuing *a posteriori* diagnosis: the proof of each person's own balance is the level he or she has attained of personal happiness, health and success in life. Economic development, good health, advancement to high office, all serve as effective signs of grace; the course of events for better or worse reveals one's innate vital force. Finally, while the idiom of heat and accompanying soul concepts enjoins an active role for the individual in discovering, carrying out and continually checking his or her spiritual and social place, there is no escape from the destiny implied by one's innate balance. Life consists of coping with the inevitable. The idiom is used as a secondary rationalization of good and bad fortune, and thus not only describes but justifies differences between people and the institutions of the social order which perpetuate these differences.

The principle of heat contains in outline a traditional theory of the nature and sources of vitality, both individual and collective. Mayan communities, not only in Chiapas, identify sterility and other procreative problems with abnormal states of coldness, and fertility (entailing fecund capacity and its manifestations) with an appropriate level of heat (e.g. Guiteras Holmes, 1969; Paul, 1971; Logan, 1973; Cosminsky, 1976). Conception requires the right proportion of heat, but childbirth, as a period of intense danger, is pervaded by cold. The development of these ideas, or rather, the system of which Mayan ideas about fertility and sterility are a part, may be illustrated by the role of the myth of Creation in Chamula.

The life and attributes of Christ have been assimilated to the Sun or High God, according with pre-Colombian Mayan cosmology. Images of heat, life and life-giving pervade all aspects of community and domestic activity, in essentially the same way that Christ's intervention (via the mediation of saints) pervades potentially every detail of life in a Christian community. The Chamula, however, have their own system of interpreting divine and saintly action. The Sun ('Our Father Heat') was born of the cold moon.

> 'Day and night, the yearly agricultural and religious cycles, the seasons, the divisions of the day, most plants and animals, the stars, and the constellations all are the work of the creator, the life-force itself. Only demons, monkeys, and Jews preceded and were hostile to the coming of order. These forces killed the sun early in the First Creation and forced him to ascend into the heavens, where he provided heat, light, life and order' (Gossen, 1974, pp.30-1).

The general movement from cold to heat and life contained in the myth is reflected in the human life cycle. In the course of life each person acquires more and more heat, the hottest period coming a little before death. Prayer and ritual assist the control and application of vital heat to best effect by enlisting saintly or other supernatural support.

The mapping of the notion of heat and the possibilities of its control onto the life cycle gives it explanatory properties in the manner of an age and sex structure. These appear in three aspects: seniority, male priority and, as already remarked, social aetiology.

Length of life is determined by the size of the heavenly candle that the Sun-Christ lights upon each person's birth. The respect and power which accrue to senior men in a community is due in part to their age or accumulated heat. Generally, holders of the highest religious offices are older men, but not all old men accede or aspire to them, and there are many different paths through the hierarchy. Different life histories are seen by members of the community as evidence confirming relative social and spiritual position, or the inherent vital force, of different men. Life history also reflects the extent to which men are able to carry out Chamula family and reproductive strategies; in short, a man relies on his wife and children for labour and for connections (via baptism, marriage, and office) which create obligations among a wider group of kin, and which may perhaps be turned to advantage. Sterility strikes at the basis of all efforts to prove the greatness of one's heat - social, economic, and spiritual - and is thus appropriately represented by the Chamula as excessive coldness.

According to the myth of creation, the Sun was born of the Moon, as Christ was born of Mary. Their subsequent relationship however, is very different from the Christian account. The clever Sun blinded his mother shortly after his birth, and the Moon has since then followed behind him, providing him with meals, and providing humans with relatively less heat, light, and other gifts. As Gossen remarks, 'her relationship to her son is like that of the female principle to the male principle in Chamula life: submissive within a wider sphere of economic interdependence' (1974, p.40). Coldness, lowness and femininity are opposed generally to heat, masculinity and altitude. As the Sun and Moon traverse the sky they mark out the basic categories of space and time which describe Chamula orientation to the outside world. As the highest Indian township, the one closest to the Sun, and the 'navel of the earth', Chamula is considered to be spiritually the most vital place in the world. As one gets further and further away from Chamula centre, danger increases and access to the gods and saints (and to the *shamans* who assist laymen in praying to them) decreases.

A Frame of Vital Reference

The frame of vital reference in Chamula may be summarized schematically as the application of the diagnostic device of relative heat and cold (and attendant soul concepts) to the elements of birth, age, sex, parentage, marriage, group affiliation, death, and movement. These elements become a spatial and temporal grid in which the meaning, force, right and wrong of any course of action or events may be located. In the course of history this framework has evolved into a particular set of vital limits and alternatives. Following Douglas (1966), we can recognize certain elements as marking the 'external boundaries' of Chamula society, and others which specify 'internal lines' along which social tensions tend to be organized and resolved. A set of vital limits are characterized and maintained as much by the selective ways in which they are broken or redressed, as by strict adherence. As Douglas remarks:

> '...we enter the sphere which lies between that behaviour which an individual approves for himself and what he aproves for others: between what he approves as a matter of principle and what he vehemently desires for himself here and now in contradiction of the principle; between what he approves in the long term and what he approves in the short term. In all this there is scope for discrepancy' (p.130).

Description of Chamula institutions has shown that the primacy of heat, seniority and male principles is repeated and elaborated extensively in mutually supporting domestic, religious, political, and economic fields of activity. The pressure to conform implied by this redoubling of supernatural, moral and economic values leads to well-defined roles or types of behaviour expected of men, women, wives, sons, office holders, debtors, witches, penitents, and so forth. The impression might well be created that Mayan townships like Chamula are rigorous, efficient, puritanical little organisms.

Such an impression should, however, be dispelled by the four properties of decision-making, outlined earlier. The Chamula do not see themselves as controlling their own daily lives very well, and the possibilities for social and material misfortune are manifest to them in the chequered careers of their fellows. The great quantity of ritual performed by Chamulas and the complexity of their aetiology of soul concepts, are some index of the importance of right conduct and of its difficulty owing to weakness, error, or the malevolence of others. While the true nature of one's actions may only be known after the fact, and the precise nature of illness is subject to interpretation, the boundaries of acceptable behaviour - of being a Chamula - coincide explicitly with the limits of life.

All serious morbidity is attributable to witchcraft. When a *shaman* is called in to divine the cause of illness he may describe, upon examining the sufferer, how a witch has sold his soul to the Earth Lord, how his animal soul has wandered away from its safe 'corral' or been attacked by that of stronger person/animal spirit, or how some particular part of the soul has been lost. If the causes of death are sought, they will be extensions of these explanations: no one dies a natural death but that someone else or some intended agency is responsible. If, on the other hand, we consider the beginning of life, the same principles apply. Conception cannot occur, nor pregnancy take its natural course, if norms are not followed, especially performance of the right ritual. Witches have the power to take the foetus from the womb, to transfer it to the wombs of other women, to cause miscarriage and premature births, and so forth. It is accepted that the wealthy who do not perform their social obligations are a legitimate object of witchcraft. A reputation for malevolent witchcraft or murder may make it necessary for individuals to flee the community to save their own lives. Socially defined sterility, death, and departure thus define the limits of behaviour in Chamula.

As Gossen has shown, Chamula is in essence a spiritual home, radically contrasted to lowland Ladino territory (associated with demons) and Ladino behaviour (likened to animals). Death occurs when the soul wanders off or is spirited away; labour migration is confined to the highlands or adjacent lowland areas, never too far from Chamula centre. Permanent departure is the exception, and such persons do not pose a threat to the system insofar as they effectively define themselves out of it. There is some reason to think, however, that this process may be an important and recurring demographic mechanism.

> 'Chamulas, in a small but steady stream, are always finding ways to opt out of the whole *municipio* system. A home in one of the various Chamula *colonias* outside the *municipio*, or a permanent position on a *finca* achieve just this result' (Crump, 1976, p.214).

The pattern of Chamula movement to new settlements, either on lands provided by government schemes, or on lands they have effectively seized from neighbouring townships has existed since the 1930s. It is not unknown for Chamulas to leave, permanently or temporarily, when faced with appointment to office, and some flee in the middle of their terms, leaving a tangle of debts and responsibilities for their families and *compadres* to sort out (Linn, 1977, p.64). Chamulas may marry into other Indian communities, or adopt neighbouring Indian identities. The numbers involved in each of these options appear to be relatively small, and residence outside the township, whether short or long term, does not prevent many Chamulas from returning to participate in the hierarchy. As in other highland communities, there is little evidence that work on the *fincas* leads directly to adoption of Ladino identity; Indians take up Ladino technology, dress or methods piecemeal, as it suits them, without wishing to become Ladinos as such.

The forces pushing Chamulas out of their township may reflect the pressure of numbers, but they are the direct result of internal differences and the sanctions that enforce them. Economic and spiritual dimensions are inextricable, for example, in the action of a man who forecloses on a debt in order to obtain a piece of land, such action being evidence of his greater heat. Foreclosure may have ramifications, in turn, on the power relations of local descent groups, and on their internal dissensions, as the land foreclosed may, for example, have been a pawn in a son's expected inheritance, already committed in marriage negotiations with another descent group. The 'internal lines' of force along which differences of heat and wealth are made manifest, are articulated by the major life events and relations which they positively or adversely influence: nuptiality; entry to office; seniority in a descent group, settlement, or *barrio*; divorce; and the maintenance of all of the obligations of kinship, marriage, and godparenthood necessary to any political, economic and ritual undertaking. The man of strong, proven vital force will have to hand the necessary cash or credit to pay for rituals, including both those needed in defence or cure of witchcraft, and those that are a responsibility of office.

Well-performed ritual is itself a manifestation of heat, and a means to guarantee individual and collective well-being: it converts wealth to community service of the saints and spirits. The form and language of ritual reiterates the frame of vital reference; as Linn shows, people's relation to the saints is expressed in a family idiom (1977, pp.521-62), and also repeats the themes of debt and credit (1977, pp.417-31). Ritual is underwritten by rules of sexual abstinence, and by gossip and festivities which seize upon the sexual and other transgressions of office holders (Bricker, 1973). Indian court procedure, as described in Collier's study of Zinacantan (1973), also entails a highly ritualized play upon moral and spiritual transgressions, the cases of which are predominantly marital problems, disrupted bride-price and courtship, and property disputes amongst kin. In marital conflicts, for example, wives typically petition the courts to reprimand their husbands and to obtain redress for wrongdoings. Husbands usually are shamed readily into making concessions: misbehaviour reflects upon their reputation, remarriage is expensive, and divorce may strike at the basis of the complex network of obligations a man has established over a long period. It is shameful for a man not to have a woman to cook and care for him, and here again the bounds of identity coincide with vital limits: a man with a mother, an adult daughter, or daughter-in-law may manage without a wife, but otherwise a man who cannot persuade a woman to marry must leave the community (Collier, 1973, p.199).

Continuity in Change

In this chapter I have tried to show how conventional ethnographic and historical sources can answer a fundamental and longstanding problem in population studies, namely, the deployment of local populations according to the logic of their own purposes. While detailed micro-studies are the essence of these sources, it is clear that the study of recruitment and identity addresses institutions and strategies likely to be relevant at national and regional levels, over long periods of time. It may be wondered whether the label 'micro-studies' is sufficient to an approach which effectively dissolves the hiatus of macro- and micro-levels, in favour of the comparative study of social institutions.

Chamula township gives evidence of many features described elsewhere of populous, economically underdeveloped, rural areas: a shortage of land; steady population growth; stratification, exploitation and impoverishment; moral sanctions linked to differences in age and sex, and backed up by gossip, religion, and status; and so forth. The Chamula are aware of all of this, but the distinctive institutions and values in which these facts are manifest to them, and the behaviour Chamulas consider appropriate in response, could not be anticipated on the basis of any existing general theory of social or political economy. Chamula society may be said to rest on their interpretations of four population elements: morbidity, or their 'theory' of vital energy; recruitment to key roles in the social structure, or the demography of religious office; family and kinship, organized as local descent groups in support of office holders' vital energy; and migration and temporary employment outside the township, which perpetuates the economic and cultural differences and interdependence of Indian and Ladino populations. These four points comprise a demographic regime which translates social and economic structures in terms of local evaluations of basic life events and recruitment processes. Basically, analysis proceeds by considering how institutions of hierarchy, family and movement are deployed to sustain, and where necessary adjust and revise, the vital principles which are the core of Chamula identity. It then becomes possible to inquire into the implications for local population processes of variables favoured in other approaches - differential accumulation of wealth, proximate determinants of fertility, relations between generations - without denying the primary relevance of Indian experience and institutions.

Put another way, the regime traces distributions of conscious choice in a social system, without restricting choice to demographic preconception, and while enabling us to retain the essential fact that the members of the society have a restricted vision of the aggregate implications of their choices. It is very important to remember that the regime is, as with any model, a tremendous simplification and codification. The resulting picture, however, is neither static nor patronizing. The study of population composition and decomposition, as an aspect of the historical identity of groups, enables us to get at the elasticity of social structures inherent in the diversity of responses of which they are capable to any given problem.

For example, probably the greatest material threat to the Chamula regime as it stands would be a severe reduction in the need for labour in the Chiapas economy. Displacement of this source of subsistence and capital would have repercussions at each of the other points in the regime. A number of lines of action in response to such a problem are listed in Table 23.1.

With the exception of the last point in the Table, all of the options listed are indicated because they may be found at work already in Chamula. Wasserstrom (1978), for instance, argues that exploitation of marginal lands has greatly increased in recent decades. Crump, in addition to his discussion of land transactions and foreclosure (1976, pp.153-4, 179, 214), remarks on the growing advantages of civil office to members of the oligarchy (p.223), and several patterns of economic diversification

Table 23.1 Responses to Reduction in Demand for Labour: Some Chamula Alternatives

MIGRATION

- search for employment in more distant areas;
- agree to move to more distant colony schemes promoted by the government;
- rent lands outside the township, and farm them commercially.

LOCAL DESCENT GROUPS

- farm their own lands more intensively, and bring even more marginal lands into production;
- sell their land; acquire more local land by rent or purchase;
- give more attention to the allocation of land by inheritance; become involved in more court cases and land disputes;
- delay marriage; reduce the cost of courtship;
- diversify economic activities (e.g. commercial agriculture, crafts, trading in other Chiapas townships).

RECRUITMENT TO OFFICE

- renegotiate or foreclose on debts;
- reduce the cost of more expensive religious offices;
- attach greater importance to civil offices, using them to negotiate government assistance.

SOCIAL AND SUPERNATURAL CONTROL

- intensify use of *shamans*, who discover increasing amounts of serious witchcraft;
- increase sanctioned violence with respect to apparently asocial uses of wealth and power;
- emphasize certain avenues of supernatural assistance, while devaluing others;
- accept that religious and ritual practice permit wider movement outside the township in search of employment;
- accept a greater Ladino presence in Chamula.

(pp.174-89), including the renting of fields for commercial purposes outside the township (p.225). Colonization is noted by Collier (1975, pp.160-1), who argues that as land becomes scarce and subject to dispute, local descent groups become more important as means of retaining control over property. The expansion of road networks has already increased the scope of Chamula movement. Recourse to the courts, cheaper marriage and office arrangements, and the selection of saints and spirits appropriate to a given problem, have always been options in the system. In addition to the remarkable figures for homicide cited by Favre (1964), both Crump (1976, pp.252-3) and Linn (1977, pp.34-5) give examples of recent violence.

Evidently the response of a complex society to changes of potentially structural significance will be manifold. Interest attaches to the ways in which the several points (or, more likely, some selection of them) are connected, since these series begin to look like alternative strategies encompassed by the demographic regime. The four points of the demographic regime comprise a framework for the study of concomitant variation, within which change in Chamula may be compared to that of Mayan townships having related institutions, elsewhere in Mexico and Guatemala.

Acknowledgements

I thank Thomas Crump and Priscilla Rachun Linn for permission to cite their unpublished doctoral theses. This chapter was written with the assistance of the Population Council's International Research Awards Program on the Determinants of Fertility; the Program is supported by USAID.

24

THE SOCIAL, ECONOMIC AND CULTURAL CONTEXT OF WOMEN'S HEALTH AND FERTILITY IN RURAL NORTH YEMEN

Cynthia Myntti

'...The profound human reality is a synthesis of biological function, cultural definitions and rules, and social action'.

Carol MacCormack (1982)

Introduction

Recent work by Bongaarts (1978) provided a powerful analytical framework for understanding how fertility levels are reached and how they change. He isolated what he calls 'proximate determinants' or behavioural and biological factors through which socioeconomic and other variables affect fertility. One of these proximate determinants, contraceptive use, is the subject of this chapter.

The main part of the chapter provides evidence as to why rural Yemeni women might make the decision to contracept. It suggests that the decision to control their fertility is the result of a complex array of socioeconomic and cultural factors, only understood by in-depth research into the world in which these women live - their social values and institutions, a rural economy which demands their labour, and a conceptual or cultural order which strictly delimits good from bad, pure from impure and healthy from harmful.

Even in one small community in rural Yemen, women are not an indifferentiated group, for they have not only different personalities and experience but also come from contrasting social strata. One can therefore talk about all Yemeni women only with utmost caution. Furthermore it is almost impossible to make meaningful statements about 'Middle Eastern women'. When it comes to fertility behaviour, it is more important to understand why the differences exist among women in the Middle East than to fall into the powerful - and usually incorrect - stereotypes about Middle Eastern women.

The final section of the chapter considers women's perceptions of specific contraceptive methods. It tries to answer the question, if women do in fact have stated reasons for limiting their fertility, why is contraceptive prevalence so low? The answer is not the usual one - that women are ignorant of contraceptive methods or that services are not available.

Data presented here are drawn from anthropological fieldwork conducted in 1977-1979 in a rural community in the Yemen Arab Republic, or as it is commonly called, North Yemen.

Findings of the research are presented, rather than an exposition of the research method. Participant observation generated qualitative data on the community which was supplemented by a demographic survey of all ever-married women in the village (see Myntti, 1979) and systematic interviews with doctors and patients at the nearest hospital.

The chapter is further limited in its scope, concentrating on first-hand observations of Yemeni women, and drawing on unpublished and published sources on other Middle Eastern women. To this extent, it ignores rich comparative material such as that presented in Carol MacCormack's (1982) *Ethnography of Fertility and Birth* and the WHO-sponsored study on menstruation (Snowden and Christian, 1983). Moreover, it ignores the theoretical contributions of symbolic anthropology on the subject of the body. While their writings have not been quoted directly, the works of Douglas (1966), Loudon (1977) and Skultans (1970) have been influential in the present study.

The Ethnographic Context of Reproductive Health and Fertility

North Yemen usually catches people by surprise. It does not fit the mind's eye view of the Arabian Peninsular with barren emptiness and flatness broken only by sand dunes. According to Yemenis and historians of antiquity, Yemen was the home of the Queen of Sheba who ruled over a State with an economy based on irrigated agriculture. Indeed the Romans called Yemen *Arabia Felix*, happy and prosperous from agricultural production in lush green valleys and carefully worked mountain terraces. Until today, produce includes a wide range of cereals, vegetables, fruits and the famous Mokha coffee, named after the Yemeni port from which it was exported.

North Yemen, with a population estimated at just over 5.3 million in 1975, is predominantly rural. Approximately 85 per cent of all Yemenis live in small villages and derive their livelihood from agriculture as owners and cultivators of rainfed plots. In recent years the phenomenon of labour migration of adult males to the adjacent wealthy oil-producing countries has influenced significantly both national and household economies. In the poorly endowed areas of the countryside, farmers cannot produce cash crops and instead cultivate drought-resistant sorghum and millet on rainfed lands. In such areas remittances from migration appear to be subsidizing agriculture. That is, only families who have a steady inflow of cash can afford key agricultural inputs like ploughing.

The community studied is situated in a poorly endowed agricultural zone, with agricultural production and labour migration the basis of the domestic economy. Here, as elsewhere in Yemen, the household is the main unit of production and consumption. The normative household is structurally the partrilineally extended family of three generations (grandparents, married sons, their wives and children). However, at any point in time, one finds a variety of living arrangements in the community. Indeed, the most useful way to understand the 'household' as an economic and social unit is to view it passing through time; children age, marry, sons bring wives, some segment into their own households, and eventually the senior generation passes on. By viewing the household in a developmental cycle, it is clear that the availability of labour for agriculture varies through time. Labour availability depends not only on the sex and age composition of the household, but the vagaries of health and illness which affect each member's physical capacity to work.

Agricultural production in Yemen has always functioned on division of labour based on sex and age. The youngest and oldest household members perform the lightest tasks such as sowing and weeding. Men have major responsibility for ploughing and threshing for short periods in the spring and autumn. Women, particularly those aged 15 to 45, have the major role in agricultural production, working long hours over the entire year. Their tasks include land preparation in winter, collecting and applying manure, sowing, thinning weeding, harvesting, assistance with threshing, cleaning, storing and finally milling. With the exception of milling, none of these tasks is mechanized. And even the mill is a recent addition; previously women ground all grains by hand on circular stone mills.

Children are also vital in the traditional work equation. They help with sowing and weeding. In the winter, girls help with land preparation by beating the hard soils into smaller clods. Older children help run the household while women are at work in the fields. Sons take donkeys with water tins to the well to procure domestic water needs. Daughters perform a wide range of tasks, from caring for younger siblings, to cleaning, washing clothes and cooking. Until recently, teenaged daughters also collected fuel wood, an extremely arduous task.

The fundamental economic ratio is labour to land. In much of Yemen the land tenure situation is fluid, with many households both owning, renting in and renting out lands through time. For example, a household with excess labour might take lands in on a rental basis. A household with labour shortage might either rent lands out, or hire day workers at peak periods. The latter option, of course, demands the ability to pay the cash wages now demanded by the rural labour force.

In other cases, land and labour are in good balance, and household members themselves are physically fit and in optimal working condition. Households may even find themselves in the enviable position of excess labour to land through the good fortune of sons marrying strong, fertile women. In these circumstances, women are likely to help others in similar household situations during the peak work periods; extra-household reciprocal labour is particularly common during the periods of planting, weeding and harvesting. Women take turns on each other's lands, working as a group. However, only those who are in a position to give labour are able to take labour.

Some households are not so fortunate. They require labour but are not in a position to reciprocate. This often happens to smaller households, particularly nuclear ones where a women has only very small children, or in larger households with either sickly or pregnant women. Such a situation is disastrous if the family has limited cash resources because it cannot then even hire labour.

In any case a few men can keep the agricultural system functioning as long as their labour is complemented by the continuous work of many women and children. Thus it is necessary to have a distribution of household labour by age and sex which favours young women; and the healthy physical condition of individual members, particularly its women.

Put another way, the crux of the issue is that the economic success of an agricultural household in rural North Yemen is dependent on two important dimensions of women's roles - reproduction and production. It is the balance between them that is important.

In rural Yemen, one is struck continually by the necessity to preserve a woman's productive capacity. In the eyes of women, the issues of health - their ability to be productive - and fertility are inextricably related. The discussion now turns to these links by beginning with general folk conceptions of health.

Body Balance and the Maintenance of Health

Many folk concepts of health in rural North Yemen today appear to derive from the humoural theory of health and illness found in classical Arabic medicine and before it, the humoural Greek theories. Judging by what villagers say and do, however, such folk concepts are modified and simplified versions of the classical theories. Of fundamental importance in both the classical and folk theories is the concept of internal body balance. A healthy body is in rough equilibrium, whereas an unhealthy body contains excesses of certain harmful substances.

In the folk theories the first principle of good health is the necessity of a balanced diet. Here the folk theory differs slightly from the classical theory. It gives less emphasis to qualities of foods which produce internal equilibrium than the classical theories and more emphasis to foods which are specifically blood-producing. Blood is viewed as the only good product of digestion and the other products, yellow bile, black bile and phlegm are harmful. Blood is widely represented in local symbolism as strength and life. For example, a paralyzed limb is 'dry' and 'without blood'. The sun, thought to cause insomnia and fevers, 'dries the brains' and 'takes the blood from the head'.

The second folk principle of health builds on the first. Digestion is the key process in body health, and its efficiency is maintained through the routine use of purges. Here purity and health are interrelated and, as shall be shown below, purity is an important theme in other aspects of health. Traditional cures, it is said, will work only if the person has a pure heart and body. Thus, prior to a visit to a healer, the patient uses a purge such as castor oil senna, or the resin of aloe. Similarly, one must be pure before going on the pilgrimage to Mecca. The specific purge is called *Sharba sanna makka* or the senna of Mecca purge. Finally the Ramadan fast is itself likened to a purge for it is a visceral purifier. Ramadan is also a time when new clothes are prepared, houses are cleaned and renovated, and people engage in, as they say, 'pure acts of charity'.

Female Health

In promoting their own health females are subject to the same concerns as the population at large - seeking a good diet with special attention to blood-producing foods, and promoting the efficient functioning of the digestive system through routine use of purgatives. In addition, females have their own specific set of concerns to do with their reproductive system. These concerns draw the conceptual link between overall health, reproductive health and fertility.

Yemeni women have a simplified understanding of their reproductive system. It consists mainly of the *al-mahbila* (uterus), which is described as a hollow inverted flask. They do not know of the ovaries and the fallopian tubes. Others who have written on perceptions of the reproductive system by Middle Eastern women have also commented on the emphasis on the uterus as a vaguely defined vessel (see Khattab 1975, p.28) writing on Egypt; Good (1980) writing on Iran; and Granquist (1947) on Palestine in the 1930s.

However, unlike other Middle Eastern women who think that women contribute only the vessel for foetal growth, Yemeni women understand that conception takes place in the uterus with the union of the female *dhariyya* (egg) with the *dhari* (sperm) presented in *mani* (semen) through intercourse. Thus both males and females are perceived to contribute physiological material to conception. Each conception also has a supernatural dimension to it. That conception 'does' occur through one 'specific' sexual act is viewed as the will of God since man can always 'give his seed' but only God can create.

Infertility is, therefore, ultimately God's will. However, it can occur because the male partner has no sperm or not enough of them. It can also occur because the woman has no ova or because the uterus is twisted or 'locked'. To women, the twisting of the uterus can occur naturally and is remedied through massage. Throughout Yemen there are female massage specialists who manipulate the abdomen to untwist the uterus. Other writers on the health of Yemeni women have also alluded to this practice (see Adra, 1983, p.12 and Ansell, 1981, p.6).

Great care is given following childbirth to ensure that the uterus is in its proper place, and in particular that it is not twisted, fallen, or on its side. For if it is, it will be impossible for the woman to conceive again. Some women claim that all that is required is that they put their feet up in the air and jiggle their torso: others claim that only the masseuse can ensure that the uterus is in its proper place.

In some Middle Eastern societies, infertility is explained as the result of black magic. In rural Yemen, this is never the explanation. Rather the woman herself bears great responsibility for infertility due to personal negligence in ritual cleansing after periods of pollution. The result is a 'locked' uterus. Women are considered impure as long as they are expelling sexual substances. Menstrual blood ('red filth') is one, as is bleeding following childbirth. Other sexual fluids ('white filth') include postpartum flows and vaginal secretions. Women must wash themselves carefully following each occasion of ritual impurity.

A necessary precondition to regaining a pure state is the total expulsion of the polluting substances. However, before discussing means used to encourage expulsion, the seemingly contradictory attitudes about blood need to be clarified. It has already been stated that, in local view, blood is the only good product of digestion and the essence of life. A human being cannot have too much blood. Yet how is it that menstrual blood is not only highly polluting but that folk health practices encourage its complete and rapid expulsion?

Yemeni women say that menstrual blood originates from a *carq al-gidham* (vein) which only females have. It is completely different from blood *asli* ('original') to the human system. Unlike ordinary body blood, menstrual blood is highly polluting, and contact with it can cause physical problems. Intercourse during menstruation can cause severe harm to the man. A village woman with a serious skin infection claimed she had washed in water used by a menstruating woman. A menstruating woman cannot participate in ritual activities that necessitate a pure state: the Pilgrimage, prayer and the Ramadan feast.

While the substance is highly polluting, menstruation itself is cleansing. Khattab (1975, p.28) and Wassef (1981, p.101), anthropologists who studied perceptions of the human body in Egypt, report similar views. In Yemen the expression for 'she had her period' is the same as *hia sabunat* (she washed). A period of 5 to 7 days is considered normal, and allows all the *waskha* (impurities) to be expelled. If a woman has light, short, or irregular periods, she will fall ill. Thus, women use many home remedies to encourage a heavy flow. Remedies include mixtures of ghee and honey, dates, infusions of thyme, barley, jujube fruit, or cloves and cinnamon with raw sugar. The sap of the jujube tree (*Zizyphus spina-Christi*) is also boiled and drunk to regulate periods. Women believe that they are necessary because they hasten the cleansing process.

In spite of home-based 'preventive medicine' measures to encourage menstrual flow, problems can arise. Hospitals report women seeking treatment for general body pains which they claim are due to insufficient expulsion of menstrual impurities. They say their bodies have become dense and full of pain.

Among Yemeni women, there appears to be little understanding of the relationship between menstruation and the intra-uterine growth of the foetus. During pregnancy, the lack of menstrual flow is problematic. Adra (1983, p.15) writing on women in al-Ahjur Yemen, reports that women claim oedema is from the build-up of menstrual blood during pregnancy. Other Yemeni women attribute varicose veins to the build-up of menstrual blood over the gestation period.

By observing the practices of women concerning menstruation, it is clear that they take an active role in what they understand to be promoting their own health. The recurring themes are the expulsion of impurities and the promotion of bodily balance. Active health promotion is also equally clear in practices surrounding pregnancy, birth and the postpartum period, particularly the latter.

The main concern among women during pregnancy is to ensure safe delivery by keeping the foetus small. Thus they usually restrict dietary intake. Dorsky (1981, pp.176–7) found this practice among women in the Yemeni town of Amran as well. In a country where women give birth at home and emergency hospital services are far distant, fear of death during childbirth is amply justified. In her study of Yemeni women Adra (1983, p.19) found that birth is likened to the Pilgrimage, a risky journey with safe return uncertain; 'the grave is open and ready'. Women are terrified of long labour, and they say that one of the most common curses put on a woman is one which delays delivery, causing the expansion of the foetus and eventual death of the woman.

Childbirth usually takes place in secrecy, in the presence of only the senior women of the household. It is they who look after the new mother during her 40-day confinement period. This period has less specifically to do with the outcome of the birth (i.e., live male or female, or stillbirth), than with the condition of the mother. All actions during this period are meant to counteract the weakening effects of birth on the mother, and actively promote her return to health and fertility.

The first set of actions aims to encourage the expulsion of all impurities. Substances similar to those used during menstruation are made into infusions. One special herbal mixture called *qahwat al-wilada* (birth coffee) is drunk to promote bleeding. In recent years modern medical practitioners have encouraged village women in Yemen to take an injection to stop bleeding in the postpartum period. This the women are adamantly against, for they feel it is extremely harmful. They state that impurities must be expelled for at least 7 days.

The neonate is also moved from an impure to a pure state. The umbilicus is allowed to bleed to allow impure substances out. Ingrams (1946, p.99), writing about rural South Yemen during the 1940s, reported that it was also common to shave the hair of the baby after birth; 'the hair of the (mother's abdomen)', as it was called, was viewed as impure.

Normally a cloth is wrapped tightly around the woman's abdomen following childbirth to aid expulsion of impurities. Ingrams (1946, p.98) found that binding was to prevent the dangerous afterbirth substances from rising and killing the women. Ansell (1981, p.10) reports the practice among women in Mahweit, Yemen, as a method of restoring visceral organs to their proper places, and also to relieve pain.

A second set of actions is meant to strengthen the woman. She is fed chicken, raisins and dates, milk with myrrh. Many Middle Eastern women are fed special strengthening foods in the period of confinement. Chicken is universal as are foods with a high sugar content.

Finally the woman's reproductive organs must be returned to their proper position. She squats over incense which is said to tighten the vagina. Then, specialists begin a series of massages to put the uterus in place. Ingrams (1946, p.98) reported that poultices of tumeric, myrrh, gum and oil were put on the woman's back in South Yemen, and others report the importance of abdominal massage among Yemeni women (Ansell, 1981, p.19). In many parts of Yemen women also seek vacuum cupping on the abdomen to avoid a twisted uterus (see also Hunte (1980) on postpartum practices in Afghanistan).

The conscientious and systematic encouragement of the expulsion of impurities, the strengthening of the body with special foods, and the realignment of the reproductive organs through massaging, cupping and incense: these actions are all performed by women to ensure reproductive health and, indeed, their own future fertility.

Fertility and Health in a Yemeni Agricultural Community

Village women strive for a balance between their overall health, which has a bearing on their production functions, and their ability to produce and raise healthy offspring.

On the face of it, fertility is highly valued. Having children secures the woman's place as a wife and elevates her to motherhood, venerated in Yemen as elsewhere in the Middle East. Children are a natural and desired outcome of sexual relations between husband and wife. 'If' calculations are made for future security, children may have a perceived economic value as extra hands in farm work and/or for their income earning potential as workers in town. Whatever aspect is given emphasis at any point in time, there are many reasons why village women in Yemen desire to have children.

However, concern for their own personal health status limits their enthusiasm for uncontrolled reproduction. Women are adamantly against having 'one child on top of the next', as they say. They claim it makes the woman herself constantly tired, 'the uterus cries from too many pregnancies', 'the uterus becomes thin and in a dangerous condition'. Back pains and general fatigue come from a 'worn out womb'.

At issue is not only the desired overall number of children but the interval between each birth. Infant mortality remains high in Yemen, anywhere from 159-175 per 1,000 live births according to various estimates. (See Table 24.1 for basic demographic parameters for the country.) Yemeni women recognize that not all the children they bear will survive to adulthood. Thus to ensure the desired number of males and females, women are likely to need to be pregnant a few more times than the total number of children desired. If at all possible, they start childbearing in the first year of marriage, when they are on average about 17 years old.

While the desired number of children may vary from woman to woman, all agree on the importance of spacing births to promote their own health and that of the newborn. In the past this was accomplished by prolonged breastfeeding, up to 21 months in some instances. While amenorrhoea is generally viewed as harmful, lactational amenorrhoea is seen as 'a gift from God' promoting the desired longer birth intervals (see Khattab, 1975, p.22). In spite of the many cultural factors which encourage Yemeni women to breastfeed, women are now breastfeeding less. This is due primarily to the increase in use of milk powders and in bottle feeding, promoted in the media and offered to women in clinics (see Firebrace, 1981, and Melrose, 1981). It is probable, moreover, that the use of modern contraceptives has not been able to fully substitute for the birth spacing that once was the effect of lactation.

Modern contraceptives are available in Yemen, even in the remotest mountain villages. Though the government of Yemen is officially pronatalist, family planning services are available in all government hospitals and health centres. Physicians, who tend to work in rural market towns and in the cities, offer contraceptives in their private clinics. Women who travel in from rural areas are a high proportion of their clients. Finally, most pharmacies, which are found in rural as well as urban locations,

Table 24.1 North Yemen: Basic Demographic Parameters Estimated by Various Authorities

	Swiss API 3% sample 1975 census (1978)	Hill (1980)	World Bank (1980)	WHO (1983)
Per capita income				$410
Population	*de jure* 5.3 million	*de jure* 5.3 million	5.8 million end 1979	6.8 million end 1980
Population Density			30 per sq.km.	
Adult Literacy			13%	15% males 4% females
Occupied Dwellings Without Safe Water			96%	70%
Dwellings without Hygenic Waste Disposal				88%
Crude Birth Rate	46%	47 - 50%	48	47.3
Crude Death Rate	22%	26%	25	28.7
Rate of Natural Increase	2.4%	2.7 - 3.0%	2.9%	1.86%
Infant Mortality Rate	159 per 1,000	175 per 1,000		159
Total Fertility Rate (per woman)		6.5 - 7.2		

stock oral contraceptives at a minimum. A survey conducted in 1980 by the Yemen Family Planning Association found that 'contraceptives are used, sold, and bought on a much wider scale than we previously thought...' (Yemen FPA, 1980). In the community studied, ten out of the 160 adult males had had vasectomies.

Thus couples do utilize modern contraceptives; and they do so, they say, to protect the health of the mother. By limiting fertility the couple consciously favours the continued health of the mother in the balance between two desired ends: health and production on one hand, and fertility and reproduction on the other.

Yet despite a seeming willingness to limit their fertility, contraceptive use is not high among Yemeni women in the reproductive ages. The Yemen Family Planning Association found that 13.1 per cent of the couples they interviewed were using contraceptives (Yemen FPA, 1980). What accounts for the discrepancy between the apparent readiness to contracept and the relatively low use of contraceptives? It is here where cultural factors come into play, particularly those which underlie concepts of health and fertility. For if a woman chooses to contracept to protect her own health, she will not be inclined to use a method that might have an equally negative effect on her health.

Therefore, some of the imputed and actual side effects of available birth control methods may discourage women from becoming users. To Yemeni women, bleeding and increased secretions in between periods renders the woman impure and limits her ritual and sexual activity. Too little bleeding during periods causes a build-up of impurities and will lead to a dense body and pains. Or, no period for several months would be a disaster to body balance and health.

In part, reluctance to use the methods available, mainly the pill and Depo-Provera, is due to misinformation. When husbands or relatives purchase pills in pharmacies, for example, they receive few or no instructions as to their proper use and possible side effects. Moreover doctors rarely take time to explain these things to women who seek contraceptives from them in their clinics or at Maternal-Child Health Centres. Women are forced to draw their own health conclusions from the side effects they experience.

Of the women who use pills, many complain of irregular menstruation, headaches, dizziness and fatigue. Those who have tried the injectible contraceptive Depo-Provera complain of pains and bleeding and menstrual disturbances. Clearly these side effects strike the central core of a woman's health: her regular bleeding and internal body balance. Women therefore cannot use, or will not use, contraceptives with any confidence unless they know that in so doing, they are truly preserving their health.

In the Yemeni context, then, evidence suggests that women cannot afford to be pregnant continually. They are conscious about the fine balance between their own ability to work and their role in producing the next generation of workers. They are aware that too many pregnancies, or being pregnant too soon, has a deleterious immediate effect on their own health. The conditions are right for acceptance of modern contraceptives, particularly since breastfeeding is declining and birth intervals are likely to shorten if the spacing once achieved by lactation is not substituted for by contraceptive use.

Family planning strategies are too often guilty of a single-minded pursuit of the goal of reduced fertility. By failing to place this desired outcome within a broader context of women's total health concerns, many well-intentioned programs flounder. The Yemeni case shows that the active concern women show for preserving their health and well-being could, with sensitive and informed planning, become the basis for truly effective health and family planning programs. Women's concerns about the side-effects of various contraceptive methods should, therefore, become the starting point of a program, rather than be dismissed as irrational or non-medical. Researchers and family planning program personnel alike would do well to recognize the fact that most women, even uneducated rural women in a traditional society such as Yemen, are not passive about matters of life that concern them the most.

Lay Concepts of Reproductive Physiology Related to Contraceptive Use: A Method of Investigation*

Carol P. MacCormack

Extensive and Intensive Methods of Investigation

Knowledge about relatively safe and effective methods of contraception are widely known in some countries. The proportion of the adult population with this knowledge can be quickly known using questionnaire survey methods. Some countries also have family planning services which provide good coverage of the population. Coverage can be known by looking at Ministry of Health statistics and verifying them by direct observations of clinics and their function. Yet even when contraceptive knowledge and coverage in a country are good, actual utilization rates are sometimes low. A significant proportion of women in their reproductive years have never used contraceptive services, or of those who have ever used them, some use contraceptives sporadically and ineffectually. In such a situation, the survey questionnaire is usually not an adequate data collection technique for understanding why women are making particular choices.

Intensive qualitative methods are of two types: sociological and cognitive. Sociological investigations measure behaviour affected by social structures such as class or family type. Sociological studies, for example, would seek to understand if women of a particular class, caste, ethnic group, age group, or other social category are being left out of services and educational opportunities. Sociological investigations might also attempt to answer more subtle questions. For example, why are a significant number of women seeking high-risk late term abortions in a country where abortion is illegal except on medical grounds? A possible reason in countries where marriage rates are low (usually with concomitant high male unemployment) is that only by becoming pregnant can a woman test the baby's father's promise of financial support. Should he renege, then an abortion may be preferred by the mother to solitary support of another child.

Investigations into the conceptual domain are also necessary. This paper gives a technique for exploring the cognitive system of a sample of women. What images and concepts do they have of their bodies, and how do they think the pill, an intra-uterine

---

*An updated version of this chapter appears in the *Journal of Tropical Medicine and Hygiene*, 1986.

device, Depo-Provera, or other methods actually work? Their lay concept of reproductive physiology will affect the way they actually use or do not use contraceptives.

This method of cognitive analysis was developed in a study of 300 urban and rural Jamaican women in 1983 and 1984. It was also tested on a small sample of women attending health centres in central Sudan, American undergraduates reading anthropology, British undergraduates reading social anthropology, and British second-year medical students.

Methods: A Jamaican Example

Interviews were structured by a schedule of open-ended questions, and an outline drawing of a matronly female figure. Interviews were conducted in a conversational rather than a formal style, and questions could be put in a variety of ways, interspersed with a good deal of small talk and even jokes. The object was (i) to put women at ease; (ii) let them know we understood and were interested in their concepts; and (iii) convey that we were not looking for medically correct responses only. Thus, when a woman said she could not remember the biology she had been taught in school, we reassured her that we were not school examiners but were only interested in what 'she' thought her own body was like inside. We were careful not to ask leading questions that would pre-suppose a medical textbook type of answer. For example, from my previous work in Sierra Leone I knew that many women did not think of the uterus as a bag, but visualized the vagina/uterus as a central tube, sometimes open at both ends. Therefore, we did not say 'please draw your uterus (womb)', but 'please draw the place where the baby grows'.

The quality of interviewers is crucial to the success of this type of investigation. They must be intelligent, have a degree of social grace, be interested in the topic, and be women - preferably mature women with children. In Jamaica, women university students, especially mature students, earning money in holidays, helped with interviewing. To minimize variation between interviewers we initially did interviews together, holding a small group discussion with a woman. Then we split into pairs of interviewers and I paired with each interviewer in turn. When satisfied that we were all giving similar encouragements, had found the best way to put questions without giving offence and all were avoiding leading questions, we began to interview singly. Each day I interviewed on site with the others. At the end of each day (or each week) I read the interview sheets to look for signs of interviewer bias.

Each interview took at least a half-hour, but with some women an amiable conversation easily went on for an hour. Because of the length of time needed for a conversation, and because of the need for the principal investigator to participate closely in the interviewing, the sample size was a relatively small 300 women. We drew part of our sample from women attending ante-natal clinics in various locations in Kingston. However, that on its own did not constitute an adequate sample. It was a self-selected sample of women using health services, and might not be characteristic of the country at large. We particularly wanted to know about women who are not using health services as planned. Therefore we also sampled women who came to fruit and vegetable markets in various locations. The open markets attract a broad cross-section of Jamaican women in Kingston. We had a 98 per cent compliance rate. Two rather depressed women attending ante-natal clinic did not make drawings, and a few shoppers were too busy to be bothered. Most women found the task and concomitant conversation enjoyable.[1]

The Interview Schedule

The interview ended with objective questions about the woman's age, the last year she completed in school, and a three-part question giving an indication of socioeconomic status.[2] The interview began with questions that were less objective, and were easier to chat about, even joke about. For example, 'Is it possible for a woman to become pregnant if she has sex while she is menstruating?' (Many Jamaicans suspect that an albino child may result.) Follow-up questions probed to see if women knew of any safe period during the menstrual cycle.

We offered the outline drawing by saying we were curious to know what women are like inside. 'Where does the baby grow?' (gentle persuasion to draw). 'Where does the baby egg come from?' (jokes about whether women are like hens with eggs inside - or do all the eggs come from the father?). 'Where does menstrual blood come from?'. 'Why do women bleed every month?'. We continued questioning in this way until the woman had made the most complete drawing she was inclined to do.

After they had finished the drawing, women were asked if they had ever used contraceptives. If they had ever used them, we asked the method(s) they had used. 'Do you like the method (named) you used?'. We probed for their concept of how the device or chemical functioned, and also sought any factors that might affect the social relationship between the woman and her partner. We asked what she liked about the method(s), then invited conversation about what she did not like.

To broaden the inquiry to include all concepts that might prevent a woman from ever using a method, we asked if they knew of any other methods, probing for all family planning service methods they knew about, all traditional methods, and modern non-medical lay methods. Then, one by one, we took up the methods, referred the woman back to her drawing, and asked her to explain how she thought the method worked in her body to prevent conception.

Brief Findings

The most common reason for not using, or not continuing to use, an intra-uterine device was the fear that it would become lost in the body. Figures 25.1 and 25.2 indicate the concept held by some women that the vagina and uterus are a single tube. The tube may be open at both ends (Figure 25.2). Thus women tie a binder below the breasts in late pregnancy and sometimes in birth 'to keep the baby from coming up and choking me', or 'to keep the placenta from coming up'. To insert a coil in this tube is to risk it drifting upward, becoming lost in the body.

An equally frequent complaint was that the coil caused pain to the woman and her partner. Virtually every woman who knew about the coil drew it in the vagina (Figures 25.3, 25.4 and 25.6). They thought of it as a blocking device that kept the sperm from entering the uterus. Therefore women readily acquiesced to their partner's complaint that the coil poked him and interfered with his pleasure.

Some women told us of their fear that the coil might enter the uterus where it would adversely affect the baby in the event of pregnancy. It would take space where the baby would grow, and might become implanted in the growing foetus, or block the cervix when birth began. Some women worried that if the coil did enter the uterus, it was difficult to remove, requiring an operation. Others spoke of it causing pain and pelvic infection which might lead to blocked tubes and sterility.

A related complaint was that the coil caused an unpleasant smell. The only aspect of the coil they actually saw was the strings hanging down, like the strings of a tampon. But unlike a tampon which is frequently changed, the coil remained in place for months or years, absorbing sperm, in contact with menstrual blood, but never removed, washed or changed.

A few women mentioned the coil coming out spontaneously, or not being reliable, and 75 per cent of the women who had used the coil complained that it caused heavy bleeding.

Depo-Provera, on the other hand, caused worry because women went for months or years without menstrual bleeding. They regarded regular menstruation as a sign of good health. It is also a time of bodily cleansing, sometimes enhanced by use of a laxative at the end of the menstrual period for 'a good wash-out'. Months without bleeding also caused women to worry about permanent loss of fertility. No menstruation was interpreted as a sign that Depo-Provera had 'blocked up the tubes'. Women were also concerned about developing high blood pressure. With Depo-Provera they would have too much blood accumulating in the body if they did not menstruate a satisfactory amount every month. (In pregnancy the accumulating blood is used up making the baby, and was not therefore thought to cause a high blood pressure problem.)

Many women thought of the birth control pill working mechanically, not chemically. Pills went to the cervix and blocked the sperm from entering the uterus. But one might have too large a build-up of pills over time, so women either used castor oil at regular intervals to have a good wash-out, or stopped taking the pill for a time to allow the load of pills to reduce itself. Women also said they feared the pill 'because it caused clots'. When asked to indicate where the clots were, they replied, 'you know, the clots you have with your menstrual period'.

Women talked a great deal about their 'tubes' and the need to keep them open. We asked them to draw their tubes. For some the essential 'tube' was the same as the vagina, and the proposition to 'have their tubes tied' was interpreted as having the vagina tied, with no more sex, and a worry about menstrual flow (Figure 25.5).

As with the coil, women feared that condoms would come off and become lost in their body or block up their tubes and cause sterility. There was also a very widely-held fear that condoms easily burst and were therefore unreliable. Men also complained to their partner that the condom was not natural, preferring direct skin to skin contact.

When women talked of contraception being 'unnatural' some indicated that they had a specific number of eggs, and contraception could delay their development, but they might as well just go ahead and live out their destiny (Figure 25.6). But they did not particularly object to contraception on religious grounds or regard the use of contraceptive methods in themselves as an unnatural act. Indeed, most women knew of indigenous methods of fertility regulation, such as drinking laundry blue to keep their menstrual periods from coming.

Discussion and Recommendations

Women in Kingston, Jamaica are interested in their reproductive health, and monitor the state of their health by noting the time, quantity, and quality of menstrual bleeding. Deviation from their normal flow caused worry and contributed to underutilization, or irregular use, of services which provided relatively safe methods of fertility control.

Women recognized pelvic pain, inflammation, and unpleasant-smelling discharge as signs of a condition which might lead to sterility. This investigation suggests that women are confusing sexually transmitted disease with possible complications from intra-uterine devices.

When an intra-uterine device is inserted, care must be given to show what it looks like, explain where it is placed, and how it works to prevent conception. Information on prevention and treatment of sexually transmitted disease might be given at the same time. Once signs and symptoms of disease, and explanations

Cognitive Analysis Developed in a Study of 300 Urban and Rural Jamaican Woman. 1983/84

Fig.25.1

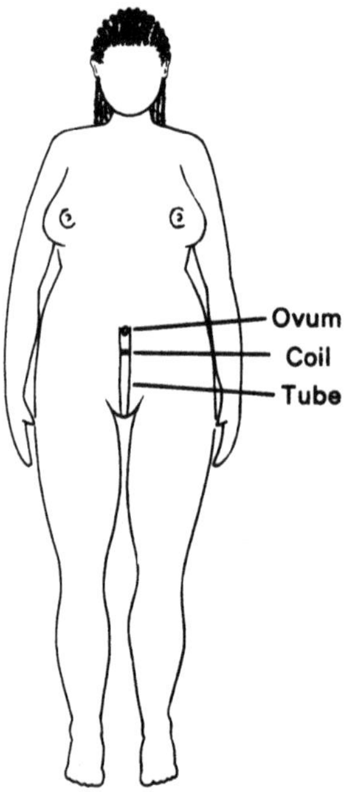

Fig.25.2

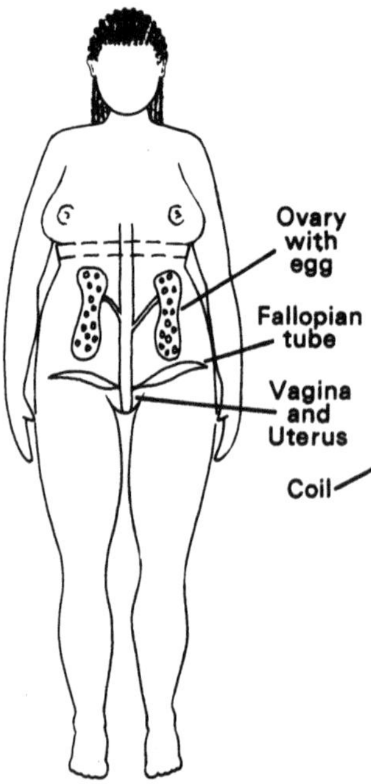

Fig.25.3

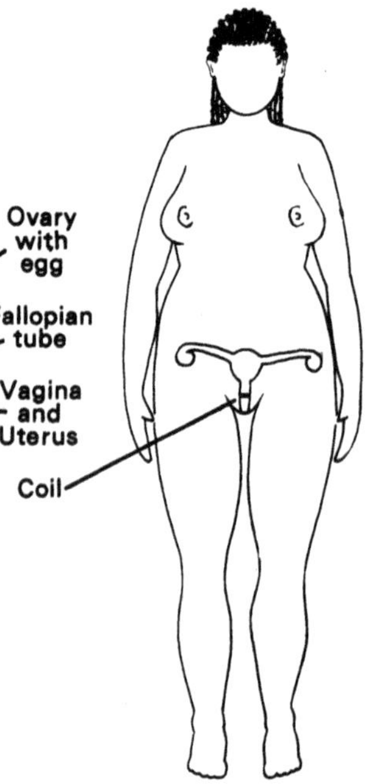

Fig.25.4

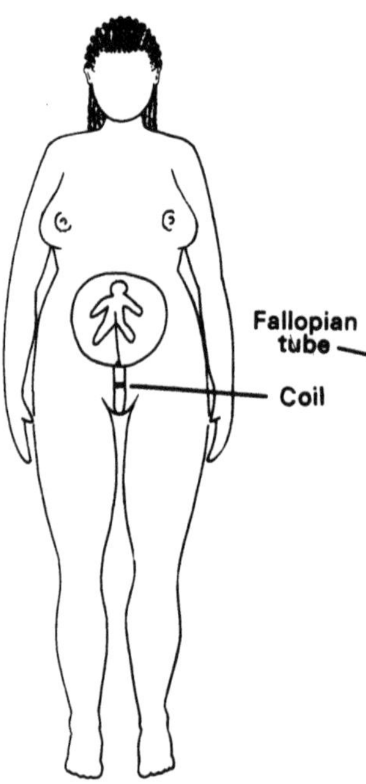

Fig.25.5

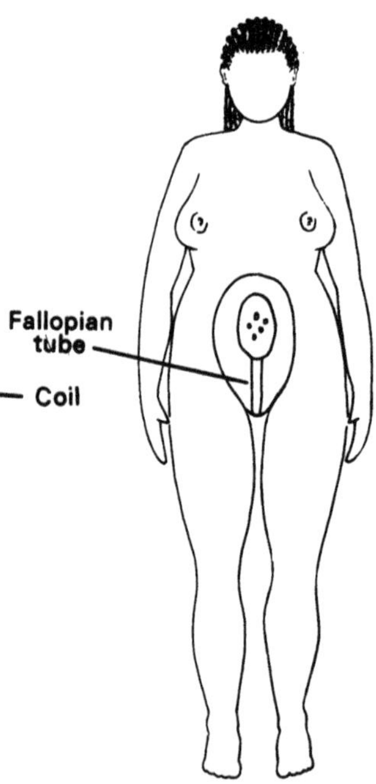

Fig. 25.6

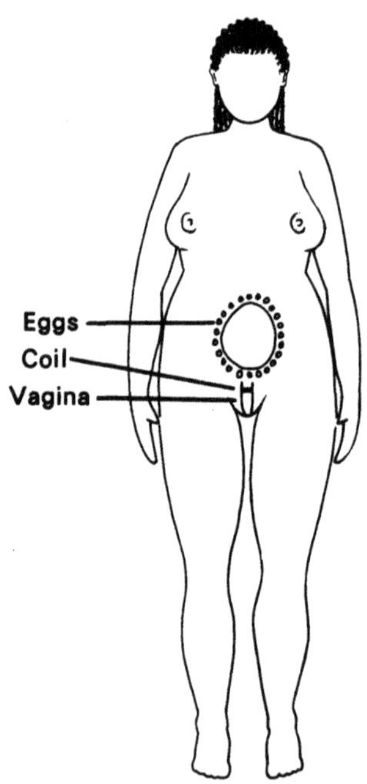

of possible complications from the use of an intra-uterine device are described, the two phenomena may be kept conceptually distinct by women. But if careful explanation is not given, women may continue to blame contraceptives for illness and discomforts with different aetiologies.

If a contraceptive might change the pattern of menstruation, care must be taken to explain why, and to reassure women that the change will not harm them or make them infertile for life. Indeed, women might come to understand that consistent use of the pill can regulate cycles and enhance potential fertility, at the same time it might diminish the amount of menstrual flow. Such explanations would be given in ordinary lay language, not in medical language.

Family planning clinics are a great potential resource, where women might learn, on a one-to-one basis, about gynaecological health. The 'quality' of interaction between staff and patients must be assessed as well as the 'efficiency' of numbers seen. In-service courses to improve staff skills in health education would probably be cost-effective.

Most women said they learned about contraception from other women, and from newspapers. Newspapers, however, often seek to increase their readership through sensationalism. Thus women are told of the danger of stroke from using the pill, and when they see clots in menstrual blood they feel they are at risk. Newspapers might be requested to provide more informative articles, perhaps written in collaboration with physicians as is now done with some radio broadcasts. Furthermore, attempts might be made to improve the practical content of health education in schools. This would help women to assess the validity of sensationalized mass media accounts.

Conclusion

There was little correlation between anatomically correct drawings and years of education; an old woman with the notional age of 70, who had never been to school, produced one of the most accurate drawings and explanations. In analysis of these drawings we are not interested in correctness, but in insights into what people think about reproductive function. What they think is a fact that influences actual health behaviour. Effective health education acknowledges lay concepts and seeks to bridge constructively from the way ordinary people think, to a more effective understanding of physiological function. Furthermore, we must understand why people are 'not' using health services as intended so that clinical practices might be improved to make them more attractive.

Notes

1. In doing a similar Jamaican study, on treatment for diarrhoea in children, mothers found the digestive system much less

interesting to draw or talk about. The digestive system produces waste, but the reproductive system yields a child and a degree of social power for the mother.

2. Women were asked:

   Do you own ___ or rent ___ the place where you live?

   How many rooms do you own/rent? ___

   How many people live in those rooms? ___

   We then constructed a socioeconomic scale based on ownership of capital and crowding. This method, however, would not work in some parts of the world, for example rural Africa.

Concluding Observations

26

The Use of the Method of Participant Observation in the Study of Demographic Phenomena

M.N. Srinivas

At the outset, I should make it clear that I am a social anthropologist and 'not' a demographer. I am also an odd kind of social anthropologist: I have not studied tribal groups isolated from the mainstream of national life and culture but peasants who are an integral part of the wider, encompassing culture and society.

Further, the groups and communities that I have studied have all been, very broadly speaking, members of my own culture and society. This, however, goes against the current dogma that anthropology is the study of the 'other', the other being conceived of as an exotic group living many seas away from the anthropologist's university. In practice, it meant, until recently at any rate, Western anthropologists studying non-Western groups living in the Third World. Since Westerners were also conquerors a hierarchical bias of the anthropologist's superiority to the natives was built into the discipline. Also, since most anthropologists are men, andro-centrism was also integral to social anthropology.

However, it is necessary to note in this context that since the end of World War II, a major change has begun to take place in the composition of social anthropologists and this is likely to result in radical changes in the discipline. Social anthropology and sociology are becoming popular in Third World countries; already, in countries such as India, Sri Lanka and Japan, indigenous anthropologists (and sociologists) are busy studying sections of their own societies. Even if these scholars are not as thoroughly trained as scholars in some western universities, their knowledge of the field language is likely to be far more intimate, and the time at their disposal greater. They can also get back to the field with greater ease when necessary. These scholars are likely to be anti-colonialist in their general approach, and in spite of the fact of stratification in indigenous society, they are culturally closer to the people they study.

In this connection, the point needs to be made that though the use of the method of participant observation in its strictest sense requires a sound knowledge of the language of the community to be studied, in my experience, very few Western anthropologists are able to achieve it. For instance, I do not think any of the Western anthropologists who have worked in South India would read for pleasure a novel in the language of their field area. I think this kind of skill is necessary especially if the anthropologist is writing on such sensitive areas as religion, morals, and world-view, intra-familial relations, and indebtedness and assets.

I would like to discuss here, though very briefly, the wide-spread belief that anthropology is the study of other cultures, even if its ultimate aim is the understanding of one's own (Evans-Pritchard, 1951, pp.128-9). In this connection, the 'other' has been conceived of as a faraway, primitive community, as exotic as possible. There may be some historical justification for this but during the last 50 years or so anthropologists have studied communities encysted in the great civilizations, and even more importantly, many anthropologists in the Third World have studied villages, slums and so on, in their own countries. In societies which are stratified, and which also exhibit other forms of differentiation, the 'other' might well be a village situated a few miles away, or even a slum a few hundred yards from the anthropologist's house. Anthropological studies of one's own societies are beginning to be a flourishing enterprise.

The shift from the study of the exotic and faraway 'other' to the study of the backyard 'other' is important from the point of view of collaboration between social anthropologists and demographers. It has occurred largely in Third World countries, though, to be fair, a few scholars in Western countries, particularly the USA,[1] are involved in the study of their own societies. Further, rapid population growth is a feature of Third World countries and social anthropologists living in them cannot afford to ignore population growth, either as scholars or as citizens. As Professors Shah and Ramaswamy (n.d., p.1) have remarked:

> 'Increasing unemployment, pressure on land, shortage of housing, inadequate school and health facilities, and shortages of every kind of resource have made the population problem very much a part of the daily experience of the laymen'.

Every anthropologist knows that participant observation is not only a method, but a method bound up with certain ideas: the idea that culture is a whole made up of inter-related parts is basic to participant observation. Under Radcliffe-Brown culture was replaced by social structure or system, but the concept of the system being a whole consisting of inter-dependent parts was integral to his thinking as is generally well known.

To turn specifically to the method of participation observation, it does make for the collection of more accurate data than is possible through large scale surveys even when the latter are conducted very well, and additionally, the investigators are not only competent but committed. This statement has special force when accurate numerical data are sought from illiterates. My own experience in rural south Karnataka is relevant in this connection. When I had to record the ages of elderly villagers, I first tried to find out how old they were when one or other major community event (flood, epidemic) had occurred, and calculated their present age from that figure. The end figure was fairly accurate especially as during the interview there were present knowledgeable villagers who intervened when they thought the interviewer was gaining incorrect information. Several of my men informants did not know the real names of their young children. Not infrequently, men were wholly ignorant of the female side of the culture, and sustained interviewing, preferably by women, would be necessary to remedy this.

The data that came during the first few weeks of my stay were not always accurate, and sometimes even misleading. It was only after I had been accepted as a friend by several leading villagers, and had done a census of the village, that accurate information started to flow. Here I should stress that the kind of rapport that the anthropologist builds up by living amongst the people, communicating with them in their own language, and forming deep friendships amongst them, is the key to the securing of accurate data, particularly on very sensitive matters. No other method can guarantee the same quality of data. Demographers are usually very concerned about the accuracy of the information collected for their studies, but participant observation can only be of limited use to them because its use is confined to small communities whereas demographers generally rely on large surveys.

Underlying the use of the participant observation method is also the belief that 'knowledge' about a community is different from 'understanding', and that the latter can only be obtained by actually living in it as an ordinary member for a sufficiently long period of time, using the local language in dealings with the indigenes, and finally, by the anthropologist making a sustained effort to put himself or herself in the shoes of the people studied. Understanding comes, or appears to come, suddenly, and the anthropologist grasps the logic of the institutions of the indigenes, and what is more, feels that that logic is right. The anthropologist then becomes a champion of the indigenes' culture, and simultaneously, a critic of his or her own. Every anthropologist has been through this and the mature ones pass from this new subjectivity to a position where they have achieved some distance both from their natal culture and the culture of the group they have studied.

I have no time to develop this point further, but it should be obvious that participant observation in its fullest sense is not needed for the general run of demographic studies. But prolonged stay in the community of study, the cultivation of the friendship of the people, and participating in their activities will result in access to accurate information in such sensitive areas as sex customs and practices, conceptions, births, miscarriages and abortions, conjugal relations and contraceptive practices. When large numbers of people to be studied are illiterate, quantification of information is a slippery task, to say the least, and the fullest rapport needs to be established with the community of study to minimize error. In this connection, the collection of genealogies may be recommended to demographers for the collection of more reliable data on matters such as birth, death, marriage and similar data. Anthropologists regard genealogies as basic to their fieldwork.[2]

The idea that each society is a whole and that its various points or aspects are linked to each other, and that changes in any one institution or institution-set produce changes in other institutions, was elaborated in structural-functionalism which began to replace functionalism in British anthropology in the 1940s. I suggest that the idea of the inter-relatedness of the different institutions of a society, and the linked idea that particular institutions need to be viewed in relation to the total society may prove to be heuristically fruitful in demographic research also. It is possible, however, that they are already being used in demographic research without any theroetical discussion of the utility of these ideas.

Linkages between one area of culture/society and another are a commonplace particularly in peasant societies. For instance, all over India tremendous importance is attached to fertility in women. One could say that fertility is a part of femininity, and correspondingly, there is a dread of barrenness. When a couple is childless in rural India the fault is assumed to be the woman's until the contrary is proved. She can be set aside by her husband and another wife taken. Endless pilgrimages are undertaken, and vows made, to favourite dieties in the hope of obtaining children. The Abbé Dubois for instance, reports of such pilgrimages being undertaken by peasants in Mysore, and he describes in some detail a particularly nauseous custom practised by pilgrims to the great temple in Nanjanagud (as quoted in Srinivas, 1942, pp.175-6). In southern Karnataka, the barren woman was despised, and mendicants from the high castes did not accept food or grain offered by her.

Contrariwise, it was through her fertility that a woman was accepted in her husband's house, became a mother, mother-in-law and grandmother, earning the respect of her affinal as well as natal kinsfolk. The birth of a son to a woman ensured that the family's land would be cultivated, the lineage would continue, and the dead ancestors of the lineage receive periodic propitiations which were essential for their sustenance. They also looked after the welfare of the living members of the lineage.

The point that I am making is a simple one: the question of fertility cannot be considered at merely the individual or even conjugal level. At least two lineages have a vested interest in a woman's fertility, and even more important, fertility as a value is stresssed by the culture as a whole. In short, fertility cannot be considered without taking the entire community and its culture into account. Looking at it as an affair of the couple only would be to import what Dumont castigates as Western 'sociocentrism'.

In other words, knowledge of the community's culture, its internal structure and its relations with other groups or communities, is essential in order to understand fertility behaviour. It can only be obtained through the use of micro-methods including participant observation and intensive case studies. Much closer co-operation is therefore called for between anthropologists and demographers than exists at present. I must admit here that the co-operation is likely to benefit the anthropologist more than the demographer, for cultural and social change has forced itself to the centre of attention of anthropologists, and it cannot be considered without some attention to rapid population growth and its effects on institutions and behaviour.

It is commonplace that some tension if not opposition exists between macro-surveys and micro-studies, between the practitioners of the bird's eye-view and of the worm's eye-view, and the advocates of each are critical of the other. Macro-surveys produce gross correlations but they do not explain the nature of the linkage between the variables. Too often, a relation of causality is imposed on the linkage in order to enable remedial action to be taken by concerned agencies. It is necessary to add here that the nature of the linkage is best examined in a micro-study. Such a course was taken by Monica Das Gupta in her demographic study of Rampur, a village near Delhi, which had been previously investigated by the anthropologist Oscar Lewis in the fifties. The conclusions of her study are best stated in her own words:

> 'I examined the relationship between the very significant differences in the growth rate of different sections of Rampur on the one hand, and the different economic opportunities open to the villagers, on the other. The Brahmins, who have for the longest period been dependent on the urban economy for much of their income, have had a considerably lower growth rate than those who remained in the village economy. With the growth of population and the mechanization of agriculture, an increasing proportion of villagers is seeking urban employment.
>
> 'However, the various rural strata are differentially equipped to avail themselves of the external employment opportunities, which is neglected in the rationale of their fertility behaviour. The upper strata find it easier to secure the better-paid, permanent jobs, simply because they are in a position to meet the heavy but necessary investment in education and bribes. The volume of investment thus required puts a premium on lower fertility and helps to explain the increasing interest among this group to limit their family size.
>
> 'Of the lower strata, only some have struggled to make these investments and thereby managed to get a foothold on the upward spiral to economic success. However, the bulk of the poorer strata cannot afford such heavy expenditure and have to rely on their traditional village occupations and casual jobs for their subsistence. These people hope to maximize their potential income by having numbers of children, which in turn

makes it increasingly difficult for them to get onto the upward spiral' (Das Gupta, 1977, p.119).

Her micro-study enabled Das Gupta to 'delineate the actual mechanisms through which education and industrialization are influencing fertility in Rampur' (Das Gupta, 1977, p.119).

If micro-studies enable us to understand the nature of the linkage between different variables then they ideally complement macro-studies which give us correlations between the variables. It is necessary that the insights obtained by micro-studies are further tested by appropriately-designed surveys, meso and macro. In this connection, a common and utterly unjustified criticism of micro-studies is that they do not yield generalizations. 'What can a single village teach one about rural India?' is a comment that is only too frequently levelled by critics of village studies in India. The answer is that it can teach a great deal if one is 'not' looking for generalizations about rural India. It can tell one about the quality of life in rural India, the nature of relationships between groups and individuals, besides telling a great deal about the peasants, their preoccupations, problems, world-view, and so forth. In the case of many anthropologists their village studies have provided them with a framework of reference, as to facts as well as relationships, against which new knowledge from other studies could be tested, and then help to build up a picture of a region, even of India as a whole. A village study is only the beginning of a creative process and not its end.

Until very recently, demographers have relied heavily on large-scale surveys, and also their scholarly efforts have been frequently linked to the desire to control rapid population growth. At least that is the perspective one gets living and functioning in India. Dr Kamala Gopala Rao, who abstracted 550 KAP studies, i.e., a series of studies carried out to discover the linkage between family planning knowledge (K), attitude (A) and the practice of contraception (P) during the period 1951-1974, comments:

> 'This survey has indicated that the majority of studies have used questionnaires or schedules and interviews, either guided or open-ended... Out of a total of 550 studies reported here only two studies have indicated observation as the method employed for the study... An intimate problem like family planning cannot be fully understood by asking questions... Case studies, genealogical approaches, depth interviews and participant observation would throw more light on several crucial areas. Not even a single study has so far used these approaches' (as quoted in Shah and Ramaswamy, n.d., pp.3-4).

The case for micro-studies then does need pleading, not as supplanting macro-studies but as supplementing them, not only in the interests of greater understanding but in devising effective family planning programs. Perhaps the time has come to think of micro-studies as a 'necessary adjunct' to macro-studies. That is, when planning a large scale survey a few micro-studies should be undertaken simultaneously, if not earlier, so that the correlations of the macro-studies could be subjected to examination in the micro. Contrariwise, any relationship that emerges as significant in a micro-study should be tested for its range of prevalence through a macro-study. This calls for careful planning that provides for considerable flexibility in the research design. This is very difficult indeed but well worth attempting.

It would be a mistake, common enough though it is, to equate community studies with micro-studies. There can be micro-studies 'below' the community level. Intensive case studies of the experience of particular households with reference to fertility and family planning would be essential to understand in-depth fertility behaviour, and the factors which go to influence it. If households are chosen from different sections of the local community, a cross-sectional view of fertility behaviour will be obtained. Insights from these studies can be translated into hypotheses for testing at the level of community, locality, region and state.

Notes

1. See in this connection Messerschmidt (1981).

2. See in this connection W.H.R. Rivers (1971).

27

Micro-Approaches: Similarities and Differences, Strengths and Weaknesses

John C. Caldwell

In the Conference Papers, most of which are included in this book, researchers record their experiences, methodologies and findings. Insofar as these authors represent a substantial proportion of all persons known at present to be using such methods to understand population phenomena, it is appropriate to examine these contributions to see what generalizations can be made about the approach. Most of the emphasis will be on work in the contemporary Third World in order to achieve maximum comparability. Thus, exciting though their work often is, this concluding chapter will make little reference to the findings of historians, or those working on industrialized countries; it will also omit the specialized work being done in the migration field, and some of the work which is currently in progress by the group at the Australian National University. However, in order to make comparisons relevant to his own experience, the author will draw parallels with work reported elsewhere that he and his wife and colleagues have carried out in both India (Caldwell, Reddy and Caldwell, 1982b) and Africa (Caldwell, 1974; Caldwell, 1982, pp.11-80).

When demographers first began to feel the inadequacy of large scale surveys for identifying the context of population change and the forces lying behind it, they wondered whether they could identify some of the very large numbers of practising anthropologists as having population interests. Angela Molnos (1973) had achieved considerable success in converting East African anthropologists to respondents and inducing them to respond to questionnaires about the demographic behaviour of the populations which they had studied. However, it was clear that such behaviour had, at the best, been a peripheral interest for many of them and that there was much of concern to the demographer which they had not pursued. In early 1981 a Panel on Fertility Determinants of the American National Research Council (Bulatao and Lee, 1983) met in Washington to consider the anthropological contribution to the understanding of population change. The meeting consisted mostly of demographers and sociologists with the addition of some anthropologists who had worked closely with demographers and often employed demographic methods of analysis. In late 1981 a meeting was held in Los Angeles of anthropologists interested in population (Handwerker, 1986), but many of them were more interested in employing small scale surveys in anthropological research or in relating population and anthropological theories than they were in applying traditional methods of anthropological research to exploring demographic behaviour in the context of demographic change (Caldwell, 1985). The IUSSP workshop in Canberra in 1984 anticipated securing a high proportion of field anthropologists. In the event, however, although most of the twenty-eight researchers reporting the findings of their projects had partly or wholly employed anthropological approaches, very few would have described themselves as primarily anthropologists. Those most likely to do so included Oppong, Abu, Das Gupta, Myntti, Aaby, Fulton, Singarimbun, Mougne, Nag and Kak. Yet nearly everyone in this group has worked professionally in population programs. A greater number of those attending the meeting would have described their field as population or demography.

What generalizations can be drawn about micro-approach field methodology? The first is that the research sites were not randomly chosen but, as in traditional anthropology, the opportunity was usually seized when some favourable circumstances made it possible to work in a particular area. Sometimes, as with the Caldwells and Reddy in South India, characteristics were first specified and lists of villages were drawn from censuses and other official documents to narrow the choice. Sometimes, as in the work of Das Gupta, Vlassoff, and Nag and Kak, the village was predetermined by the fact of an earlier researcher having worked there. Chen's six villages were determined by the fact that they were part of the Matlab diarrhoeal diseases research area, but they may have been randomly chosen within it. However, an interesting subgroup has emerged where the population studied had already been included in a larger demographic survey. This was the case in the work of van de Walle, Hill and Thiam, and Fulton and Randall. Van de Walle studied in depth a fraction of those who had been respondents in the larger survey, but all the others appear to have investigated a wider range of people in the communities or households from which the survey respondents had been drawn.

At least nine of the studies could be described as community studies within the general canon of anthropology: Jeffery, Jeffery and Lyon; Mougne; Vlassoff; Nag and Kak; Hull, Hull and Singarimbun; Myntti; Shariff; Das Gupta; and Caldwell, Reddy and Caldwell. To these should be added the work of Lindenbaum described by Chen. A distinctive case was that of Fulton and Randall, where one of the communities was not geographically fixed, and where the researchers moved with the nomadic community. Adeokun's work involved the visiting of a number of areas in Nigeria with periods of investigation. In all of these studies there was emphasis on local residence, broad knowledge of the community and its people, participant observation, much unstructured conversation, and the use of anthropological notebooks.

Nearly all other work required intensive and continuing experience with an area or with an ethnic group. This was true both when long probing interviews were undertaken by Oppong and Abu, Hull, Hull and Singarimbun, Fulton and Randall, Hill and Thiam, and Knodel and colleagues, and also when the studies were essentially small scale demographic surveys or the results of health experiments, but where the work or its analysis was illuminated or made possible by local residence and experiences, as in the case of Pison, Carael, Garenne and Aaby.

For most of the researchers, a quantitative social science background influenced the way they undertook their micro-approach research. One example was an emphasis on initial mapping, a baseline census or even extended survey of the whole population, followed by further ecological mapping of the community from the collected census or survey data. This was a prominent feature in the work of Caldwell, Reddy and Caldwell; Hull, Hull and Singarimbun; Vlassoff; Jeffery, Jeffery and Lyon; Shariff; and Guruswamy. An even more specific hallmark of this work was the decision to predetermine the households which would be studied in greatest depth according to some characteristic of primary interest. Thus, Caldwell, Reddy and Caldwell, when examining sterilization in their earliest South Indian work, chose households containing at least one woman 30-39 years of age, currently married and cohabiting with her spouse, and with three or more surviving children. Similarly, Vlassoff's households contained a married woman, 15-49 years of age, and Chen's one with children under school age. Van de Walle interviewed seventy-four women in Bobo-Dioulasso who had recently given birth and were either in the earlier part of the reproductive span at 20-24 years of age or in the later part at 35 or more years of age.

Probably to a greater extent than most anthropologists, the micro-approach demographers take heed of larger statistical frameworks and attempt to explain demographic trends or other phenomena shown to exist by censuses or large scale surveys. Quite often the major framework, or at least an important element in that framework, is survey work with which the researchers have been associated. Examples of this are provided by the work of Knodel in Thailand, van de Walle in Bourkina-Fasso (formerly Upper Volta), Chen in Bangladesh, and Fulton and Randall, and Hill and Thiam in Mali. It is precisely this larger framework that makes it unnecesssary for the researcher to demonstrate that the relationship that has been established within an individual village exists in other villages. As long as it can be shown that the village fertility or mortality trend has paralleled that of the region or nation, then research efforts can focus on the causes of the change in the village with reasonable assurance that these causes are likely to be operative over a much wider population. If there are local idiosyncrasies, a knowledge of the broader region and its statistics provides a good chance of identifying them as such.

One other quantitative characteristic appears to be common to nearly all the studies. They measure local demographic events by means of a registration system, or a periodic survey, or both. Where such a system is carried on by the government or a larger institution, such as the International Diarrhoeal Diseases

Research Centre (Bangladesh) in the Matlab project, then these are utilized, but most research reported here is in countries where such systems do not exist. In some cases the vital events recording system lies at the heart of the project and the anthropological work explains the data collected or assists in improving the data. This is true of the work described by Pison, Garenne, and Carael, and, to a lesser extent, that of Hill and Thiam, and Fulton and Randall.

Either because demographers are accustomed to surveys and hence to comparable surviving records, or because they work in teams, some investigations have maintained transcripts of semi-structured interviews and have later employed these for analysis. Caldwell, Reddy and Caldwell used this method as a supplementary form of data, particularly at an early stage in the research. Much of the analysis by Knodel, Pramualratana and Havanon was carried out subsequent to the focus group field work employing both Thai and translated English transcripts. Van de Walle's interviews were tape-recorded in Bobo or Mossi,[1] translated into French, and finally entered into a computer. The Caldwells employ transcripts to search for patterns, to generate hypotheses, and to evaluate other hypotheses. The other researchers apparently use them in a similar fashion. However, van de Walle's computer program records the various topics referred to and subsequently groups together selections from interviews when asked to recall specific topics.

Micro-approach researchers are more likely to use a team approach than traditional anthropologists who tended to operate as one person, or possibly a couple, usually employing at least one informant. Micro-approach research often involves collaboration between more developed country and less developed country researchers. The latter typically come from outside the village but are usually from the country being researched and are commonly younger than the more developed country investigator. Often the less developed country researchers either are graduate students in social science or have previously studied in the social sciences. This was the model followed by Knodel in his collaboration with Pramualratana and Havanon, and by the Caldwells and Reddy. When societies have fewer educated persons, then the academic qualifications may be somewhat lower and this modified research model is frequently employed in Africa, as in the research of Oppong and Abu, van de Walle, Fulton and Randall, and Hill and Thiam. In Bangladesh, Chen was able to work with the experienced Matlab professional staff. Such team research makes it necessary to devise new methodologies. In both Africa and India the Caldwells have laid stress on nightly meetings of the research team to discuss the findings of the day. These discussion groups, like the interviews themselves, are a source of material for the anthropologist's notebook.

Even more than most anthropologists, micro-approach researchers pursue a specific topic by long, probing interviews. In contrast to traditional survey interviews, these are wide-ranging and of lengthy and uncertain duration. One of their characteristics is that they seize on new pieces of information and dart off in previously unexpected directions. These new investigations may add a permanent item to the probing lists. The probing lists are little more than *aide-memoires*. They underlie a conversation and are never put forward as a battery of questions. They may be asked in any order and supplemented where necessary. They need not all be asked at the same time but are a guide to the information which should be built up on a family or household over time. This type of interview was fundamental to the research of Oppong and Abu; van de Walle; Hull, Hull and Singarimbun; Shariff; Hetler; Cameron; Vlassoff; Nag and Kak; Jeffery, Jeffery and Lyon; Caldwell, Reddy and Caldwell; and, in a specialized form, Knodel, Pramualratana and Havanon. The Caldwells and Reddy found that interviews by the principal investigators who inevitably felt fewer restrictions, tended to be those which were most free-wheeling and hence were most likely to break into new areas.

Most micro-approach researchers are profoundly interested in change and innovation. This marks them off from those anthropologists who stress the delineation of those aspects of a society which have survived recent modernization. Most field demographers are deeply imbued with an interest in studying demographic transition, and are likely to treat even stable high-fertility, high-mortality societies as examples of a pre-transitional situation. Thus, many of the questions posed by micro-approach researchers deal with change. They often devote particular attention to very old people in order to establish both what the aged claim to have been the pre-existing situation and the subsequent changes. They frequently use these interviews, supplemented by local records and provincial or national archival documents, to establish a picture of change over decades or even generations. Clearly, there is a problem that the memory of the old may have become defective or that recent change may have led to a re-evaluation of the past. Most researchers do not believe that this has been a serious problem and claim that the documentary evidence usually supports the evidence from memory. With regard to some matters, there may be little in the way of documentation. For instance, in their research area, the Caldwells and Reddy found only a few decades earlier a substantial duration of post-partum sexual abstinence and of weaning being determined by the fact of another pregnancy, but these are not matters which appear in the health reports or in the older documents on the society prepared for the East India Company (Dubois, 1906; Buchanan, 1807; Wilks, 1810). Other researchers whose framework was essentially one of change over time include Mougne, who built up a whole local history; Vlassoff; Knodel, Pramualratana and Havanon; Nag and Kak; Oppong and Abu; and, perhaps to a lesser extent, the Hulls and Singarimbun, and the Jefferys and Lyon.

Anthropologists usually do not record the exact circumstances in which they obtain information; particularly whether they were completely alone with the respondent or whether others were present. Perhaps because of their association with survey methodology, these matters concern micro-approach researchers, and they usually specify the technique which was used and report on its success. Vlassoff placed great emphasis on talking individually to women, largely because she was mostly concerned with reproduction and birth control and believed that the women would be reluctant to disclose much of the information if overheard. For the same reason, the Caldwells and Reddy aimed at individual interviews on these matters. However, as their interest moved to household partition, marriage, and the treatment of sickness, they found that discussions with several people at one time often elicited much more information. This was partly because no single individual knew all the facts, but more important was the interaction between individuals which often led to far more information being divulged than any individual would have been likely to proffer. Group interviews were of particular value when discussing changes over time and every memory revealed by one person sparked off trains of thought in others, particularly in the important case of the very old. Groups often varied in composition as some members departed to undertake work that could not wait while others joined the group either because they had just completed a task or because of curiosity or, even more importantly, because they had been contacted as persons with important experiences or information. This approach has been taken further and systematized by Knodel, Pramualratana and Havanon in the focus group work undertaken in Thailand. Groups are set up beforehand and the discussion is led by a moderator, although there is still flexibility to pursue matters as they arise. He places far more importance on securing a considerable measure of social homogeneity within groups than is the case in the less formal interviews in South India, but the latter may achieve a measure of this through caste exclusiveness. In India and elsewhere there are occasions when one wishes to interview a mixed group such as the village *panchayat* (council), and other occasions when much is to be learnt through friction within the group, even to the extent of verbalized class warfare. The reports appear to indicate that group interviews were employed for some purposes by at least Jeffery, Jeffery and Lyon; Mougne; and Myntti. Adeokun and his colleagues in Nigeria discussed birth spacing with women during quasi-social gatherings, such as the maternal and child health clinics, and more easily at the annual harvest festival when sexuality is joked about and openly discussed.

Some micro-approach researchers have borrowed from the anthropologists the life history approach whereby detailed biographies are secured from specified types of individuals, at least with regard to certain areas of behaviour and experience. This has been central to the work of Oppong and Abu, and has also been extensively employed by Fulton and Randall. The Caldwells and Reddy have used it for marriage histories and the record of child illness and treatment, and have attempted to assemble family histories from the often conflicting evidence provided by different respondents within the family in respect of fertility control decision-making. The Jefferys and Lyon appear to have used such histories of the movements of women between households and their contacts with relatives since marriage.

Many micro-approach researchers stress the flexibility of their fieldwork and criticize large scale surveys on the grounds of their rigidity once fieldwork begins and of the extent to which a restricted number of questions and a specific type of wording tend to constrain and even pre-ordain answers. They cherish their own flexibility. Some employ as a central part of their research a series of small scale surveys or complete village censuses which are highly focused on specific behaviour and which are developed only in the course of the research as all the relevant matters become known. Their chief purpose is to provide numerical patterns and to allow certain hypotheses to be supported or refuted by statistical tests. Most research reported in the seminar appears to have placed some emphasis on methodology of this kind.

Micro-approach research is ideally suited to the examination of the working of institutions such as health and family planning programs. The mixture of participant observation, interviewing of major actors and small scale surveys of what is actually relevant in the area allows an understanding of institutional strengths and weaknesses to an extent that is impossible through official reporting systems or predesigned large scale surveys. No chapter here is specifically an institutional study but the operation of the health system is central to the work of Chen and Myntti while that of the family planning program plays a significant role in the studies of Knodel, Pramualratana and Havanon, Mougne, Vlassoff, Nag and Kak, the Hulls and Singarimbun, and the Caldwells and Reddy. Those involved in more traditional demographic research are often deeply suspicious of the micro-approach because they hold that nothing can be conclusively proved in the sense that a high degree of probability can be shown for the statisitcal association of two measures in a survey. Most of the chapters in this volume show very little concern for the validity of this attack. The fundamental reason seems to be a profound scepticism on two different points. The first is whether the statistical association, though significant, is meaningful. They feel that many of the variables are responses to questions which either were not asked about matters of fundamental importance or were asked in such a way as to distort reality by measuring only part of it. The second point is a feeling that the macro-approach presents only a cross-sectional view and is deficient in the measurement of change and quite incapable of explaining change. They value macro-approach work insofar as it provides quantitative parameters but believe that the micro-approach is a better instrument for explaining those parameters. Most were not particularly concerned with using their work to construct better large scale surveys, although this is an argument that has often been put forward to justify the micro-approach.

More surprisingly, little attention was given to the nature of proof in micro work. The Caldwells and Reddy explained that they believed that the validation of the work rested on the same premise as does that of anthropology. Hypotheses are built up within the field and successive research tends to support or disprove them. In practice the scientific method demands survival from being disproved, but qualitative work in the social sciences can never achieve such absolutes, and field workers think much more in terms of increasing plausibility than of disproving null hypotheses. Anthropology has in certain sub-fields built up a larger theoretical structure than has as yet been possible in the micro-approach field with regard to demographic change. Thus, micro-approach researchers experience much greater pressure to generate their own testable hypotheses, although such hypotheses can also frequently be inferred from pre-existing statistical or historical analyses. Certainly, most micro-approach researchers place great importance on the ability of their work to produce theory. How, then, do the researchers move from their transcripts and notes to theory? The Caldwells employ successive household visits to build up files on each household. They repeatedly read these files and their notebooks to suggest testable hypotheses. These hypotheses also come into existence very suddenly from illuminating insights during interviews or during nightly discussions. The hypotheses are discussed and made more rigorous and are subsequently formulated in writing. They are tested in interviews and the results are brought back for further discussion. Increasingly they have treated the population being investigated as co-researchers and have put the hypotheses directly to them for comment, support and refutation. This is also done by Knodel, Pramualratana and Havanon, who agree that the participants in social change are well aware of what has happened to them and are often very sophisticated in the reasons they ascribe for change and the results they see flowing from it. Most of the community-based research seems to have operated in this general fashion.

Most of the seminar participants would agree with Chen and Guruswamy that a micro-approach was needed for time budget studies, and most would agree that this was also true with regard to ill-health and its treatment. The researchers have constantly emphasized that they are interested not only in patterns but also in processes. The analysis of processes produced by Fulton and Randall is culturally solid and complex and could not have been achieved solely through a large scale survey. It is possible that many macro-approach analysts, seeking broad generalizations over a sweep of peoples and the parsimony favoured by economists, would regard this rich texture as a condemnation of the micro-approach. The answer may be that the simple generalizations, in the area of social behaviour, may never be wholly right and may well not be worth pursuing. Many of the researchers would agree with Hill and Thiam that there is no direct economic determination of demographic patterns and hence the demonstration that there is some significance in the correlation is probably more dangerous than helpful. Knodel, Pramualratana and Havanon concluded that social indices do not capture the nature of socioeconomic change and consequently that an analysis employing such measures would almost certainly be highly misleading. In a single chapter, micro-approachers might well feel the space too limited to pursue all their findings. Thus, the Jefferys and Lyon established the almost horrifying degree of social isolation of young married women in the rural area where they were working in North India. Here they report on statistical efforts to show that this might vary according to the distance between their new residence and the home of origin, and went far toward showing that the hypothesized variation did not hold good. Yet, the more immediate conclusion that would be drawn by most readers is that the only protection for such women is to buttress their situation by producing as many descendants, especially sons, as they can and that this goes far toward explaining continuing high fertility.

Finally, it is clear that most of the micro-approach researchers felt that they had established a method for identifying previously unsuspected information and that large scale surveys have almost guaranteed themselves protection from such upsets. Most would support Aaby in his statement: 'Science seems to be most fruitful when it is confronted by new or contradictory evidence'.

We should now proceed briefly to see if there is any relationship between the pictures of demographic change and its origins drawn by the various researchers.

One of the points most widely agreed upon, and indeed uncontested in these chapters, is that there was until recently little effective control of fertility in the societies studied. Where attempts were made to procure abortion this was generally because of conceptions which should not have taken place as in the case of premarital or adulterous sexual relations or incest. The major constraint on fertility was provided by mechanisms which had social ends other than the control of fertility or which aimed at minimizing child and maternal mortality. The former included constraints on the age of marriage, the remarriage of widows and sexual relations once grandmaternal status had been achieved. The latter took the form of prolonged lactation and, in some areas, of post-partum sexual abstinence. There is widespread agreement on three points. None of these mechanisms was consciously or primarily intended to limit family size. Human milk was regarded as a free gift and long lactation was regarded as natural and economical and was not seen as a method of contraception or even usually of birth spacing. When family planning programs came, at least in Asia, the decline in fertility could technically be ascribed to their services and would have been slower or nonexistent without them. This is essentially the picture of Asia provided by the Caldwells and Reddy, Nag and Kak, the Hulls and Singarimbun, Knodel, Pramualratana and Havanon, and Mougne and Mynnti; as it is also of Africa, as described by van de Walle, and Oppong and Abu, except in so far as family planning where it exists at all may have reached only the elites. Those who have studied the matter also agree that rising ages at first marriage are in no way a product of any increasing desire to control ultimate family size, but are a product of quite different social forces. This is clear in the reports of Knodel, Pramualratana and Havanon, the Hulls and Singarimbun, and in the work of the Caldwells and Reddy. Greater indecision marked the interpretation of the institution of child fostering, usually between relatives. The Caldwells concluded in Africa that this showed the net economic value of children, but, in Thailand where it is also practised, Mougne; and Knodel, Pramualratana and Havanon were less certain. Another important point is that Knodel, Pramualratana and Havanon and the Caldwells have specifically reported that the reduced probability of child death is rarely cited by families as a reason for restricting fertility; equally significant is the silence on the topic in the other reports, evidencing apparently the failure of respondents to discuss family planning in these terms. Finally, some of the reports show that a failure of respondents to employ contraception arises not only from perceiving no economic advantage in doing so but also a deep apprehension of the effect on comfort, health or even life of the means employed. In India this has been reported by the Jefferys and by the Caldwells and Reddy. Vlassoff reported almost a lack of relation between sterilization and the desire to limit family size when she noted that women preferred to be sterilized only at a time when they would have traditionally begun to abstain from sexual relations. Whether this is evidence of coping with the pressures of the Emergency, or of securing the incentives without affecting fertility, or of sexual revolution is unclear. One point with regard to pre-transitional fertility control remains somewhat controversial, at least in the thoughts of the present writer. Mougne presents evidence to show that womb drying in Thailand is intended to prolong the birth interval. Yet it is so parallel to similar actions in Africa and elsewhere that are meant to return the womb to its normal condition that one would like to encourage further research.

Although the onset of fertility decline may owe its timing in Asia to the provision of family planning services, nearly all researchers agree that the success of the programs was also due to massive social and economic change. What is striking is the consensus with regard to these changes. Knodel, Pramualratana and Havanon identify in Thailand the declining access to land and subdivision of holdings; the penetration of the society by the market economy; a reduction in the amount children contribute in labour and an increase in expenditures for children; the rising cost of schooling and an increasing dilemma posed by the current cost of schooling several children at once threatening to shorten the potential schooling period of each so that the maximum returns possible in later life from educated children may not be received; a changing culture partly induced by the messages from radio, television and the cinema; and a context in which the locus of family planning decision-making is largely that of the conjugal couple with the wife having considerable say. They pointed out that one inducement to educate children was to secure for them non-agricultural jobs so as to escape from unstable farm incomes, and that, as the government provides more schools, there is ever less option with regard to giving children at least some schooling. This is a picture of the preconditions for fertility decline in Thailand that is in essential agreement with Mougne's analysis. She stresses that women play a major role in agriculture and control local trade and that repeated pregnancies and caring for young children disrupt these activities. There is a temptation to prevent additional births in a society where fertility above what was considered an adequate family size did not bring extra prestige. These identifications of the major factors involved in destabilizing a society with previously stable high fertility is essentially the same as that identified by the Caldwells and Reddy in India, not only with regard to the main factors but even to their ordering by degree of importance. Very similar conclusions have also been drawn by Shariff for another locality in South India. Nor are they dissimilar from the findings of Nag and Kak in Punjab. They and the Caldwells and Reddy have both identified a declining demand for child labour related to reduced farm size, technological change and an increasing propensity by large farmers not to employ as agricultural labour either whole families or young children, but preferably adults. Both the Caldwells and Mougne found that landless labourers were less certain about the advantages of family planning because their only hope for improving their living conditions lies in the possibility that one of their children might make the breakthrough into greater affluence for the whole family. The major emphasis on education was on the impact of the cost of raising children. Nevertheless, some attention was paid to the effects brought about by girls going to school and growing to be educated mothers. Chen reported Lindenbaum's findings in Bangladesh that the community perceived education as a key element in a woman's social identity, that she was more self-sufficient and was expected by the community to act in this way, and that this induced mothers to seek modern health treatment for their children at an earlier time and changed behaviour in the home. This is very similar not only to what the Caldwells and Reddy found in South India but also to the Caldwells' findings in Nigeria and Ghana. Africa is often different; in much of it there is no private land, education costs are more widely diffused, wealth flows are protected by lineage and even ancestral interests in the rights of the old, and reproductive decision-making is rendered complex by the concept of bride wealth conferrring the major rights in this domain on the husband and his family (Caldwell and Caldwell, 1985). Nevertheless, Oppong and Abu found that among the professional elites in Ghana conflict between women's work and problems of child care is beginning to encourage limitation of family size. Fulton and Randall in the Sahel discovered a situation among agriculturalists not very different from that described elsewhere for sub-Saharan Africa, but among nomadic pastoralists they described a situation where class differences and important reasons for controlling marriage mean that there is not strong emphasis on very high fertility and indeed no attainment of it.

The situation found in this analysis is that most micro-approach researchers work in much the same way, and with much the same perspectives. Their work is small scale and low cost although most would probably not object to the setting up of a more expensive network of such projects providing that competent researchers could be found. The studies are intensive and give great attention to the cultural, social and economic context. There is a diversity of research methods although the main division is between those who place the emphasis on demographic measurements and use the more qualitative approach to explain their demographic rates and those who seek to explain changing society including demographic behaviour. Among all, there is a flexibility of approach and usually a continuity of researcher involvement from data collection to analysis and publication. Most have a deep suspicion that without personal continuity the essential truth of demographic change might be misunderstood or omitted, much as the great detective discovers when visiting the scene of the crime that the key element had nearly been overlooked.

We are probably coming close to understanding why fertility declined in Southeast and South Asia. Micro-approach workers have established a framework which will set an agenda both for social and demographic historians and also for contemporary quantifiers. An equally clear agenda has not yet been drawn up for the area of morbidity and mortality decline. Where the fertility situation is essentially different as in sub-Saharan Africa or in the Islamic societies stretching from Mauritania to Bangladesh, the task is just beginning and a great deal of good micro-approach work is desperately needed.

Perhaps a last admonitory note is appropriate. The heart of the micro-approach work is the direct and continuing contact between the principal investigators and the people they are investigating. This should be the case with all good social science. Even large scale surveys should be preceded by semi-structured investigations ranging from conversation to long probing interviews and subsequently by a series of field tests as the questionnaire is put together - not primarily tests of the logistic system but of whether the questions are meaningful, whether they are understood and answered adequately by the respondents, and whether they are all the questions necessary to investigate fully the matter being studied in that society. These are not tasks that can be satisfactorily delegated; the best surveys and the best subsequent analyses are those where the senior researchers are fully involved in every aspect of the interviewing and later work. The micro-approach will always be able to accommodate variations, be they focus group work or better collection of vital statistics through immersion in a specific society. Nevertheless, the central tradition of the work should remain community studies. There will be dangers. With greater funding and more comparative work, the temptation felt by the principal investigators to be organizers, co-ordinators and interpreters of results will grow. Some will allow their assistants to do nearly all - or even all - the interviewing, although this will not always be clear in the published reports of the work. If this happens, then the real value of the work is largely lost. Genuine insights come from undertaking and being in control of every stage of the investigation. It is only during the interviewing (and not while reading the reports) that chance remarks are heard, that new leads can be spontaneously followed, that nascent hypotheses begin to emerge, and that sufficient change in balance occurs to introduce a whole new emphasis into the study. The worthwhile studies will remain those where one person or a small group of people assumes full intellectual responsibility at every stage of the investigation from interviewing to developing new testable hypotheses, and through the analysis to the writing up and publication.

Notes

1. Known by linguists as 'moré' but usually referred to outside Africa by the name of the speakers, the Mossi.

REFERENCES

Aaby, P. (1984), 'Epidemics among Amerindians and Inuits. A Preliminary Interpretation', unpublished manuscript. [16]

Aaby, P., Bukh, J., Lisse, I.M. and Smits, A.J. (1981a), 'Measles Vaccination and Child Mortality', ***Lancet***, vol.2, p.93. [16]

Aaby, P., Bukh, J., Lisse, I.M., Smits, A.J., Smedman, L., Jeppsson, O. and Lindberg, A. (1981b), 'Breastfeeding and Measles Mortality in Guinea-Bissau', ***Lancet***, vol.2, p.1231. [16]

Aaby, P., Bukh, J., Smits, A.J. and Lisse, I.M. (1981c), ***Child Mortality in Guinea-Bissau: Malnutrition or Overcrowding?***, Institute of Ethnology and Anthropology, Copenhagen. [16]

Aaby, P., Bukh, J., Lisse, I.M. and Smits, A.J. (1983a), 'Measles Mortality, State of Nutrition, and Family Structure: A Community Study from Guinea-Bissau', ***The Journal of Infectious Diseases***, vol.147, no.4, pp.693-701. [16]

Aaby, P., Bukh, J., Lisse, I.M. and Smits, A.J. (1983b), 'Spacing, Crowding, and Child Mortality in Guinea-Bissau', ***Lancet***, vol.2, p.161. [16]

Aaby, P., Bukh, J., Lisse, I.M. and Smits, A.J. (1984a), 'Measles Vaccination and Reduction in Child Mortality: A Community Study from Guinea-Bissau', ***Journal of Infection***, vol.8, pp.13-21. [16]

Aaby, P., Bukh, J., Lisse, I.M. and Smits, A.J. (1984b), 'Overcrowding and Intensive Exposure as Determinants of Measles Mortality', ***American Journal of Epidemiology***, vol.120, pp.49-63. [16]

Aaby, P., Bukh, J., Lisse, I.M. and Smits, A.J. (1984c), 'Severe Measles in Sunderland, 1885. A European-African Comparison of Causes of Severe Infection', unpublished manuscript. [16]

Aaby, P., Bukh, J., Lisse, I.M., Smits, A.J., Gomes, J., Fernandes, M.A., Indi, F. and Soares, M. (1984d), 'Determinants of Measles Mortality in a Rural Area of Guinea-Bissau: Crowding, Age, and Malnutrition', ***Journal of Tropical Pediatrics***, vol.30, pp.164-8. [16]

Adams, R.N. and Rubel, A.J. (1967), 'Sickness and Social Relations', in M. Nash (ed.), ***Handbook of Middle American Indians***, vol.6, pp.333-56. [23]

Addo, N., Gaisie, S.K. and Nabila, A. (1978), 'Determinants of Fertility Patterns and Their Implications for the Ghana Population Policy', paper presented at a Review Workshop of the Committee of Population Policies in Developing Countries, Cairo, Case Studies on Population Policies in Developing Countries, Liège, IUSSP, mimeo. [9]

Adeokun, L.A. (1981), 'The Next Child: Spacing Strategy in Yorubaland (with Translations from Taped Interviews)', African Demography Working Papers No.8, Population Studies Center, Philadelphia. [8]

<u>Note</u>: For easy reference nos. in [] denote chapter(s) of origin in this volume.

Adeokun, L.A. (1982), 'Marital Sexuality and Birth Spacing among the Yoruba', in C. Oppong (ed.), ***Female and Male in West Africa***, George Allen and Unwin, London, pp.127-37. [8]

Adeokun, L.A. (1983a), 'Early Child Development and the Next Child Decision', ***Genus***, vol.39, nos. 1-4, pp.115-40. [8]

Adeokun, L.A. (1983b), 'Fertility-Inhibiting Effects of the Intermediate Fertility Variables Among the Ekiti and Ikale Yoruba in Nigeria', paper presented at the Second Annual Conference of the Population Association of Nigeria, University of Ife, Ile-Ife, November. [8]

Adeokun, L.A. (1984), 'Socio-Economic Determinants of Child Development and Child Spacing', Department of Demography and Social Statistics Seminar Series, University of Ife, Ile-Ife, March. [8]

Adra, N. (1983), 'Local Perception of Breastfeeding, Fertility and Infant Care in Ahjur, Yemen Arab Republic', unpublished report, ME Awards, The Population Council, Cairo. [24]

Ahmad, S. (1984), 'Quality of Age Data in 1971 and 1980 Censuses of Indonesia', Research Note No.19, International Population Dynamics Program, Department of Demography, ANU, Canberra. [4]

Anker, R., Buvinic, M. and Youssef, N. (1981), ***Women's Roles and Population Trends in the Third World***, Croom-Helm, London. [18]

Ansell, C. (1981), 'Women and Health in Mahweit Town', unpublished report, American Save the Children/Yemen, Sanaa. [24]

Appleby, A.B. (1979), ***Famine in Tudor and Stuart England***, Stanford University Press. [13]

Appleyard, R.T. (1964), ***British Emigration to Australia***, ANU Press, Canberra. [21]

Arthur, W.B. and McNicoll, G. (1978), 'An Analytical Survey of Population and Development in Bangladesh', ***Population and Development Review***, vol.4, no.1, pp.23-80. [Intro]

Asian Development Bank (1978), ***Rural Asia: Challenge and Opportunity***, Preager, New York. [1]

Aycock, W.L. and Eaton, P.A. (1925), 'A Comparison Between Multiple Cases of Measles, Scarlet Fever and Infantile Paralysis', ***American Journal of Hygiene***, vol.5, pp.733-41. [16]

Ayer, A.J. (1946), ***Language, Truth and Logic***, Gollancz, London. [Intro]

Azu, D.G. (1974), ***The Ga Family and Social Change***, African Social Research Documents, Leiden. [9]

Bailey, K.D. (1978), ***Methods of Social Research***, The Free Press, New York. [22]

Bastin, R. (1985), 'Weasisi Mobility: A Committed Rural Proletariat?', in M. Chapman and R.M. Prothero (eds), ***Circulation in Population Movement: Substance and Concepts from the Melanesian Case***, Routledge and Kegan Paul, London, pp.175-90. [22]

Bathgate, M.A. (1975), 'Bihu Matena Golo: A Study of the Ndi-Nggai of West Guadalcanal and Their Involvement in the Solomon Islands Cash Economy', unpublished Ph.D. thesis, Department of Geography, Victoria University, Wellington. [22]

Bathgate, M.A. (1985), 'Movement Processes from Precontact to Contemporary times: the Ndi-Nggai, West Guadalcanal, Solomon Islands', in M. Chapman and R.M. Prothero (eds), ***Circulation in Population Movement: Substance and Concepts from the Melanesian Case***, Routledge and Kegan Paul, London, pp.83–118. [20,22]

Becker, G.S. (1976), ***The Economic Approach to Human Behavior***, University of Chicago Press. [1]

Bedford, R.D. (1971), 'Mobility in Transition: An Analysis of Population Movement in the New Hebrides', unpublished Ph.D. thesis, Department of Human Geography, ANU, Canberra. [22]

Bedford, R.D. (1973), 'New Hebridean Mobility: A Study of Circular Migration', Department of Human Geography Publication HG/9, ANU, Canberra. [22]

Bedford, R.D. (1985), 'Population Mobility in a Small Island Periphery: The Case of Eastern Fiji', in M. Chapman and R.M. Prothero (eds), ***Circulation in Population Movement: Substance and Concepts from the Melanesian Case***, Routledge and Kegan Paul, London, pp.333–59. [22]

Bennett, J.A. (1974a), 'Cross-Cultural Influences on Village Relocation on the Weather Coast of Guadalcanal, c1870–1953', unpublished M.A. thesis, University of Hawaii, Honolulu. [20]

Bennett, J.A. (1974b), 'Population Distribution and Village Relocation 1870–1950', in M. Chapman and P. Pirie (eds), ***Tasi Mauri: A Report on Population and Resources of the Guadalcanal Weather Coast***, East-West Population Institute and University of Hawaii, Honolulu, pp.2.1–69. [20]

Bennett, J.A. (1979), 'Wealth of the Solomons: A History of Trade, Plantations and Society in the Solomon Islands, c1800–1942', unpublished Ph.D. thesis, ANU, Canberra. [20]

Bennett, J.A. (1981), 'Personal Work Histories of Solomon Islands Plantation Labourers - Methodology and Uses', ***Pacific Studies***, vol.5, pp.34–56. [20]

Bennett, J.A. (1987), ***Wealth of the Solomons: A History of a Pacific Archipelago, 1800–1978***, Pacific Islands Monograph Series 3, University of Hawaii Press, Honolulu. [20]

Bequele, A. (1980), 'Poverty, Inequality and Stagnation: The Ghanaian Experience', World Employment Programme Research Working Paper, ILO, Geneva, mimeo, (restricted). [9]

Bernus, E. (1981), ***Touaregs Nigériens***, ORSTOM, Paris. [12]

Bertaux, D. (ed.), (1981), ***Biography and Society: The Life History Approach in the Social Sciences***, Sage Publications, London. [9,22]

Bertaux-Wiamé, I. (1981), 'The Life History Approach to the Study of Internal Migration', in D. Bertaux (ed.), ***Biography and Society***, Sage Publications, London, pp.249–65, 29–35. [9,22]

Bertaux, D. and Bertaux-Wiamé, I. (1981), 'Life Stories in the Baker's Trade', in D. Bertaux (ed.), ***Biography and Society***, Sage Publications, London, pp.169–89. [9]

Bertin, R.F. (1928), 'Village Chrétiens de Guadalcanal dans le District de Tangarare', ***Les Missions Catholiques***, pp.550–74. [20]

Bertrand, J.T., Pineda, M.A. and Santiso G. R. (1979), 'Ethnic Differences in Family Planning Acceptance in Rural Guatemala', ***Studies in Family Planning***, vol.10, nos 8/9, pp.238–45. [23]

Bhat, P.N.M., Preston, S. and Dyson, T. (1984), ***Vital Rates in India, 1961-1981***, Committee on Population and Demography, Report No.24, National Academy Press, Washington D.C. [14]

Billewicz, W.Z. and McGregor, I.A. (1981), 'The Demography of Two West African (Gambian) Villages, 1951-75', ***Journal of Biosocial Science***, vol.13, pp.219-40. [16,17]

Bilsborrow, R.E. (1981), ***Surveys of Internal Migration in Low Income Countries: The Need for and Content of Community Level Variables***, International Labour Office, Geneva. [21]

Black, F.L., Pinheiro, F.P., Heirholzer, W.J. and Lee, R.V. (1979), 'Epidemiology of Infectious Disease: The Example of Measles', in ***Health and Disease in Tribal Societies***, Elsevier, New York. [16]

Blacker, J.G.C. (1977), 'The Estimation of Adult Mortality in Africa from Data on Orphanhood', ***Population Studies***, vol.31, no.1, pp.107-28. [17]

Blalock, H.M. (1969), ***Theory Construction***, Prentice Hall, Englewood Cliffs, N.J. [Intro]

Blalock, H.M. and Blalock, A.B. (eds), (1968), ***Methodology in Social Research***, McGraw-Hill, New York. [Intro]

Bolte, K.M. (1980), 'On Analytic Problems of Modern Reproductive Behaviour Types of Reproductive Decision Making: A Step Towards a Predictive Population Theory', paper presented to the Seminar on Determinants of Fertility Trends, Major Theories and New Directions for Research, Bad Homberg, IUSSP, Liège. [9]

Bongaarts, J. (1978), 'A Framework for Analysing the Proximate Determinants of Fertility', ***Population and Development Review***, vol.4, no.1, pp.105-32. [8,24]

Bongaarts, J. (1982), 'The Fertility-Inhibiting Effect of the Intermediate Fertility Variables', ***Studies in Family Planning***, vol.13, pp.179-89. [8]

Bongaarts, J., Burch, T. and Wachter, K., ***Family Demography: Methods and Their Application***, (in press). [19]

Bongaarts, J. and Potter, R.G. (1983), ***Fertility, Biology and Behavior: An Analysis of the Proximate Determinants***, Academic Press, New York. [Intro,11]

Bonnemaison, J. (1976), 'Circular Migration and Uncontrolled Migration in the New Hebrides', ***South Pacific Bulletin***, vol.4, pp.7-13. [22]

Bonnemaison, J. (1977), 'The Impact of Population Patterns and Cash-Cropping on Urban Migration on the New Hebrides', ***Pacific Viewpoint***, no.18, pp.119-32. [22]

Bourgeois-Pichat, J. (1981), 'Recent Demographic Change in Western Europe: An Assessment', ***Population and Development Review***, vol.7, pp.19-42. [1]

Brass, W. and Coale, A.J. (1968), 'Methods of Analysis and Estimation', in W. Brass ***et al.*** (eds), ***The Demography of Tropical Africa***, Princeton University Press, pp.88-139. [17]

Brass, W. and Hill, K.H. (1973), 'Estimating Adult Mortality from Orphanhood', in ***Proceedings of the International Population Conference, Liège 1973***, IUSSP, Liège. [17]

Brass, W. and Macrae, S. (1984), 'Childhood Mortality Estimated from Reports on Previous Births Given by Mothers at the Time of a Maternity: I. Preceding-Births Technique', ***Asian and Pacific Census Forum***, vol.11, no.2, pp.5-8. [Intro]

Breckenridge, M.E. and Murphy, M.N. (1969), ***Growth and Development of the Young Child*** (8th edition), W.B. Saunders Company, Philadelphia. [8]

Bricker, V.R. (1973), ***Ritual Humor In Highland Chiapas***, University of Texas Press, Austin. [23]

Bricker, V.R. (1981), ***The Indian Christ, The Indian Kings***, University of Texas Press, Austin. [23]

Bronowski, J. (1951), ***The Common Sense of Science***, Pelican, London. [Intro]

Bryant, N.A. (1973), 'Population Pressure and Agricultural Resources in Central Java: The Dynamics of Change', unpublished Ph.D. thesis, Michigan State University, E. Lansing. [21]

Buchanan, F.H. (1807), ***A Journey from Madras through the Countries of Mysore, Canara and Malabar Performed under the Orders of the Most Noble the Marquis Wellesley Governor General of India for the Express Purpose of Investigating the State of Agriculture, Arts and Commerce; Religion, Manners and Customs; the History Natural and Civil and Antiquities in the Dominions of the Rajah of Mysore and the Countries Acquired by the Honorable East India Company***, T. Cadell and W. Davies, London. [27]

Bulatao, R.A. and Lee, R.D. (eds), (1983), ***Determinants of Fertility in Developing Countries***, Academic Press, New York. [1,27]

Bumpass, L.L. and Westoff, C.F. (1970), ***The Later Years of Childbearing***, Princeton University Press. [Intro]

Cain, M.T. (1977), 'The Economic Activities of Children in a Village in Bangladesh', ***Population and Development Review***, vol.3, no.3, pp.201-27. [Intro,6,8,14]

Cain, M.T. (1978), 'The Household Life Cycle and Economic Mobility in Rural Bangladesh', ***Population and Development Review***, vol.4, no.3, pp.421-38. [Intro]

Cain, M.T. (1981), 'Risk and Insurance: Perspectives in Fertility and Agrarian Change in India and Bangladesh', ***Population and Development Review***, vol.7, no.3, pp.435-74. [6,13,14]

Cain, M.T. (1982), 'Perspectives on Family and Fertility in Developing Countries', ***Population Studies***, vol.36, no.2, pp. 159-76. [13]

Cain, M.T. (1983a), 'Intensive Community Studies', Paper 1, Session W, World Fertility Survey Seminar on Collection and Analysis of Data on Community and Institutional Factors, International Statistical Institute, Voorburg. [13]

Cain, M.T. (1983b), 'Fertility as an Adjustment to Risk', ***Population and Development Review***, vol.9, pp.688-702. [13]

Cain, M.T., Khanam, S.R. and Nahar, S. (1979), 'Class, Patriarchy and Women's Work in Bangladesh', ***Population and Development Review***, vol.5, no.3, pp.405-38. [13]

Cain, M.T. and Lieberman, S. (1982), 'Development Policy and the Prospects for Fertility Decline in Bangladesh', Working Paper No.91, Center for Policy Studies, the Population Council, New York. [1]

Calder, B. (1977), 'Focus Groups and the Nature of Qualitative Marketing Research', ***Journal of Marketing Research***, no.14, pp. 353-64. [3]

Caldwell, J.C. (1968), ***Population and Family Change in Africa: The New Urban Elite in Ghana***, ANU Press, Canberra. [9]

Caldwell, J.C. (1969), ***African Rural-Urban Migration***, ANU Press, Canberra. [21]

Caldwell, J.C. (1974), 'The Study of Fertility and Fertility Change in Tropical Africa', Occasional Papers no.7, World Fertility Survey/Intl. Statistical Institute, Voorburg. [27]

Caldwell, J.C. (1976), 'Toward a Restatement of Demographic Transition Theory', ***Population and Development Review***, vol.2, nos 3-4, pp.321-66. [6,13]

Caldwell, J.C. (1977), 'Towards a Restatement of Demographic Transition Theory', in J.C. Caldwell (ed.), ***The Persistence of High Fertility***, Department of Demography, ANU, Canberra, pp.25-119. [12]

Caldwell, J.C. (1978), 'A Theory of Fertility from High Plateau to Destabilization', ***Population and Development Review***, vol.4, no.4, pp.553-77. [13]

Caldwell, J.C. (1979), 'Education as a Factor in Mortality Decline: An Examination of Nigerian Data', ***Population Studies***, vol.33, no.3, pp.395-413. [15]

Caldwell, J.C. (1981), 'The Mechanisms of Demographic Change in Historical Perspective', ***Population Studies***, vol.35, no.1, pp. 5-27. [6]

Caldwell, J.C. (1982), ***Theory of Fertility Decline***, Academic Press, London. [1,6,10,27]

Caldwell, J.C. (1983a), 'In Search of a Theory of Fertility Decline for India and Sri Lanka', in K. Srinivasan and S. Mukerji (eds), ***Dynamics of Population and Family Welfare 1983***, Himalaya Publishing House, Bombay, pp.103-37. [2,14]

Caldwell, J.C. (1983b), 'Direct Economic Costs and Benefits of Children', in R.A. Bulatao and R.D. Lee (eds), ***Determinants of Fertility in Developing Countries***, Academic Press, New York, vol.1, pp.458-93. [Intro,6]

Caldwell, J.C. (1985), 'Strengths and Limitations of the Survey Approach for Measuring and Understanding Fertility Change: Alternative Possibilities', in J. Cleland and J. Hobcraft (eds), ***Reproductive Change in Developing Countries: Insights from the World Fertility Survey***, Oxford University Press, pp.45-63. [2,22,27]

Caldwell, J.C. and Caldwell, P. (1977), 'The Role of Marital Sexual Abstinence in Determining Fertility: A Study of the Yoruba in Nigeria', ***Population Studies***, vol.31, no.2, pp.193-217. [Intro]

Caldwell, J.C. and Caldwell, P. (1985), 'Cultural Forces Tending to Sustain High Fertility in Tropical Africa', PHN Technical Note 85-116, Population Health and Nutrition Department, World Bank, Washington, D.C. [2,27]

Caldwell, J.C., Reddy, P.H. and Caldwell, P. (1982a), 'The Micro Approach in Demographic Investigation: Toward a Methodology', paper presented at an International Seminar on Demographic Change in the Social Context, organized by the Population Centre, Bangalore, September. [2,3,5,21,22]

Caldwell, J.C., Reddy, P.H. and Caldwell, P. (1982b), 'The Causes of Demographic Change in Rural South India: A Micro Approach', ***Population and Development Review***, vol.8, no.4, pp.689–727. [Intro,2,7,14,27]

Caldwell, J.C., Reddy, P.H. and Caldwell, P. (1983a), 'The Social Component of Mortality Decline: An Investigation in South India Employing Alternative Methodologies', ***Population Studies***, vol. 37, no.2, pp.183–205. [Intro,2]

Caldwell, J.C., Reddy, P.H. and Caldwell, P. (1983b), 'The Causes of Marriage Change in South India', ***Population Studies***, vol.37, no.3, pp.343–61. [Intro,2]

Caldwell, J.C., Reddy, P.H. and Caldwell, P. (1984a), 'The Determinants of Family Structure in Rural South India', ***Journal of Marriage and the Family***, vol.46, no.1, pp.215–29. [Intro,2]

Caldwell, J.C., Reddy, P.H. and Caldwell, P. (1984b), 'The Determinants of Fertility Decline in Rural South India', in T. Dyson and N. Crook (eds), ***India's Demography: Essays on the Contemporary Population***, South Asian Publishers, New Delhi, pp. 187–208. [2]

Caldwell, J.C., Reddy, P.H. and Caldwell, P. (1985), 'Educational Transition in Rural South India', ***Population and Development Review***, vol.11, no.1, pp.29–51. [Intro]

Caldwell, J.C., Reddy, P.H. and Caldwell, P. (1986), 'Periodic High Risk as a Cause of Fertility Decline in a Changing Rural Environment: Survival Strategies in the 1980–1983 South Indian Drought', ***Economic Development and Cultural Change***, vol.34, no.4, pp.677–701. [Intro,2]

Caldwell, J.C. and Ruzicka, L.T. (1985), 'The Determinants of Mortality Change in South Asia', in K. Srinivasan and S. Mukerji (eds), ***Dynamics of Population and Family Welfare: 1985***, Himalaya Publishing House, Bombay. [2]

Caldwell, P. and Caldwell, J.C. (1981), 'The Function of Child-Spacing in Traditional Societies and the Direction of Change', in H.J. Page and R. Lesthaeghe (eds), ***Child Spacing in Tropical Africa***, Academic Press, London. [Intro,10]

Camargo, A.A. de (1981), 'The Actor and the System: Trajectory of the Brazilian Political Elites', in D. Bertaux (ed.), ***Biography and Society***, Sage Publications, London, pp.191–201. [9]

Cameron, J. (1984), 'Notions of Biology in Value of Children. Research Application of an Interpretive Perspective to a Demographic Problem', paper presented at the IUSSP Seminar on Micro-Approaches to Demographic Research, ANU, Canberra, 3–7 September. [Intro,27]

Campbell, B.M.S. (1983), 'Agricultural Programs in Medieval England: Some Evidence from Eastern Norfolk', ***Economic History Review***, vol.36, no.1, pp.26–46. [13]

Cancian, F. (1972), ***Change and Uncertainty in a Peasant Economy***, Stanford University Press. [23]

Cantrelle, P. (1969), ***Etude Démographique dans la Région du Sine-Saloum (Senegal). Etat Civil et Observation Démographique***, Travaux et Documents 1, ORSTOM, Paris, 121p. [17]

Caraël, M. (1981), 'Child-spacing, Ecology and Nutrition in the Kivu Province of Zaire', in H.J. Page and R. Lesthaeghe (eds), ***Child-Spacing in Tropical Africa: Traditions and Change***, Academic Press, London, pp.275–86. [11]

Catani, M. (1981), 'Social-Life History as a Ritualized Oral Exchange', in D. Bertaux (ed.), ***Biography and Society***, Sage Publications, London, pp.211-22. [9]

Census of India (1981), ***Report and Tables based on 5 per cent Sample Data, Part 11 Special, Series 6***, Haryana Government of India. [6]

Chalmers, A.K. (1930), ***The Health of Glasgow, 1818-1925***, Glasgow. [16]

Chandrasekaran, C. (1959), 'Cultural Factors and Propagation of Family Planning in the Indian Setting', ***Journal of Family Welfare***, vol.5, no.3, pp.43-51. [5]

Chapman, M. (1966), 'Field Report: October 1965 - February 1966', Duidui, Solomon Islands, typescript. [20]

Chapman, M. (1969), 'A Population Study in South Guadalcanal: Some Results and Implications', ***Oceania***, vol.40, pp.119-47. [20,21,22]

Chapman, M. (1970), 'Population Movement in Tribal Society: The Case of Duidui and Pichahila, British Solomon Islands', unpublished Ph.D. thesis, University of Washington, Seattle. [20,22]

Chapman, M. (1971), 'Population Research in the Pacific Islands: A Case Study and Some Implications', Working Paper No.17, East-West Population Institute, Honolulu. [20,21]

Chapman, M. (1975), 'Mobility in a Non-Literate Society: Method and Analysis for Two Guadalcanal Communities', in L.A. Kosiński and R.M. Prothero (eds), ***People on the Move***, Methuen, London, pp.129-45. [20,22]

Chapman, M. (1976), 'Tribal Mobility as Circulation: A Solomon Islands Example of Micro/Macro Linkages', in L.A. Kosiński and J.W. Webb (eds), ***Population at Microscale***, New Zealand Geographical Society and the Commission on Population Geography, International Geographical Union, Christchurch, pp.127-42. [20,22]

Chapman, M. (1985), 'Me Go "Walkabout"; You Too?', in M. Chapman and R.M. Prothero (eds), ***Circulation in Population Movement: Substance and Concepts from the Melanesian Case***, Routledge and Kegan Paul, London, pp.429-43. [20]

Chapman, M. and Bennett, J. (1980), 'Method and History of a Multidisciplinary Field Project: Population and Resources of South Guadalcanal, 1971-75', ***Yagl-Ambu*** (Papua New Guinea Journal of the Social Sciences and Humanities), vol.7, pp.47-76. [20]

Chapman, M. and Pirie, P. (1974), 'Tasi Mauri: A Report on Population and Resources of the Guadalcanal Weather Coast', East-West Population Institute and University of Hawaii, Honolulu, multilith. [20]

Chen, L.C., Ahmed, S., Gesche, M. and Mosley, W.H. (1974), 'A Prospective Study of Birth Interval Dynamics in Rural Bangladesh', ***Population Studies***, vol.28, no.2, pp.277-96. [11]

Chen, L.C., Chowdhury, A.K.M.A. and Huffman, S.L. (1980), 'Anthropo-metric Assessment of Energy-Protein Malnutrition and Subsequent Risk of Mortality among Preschool Aged Children', ***American Journal of Clinical Nutrition***, vol.33, pp.1836-45. [16]

Chen, L.C., Huq, E. and D'Souza, S. (1981), 'Sex Bias in the Family Allocation of Food and Health Care in Rural Bangladesh', ***Population and Development Review***, vol.7, no.1, pp.55-70. [15]
Chen, L.C., Rahman, M. and Sarder, A.M. (1980), 'Epidemiology and Causes of Death among Children in a Rural Area of Bangladesh', ***International Journal of Epidemiology***, vol.9, pp.25-33. [15]
Chen, L.C. and Scrimshaw, N.S. (eds), (1983), ***Diarrhea and Malnutrition***, Plenum Press, New York and London. [15]
Chowdhury, A.K.M.A. and Chen, L.C. (1977), 'The Interaction of Nutrition, Infection, and Mortality during Recent Food Crisis in Bangladesh', ***Food Research Institute Studies***, vol.16, pp. 1-23. [15]
Chiang, C.L. (1968), ***Introduction to Stochastic Processes in Biostatistics***, John Wiley and Sons, New York. [17]
Cicourel, A.V. (1973), ***Cognitive Sociology***, Penguin Books, Harmondsworth. [1]
Cicourel, A.V. (1974), ***Theory and Method in a Study of Argentine Fertility***, Wiley, New York. [1]
CICRED (1984), 'Demography of the Family, Project No.2, Final Report', CICRED, Paris. [19]
Clarke, P.B. (1982), ***West Africa and Islam***, Edward Arnold, London. [19]
Coale, A.J. (1967), 'Factors Associated with the Development of Low Fertility: An Historic Summary', ***World Population Conference 1965***, United Nations, New York, vol.2. [7]
Coale, A.J. (1973), 'The Demographic Transition', in ***The Population Debate: Dimensions and Perspectives***, United Nations, New York, vol.1. [1]
Coe, M. (1966), ***The Maya***, Thames and Hudson, London. [23]
Colby, B.N. (1965), ***Ethnic Relations in Highland Chiapas***, University of New Mexico Press, Santa Fe. [23]
Colby, B.N. and van den Berghe, P. (1969), ***Ixil Country***, University of California Press, Berkeley. [23]
Colle, P. (1937), ***Essai de Monographie des Bashi***, Polycopié, Bukavu. [11]
Collier, G.M. (1975), ***Fields of the Tzotzil***, University of Texas Press, Austin. [23]
Collier, J.F. (1973), ***Law and Social Change in Zinacantan***, Stanford University Press. [23]
Collier, J.F. (1974), 'Women in Politics', in M.Z. Rosaldo and L. Lamphere (eds), ***Women, Culture and Society***, Stanford University Press, pp.89-96. [23]
Collier, W.L. (1981), 'Agricultural Evolution in Java', in G. Hansen (ed.), ***Agricultural and Rural Development in Indonesia***, Westview Press, Boulder, pp.147-73. [21]
Connell, J. (1985), 'Copper, Cocoa and Cash: Terminal, Temporary and Circular Mobility in Siwa, North Solomons', in M. Chapman and R.M. Prothero (eds), ***Circulation in Population Movement: Substance and Concepts from the Melanesian Case***, Routledge and Kegan Paul, London, pp.119-48. [22]
Connell, J., Dasgupta, B., Laishley, R. and Lipton, M. (1976), ***Migration from Rural Areas: The Evidence from Village Studies***, Oxford University Press. [21]

Conning, A.M. (1972), 'Rural-Urban Destinations of Migrants and Community Differentiation in a Rural Region of Chile', ***International Migration Review***, vol.6, no.2, pp.148-57. [21]
Coovadia, H.M., Kiepiela, P. and Wesley, A.G. (1984), 'Immunity to and Infant Mortality from Measles', ***South African Journal of Medicine***, vol.65, pp.918-21. [16]
Cox, P.S.V. (1973), 'Geographical Variation in Disease Within a Single District', ***East African Medical Journal***, vol.50, pp. 712-9. [16]
Cosminsky, S. (1976), 'Birth Rituals and Symbolism: A Quiche Maya - Black Carib Comparison', in P. Young and J. Howe (eds), ***Ritual and Symbol in Native Central America***, University of Oregon Press, Eugene, pp.107-23. [23]
Crump, S.T. (1976), 'Boundaries in the Function of Money', unpublished Ph.D. thesis, University of London. [23]
Curtain, R. (1980a), 'The Structure of Internal Migration in Papua New Guinea', ***Pacific Viewpoint***, vol.21, no.1, pp.42-61. [22]
Curtain, R. (1980b), 'Sepik Labour Migration: Causes and Consequences', unpublished Ph.D. thesis, Department of Geography, ANU, Canberra. [22]
Darling, M. (1947), ***The Punjab Peasant in Prosperity and Debt***, Oxford University Press. [6]
Das Gupta, M. (1977), 'From a Closed to an Open System: Fertility Behaviour in a Changing Indian Village', in T.S. Epstein and D. Jackson (eds), ***The Feasibility of Fertility Planning***, Pergamon Press, Oxford, pp.97-121. [26]
Das Gupta, M. (1978), 'Production Relations and Population: Rampur', ***Journal of Development Studies***, vol.14, no.4, pp. 177-85. [14]
Das Gupta, M. (1981), 'Population Trends and Changes in Village Organization: Rampur Revisited', unpublished Ph.D. thesis, University of Sussex. [6]
Davis, K. and Blake, J. (1956), 'Social Structure and Fertility: An Analytical Framework', ***Economic Development and Cultural Change***, vol.4, no.4, pp.211-35. [Intro,8]
Davis, R. (1974), 'Muang Metaphysics: A Study of Northern Thai Myth and Ritual', unpublished Ph.D. thesis, University of Sydney. [7]
Debroise, A. Sy I. and Satgé, P. (1967), 'La Rougeole en Zone Rural', ***L'Enfant en Milieu Tropical***, vol.38, pp.20-36. [16]
Delvoye, P., Demaegd, M., Delogne-Desnoeck, J. and Robyn, C. (1977), 'The Influence of the Frequency of Nursing and of Previous Lactation Experience on Serum Prolactin in Lactating Mothers', ***Journal of Biosocial Science***, vol.9, pp.447-52. [11]
Denzin, N.K. (1981), 'The Interactionist Study of Social Organization: A Note on Method', in D. Bertaux (ed.), ***Biography and Society***, Sage Publications, London, pp.149-67. [9]
Dinan, C. (1983), 'Gold Diggers and Sugar Daddies', in C. Oppong (ed.), ***Female and Male in West Africa***, George Allen and Unwin, London, pp.344-66. [9]
Dorsky, S. (1981), 'Women's Lives in a North Yemeni Highlands Town', unpublished Ph.D. thesis, Department of Anthropology, Case Western Reserve University. [24]

Douglas, M. (1966), ***Purity and Danger: An Analysis of the Concepts of Pollution and Taboo***, Routledge and Kegan Paul, London. [23,24]

Dover, A.S., Escobar, J.A., Duenas, A.L. and Leal, E.C. (1975), 'Pneumonia associated with Measles', ***Journal of the American Medical Association***, vol.234, pp.612-4. [16]

Drinkwater, H. (1885), ***Remarks upon the Epidemic of Measles Prevalent in Sunderland. With Notes upon 311 cases from middle of January to end of March 1885***, James Thin, Edinburgh. [16]

D'Souza, S. and Bhuiya, A. (1982), 'Socioeconomic Mortality Differentials in a Rural Area of Bangladesh', ***Population and Development Review***, vol.8, no.4, pp.753-9. [15]

D'Souza, S. and Chen, L.C. (1980), 'Sex Differentials in Mortality in Rural Bangladesh', ***Population and Development Review***, vol.6, no.2, pp.257-70. [15]

Dubois, J.A. (1906), ***Hindu Manners, Customs and Ceremonies***, Third Edition, trans. by H.K. Beaumont, Clarendon Press, Oxford. [27]

Duby, G. (1968), ***Rural Economy and Country Life in the Medieval West***, Edward Arnold, London. [13]

Dyson, T. (1979), 'A Working Paper on Fertility and Mortality: Estimates for the States of India', paper presented at the New Delhi Workshop of the Panel on India, Cttee on Population and Demography, Nat. Academy of Sciences, Washington, D.C. [6]

Dyson, T. and Moore, M. (1983), 'Kinship Structure, Female Autonomy, and Demographic Behaviour in India', ***Population and Development Review***, vol.9, no.4, pp.35-60. [7,18]

Dyson, T. and Somawat, G. (1983), 'An Assessment of Fertility Trends in India', paper presented at the Conference on Recent Population Trends in South Asia, New Delhi. [6]

Early, J.D. (1974), 'Revision of Ladino and Maya Census Populations of Guatemala, 1950 and 1964', ***Demography***, vol.11, no.1, pp.105-17. [23]

Easterlin, R. (1975), 'An Economic Framework for Fertility Analysis', ***Studies in Family Planning***, vol.6, no.3, pp.54-63. [10]

Echols, J.M. and Shadily, H. (1970), ***An Indonesian-English Dictionary***, Cornell University Press, Ithaca. [21]

Eddington, A. (1935), ***Space, Time and Gravitation***. [20]

Evans-Pritchard, E.E. (1951), ***Social Anthropology***, Cohen and West, London. [26]

Ewbank, D.C. (1981), 'Age Misreporting and Age-Selective Underenumeration: Sources, Patterns and Consequences for Demographic Analysis', Committee on Population and Demography, Report 4, National Academy Press, Washington, D.C. [17]

Favre, H. (1964), 'Notas Sobra el Homicido entre los Chamulas', ***Estudios des Cultura Maya***, vol.4. [23]

Fawcett, J.T. (1983), 'Perceptions of the Value of Children: Satisfaction and Costs', in R.A. Bulatao, R.D. Lee, P.E. Hollerbach and J. Bongaarts (eds), ***Determinants of Fertility in Developing Countries*** , vol.1, ch.13, Academic Press, London. [Intro]

Fawcett, J.T. and Bornstein, M.H. (1973), 'Modernization, Individual Modernity, and Fertility', in J.T. Fawcett (ed.), ***Psychological Perspectives on Population***, Basic Books, New York, pp.106-31. [5]

Ferry, B. (1976), 'Le Fichier Evénements. Une Nouvelle Méthode d'observation Rétrospective', ***L'Observation Démographique dans les Pays à Statistiques Déficientes***, Chaire Quetelet 76, Université Catholiques de Louvain, pp.137-63. [17]

Field, M.J. (1940), ***Social Organization of the Ga People***, Crown Agents for the Colonies, Accra. [9]

Findley, S.E. (1982), 'Migration Survey Methodologies: A Review of Design Issues', Paper No.20, IUSSP, Liège. [20]

Firebrace, J. (1981), ***Infant Feeding in the Yemen Arab Republic***, Catholic Institute for International Relations and War on Want, London. [24]

Fortes, M. (1949), ***The Web of Kinship among the Tallensi***, Oxford University Press. [9]

Fortes, M. (1950), 'Kinship and Marriage among the Ashanti', in A. Radcliffe-Brown and D. Forde (eds), ***African Systems of Kinship and Marriage***, Oxford University Press. [9]

Fortes, M. (1954), 'A Demographic Field Study in Ashanti', in F. Lorimer (ed.), ***Culture and Human Fertility***, UNESCO, Paris, pp. 253-95. [8,9]

Frazer, I. (1981), 'Man Long Taon', unpublished Ph.D. thesis, Department of Anthropology, ANU, Canberra. [22]

Frazer, I. (1985), 'Circulation and the Growth of Urban Employment Amongst the Toombaito, Solomon Islands', in M. Chapman and R.M. Prothero (eds), ***Circulation in Population Movement: Substance and Concepts from the Melanesian Case***, Routledge and Kegan Paul, London, pp.225-48. [22]

Freedman, R. (1974), 'Examples of Community-Level Questionnaires', WFS Occasional Papers No.9, World Fertility Survey, London. [4]

Freedman, R. and Hermalin, A.I. (1975), 'Do Statements About Desired Family Size Predict Fertility? The Case of Taiwan 1967-79', ***Demography***, vol.12, no.3, pp.407-16. [Intro]

Freedman, R., Fan, T.-H., Wei, S.-P. and Weinberger, M.B. (1977), 'Trends in Fertility and in the Effects of Education on Fertility in Taiwan 1961-74', ***Studies in Family Planning***, vol. 8, no.1, pp.11-18. [Intro]

Friesen, W. (1983), 'Accessibility and Circulation in the Western Solomon Islands', paper presented at the 15th Pacific Science Congress, Dunedin. [22]

Gagnon, N. (1981), 'The Analysis of Life Accounts', in D. Bertaux (ed.), ***Biography and Society***, Sage Publications, London, pp. 47-60. [9]

Gallais, J. (1984), ***Hommes du Sahel***, Flammarion, Paris. [19]

Gardner, R.W. (1981), 'Macrolevel Influences on the Migration Decision Process', in G.F. De Jong and R.W. Gardner (eds), ***Migration Decision Making***, Pergamon Press, New York, pp.59-89. [21]

Garenne, M. (1981), 'Size of Households in Tropical Africa', Working Paper No.5, African Demography Program, University of Pennsylvania, Philadelphia. [19]

Garenne, M. (1982), 'Variations in the Age Pattern of Infant and Child Mortality with Special Reference to a Case Study in Ngayokheme (Rural Senegal)', unpublished Ph.D. thesis, University of Pennsylvania. [17]

Garenne, M. (1984), 'The Concept of Follow-up Survey and its Implications for Data Collection: Example of using a Computerized Questionnaire for Improving the Recording of Early Deaths in Rural Senegal', paper presented at the IUSSP Seminar on Micro-Approaches to Demographic Research, ANU, Canberra, 3-7 September. [Intro,27]

Garfinkel, A. (1981), ***Forms of Explanation: Rethinking the Questions in Social Theory***, Yale Univ. Press, New Haven. [1]

Garnaut, R., Wright, M. and Curtain, R. (1977), 'Employment, Incomes and Migration in Papua New Guinea Towns', IASER Monograph No.6, Papua New Guinea. [22]

Geertz, C. (1963), ***Agricultural Involution***, University of California Press, Berkeley. [23]

Gendrau, F. and Nadot, R. (1967), 'Afrique Noire, Madagascar, Comores. Démographie Comparée', Tome 3, 'Structure par Age, Actuelle et Future', DGRST, Paris. [17]

Gideon, H. (1962), 'A Baby is Born in Punjab', ***American Anthropologist***, vol.64, pp.1220-34. [18]

Glaser, B.G. (1978), ***Theoretical Sensitivity: Advances in the Methodology of Grounded Theory***, The Sociology Press, Mill Valley, California. [3]

Glaser, B.G. and Strauss, A.L. (1967), ***The Discovery of Grounded Theory, Strategies for Qualitative Research***, Aldine Publishing Company, Chicago. [3,22]

Gluckman, M. (1961), 'Ethnographic Data in British Social Anthropology', ***Sociological Review***, no.9, pp.5-17. [20]

Godfrey, E.S. (1928), 'Measles in Institutions for Children', ***Journal of Preventive Medicine***, vol.2, pp.1-33, 251-72. [16]

Goldstein, S. and Goldstein, A. (1981), 'Surveys of Migration in Developing Countries: A Methodological Review', Paper No.71, East-West Population Institute, Honolulu. [20]

Good, M.-J. Del V. (1980), 'Of Blood and Babies: The Relationship of Popular Islamic Physiology to Fertility', ***Social Science and Medicine***, vol.148, pp.147-56. [24]

Goodman, L.A. (1961), 'Statistical Methods for the Mover-Stayer Model', ***Journal of the American Statistical Association***, vol.56, pp.841-68. [20]

Goody, E.N. (1973), ***Contexts of Kinship***, Cambridge University Press. [9]

Goody, E.N. (1978), 'Some Theoretical and Empirical Aspects of Parenthood in West Africa', in C. Oppong, G. Adaba, M. Bekombo-Priso and J. Mogey (eds), ***Marriage, Fertility and Parenthood in West Africa***, Changing African Family Project No.4, Department of Demography, ANU, Canberra, pp.227-72. [9]

Goody, E.N. (1982), ***Parenthood and Social Reproduction: Fostering and Occupational Roles in West Africa***, Cambridge University Press. [9]

Goody, J.R. (1956), ***The Social Organization of the Lowiili***, London. [9]

Goody, J.R. (1958), 'The Development Cycle in Domestic Groups', Cambridge Papers in Social Anthropology, no.1, Cambridge University Press. [Intro]

Goody, J.R. and Tambiah, S.J. (1973), 'Bridewealth and Dowry', Cambridge Papers in Social Anthropology no.7, Cambridge University Press. [Intro,12]

Gossen, G. (1974), ***Chamulas in the World of the Sun***, Cambridge, Mass. [23]
Gossen, G. (1975), 'Animals Souls and Human Destiny in Chamula', ***Man***, vol.10, pp.448-61. [23]
Granquist, H. (1947), ***Birth and Childhood Among the Arabs: Studies in a Muhammadan Village in Palestine***, Soderstrom and Company, Helsingfors. [24]
Gubry, P. (1975), 'Une Confrontation entre Deux Méthodes de Détermination des Ages au Cameroun', Cahiers ORSTOM, Série Science Humaines, vol.12, no.4, pp.325-37. [17]
Guiteras Holmes, C. (1969), 'La Magia en las Crisis del Embarazo y Parto en los Actuales Grupos Mayances de Chiapas', ***Estudios de Cultura Maya***, vol.1, pp.159-66. [23]
Guruswamy, M. (1984), 'Nature of Activity in a Village Setting: Methods of Data Collection', paper presented at the IUSSP Seminar on Micro-Approaches to Demographic Research, ANU, Canberra, 3-7 September. [Intro, 27]
Haberkorn, G. (1985), 'Recent Population Trends in Vanuatu', Australia Island Working Paper No.85/4, National Centre for Development Studies, ANU, Canberra. [22]
Haberkorn, G. (1987), 'Port Vila - Transit Station or Final Stop? Recent Developments in Vanuatu Population Mobility', unpublished Ph.D. thesis, Department of Demography, ANU, Canberra. [22]
Hajnal, J. (1982), 'Two Kinds of Preindustrial Household Formation System', ***Population and Development Review***, vol.8, no.3, pp. 449-94. [19]
Handwerker, W.P. (ed.), (1986), ***Culture and Reproduction: An Anthropological Critique of Demographic Transition Theory***, Westview Press, Boulder USA. [27]
Hankiss, A. (1981), 'Ontologies of the Self: On the Mythological Rearranging of One's Life History', in D. Bertaux (ed.), ***Biography and Society***, Sage Publications, London, pp.203-9. [9]
Harsojo (1971), 'Kebudajaan Sunda (Sundanese Culture)', in Koentjaraningrat (ed.), ***Manusia dan Kebudajaan di Indonesia (Peoples and Cultures of Indonesia)***, Penerbit Djambatan Jakarta, pp.305-26. [21]
Haviland, J.B. (1977), ***Gossip, Reputation and Knowledge in Zinacantan***, Chicago. [23]
Heer, D.M. and Smith, D.O. (1968), 'Mortality Level, Desired Family Size, and Population Increase', ***Demography***, vol.5, no.1, pp.104-21. [16]
Hendrickse, R.G. (1975), 'Problems of Future Measles Vaccination in Developing Countries', ***Transactions of the Royal Society of Tropical Medicine and Hygiene***, vol.69, pp.31-4. [16]
Henin, R.A. (1968), 'Fertility Differentials in the Sudan', ***Population Studies***, vol.22, no.1, pp.147-64. [12]
Henin, R.A. (1969), 'The Patterns and Causes of Fertility Differences in the Sudan', ***Population Studies***, vol.23, no.2, pp. 171-98. [12]
Hennart, P. (1983), 'Allaitment Maternal en Situation Nutritionnelle Critique', thèse d'aggrégation, Université Libre de Bruxelles. [11]

Hennart, P., Delogne-Desnoeck, J., Vis, H. and Robyn, C. (1981), 'Serum Levels of Prolactin and Milk Production in Women During a Lactation Period of Thirty Months', ***Clinical Endocrinology***, vol.14, pp.349-53. [11]

Henry, L. (1960), 'Mesure Indirect de la Mortalité des Adultes', ***Population***, vol.15, pp.457-66. [17]

Henry, L. (1961), 'Some Data on Natural Fertility', ***Eugenics Quarterly***, vol.8, no.2, pp.81-91. [10]

Héritier, F. (1968), 'L'enquête ethno-démographique', in J. Poirier (ed.), ***Ethnologie Générale***, Gallimard, Paris. [12]

Hess, C., Thiam, A., Fowler, C. and Swift, J. (1984), 'A Fulani Agro-Pastoral Production System in the Malian Gurma', Report to the International Livestock Centre for Africa. [19]

Hetler, C. (1984), 'Female Headed Households in Indonesia', paper presented at the IUSSP Seminar on Micro-Approaches to Demographic Research, ANU, Canberra, 3-7 September. [27]

Heyworth, B. (1973), 'Pathogenesis of Measles', ***British Medical Journal***, vol.3, p.693. [16]

Hilderbrand, K. (1984), 'Assessing the Components of Seasonal Stress Amongst the Seno-Mango Fulani', in A.G. Hill (ed.), ***Population, Health and Nutrition in the Sahel***, Kegan Paul International, London, ch.12. [19]

Hilderbrand, K., Hill, A.G., Randall, S. and van der Eerenbeemt, M.-L. (1985), 'Child Mortality and Care of Children in Rural Mali', in A.G. Hill (ed.), ***Population, Health and Nutrition in the Sahel***, Kegan Paul Intnl., London, pp.184-204. [Intro, 12]

Hill, A.G. (1980), 'Levels and Trends of Fertility and Mortality in the Yemen Arab Republic', in K. Abu Jaber (ed.), ***Levels and Trends of Fertility and Mortality in Selected Arab Countries of West Asia***, The Population Studies Programme, University of Jordan, Amman, pp.91-104. [24]

Hill, A.G. (ed.), (1984), ***Population, Health and Nutrition in the Sahel***, Kegan Paul International, London. [19]

Hill, A.G. and Randall, S. (1984), 'Différences Géographiques et Sociales dans la Mortalité Infantile et Juvénile au Mali', ***Population***, vol.39, no.6, pp.921-46. [12]

Hill, A.G., Randall, S.C. and Sullivan, O. (1982), 'The Mortality and Fertility of Farmers and Pastoralists in Central Mali 1950-81', Research Paper 82-4, Centre for Population Studies, London School of Hygiene and Tropical Medicine. [19]

Hill, A.G., Randall, S.C. and van der Eerenbeemt, M.-L. (1983), 'Infant and Child Mortality in Rural Mali', Research Paper 83-5, Centre for Population Studies, London School of Hygiene and Tropical Medicine. [Intro,12,16,19]

Hirsch, A. (1883), ***Handbook of Geographical and Historical Pathology***, The New Sydenham Society, London. [16]

Hofsteede, W.M.F. (1971), 'Decision Making Processes in Four West Javanese Villages', unpublished Ph.D. thesis, Katholieke Universiteit, Nijmegan. [21]

Howell, N. (1979), ***Demography of the Dobe !Kung***, Academic Press, New York, 389p. [17]

Howie, P.W. and McNeilly, A.S. (1982), 'Effect of Breastfeeding on Human Birth Intervals', ***Journal of Reproduction and Fertility***, vol.65, pp.545-57. [11]

Howlett, D. (1980), 'When a Peasant is Not a Peasant: Rural Proletarianization in Papua New Guinea', in G.J. Linge (ed.), ***Of Time and Place***, ANU Press, Canberra, pp.193-210. [22]
Huffman, S.L., Chowdhury, A.K.M.A., Chakraborty, J. and Simpson, N. (1980), 'Breast-Feeding Patterns in Rural Bangladesh', ***American Journal of Clinical Nutrition***, vol.33, pp.144-54. [11]
Hugo, G.J. (1975), 'Population Mobility in West Java, Indonesia', Ph.D. thesis, Department of Demography, ANU, Canberra. (Published 1978, Gadjah Mada University Press, Yogyakarta.)[21]
Hugo, G.J. (1976), 'Research Proposal for a Study of Rural-Urban Migration in West Java', in M. Singarimbun (ed.), ***Pedoman Praktis Membuat Usul Proyek Penelitian (A Practical Guide for Making Research Proposals)***, Methodology Series No.1, Population Institute, Gadjah Mada University, Yogyakarta, pp. 28-53. [21]
Hugo, G.J. (1981), 'Village-Community Ties, Village Norms and Ethnic and Social Networks: A Review of Evidence from the Third World', in G.F. De Jong and R.A. Gardner (eds), ***Migration Decision Making***, Pergamon Press, New York, pp.186-224. [21]
Hugo, G.J. (1982a), 'Sources of Internal Migration Data in Indonesia: Their Potential and Limitations', ***Indonesian Journal of Demography***, vol.17, p.35. [21]
Hugo, G.J. (1982b), 'Circular Migration in Indonesia', ***Population and Development Review***, vol.8, no.1, pp.59-83. [21]
Hugo, G.J. (1982c), 'Evaluation of the Impact of Migration on Individuals, Households and Communities', in ESCAP, ***National Migration Surveys No.x, Guidelines for Analyses***, United Nations, New York, pp.189-215. [21]
Hugo, G.J. (1985a), 'Investigating Community Level Effects on Population Movement', in J.B. Casterline (ed.), ***The Collection and Analysis of Community Data***, International Statistical Institute, Voorburg, pp.157-75. [21]
Hugo, G.J. (1985b), 'Structural Change and Labour Mobility in Rural Java', in C. Standing (ed.), ***Labour Circulation and the Labour Process***, Croom Helm, London, pp.46-88. [21]
Hull, H.F. (1983), personal communication. [16]
Hull, H.F., Williams, P.J. and Oldfield, F. (1983), 'Measles Mortality and Vaccine Efficacy in Rural West Africa', ***Lancet***, vol.1, pp.972-5. [16]
Hull, T.H. (1975), 'Each Child Brings its Own Fortune: An Inquiry into the Value of Childen in a Javanese Village', unpublished Ph.D. thesis, Department of Demography, ANU, Canberra. [4]
Hull, T.H. (1976), 'An Improved Technique of Using Time Lines in Determining Ages for Demographic and Health Surveys', Working Paper No.4, Population Institute, Gadjah Mada University, Yogyakarta. [4]
Hull, T.H. (1977), 'The Influence of Social Class on the Need and Effective Demand for Children in a Javanese Village', in L.T. Ruzicka (ed.), ***The Economic and Social Supports for High Fertility***, Family and Fertility Change Series No.2, Department of Demography, ANU, Canberra. [4]
Hull, T.H. and Hull, V.J. (1977a), 'The Relation of Economic Class and Fertility: An Analysis of Some Indonesian Data', ***Population Studies***, vol.31, no.1, pp.43-57. [4]

Hull, T.H. and Hull, V.J. (1977b), 'Indonesia', in J.C. Caldwell (ed.), ***The Persistence of High Fertility: Population Prospects in the Third World***, Changing African Family Project Series No.1, Department of Demography, ANU, Canberra. [4]
Hull, V.J. (1975), 'Fertility, Socioeconomic Status, and the Position of Women in a Javanese Village', unpublished Ph.D. thesis, Department of Demography, ANU, Canberra. [4]
Hull, V.J. (1977), 'Fertility, Women's Work, and Economic Class: A Case Study from Southeast Asia', in S. Kupinsky (ed.), ***The Fertility of Working Women: A Synthesis of International Research***, Praeger, New York. [4]
Hull, V.J. (1980), 'Intermediate Variables in the Explanation of Differential Fertility', ***Human Ecology***, vol.8, pp.213-43. [4]
Hunte, P. (1980), 'The Socio-Cultural Context of Perinatality in Afghanistan', unpublished Ph.D. thesis, Department of Anthropology, University of Wisconsin, Madison. [24]
India, Census of (1981), ***Report and Tables based on 5 per cent Sample Data, Part 11 Special, Series 6***, Government of India, Haryana. [6]
India, Government of, Department of Family Welfare (1982), ***Family Welfare Programme in India, Year Book, 1980-81***, Ministry of Health and Family Welfare, New Delhi, p.29. [2]
India, Operations Research Group, Baroda, (1983), 'Family Planning Practices in India - Second All-India Survey', Baroda, ORG, mimeo. [6]
India, Registrar General (1982), ***Levels, Trends and Differentials in Fertility 1979***, Government of India, New Delhi. [6]
India, Registrar General (1983), ***Sample Registration Bulletin***, New Delhi, Ministry of Home Affairs, Government of India, vol.17, no.1, pp.3-4. [2]
Ingrams, D. (1946), ***A Survey of the Social and Economic Conditions of the Aden Protectorate***, Government Printer, Eritrea. [24]
Inkeles, A. and Smith, D.H. (1974), ***Becoming Modern. Individual Change in Six Developing Countries***, Harvard University Press, Cambridge, Mass. [5]
International Planned Parenthood Federation (n.d.), ***Family Planning in Guatemala: A Profile***, IPPF, London. [23]
Jackson, K.D. (1971), 'Traditional Authority and National Integration, The D'Arul Islam Rebellion in West Java', unpublished Ph.D. thesis, Massachusetts Institute of Technology, Boston. [21]
Jay, R. (1969), ***Javanese Villagers: Social Relations in Rural Modjokuto***, MIT Press, Cambridge, Mass. [4]
Jeffery, P.M. (1979), ***Frogs in a Well***, Zed Press, London. [18]
Jelliffe, D.B. (1966), ***The Assessment of the Nutritional Status of the Community***, WHO, Geneva. [16]
Kahl, J.A. (1968), ***The Measurement of Modernism, a Study of Values in Brazil and Mexico***, University of Texas Press, Austin. [5]
Karpati, Z. (1981), 'The Methodological Uses of the Life History Approach in a Hungarian Survey on Mobility and Urbanization', in D. Bertaux (ed.), ***Biography and Society***, Sage Publications, London, pp.133-48. [9]
Kasarda, J.D. (1971), 'Economic Structure and Fertility', ***Demography***, vol.8, no.3, pp.307-18. [14]

Kasongo Project Team (1981), 'Influence of Measles Vaccination on Survival pattern of 7-35-month-old Children in Kasongo, Zaire', ***Lancet***, vol.1, pp.764-7. [16]
Kasongo Project Team (1983), 'Anthropometric Assessment of Young Children's Nutritional Status as an Indicator of Subsequent Risk of Dying', ***Journal of Tropical Pediatrics***, vol.29, pp. 69-75. [16]
Kemp, J. (1970), 'Initial Marriage Residence in Rural Thailand', in T. Bunnag and M. Smithies (eds), ***In Memorium Phya Anuman Rajadhon***, Siam Society, Bangkok. [7]
Keyes, C.F. (1975), 'Kin Groups in a Thai-Lao Community', in G.W. Skinner and A.T. Kirsch (eds), ***Change and Persistence in Thai Society***, Cornell University Press, Ithaca. [7]
Keyfitz, N. (1977), ***Introduction to the Mathematics of Population***, Addison-Wesley, Reading, Mass. [17]
Khalifa, A.M. (1973), 'A Proposed Explanation of the Fertility Gap Differentials by Socio-Economic Status and Modernity: The Case of Egypt', ***Population Studies***, vol.27, no.3, pp.431-42. [5]
Khattab, H.A.S. (1975), 'Patterns and Perception of Vaginal Bleeding: A Survey of Knowledgeable Sources in Egypt', unpublished report, WHO Human Reproduction Unit, Geneva. [24]
Khoo, S.-E., Suharto, S., Tom, J.A. and Supraptilah, B. (1980), 'Linking Data Sets: The Case of Indonesia's Intercensal Population Surveys', ***Asian and Pacific Census Forum***, vol.7, no.2, pp.1-2, 9-12. [21]
Khuda, B.-e- (1979), 'Land Utilisation in a Village Economy in Bangladesh', unpublished Ph.D. thesis, Department of Demography, ANU, Canberra. [Intro]
Kilson, M. (1974), ***African Urban Kinsmen: The Ga of Central Accra***, C. Hunt and Co, London. [9]
Knodel, J. and Debavalya, N. (1978), 'Thailand's Reproductive Revolution', ***International Family Planning Perspectives***, vol.4, no.2, pp.34-49. [7]
Knodel, J., Havanon, N. and Pramualratana, A. (1983), 'A Tale of Two Generations: A Qualitative Analysis of Fertility Transition in Thailand', Research Report no.83-44, Population Studies Center, University of Michigan, Ann Arbor. [7]
Knodel, J. and Pitaktepsombati, P. (1973), 'Thailand: Fertility and Family Planning among Rural and Urban Women', ***Studies in Family Planning***, vol.4, no.9, pp.229-55. [7]
Kohl, M. (1981), 'Biography: Account, Text, Method', in D. Bertaux (ed.), ***Biography and Society***, Sage Publications, London, pp. 61-75. [9]
Kreager, P. (1982), 'Demography in situ', ***Population and Development Review***, vol.8, no.2, pp.237-66. [Intro]
Kreager, P. (1983), 'Interim Report to the Population Council', unpublished manuscript. [23]
Krier, D.F. (1969), 'Population Movement in England 1650-1812: A Family Reconstitution Study of Three Eighteenth Century Lancashire Parishes', unpublished Ph.D. thesis, Boston College Graduate School, Boston. [21]
Lancet (1968), 'Editorial: Measles in Africa', ***Lancet***, vol.1, p. 239. [16]
Lancet (1983), 'Editorial: Measles Mortality and Malnutrition', ***Lancet***, vol.2, p.661. [16]

Langaney, A., Dallier, S. and Pison, G. (1979), 'Démographie sans Etat Civil: Structure par Age des Mandenka du Niokholo', ***Population***, vol.34, no.4-5, pp.909-15. [17]

Larson, A. (1984), 'Life Course Transitions in Late Nineteenth Century Melbourne: An Outline of a Micro-Approach to Historical Demography', paper presented at the IUSSP Seminar on Micro-Approaches to Demographic Research, ANU, Canberra, 3-7 September. [Intro]

Lasaqa, I.Q. (1972), ***Melanesians' Choice: Tadhimboko Participation in the Solomon Islands Cash Economy***, New Guinea Research Bulletin no.45, New Guinea Research Unit, Port Moresby, and ANU, Canberra. [20]

Laslett, P. and Wall, R. (1972), ***Household and Family in Past Time***, Cambridge University Press. [19]

Lauro, D.J. (1979), 'Life History Matrix Analysis: A Progress Report', in R.J. Pryor (ed.), ***Residence History Analysis***, Studies in Migration and Urbanization 3, Department of Demography, ANU, Canberra, pp.135-54. [20]

Lee, R.B. (1979), ***The !Kung San: Men, Women, and Work in a Foraging Society***, Cambridge University Press. [8]

Lee, R.B. and DeVore, I. (eds), (1978), ***Kalahari Hunter-Gatherers: Studies of the !Kung San and Their Neighbors***, Harvard University Press, Cambridge, Mass. [8]

Leibenstein, H. (1957), ***Economic Backwardness and Economic Growth***, John Wiley and Sons, New York. [14]

Leridon, H. (1977), ***Human Fertility: The Basic Components***, University of Chicago Press. [11]

Leridon, H. and Menken, J. (eds), (1979), ***Natural Fertility***, Ordina, Liège. [8]

Lerner, D. (1958), ***The Passing of Traditional Society***, Free Press of Glencoe, New York. [5]

Lesthaeghe, R. (1980), 'On the Social Control of Human Reproduction', ***Population and Development Review***, vol.6, pp.527-48. [1]

Lesthaeghe, R., Vanderhoeft, C., Becker, S. and Kibet, M. (1983), 'Individual and Contextual Effects of Education on the Proximate Determinants and on Lifetime Fertility in Kenya', IPD Working Papers 83-2/9, Vrije Universiteit, Brussels. [Intro]

Levine, R.A. (1978), 'Comparative Notes on the Life Course', in T.K. Harevan (ed.), ***Transitions***, Academic Press, London, pp. 287-96. [9]

Levine, R.A. (1980), 'Influences of Women's Schooling on Maternal Behavior in the Third World', ***Comparative Education Review***, vol.24, no.2 (part 2), pp.S78-S105. [15]

Levine, R.A. (1984), 'Maternal Behavior and Child Development in High Fertility Populations', Fertility Determinants Research Notes No.2, The Population Council, New York. [9]

Levine, S. (1982), ***Mothers and Wives***, Chicago University Press.[9]

Lindenbaum, S. (1983), 'The Influence of Maternal Education on Infant and Child Mortality in Bangladesh', Report for the International Centre for Diarrhoeal Disease Research, Dhaka. [Intro,15]

Linn, P.R. (1977), 'The Religious Office Holders in Chamula', unpublished D.Phil. thesis, Oxford University. [23]

Logan, M.H. (1973), 'Humoral Medicine in Guatemala and Peasant Acceptance of Modern Medicine', ***Human Organisation***, vol.32, pp. 385-95. [23]

Logan, M.H. (1977), 'Anthropological Research on the Hot-Cold Theory of Disease', ***Medical Anthropology***, vol.1, pp.87-112. [23]

Loudon, J.B. (1977), 'On Body Products', in J. Blacking (ed.), ***The Anthropology of the Body***, Academic Press, London, pp.161-78. [24]

Lucas, A., Lucas, P.J. and Baum, J.D. (1979), 'Pattern of Milk Flow in Breastfed Infants', ***Lancet***, vol.2, p.57. [11]

McArthur, N. (1961), ***Report on the Population Census of 1959 (B.S.I.P.)***, Western Pacific High Commission, Honiara. [20]

McCall, R.B. (1980), ***Infants - the New Knowledge about the Years from Birth to Three***, Vintage Books, New York. [8]

MacCormack, C.P. (ed.), (1982), ***Ethnography of Fertility and Birth***, Academic Press, London. [24]

McDaniel, E.B. and Pardthaisong, T. (1973), 'Evaluating the Effectiveness of a Two-Year Family Planning Action Program at Ban Pong Village in Northern Thailand', Paper no.5, Institute of Population Studies, Chulalongkorn University, Bangkok. [7]

Macfarlane, A. (1976), ***Resources and Population***, Cambridge University Press. [7]

McNeilly, A.S., Glasier, A., Howie, P., Houston, M., Cook, A. and Boyle, H. (1983), 'Fertility after Childbirth: Pregnancy Associated with Breastfeeding', ***Clinical Endocrinology***, vol.18, pp.167-73. [11]

McNicoll, G. (1968), 'Internal Migration in Indonesia', ***Indonesia***, vol.5, pp.29-92. [21]

McNicoll, G. (1975), 'Community-Level Population Policy: An Exploration', ***Population and Development Review***, vol.1, pp. 1-21. [1]

McNicoll, G. (1980a), 'Institutional Determinants of Fertility Change', ***Population and Development Review***, vol.6, no.3, pp. 441-62. [1,13,23]

McNicoll, G. (1980b), 'Review of S. Hong, 1979. Community Development and Human Reproductive Behaviour', ***Population and Development Review***, vol.6, no.3, pp.502-3. [21]

McNicoll, G. (1983), 'The Nature of Institutional and Community Effects on Demographic Behaviour: An Overview', Working Paper No.101, Center for Policy Studies, The Population Council, New York. [13]

McNicoll, G. (1984), 'Adaptation of Social Systems to Changing Mortality Regimes', Working Paper No.108, Center for Policy Studies, The Population Council, New York. [6]

McNicoll, G. and Singarimbun, M. (1983), ***Fertility Decline in Indonesia: Analysis and Interpretation***, National Academy Press, Washington. [1]

Mamdani, M. (1972), ***The Myth of Population Control***, Monthly Review Press, New York and London. [6,7,14]

Manautou, J.M. (ed.), (1982), ***The Demographic Revolution in Mexico, 1970-1980***, Inst. of Social Security, Mexico City. [23]

Manshande, J.P. and Vuysteke, J. (1981), 'Faltering Infant Growth', ***Lancet***, vol.1, pp.779-80. [16]

Mantra, I.B. (1981), ***Population Movement in Central Java***, Gadjah Mada University Press, Yogyakarta. [21]

Marriott, T. (n.d., c1969), 'Chronology of Events in the British Solomon Islands', Honiara, mimeo. [20]

Melrose, D. (1981), ***The Great Health Robbery: Baby Milk and Medicines in Yemen***, OXFAM, Oxford. [24]

Messerschmidt, D.A. (ed.), (1981), ***Methods and Issues in the Study of One's Own Society***, Cambridge University Press. [26]

Meunier, H. (1898), 'Sur un Symptome Nouveau de la Période Précontagieuse de la Rougeole et sur sa Valeur Prophylactique', ***Gazette Hebdomadaire de Médicine et de Chirurgie***, pp.1057-61. [16]

Miller, D. (1980), 'Settlement and Diversity in the Solomon Islands', ***Man***, vol.15, pp.451-66. [20]

Mitchell, J.C. (1967), 'On Quantification in Social Anthropology', in A.L. Epstein (ed.), ***The Craft of Social Anthropology***, Tavistock, London. [4]

Mitchell, J.C. (1983), 'Case and Situation Analysis', ***Sociological Review***, no.31, pp.187-211. [20,22]

Mitchell, J.C. (1985), 'Towards a Situational Sociology of Wage-Labour Circulation', in R.M. Prothero and M. Chapman (eds), ***Circulation in Third World Countries***, Routledge and Kegan Paul, London, pp.30-53. [20,22]

Molnos, A. (1973), ***Cultural Source Materials for Population Planning in East Africa***, especially Volume 2, ***Innovation and Communication*** and Volume 3, ***Beliefs and Practices***, East African Publishing House, Nairobi. [27]

Morley, D. (1963), 'A Medical Service for Children Under Five Years of Age in West Africa', ***Transactions of the Royal Society of Tropical Medicine and Hygiene***, vol.57, pp.79-94. [16]

Morley, D. (1976), ***Paediatric Priorities in the Developing World***, Butterworth, London. [8]

Morley, D., Martin, W.J. and Allen, I. (1967), 'Measles in West Africa', ***West African Medical Journal***, vol.16, pp.24-31. [16]

Morrison, P.A. (1983), 'Introduction and Overview', in P.A. Morrison (ed.), ***Population Movements: Their Forms and Functions in Urbanization and Development***, Ordina, Liège, pp.1-16. [20]

Moser, C.B. and Kalton, G. (1970), ***Survey Methods in Social Investigation***, Heineman, London. [21]

Mosley, W.H. (1980), 'Social Determinants of Infant and Child Mortality: Some Considerations for an Analytical Framework', in 'Health and Mortality in Early Childhood', Report on a Study Group, The Population Council, Cairo. [Intro]

Mosley, W.H. (1983), 'Will Primary Health Care Reduce Infant and Child Mortality? A Critique of Some Current Strategies with Special Reference to Africa and Asia', paper delivered at the IUSSP Seminar on Social Policy, Health Policy, and Mortality Prospects, Paris, 28 February - 4 March. [15,16]

Mougne, C.M. (1978), 'An Ethnography of Reproduction: Changing Patterns of Fertility in a Northern Thai Village', in P.A. Stott (ed.), ***Nature and Man in South East Asia***, School of Oriental and African Studies, London. [7]

Mougne, C.M. (1982), 'The Social and Economic Correlates of Demographic Change in a Northern Thai Community', unpublished Ph.D. thesis, University of London. [7]

Muller, A.S., Voorhoeve, A.M., Mannetje, W. and Schulpen, T.W.J. (1977), 'The Impact of Measles in a Rural Area of Kenya', ***East African Medical Journal***, vol.54, pp.364-72. [16]
Myntti, C. (1979), 'Population Processes in Rural Yemen: Temporary Emigration, Breastfeeding and Contraception', ***Studies in Family Planning***, vol.10, no.10, pp.282-9. [24]
Myntti, C. (1983), 'Changing Attitudes Toward Health: Observations from the Hugariyya, Yemen', in C. Nelson (ed.), ***Women, Health and Development***, Cairo Papers in Social Science, American University in Cairo, pp.121-31. [24]
Nag, M. (1968), 'Factors Affecting Human Fertility in Non-Industrial Societies: A Cross-Cultural Study', Publications in Anthropology no.66, Human Relations Area Files Press, Yale University, New Haven. [7]
Nag, M. (1979), 'How Modernization Can Also Increase Fertility', Working Paper No.49, Center for Policy Studies, The Population Council, New York. [11]
Nag, M., Peet, R.C. and White, B.N.F. (1977), 'Economic Value of Children in Two Peasant Societies', ***Proceedings of the IUSSP International Population Conference, Mexico 1977***, IUSSP, Liège, vol.1, pp.123-40. [Intro,6]
Nag, M., White, B.N.F. and Peet, R.C. (1978), 'An Anthropological Approach to the Study of the Economic Value of Children in Java and Nepal', ***Current Anthropology***, vol.19, no.2, pp.293-306.[14]
Naim, M. (1974), 'Voluntary Migration in Indonesia', Working Paper No.26, Institute of Southeast Asian Studies, Singapore. [21]
Nash, J. (1970), ***In the Eyes of the Ancestors***, Yale University Press, London. [23]
Nerdrum, J.G.B. (1901-2), 'Indtryk og Oplevelser under et 7 Aars Ophold Paa Salomon Erne', ***Norwegian Geographical Society Yearbook.*** [20]
Nerlove, M. (1974), 'Household and Economy: Toward a New Theory of Population and Economic Growth', ***Journal of Political Economy***, vol.82, pp.S200-18. [1]
Nunkunya, G. (1969), ***Kinship and Marriage among the Anlo Ewe***, Athlone Press, London. [9]
O'Neill, B.J. (1984), 'Nuptiality and Illegitimacy in Twentieth-Century Northern Portugal: An Anthropological Case Study', paper presented at the IUSSP Seminar on Micro-Approaches to Demographic Research, ANU, Canberra, 3-7 September. [Intro]
Operations Research Group, Baroda, (1983), 'Family Planning Practices in India - Second All-India Survey', Baroda, ORG, mimeo. [6]
Oppong, C. (1973), ***Growing Up in Dagbon***, Ghana Publishing Corporation. [9]
Oppong, C. (1980), 'A Synopsis of Seven Roles and Status of Women: An Outline of a Conceptual and Methodological Approach', Research Working Paper, World Employment Programme, ILO, Geneva, mimeo (restricted). [9]
Oppong, C. (1982), ***Middle Class African Marriage***, George Allen and Unwin, London (reprint of 1974). [9]
Oppong, C. (1983a), 'Paternal Costs, Role Strain and Fertility Regulation: Some Ghanaian Evidence', Research Working Paper, World Employment Programme, ILO, Geneva, mimeo (restricted).[9]

Oppong, C. (1983b), 'Women's Roles, Opportunity Costs and Fertility', in R.A. Bulatao and R.D. Lee (eds), ***Determinants of Fertility in Developing Countries***, Academic Press, London, vol.1, pp.547-89. [9]

Oppong, C. (ed.), (1983c), ***Female and Male in West Africa***, George Allen and Unwin, London. [9]

Oppong, C. (1985), 'Aspects of Anthropological Approaches to the Study of Fertility', in G. Farooq and G. Simmons (eds), ***Fertility in Developing Countries: An Economic Perspective on Research and Policy Issues***, Macmillan, London, pp.240-70. [9]

Oppong, C. (1988), ***Sex Roles, Population and Development in West Africa***, James Currey, London. [9]

Oppong, C. and Abu, K. (1985), ***A Handbook for Data Collection and Analysis on Seven Roles and Statuses of Women***, ILO, Geneva. [9]

Oppong, C. and Abu, K. (1987), ***Ghanaian Mothers: Impacts of Education, Migration and Employment***, Women, Work and Development Series, ILO, Geneva. [9]

Oppong, C., Okonjo, K. and Okali, C. (1977), 'Women's Roles and Fertility in West Africa: A Biographical Approach', Population and Development Policy Research Project, Légon, submitted to Rockefeller Foundation. [9]

Orubuloye, I.O. and Caldwell, J.C. (1975), 'The Impact of Public Health Services on Mortality: A Study of Mortality Differentials in a Rural Area in Nigeria', ***Population Studies***, vol.29, no.2, pp.259-72. [Intro]

Page, H.J. and Lesthaeghe, R. (eds), (1981), ***Child-spacing in Tropical Africa: Traditions and Change***, Academic Press, London. [11]

Palmer, A.W. (1959), 'The Sundanese Village', in G.W. Skinner (ed.), ***Local, Ethnic and National Loyalties in Village Indonesia: A Symposium***, Yale University Press, New Haven, pp. 42-51. [21]

Papineau, D. (1978), ***For Science in the Social Sciences***, Macmillan, London. [Intro]

Paravicini, E. (1931), ***Reisen in den Britischen Salomonen***, Verlag Huber, Leipzig. [20]

Pardthaisong, T. (1974), 'The Epidemiology of the Acceptance and Use of Depo-Provera as an Injectable Contraceptive in Chiang Mai, Northern Thailand', unpublished M.Sc. thesis, University of London. [7]

Paul, L. (1971), 'The Mastery of Work and the Mystery of Sex in a Guatemalan Village', in M.Z. Rosaldo and L. Lamphere (eds), ***Women, Culture and Society***, Stanford University Press, pp. 281-99. [23]

Pelto, P. (1970), ***Anthropological Research: The Structure of Inquiry***, Harper and Row, New York. [4]

Phillips, J., Stinson, W., Bhatia, S. Rahman, M. and Chakroborty, J. (1982), 'The Demographic Impact of the Family Planning Health Services Project in Matlab, Bangladesh', ***Studies in Family Planning***, vol.13, no.5, pp.131-40. [1]

Picken, R.M.F. (1921), 'The Epidemiology of Measles in a Rural and Residential Area', ***Lancet***, vol.1, pp.1349-53. [16]

Pison, G. (1980), 'Calculer l'Age sans le Demander. Méthode d'estimation de l'Age et Structure par Age des Peul Bandé (Sénégal Oriental)', *Population*, vol.35, no.4-5, pp.861-92. (Translated into English: 'Calculating Age Without Asking for it. Method of Estimating the Age and Age Structure of the Fule Bandé (Eastern Senegal)', Selected Papers on Population, no.9, INED-INSEE-ORSTOM, Ministère de la Coopération). [17]

Pison, G. (1982a), ***Dynamique d'une Population Traditionelle: Les Peul Bandé (Sénégal Oriental)***, Cahier No.99, INED Travaux et Documents, PUF, Paris, 278p. [17]

Pison, G. (1982b), 'Sous-enregistrement, Sexe et Age: Exemple d'une Mesure Directe dans Une Enquête Africaine', ***Population***, vol.38, no.3, pp.648-54. [17]

Pison, G. (1985), 'Evaluation des Méthodes Indirectes d'Estimation de la Mortalité des Enfants', actes du Séminaire du Centre International de l'Enfance, ***L'estimation de la Mortalité du Jeune Enfant (0-5 ans) en Afrique***, Paris, in press. [17]

Pison, G. and Langaney, A. (1985), 'The Level and Age Pattern of Mortality in Bandafassi (Eastern Senegal): Results from a Small-Scale and Intensive Multi-Round Survey', ***Population Studies***, vol.39, no.3, pp.387-405. [17]

Poos, L.R. and Smith, R.M. (1984), 'Legal Windows into Historical Population? Recent Research on Demography and the Manor Court in Medieval England', ***Law and History Review***, vol.2, pp.128-52. [13]

Popper, K. (1959), ***The Logic of Scientific Discovery***, Hutchinson, London. [Intro]

Population Council (1981), 'Research on the Determinants of Fertility: A Note on Priorities', ***Population and Development Review***, vol.7, pp.311-24. [13]

Potter, J.E. (1983), 'Effects of Societal and Community Institutions on Fertility', in R.A. Bulatao and R.D. Lee (eds), ***Determinants of Fertility in Developing Countries***, Academic Press, New York, vol.2, pp.627-65. [13]

Potter, J.M. (1976), ***Thai Peasant Social Structure***, University of Chicago Press. [7]

Potter, R.G. (1963), 'Birth Intervals: Structure and Change', ***Population Studies***, vol.17, no.2, pp.155-66. [11]

Premi, M.K. (1984), 'A Case for Micro-Level Studies on Internal Migration in India', paper presented at the IUSSP Seminar on Micro-Approaches to Demographic Research, ANU, Canberra, 3-7 September. [Intro]

Preston, S.H. (1979), 'Urban Growth in Developing Countries: A Demographic Reappraisal', ***Population and Development Review***, vol.5, no.3, pp.195-215. [22]

Preston, S.H. and Bhat, P.N.M. (1984), 'New Evidence on Fertility and Mortality Trends in India', ***Population and Development Review***, vol.10, no.3, pp.481-503. [6,14]

Pryor, R.J. (1975), 'Migration and the Process of Modernization', in L.A. Kosinski and R.M. Prothero (eds), ***People on the Move***, Methuen, London, pp.23-38. [21]

Punjab, Government of (1982), ***District Ludhiana at a Glance 1981***, District Gazetteer, District Statistical Office, Ludhiana. [14]

Randall, S.C. (1984), 'A Comparative Study of Three Sahelian Populations', unpublished Ph.D. thesis, University of London. [Intro,19]

Randall, S.C. and Winter, M. (1985), 'The Reluctant Spouse and the Illegitimate Slave: Marriage, Household Formation and Demo-Graphic Behaviour amongst Malian Tamasheq from the Niger Delta and the Gowna', in A.G. Hill (ed.), ***Population, Health and Nutrition in the Sahel***, Kegan Paul International, London, pp. 153–83. [Intro,12,19]

Rajadhon, P.A. (1968), 'The Story of Thai Marriage Custom', ***Essays on Thai Folklore***, The Social Science Association Press of Thailand, Bangkok. [7]

Reyna, S.P. (1975), 'Age Differential, Marital Instability and Venereal Disease: Factors Affecting Fertility Amongst the North West Barma', in M. Nag (ed.), ***Population and Social Organization***, Mouton & Co., The Hague and Paris. [12]

Richard, J. and El Awad Galal el Din, M. (1982), 'The Beginning of Family Limitation in the Three Towns of the Sudan', in ***Demographic Transition in Metropolitan Sudan***, Changing African Family Project Series Monograph No.9, Department of Demography, ANU, Canberra. [9]

Rivers, W.H.R. (1971), 'The Genealogical Method', in N. Grayburn (ed.), ***Readings in Kinship and Social Structure***, Harper Row, New York, pp.52-9. [26]

Robertson, C. (1974), 'Economic Women in Africa: Profit-Making Techniques of Accra Market Women', ***Journal of Modern African Studies***, no.12, pp.657-64. [9]

Robertson, C. (1977), 'The Nature and Effects of Differential Access to Education in Ga Society', ***Africa***, no.2, pp.208-19. [9]

Romaniuk, A. (1980), 'Increase in Natural Fertility during the Early Stages of Modernization: Evidence from an African Case Study, Zaire', ***Population Studies***, vol.34, no.2, pp.293–310. [11]

Ross, A.H. (1962), 'Modification of Chicken Pox in Family Contacts by Administration of Gamma Globulin', ***New England Journal of Medicine***, vol.267, pp.369-76. [16]

Rosenfield, A., Asavesana, W. and Mikhanorn, J. (1973), 'Person to Person Communication in Thailand', ***Studies in Family Planning***, vol.4, no.6, pp.145-9. [7]

Ruzicka, L. and Chowdhury, A.K.M.A. (1978), 'Demographic Surveillance System - Matlab, Vol.2, Census 1974', Scientific Report No.10, International Centre for Diarrheal Disease Research, Dhaka, March. [15]

Ryan, D. (1985), 'Bi-locality and Movement Between Village and Town Toaripi, Papua New Guinea', in M. Chapman and R.M. Prothero (eds), ***Circulation in Population Movement: Substance and Concepts from the Melanesian Case***, Routledge and Kegan Paul, London, pp.251-68. [22]

Ryder, N.B. (1983), 'Fertility and Family Structure', ***Population Bulletin of the United Nations***, no.15, pp.15–34. [6]

Safilios-Rothschild, C. (1982), 'Female Power, Autonomy and Demographic Change in the Third World', in R. Anker ***et al.*** (eds), ***Women's Roles and Population Trends in the Third World***, Croom Helm, London. [7]

Sanjek, R. (1983), 'Female and Male Domestic Cycles in Urban Africa: The Adabraka Case', in C. Oppong (ed.), ***Female and Male in West Africa***, George Allen and Unwin, London. [9]
Sanjek, R. and Sanjek, L.M. (1976), 'Notes on Women and Work in Adabraka', ***Urban African Notes***, vol.2, no.2, pp.1-25. [9]
Savage, F.M.A. (1967), 'A Year of Measles', ***Medical Journal of Zambia***, vol.1, pp.67-77. [16]
Schofield, R. (1983), 'The Impact of Scarcity and Plenty on Population Change in England, 1541-1871', ***Journal of Interdisciplinary History***, vol.xiv, no.2, pp.265-91. [13]
Scott, C. and Sabagh, G. (1970), 'The Historical Calendar as a Method of Estimating Age: The Experience of the Moroccan Multipurpose Sample Survey of 1961-63', ***Population Studies***, vol.24, pp.93-109. [20]
Scrimshaw, N.S., Salomon, J.B., Bruch, H.A. and Gordon, J.E. (1966), 'Measles, Diarrhea, and Nutritional Deficiency in Rural Guatemala', ***American Journal of Tropical Medicine and Hygiene***, vol.15, pp.625-31. [16]
Scrimshaw, S. (1978), 'Infant Mortality and Behaviour in the Regulation of Family Size', ***Population and Development Review***, vol.4, no.3, pp.383-403. [6]
Scrimshaw, S. (1983), 'Infanticide as Deliberate Fertility Regulation', in R.A. Bulatao and R.D. Lee (eds), ***Determinants of Fertility in Developing Countries***, Academic Press, New York, vol.2, pp.245-66. [6]
Shah, A.M. and Ramaswamy, E.A. (n.d.), 'Human Fertility and Culture', mimeographed paper. [26]
Shariff, A. (1984), 'The Changing Family System: Women's Status and Fertility Decisions - Evidence from a Micro-Study in South India', paper presented at the IUSSP Seminar on Micro-Approaches to Demographic Research, ANU, Canberra, 3-7 September. [Intro]
Sheikh, K., Sarder, A.M., Becker, S. and Chen, L.C. (1979), 'Demographic Surveillance System - Matlab, Vol.6, Vital Events and Migration - 1977', Scientific Report No.18, International Centre for Diarrheal Disease Research, Bangladesh, Dhaka, February. [15]
Singarimbun, M. and Hull, T.H. (1977), 'Social Responses to High Mortality Which Act to Support High Fertility', ***Proceedings of the IUSSP International Population Conference, Mexico City 1977***, IUSSP, Liège, vol.1, pp.225-40. [4]
Singarimbun, M. and Manning, C. (1974), 'Marriage and divorce in Mojolama', ***Indonesia***, vol.17, pp.67-82. [4]
Singarimbun, M. and Manning, C. (1976), 'Breastfeeding, Amenorrhea, and Abstinence in a Javanese Village: A Case Study of Mojolama', ***Studies in Family Planning***, vol.7, no.6, pp. 175-9. [4]
Singarimbun, M. and Penny, D. (1973), ***Population and Poverty in Rural Java: Some Economic Arithmetic from Sriharjo***, Cornell International Agricultural Development Monograph No.41, Cornell University, Ithaca. [4]
Singarimbun, M. and Penny, D. (1976), ***Penduduk dan Kemiskinan: Kasua Sriharjo di Pedesaan Jawa***, Bhratara Karya Aksara, Jakarta. (Translated from: D. Penny and M. Singarimbun (1973).) [4]

Singhanetra-Renard, A. (1981), 'Mobility in North Thailand: A View From Within', in G.W. Jones and H.V. Richter (eds), ***Population Mobility and Development: Southeast Asia and the Pacific***, Monograph 27, Development Studies Centre, ANU, Canberra, pp.137-66. [20]
Singhanetra-Renard, A. (1982), 'Northern Thai Mobility 1870-1977: A View from Within', unpublished Ph.D. thesis, University of Hawaii, Honolulu. [20]
Sinha, D.P. (1977), 'Measles and Malnutrition in a West Bengal Village', ***Tropical and Geographical Medicine***, vol.29, pp. 125-34. [16]
Siverts, H. (1969), 'Ethnic Stability and Boundary Dynamics in Southern Mexico', in F. Barth (ed.), ***Ethnic Groups and Boundaries: The Social Organisation of Cultural Difference***, George Allen and Unwin, London, pp.101-16. [23]
Skultans, V. (1970), 'The Symbolic Significance of Menstruation and the Menopause', ***Man***, vol.5, pp.639-51. [24]
Smith, R.M. (1980), 'Some Reflections on the evidence for the Origins of the European Marriage Pattern in England', in C. Harris (ed.), ***The Sociology of the Family: Sociological Review Monograph***, vol.28, pp.74-112. [13]
Smith, R.M. (1981), 'Fertility, Economy and Household Formation in England over Three Centuries', ***Population and Development Review***, vol.7, pp.595-622. [13]
Smith, R.M. (1983a), 'Hypothèses sur la Nuptialité en Angleterre aux XIIIe - XIVe Siècles', ***Annales Economies, Sociétés, Civilisations***, vol.38, no.1, pp.107-36. [13]
Smith, R.M. (1983b), 'Some Thoughts on Hereditary and Proprietary Rights in Land under Customary Law in Thirteenth and Early Fourteenth Century England', ***Law and History Review***, vol.1, no.1, pp.95-128. [13]
Smith, R.M. (ed.), (1984a), ***Land, Kinship and Life-Cycle***, Cambridge University Press. [13]
Smith, R.M. (1984b), '"Modernization" and the Corporate Medieval Village Community in England: Some Sceptical Reflections', in A.R.H. Baker and D. Gregory (eds), ***Explorations in Historical Geography***, Cambridge University Press, pp.140-79. [13]
Smith, W.R. (1977), ***The Fiesta System and Economic Change***, Columbia University Press, New York. [23]
Snowden, R. and Christian, B. (eds), (1983), ***Patterns and Perceptions of Menstruation***, Croom Helm, London. [24]
Squire, D. (1877), 'Report on the Very Fatal Epidemic of Measles in Fiji', ***Medical Times Gazette***, vol.1, pp.323-4. [16]
Srinivas, M.N. (1942), ***Marriage and Family in Mysore***, New Book Company, Bombay. [26]
Staniland, M. (1975), ***The Lions of Dagbon: Political Change in Northern Ghana***, Cambidge University Press. [9]
Stavenhagen, R. (1975), ***Social Classes in Agrarian Societies***, Anchor Books, Garden City, N.Y. [23]
Sudarkasa, N. (1973), 'Where Women Work: A Study of Yoruba Women in the Marketplace and in the Home', Anthropological Papers No.53, Museum of Anthropology, University of Michigan, Ann Arbor. [8]

Swift, J.J. (1975), 'Pastoral Nomadism as a Form of Land Use', in T. Monod (ed.), ***Pastoralism in Tropical Africa***, Oxford University Press. [12]

Swindell, K. (1979), 'Labour Migration in Underdeveloped Countries: The Case of Sub-Saharan Africa', ***Progress in Human Geography***, vol.3, no.2, pp.239-60. [22]

Swiss API (Swiss Airphoto Interpretation Team of the Swiss Technical Co-operation Service), (1978), ***Final Report of the Census (The Housing and Population Census and Supplementary Surveys)***, Department of Geography, University of Zurich. [24]

Synge, J. (1981), 'Cohort Analysis in the Planning and Interpretation of Research Using Life Histories', in D. Bertaux (ed.), ***Biography and Society***, Sage Publications, London, pp. 235-47. [9]

Tanabe, S. (1981), 'Peasant Farming Systems in Thailand: A Comparative Study of Rice Cultivation and Agricultural Technology in Chiengmai and Ayutthaya', unpublished Ph.D. thesis, University of London. [7]

Thiam, A.S. (1984), 'Le Hayire Pastoral', London School of Hygiene and Tropical Medicine, unpublished manuscript. [19]

Thompson, P. (1981), 'Life Histories and the Analysis of Social Change', in D. Bertaux (ed.), ***Biography and Society***, Sage Publications, London, pp.289-306. [9]

Tonkinson, R. (1968), 'Maat Village, Efate: A Relocated Community in the New Hebrides', Department of Anthropology, University of Oregon, Eugene. [22]

Tremlett, G. ***et al.*** (1983), 'Guidelines for the Design of National Weight-for-Age Growth Charts', ***Assignment Children***, UNICEF, no. 81/62, pp.143-75. [8]

Trens, M.S. (1957), ***Historia de Chiapas***, Mexico City. [23]

Trow, M. (1957), 'Comment on "Participant Observation and Interviewing: A Comparison"', ***Human Organization***, vol.16, no.3, pp. 33-5. [4]

Turton, A. (1976), 'Northern Thai Peasant Society: A Case Study of Jural and Political Structures at the Village Level and Their Twentieth Century Transformations', unpublished Ph.D. thesis, University of London. [7]

Tyson, J.E. and Perez, A. (1978), 'The Maintenance of Infecundity in Postpartum Women', in W.H. Mosley (ed.), ***Nutrition and Human Reproduction***, Plenum Press, New York, pp.11-28. [11]

Ukaegbu, A. (1977), 'Family Planning Attitudes and Practices in Rural Eastern Nigeria', ***Studies in Family Planning***, vol.8, no.7, pp.177-83. [10]

United Nations (1976), ***Global Review of Human Settlements***, Pergamon Press, Oxford. [22]

United Nations (1982), ***Manual 10: Demographic Estimation: A Manual of Indirect Techniques***, Population Studies No.81, New York. [17]

United Nations Fund for Population Activities, ***State of the World Population, 1984***, New York. [7]

van Rensalaar, H.C. (1974), 'Family Planning, Response and Perception Among Villagers in Bangladesh', in D.G. Jongmans and H.J.M. Claessen (eds), ***The Neglected Factor***, Van Gorcum, Assen, The Netherlands. [7]

Van Roy, E. (1971), ***Economic Systems of Northern Thailand: Structure and Change***, Cornell University Press, Ithaca. [7]
Vansina, J. (1965), ***Oral Tradition: A Study in Historical Methodology***, Aldine, Chicago. [20]
Vis, H.L., Bossuyt, M., Hennart, P. and Caraël, M. (1975), 'The Health of Mother and Child in Rural Central Africa', ***Studies in Family Planning***, vol.6, no.12, pp.437-41. [11]
Vlassoff, C. (1978), 'The Significance of Cultural Tradition for Contraceptive Change: A Study of Rural Indian Women', unpublished Ph.D. thesis, University of Poona. [5]
Vlassof, C. (1979), 'Fertility Control without Modernization: Evidence from a Rural Indian Community', ***Journal of Biosocial Science***, vol.11, no.4, pp.325-39. [5]
Vlassoff, C. (1980), 'Unmarried Adolescent Females in Rural India: A Study of the Social Impact of Education', ***Journal of Marriage and the Family***, vol.42, no.2, pp.427-36. [5]
Vlassoff, C. (1982), 'The Status of Women in Rural India: A Village Study', ***Social Action***, vol.32, no.4, pp.380-407. [5]
Walsh, J.A. (1983), 'Selective Primary Health Care: Strategies for Control of Disease in the Developing World. IV. Measles', ***Reviews of Infectious Diseases***, vol.5, pp.330-40. [16]
Wander, H. (1965), ***Die Beziehungen Zwisschen Bevolkerungsund Wirtschafsentwicklung, Dargestellt am Indonesiens***, (The Connection Between Population and Economic Development Demonstrated Through the Example of Indonesia), J.C.B. Mohr, Tubingen. [21]
Ward, E.D. (1937), ***Marriage Among The Yoruba***, Anthropological Series No.4, Catholic University of America, Washington, D.C. [8]
Ward, R.G. (1971), 'Internal Migration and Urbanization in Papua New Guinea', ***New Guinea Research Bulletin***, vol.42, pp.81-107. [22]
Ware, H. (1983), 'Female and Male Life-Cycles', in C. Oppong (ed.), ***Female and Male in West Africa***, George Allen and Unwin, London, pp.6-31. [9]
Wassef, M. (1981), 'Perception of the Human Body', unpublished M.A. thesis, Department of Anthropology, American University in Cairo. [24]
Wasserstrom (1978), 'Population Growth and Economic Development in Chiapas, 1524-1975', ***Human Ecology***, vol.6, no.2, pp.127-43. [23]
White, B.N.F. (1976), 'Production and Reproduction in a Javanese Village', unpublished Ph.D. thesis, Columbia University, New York. [6]
Whitehead, R.G., Rowland, M., Hutton, M., Prentice, A., Muller, E. and Paul, A. (1978), 'Factors Influencing Lactation Performance in Rural Gambian Mothers', ***Lancet***, vol.2, p.178. [11]
Wilks, M. (1810), ***Historical Sketches of the South of India, in an Attempt to Trace the History of Mysoor; from the Origin of the Hindoo Government of the State, to the Extinction of the Mohammedan Dynasty in 1799. Founded Chiefly on Indian Authorities Collected by the Author while Officiating for Several Years as Political Resident at the Court of Mysoor***, Longman, Hurst, Rees and Orme, London. [27]

Williams, D. (1897), 'Measles', in T.C. Allbutt and H.D. Rollestone (eds), ***System of Medicine***, London, pp.99–117. [16]

Williamson, J.B., Karp, D. and Dalphin, J. (1977), ***The Research Craft: An Introduction to Social Science Methods***, Little, Brown and Co., Boston. [22]

Wils, W., Caraël, M. and Tondeur, G. (1978), ***Le Kivu Montagneux. Surpopulation, Sous-Nutrition et Erosion du Sol***, Cemubac, Bruxelles. [11]

Wisdom, C. (1952), 'The Supernatural World and Curing', in S. Tax (ed.), ***Heritage of Conquest***, Free Press, Glencoe, pp.119–43. [23]

Woodford, C.M. (1890), ***A Naturalist among the Headhunters, Being an Account of Three Visits to the Solomon Islands - the Years 1881, 1887 and 1888***, G. Philip and Son, London. [20]

World Bank (1980), ***Yemen Arab Republic Economic Memorandum***, World Bank, Washington. [24]

World Health Organization (1983), 'Country Resource Utilization Review: Yemen Arab Republic' (draft), Geneva. [24]

World Fertility Survey, (1978), ***Indonesian Fertility Survey Principal Report***, Central Bureau of Statistics, Jakarta. [4]

Wright, G.P. and Wright, H.P. (1942), 'The Influence of Social Conditions upon Diphtheria, Measles, Tuberculosis and Whooping Cough in Early Childhood in London', ***Journal of Hygiene***, vol. 42, pp.451–73. [16]

Wrigley, E.A. (1966), 'Family Reconstitution', in E.A. Wrigley (ed.), ***An Introduction to English Historical Demography***, Basic Books, New York, pp.96–159. [21]

Wrigley, E.A. and Schofield, R.S. (1981), ***The Population History of England 1541-1871***, Edward Arnold, London. [13]

Wyon, J.B. and Gordon, J.E. (1971), ***The Khanna Study: Population Problems in Rural Punjab***, Harvard University Press, Cambridge. [14]

Yemen Family Planning Association (1980), 'A General Study of Contraceptive Use', unpublished paper, Sanaa. [24]

Young, E.A. (1977), 'Population Mobility in Agasabi/Gadsup Eastern Highlands Province', in R.T. May (ed.), ***Change and Movement***, ANU Press, Canberra, pp.173–202. [22]

Young, E.A. (1985), 'Circularity Within Migration: The Experience of Simbu and New Irelanders, Papua New Guinea', in M. Chapman and R.M. Prothero (eds), ***Circulation in Population Movement: Substance and Concepts from the Melanesian Case***, Routledge and Kegan Paul, London, pp.191–212. [22]

Young, M.W. (1983), 'Our Name is Women: We are Bought with Lime-sticks and Limepots, An Analysis of the Autobiographical Narrative of a Kalauna Woman', ***Man***, vol.18, no.3, pp.478–501. [9]

Zelditch, M. (1962), 'Some Methodological Problems of Field Studies', ***American Journal of Sociology***, vol.67, pp.566–76. [4]

For Product Safety Concerns and Information please contact our EU
representative GPSR@taylorandfrancis.com
Taylor & Francis Verlag GmbH, Kaufingerstraße 24, 80331 München, Germany

www.ingramcontent.com/pod-product-compliance
Ingram Content Group UK Ltd.
Pitfield, Milton Keynes, MK11 3LW, UK
UKHW022212190926
475702UK00003B/320
* 9 7 8 1 0 3 2 5 4 9 0 2 6 *